Figural Whiskey Bottles

by Hoffman, Potters, McCormick, Ski Country, and More

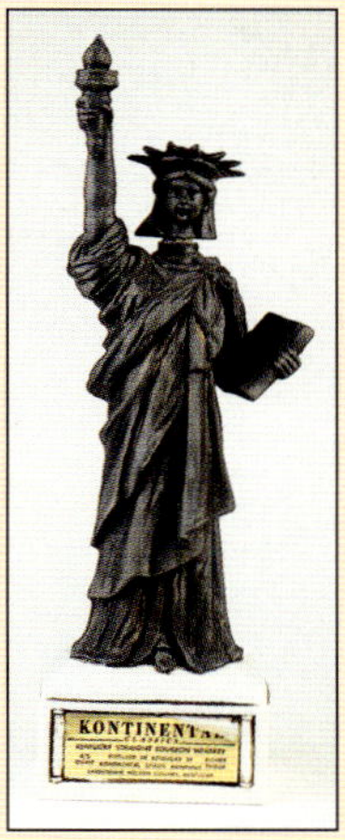

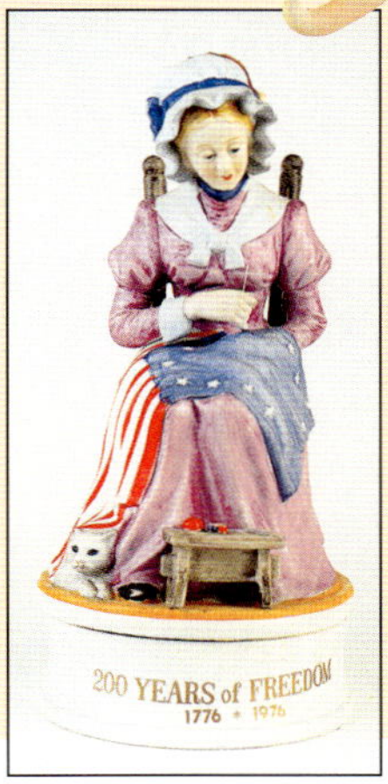

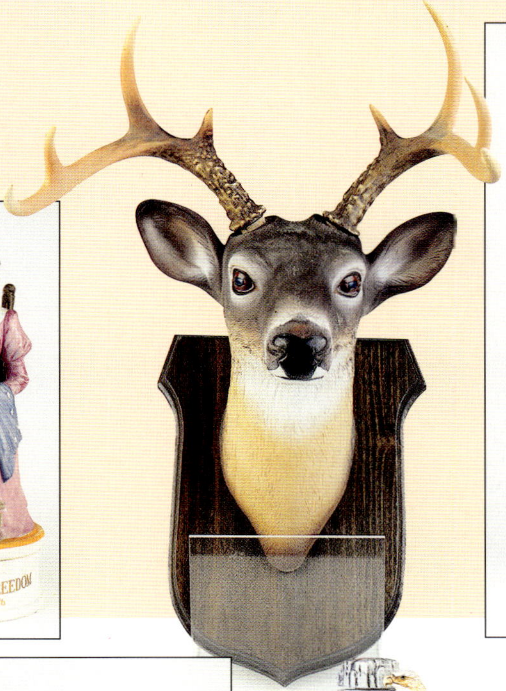

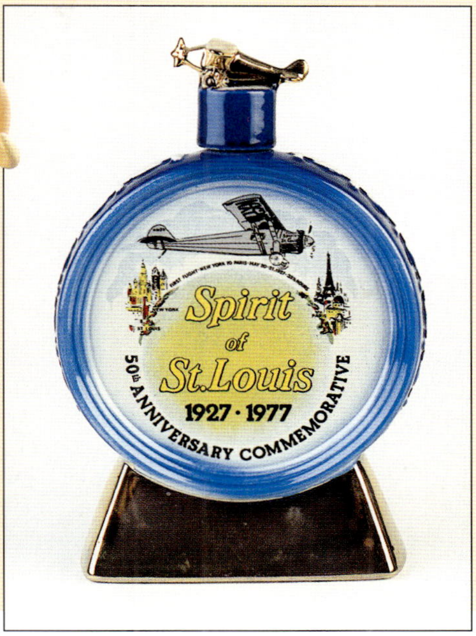

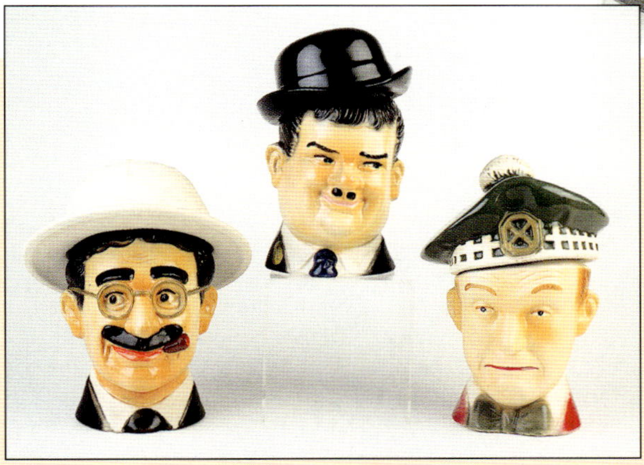

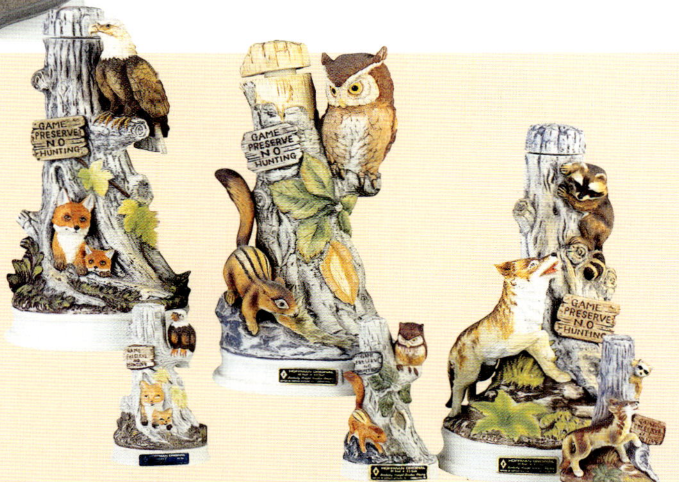

Melissa Cardona
and Ginny Parfitt

Schiffer Publishing Ltd

4880 Lower Valley Road, Atglen, PA 19310 USA

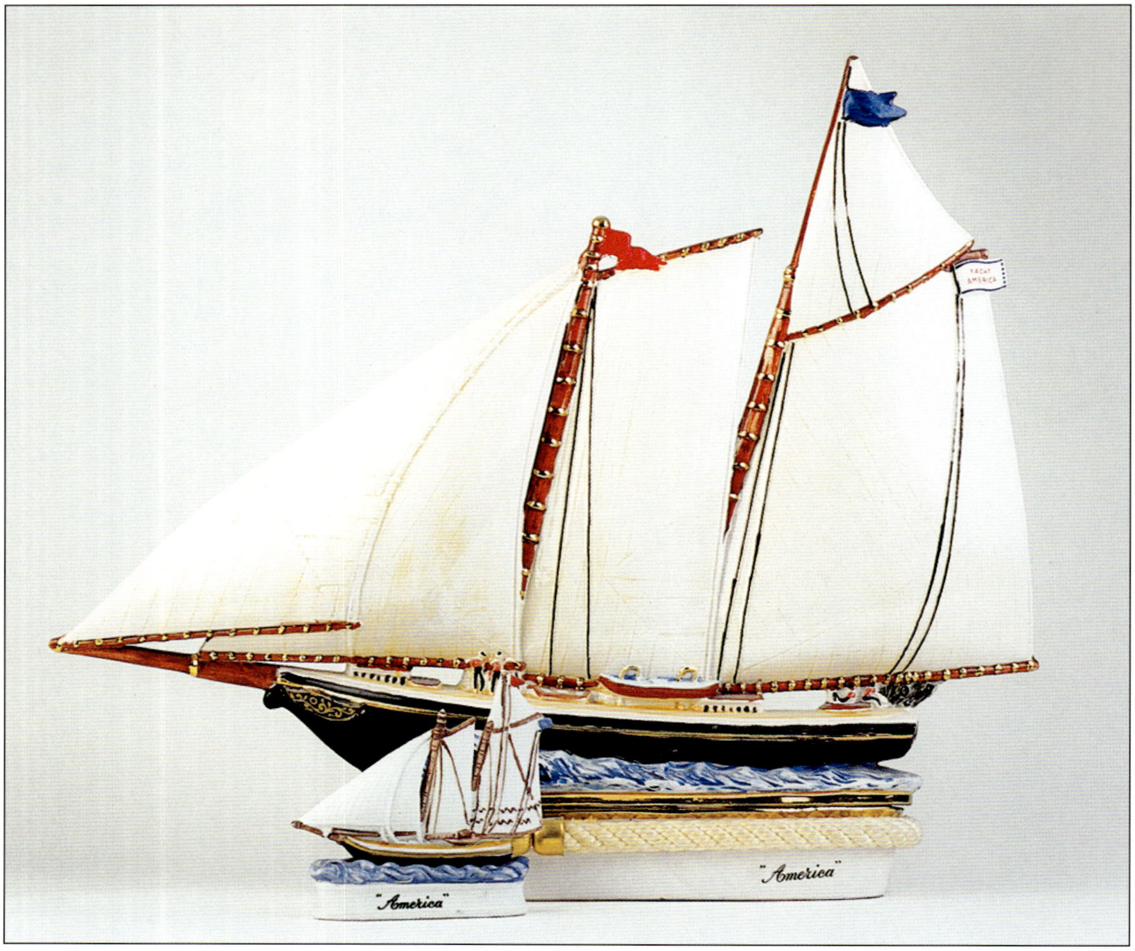

Library of Congress Card Number: 2004117728

Designed by Mark David Bowyer
Type set in Benguiat Bk BT / Humanist521 BT

ISBN: 0-7643-2169-2
Printed in China
1 2 3 4

Published by Schiffer Publishing Ltd.
4880 Lower Valley Road
Atglen, PA 19310
Phone: (610) 593-1777; Fax: (610) 593-2002
E-mail: Info@schifferbooks.com

For the largest selection of fine reference books on this and related subjects, please visit our web site at
www.schifferbooks.com
We are always looking for people to write books on new and related subjects. If you have an idea for a book please contact us at the above address.

This book may be purchased from the publisher.
Include $3.95 for shipping.
Please try your bookstore first.
You may write for a free catalog.

In Europe, Schiffer books are distributed by
Bushwood Books
6 Marksbury Ave.
Kew Gardens
Surrey TW9 4JF England
Phone: 44 (0) 20 8392-8585; Fax: 44 (0) 20 8392-9876
E-mail: info@bushwoodbooks.co.uk
Free postage in the U.K., Europe; air mail at cost.

Contents

Acknowledgments

This beautiful book could only have been produced with the help of the following individuals who are passionate and knowledgeable collectors: Bill and Dollie Bostic, whose collection we photographed for this book, have been most generous and welcoming hosts. The Bostics are active in local as well as national collectors organizations. Their amazing collection is on full display.

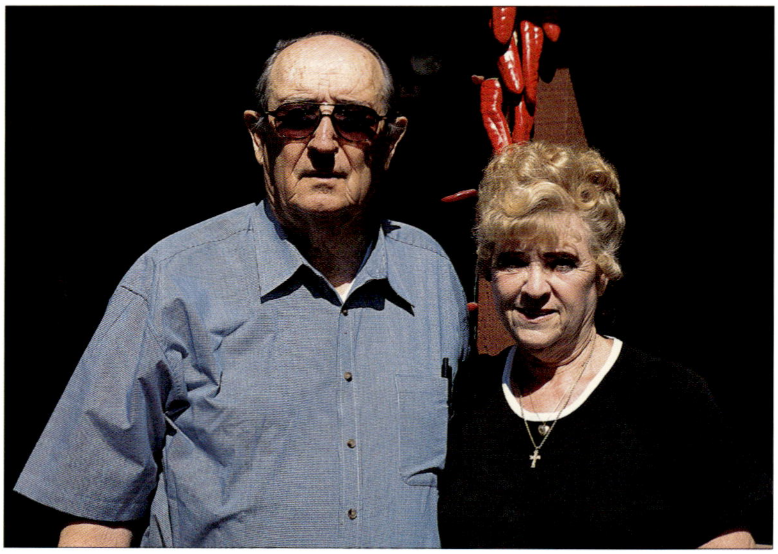

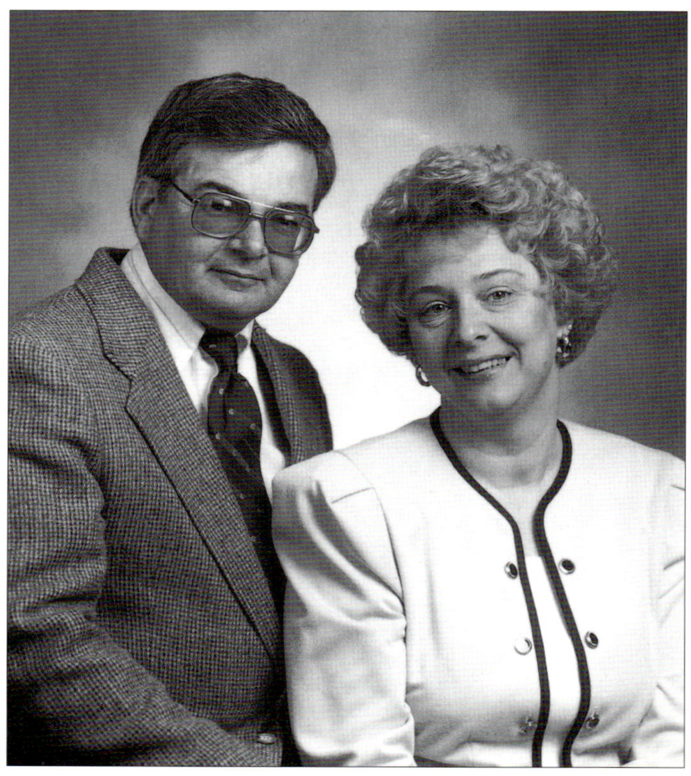

Art and Judy Turner offered a great deal of insight and assistance. The Turners have been bottle collectors and dealers for twenty-five years; their business, Homestead Collectables, is in Mill Hall, Pennsylvania. They are currently the Bottle Show Chairpersons for the International Association of Jim Beam Bottle and Specialties Clubs. They can be reached at:

Homestead Collectables
P.O. Box 173, Mill Hall, PA 17751
E-mail: jturner@kcnet.org
Website: www.homesteadcollectables.com

Introduction

Welcome to the wonderful world of collecting figural whiskey decanters. Collecting figural decanters is a rewarding hobby for novice as well as seasoned collectors.

Decanter production reached its height of popularity during the mid-1970s with over twenty companies producing figural decanters. Given the number of companies that produced decanters and the all-encompassing subject matter available, there is potential to amass a collection of thousands and thousands of bottles.

Most collectors, however, choose an area of interest and limit their collections to just those decanters. Some collectors will collect just their company of interest. Others will choose to collect wildlife, sports figures, transportation, or entertainers. There is an opportunity to amass a wonderful collection, collecting just "mini" size whiskey decanters. Mini's duplicate full size decanters, but hold only two ounces. This is a great collectible for someone with limited display space.

While the majority of figural decanters were produced in "fifth" size, a gallon figural decanter is a real find. A "fifth," of course, is one-fifth of a gallon or 4/5 quart. The United States began measuring distilled spirits in metric measurements in 1978; a "fifth" became 750ml and the "mini" became 50ml.

How Collectors Collect

Much has been written within the decanter collecting community about the wisdom of emptying the decanters in your collection. It is now widely accepted that most collectors and dealers buy, sell, and collect only empty decanters. The most compelling reasons for this are as follows:

- Unless you have a liquor license, it is illegal to sell and ship decanters that contain alcohol. There are substantial fines levied for shipping alcohol across state lines.
- In order to maintain your ceramic and porcelain decanters in top condition, it is necessary that they be empty. Ceramic and porcelain containers are not good vessels for storing liquids. Over time, small cracks appear on the glaze, through which the liquids can leak. A decanter in this less-than-pristine condition has only a small fraction of the value of a decanter in mint condition.
- If your decanter has a cork, it will, over time, dry out, allowing the contents of the decanter to first spoil, then evaporate. Decanters with dry, cracked, or broken corks are of less value than those with mint condition corks.
- You potentially risk higher home-owners insurance rates if you display or store large quantities of full liquor decanters.
- There is a substantial difference between the weight of full and empty decanters. The added weight of displaying and storing full decanters may cause display shelving to collapse, potentially causing much monetary damage to your collection.

The value of a decanter is not lessened because it has a broken or missing tax stamp. It is still considered to be in mint condition as long as all other labels and parts are in mint, unbroken condition.

Pricing Considerations

The decanters in this book are all given current market values. These values come from many sources, including dealer input, prices from recent auctions, and research, both from other publications as well as the Internet. Keep in mind that values can be regional as well as cyclical. The values in this book reflect items that are in new condition. They have been opened and emptied of their contents. Items in any other condition will have considerably less value.

Ski Country

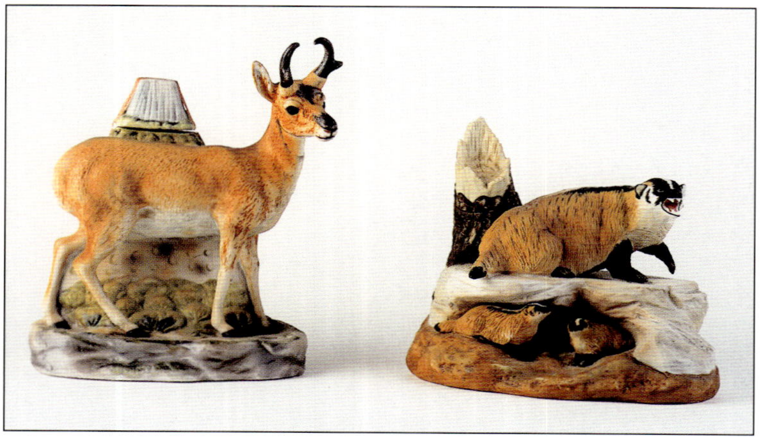

Antelope, Wyoming, 1979, $55-70. Badger, 1980, $50-59.

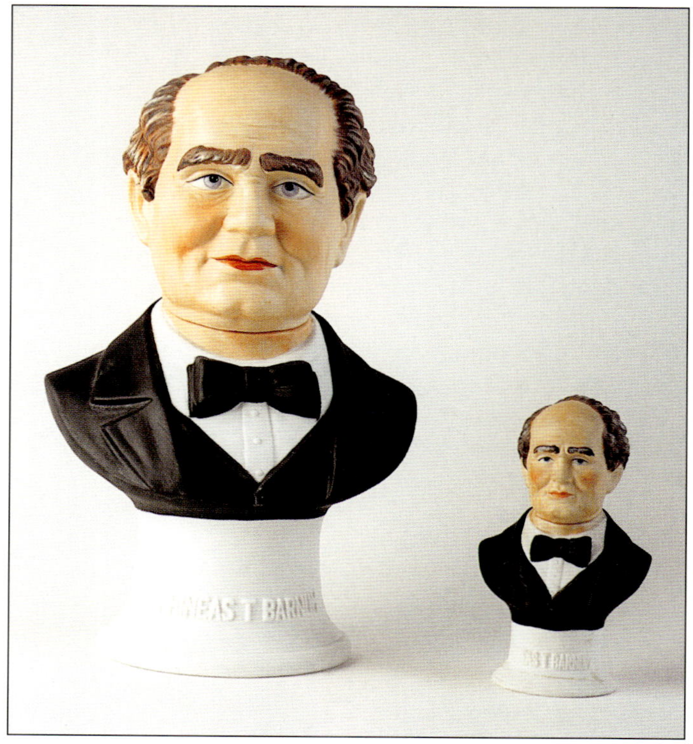

PT Barnum, 1976, fifth $53-58, mini $31-36.

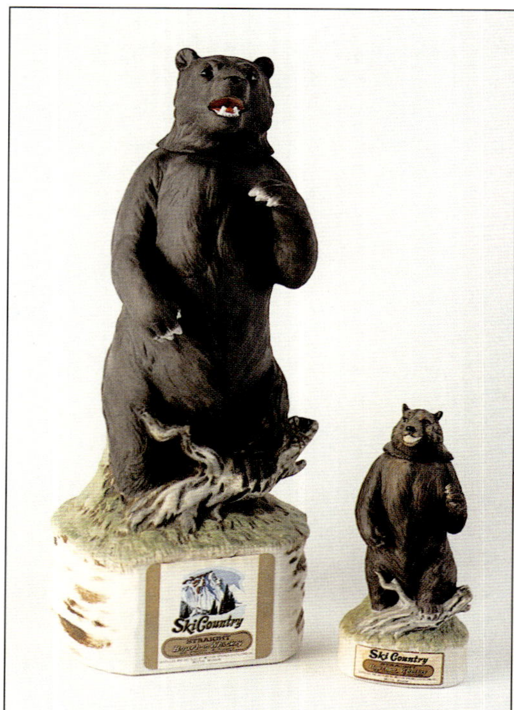

Brown Bear, 1974, fifth $39-44, mini (prototype) $85-95.

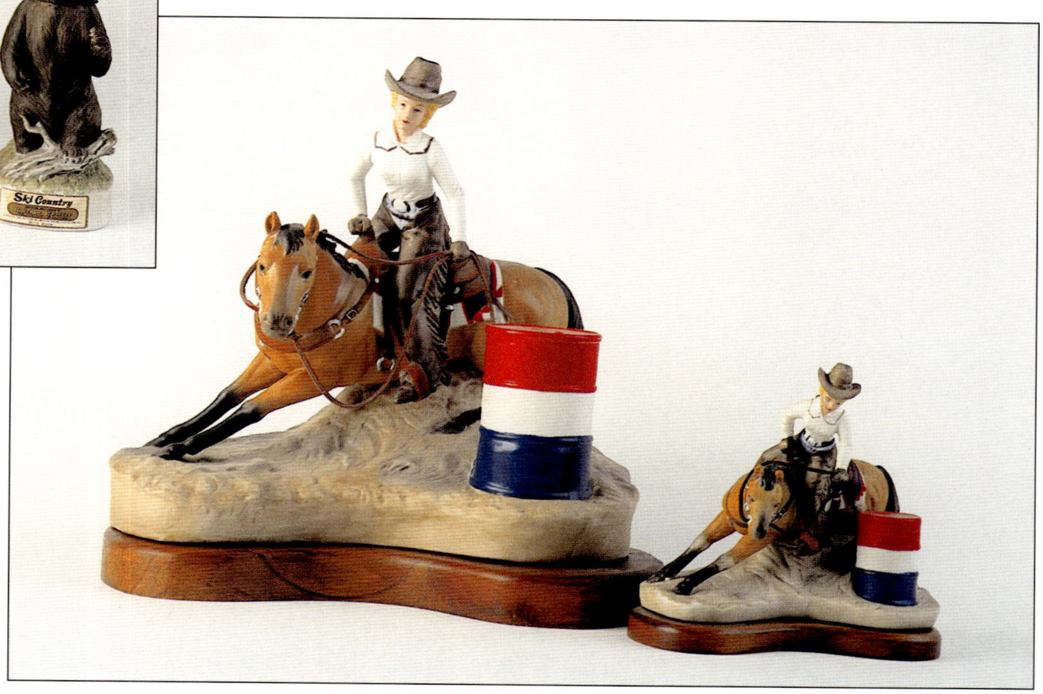

Cowgirl Barrel Racer, 1983, fifth $87-92, mini $44-46.

Bird Series

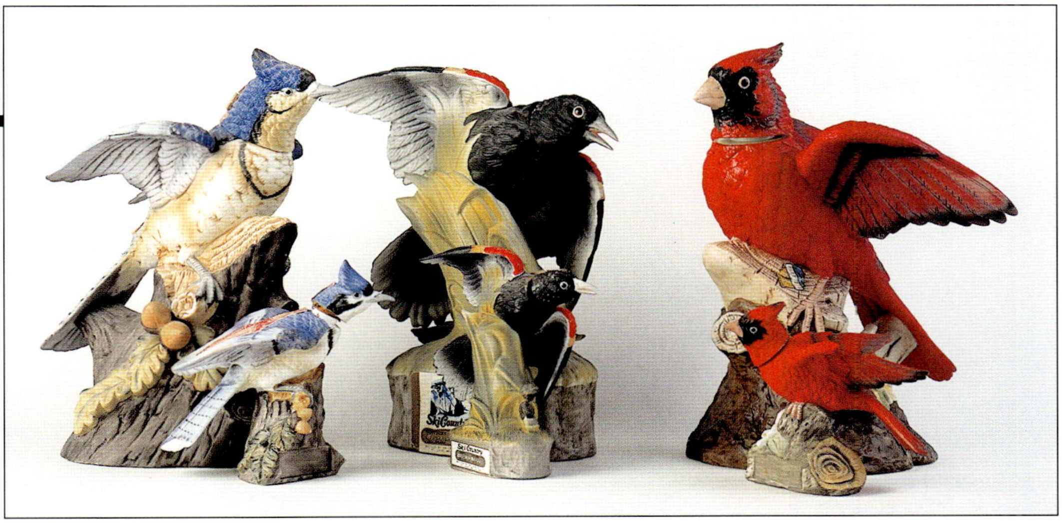

Blue Jay, fifth $89-94, mini $64-69. Black Bird Red Winged, 1977, $40-45. Cardinal, 1979, fifth $80-85, mini $58-63.

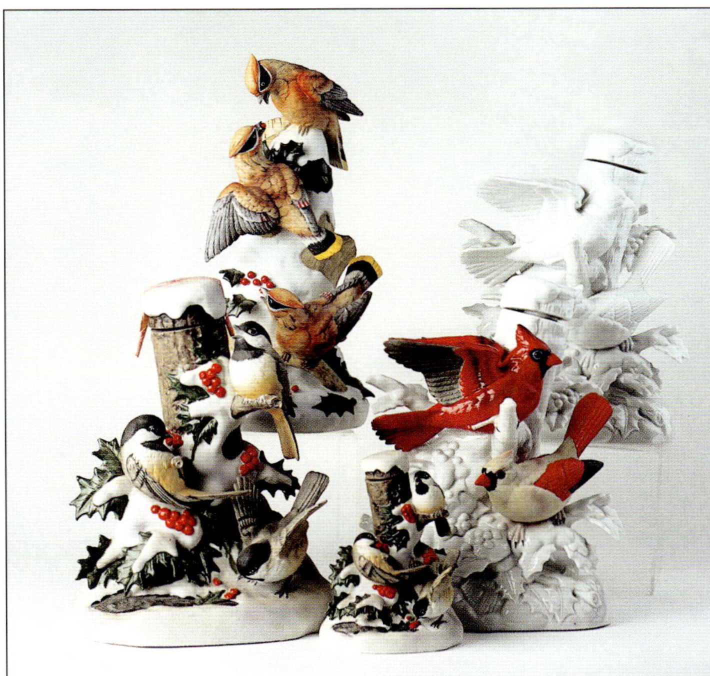

Chickadee (Christmas), 1981, fifth $75-81, mini $35-41. Cardinal (colored), 1991, $90-98. Cardinal (white), 1991, $90-98.

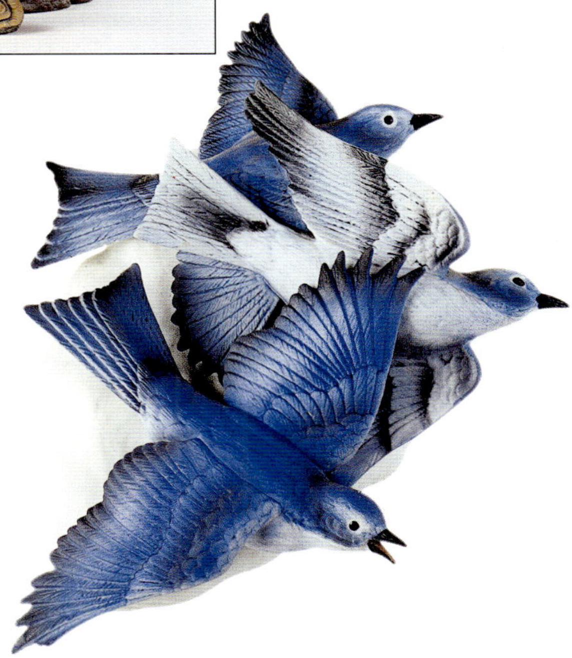

Bluebird wall plaque, 1984, $100-109.

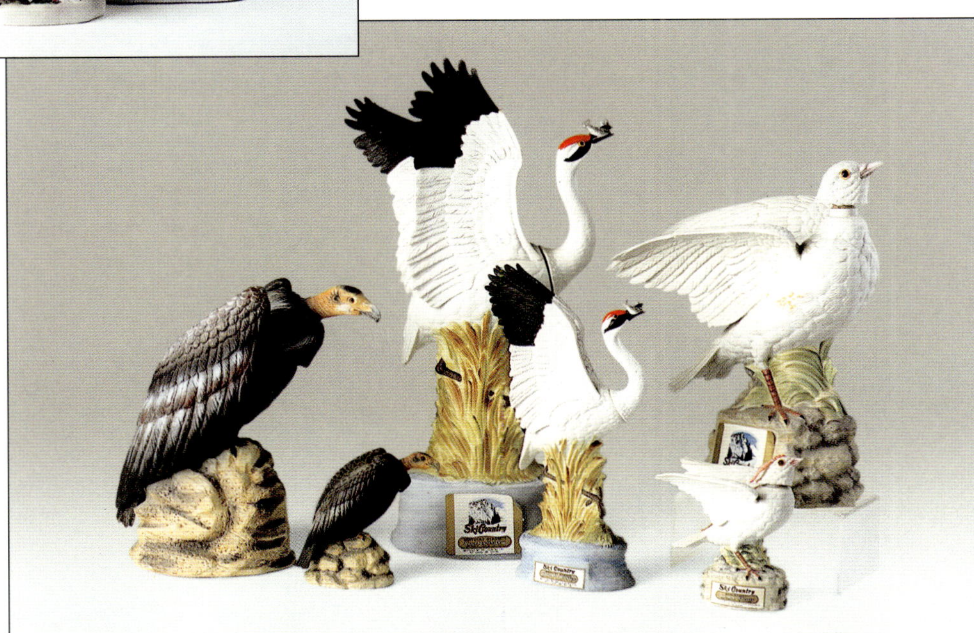

California Condor, 1973, fifth $55-63, mini $35-40. Whooping Crane, 1983, fifth $55-63, mini $50-55. Peace Dove, 1973, fifth $65-70, mini $30-38.

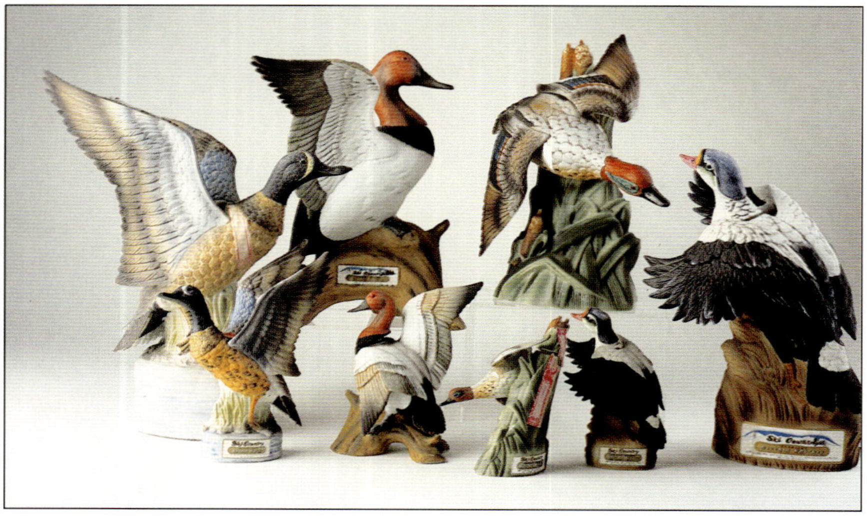

Blue Winged Teal, 1974, fifth $95-102, mini $250-259. Canvasback (Ducks Unlimited), 1981, fifth $65-70, mini $30-35. Green Winged Teal (Ducks Unlimited), 1983, fifth $195-200, mini $50-59. King Eider, 1977, fifth $65-70, mini $35-40.

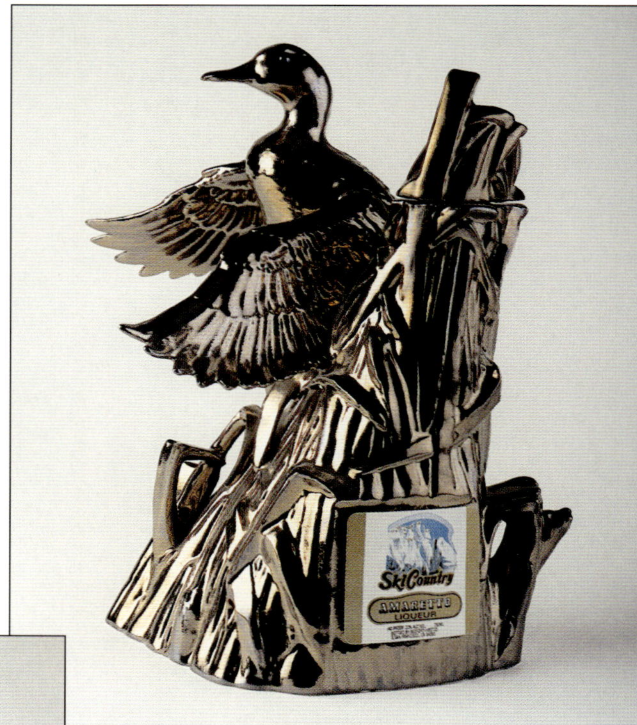

Blue Winged Teal, special limited edition bronze, 1985, fifth $125-130.

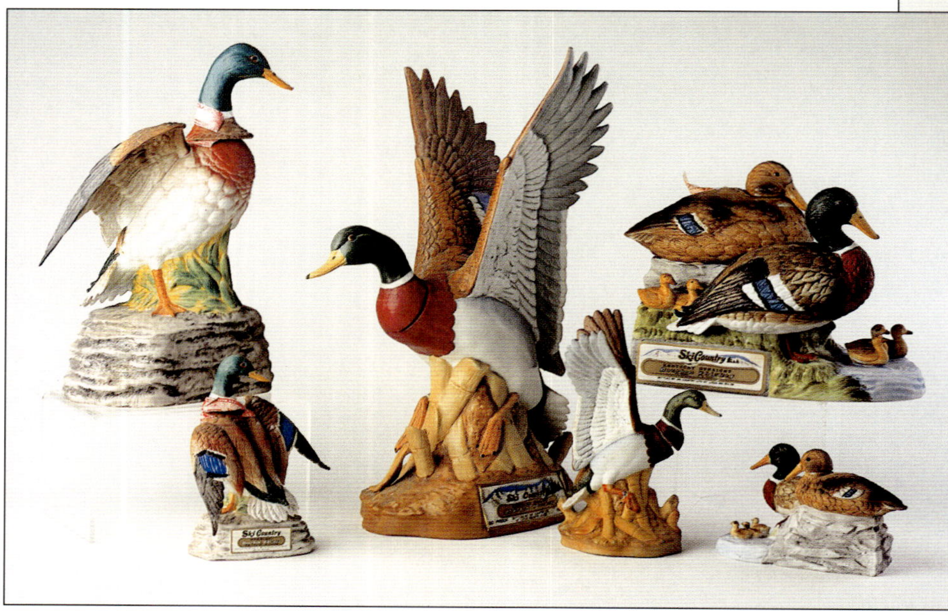

Mallard, 1973, fifth $65-70, mini $45-50. Mallard (Ducks Unlimited) 1980, fifth $81-86, mini $48-53. Mallard family, 1977, fifth $82-87, mini $53-58.

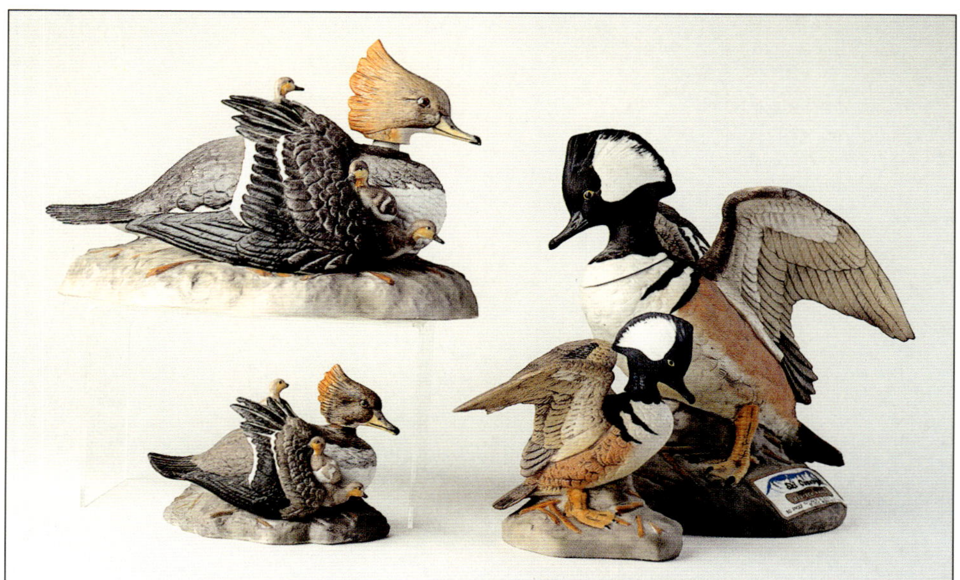

Merganzer Female, 1981, fifth $63-68, mini $30-35. Merganzer male, 1983, fifth $87-92, mini $25-30.

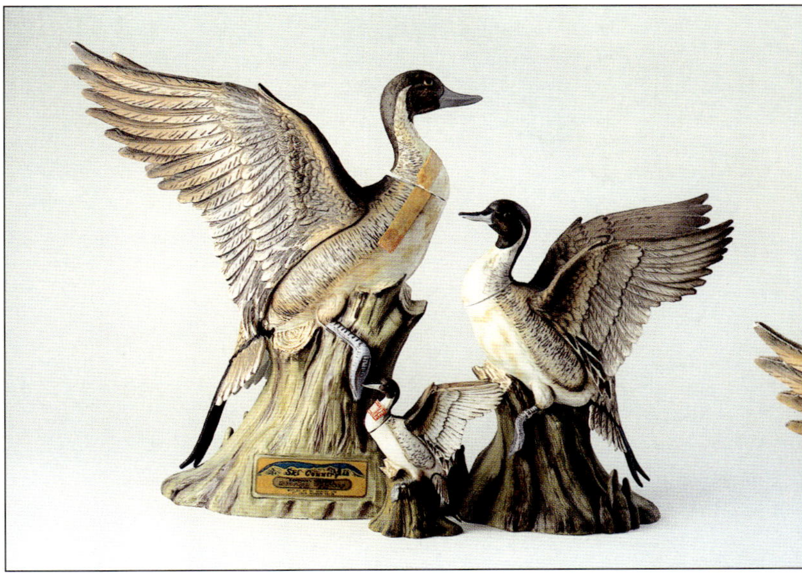

Pintail (Ducks Unlimited), 1979, fifth $115-120, mini $35-40.

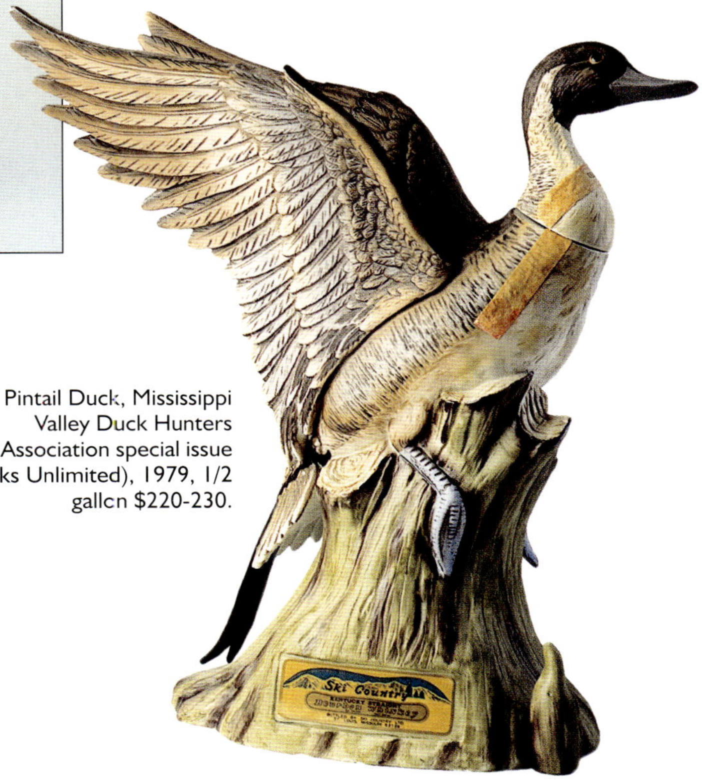

Pintail Duck, Mississippi Valley Duck Hunters Association special issue (Ducks Unlimited), 1979, 1/2 gallon $220-230.

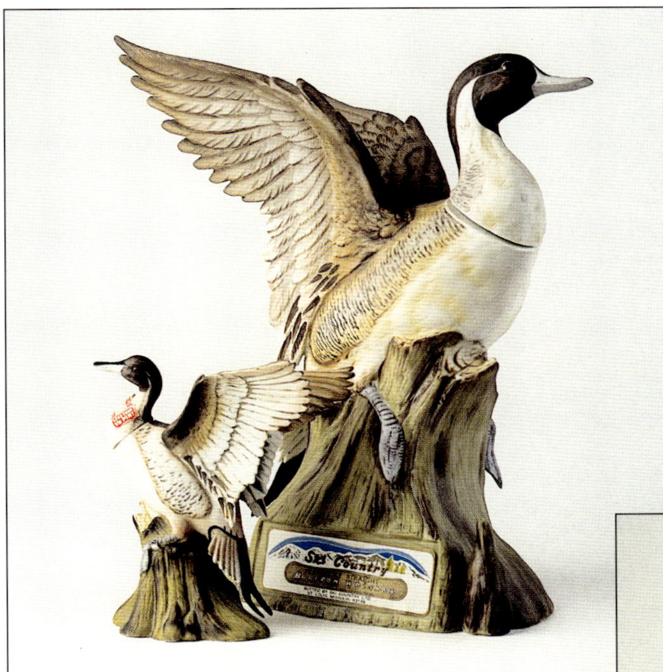

Pintail Duck, Mississippi Valley Duck Hunters Association special issue (Ducks Unlimited), fifth $115-120, mini $35-40.

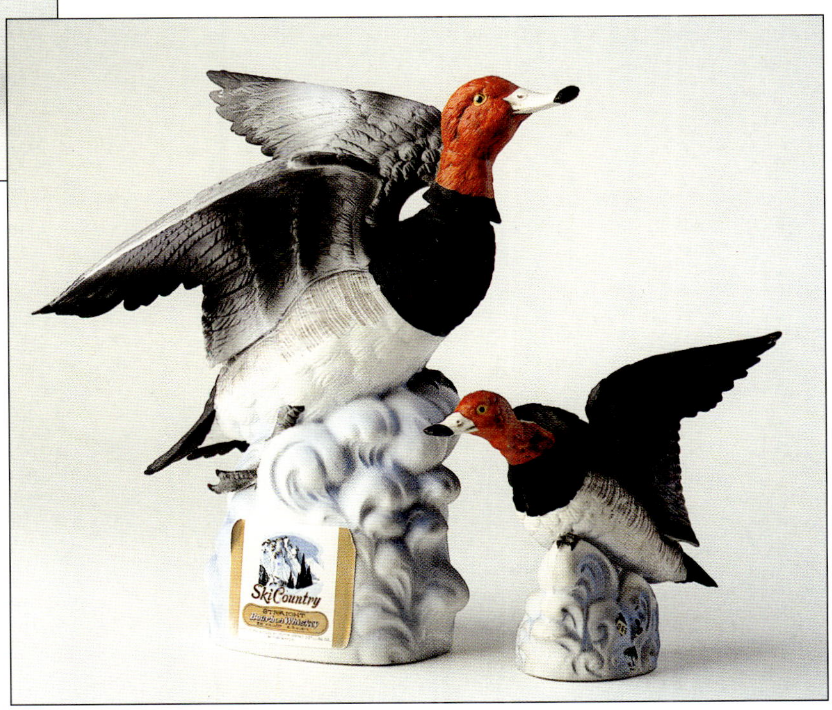

Red Headed Duck, 1974, fifth $75-83, mini $58-63.

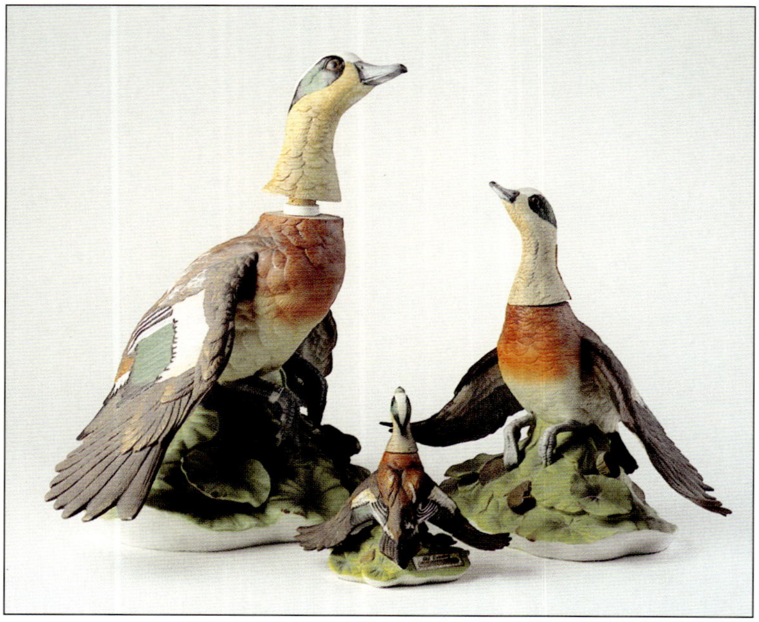

Widgeon (Ducks Unlimited), 1979, 1.75 liter $220-230, fifth $65-70, mini $28-33.

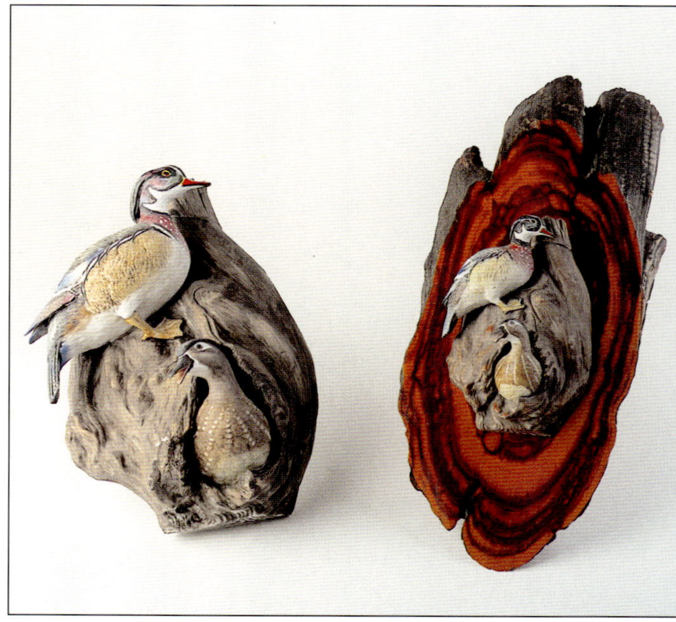

Wood Duck wall plaque, 1980, fifth $390-395, mini $87-92.

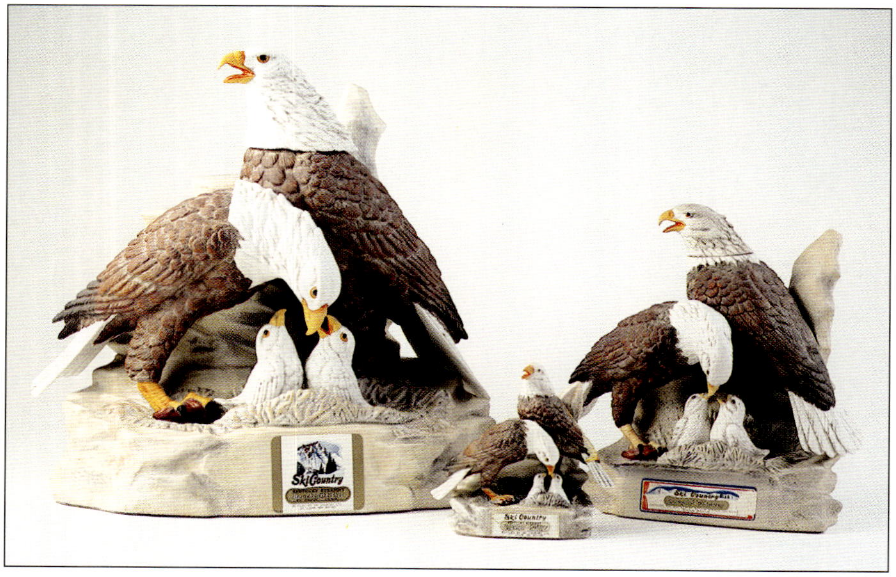

Eagle – The Birth of Freedom, 1976, gallon $2150-2179, fifth $115-120, mini $80-85.

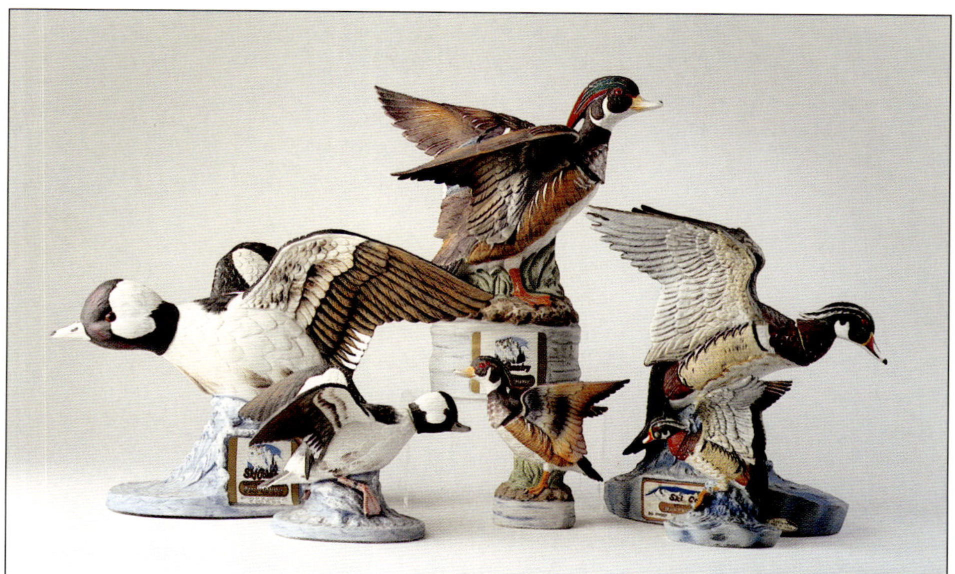

Buffalo Duck, limited edition, 1984, fifth $70-75, mini $30-35. Wood Duck, 1974, fifth $110-115, mini $50-55. Wood Duck (Ducks Unlimited), fifth $185-190, mini $150-155.

Eagle on Drum, 1976, fifth $130-138, mini $65-71. Eagle and Eaglet, 1980, fifth $135-140, mini $80-85. Eagle – Harpy, 1973, fifth $139-144, mini $105-110.

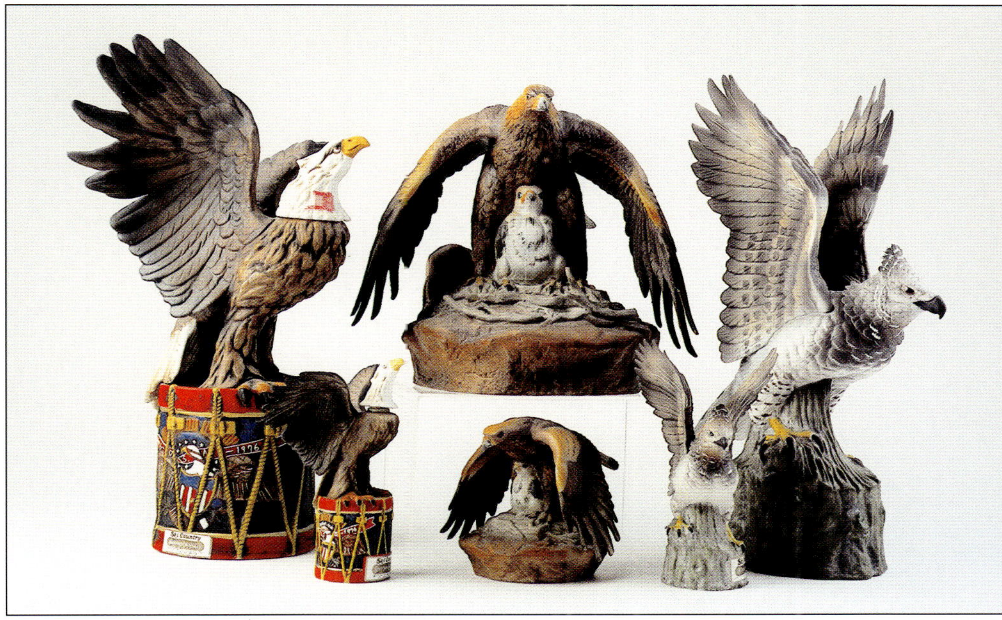

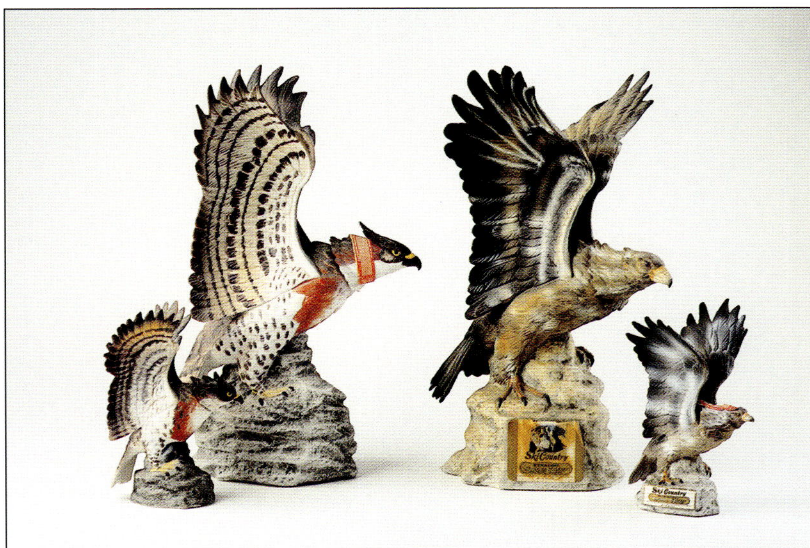

Eagle Hawk – ornate, 1974, fifth $160-169, mini $84-89. Eagle – Mountain, 1973, fifth $190-195, mini $155-162.

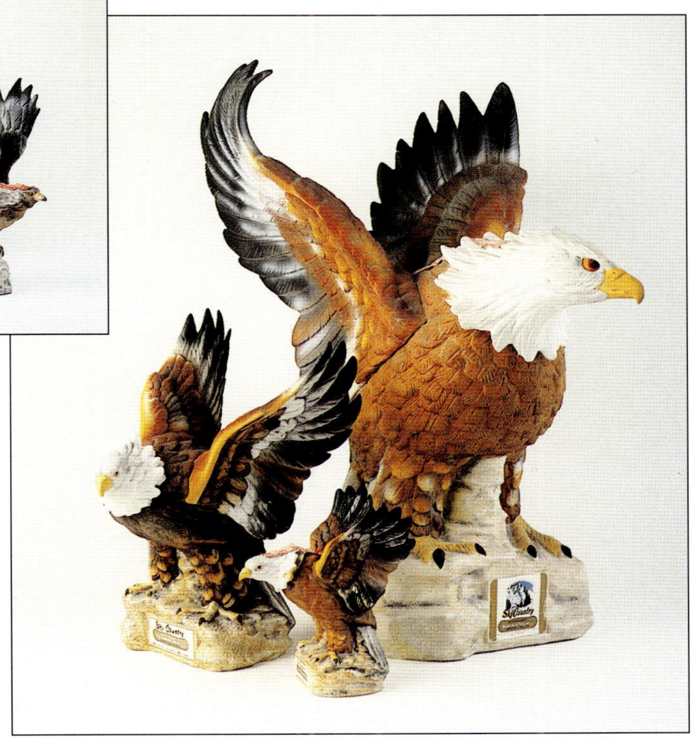

Eagle – majestic, 1972, gallon $1,850, fifth $355-362, mini $180-187.

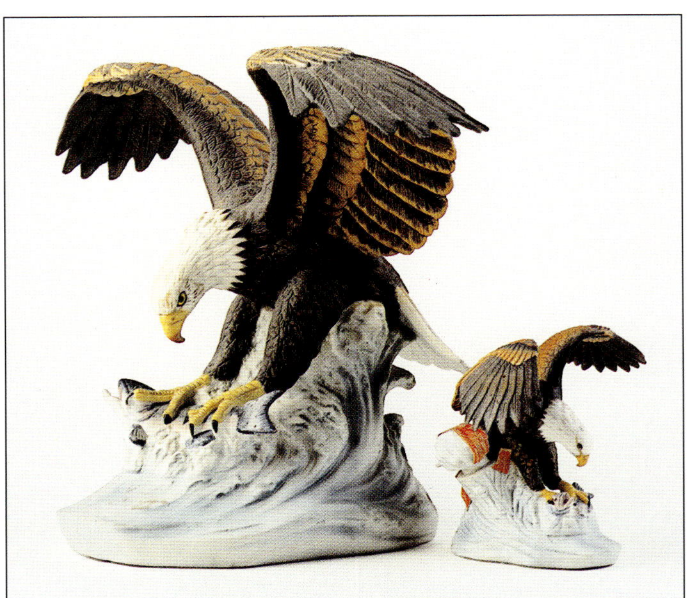

Eagle on the Water – 1981, fifth $155-160, mini $55-60.

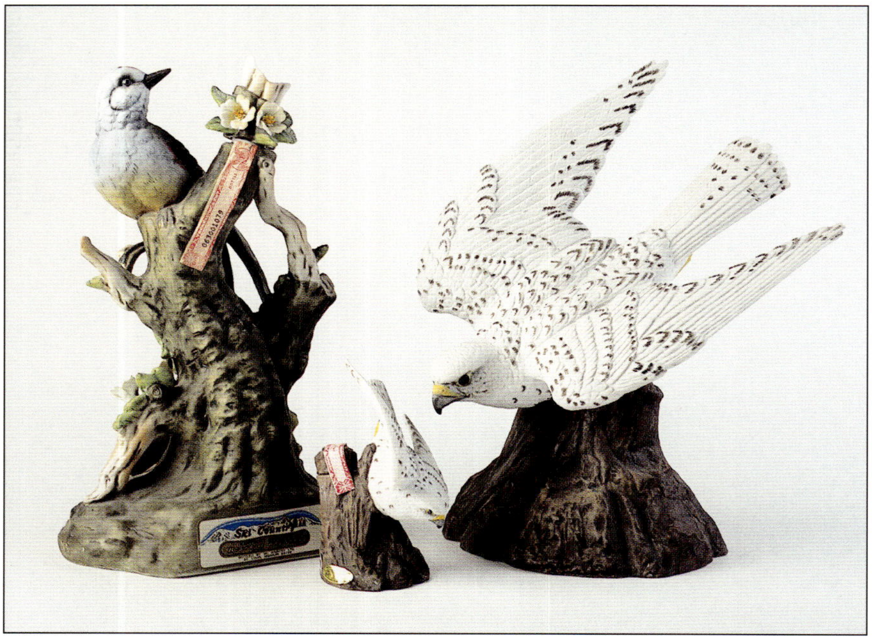

Scissor Tail Flycatcher, 1980, fifth $145-153. Falcon – Gyr, 1983, fifth $80-89, mini $30-36.

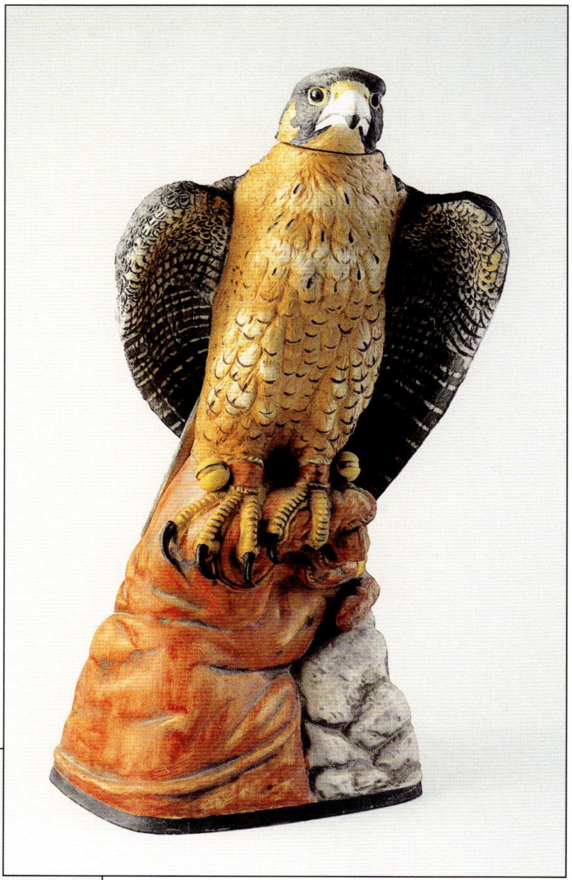

Peregrine Falcon, 1980, gallon $345-352, fifth (not shown) $95-100, mini (not shown) $50-55.

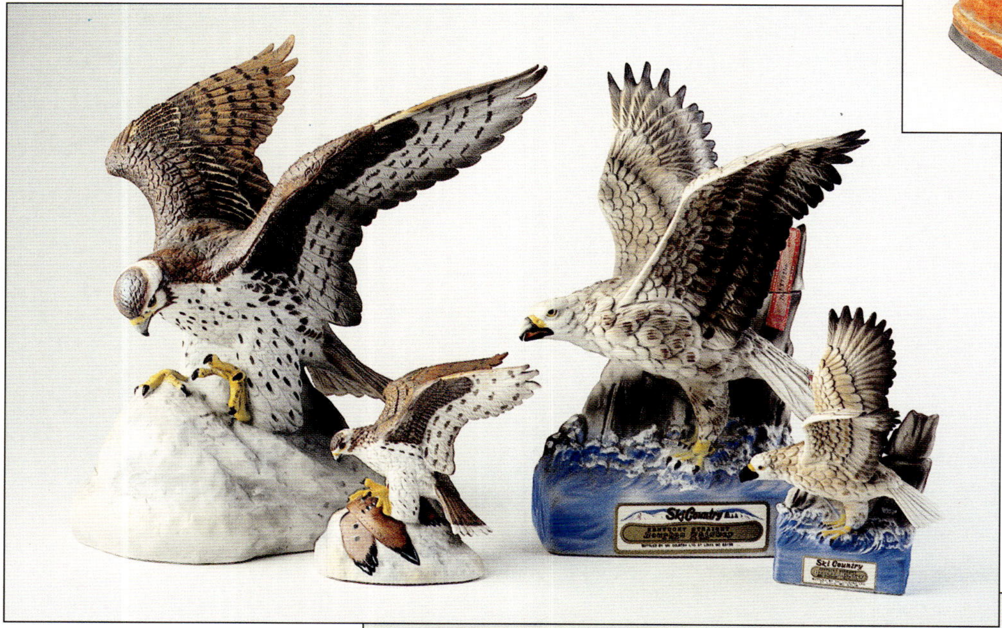

Prairie Falcon, 1980, fifth $115-120, mini $55-60. White Falcon, fifth $95-100, mini $50-55.

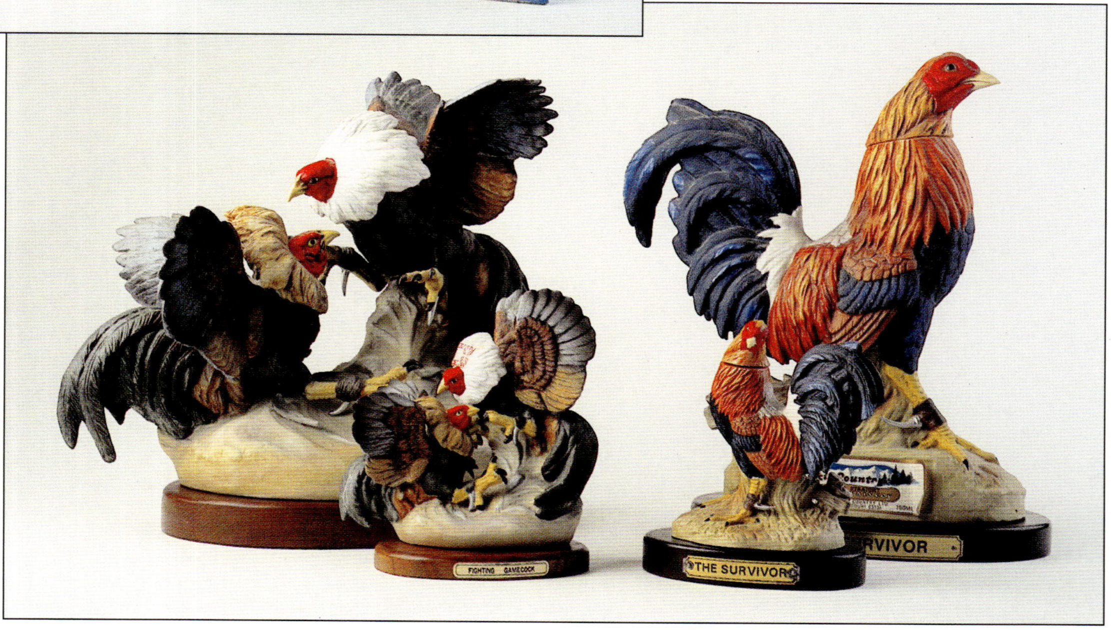

Gamecock – fighting, 1980, fifth $170-177, mini $45-52. Gamecock – survivor, 1984, fifth $80-85, mini $30-35.

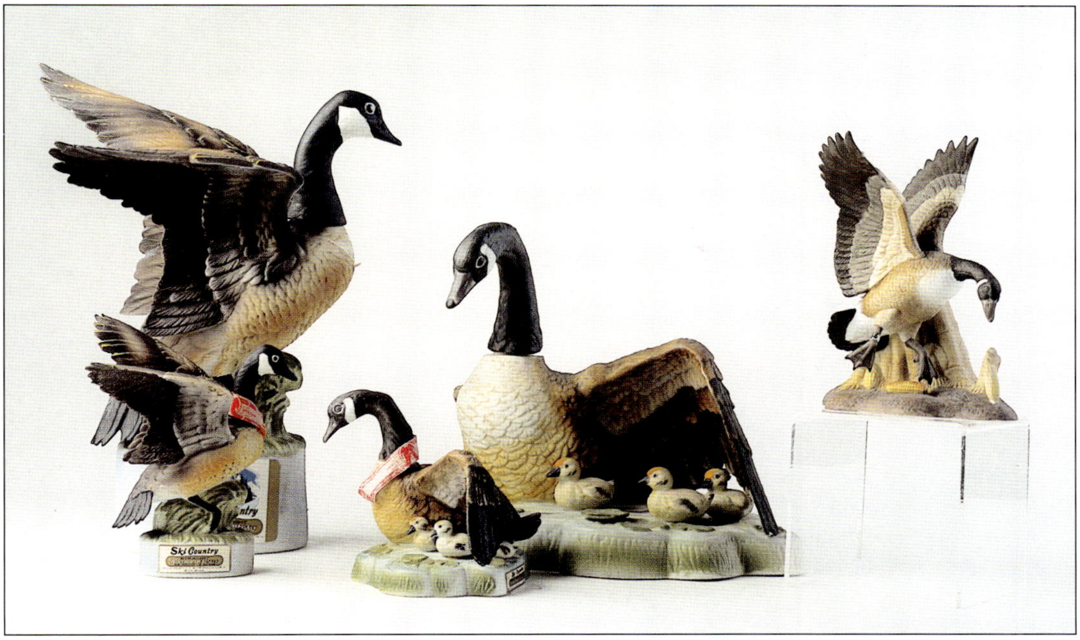

Canadian Goose, 1973, fifth $120-125, mini $40-47. Canadian Goose family, 1980, fifth $70-75, mini $30-35. Canadian Goose (Ducks Unlimited special edition), 1988, mini $95-100.

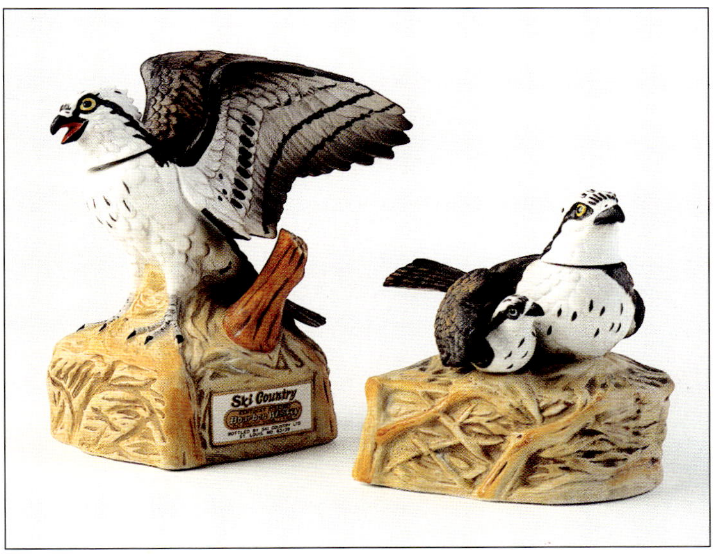

Osprey – male and female set, mini $50-55.

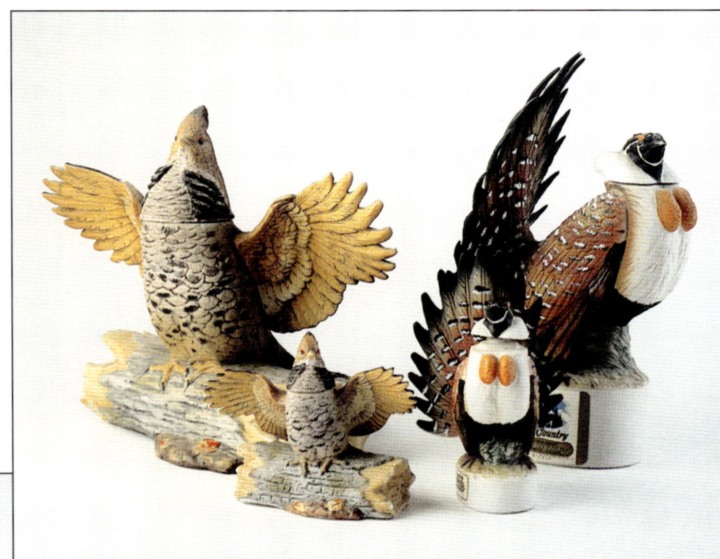

Ruffled Grouse, 1981, fifth $65-70, mini $25-32. Sage Grouse, 1974, fifth $85-90, mini $40-48.

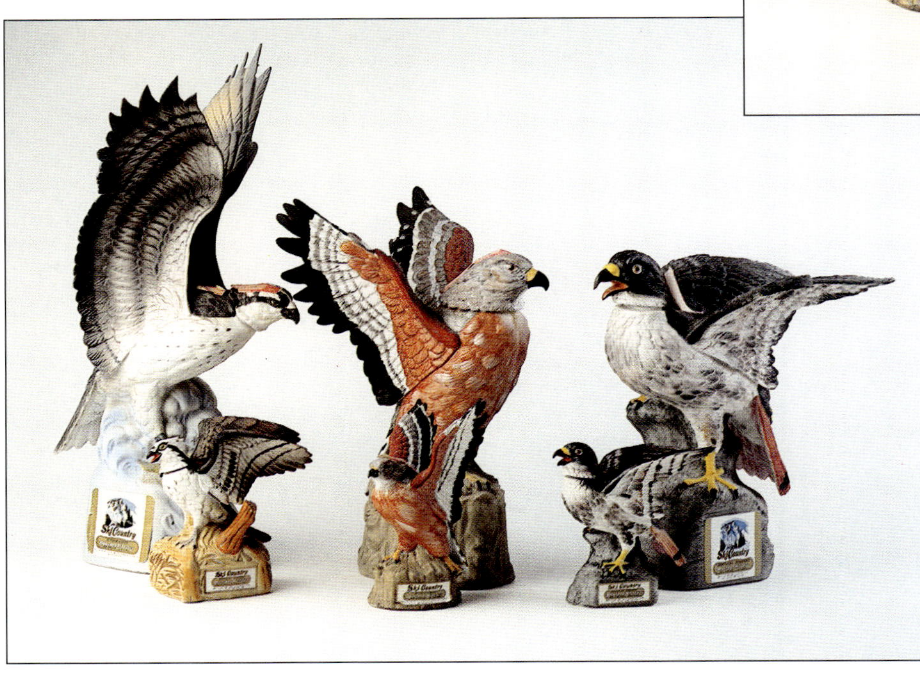

Hawk – Osprey, 1976, fifth $200-205, mini $190-195. Red Shoulder Hawk, 1972, fifth $70-76, mini $40-46. Red Tail Hawk, 1977, fifth $70-76, mini $45-52.

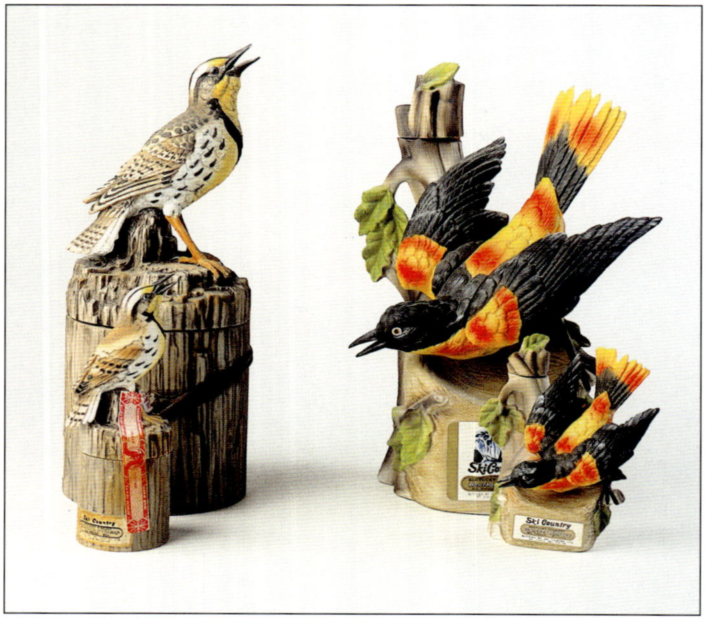

Meadowlark, 1980, fifth $55-60, mini $30-35. Baltimore Oriole, 1975, fifth $65-70, mini $28-33.

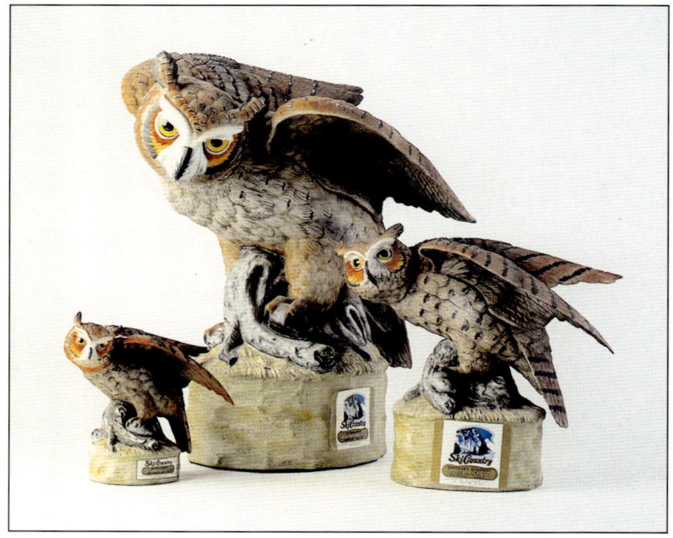

Horned Owl, 1974, gallon $1,600-1,625, fifth $90-95, mini $100-105.

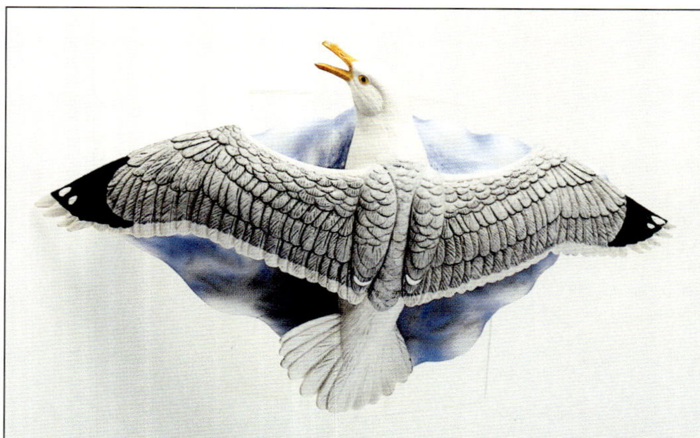

Seagull plaque, 1985 limited edition, $60-65.

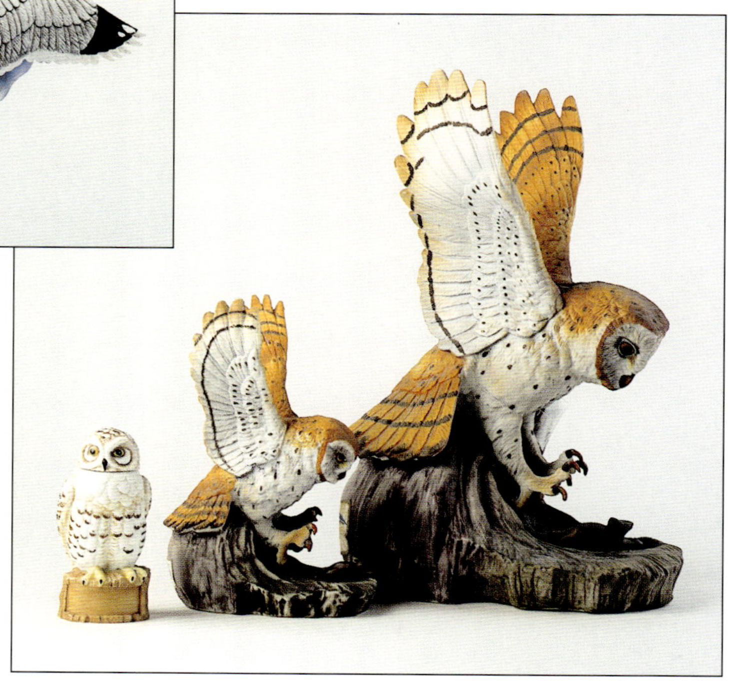

Baby Snow Owl, 1976, mini $60-70. Barn Owl "Near Miss," 1979, fifth $80-85, mini $30-35.

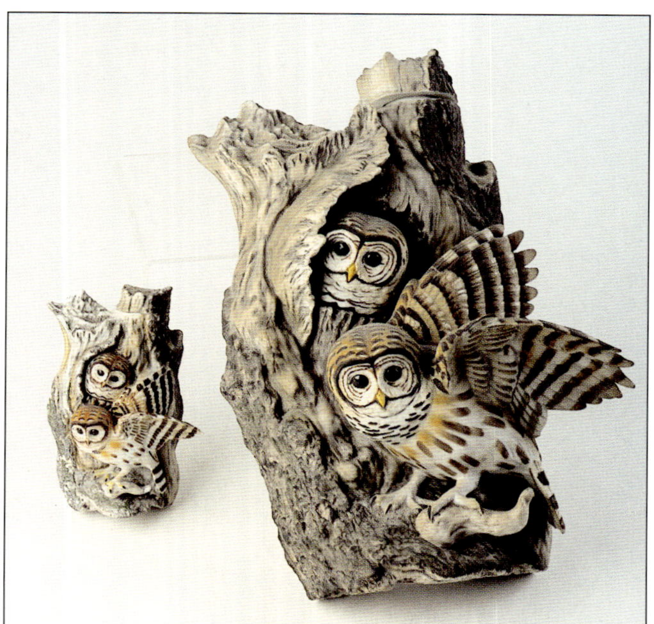

Barred Owl wall plaque, 1981, fifth $145-155, mini $90-95.

Partridge – Chucker, 1979, fifth $55-62, mini $25-30. Peacock, 1972, fifth $109-114, mini $65-70. Brown Pelican, 1976, fifth $58-63, mini $30-35. Penguin Family, 1978, fifth $65-71, mini $32-37.

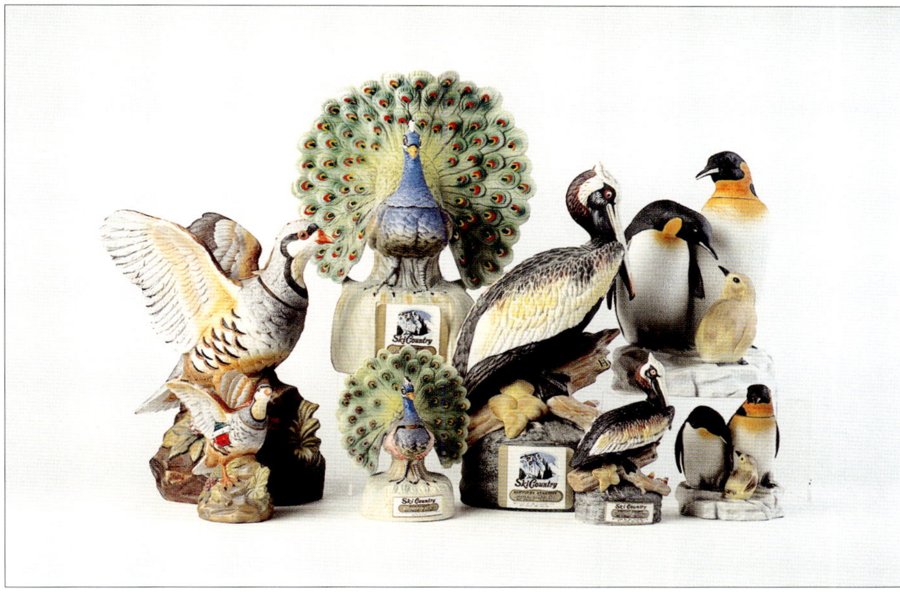

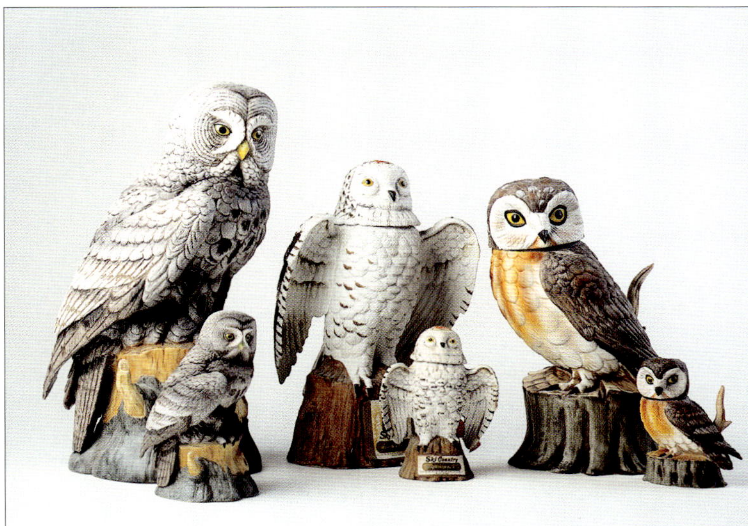

Great Gray Owl, 1985 limited edition, fifth $84-89, mini $53-58. Northern Snowy Owl, 1972, fifth $118-123, mini $94-99. Saw Whet Owl, 1977, fifth $64-69, mini $27-33.

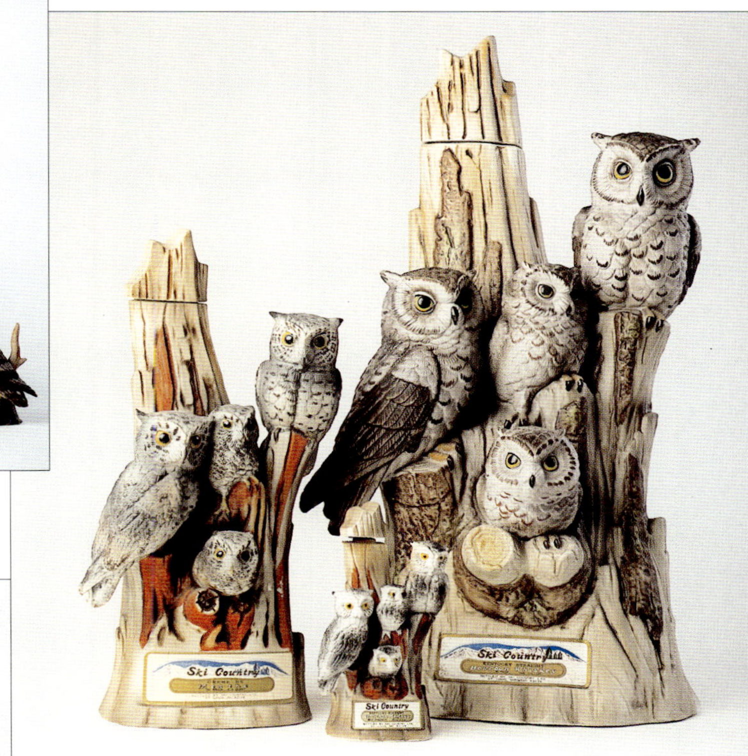

Screech Owl family, 1977, gallon $375-395 fifth, $120-125, mini $85-90.

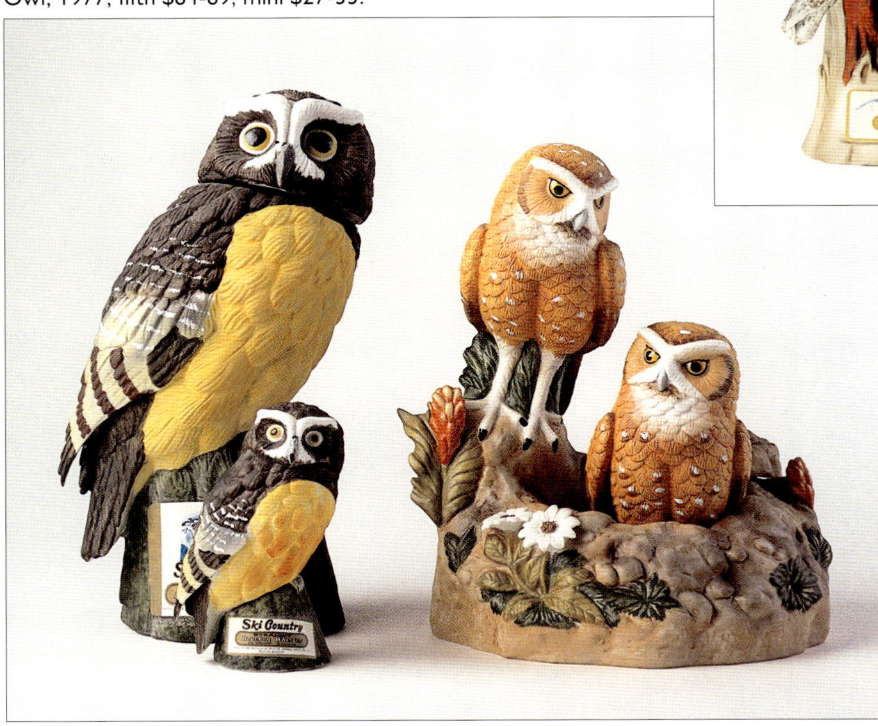

Spectacled Owl, 1975, fifth $100-108, mini $95-100. Burrowing Owl, 1986, limited edition, fifth $55-60, mini $40-45.

Golden Pheasant, 1984, fifth $60-65, mini (not shown) $35-40. Pheasant, 1977 limited edition, mini $65-70. Ring-Neck Pheasant in Corn, 1983, fifth $78-83, mini $47-52. Pheasants Fighting, 1977, fifth $108-113, mini $60-65.

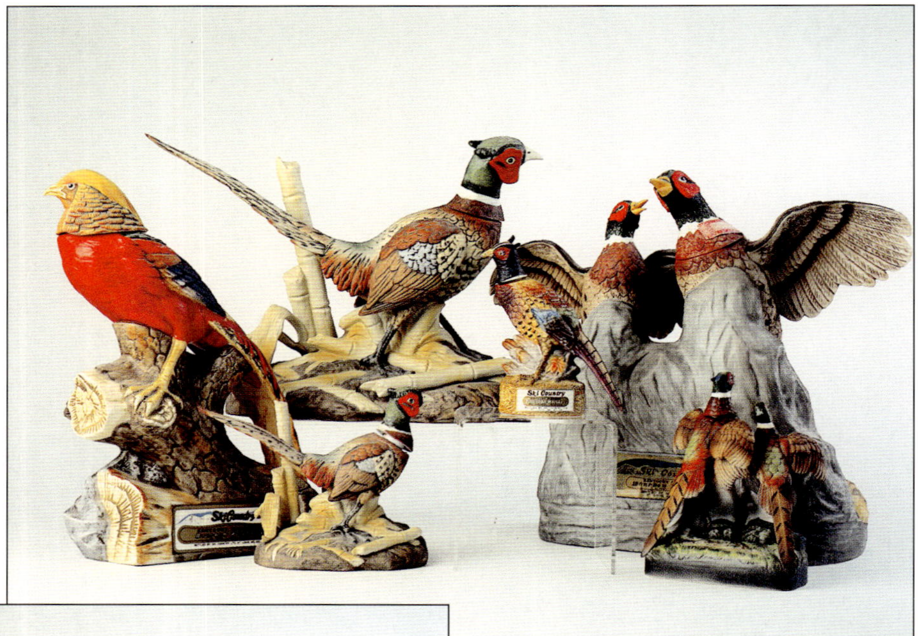

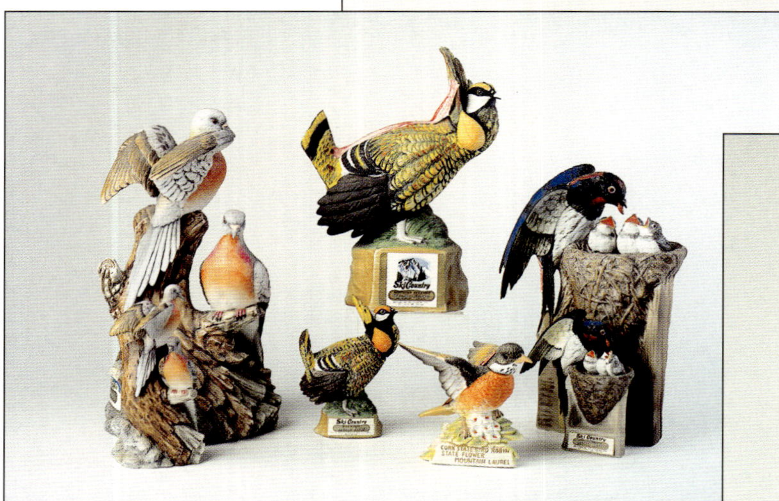

Passenger Pigeons, 1982, fifth $130-137, mini $60-67. Prairie Chicken, 1976, fifth $65-72, mini $45-53. Robin, 1975, mini $70-75. Barn Swallow, 1977, fifth $50-58, mini $40-46.

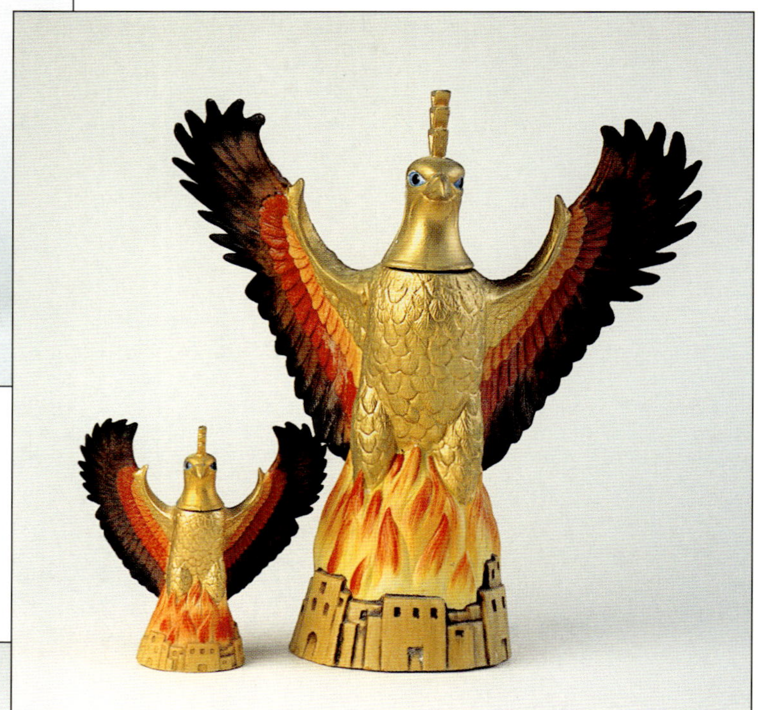

Phoenix, 1981, fifth $65-70, mini $30-35.

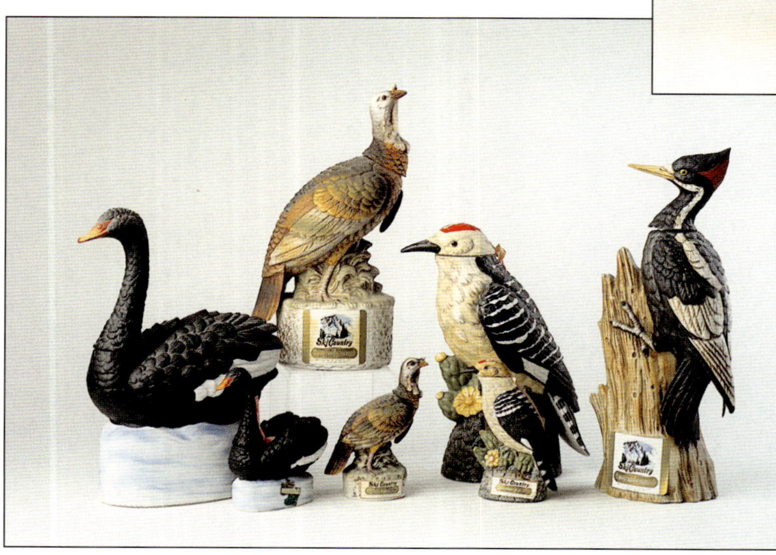

Black Australian Swan, 1974, fifth $54-59, mini $60-67. Wild Turkey, 1976, fifth $130-138, mini $139-144. Gila Woodpecker, 1972, fifth $74-79, mini $35-40. Ivory Billed Woodpecker, 1974 limited edition, fifth $49-54, mini (not shown) $40-46.

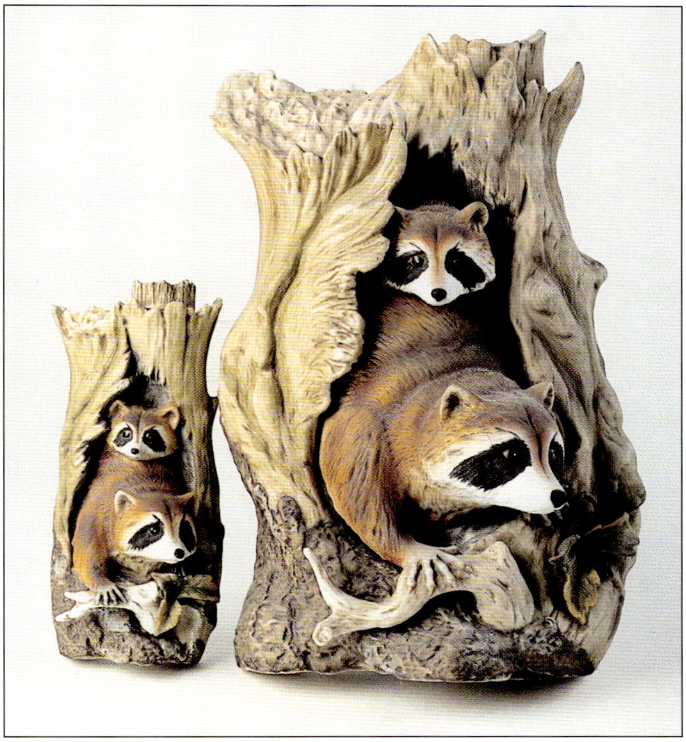

Raccoon plaque, 1981 limited edition, fifth $94-99, mini $89-94.

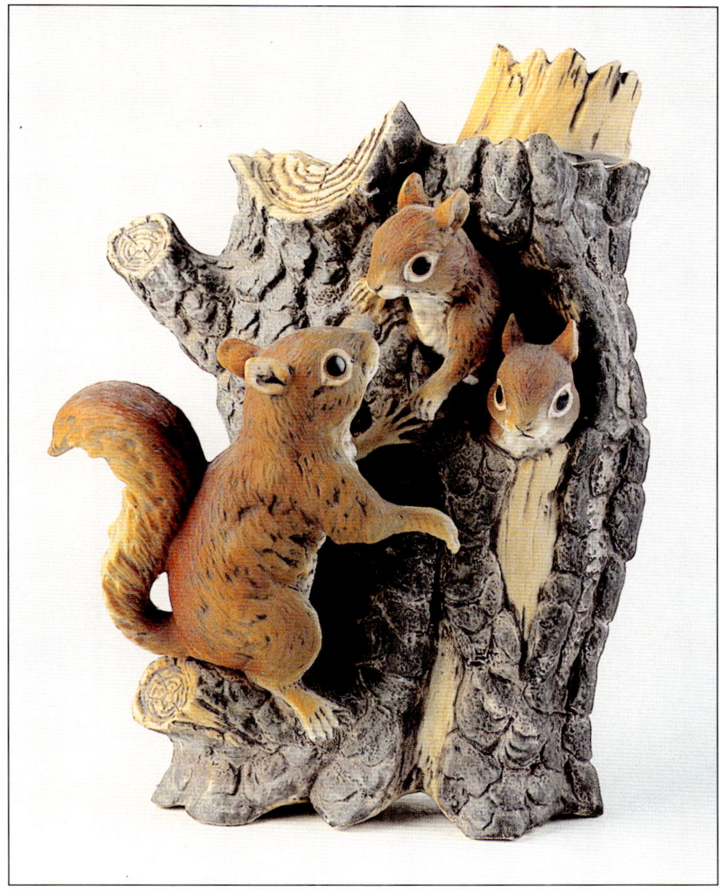

Squirrel plaque, 1983, fifth $179-184.

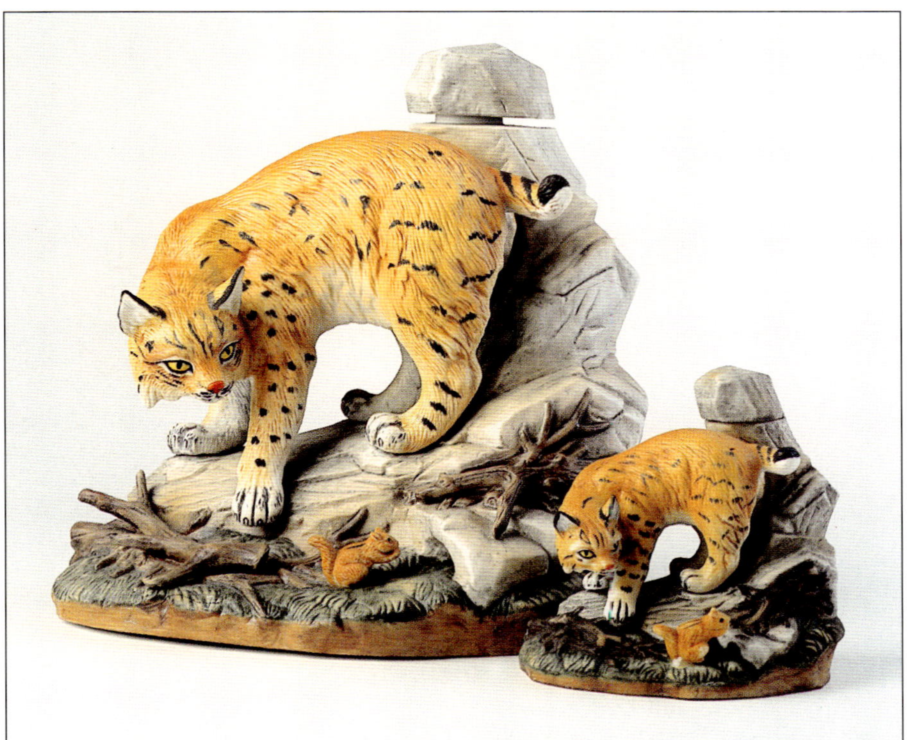

Bobcat and Chipmunk, 1980, fifth $70-75, mini $30-37.

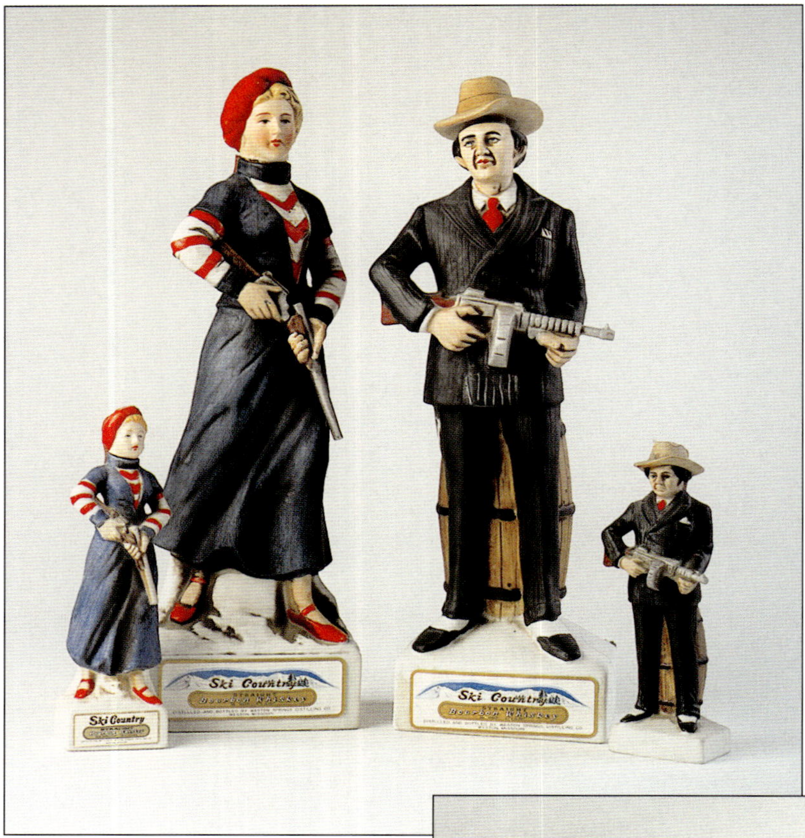

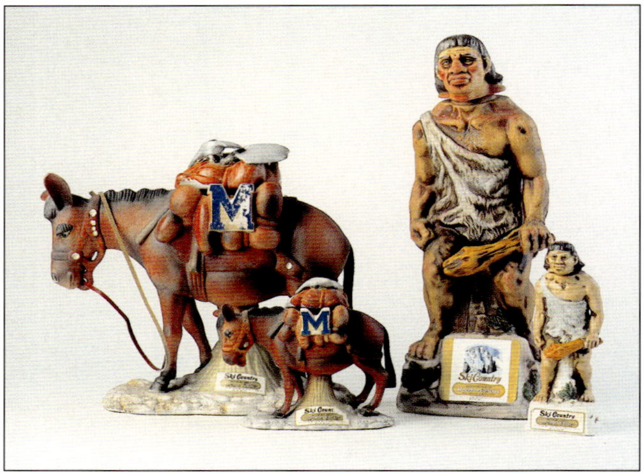

Burro – UTEP School of Mines, 1973, fifth $70-75, mini $50-55. Cave Man, 1974, fifth $25-32, mini $17-22.

Bonnie, 1974, fifth $30-38, mini $15-21. Clyde, 1974, fifth $35-43, mini $25-33.

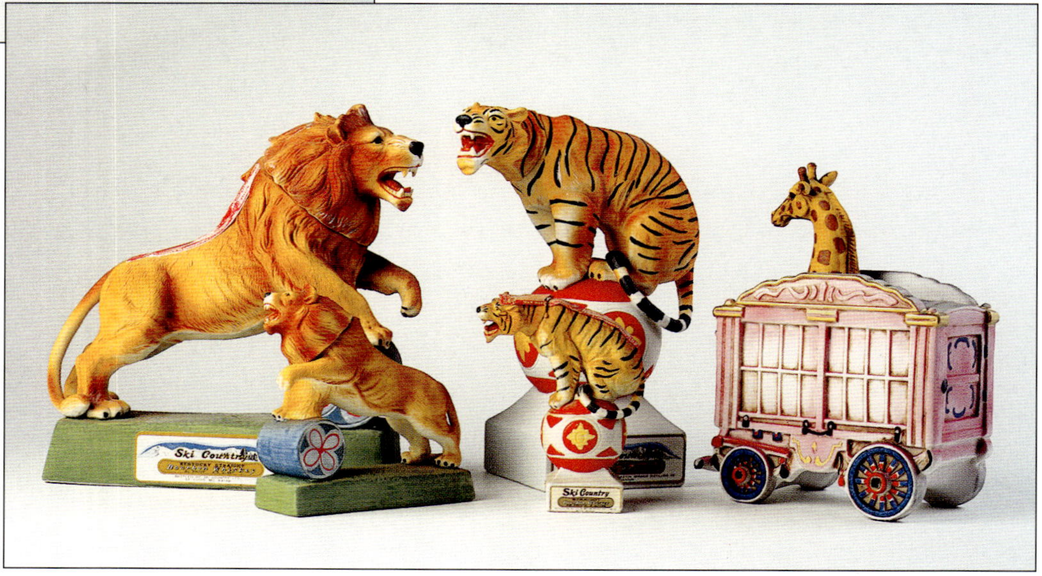

Circus Lion, 1975, fifth $45-50, mini $30-33. Circus Tiger, 1975, fifth $45-50, mini $30-35. Circus Wagon with Giraffe, 1977, fifth $50-58.

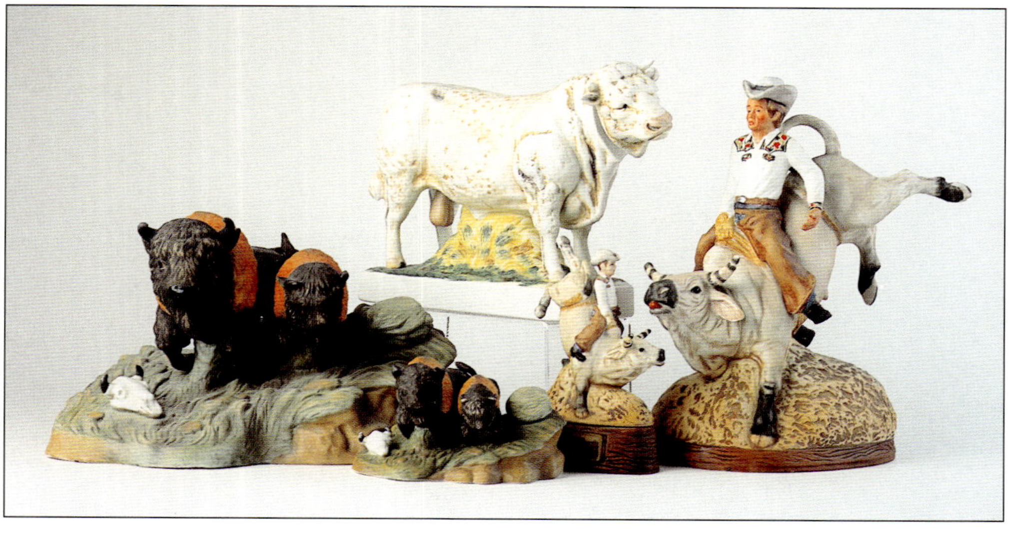

Buffalo Stampede, 1982, fifth $65-70, mini $35-40. Charolais bull, 1974, fifth $55-60. Bull Rider, 1980, fifth $80-87, mini $40-47.

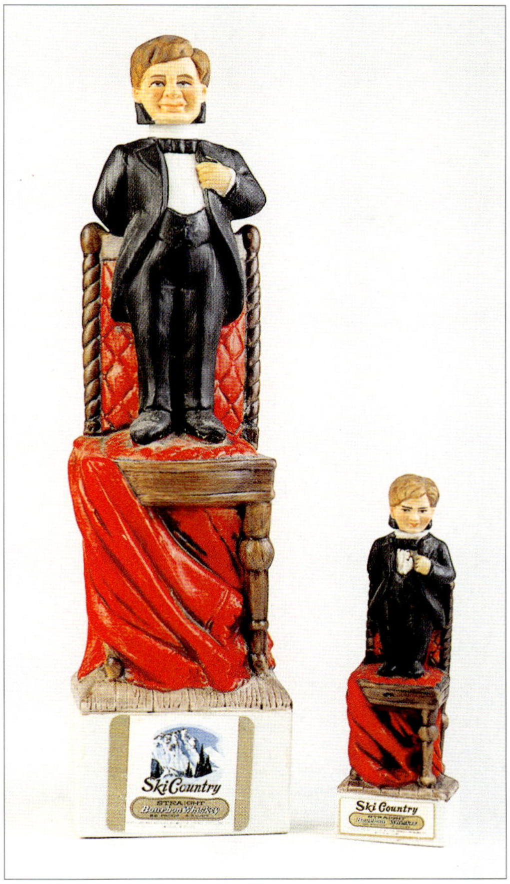

Tom Thumb, 1974, fifth $30-38, mini $19-24.

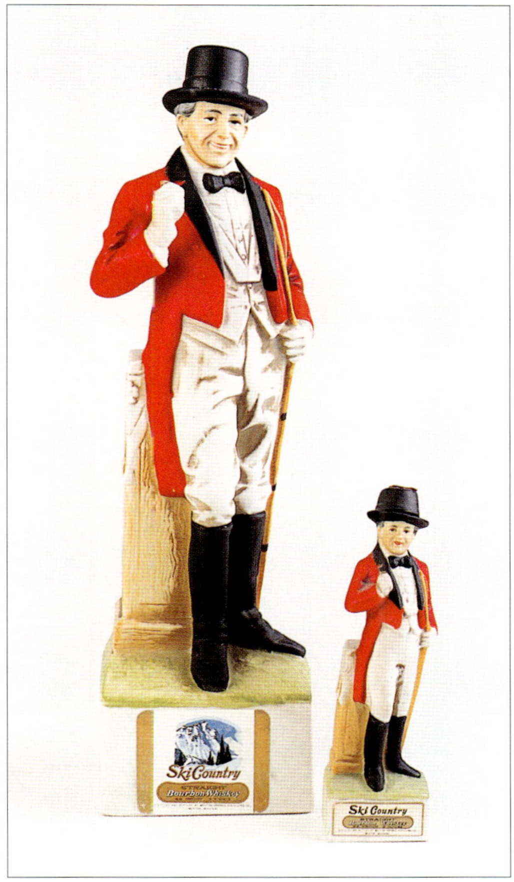

Ringmaster, 1975, fifth $35-40, mini $25-30.

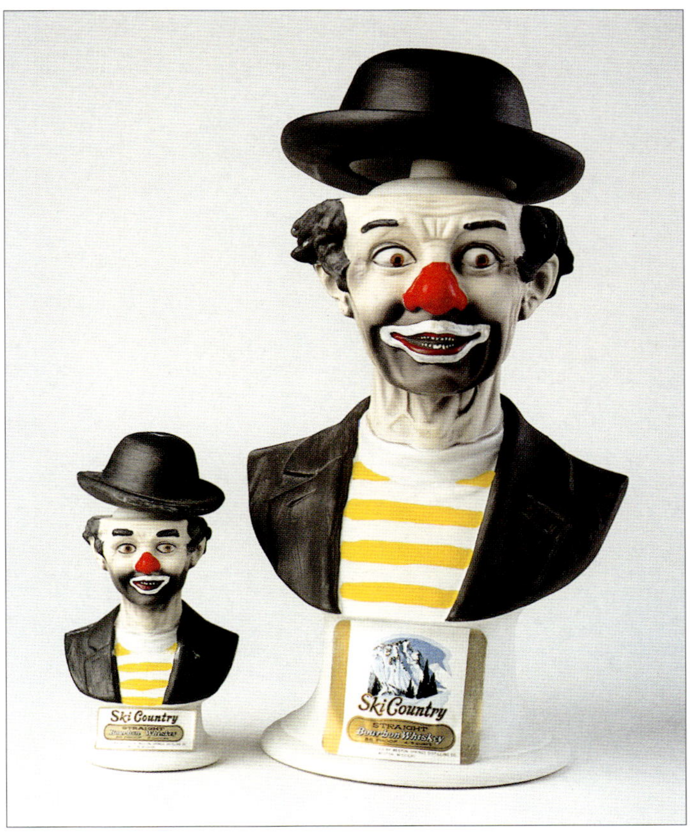

Clown bust, 1974, fifth $65-70, mini $40-45.

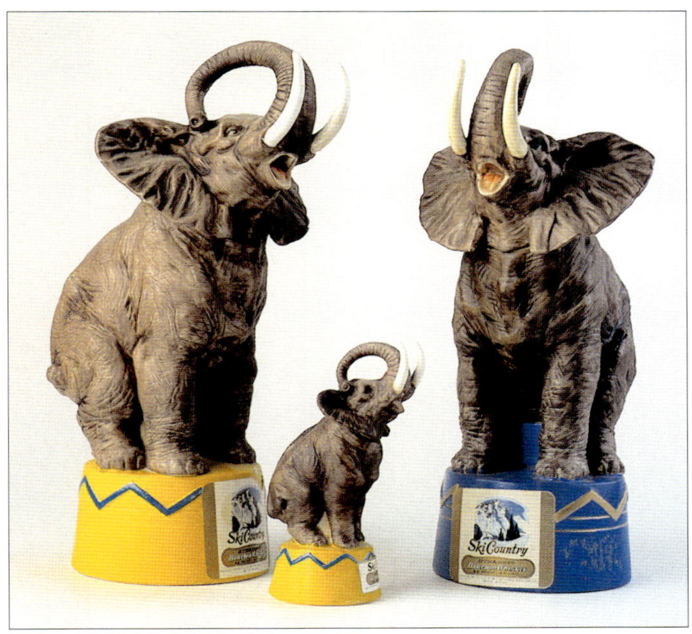

Elephant on yellow drum, 1973, fifth $45-50, mini $42-47. Elephant on blue drum, 1973, fifth $45-50.

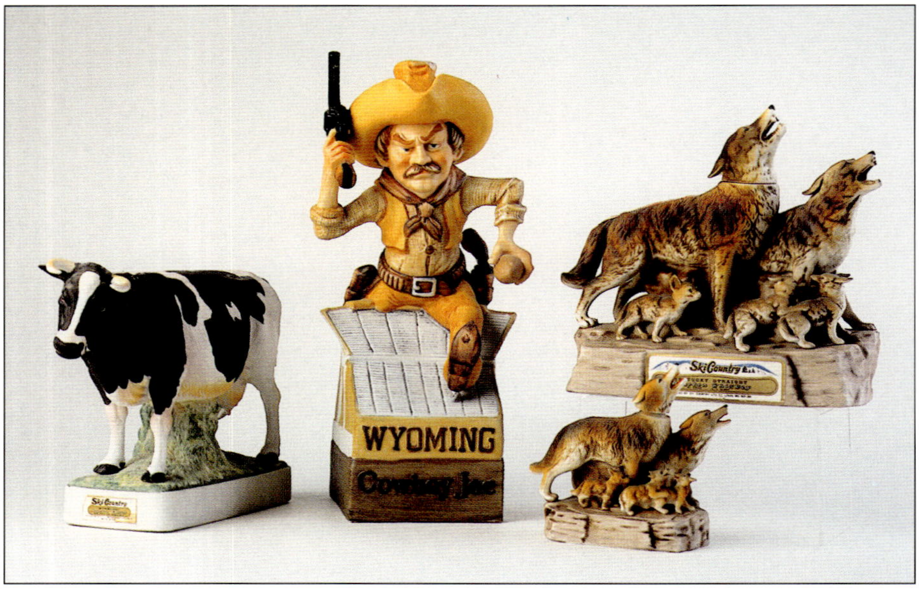

Holstein cow, 1973, fifth $70-79. Cowboy Joe, 1980, fifth $195-200. Coyote family, 1977, fifth $55-60, mini $30-35.

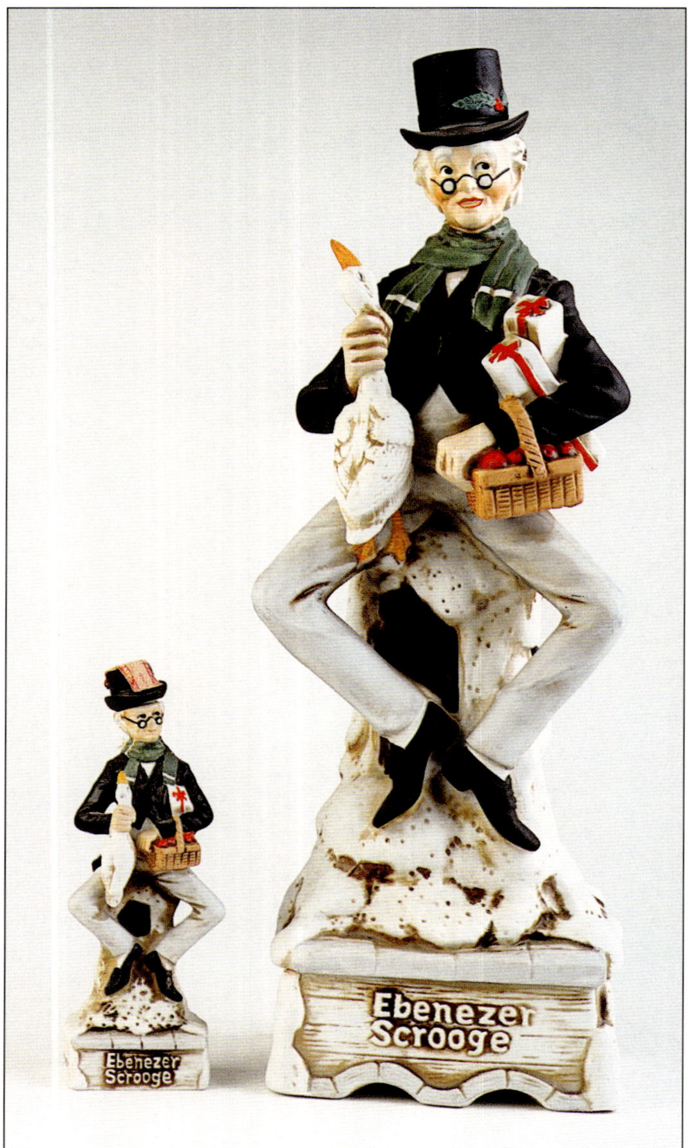

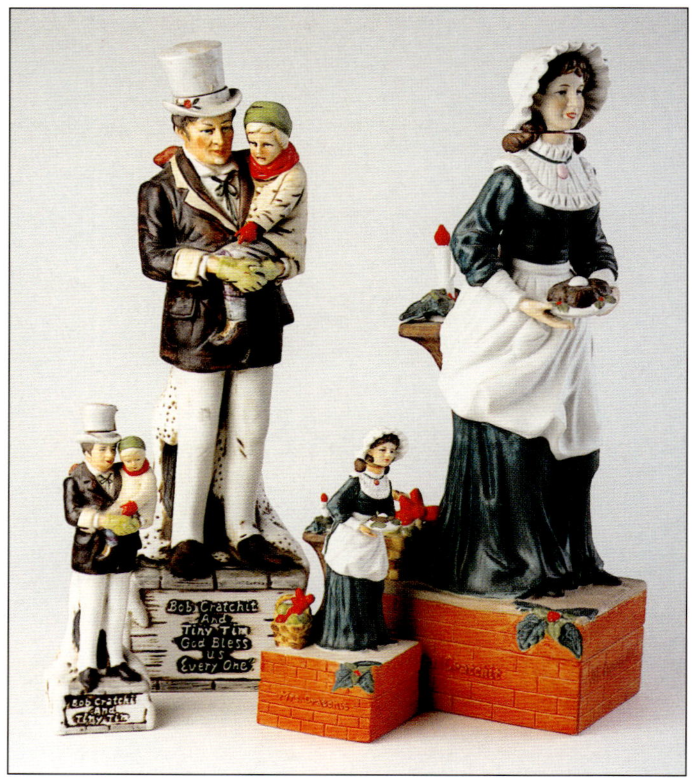

Bob Cratchit and Tiny Tim, 1977, fifth $55-62, mini $30-39. Mrs. Cratchit, 1978, fifth $70-79, mini $30-39.

Ebenezer Scrooge, 1979, fifth $60-67, mini $19-24.

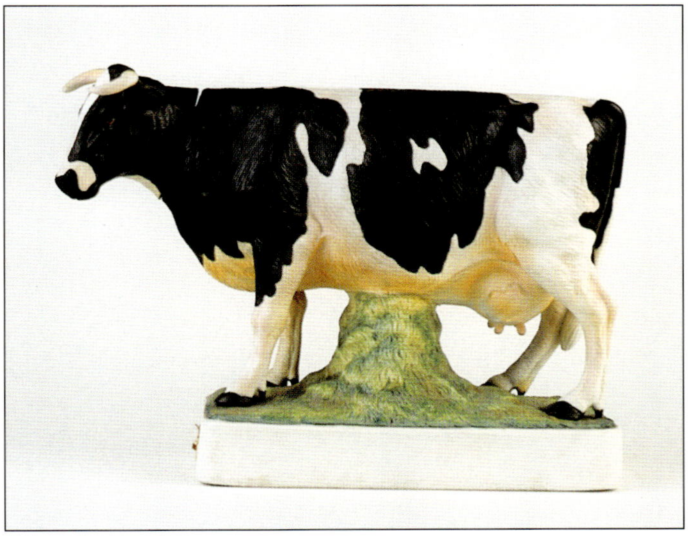

Holstein cow, mock-up, $135-145. *Courtesy of A.D. Powers.*

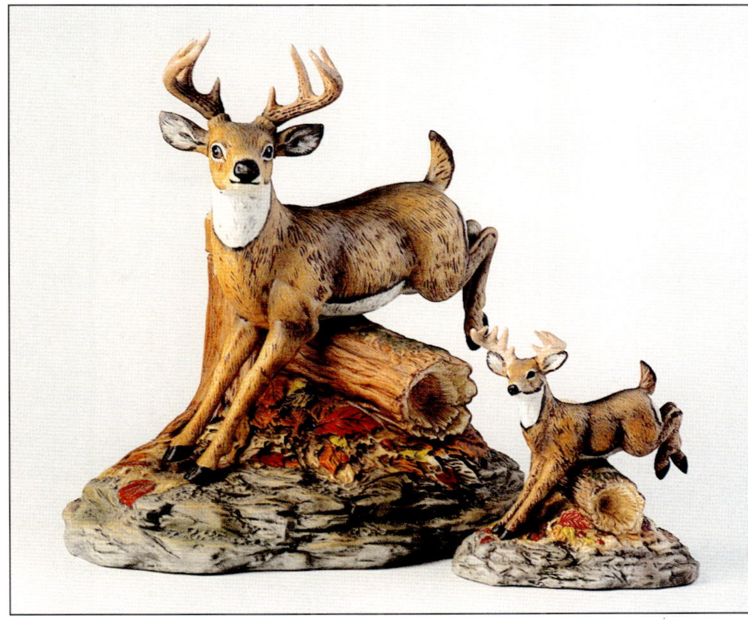

White Tailed Deer, 1982, fifth $175-182, mini $50-55.

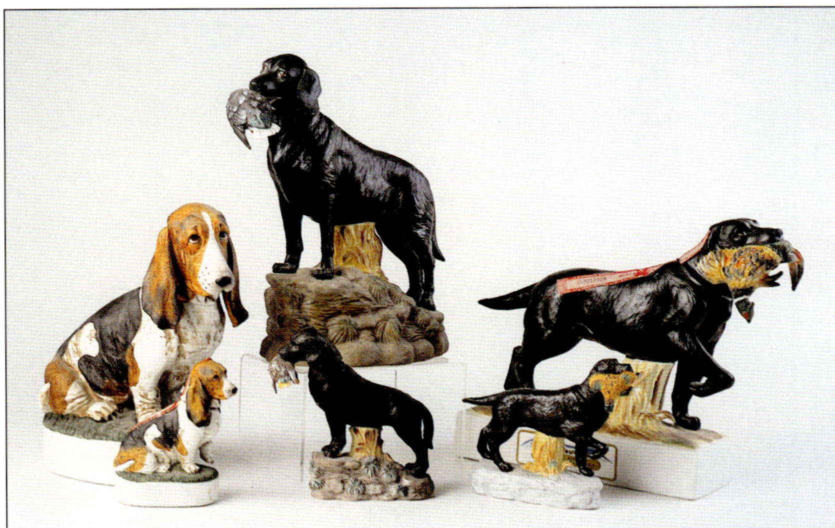

Basset Hound, 1978, fifth $55-63, mini $40-45. Labrador with mallard 1977, fifth $139-144, mini $40-47. Labrador with pheasant, 1976, fifth $90-98, mini $35-40.

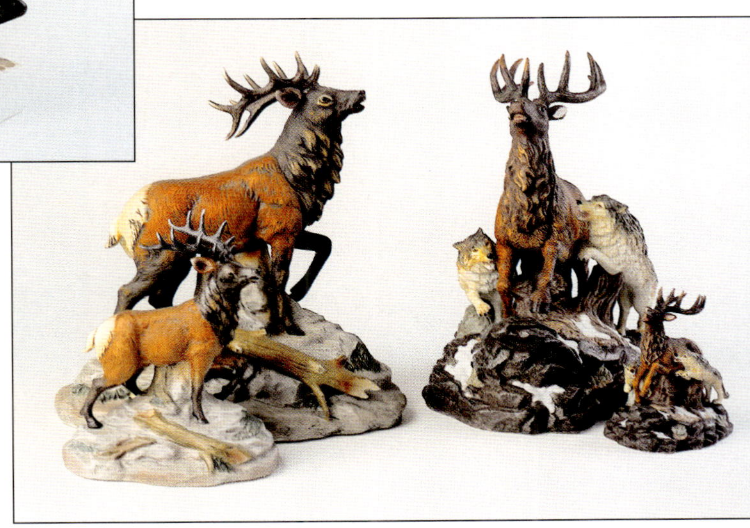

Elk, 1979, fift¬ $230-235, mini $75-81. Elk with wolves, 2003, fifth $65-70, mini $30-35.

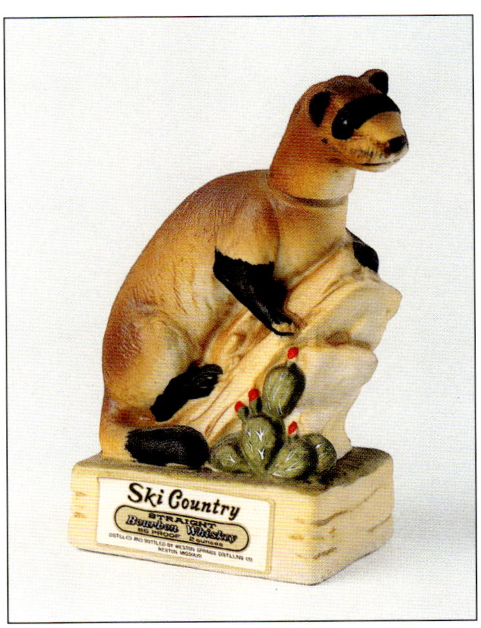

Black Footed Ferret, 1976, mini $60-66.

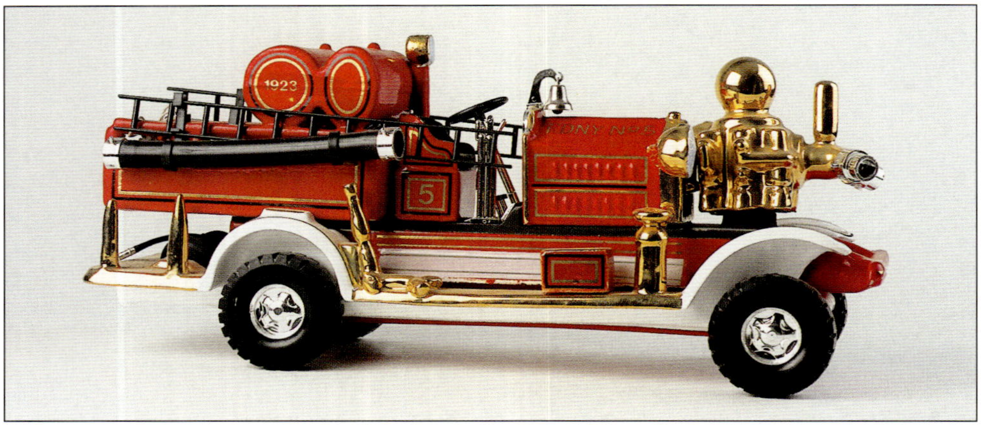

Ahrens Fox Fire engine, 1981, red and gold, fifth $255-260.

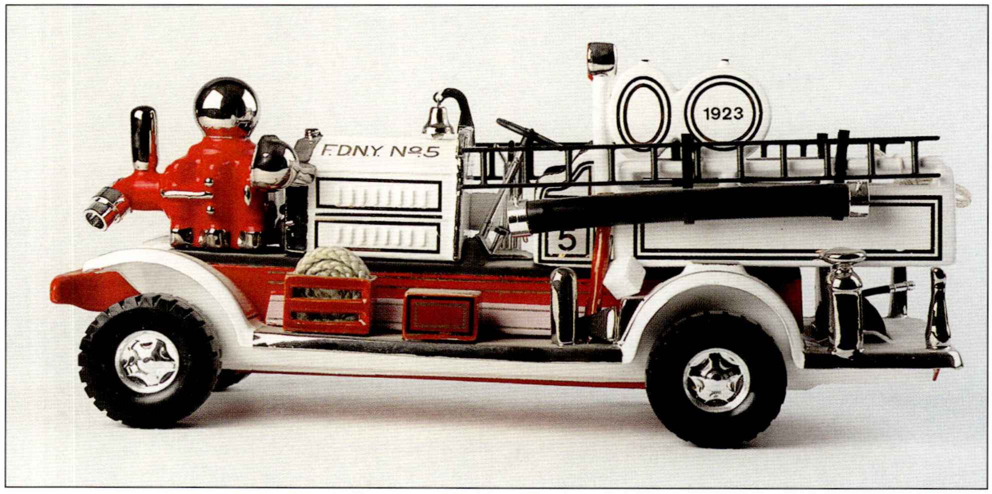

Ahrens Fox Fire engine, 1981, white and silver, fifth $255-260.

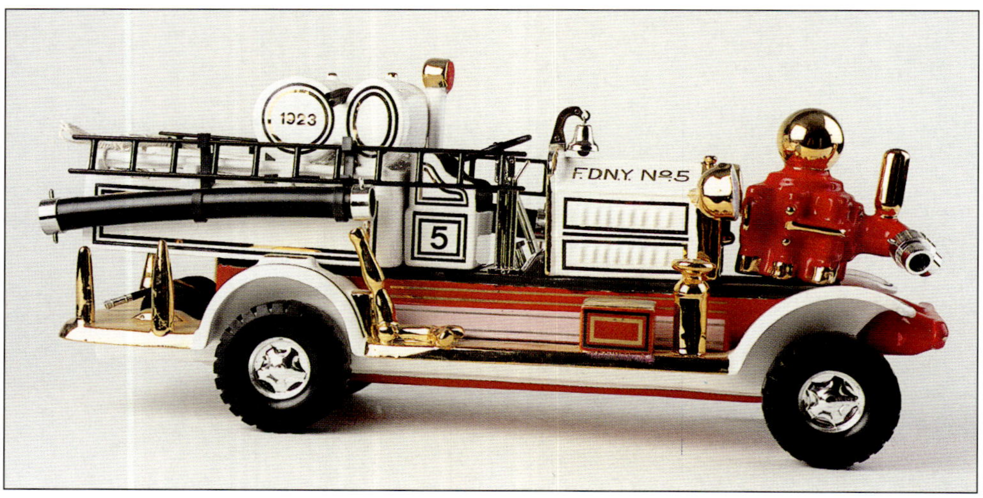

Ahrens Fox Fire engine, 1981, white and gold, fifth $255-260.

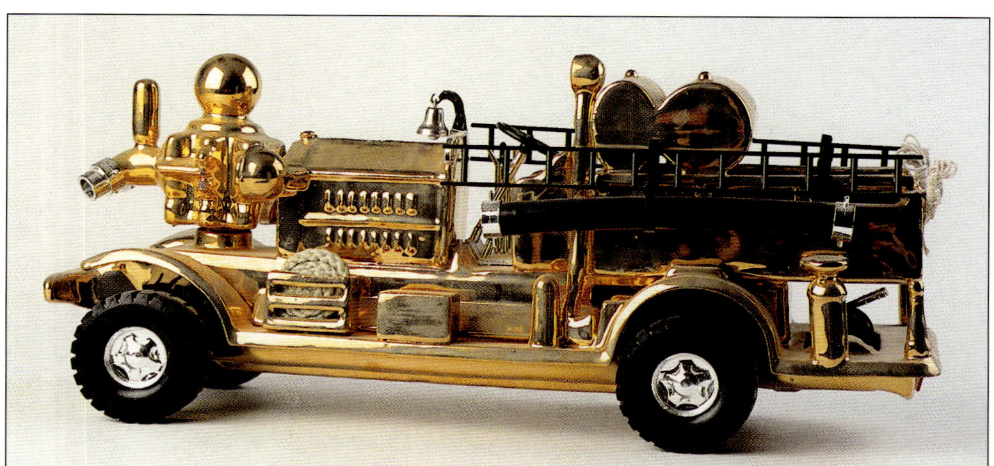

Ahrens Fox Fire engine, 1981, 14k gold plated, fifth $310-315.

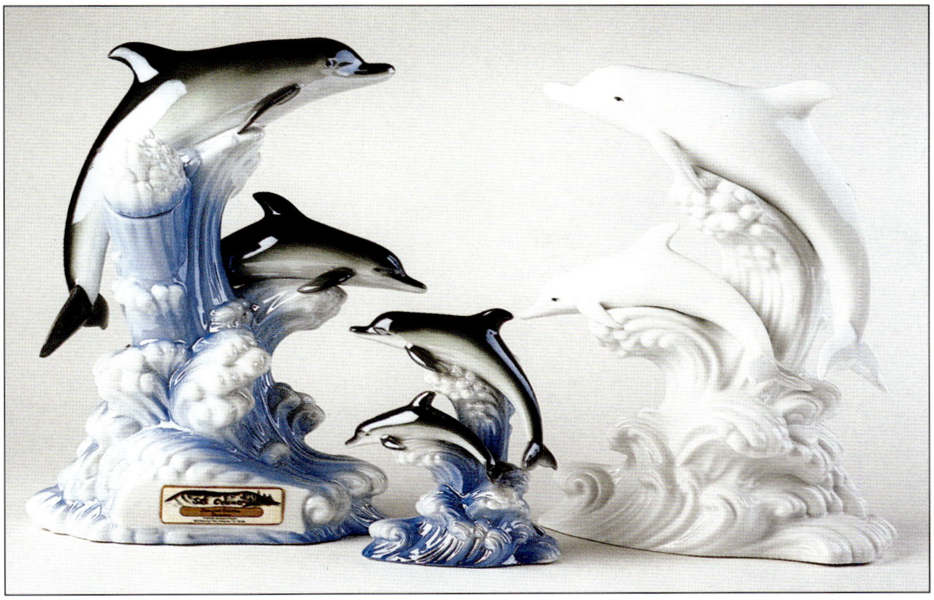

Dolphins, 2002 limited edition of 300, fifth $55-60, mini $25-30. Dolphin – white, 2003, limited edition of 100, fifth $80-85.

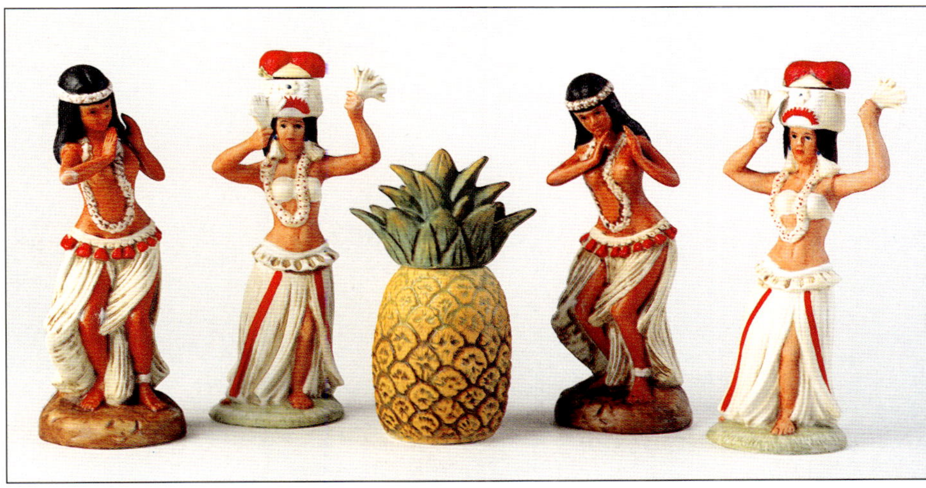

Hula dancers, 2002, pineapple 2003, Ruidoso, New Mexico district three souvenir, minis $25-30 each.

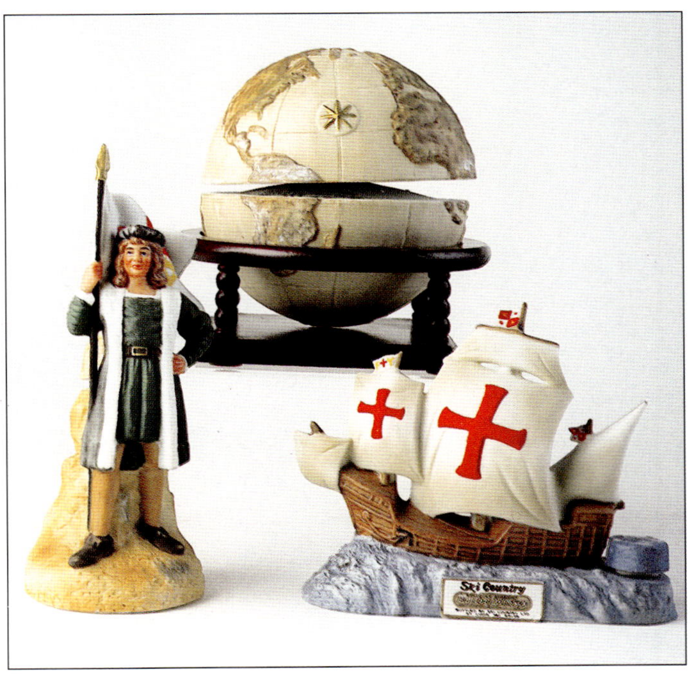

Christopher Columbus, Santa Maria, and world set, limited edition of 500, minis $310-315 set.

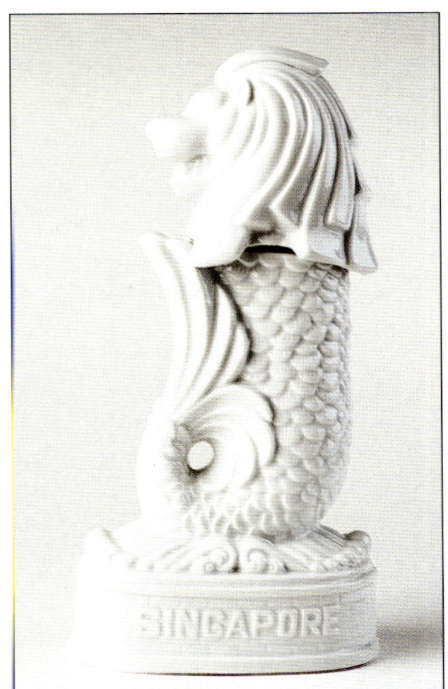

Lion's head with fish body, marked SINGAPORE, not dated, fifth $25-30.

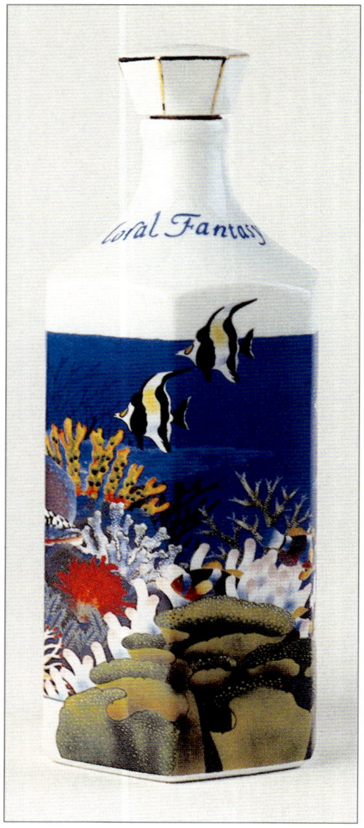

Coral fantasy collection bottle, French brandy, not dated, 500 ml $10-15.

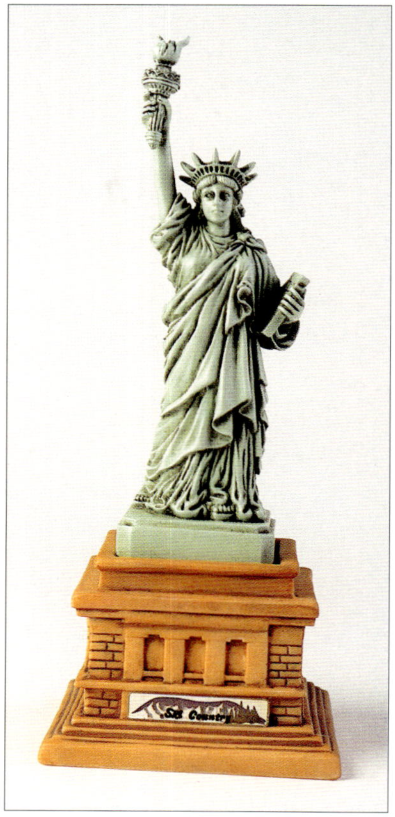

Statue of Liberty, 2002 limited edition of 500, mini $27-32.

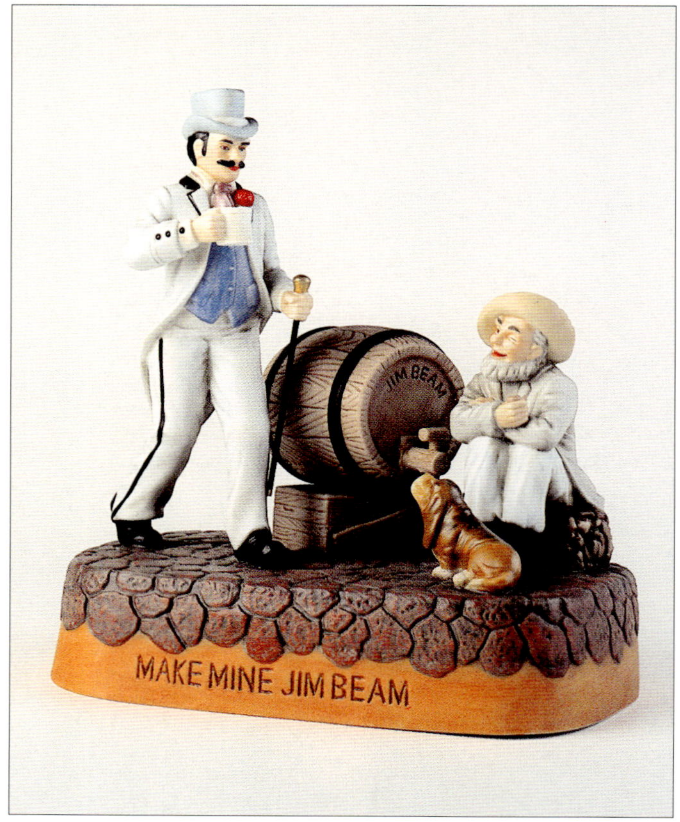

Make mine Jim Beam, 2003 limited edition of 382 for the Jim Beam Convention, fifth $95-100.

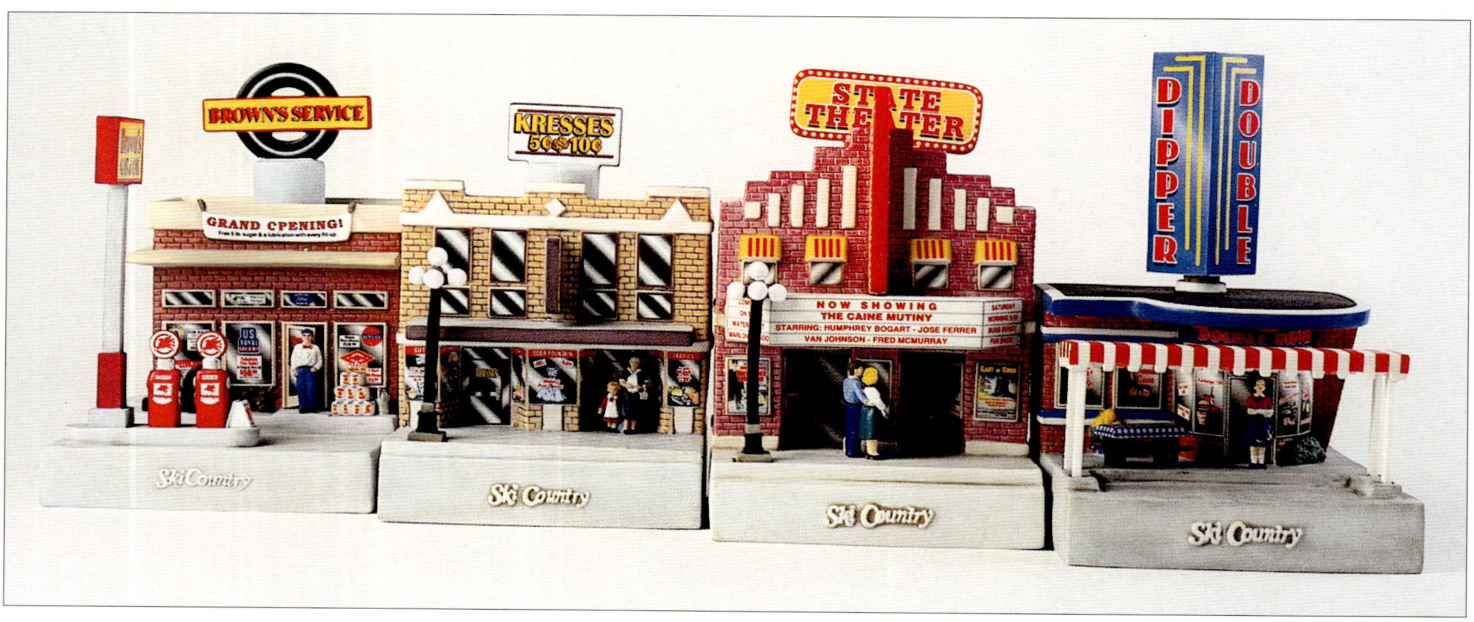

"Main Street USA." Brown's Service Station, limited edition of 700, fifth $40-48. Kress's Dime Store, limited edition of 500, fifth $40-48. State Movie Theater, limited edition of 500, fifth $40-48. Double Dipper Drive-In, limited edition of 500, fifth $40-48. Entire set $160-190.

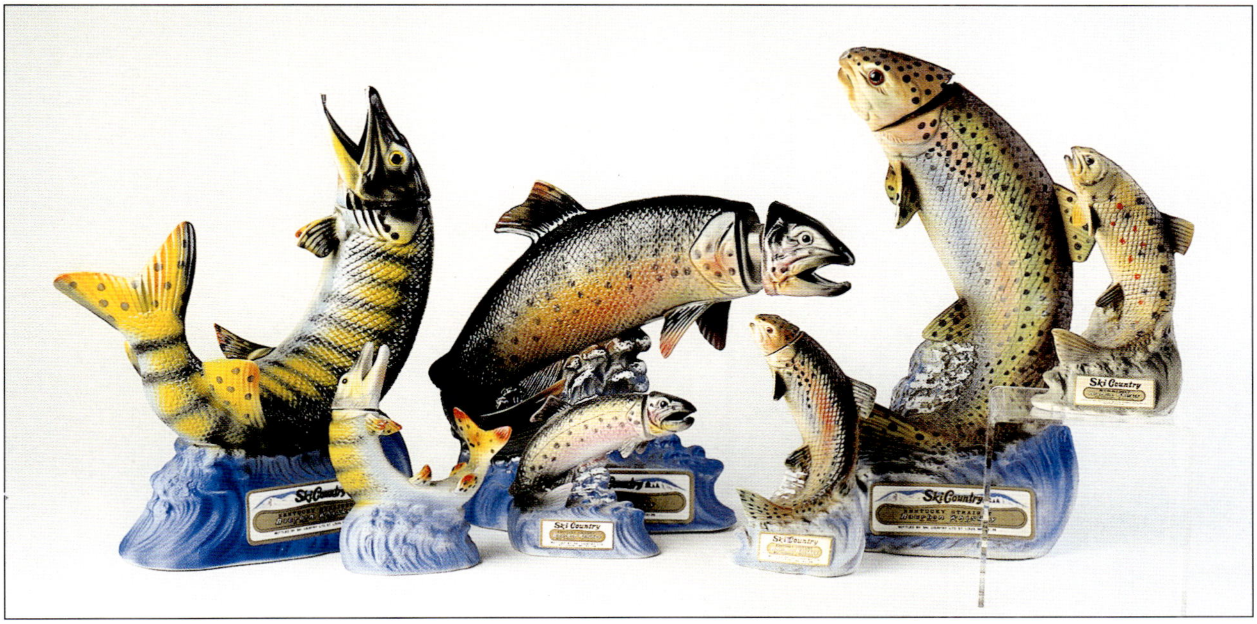

Muskie, 1977, fifth $40-46, mini $25-30. Landlocked Salmon, 1977, fifth $40-48, mini $30-36. Brown Trout, 1975, mini $50-58. Rainbow Trout, 1976, fifth $70-75, mini $35-40.

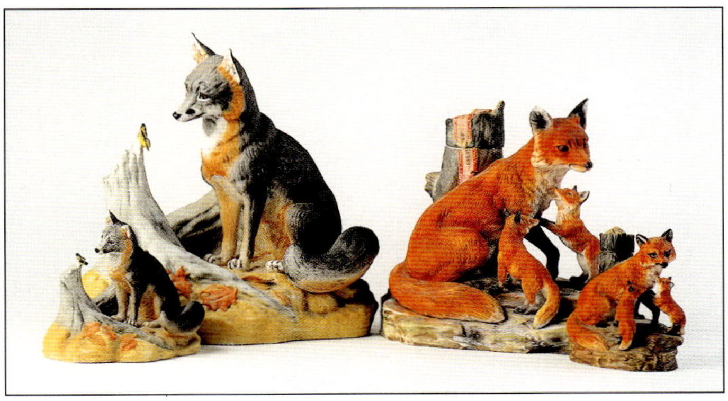

Fox and Butterfly, 1983, fifth $85-93, mini $40-47.
Fox Family, 1979, fifth $60-69, mini $40-47.

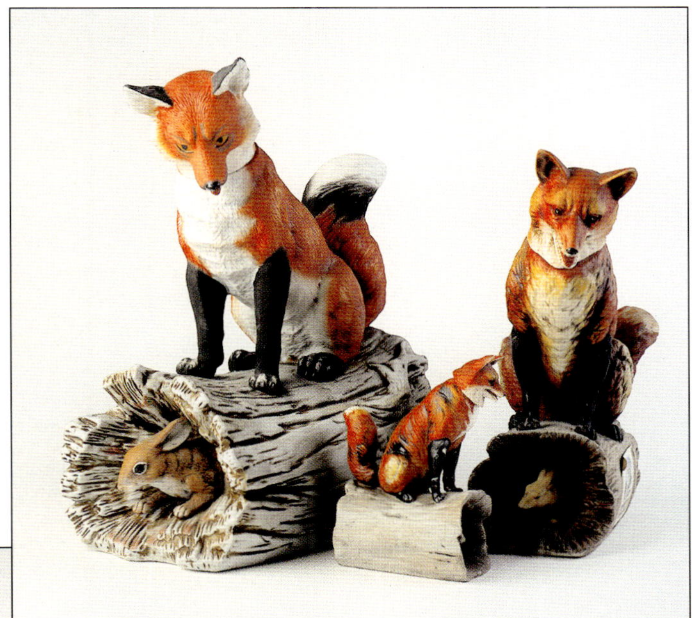

Fox on a log, 1973, 1.75 liter $250-261, fifth $105-112, mini $175-187.

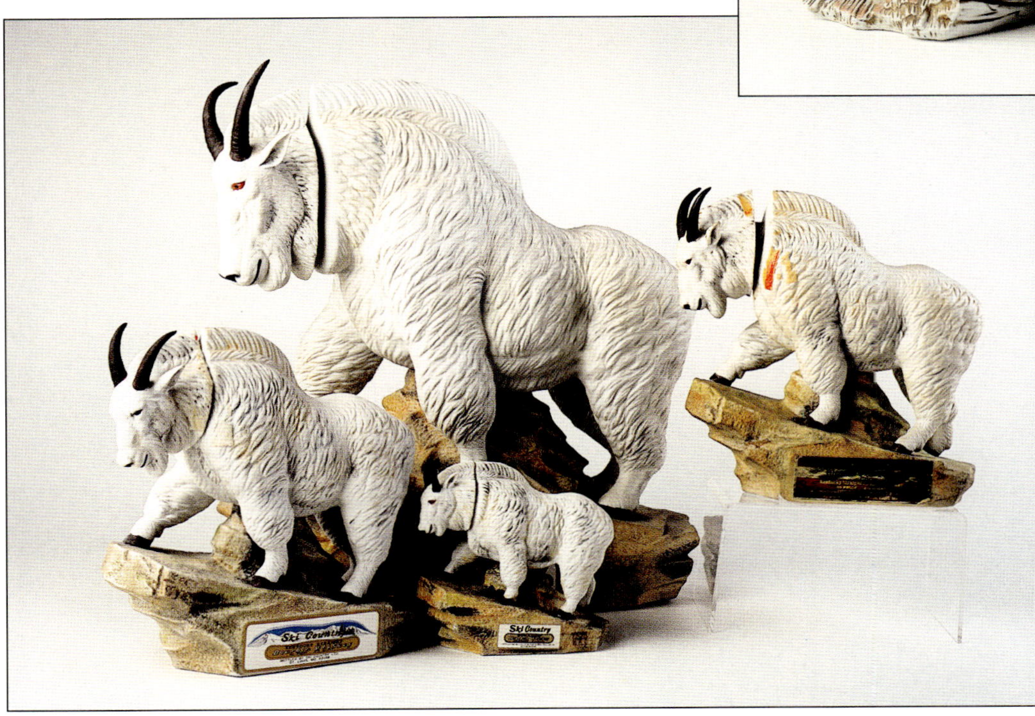

Mountain Goat, 1975, gallon $760-779, fifth $85-90, mini $50-55. Mountain Goat (Old Eastern limited edition), 1975, fifth $85-90.

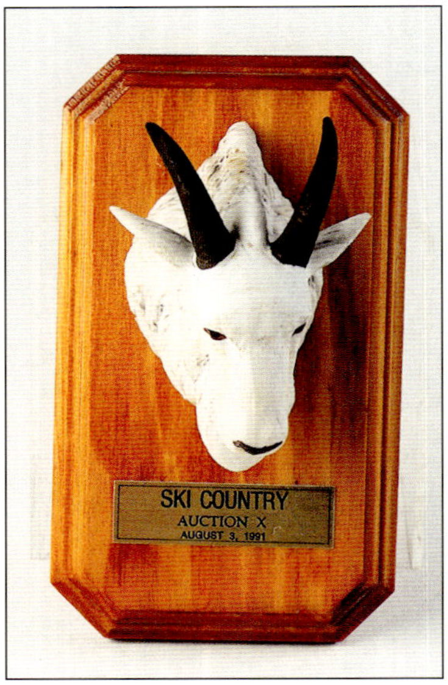

Mountain Goat plaque, 1991, mini $47-52.

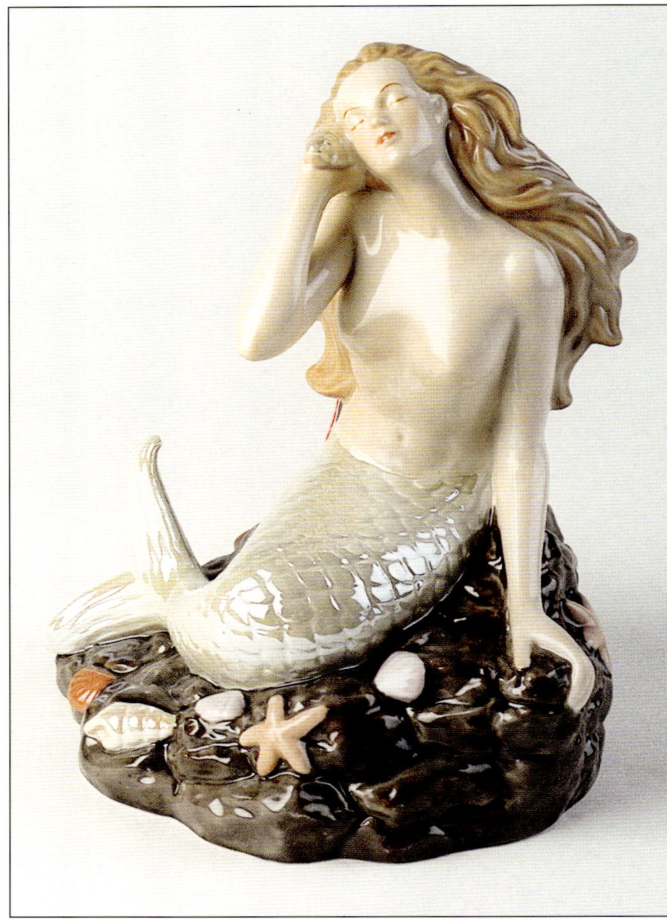

Mermaid, Coral Fantasy collection, 500ml $65-70.

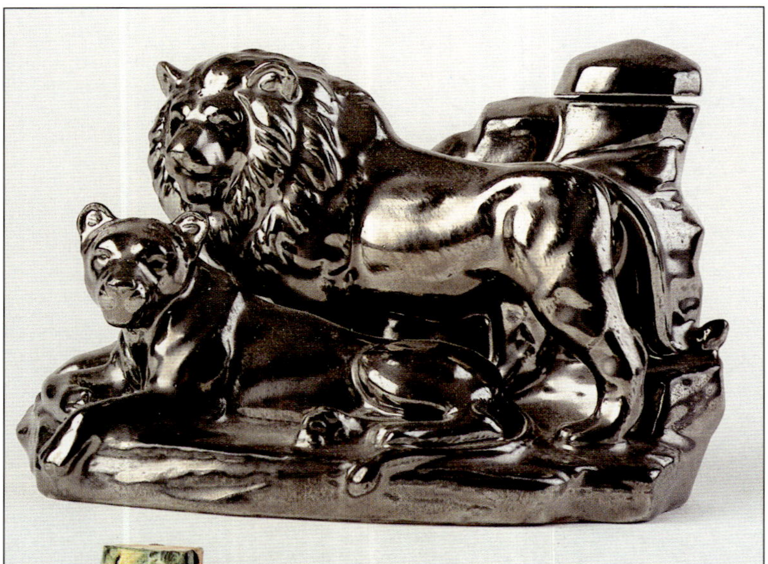

African Lions limited edition, 1987, 50ml $87-92.

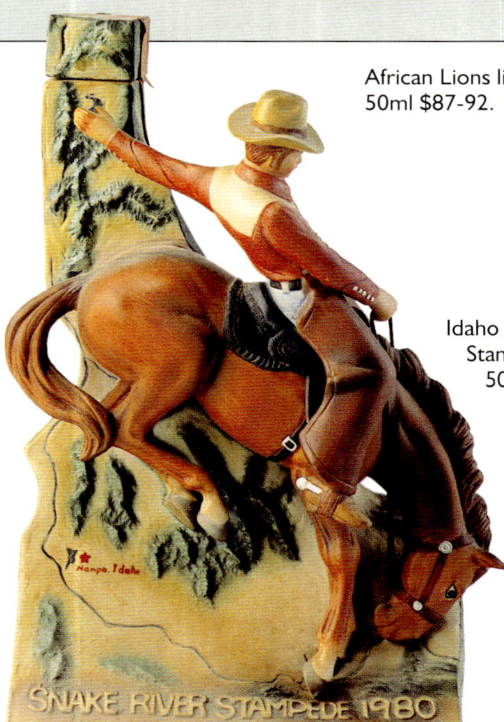

Idaho Snake River Stampede, 1980, 500ml $90-95.

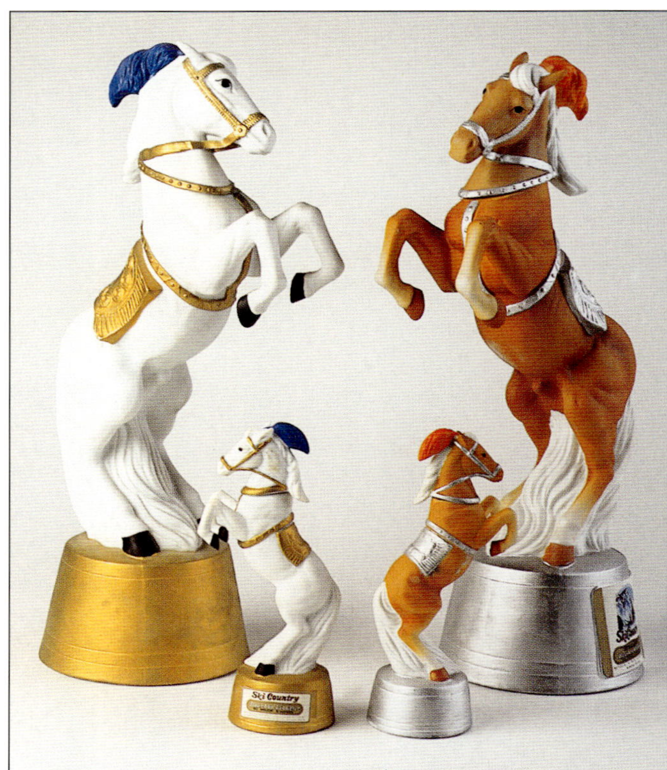

Royal Lipizzaner stallion, 1975, fifth $65-70, mini $50-55. Palomino, 1975, fifth $60-66, mini $40-45.

Indian Ceremonial Dancers

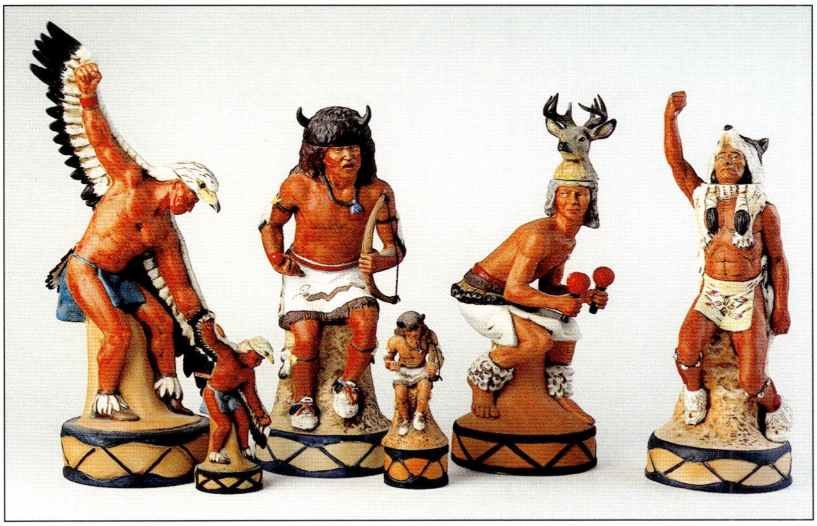

Arizona #1, Eagle Dancer, 1979, fifth $254-259, mini $34-39. Arizona #2, Buffalo Dancer, 1980, fifth $208-213, mini $42-47. Arizona #3, Deer Dancer, 1980, fifth $139-144, mini (not shown) $94-99. Arizona #4 Wolf Dancer, 1981, fifth $92-97, mini $50-55.

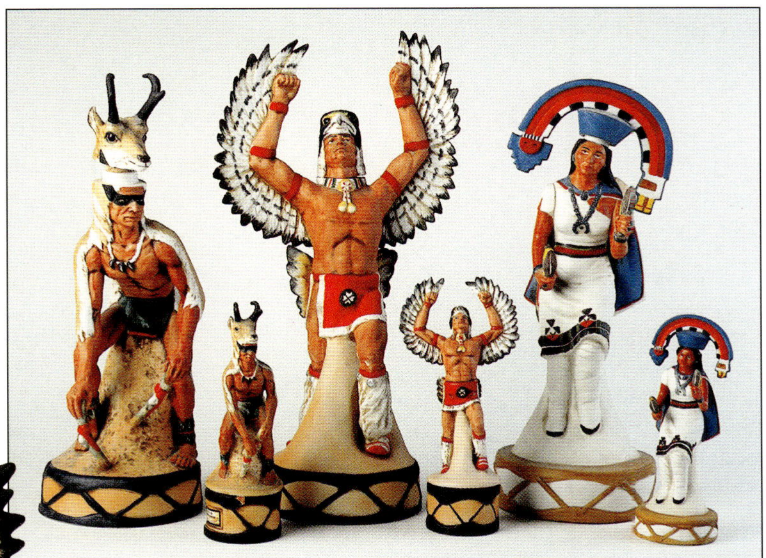

Arizona #5, Antelope Dancer, 1982, fifth $85-89, mini $43-48. Arizona #6, Falcon Dancer, 1983, fifth $155-160, mini $70-75. Arizona #7, Rainbow Dancer, 1984, fifth $94-98, mini $50-55.

Miscellaneous Ski Country Indians

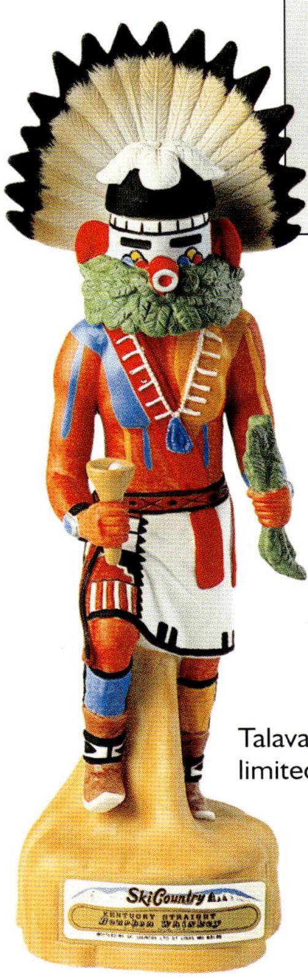

Talavai Kachina, southwest Kachina series, 1992 limited edition of 960, 750 ml $55-60.

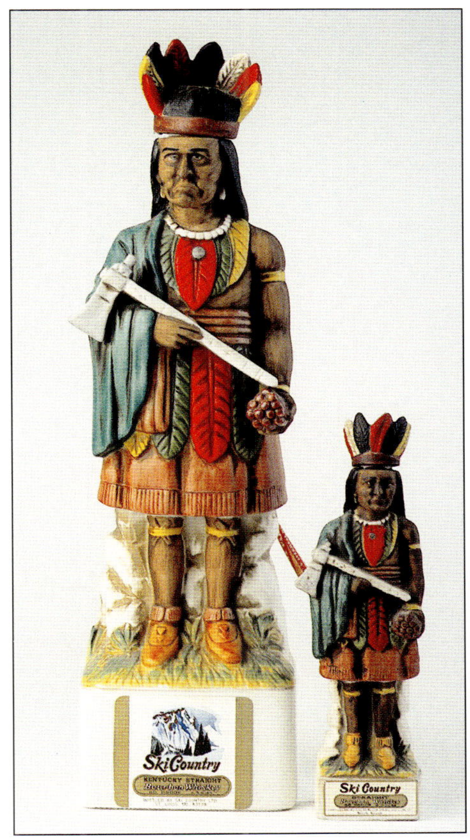

Cigar Store Indian, 1974, fifth $40-46, mini $30-38.

Indian Dancers of the Southwest

Indian – End of the Trail, 1976, fifth $265-270, mini $130-135. Indian – Great Spirit, 1975, fifth $118-123, mini $20-25. Indian – Look Out, 1977, fifth $57-63, mini $30-35.

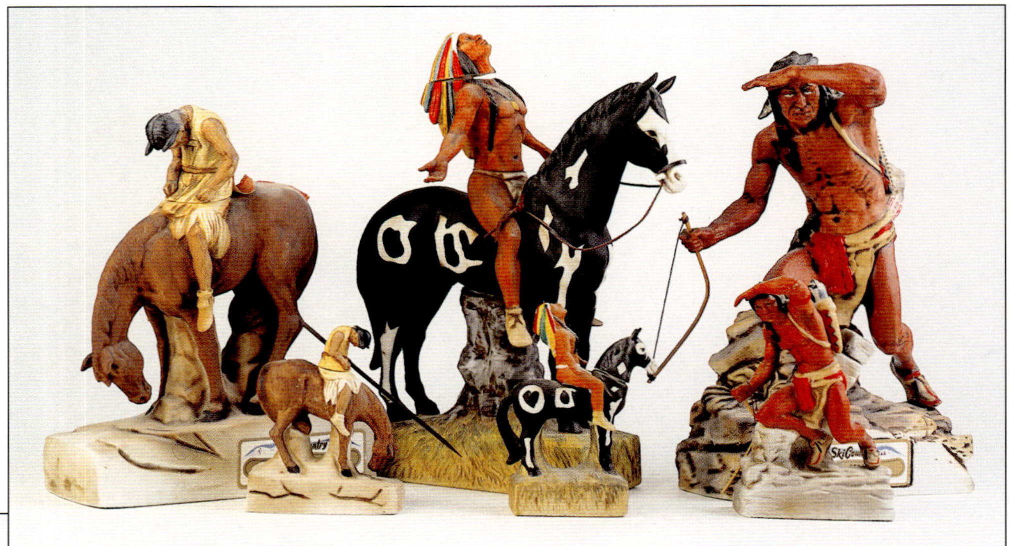

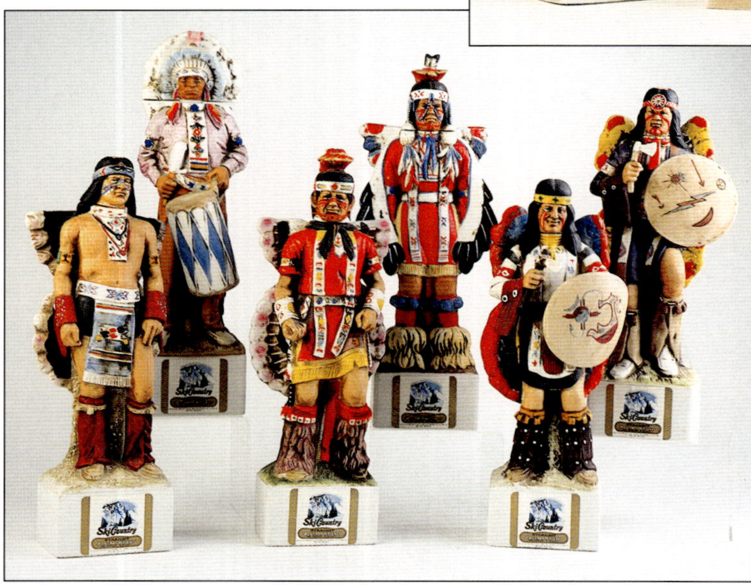

Acoma, 1975, fifth $60-65. Drummer, 1975, fifth $60-65. Eagle Dancer, 1975, fifth $60-65. Hoop Dancer, 1975, fifth $60-65. Shield Dancer, 1974, fifth $60-65. Sun Dancer, 1975, fifth $60-65. Entire set $400-410.

Indians Tribes of North American

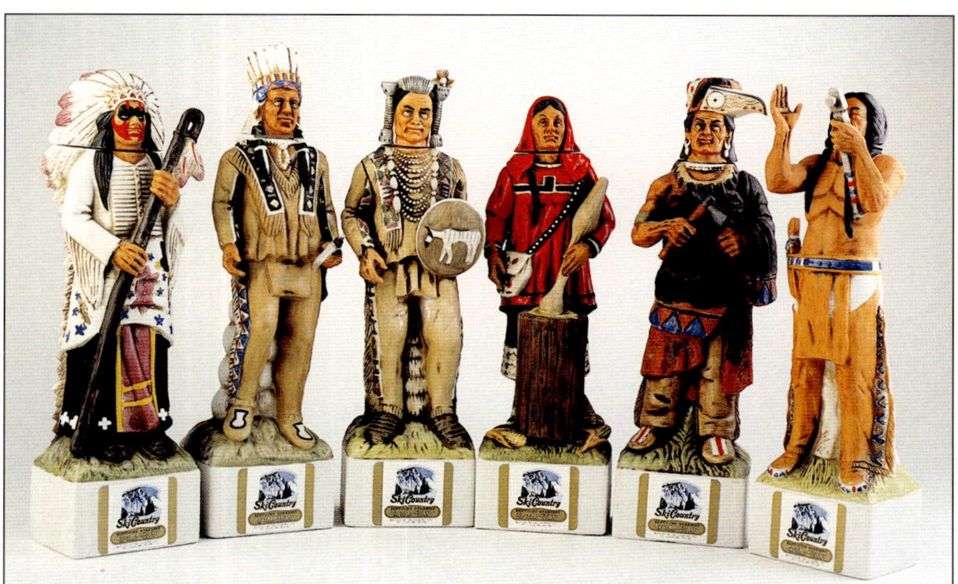

Arapahoe, 1977, fifth $40-45, mini $23-28. Blackfoot, 1977, fifth $40-45, mini $23-28. Crow, 1977, fifth $40-45, mini $23-28. Iroquois, 1977, fifth $40-45, mini $23-28. Pawnee, 1977, fifth $40-45, mini $23-28. Sioux, 1977, fifth $40-45, mini $23-28. Entire set, fifth $250-260. Entire set, mini $150-170. (Minis not shown).

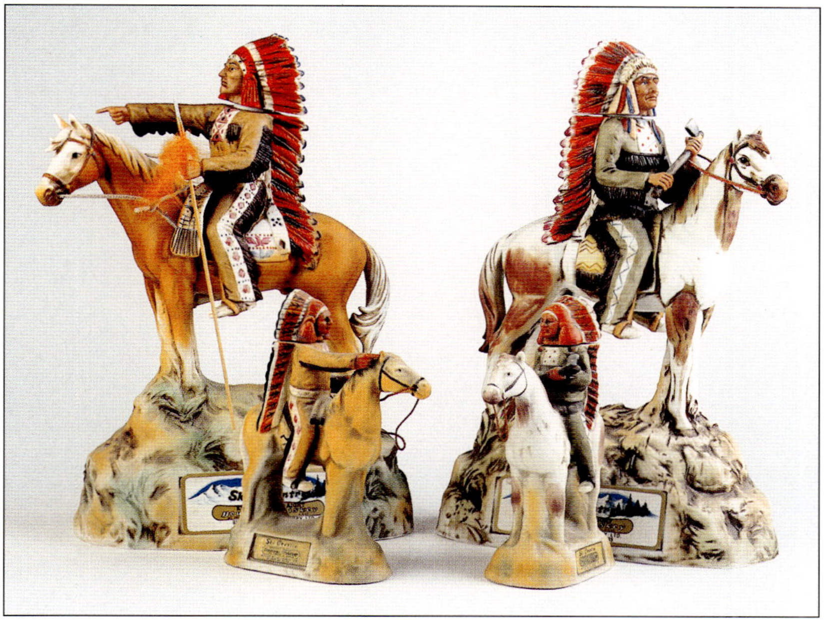

Indian Warrior # 1 with lance, 1975, fifth $155-160, mini $25-30.
Indian Warrior # 2 with hatchet, fifth $155-160, mini $25-30.

Miscellaneous Ski Country

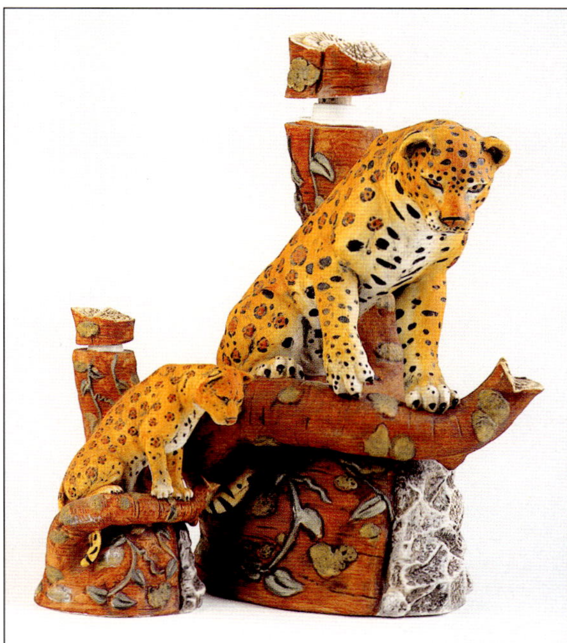

Jaguar, 1983, fifth $180-185, mini $50-55.

Jenny Lind (blue), 1976, fifth $87-93, mini $77-82. Jenny Lind (yellow), 1976, fifth $145-152, mini $159-164.

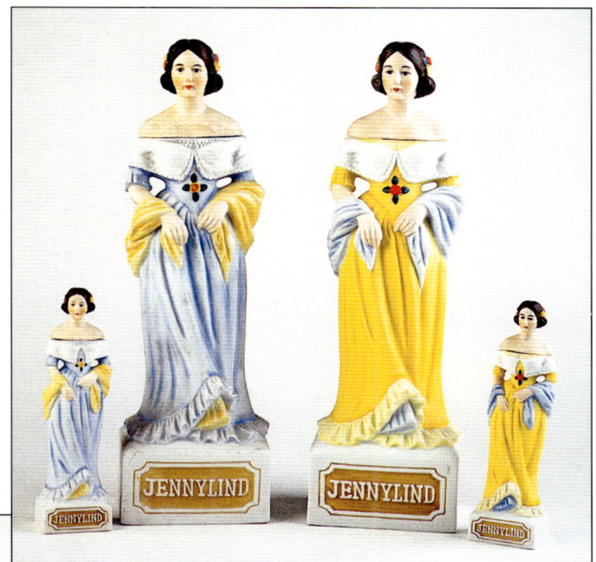

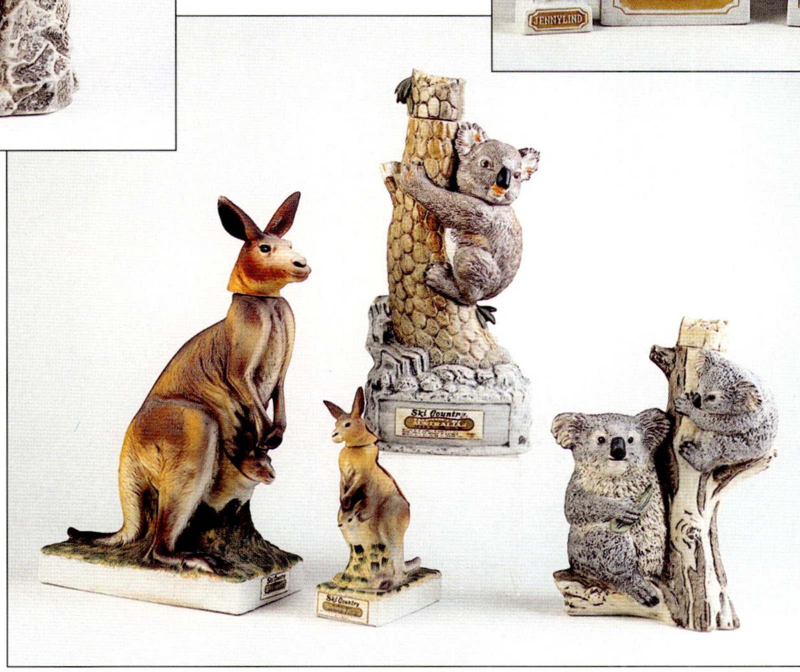

Kangaroo, 1974, fifth $35-40, mini $30-35. Koala, 1973, fifth $40-45. Double Koala, no date, fifth $55-60.

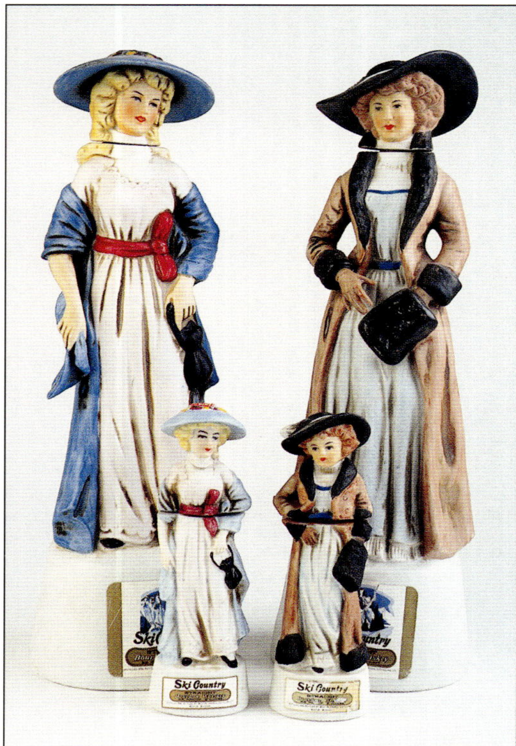

Leadville Lady (blue dress), 1973, fifth $25-30, mini $20-25. Leadville Lady (brown coat), 1973, fifth $20-25, mini $20-25.

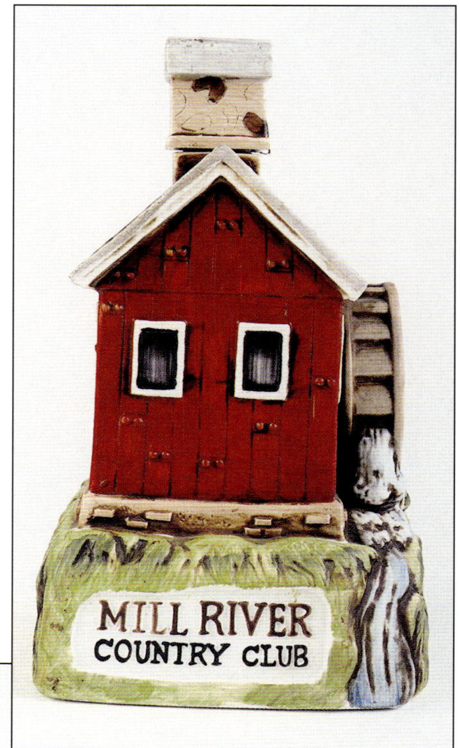

Mill River Country Club, 1977, fifth $35-40.

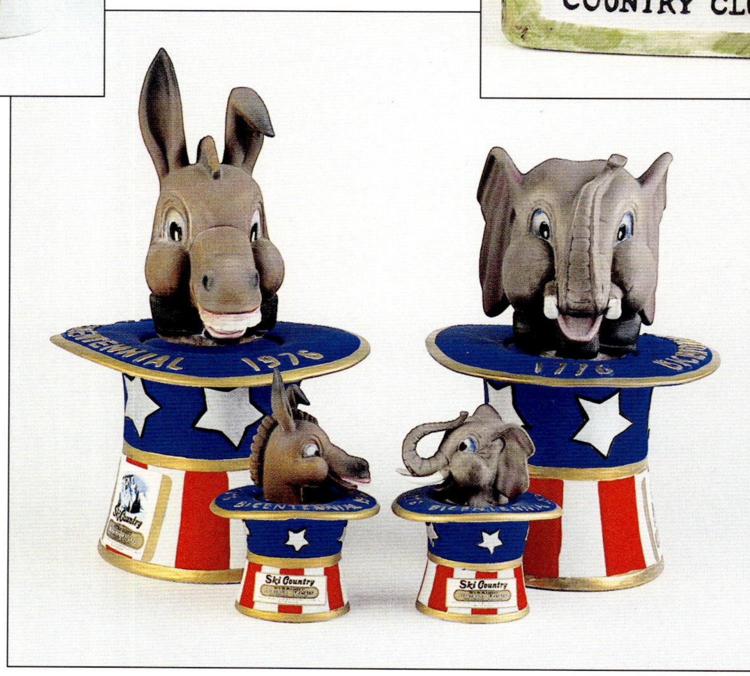

Donkey, 1976 New York Democratic National Convention, fifth $45-52, mini $20-28. Elephant, 1976 Kansas City Republican National Convention, 1976, fifth $40-48, mini $20-29.

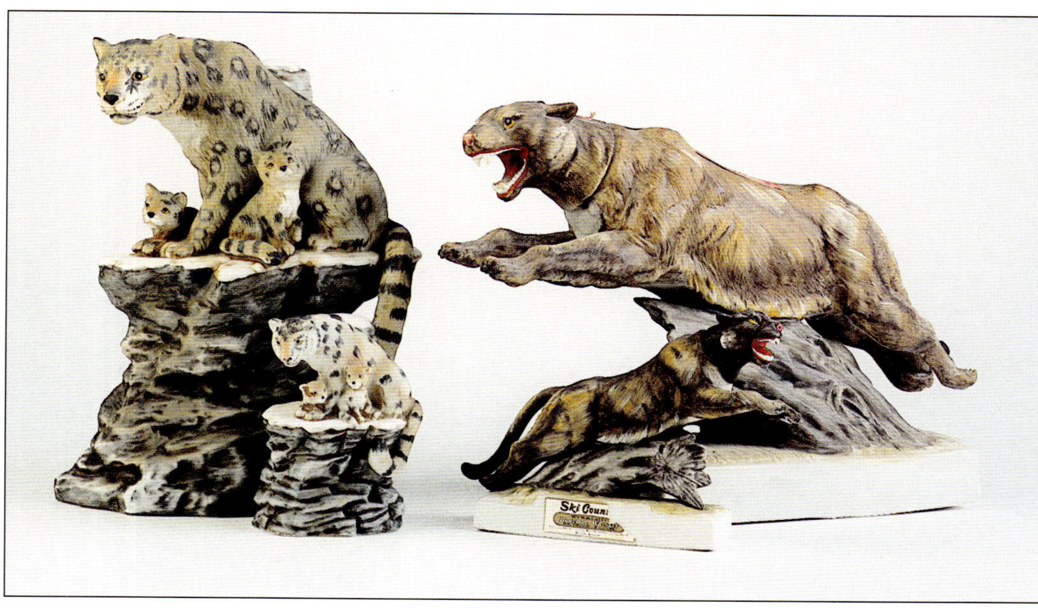

Snow Leopard, 1980, fifth $50-58, mini $30-35. Mountain Lion, 1973, fifth $60-67, mini $30-35.

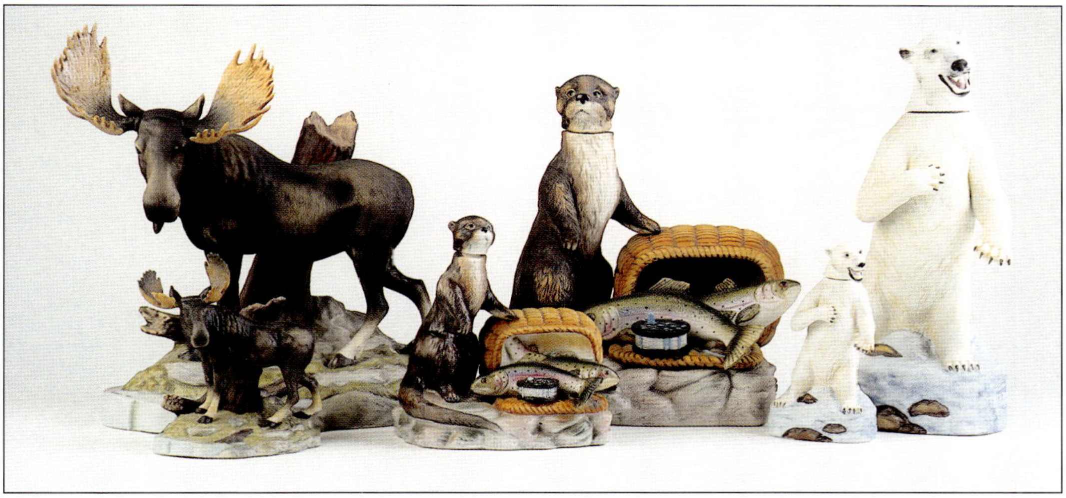

Moose, 1982, fifth $125-132, mini $40-47, River Otter, 1979, fifth $70-75, mini $30-35. Alaskan Polar Bear, 1984, fifth $60-69, mini $30-35.

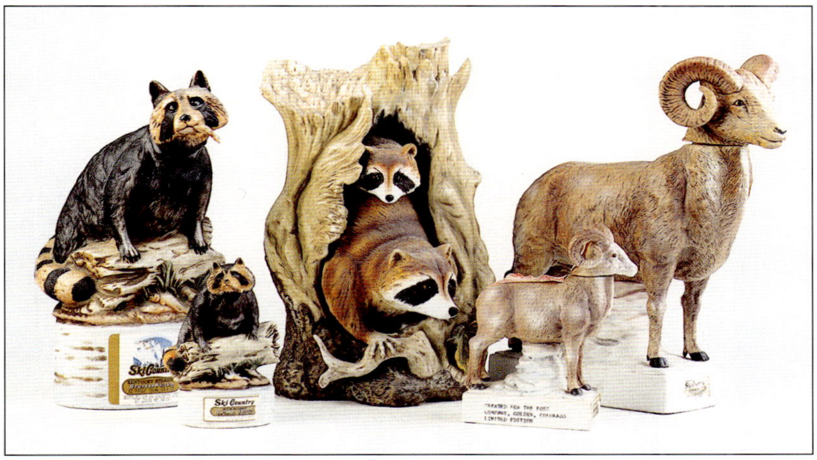

Raccoon, 1974, fifth $55-62, mini $40-47. Raccoon wall plaque, 1982, fifth $95-100. Big Horn Ram, 1973, fifth $95-100, mini $40-47.

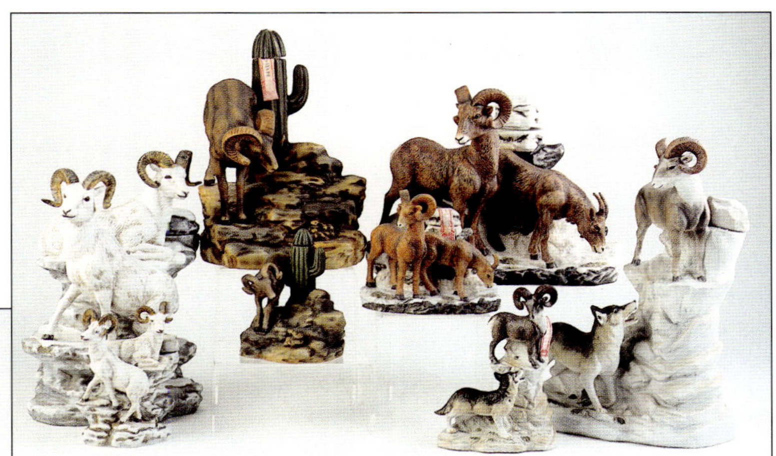

Dall Sheep, 1980, fifth $195-200, mini $53-58. Desert Sheep, fifth $125-130, mini $40-45. Rocky Mountain Sheep, 1981, fifth $75-80, mini $40-45. Stone Mountain Sheep, 1981, fifth $80-85, mini $55-60.

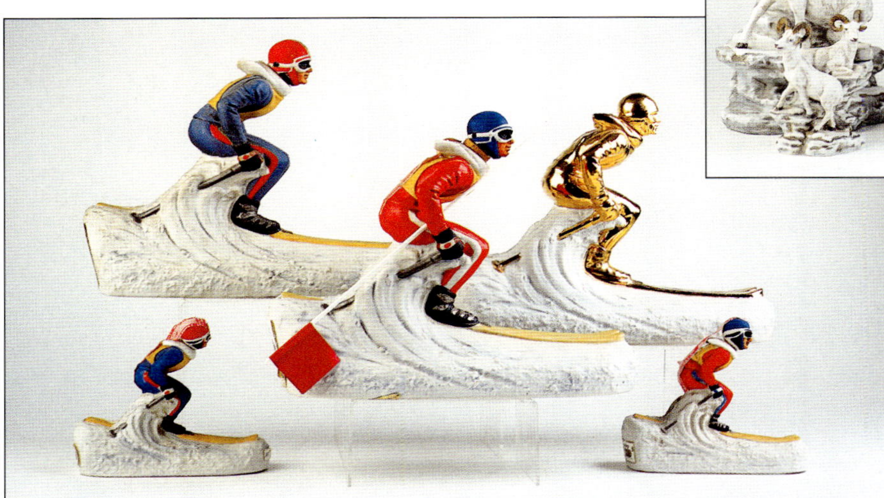

Skier (blue), 1971, fifth $40-45, mini $65-70. Skier (red), 1971, fifth $40-45, mini $55-60. Skier (gold), 1976, fifth $120-132.

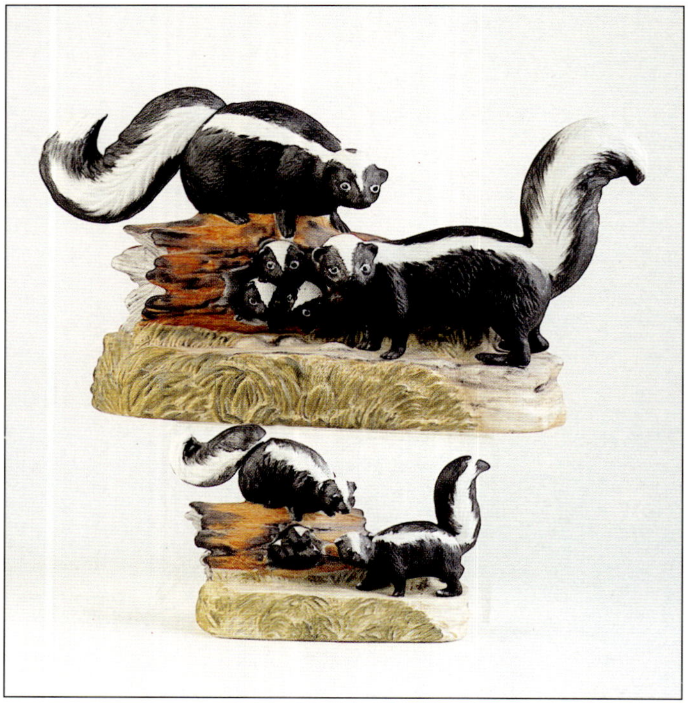

Skunk family, 1978, fifth $50-55, mini $30-35.

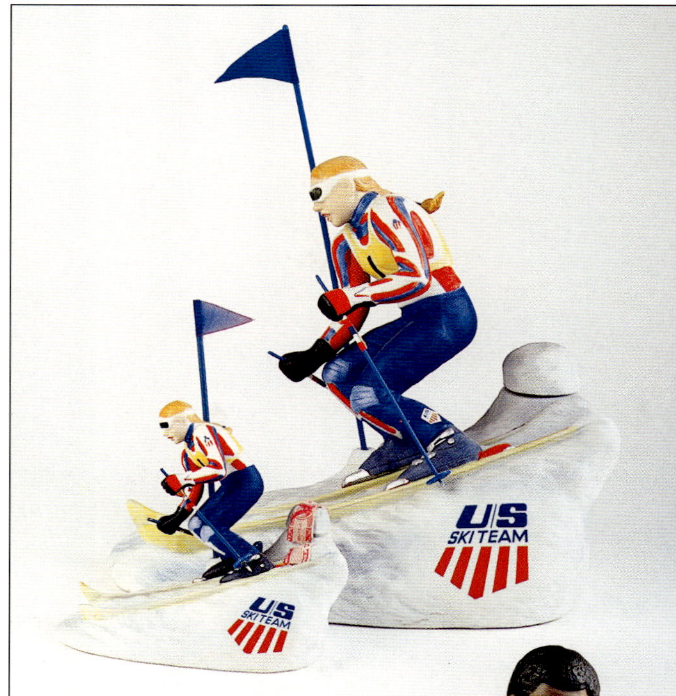

Olympic skier, 1980, fifth $45-50, mini $20-25.

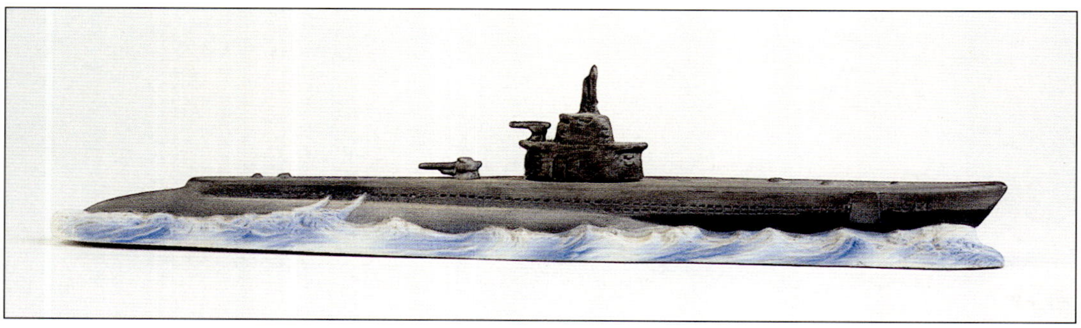

Submarine, 1976, mini $25-32.

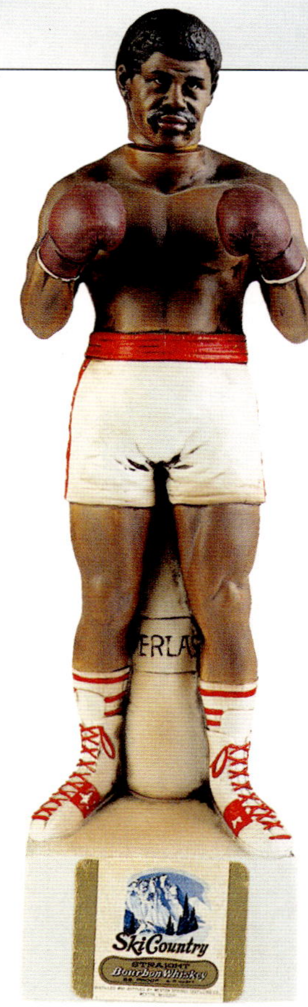

Unknown boxer, possible prototype, fifth, value undetermined.

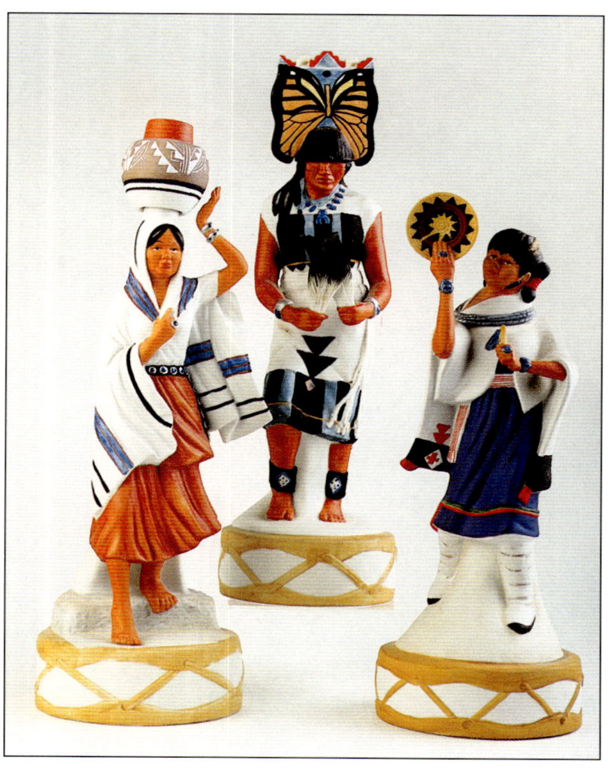

Indian series: Olla Maiden, 1985, 750 ml $80-85. Butterfly Dancer, 1985, 750 ml $95-100. Basket Dancer, 1985, 750 ml $80-85.

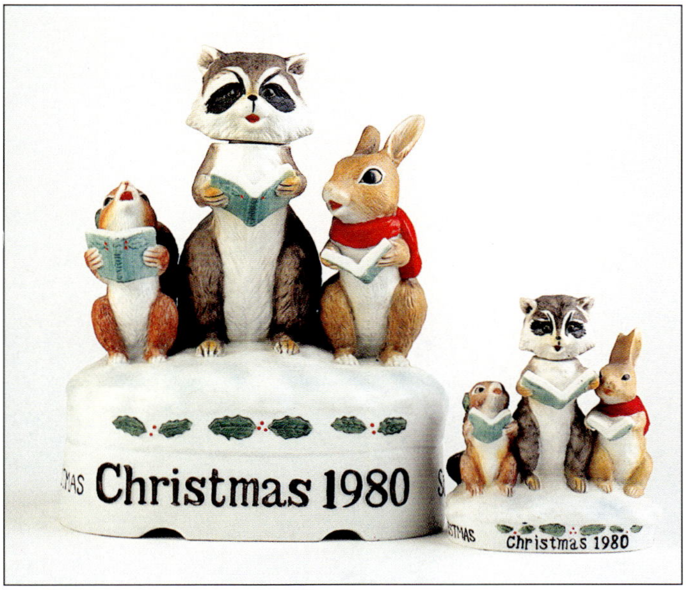

Woodland trio, Christmas 1980, fifth $74-79, mini $73-78.

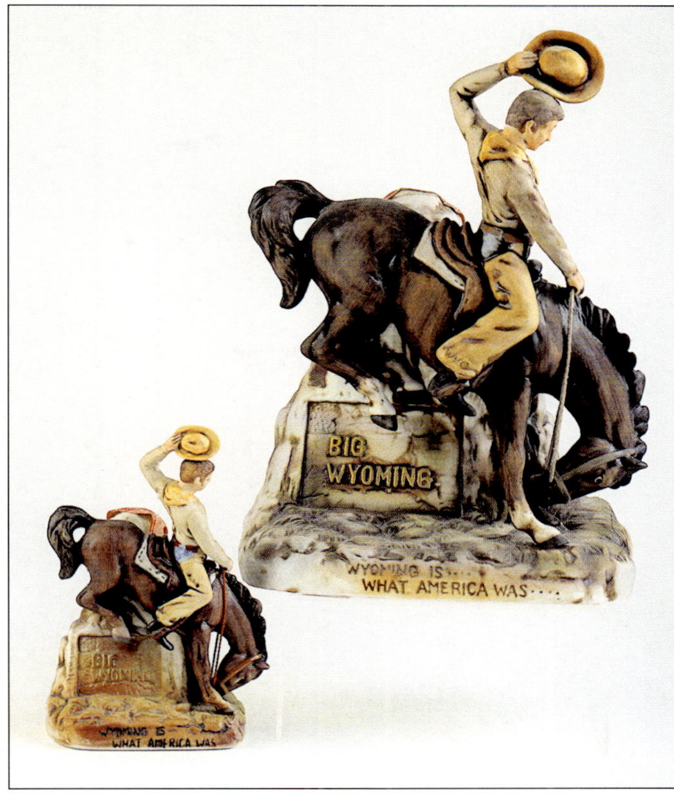

Wyoming Bronco, 1979, fifth $85-89, mini $35-43.

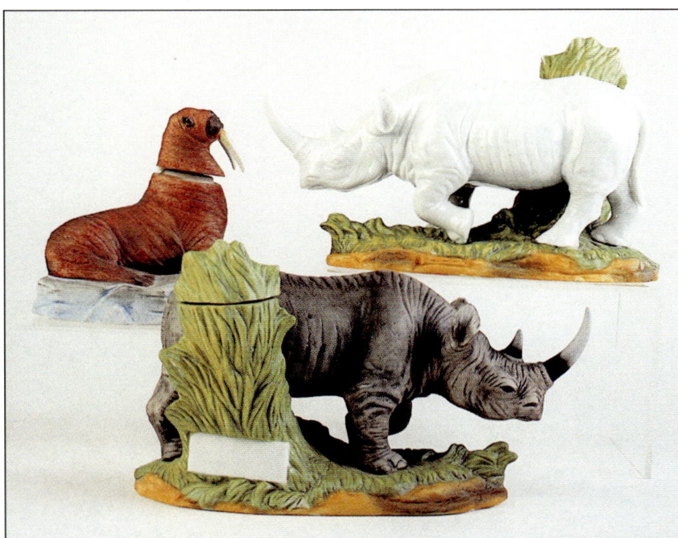

Walrus, 1985, mini $20-25. White Rhino, 1992 limited edition of 100, 50 ml $100-115. Gray Rhino, 1994 limited edition of 600, 50 ml $50-55.

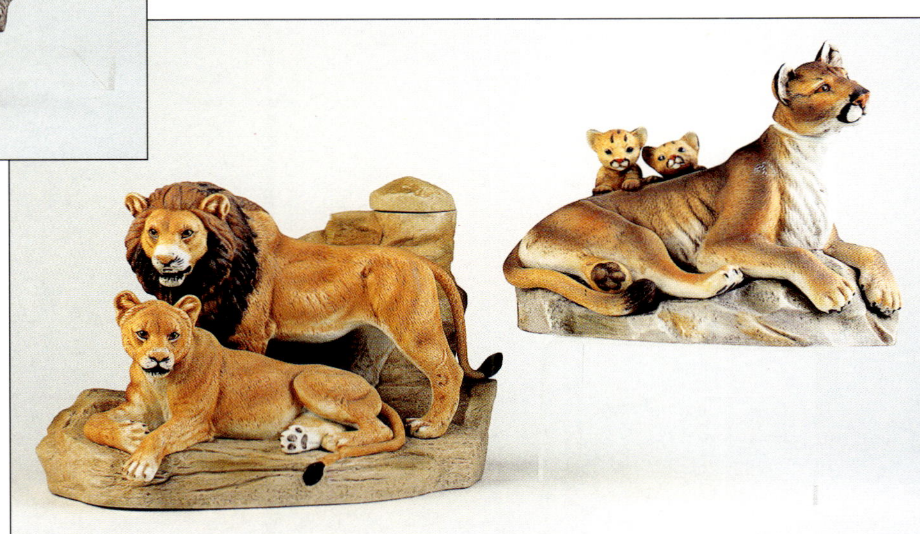

African Lion, 1987, 750ml $55-60. Mountain Lion family, 1987, 750 ml $80-85.

McCormick

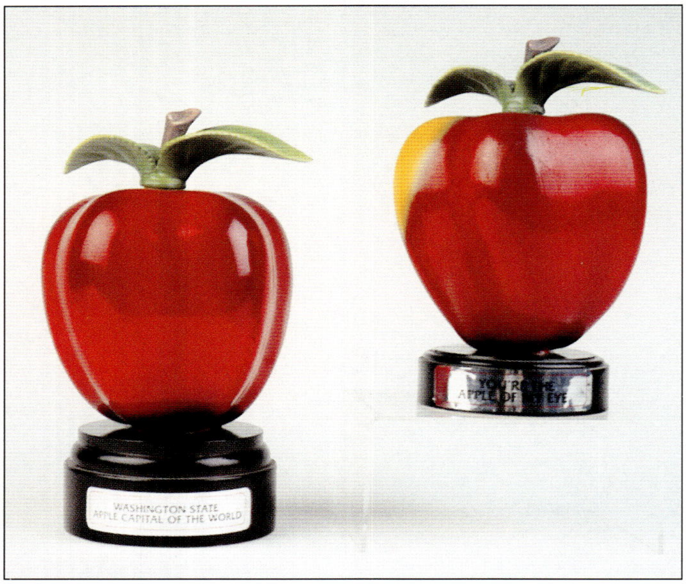

New York Apple with music, 1982, possible prototype, 50 ml, value undetermined. New York Apple without music, possible prototype, value undetermined.

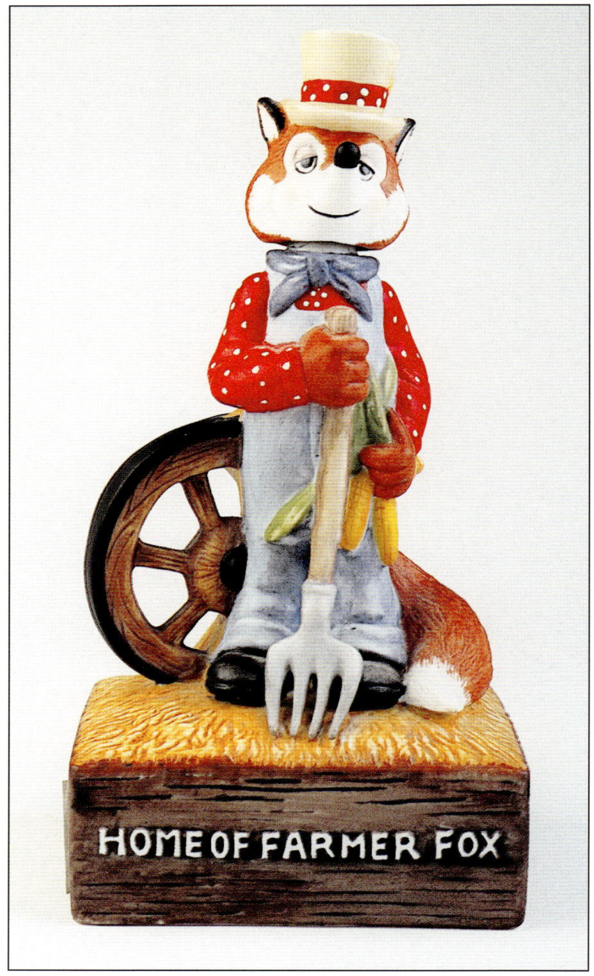

Home of Farmer Fox, music box, 50 ml $20-25.

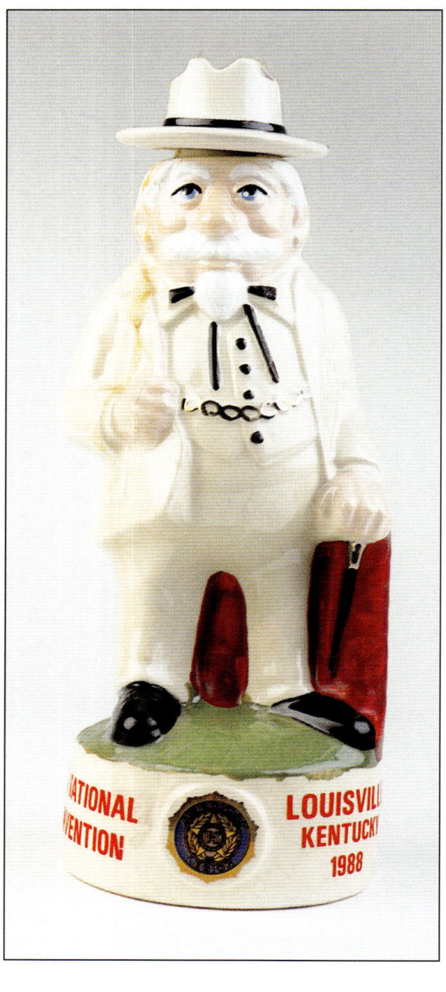

Kentucky Colonel, 1988, 70th National Convention of the American Legion, Louisville, Kentucky, 750 ml $25-30.

Automobiles and Transportation Series

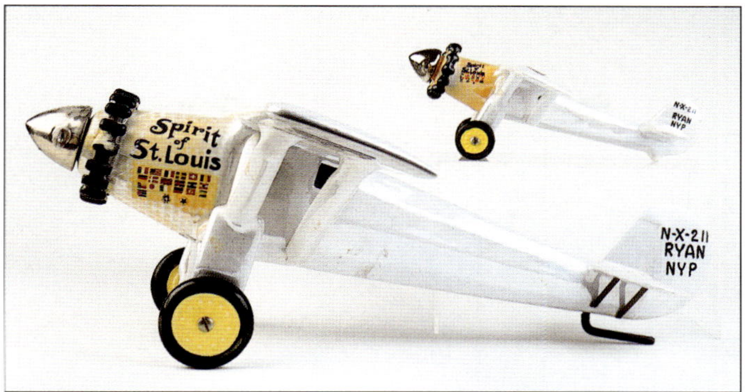

Spirit of St. Louis, 1972, fifth $75-85, mini $45-50.

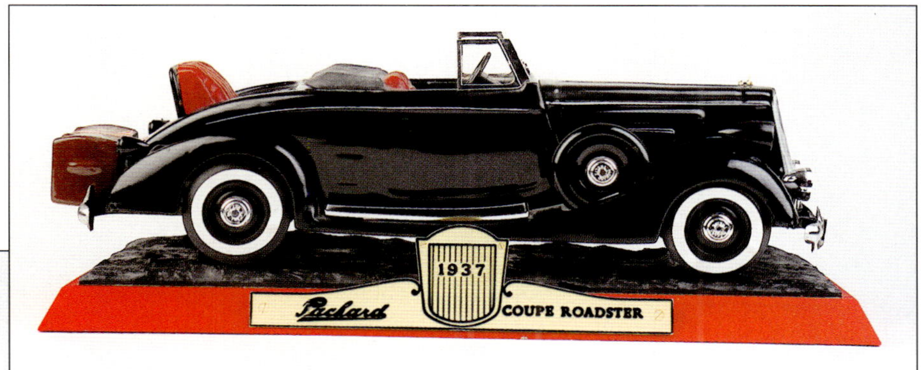

1937 Packard Coupe Roadster (black), 1980, fifth $35-40.

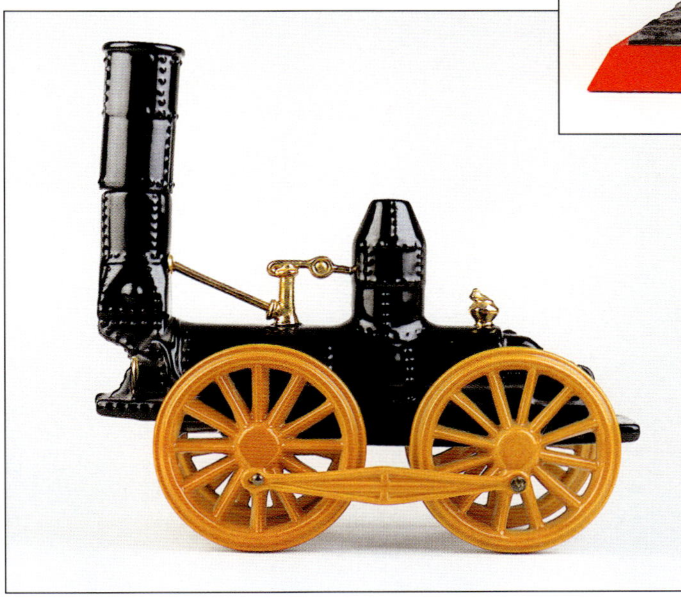

De Witt Clinton Engine, 1970, 500 ml $25-30.

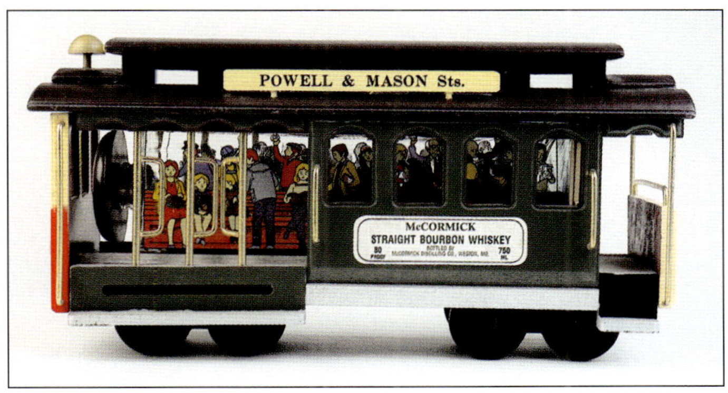

Cable Car, 1983, fifth $25-30.

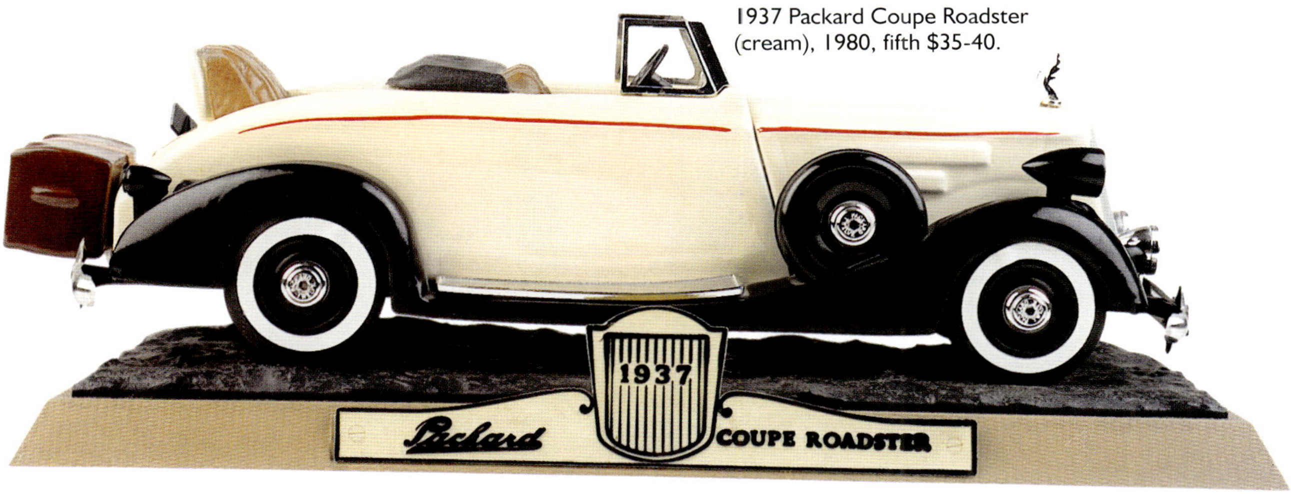

1937 Packard Coupe Roadster (cream), 1980, fifth $35-40.

Renault Racer, 1969, $45-50.

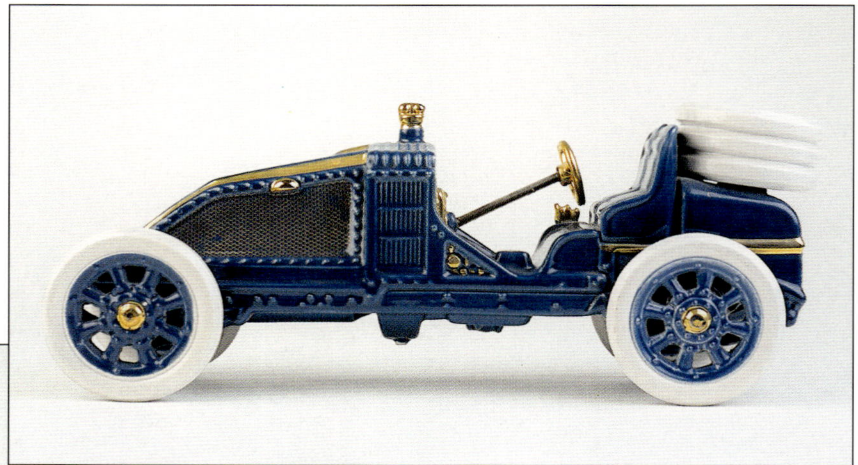

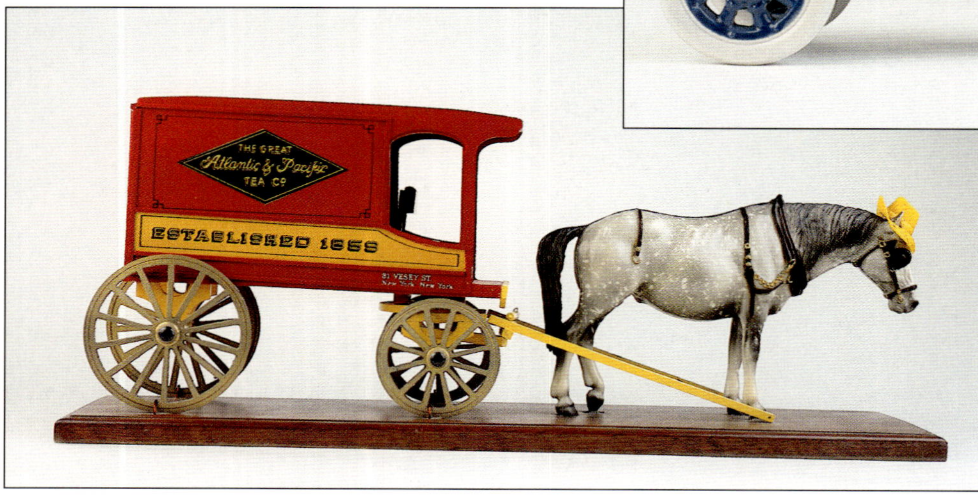

A & P Tea Company, with Briar horse, fifth $125-150.

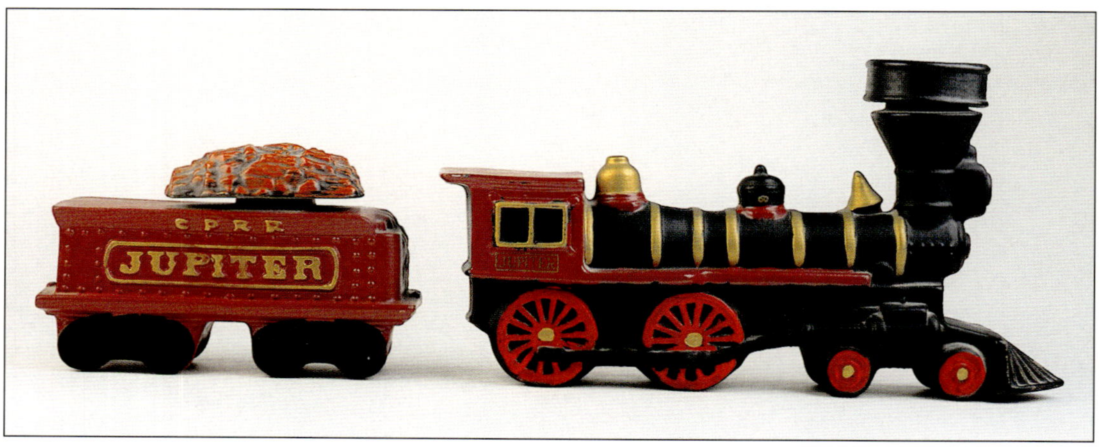

Wood Tender, 1969, pint $10-15. Jupiter Engine, 1969, fifth $25-30.

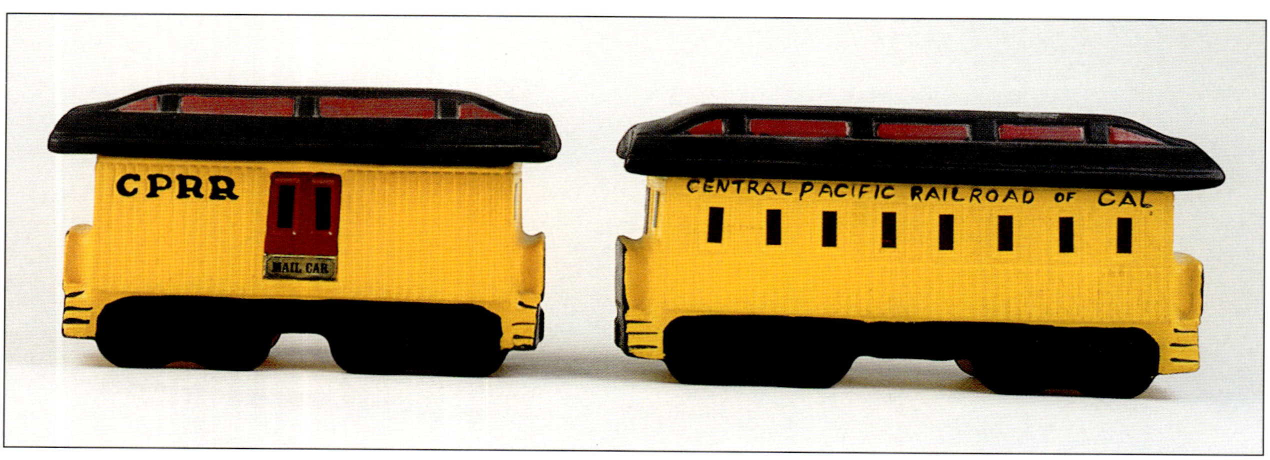

Mail Car, 1969, pint $15-20. Passenger car, 1970, fifth $15-20.

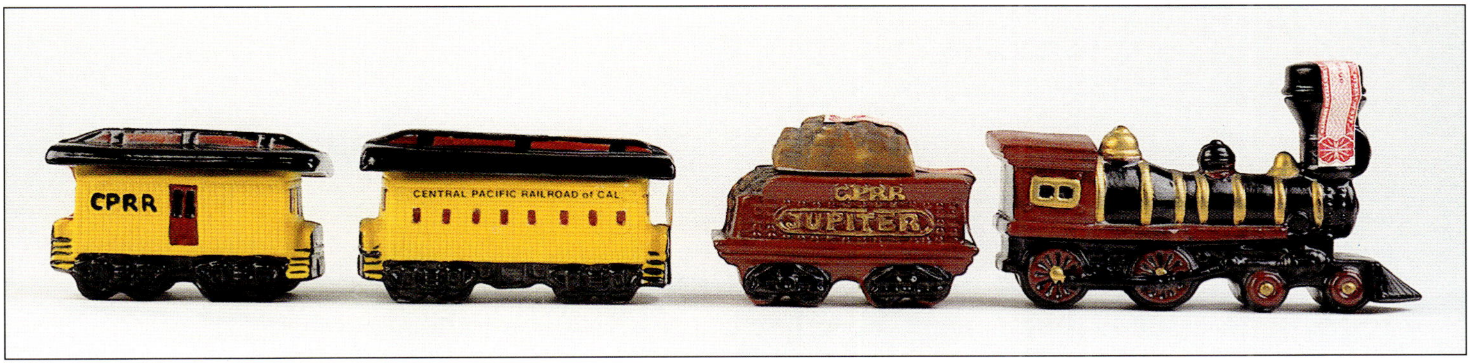

Train, 1980, mini set $45-50.

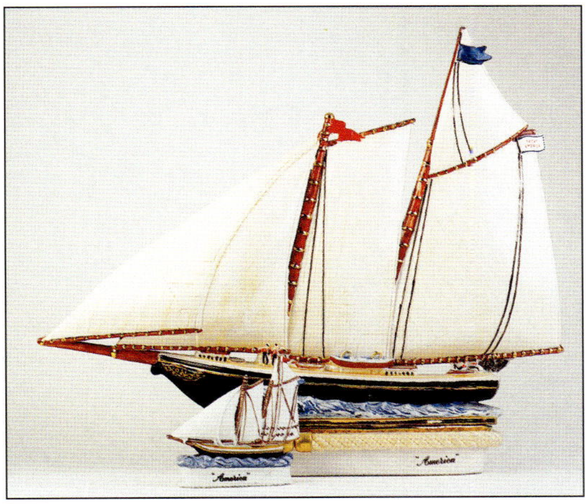

Yacht America, 1970, 13", fifth $45-50, mini $25-30.

Miscellaneous McCormick

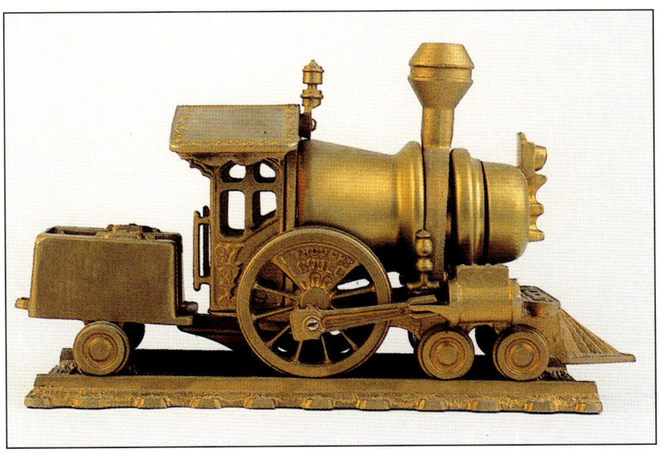

The Little Engine That Could, 1981 limited edition of 50, $45-50.

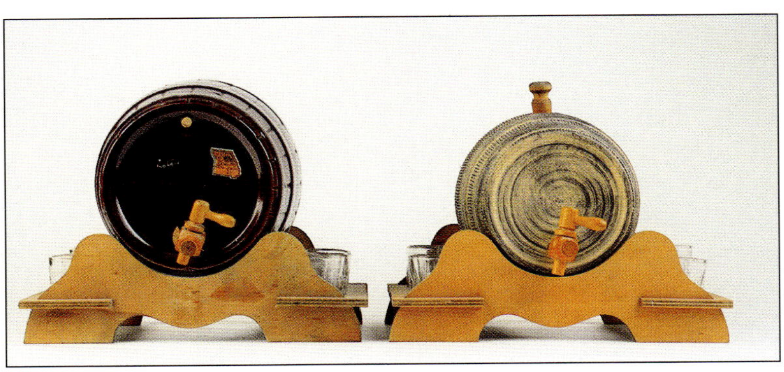

Barrel with stand and shot glasses, 1958, fifth $20-25. Barrel with stand and shot glasses, with lamp adapt kit, fifth $20-25.

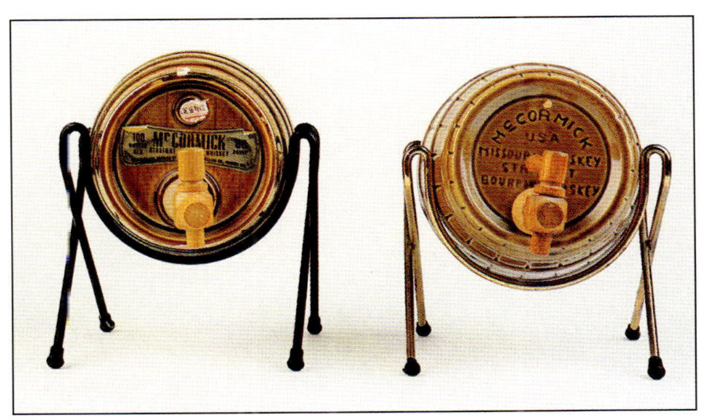

Barrel with stand (gold hoops), 1968, fifth $10-15. Barrel with stand (plain hoops), 1968, fifth $10-15.

Bicentennial Series

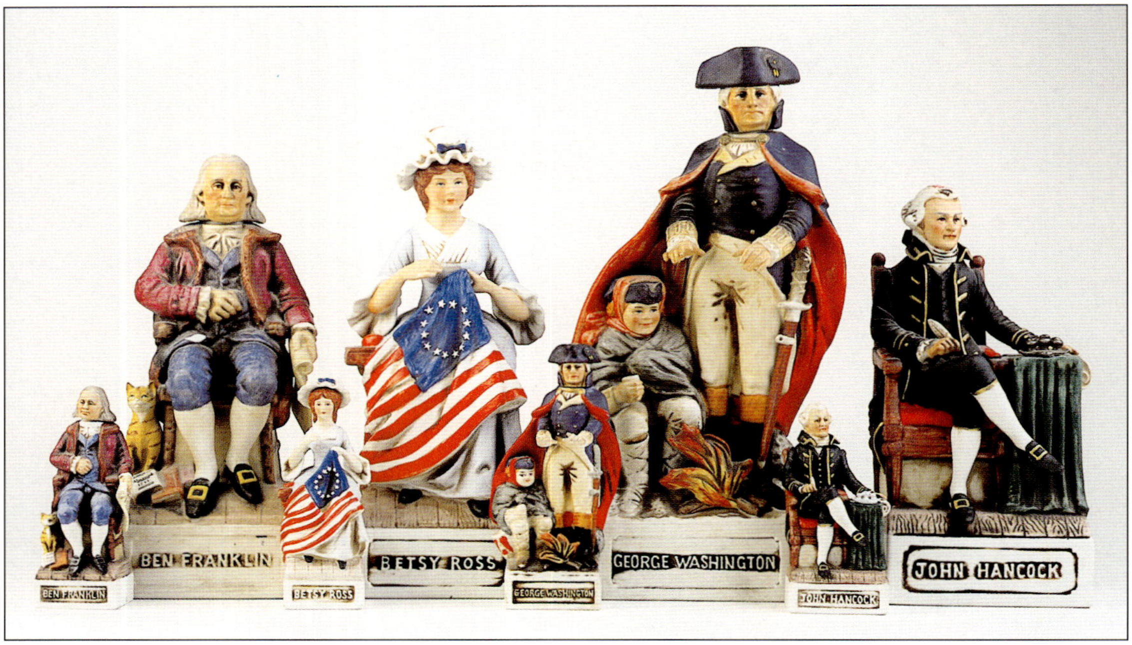

Bicentennial Series: Ben Franklin, 1975, fifth $20, mini, 1976 $10. Betsy Ross, 1975, fifth $25, mini (1976) $15. George Washington, 1975, fifth $25, mini (1976) $15. John Hancock, 1975, fifth $10, mini (1976) $5.

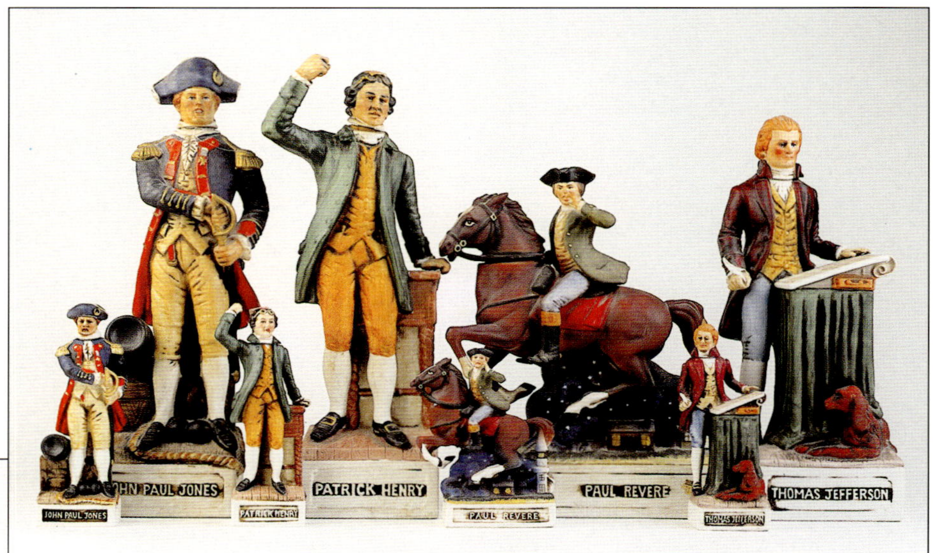

Bicentennial Series: John Paul Jones, 1975, fifth $ 20, mini (1976) $10. Patrick Henry, 1975, fifth $20, mini (1976) $10. Paul Revere, 1975, fifth $20, mini (1976) $10. Thomas Jefferson, 1975, fifth $20, mini (1976) $10.

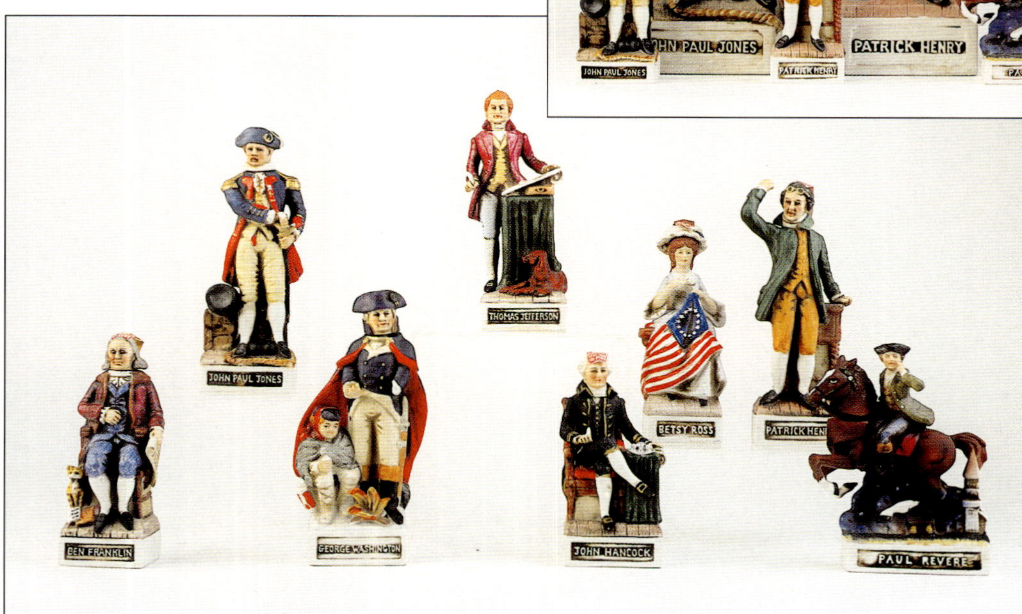

Bicentennial set of minis, 1976, $95-100.

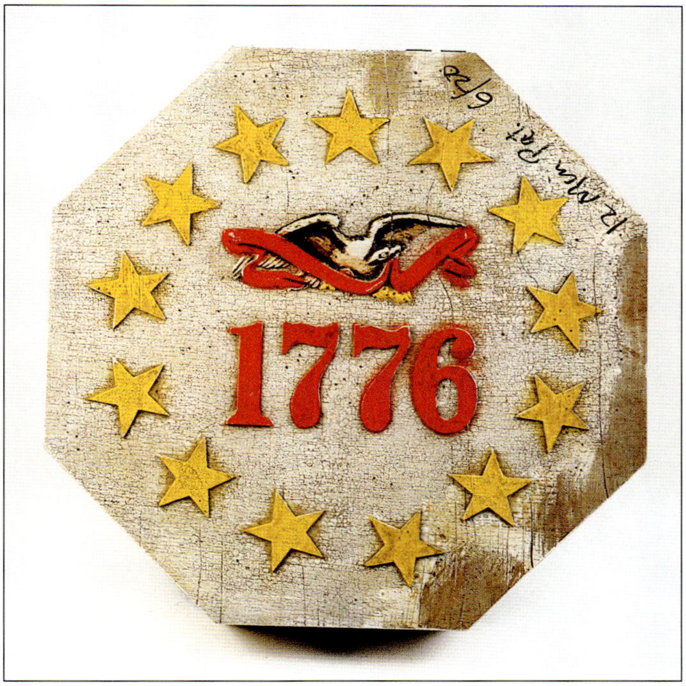

Bicentennial set case, 1976, $45-50.

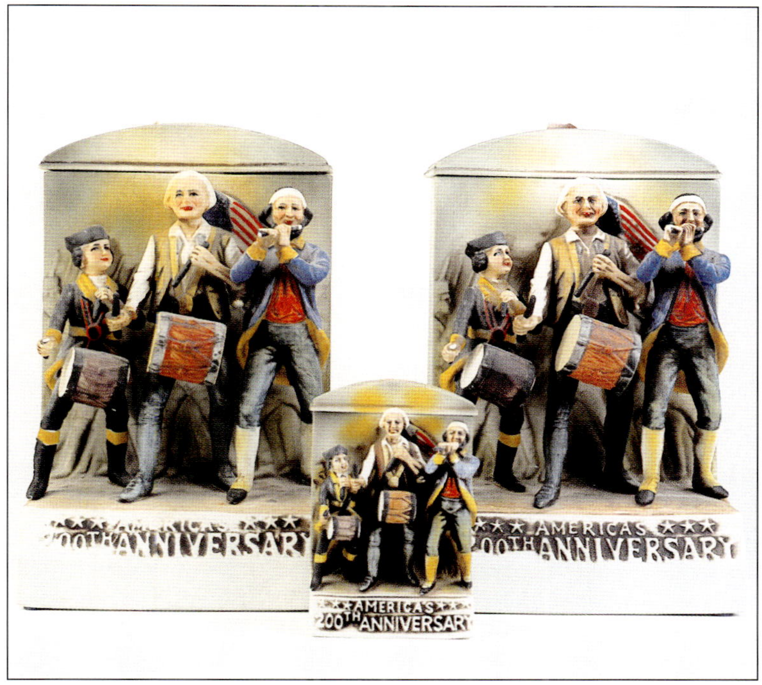

Spirit of '76, Bookends with music, 1976, fifth $40-45, mini (1977) $20.

Birds

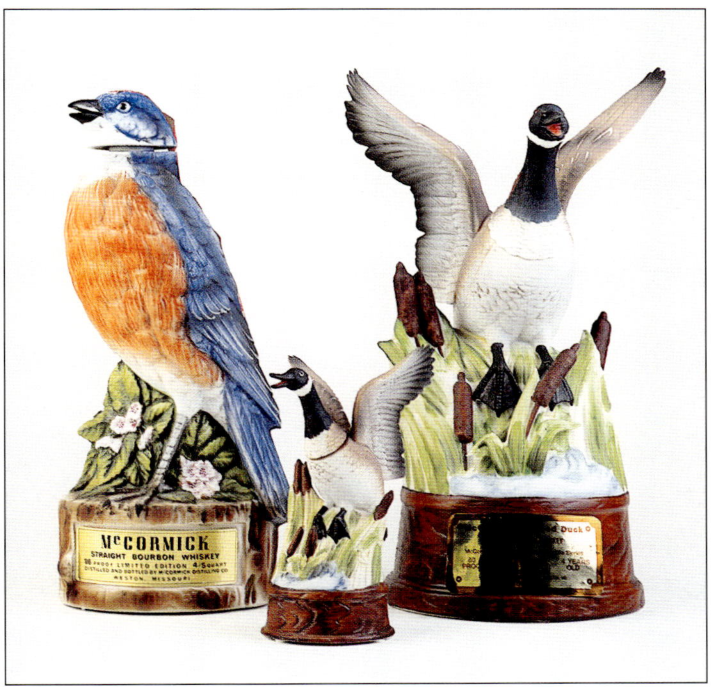

Bluebird, 1971, fifth $10-15.
Canadian Goose, 1984, fifth $20-25, mini $10-12.

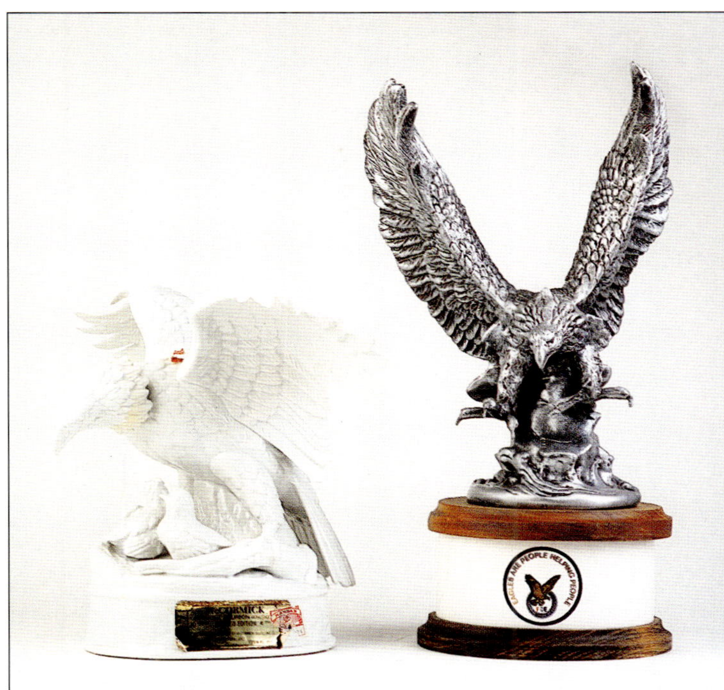

Eagle (white), 1983, fifth $45-50.
Eagle, FOE (silver), 1983, $65-70.

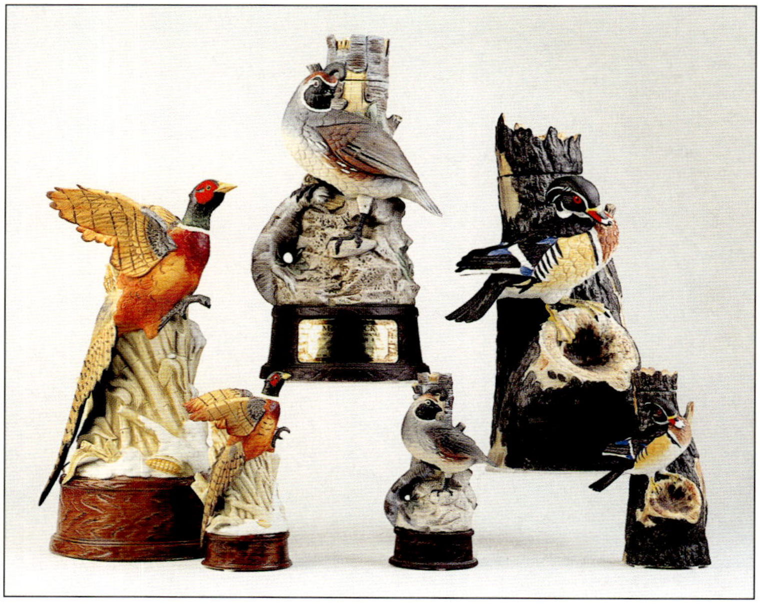

Pheasant, 1982, fifth $20, mini $10. Gambel Quail, fifth $15, mini $5. Wood Duck, 1980, fifth $15, mini $5.

Bulls

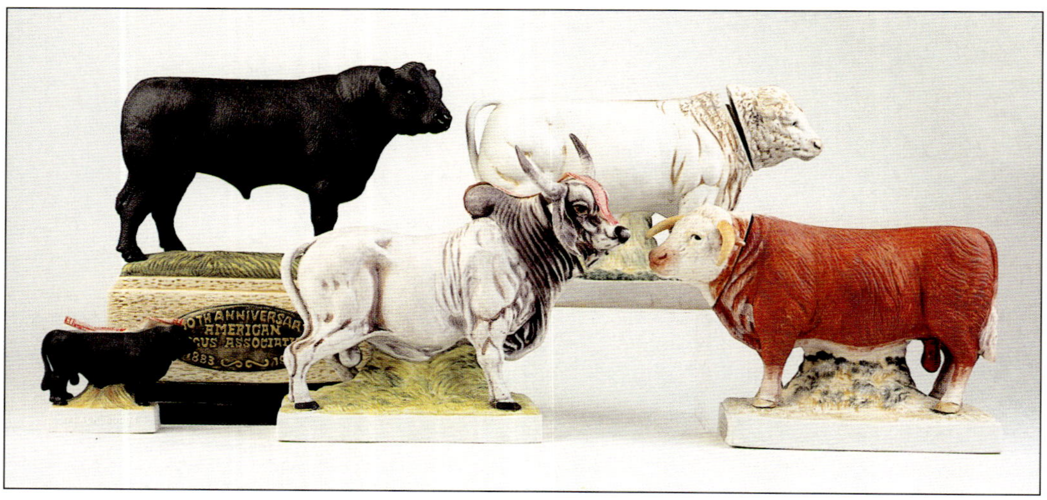

Blank Angus, Angus Assoc. 100th Anniversary, fifth, $25-30. Black Angus, 1975, mini $10-15. Brahma, 1973, fifth $20-25. Charolais, 1974, fifth $20-25. Herford, 1972, fifth $20-25.

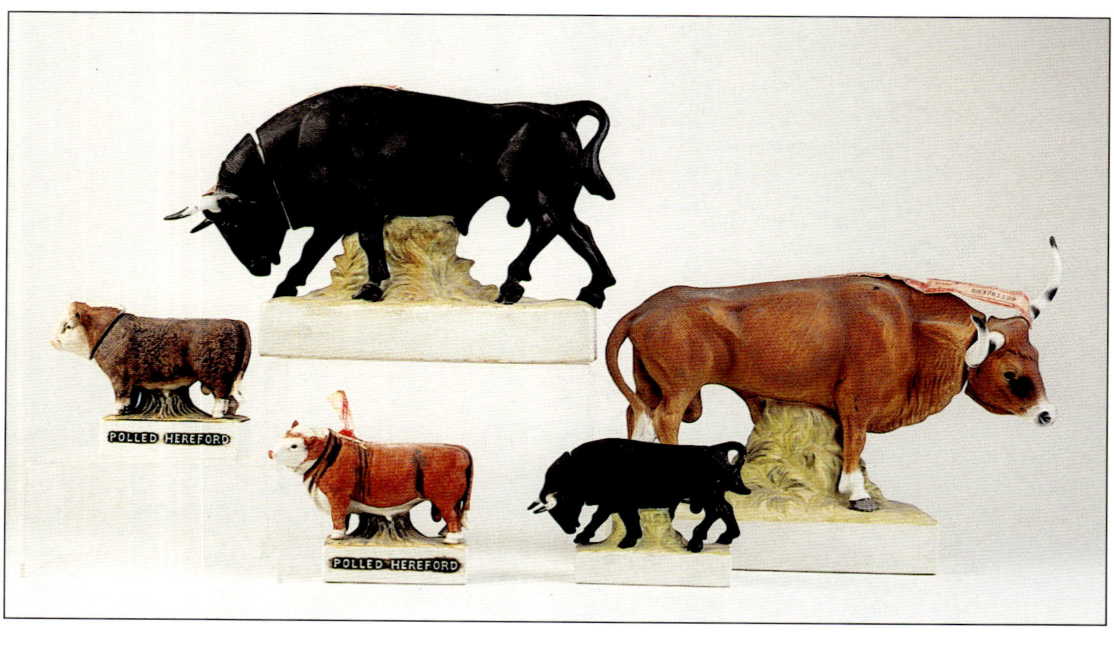

Polled Hereford (young), 1975, mini $10. Polled Hereford (old), 1975, mini $15. Mexican Fighting bull, 1974, fifth $15-20, mini $10. Texas Longhorn, 1974, fifth $15-20.

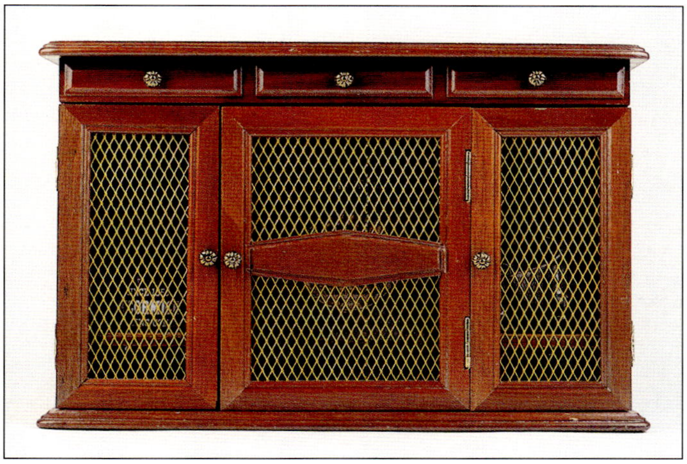

Cabinet #1, holds shot glasses inside top, 1984, fifth $25-30.

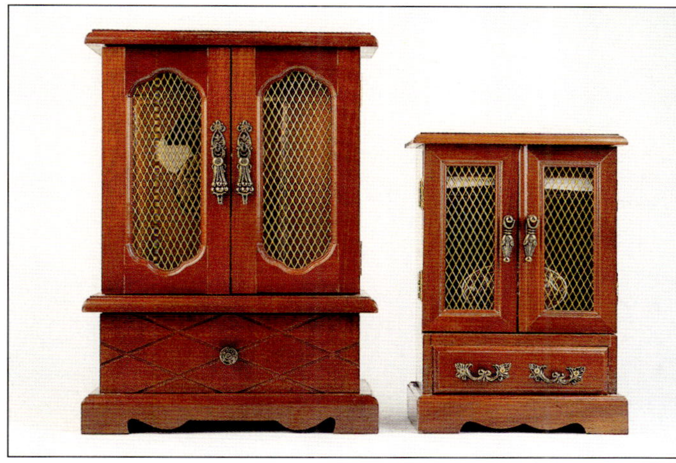

Cabinet #2, shot glass coasters in pull-out drawer, 1984, fifth $25-30. Cabinet #3, 1984, fifth $20-25.

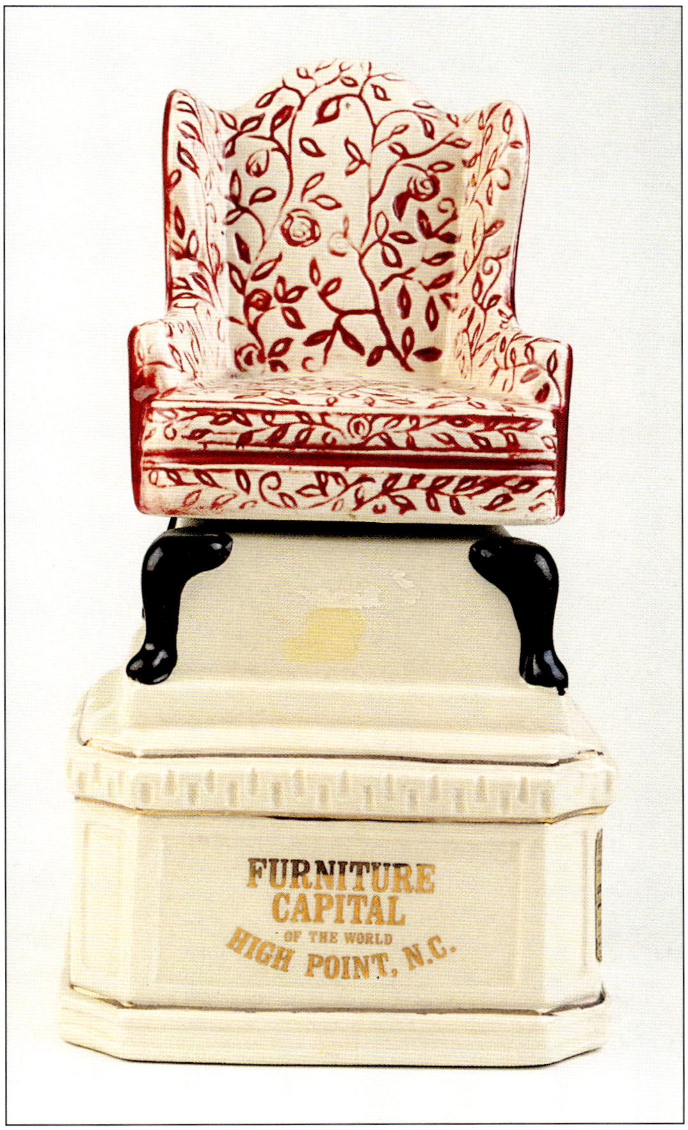

Queen Anne Chair, 1979, $20-25.

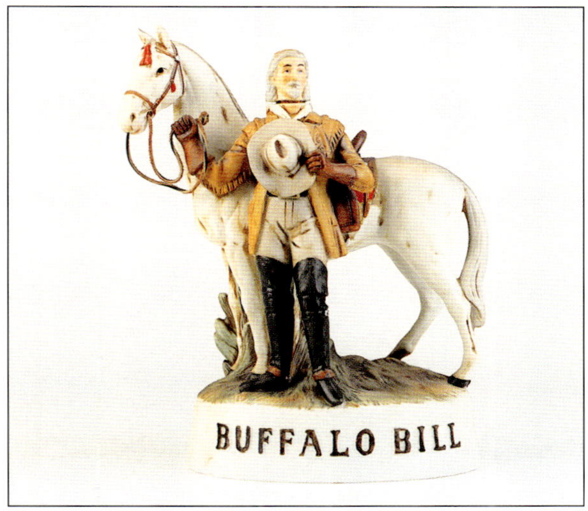

Buffalo B ll, 1979, fifth $45-50.

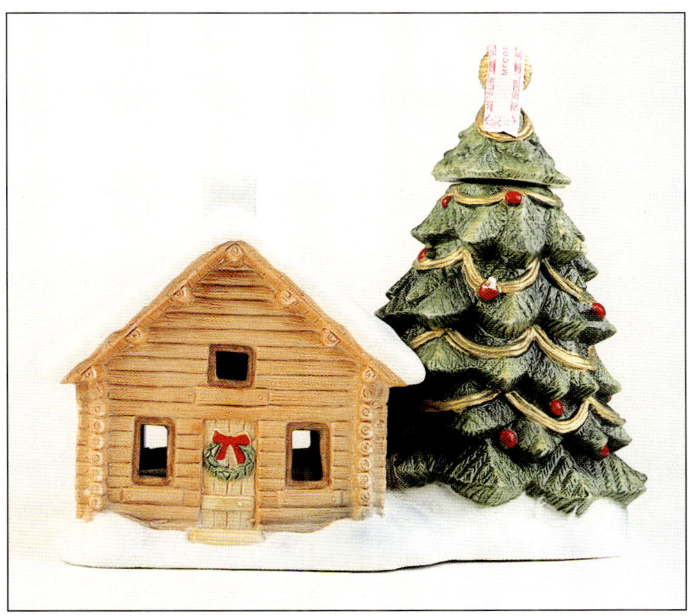

Christmas tree and cabin, with light, 1984, $25-30.

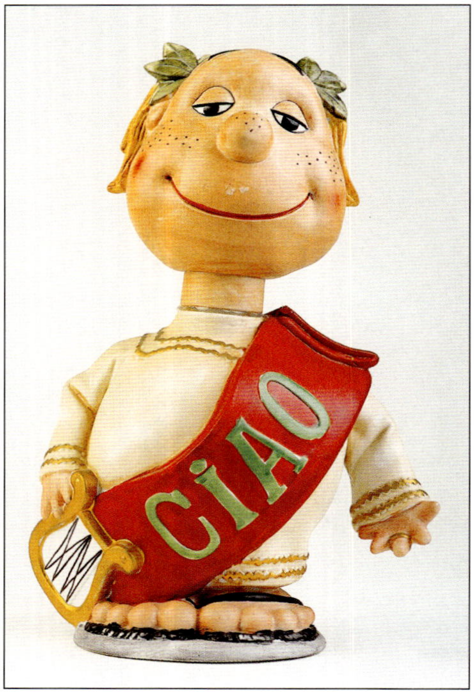

Ciao Baby, 1978, fifth $25-30.

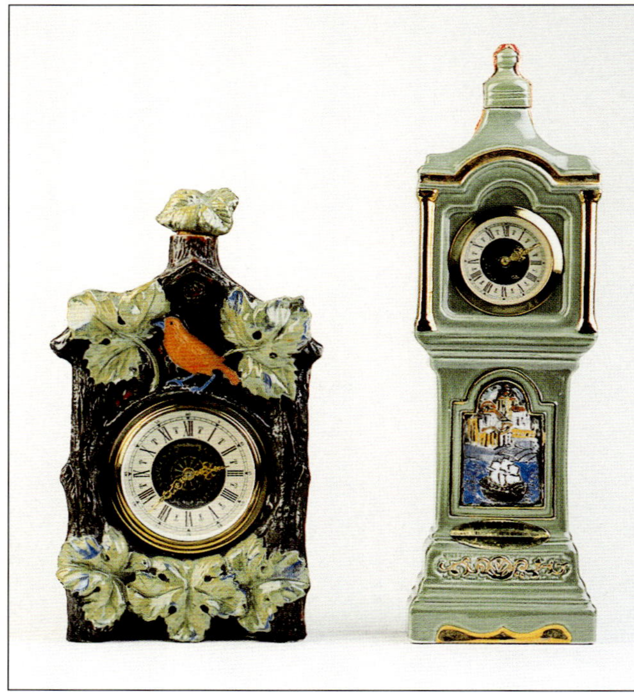

Cuckoo Clock, 1971, fifth $20-25.
Queen Anne Clock, 1979, fifth $15-20.

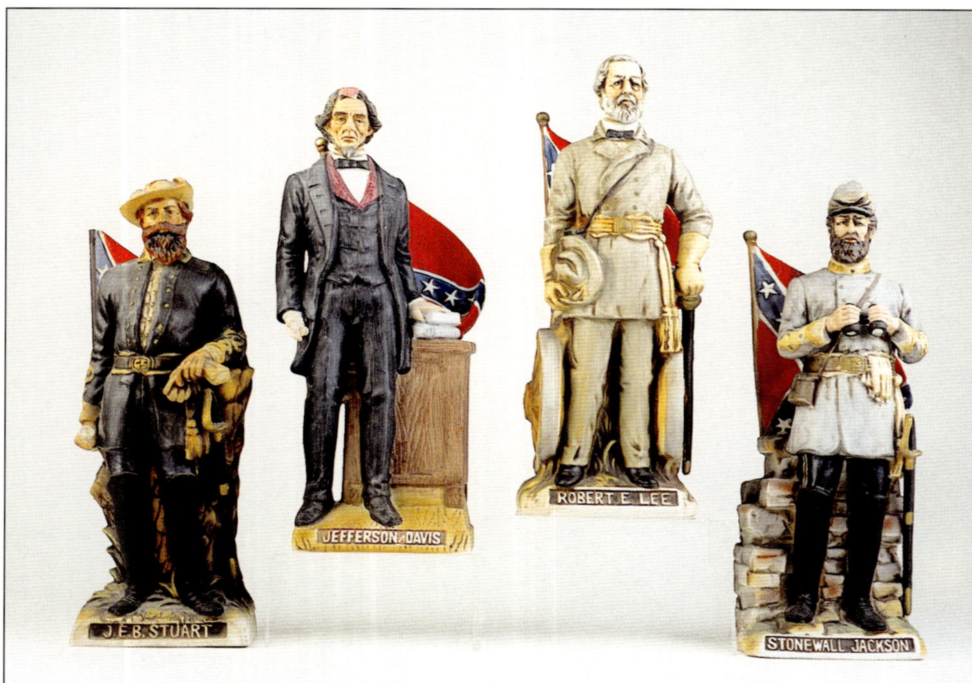

Confederate Series: Jeb Stuart, 1976, fifth $45-50. Jefferson Davis, 1976, fifth $45-50. Robert E. Lee, 1978, fifth $45-50. Stonewall Jackson, 1976, fifth $45-50.

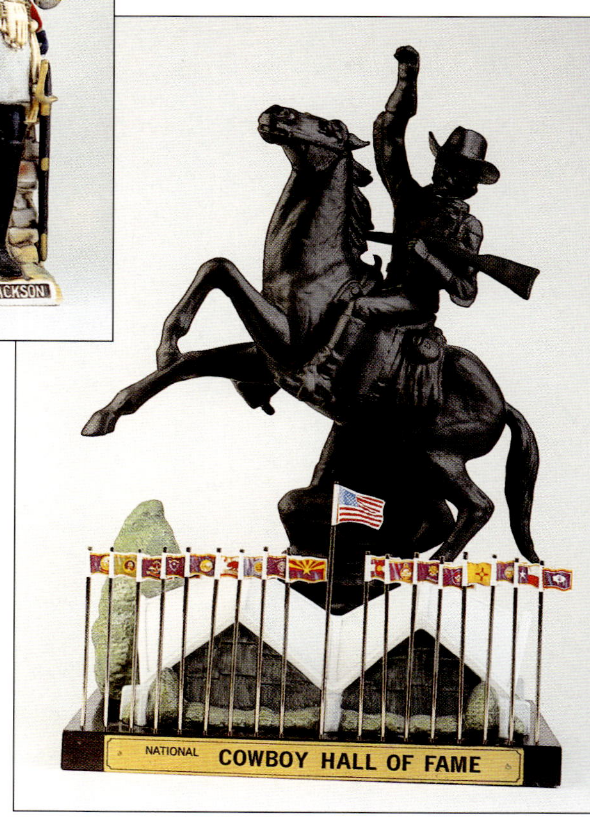

National Cowboy Hall of Fame, 1983, fifth $65-75.

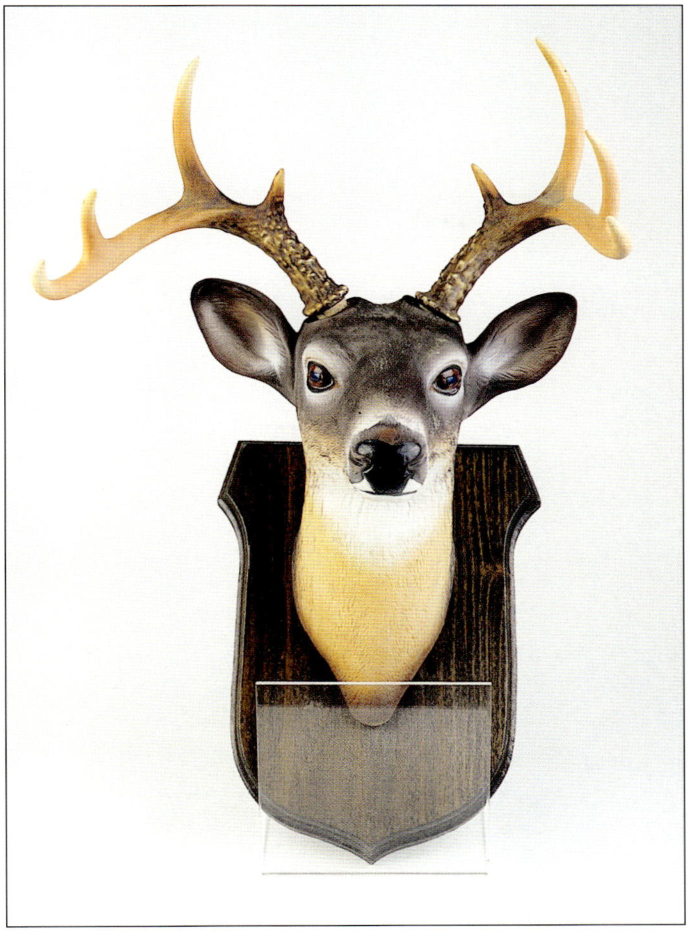

White Tail Deer trophy, 1983, fifth $25-30.

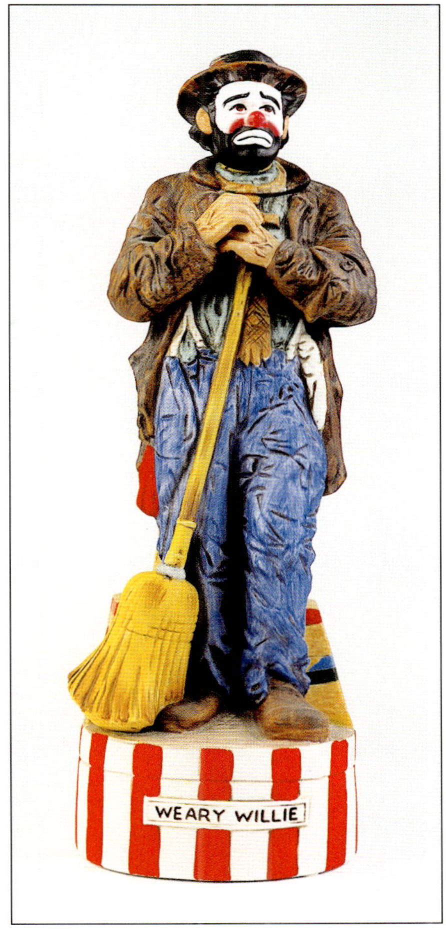

Weary Willy, 1981, music box, fifth $95-110.

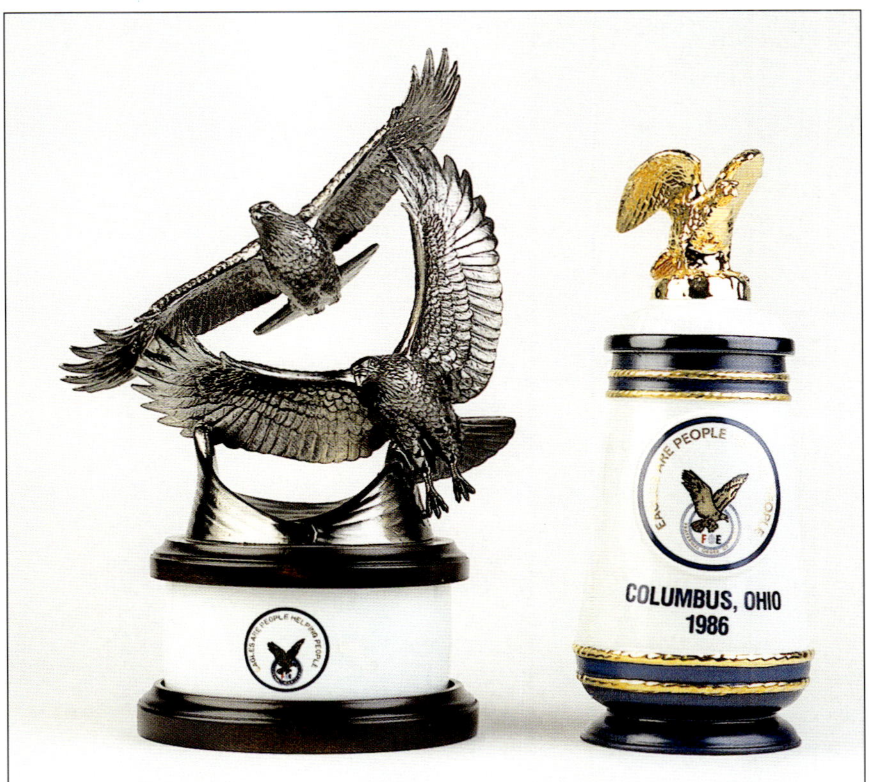

FOE convention eagles (silver), 1984, Milwaukee, Wisconsin, fifth $75-85. Gold eagle, Columbus, Ohio, 1986, fifth $45-50.

Entertainer Series

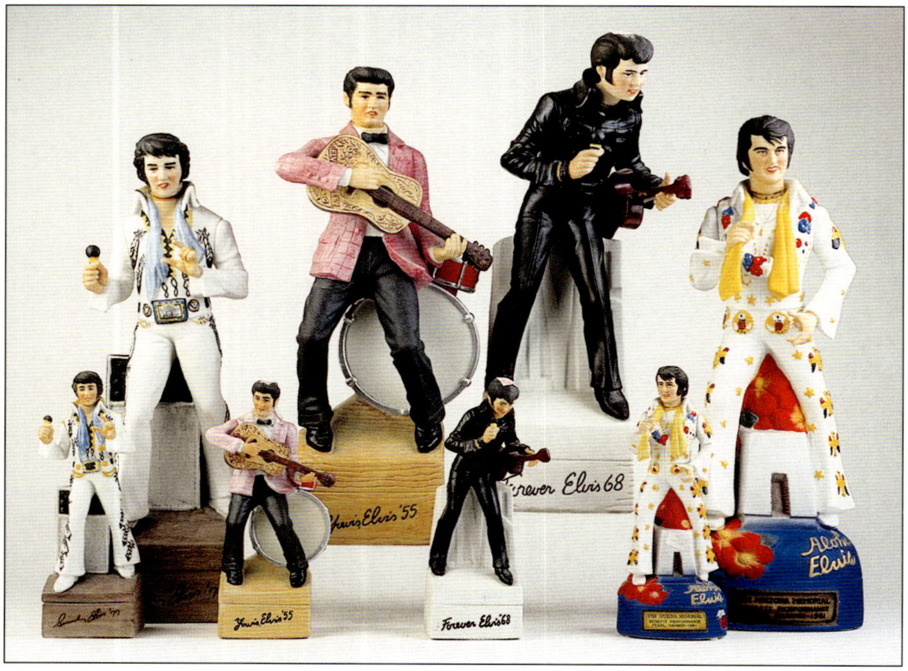

Elvis #1, music box, 1978, fifth $65-76, mini $20-25. Elvis #2, music box, 1979, fifth $65-75, mini $20-25. Elvis #3, music box, 1980, fifth $65-75, mini $20-25, Elvis Aloha, music box, 1981, fifth $110-125, mini $75-85.

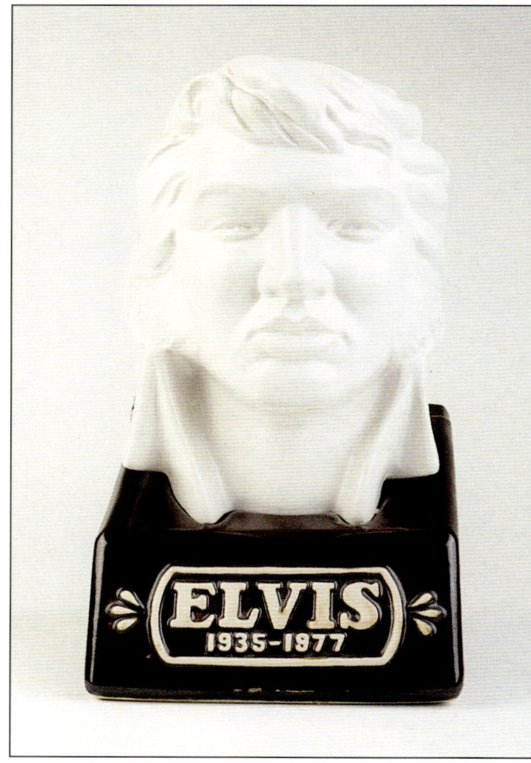

Elvis bust, 1978, fifth $35-40.

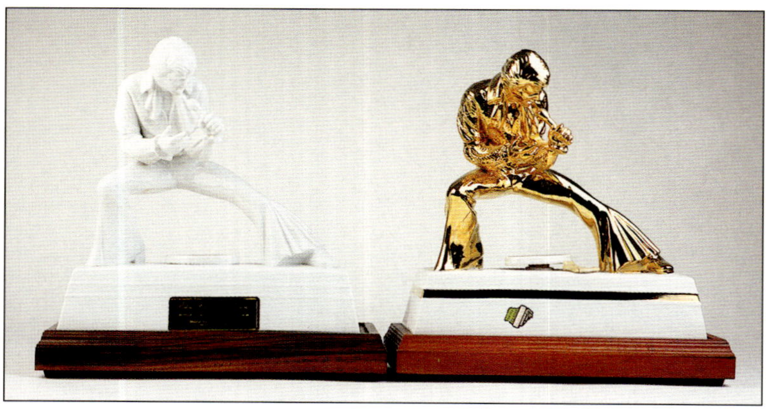

Elvis, Designer #1, music box, 1981, fifth $75-85. Elvis, Designer #1, Gold Encore, music box, 1984, fifth $125-135.

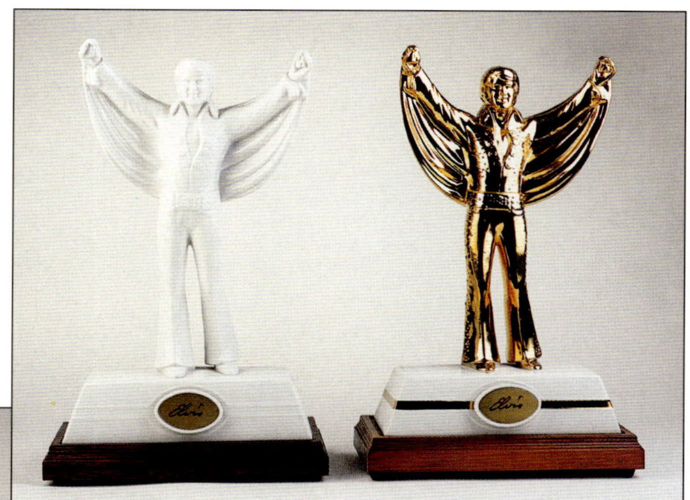

Elvis, Designer #2, music box, 1982, fifth $95-110. Elvis, Designer #2, music box (gold), 1984, fifth $125-135.

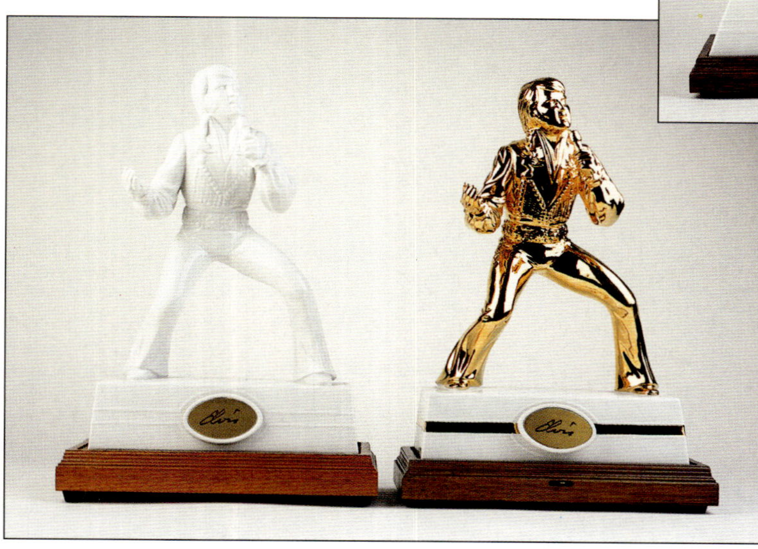

Elvis, Designer #3, music box, 1983, fifth $110-124. Elvis, Designer #3, music box, 1984, gold, fifth $150-175.

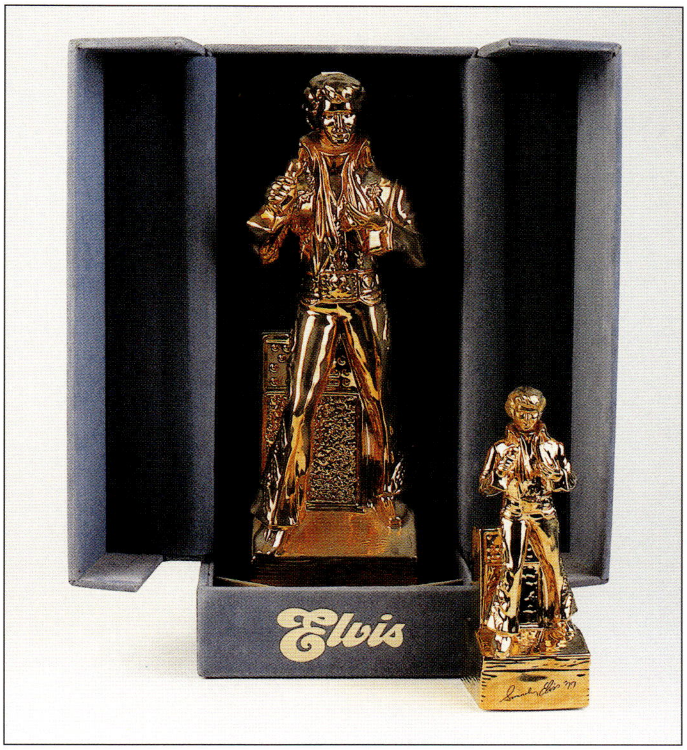

Elvis (gold), music box, 1979, fifth $90-100, mini $45-50.

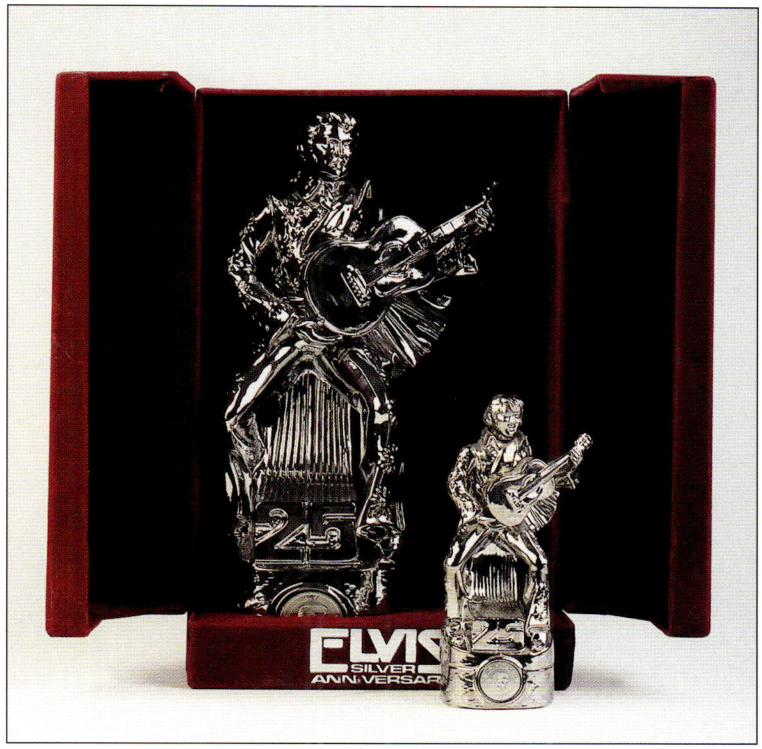

Elvis, Silver Anniversary, music box, 1980, fifth $75-85, mini $40-45.

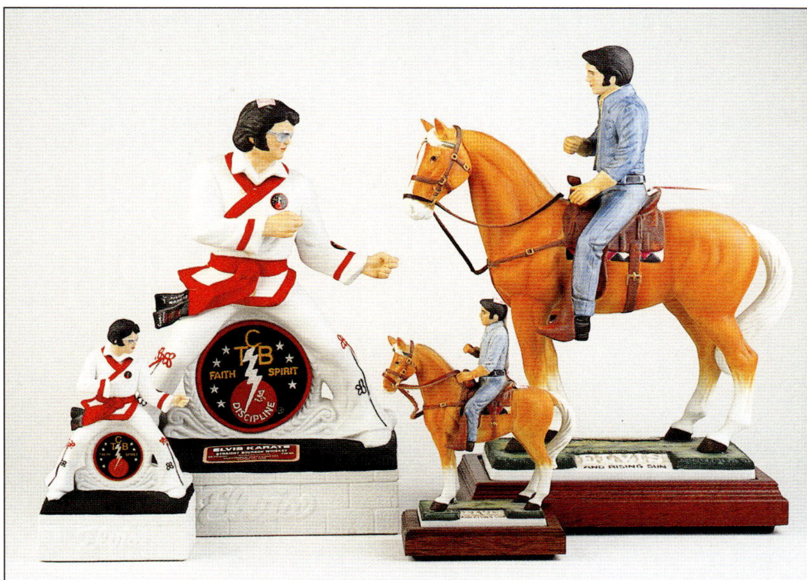

Karate Elvis, music box, 1982, fifth $145-150, mini $75-80. Rising Sun Elvis, music box, 1984, fifth $200-225, mini $150-175.

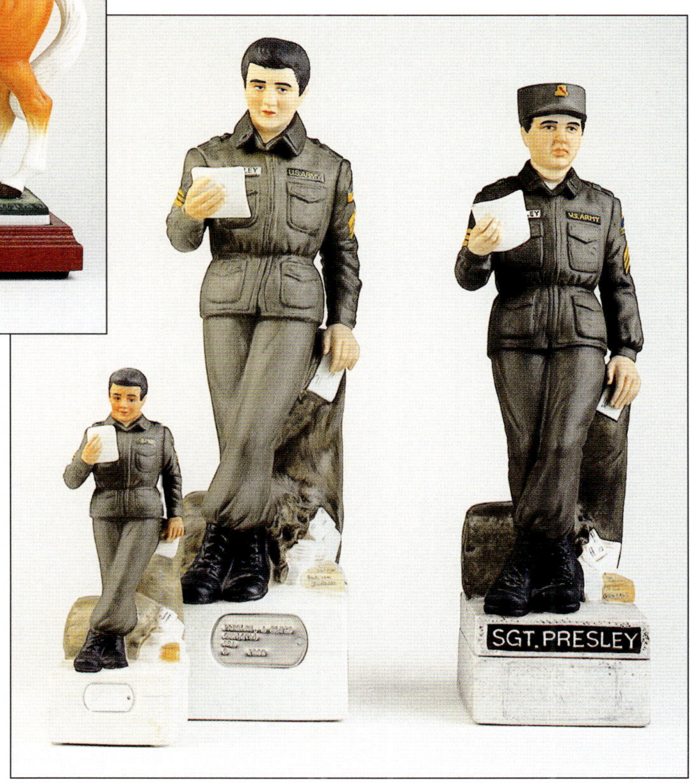

Elvis as a sergeant, music box, 1983, fifth (with dog-tags) $175-195, mini $125-135. Elvis, Sergeant Presley, one-of-a-kind prototype bottle, fifth $395-450.

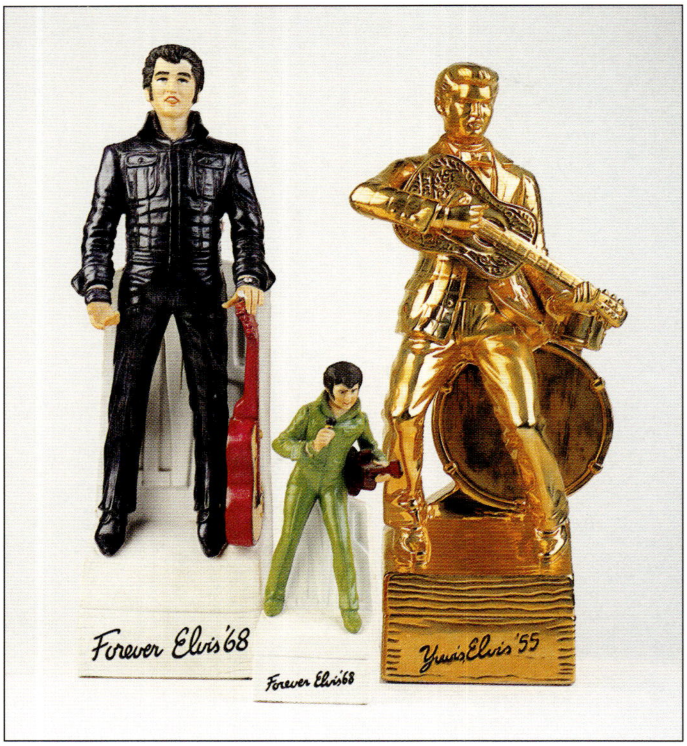

Forever Elvis '68, one-of-a-kind bottle, 1979, fifth $250-300. Forever Elvis '68, green suit, mini $150-200. Yours, Elvis '55, 14k gold plated, music box, fifth $150-195.

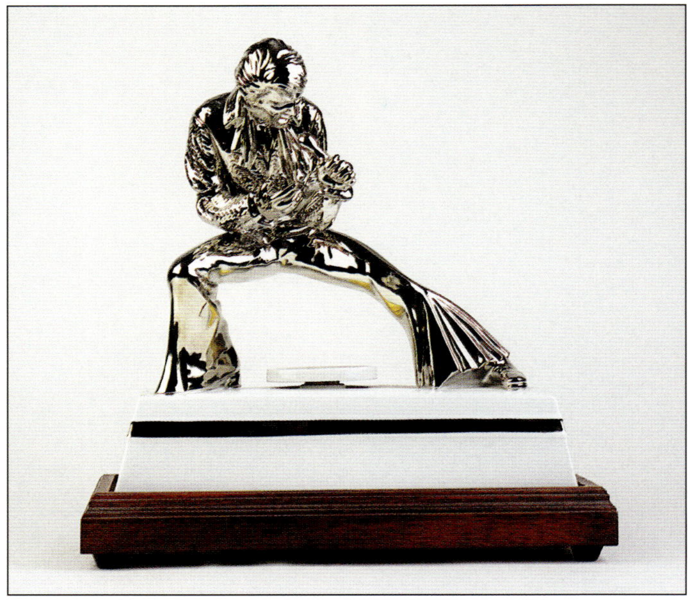

Elvis, Designer #1, one-of-a-kind silver edition, music box, fifth $250-295.

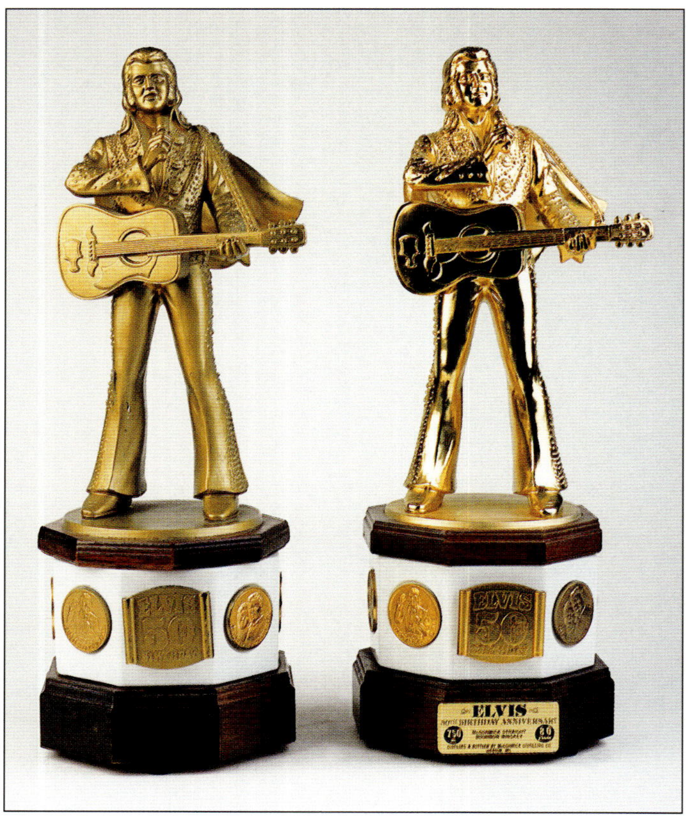

Elvis 50th birthday (bronze), one-of-a-kind, fifth $450-500. Elvis 50th birthday (gold), music box, fifth $395-425.

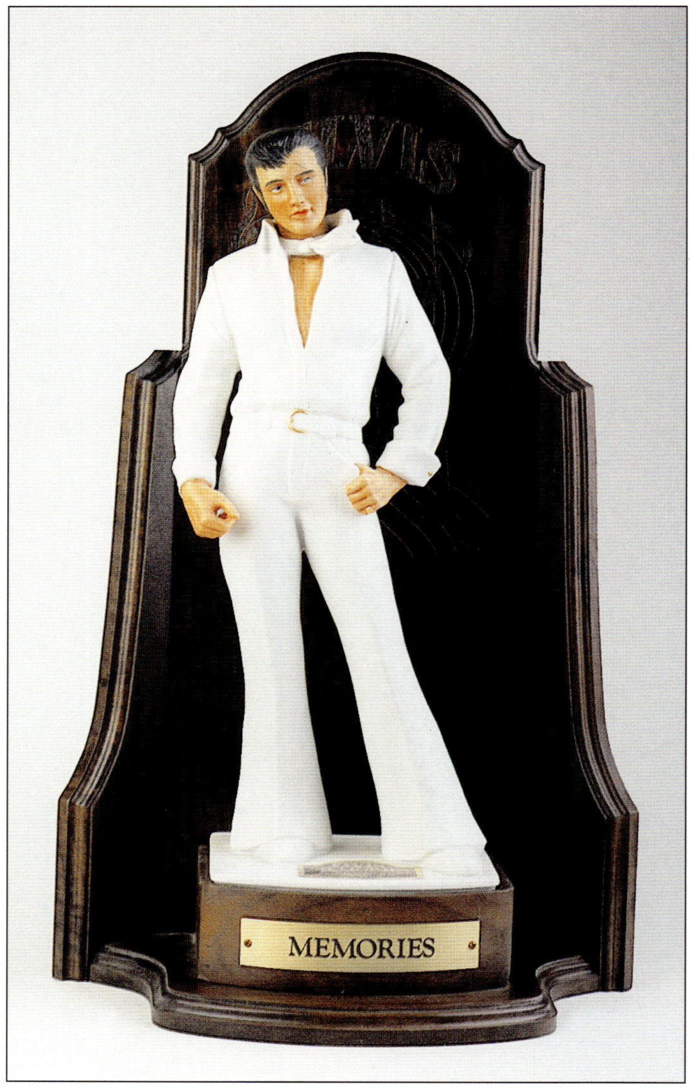

Elvis, Memories, music box, fifth $395-445.

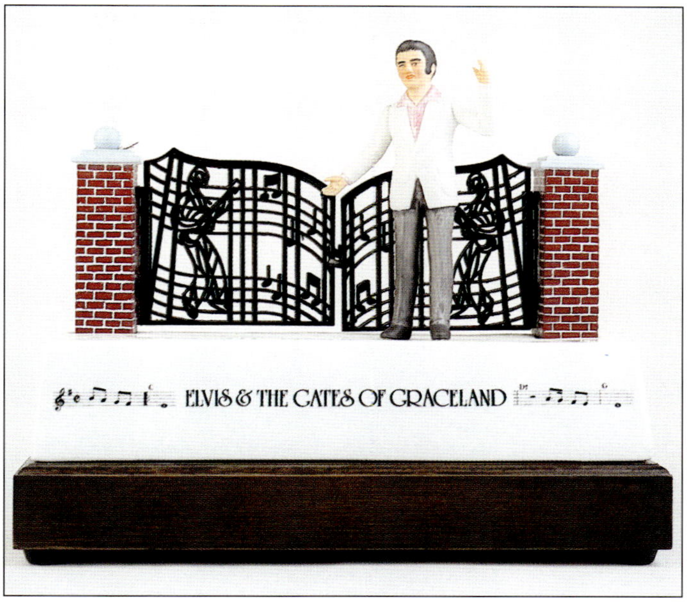

Elvis and The Gates of Graceland, music box, fifth $175-195.

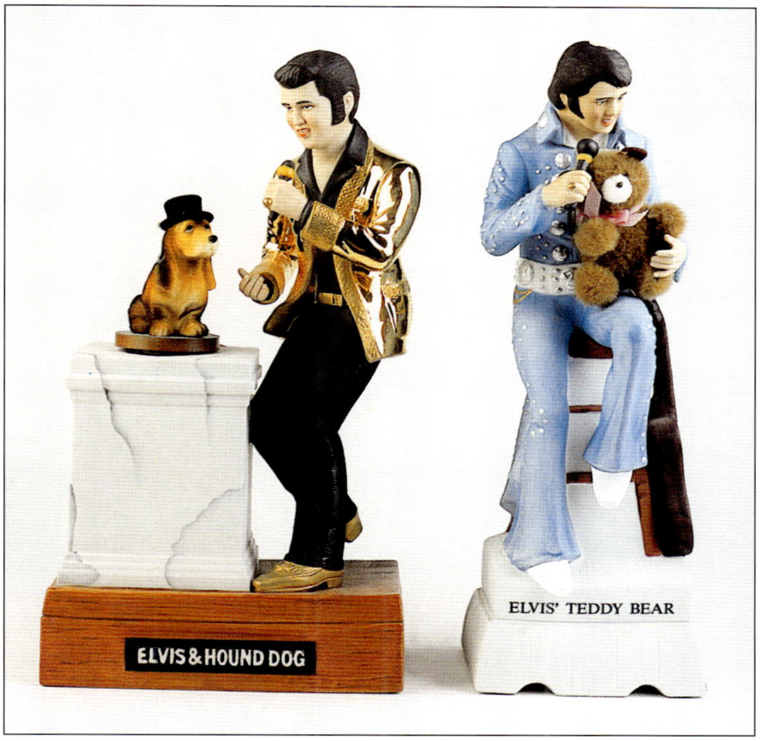

Hound Dog, music box, fifth $275-295. Elvis with Teddy Bear, music box, fifth $275-295.

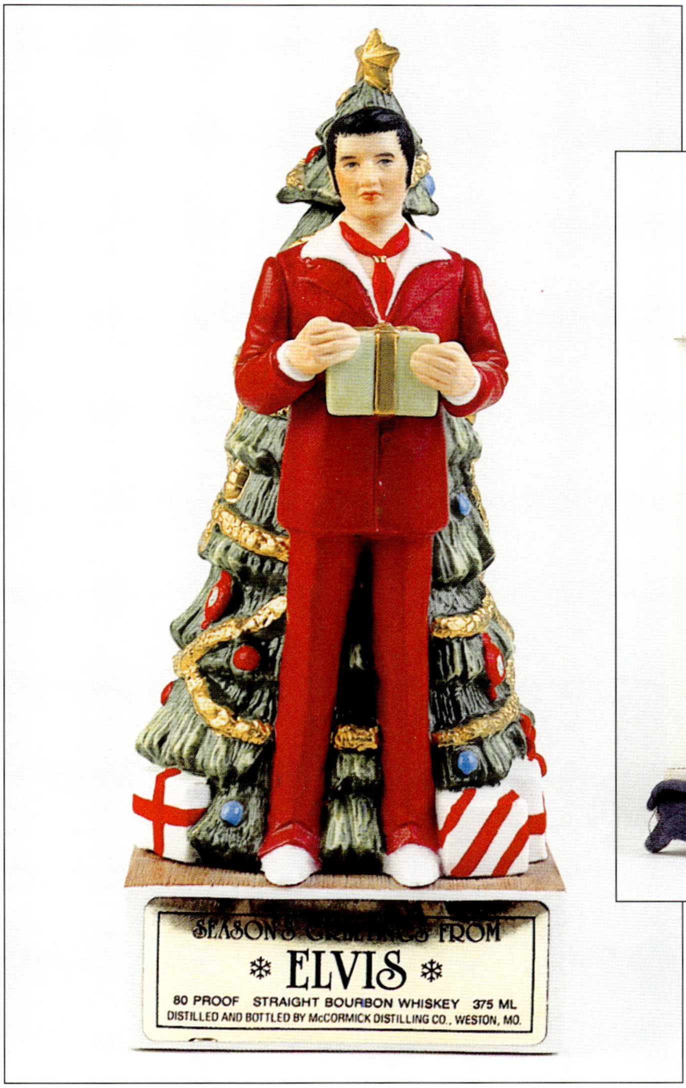

Elvis Christmas, music box, 375 ml $145-165.

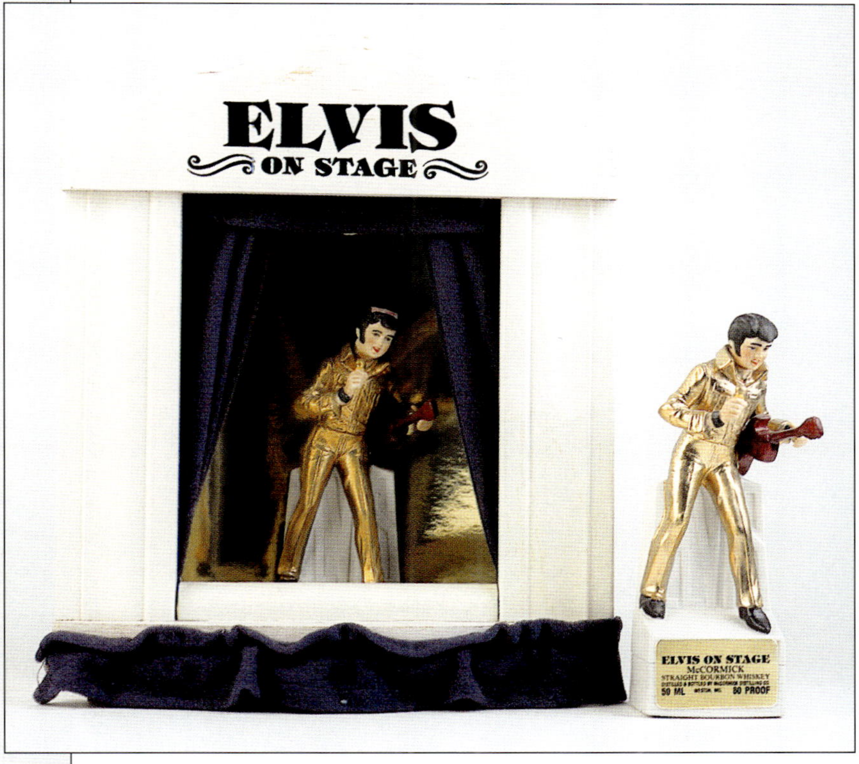

Elvis on stage (blue curtain), music box $295. Elvis on stage (red curtain), music box (not shown) $295. Elvis, mini without stage, $75-95.

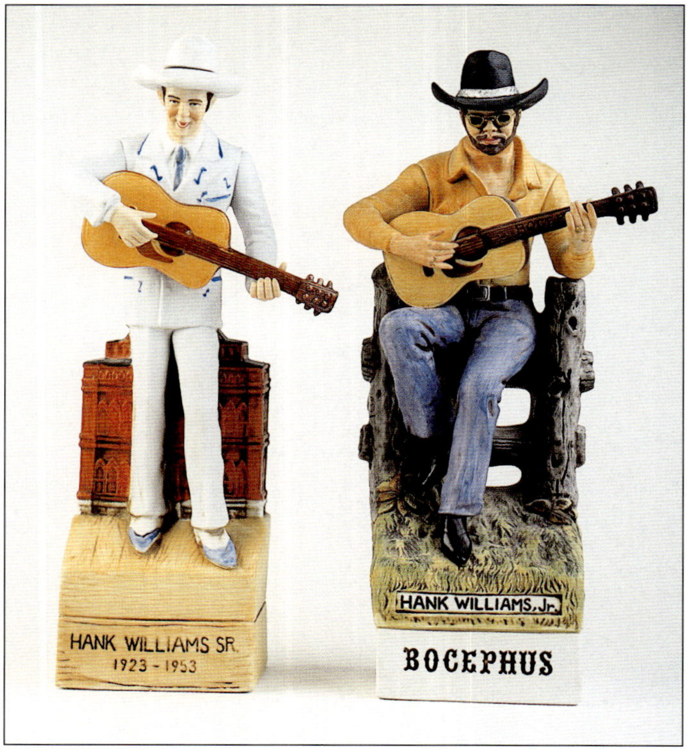

Hank Williams Sr., 1980, music box, fifth $75-95. Hank Williams Jr., 1980, music box, fifth $95-110.

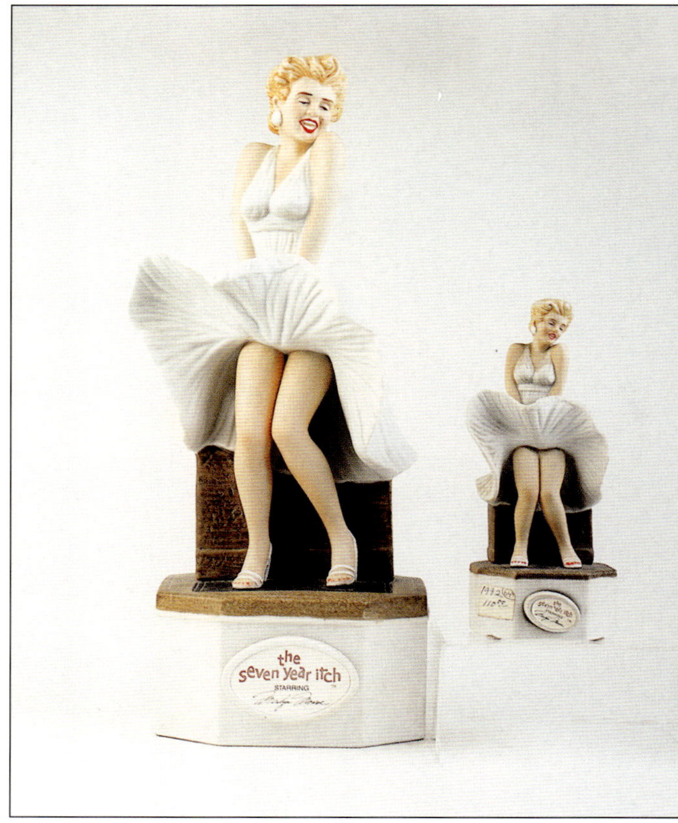

Marilyn Monroe, 1984, fifth $450-500, mini $195-225.

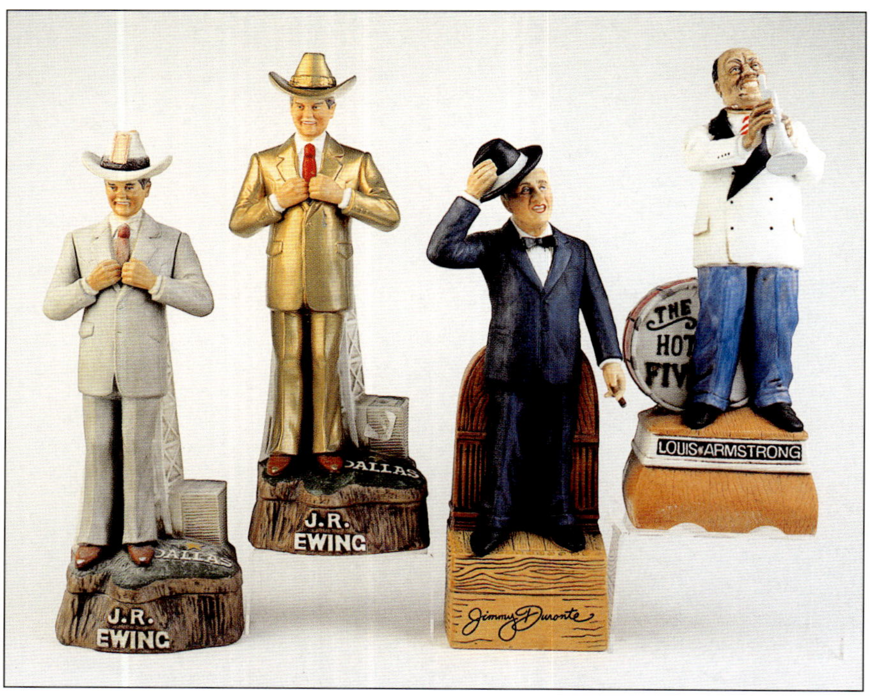

J.R. Ewing, 1980, fifth $35-45. J.R. Ewing (gold edition), 1981, fifth $45-65. Jimmy Durante, 1981, music box, fifth $65-75. Louis Armstrong, music box, 1983, fifth $85-95.

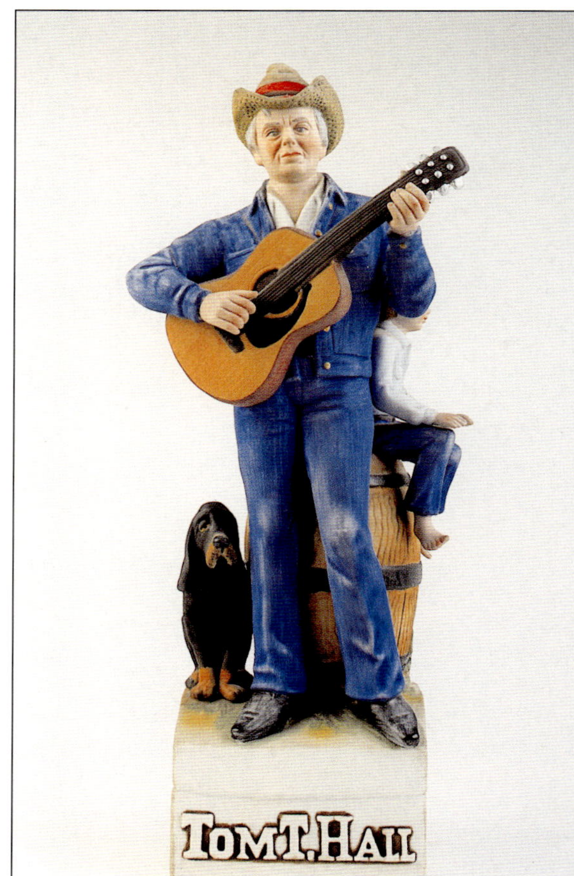

Tom T. Hall, 1980, music box, fifth $75-95.

Miscellaneous McCormick

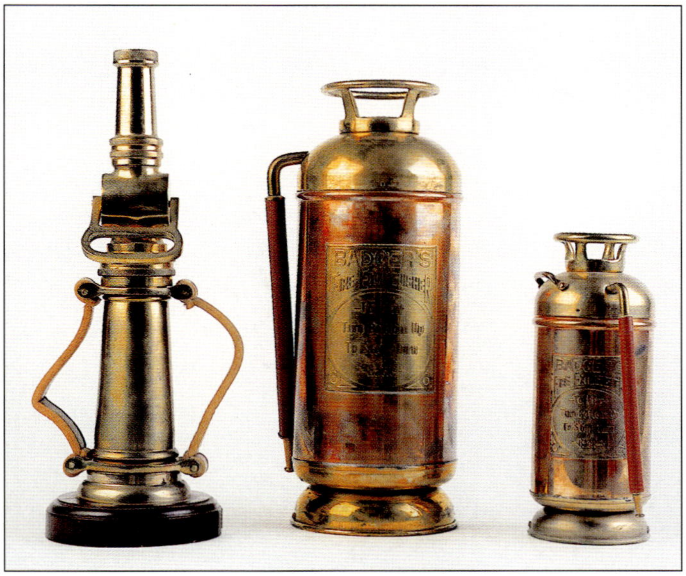

Fire nozzle, 1984, 50ml $65-75.Fire extinguisher, 1983, fifth $65-75, mini $25-35.

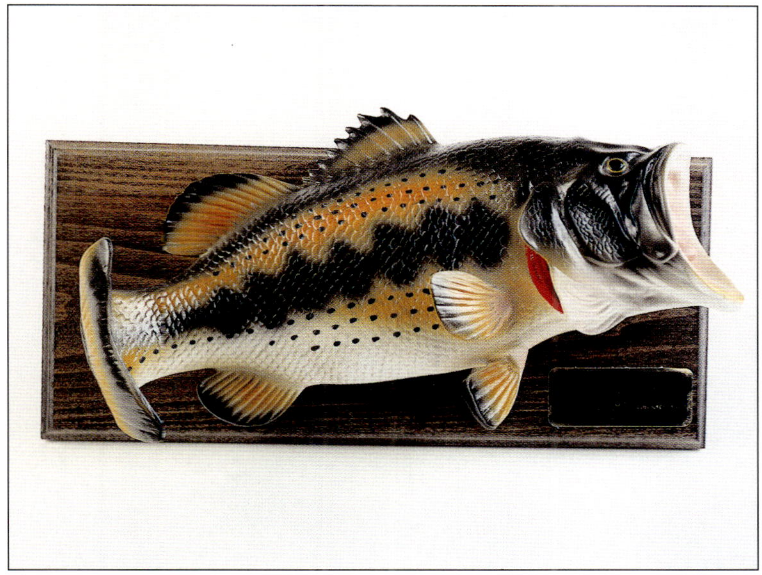

Bass wall plaque, 1982, fifth $45-55.

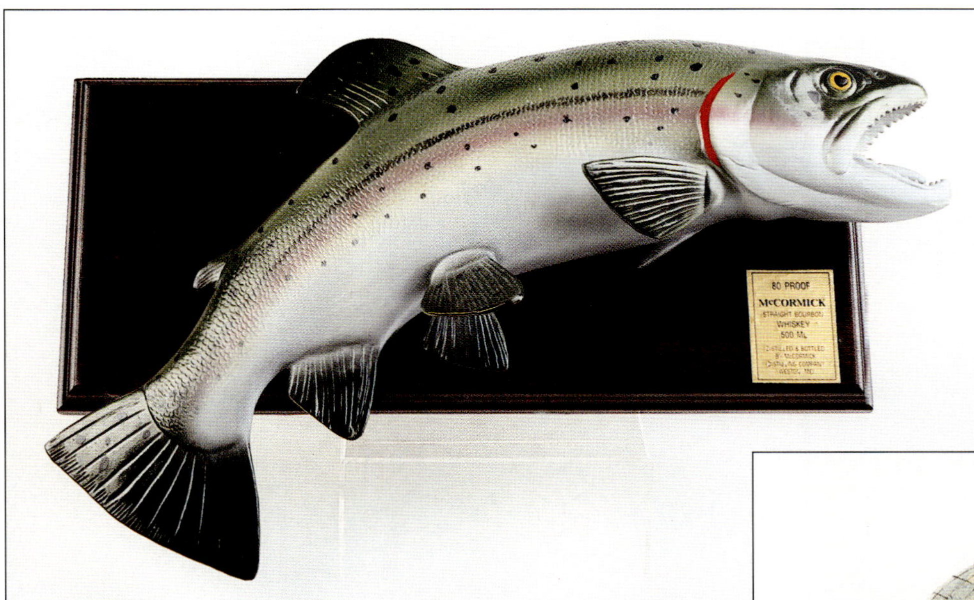

Trout wall plaque, 1984, fifth $45-55.

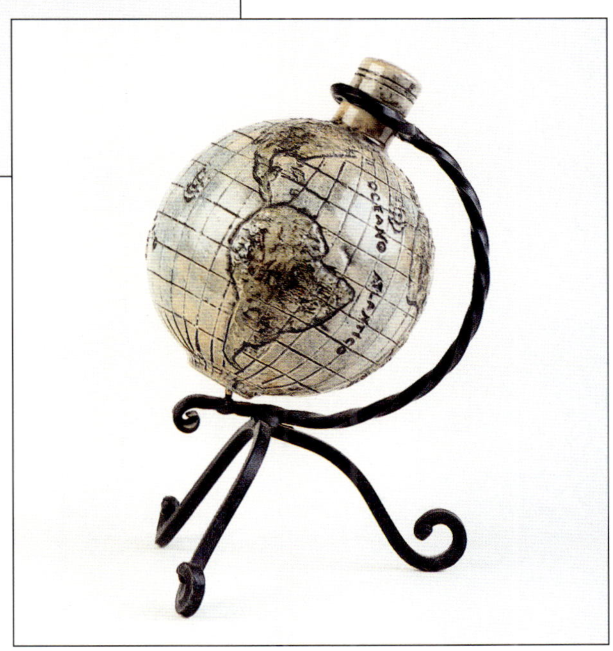

Angleica globe, 1971, fifth $15-20.

Frontiersman Series

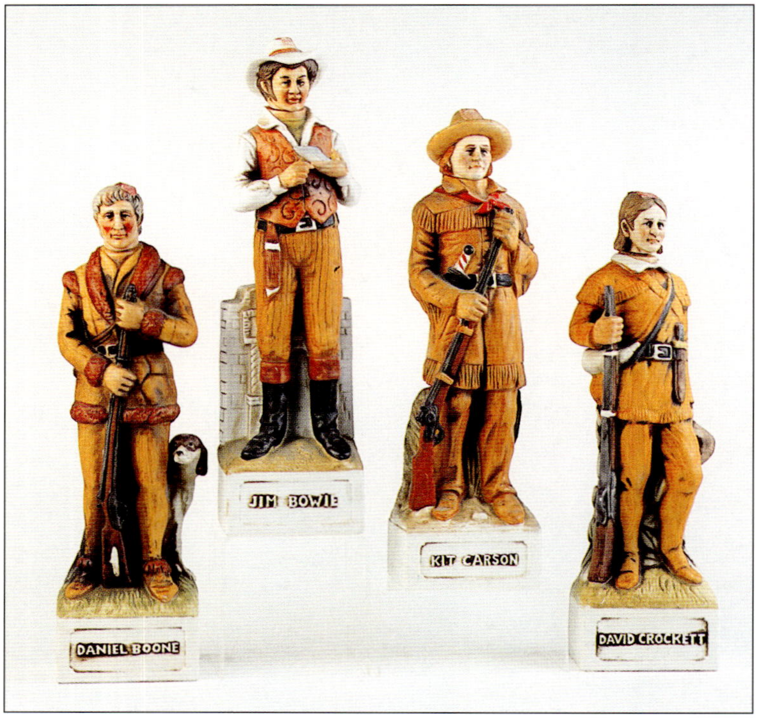

Daniel Boone, 1975, fifth $20-25; Jim Bowie, 1975, fifth $20-25; Kit Carson, 1975, fifth $20-25; Davey Crockett, 1975, fifth $20-25.

Great American Series

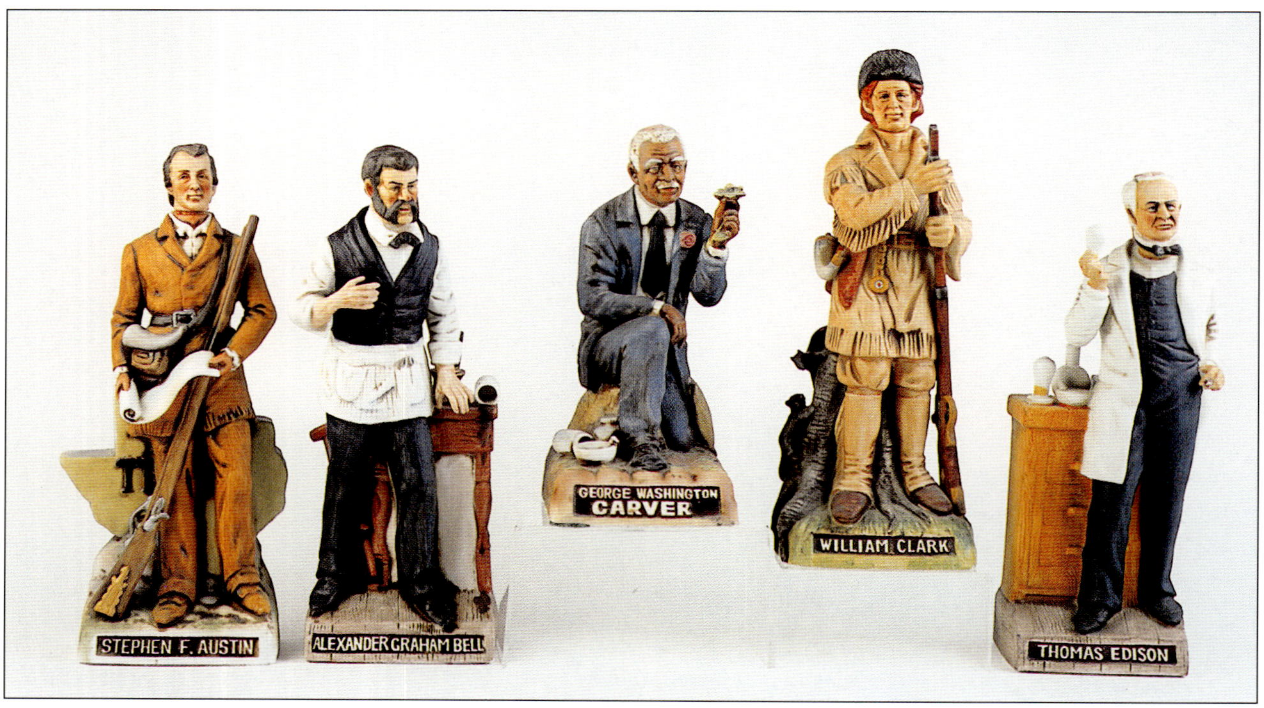

Stephen F. Austin, 1977, fifth $35-45; Alexander Graham Bell, 1977, fifth $45-55; George Washington Carver, 1977, fifth $35-45; William Clark, 1978, fifth $35-45; Thomas Edison, 1977, fifth $45-55.

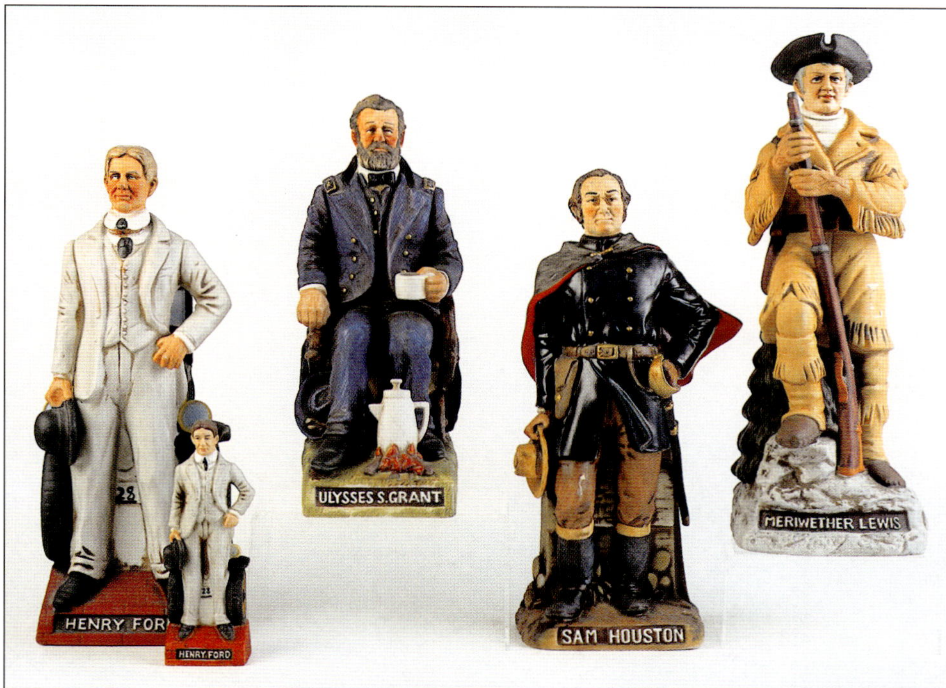

Henry Ford, 1977, fifth $45-55, mini $20-25; Ulysses S. Grant, 1976, fifth $65-75; Sam Houston, 1977, fifth $25-35; Meriwether Lewis, 1978, fifth $25-35.

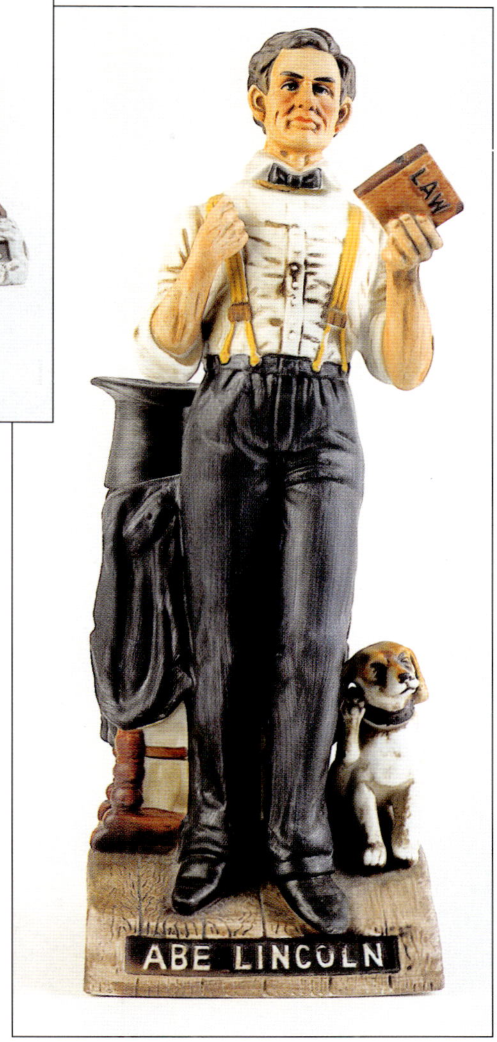

Abe Lincoln, 1976, fifth $25-35.

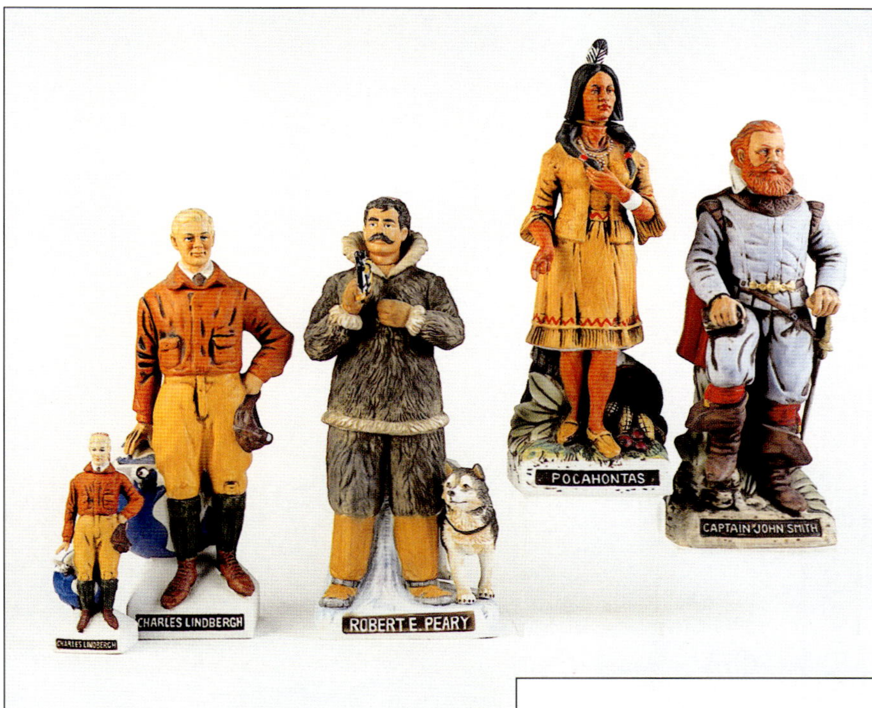

Charles Lindbergh, 1977, fifth $45-55, mini $25-30; Robert E. Peary, 1977, fifth $40-45; Pocahontas, 1977, fifth $35-40; John Smith, 1977, fifth $35-40.

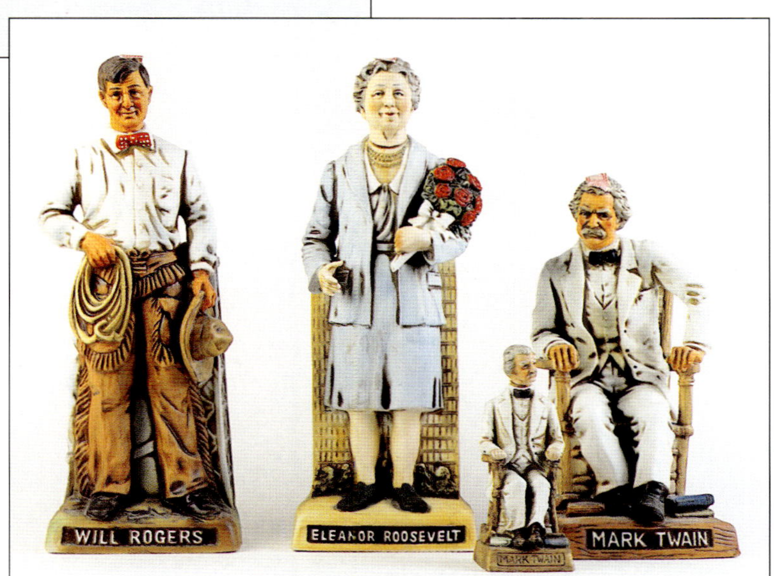

Will Rogers, 1977, fifth $40-45; Eleanor Roosevelt, 1977, fifth $20-25; Mark Twain, 1977, fifth $40-45, mini $20-25.

Gunfighter Series

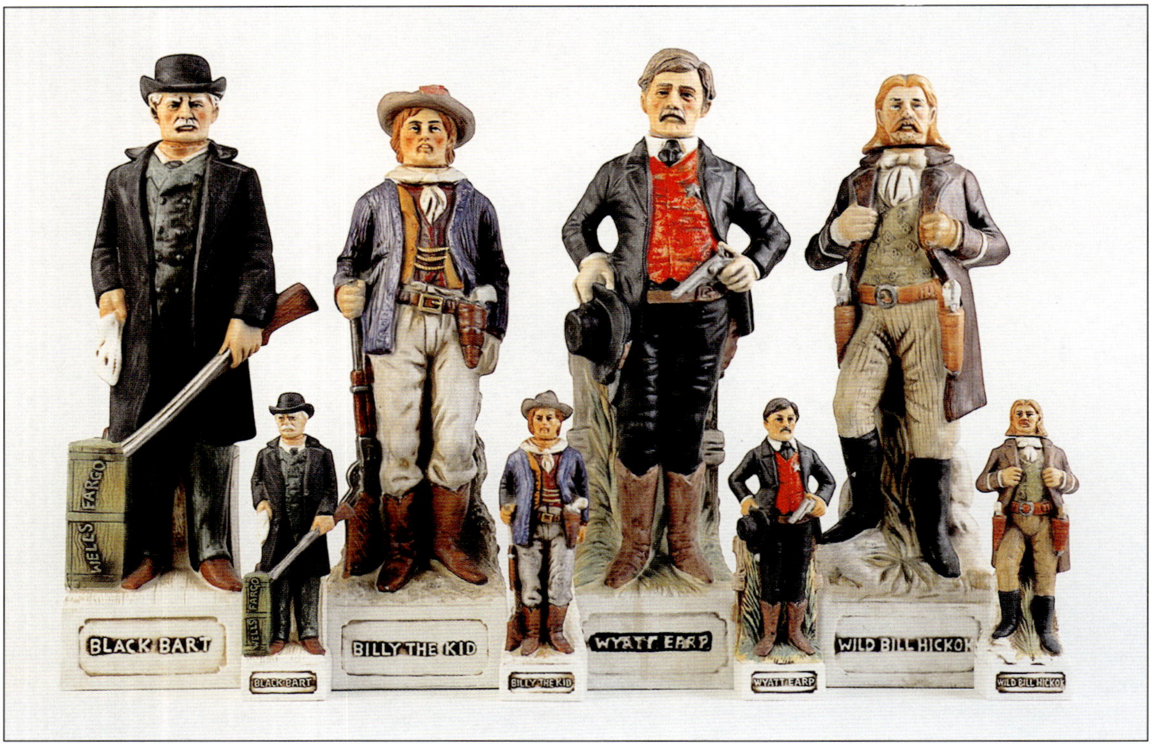

Black Bart, 1974, fifth $20-25, mini (1977) $10-15; Billy the Kid, 1973, fifth $20-25, mini (1977) $10-15; Wyatt Earp, 1972, fifth $20-25, mini $10-15; Wild Bill Hickock, 1973, fifth $20-25, mini (1977) $10-15.

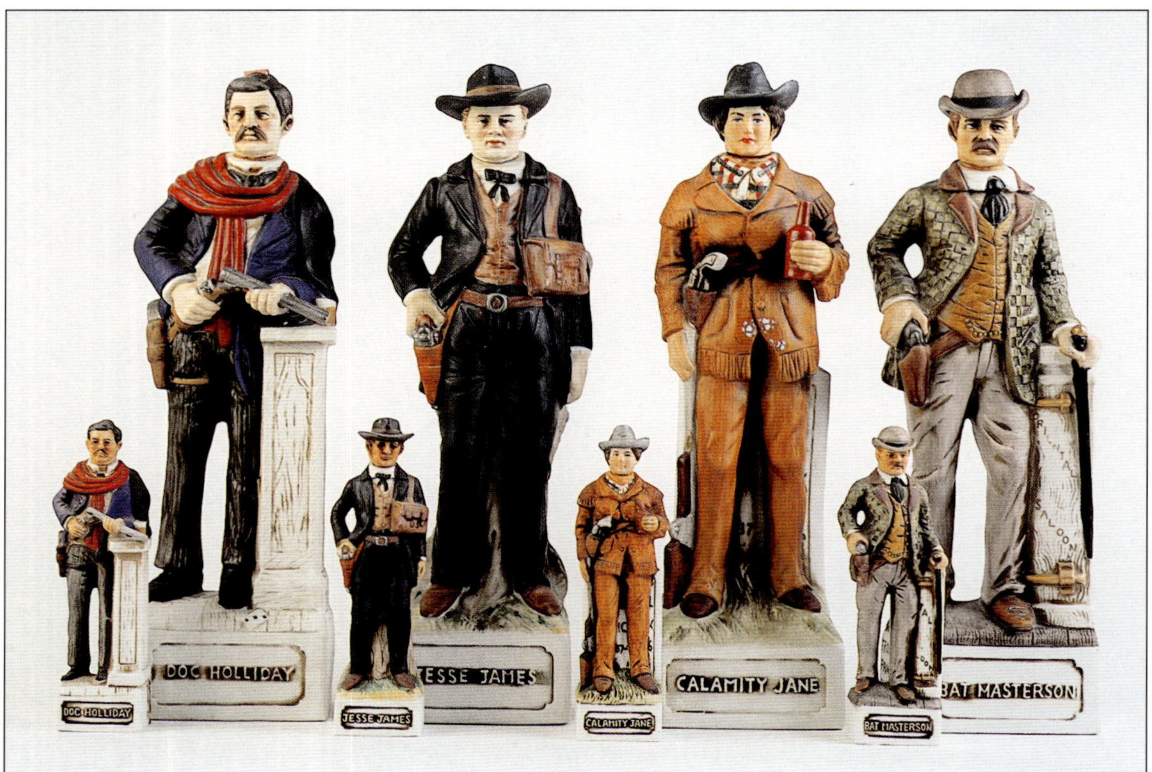

Doc Holiday, 1972, fifth $20-25, mini (1977) $10-15; Jessie James, 1973, fifth $20-25, mini (1977) $10-15; Calamity Jane, 1974, fifth $20-25, mini (1977) $10-15; Bat Masterson, 1972 fifth $20-25, mini (1977) $10-15.

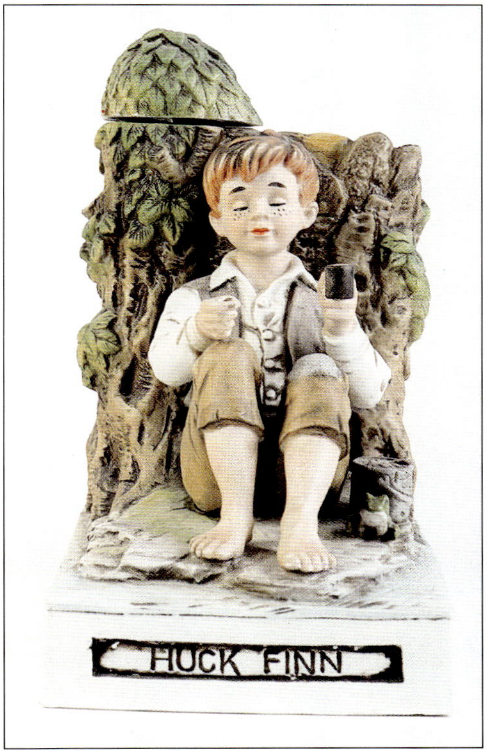

Huck Finn, 1980, fifth $20-25.

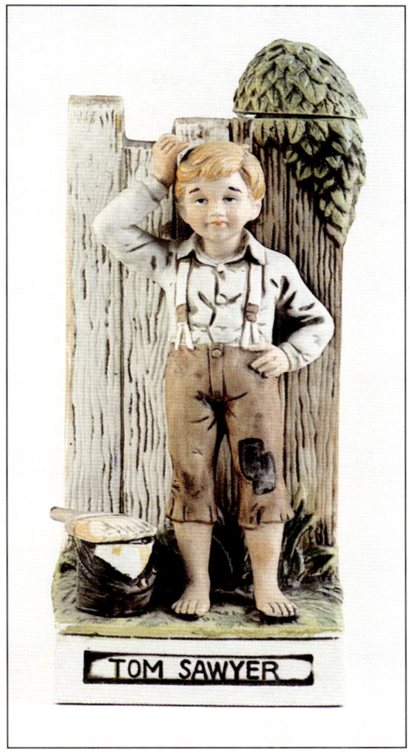

Tom Sawyer, 1980, fifth $20-25.

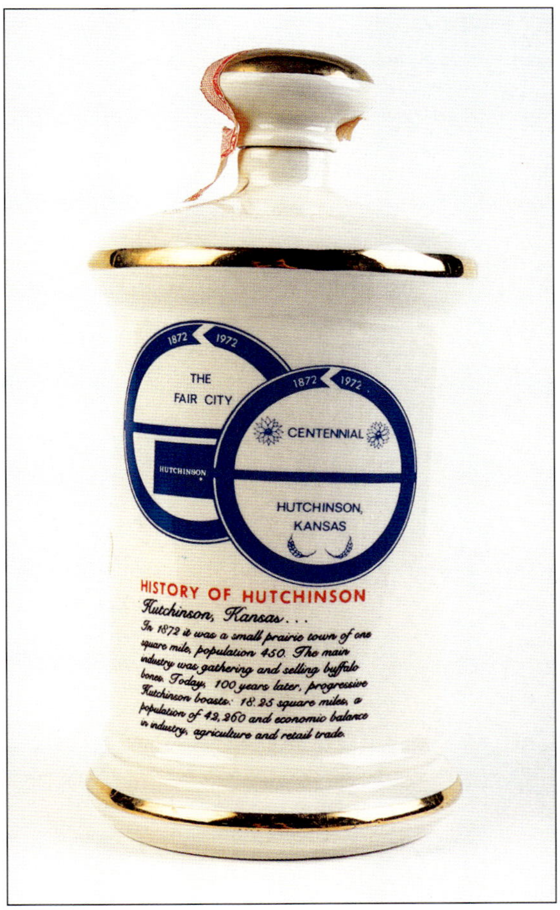

Hutchinson, Kansas Centennial, 1972, fifth $10-15.

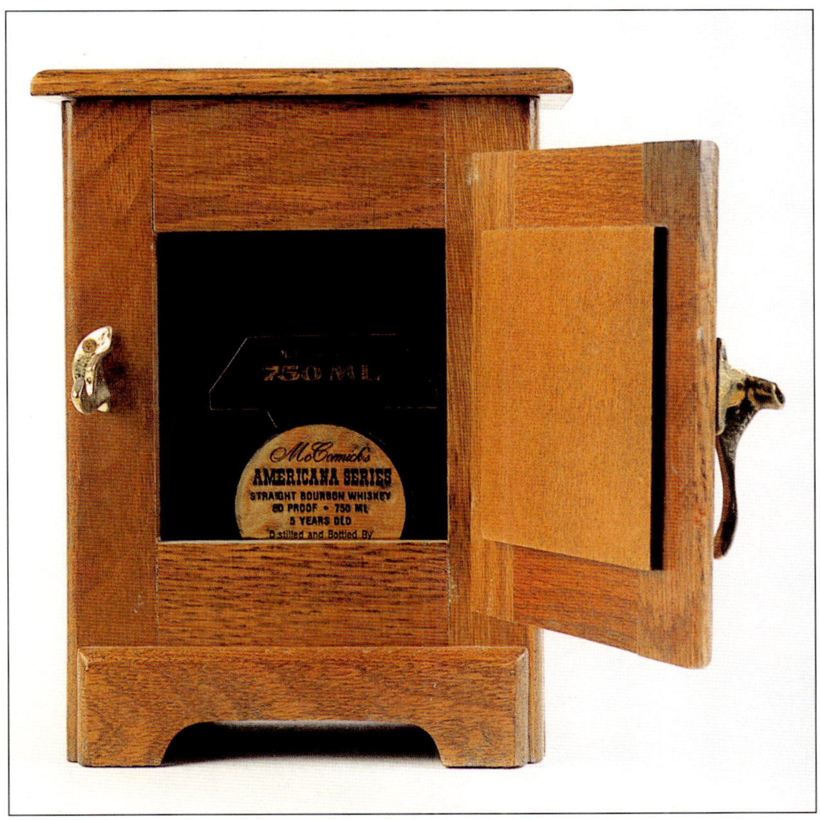

Ice Box, 1983, fifth $25-35.

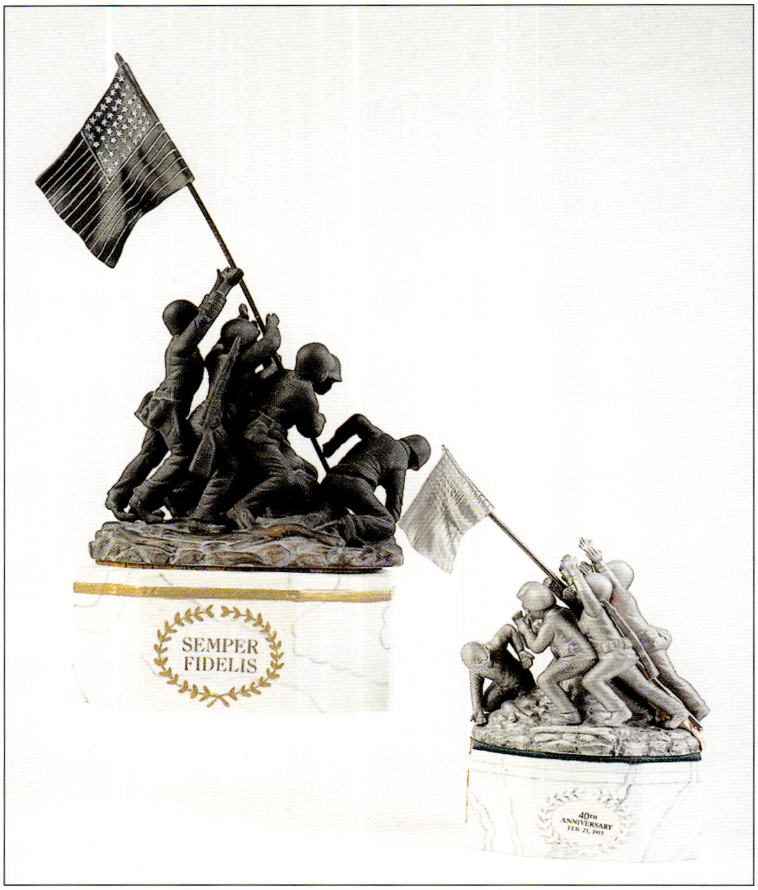

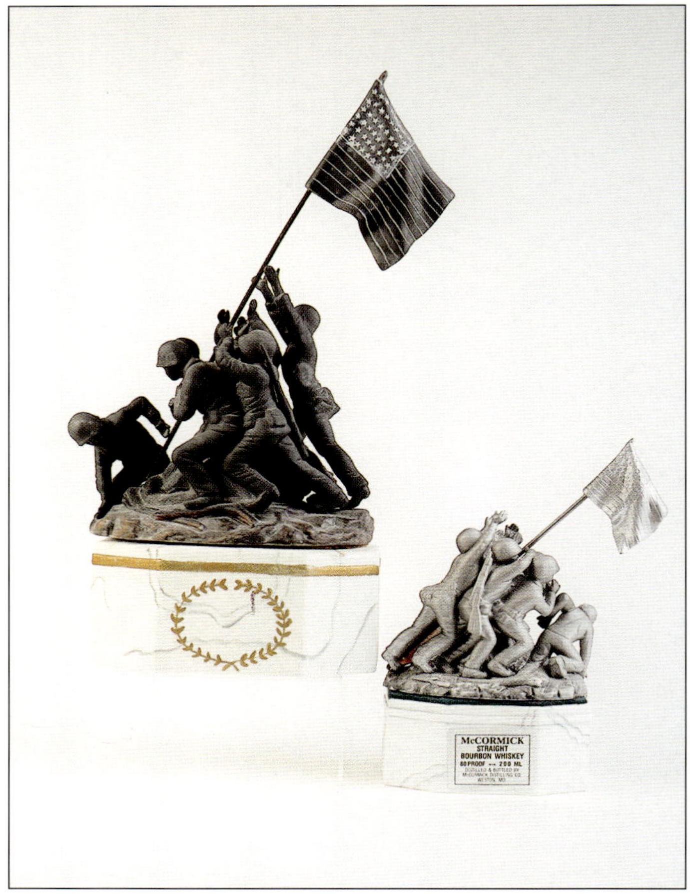

Iwo Jima, 1983, fifth $95-110, 200 ml $45-55.

Jug Series

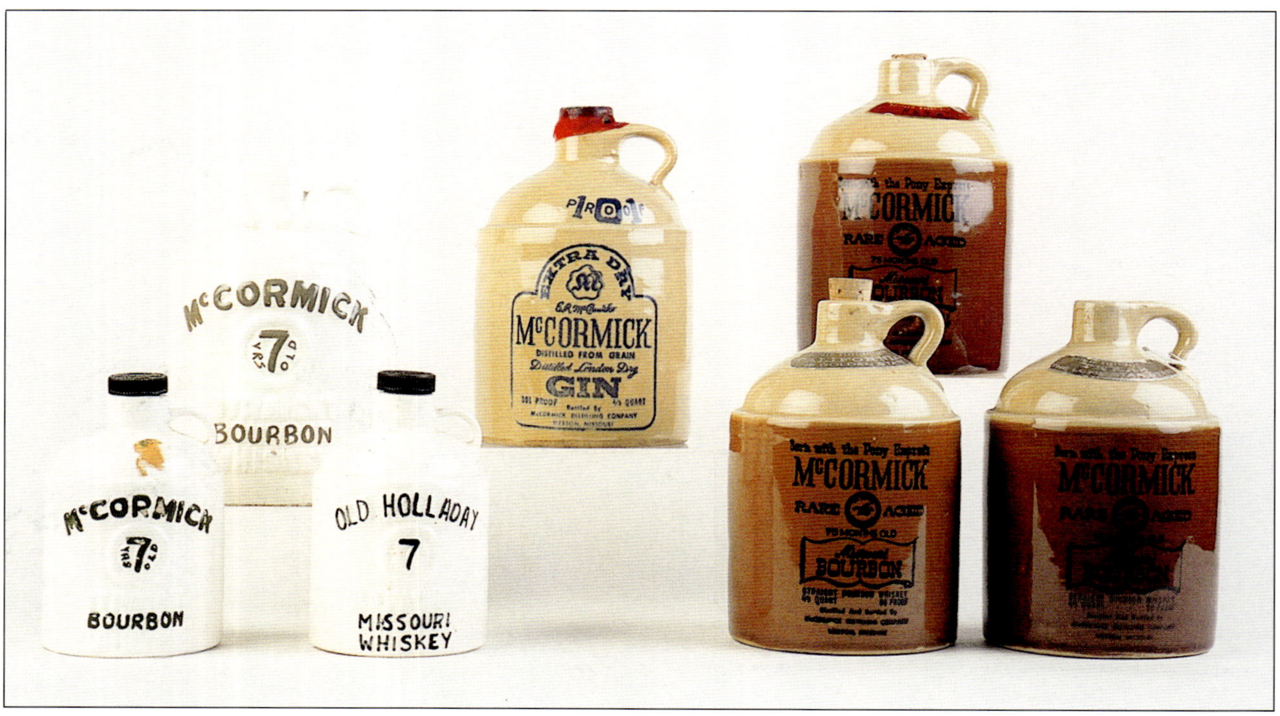

All White Jugs, 1955, $15 ea. Gin, 1967, fifth $15. McCormick Bourbon, California, 1967, fifth $25. Nevada, 1967, fifth $25. Texas, 1987, fifth $25.

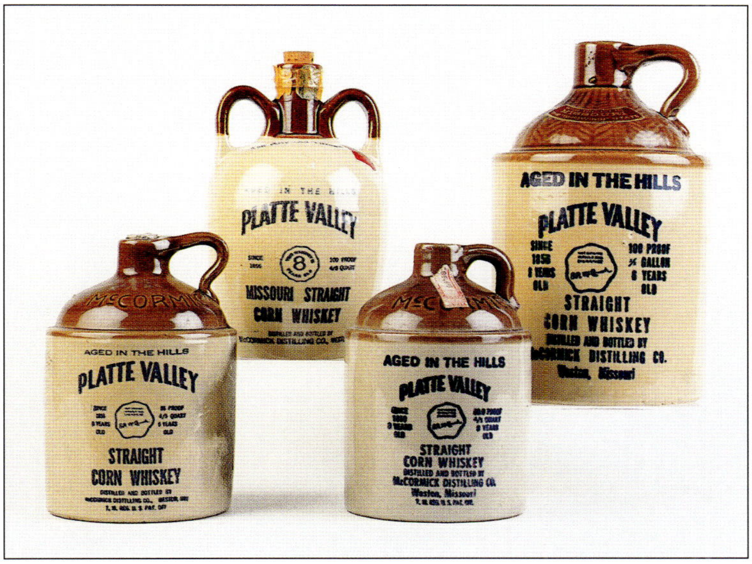

Platte Valley, 1953, two handles, fifth $10-15. Platte Valley, two tone jugs, 1967, various sizes $10-20.

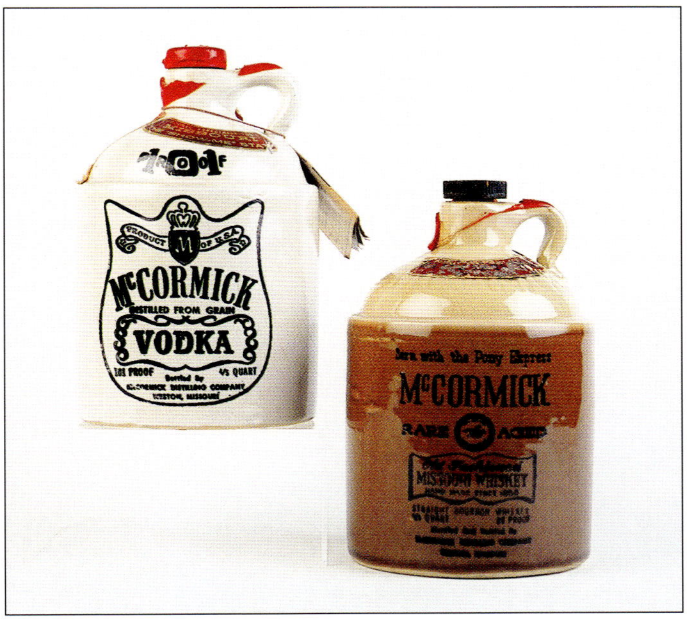

McCormick Vodka, 1967, fifth $10. Missouri, fifth $10.

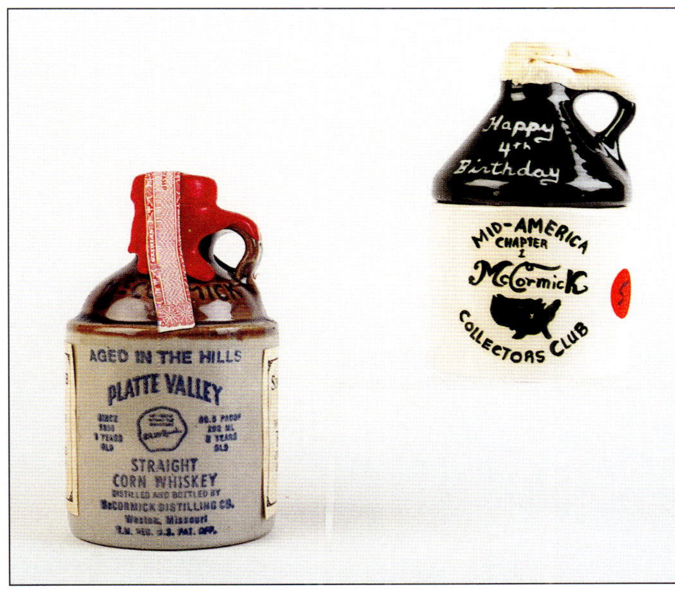

McCormick Collectors Club, Happy 1st Birthday, 1989, Happy 4th Birthday, pint $20-25.

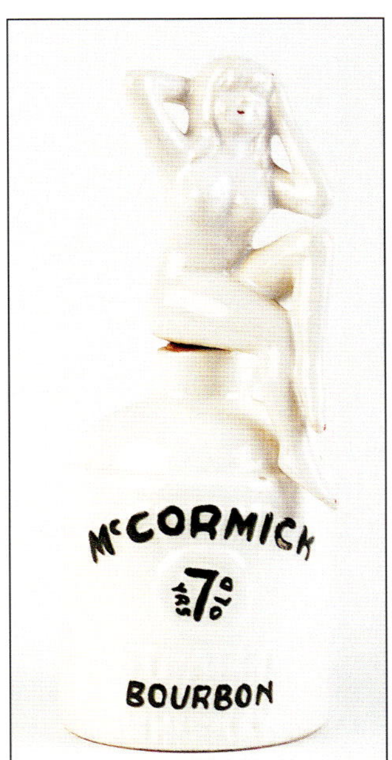

McCormick, woman nude figure, 1/2 pint $15-20.

King Arthur Series

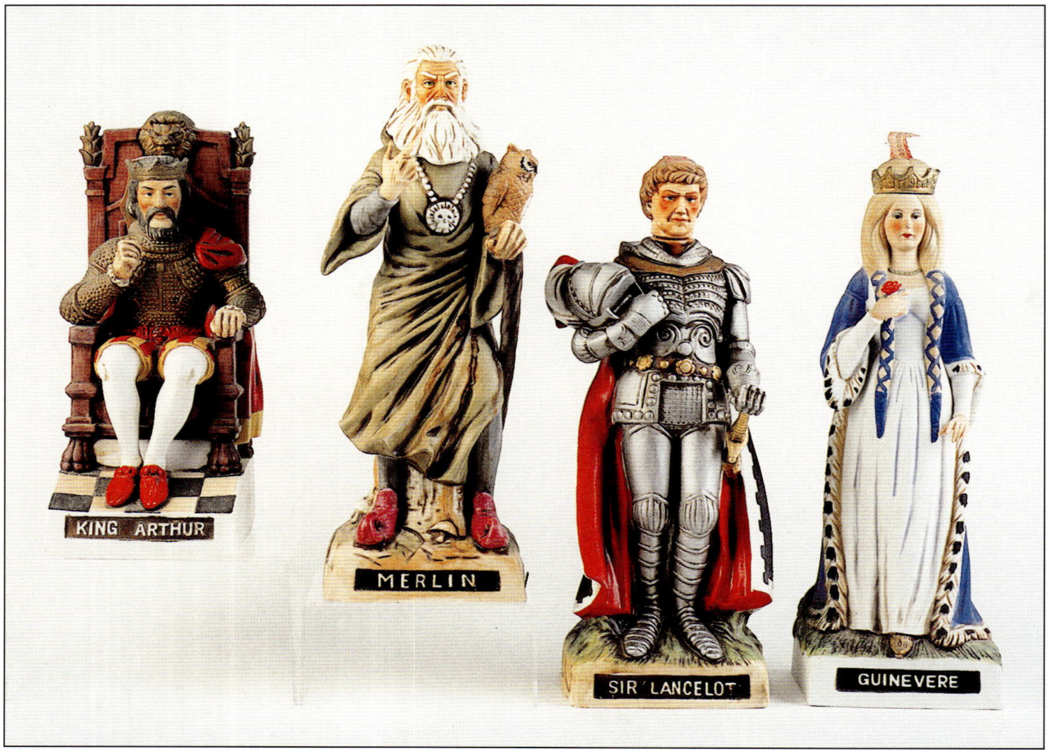

King Arthur, 1979, fifth $35-40; Merlin, 1979, fifth $30-35; Sir Lancelot, 1979, fifth $20-25; Guinevere, 1979, fifth $30-35.

Miscellaneous McCormick

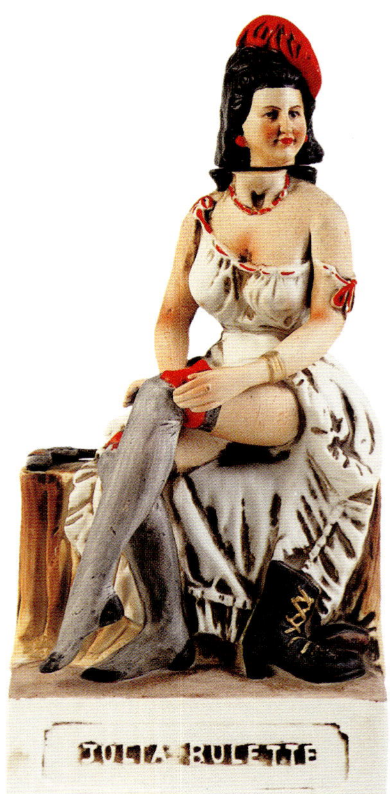

Julia Bullette, 1974, fifth $35-40.

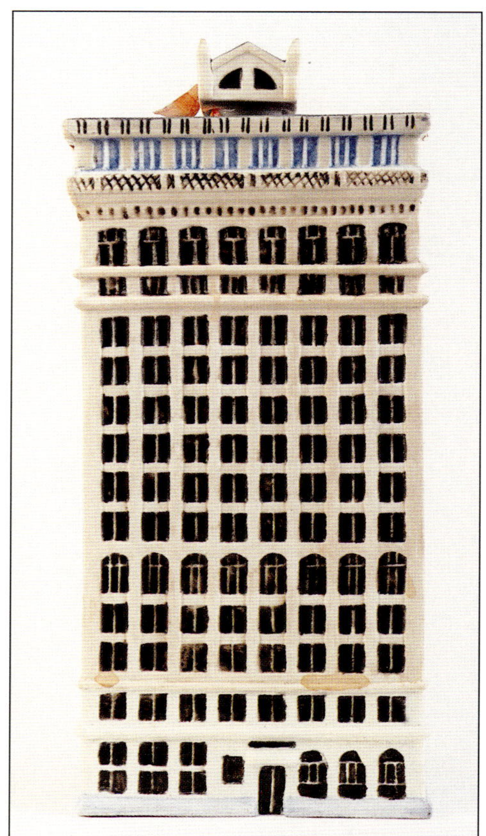

Kansas City Collectors Club, 1982, fifth $20-25.

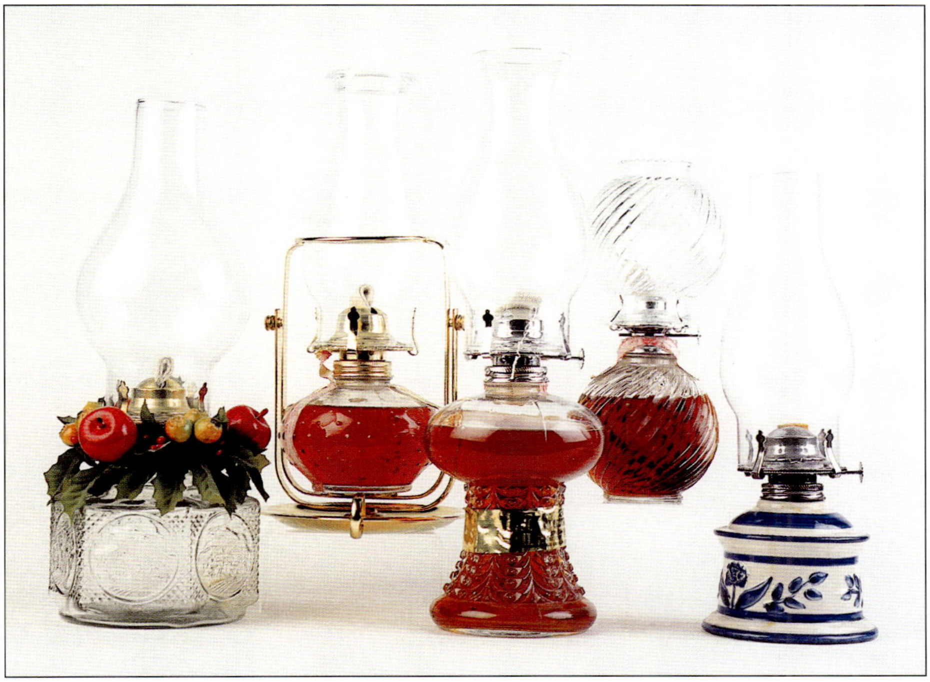

Hurricane Lamp, 1982, fifth $25-30. Captains Lamp, 1983, fifth $25-30. Country Squire lamp, 1984, fifth $25-30. Victorian Lamp, 1984, fifth $25-30. Colonial Lamp, fifth $25-30.

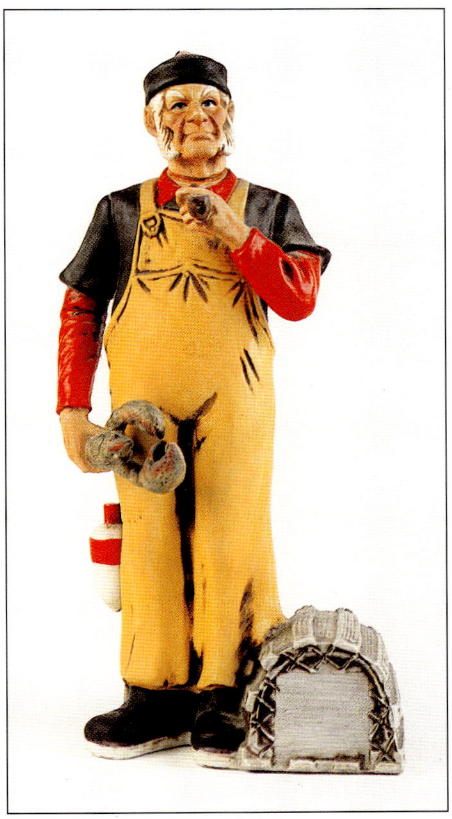

Lobsterman, 1979, fifth $10-15.

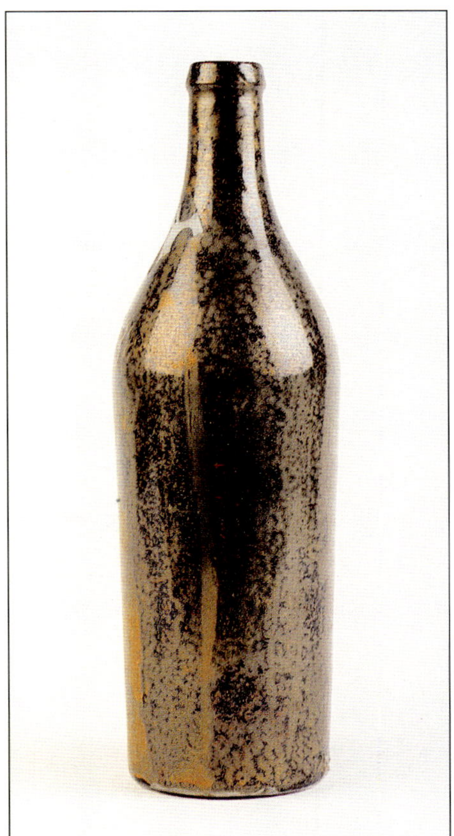

McCormick Centennial, 1956, fifth $15-20.

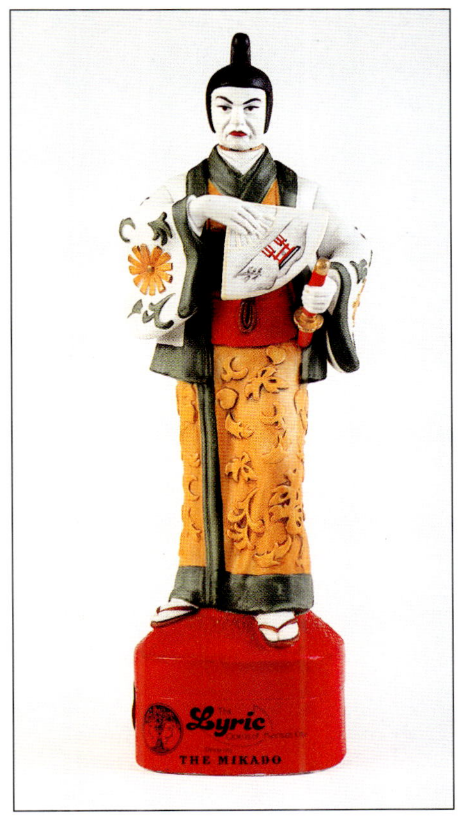

Mikado, 1980, fifth $35-40.

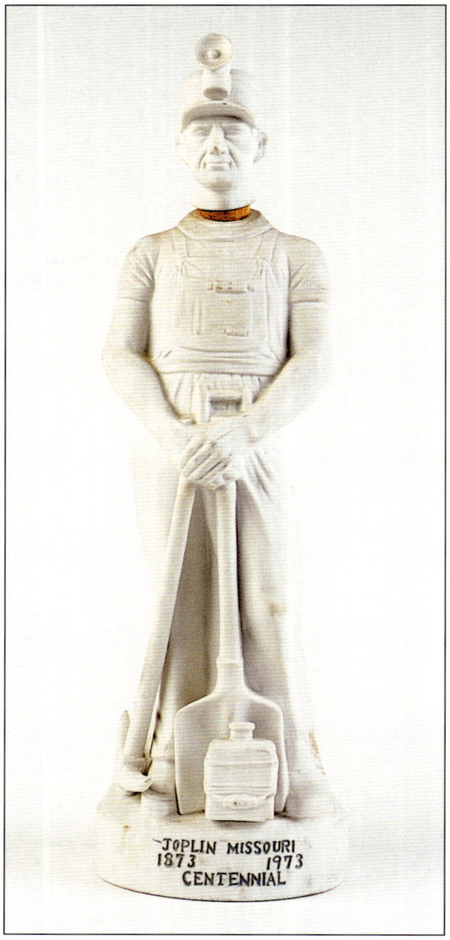

Joplin Miner, 1972, fifth $25-30.

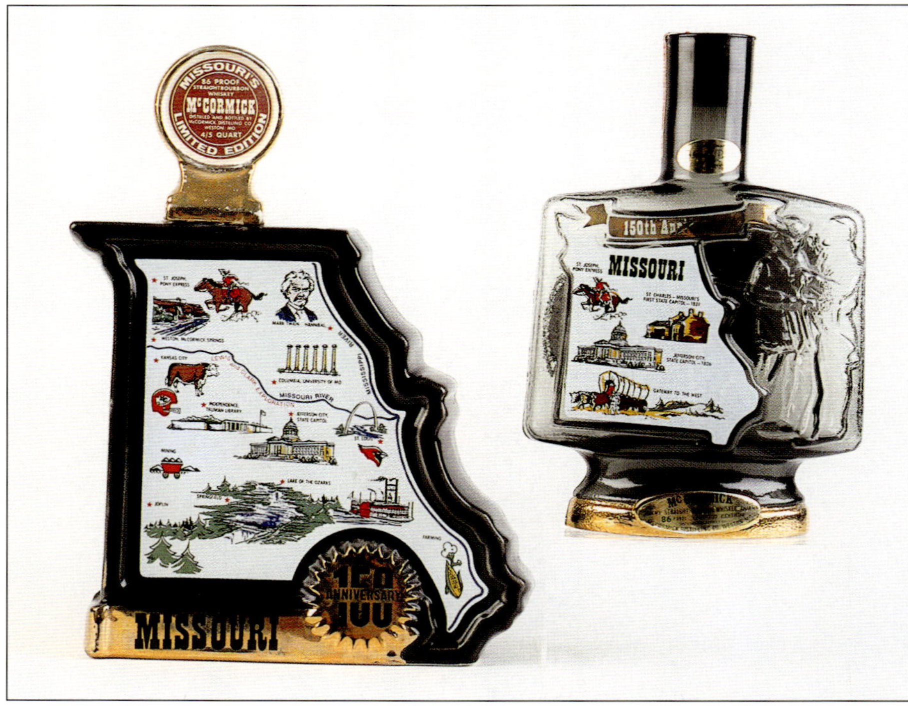

Missouri Sesquicentennial, 1970, china $10-15. Missouri Sesquicentennial, 1970, glass $10-15.

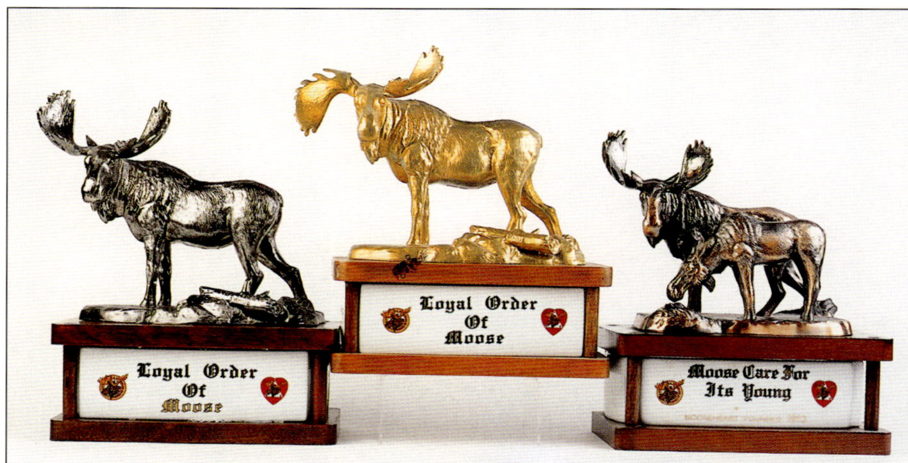

Moose Order (silver), 1984, fifth $65-75.
Moose order (gold), 1984, fifth $95-110.
Moose with female (bronze), fifth, $75-95.

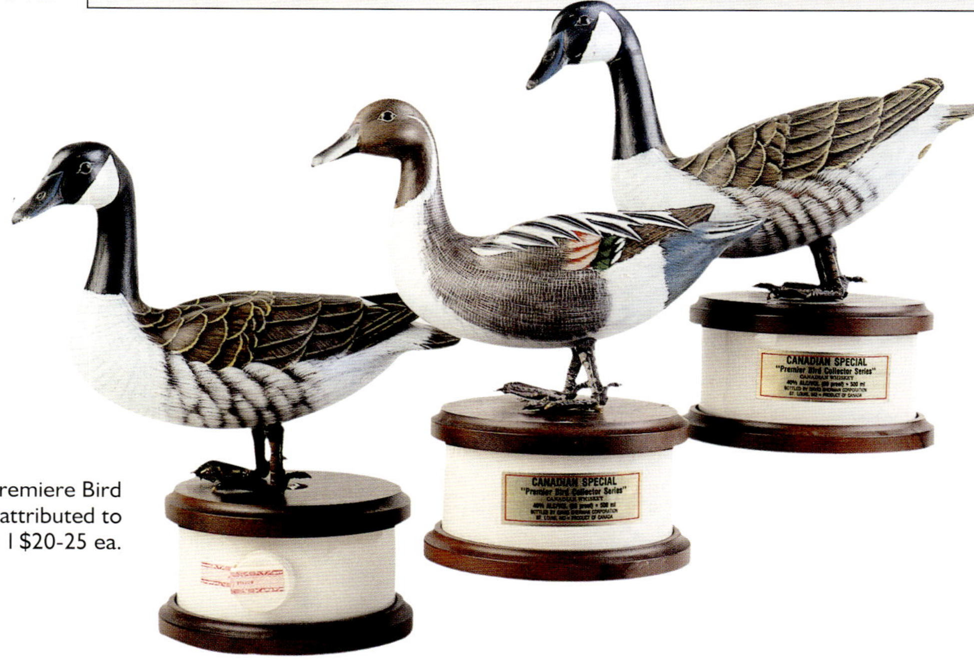

Canadian Special – Premiere Bird Collectors series: (attributed to McCormick), 500 ml $20-25 ea.

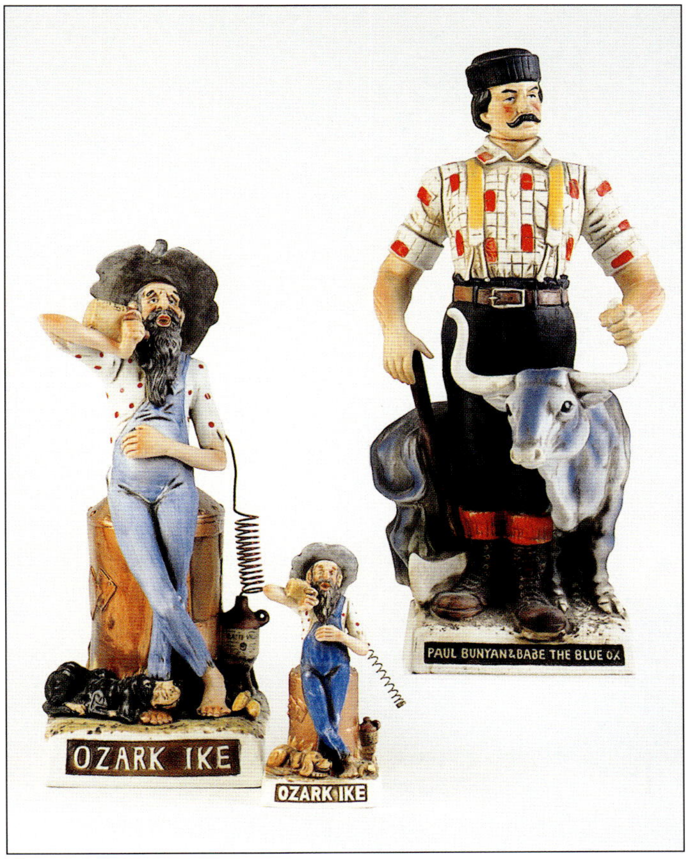

Ozark Ike, 1979, fifth $10-15, mini $5-10.
Paul Bunyan, 1979, fifth $10-15.

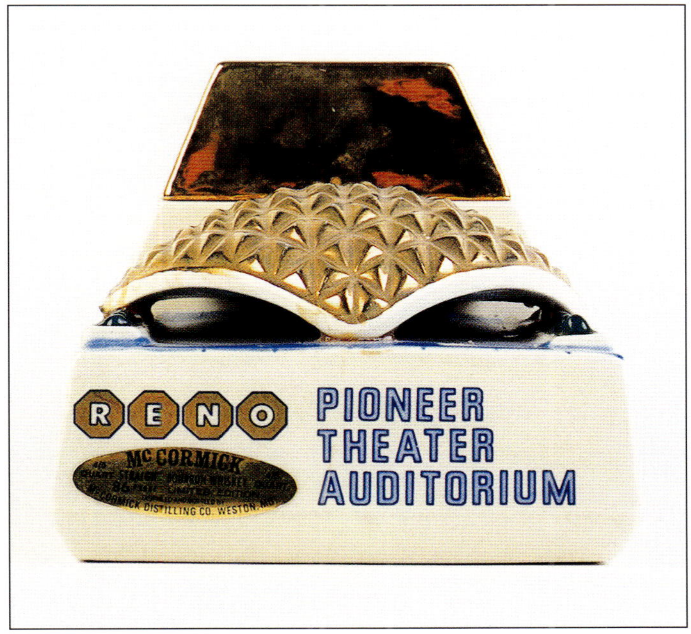

Pioneer Theatre, 1972, fifth $10-15.

Pirate Series

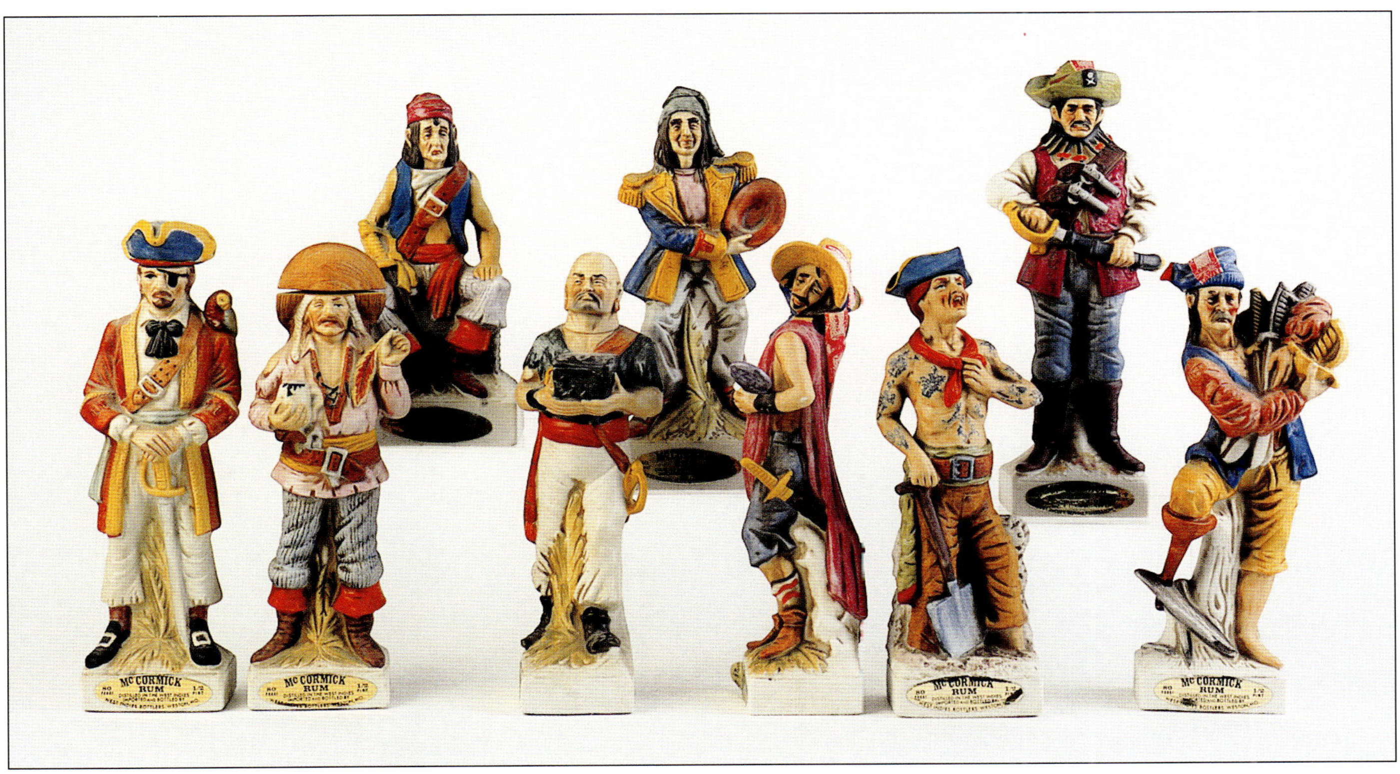

Pirates #1 through #9 (pirates 10, 11, and 12 never released), 1972, 1/2 pints $10-15 ea.

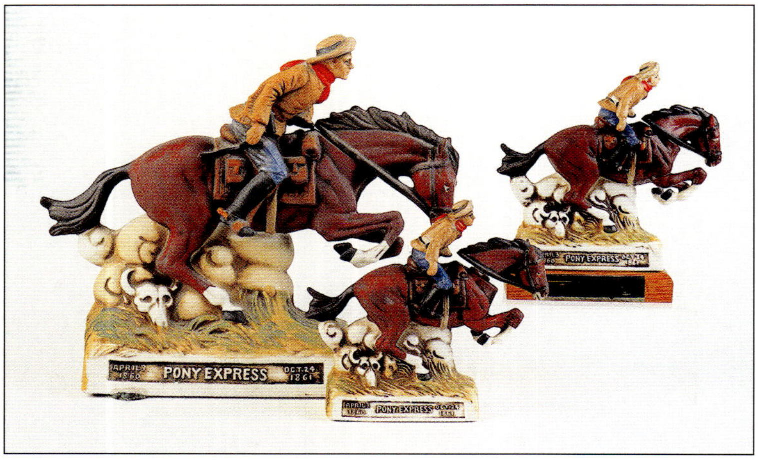

Pony Express, 1978, fifth $45-55, mini $25-30. Pony Express, Greater KC Jim Beam Club with wooden base, 1982, mini $30-35.

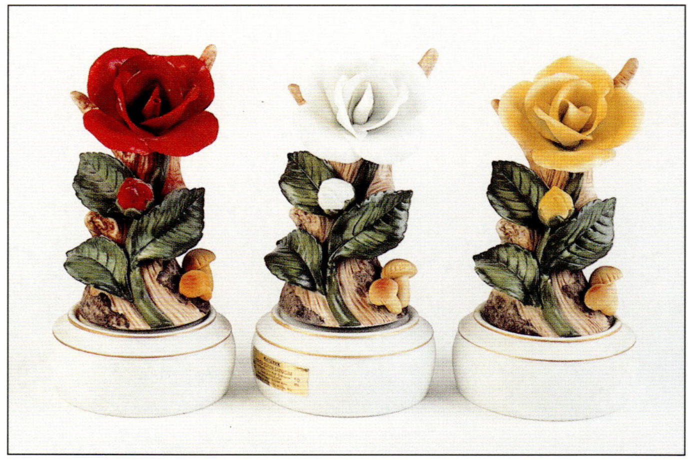

Rose Collection (red, white, and yellow), 1980, mini $10-15 ea.

Shrine Series

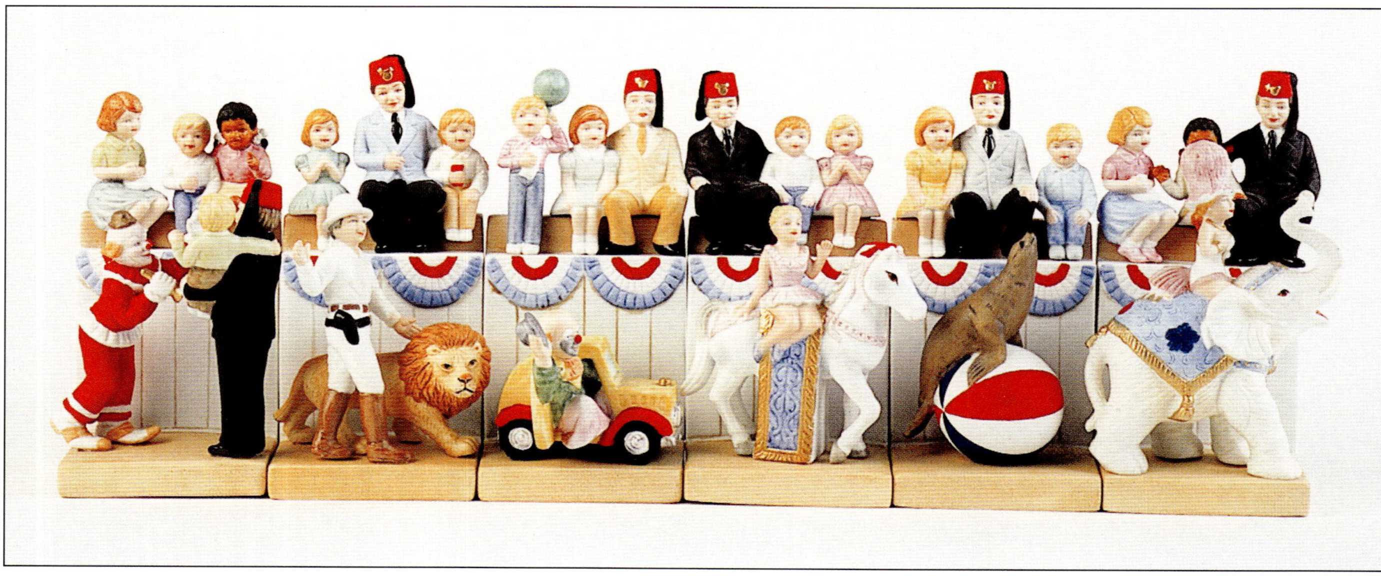

Shrine Circus – set of six, 1984, mini $125-135.

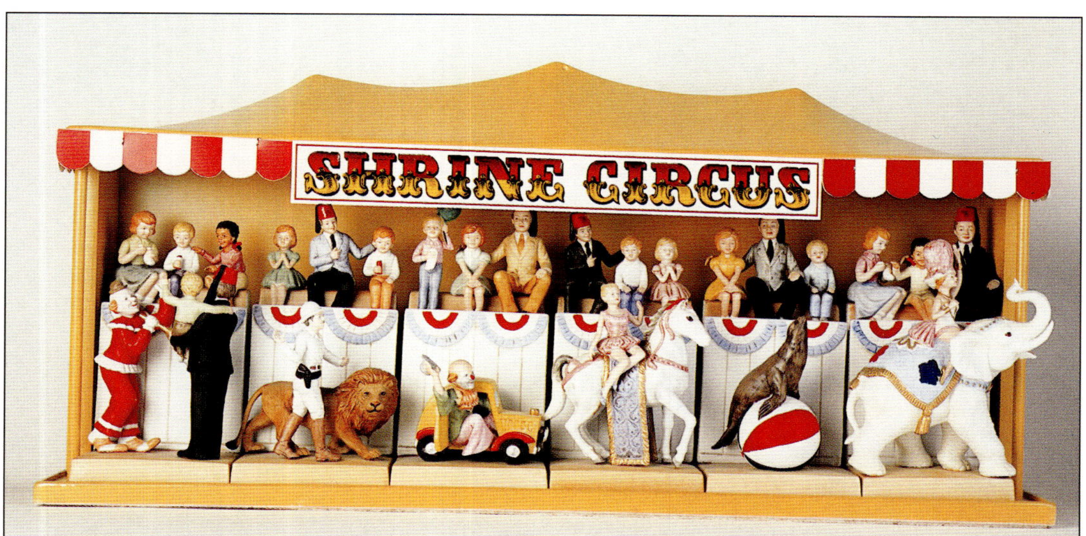

Shrine Circus – set of six with tent, 1984, 500 ml $225-250.

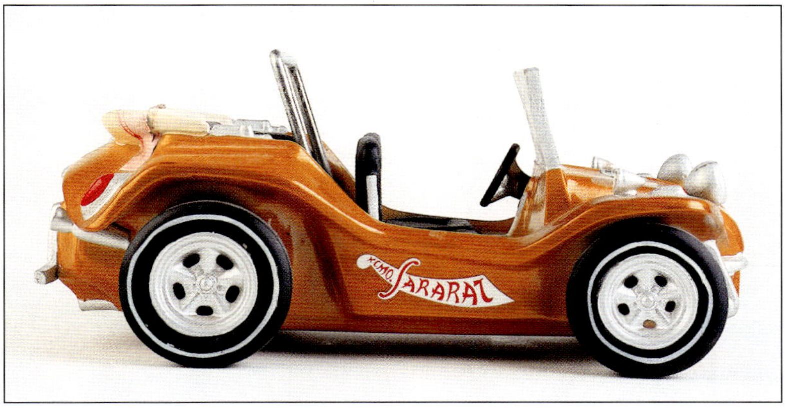

Dune Buggy, 1976, fifth $25-30.

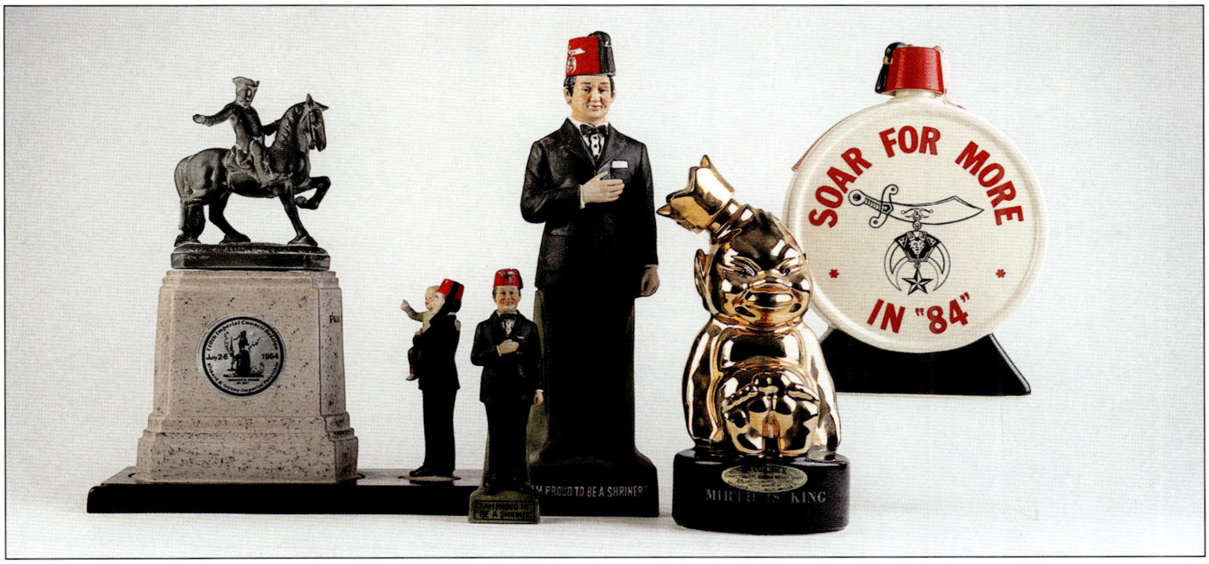

Imperial Council, 1984, fifth $45-55. The Noble, 1976, fifth $35-40, mini $20-25. Jester-Mirth King, 1972, fifth $20-25. Midian Shrine 75th Anniversary, Kansas, 1984, fifth $20-25.

Miscellaneous McCormick

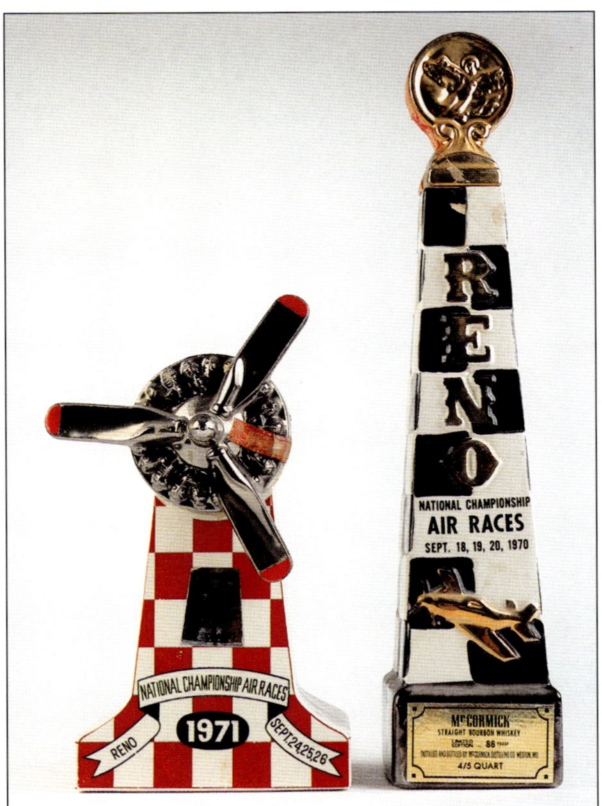

Air Race (propeller), 1971, fifth $35-40. Air Race (pylon), 1970, fifth $35-40.

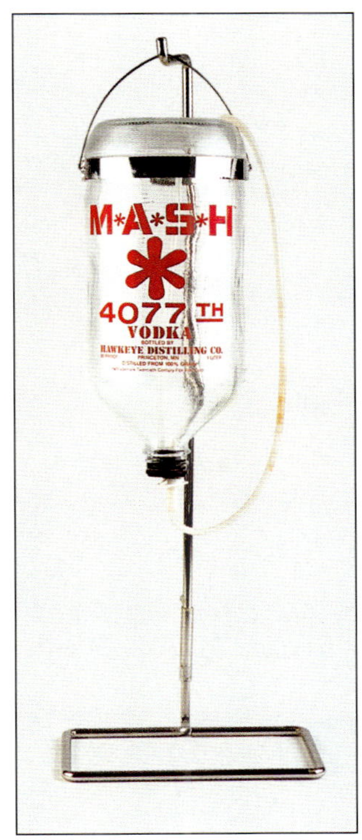

MASH – Hawkeye's Distillery, fifth $20.

Sports Series

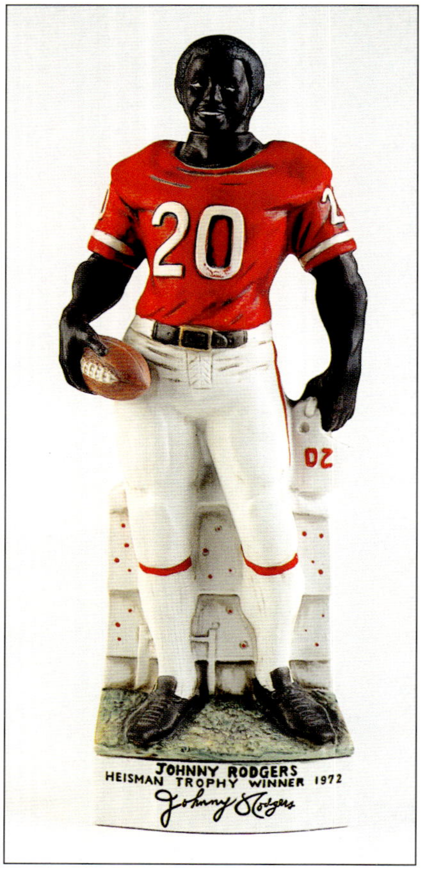

Johnny Rodgers #2, 1972, fifth $349-395.

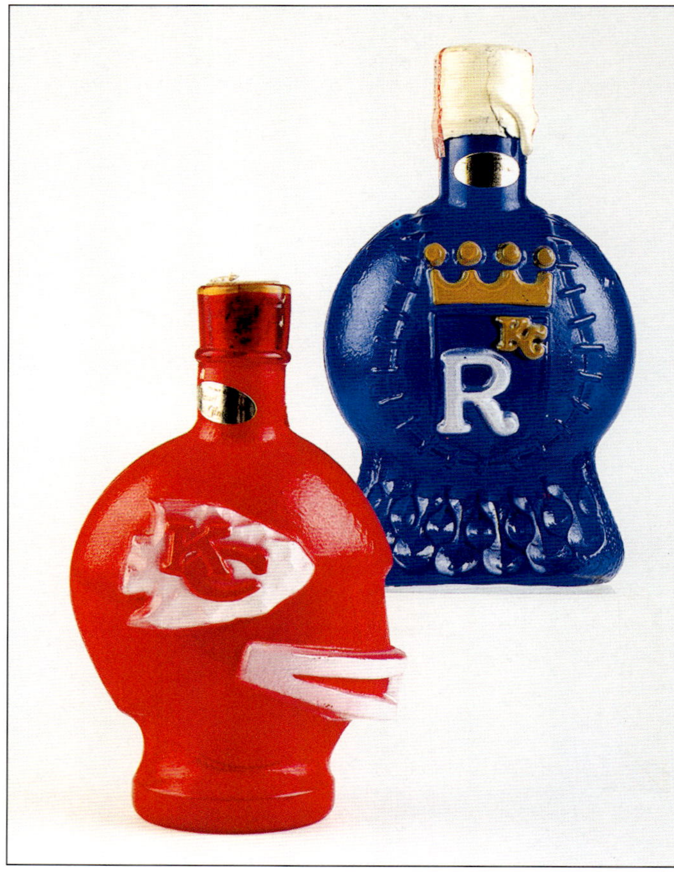

Kansas City Chiefs, 1969, fifth $35-40.
Kansas City Royals, 1971, fifth $35-40.

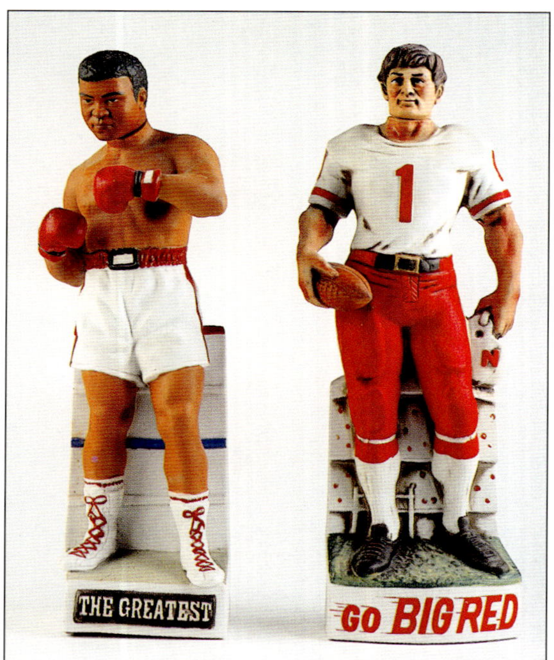

Mohammad Ali, 1980, fifth $145-165. Nebraska football player, 1972, fifth $249-295.

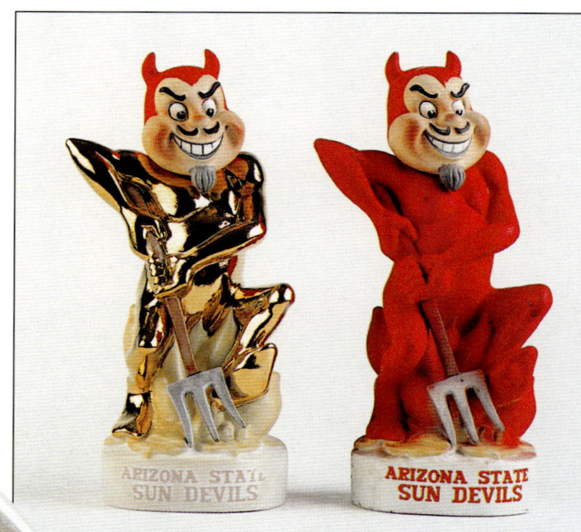

Arizona Sun Devils, gold fifth $75-95, red fifth $25-35.

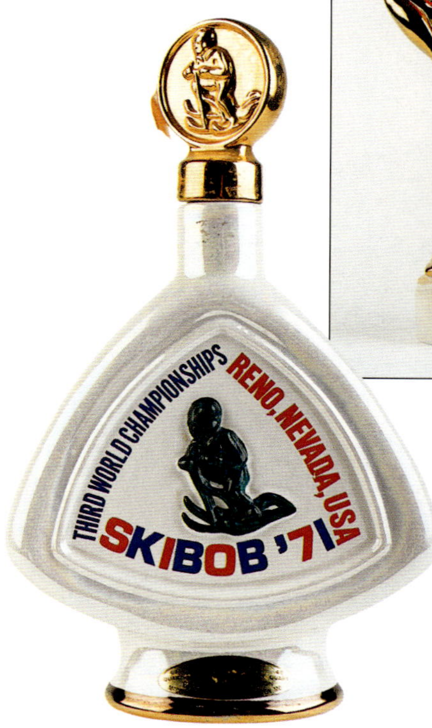

Skibob, 1971, fifth $15-20.

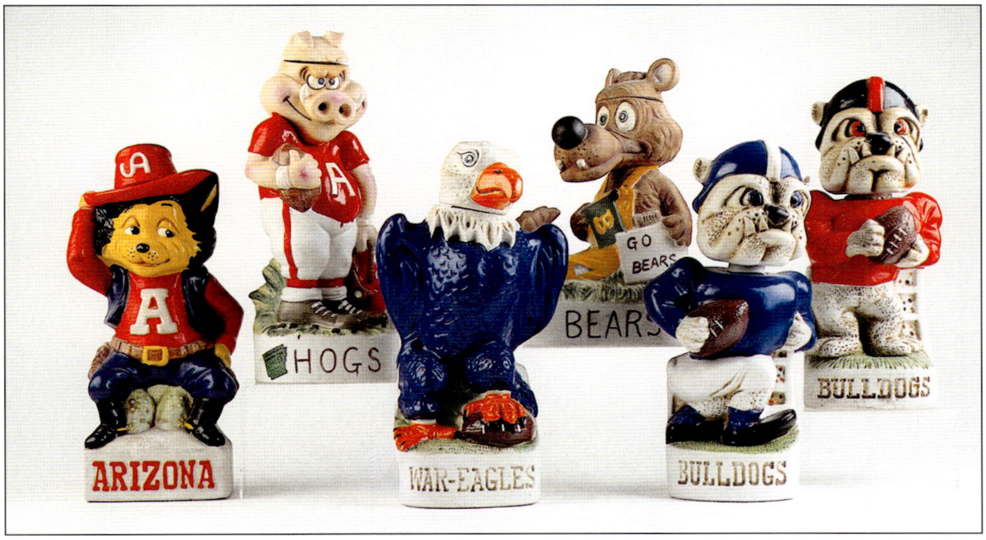

Arizona Wildcats, fifth $75-95. Arkansas Hogs, 1972, fifth $75-95. Auburn War Eagles, fifth $75-95. Baylor Bears, 1972, fifth $95-110. Brake Bulldogs (blue helmet and jersey), 1974, fifth $110-125. Georgia Bulldogs (black helmet, red jersey), fifth $110-125.

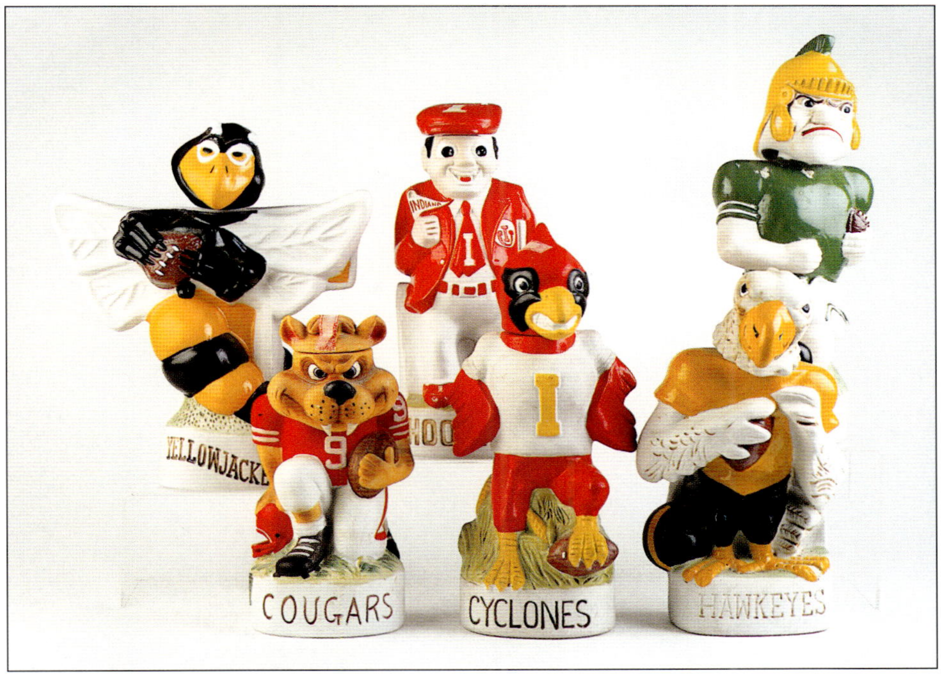

Georgia Tech Yellowjackets, fifth $110-125. Houston Cougars, 1972, fifth $95-110. Indiana Hoosiers, 1974, fifth $75-95. Iowa Cyclones, 1974, fifth $65-75. Iowa Hawkeyes, 1974, fifth $75-95. Michigan State Spartans, fifth $65-75.

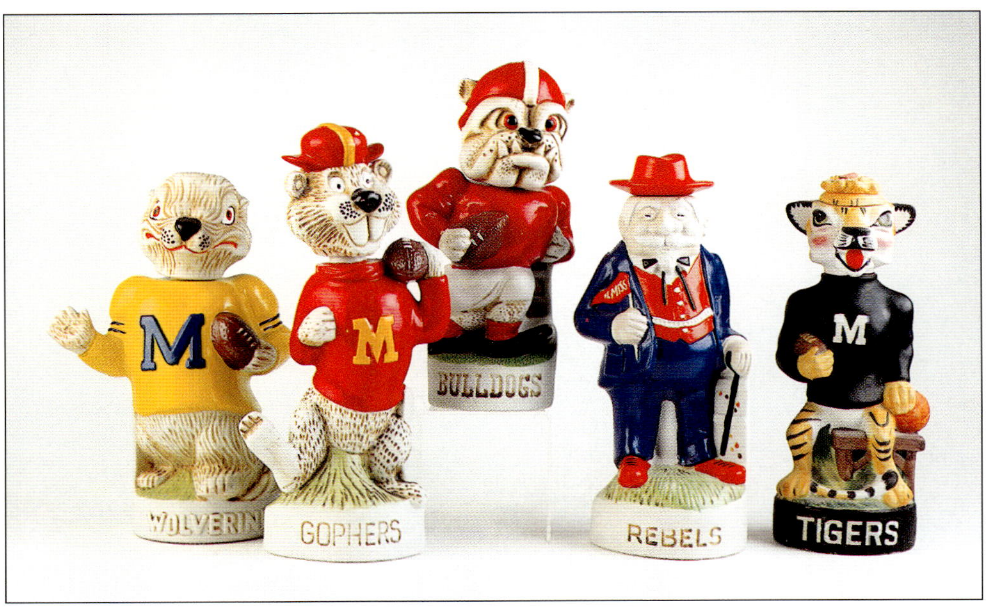

Michigan Wolverines, 1974, fifth $65-75. Minnesota Gophers, 1974, fifth $65-75. Mississippi State Bulldogs (red helmet and jersey), 1974, fifth $75-95. Mississippi Rebels, 1974, fifth $45-55. Missouri University Tigers, 1974, fifth $95-110.

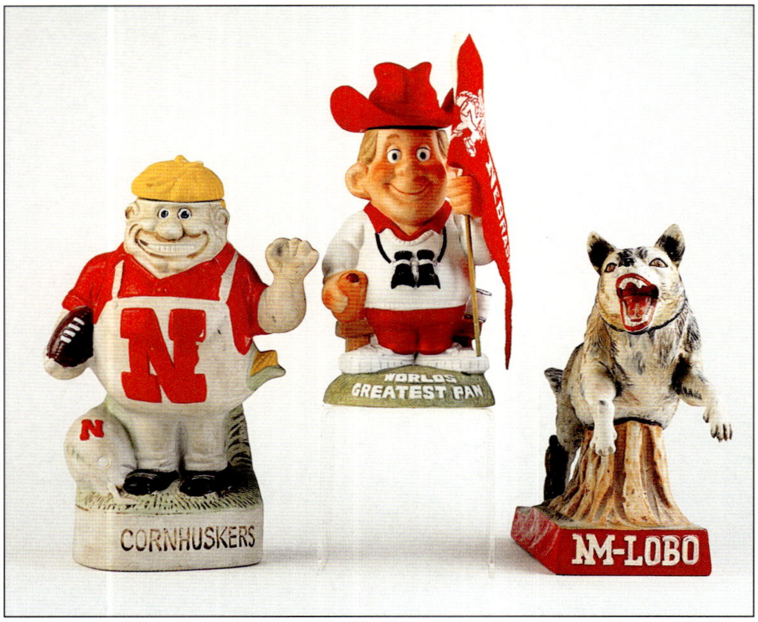

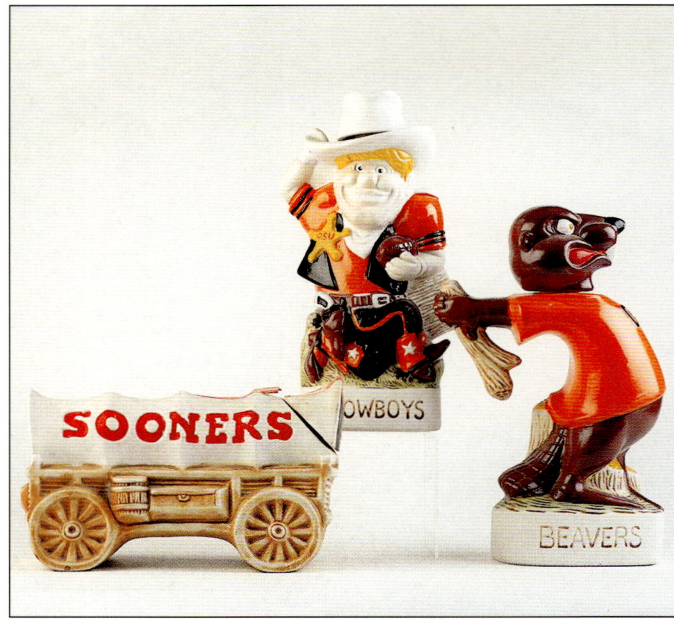

Nebraska Cornhuskers, 1974, fifth $65-70. Nebraska, World's Greatest Fan, fifth, $75-85. New Mexico Lobo, fifth $45-55.

Oklahoma Sooners Wagon, 1974, fifth $65-70. Oklahoma Southern Cowboys, 1974, fifth $75-85. Oregon Beavers, 1974, fifth $45-55.

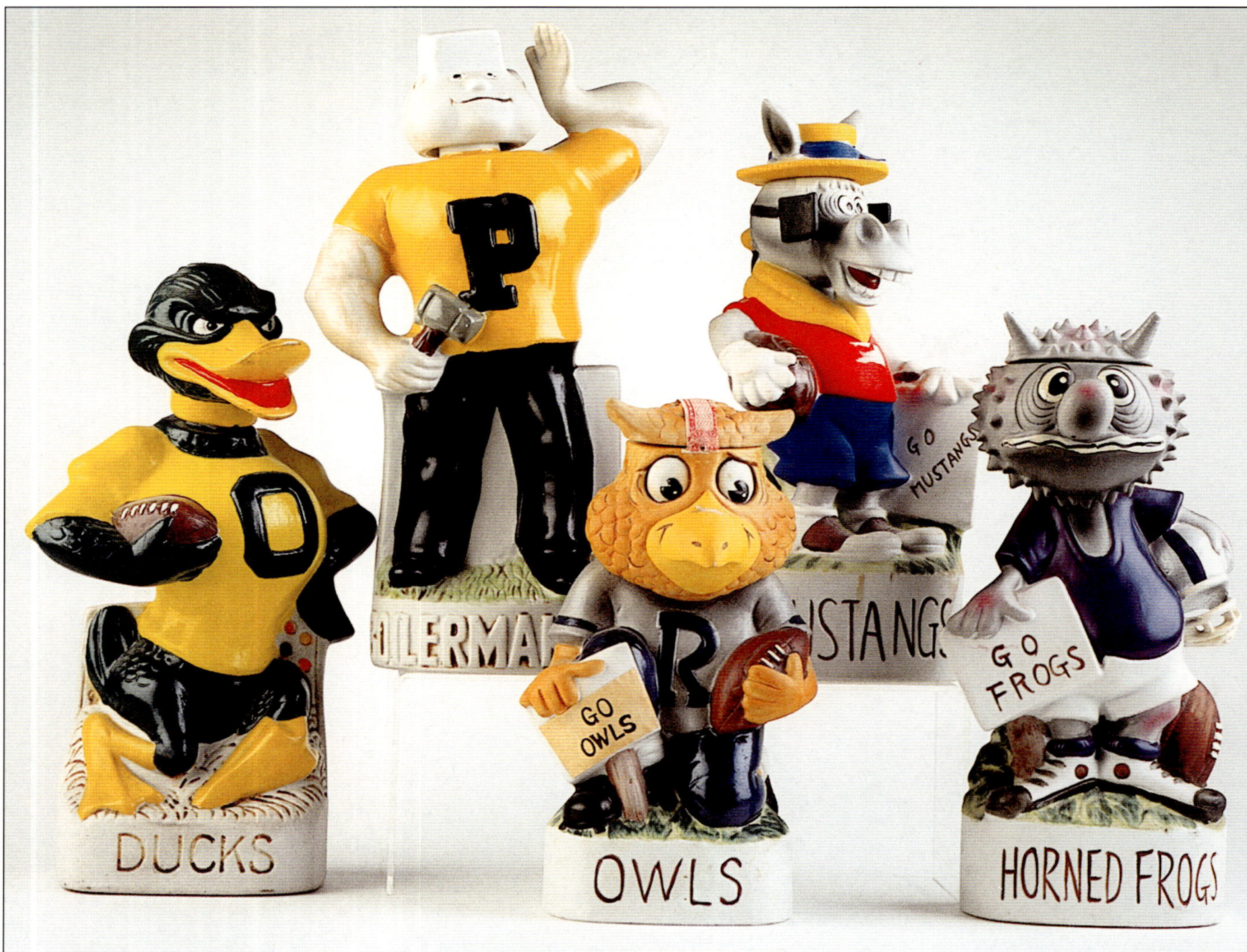

Oregon Ducks, 1974, fifth $75-85. Perdue Boilermakers, 1974, fifth $65-75. Rice Owls, 1974, fifth $80-90. SMU Mustangs, 1972, fifth $95-110. TCU Horned Frogs, 1972, fifth $95-110.

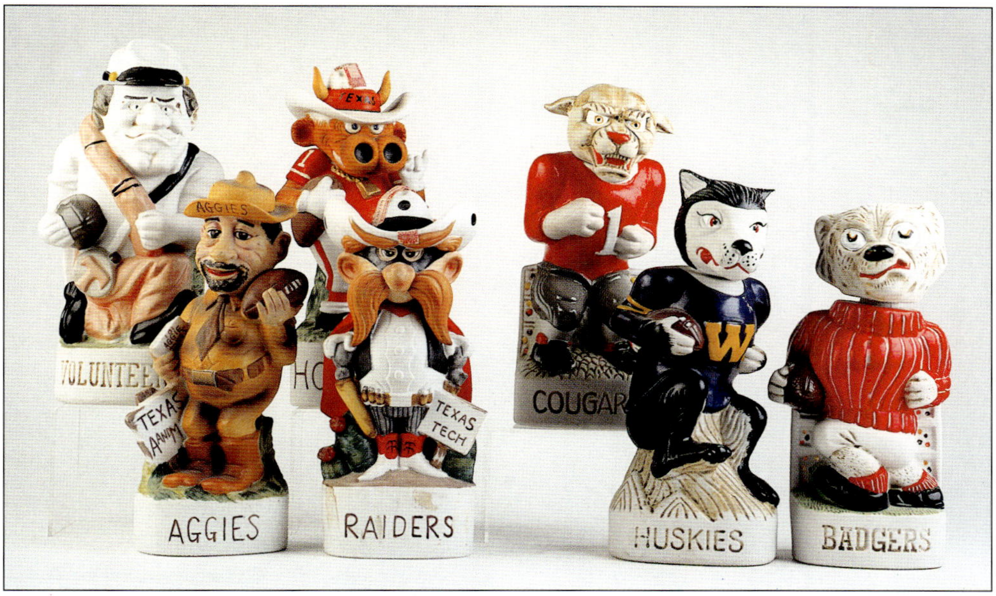

Tennessee Volunteers, 1974, fifth $65-75. Texas A&M Aggies, 1972, fifth $75-85. Texas Long Horns, 1972, fifth $85-95. Texas Tech Raiders, 1972, fifth $85-95. Washington Cougers, 1974, fifth $75-85. Washington Huskies, 1974, fifth $75-85. Wisconsin Badgers, 1974, fifth $45-55.

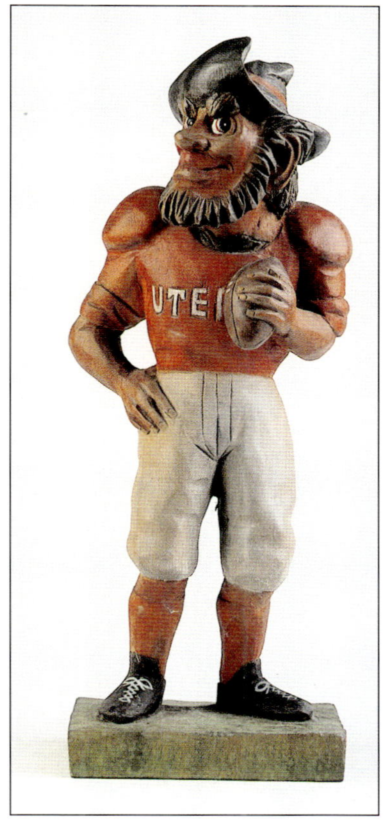

UTEP Peg Leg Pete, mock-up wooden prototype (bottle never made), $200.

Miscellaneous McCormick

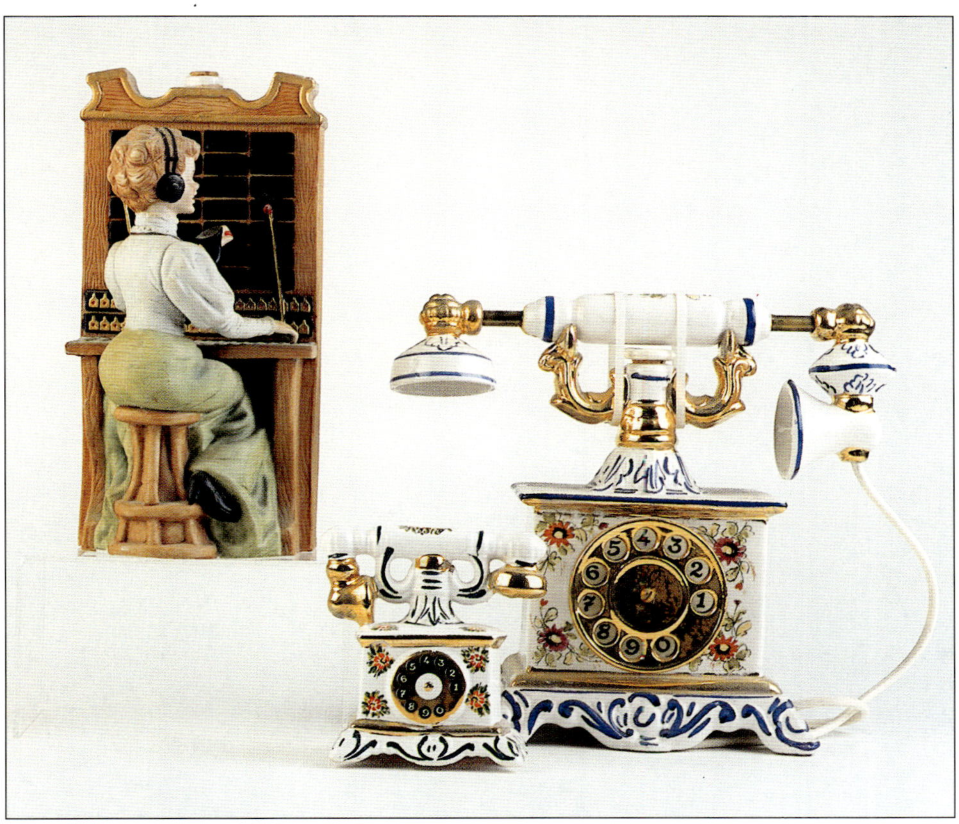

Telephone Operator, 1982, fifth $20-25. French Telephone, 1969, fifth $25-30, mini $10-15.

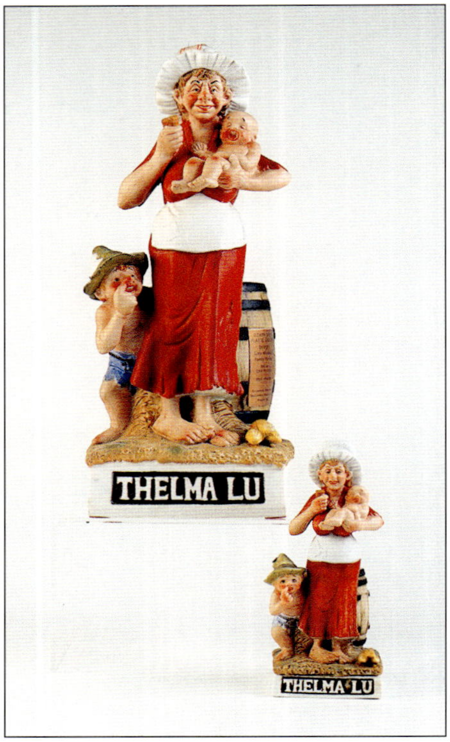

Thelma Lu, fifth $20-25, mini $10-15.

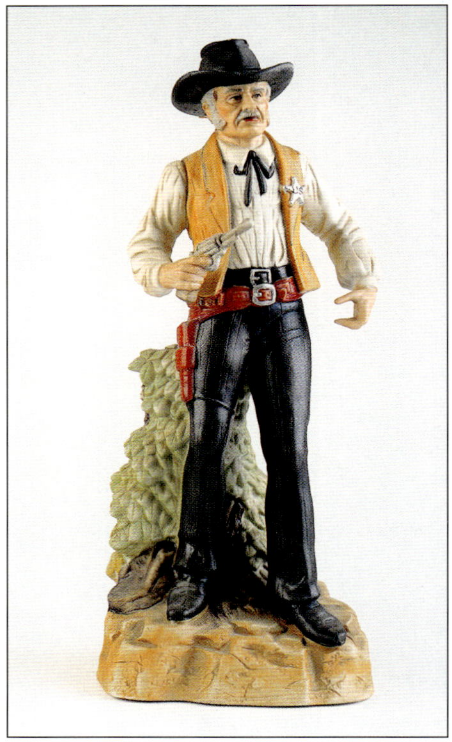

U.S. Marshall, 1979, fifth $35-45.

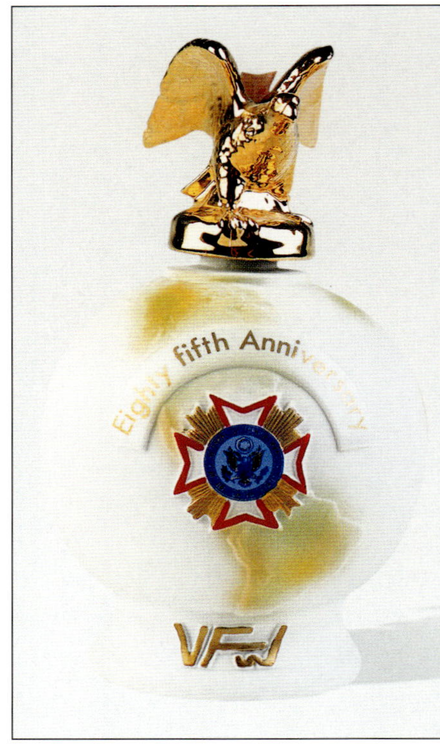

V.F.W., 1984, $25-30.

Warrior Series

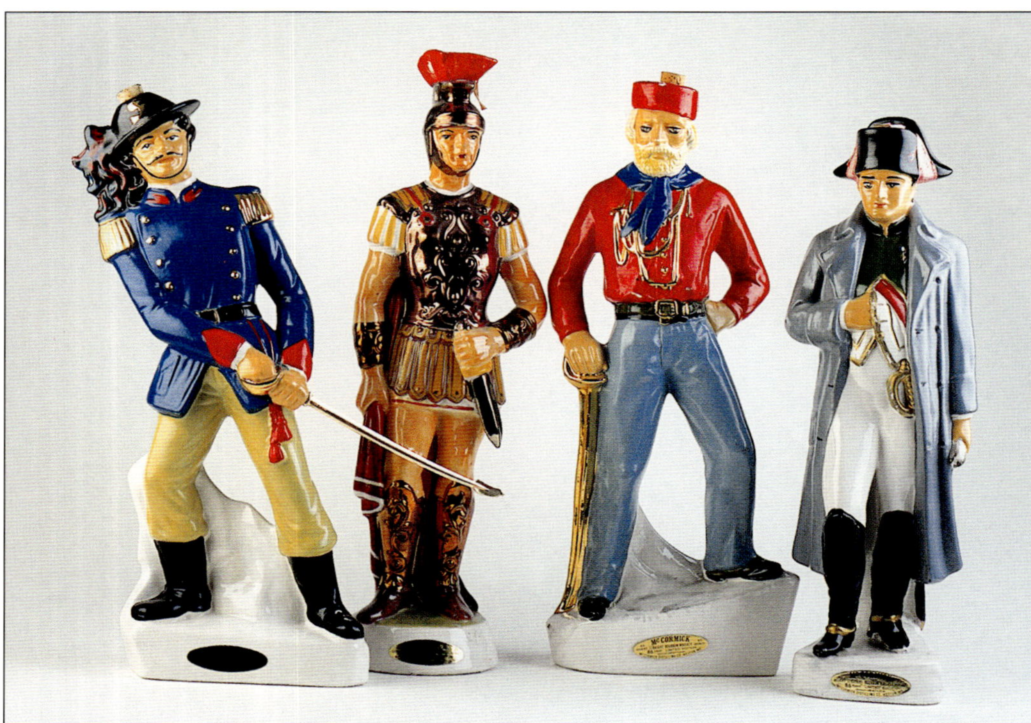

Bersaglieri, 1969, fifth $20-25; Centurion, 1969, fifth $20-25; Garibaldi, 1969, fifth $20-25; Napoleon, 1969, fifth $20-25.

Miscellaneous McCormick

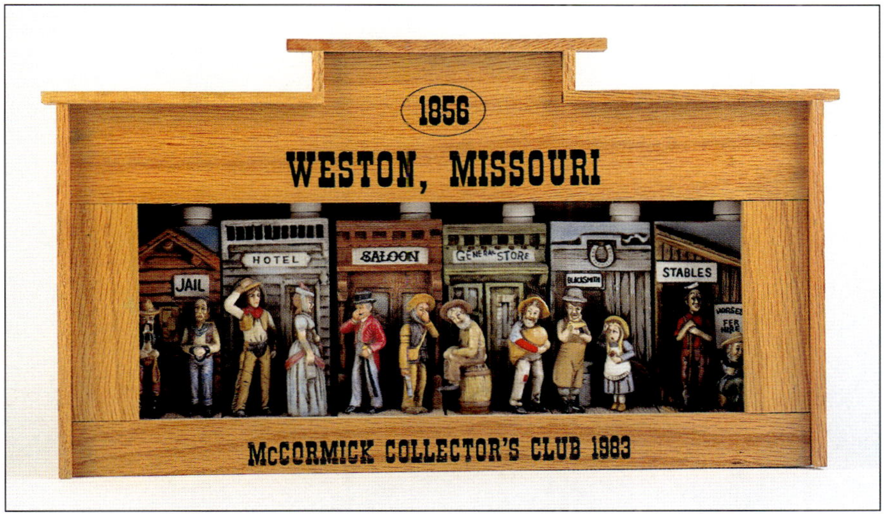

Weston, Missouri 1856, McCormick Collector's Club 1983 set of minis in frame – Hotel 1984, Saloon 1984, Jail 1984, General Store 1984, Stable 1985, Blacksmith 1985, $85-95 set.

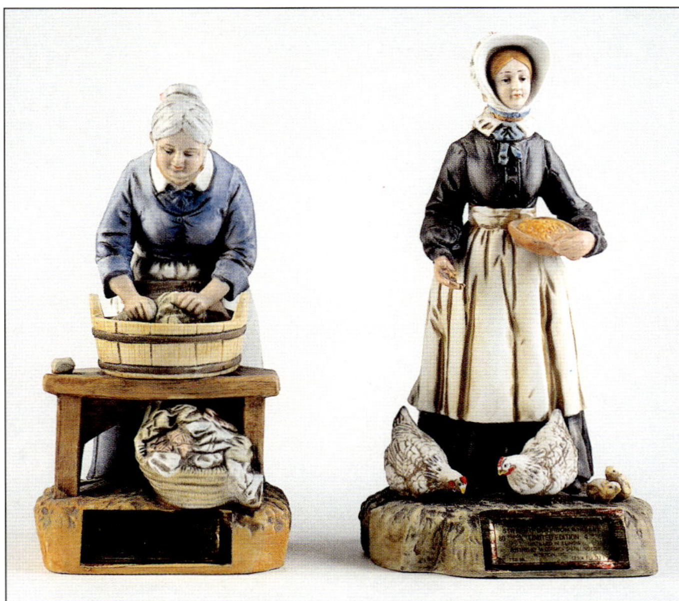

Woman Washing Clothes, 1980, fifth $20-25.
Woman Feeding Chickens, 1980, fifth $20-25.

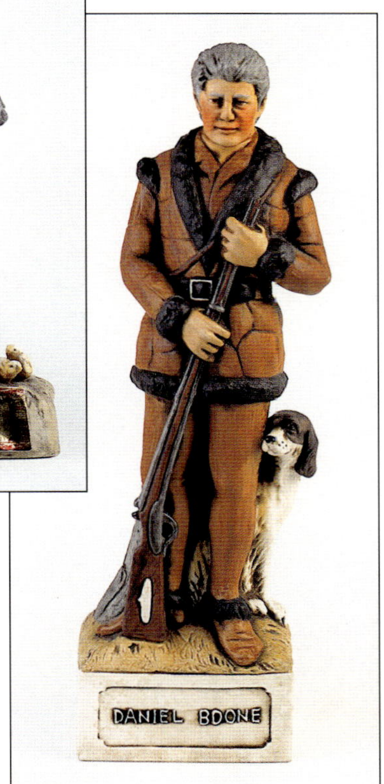

Daniel Boone, one-of-a-kind prototype, $95.

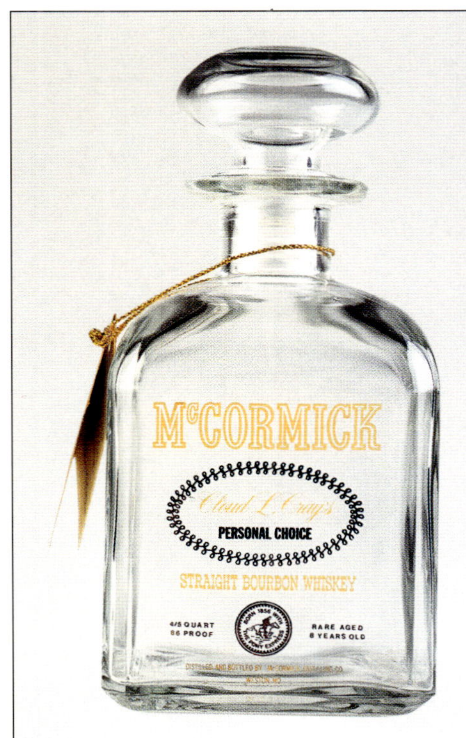

McCormick crystal decanter, $15-20.

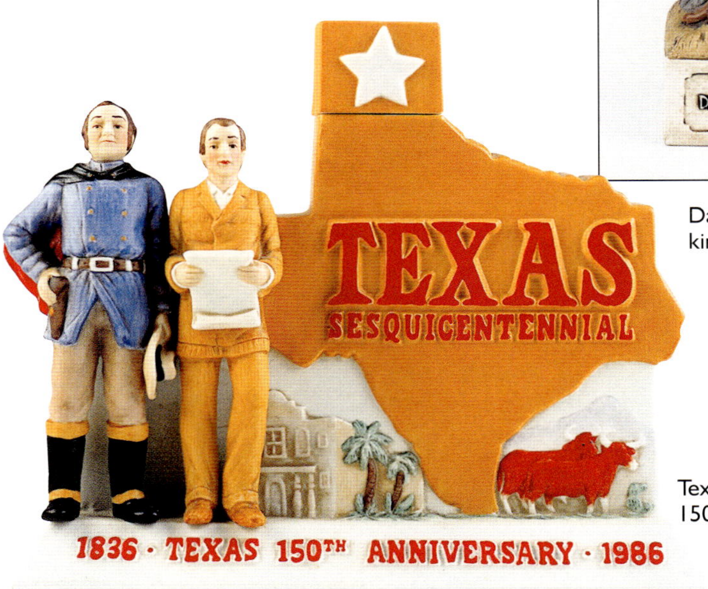

Texas of Today and Tomorrow, 150th Anniversary, $25-30.

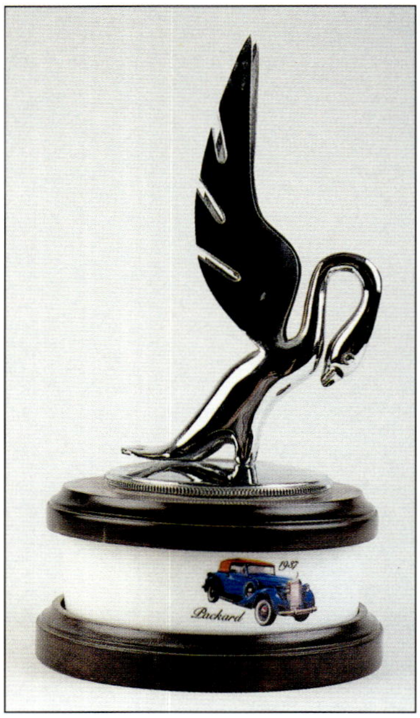

1937 Packard Hood Ornament, $45-50.

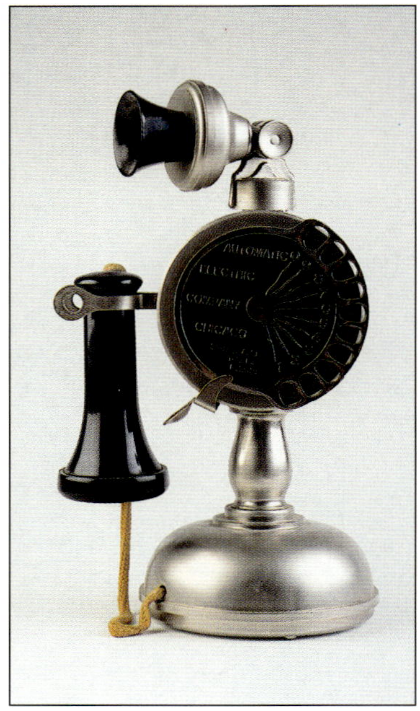

Automatic Electric Company Chicago, Telex, $20-25.

Four Aces Series

The American Cowboy, 2003 (first in a series), fifth $95-110. Made by Four Aces.

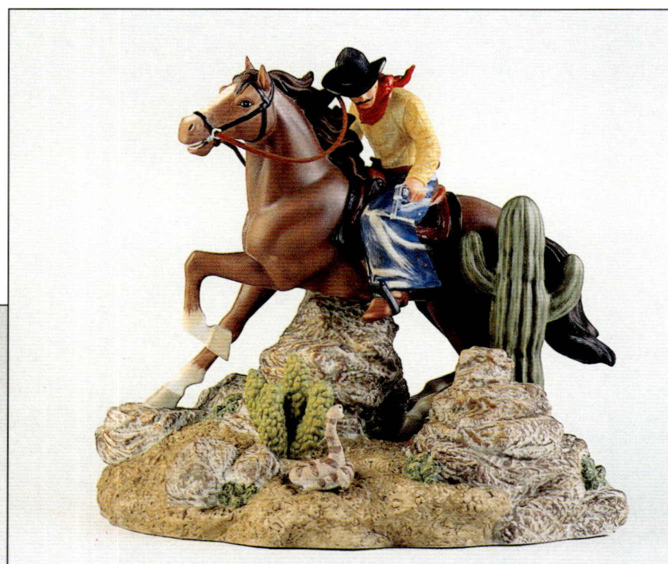

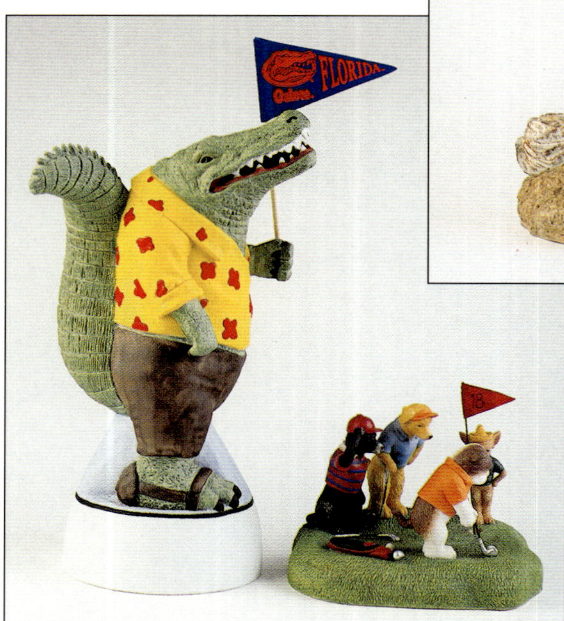

Florida Gators, 2003, fifth $45-65. Dogs Playing Golf, mini $40-45. Made by Four Aces.

We Support Our Troops, The International Association of Jim Beam Bottle and Specialties Clubs, made by the Four Aces Co., 2004, fifth $65-75.

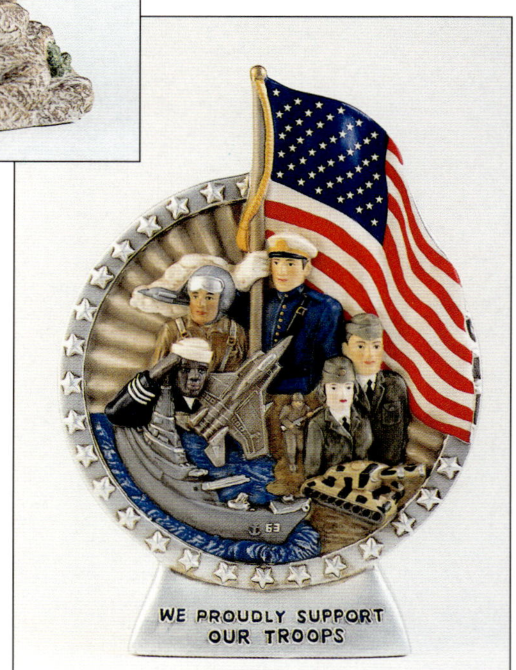

Wild Turkey

Turkey Series #1

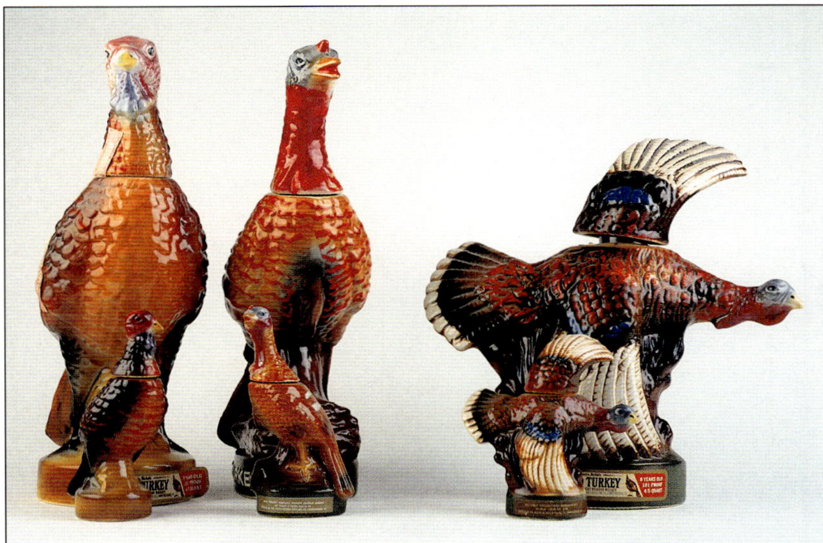

Male, 1971, fifth $125-150, mini $15; Female, 1972, fifth $75-85, mini $10; On the Wing, 1973, fifth $35-45, mini $10.

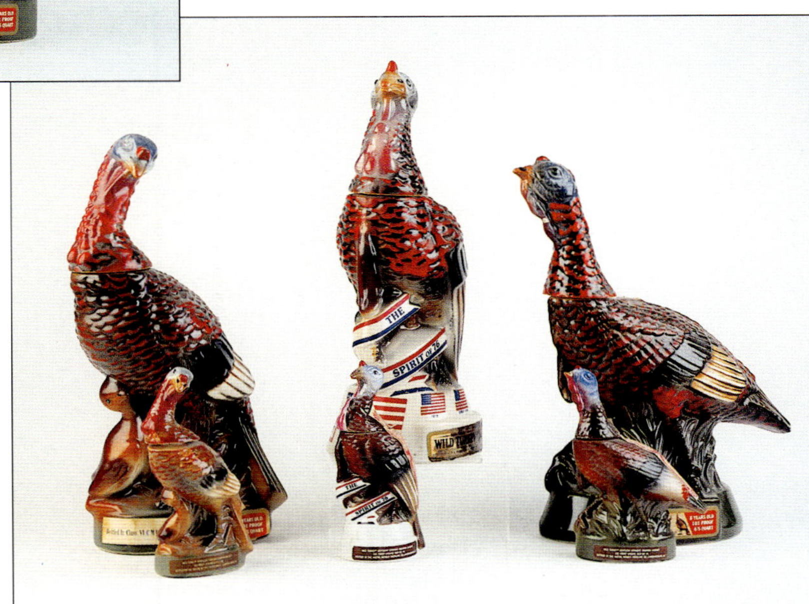

With Poult, 1974, fifth $30-35, mini $20; With Flags, 1975, fifth $25-30, mini $20; Striding, 1976, fifth $20-25, mini $20.

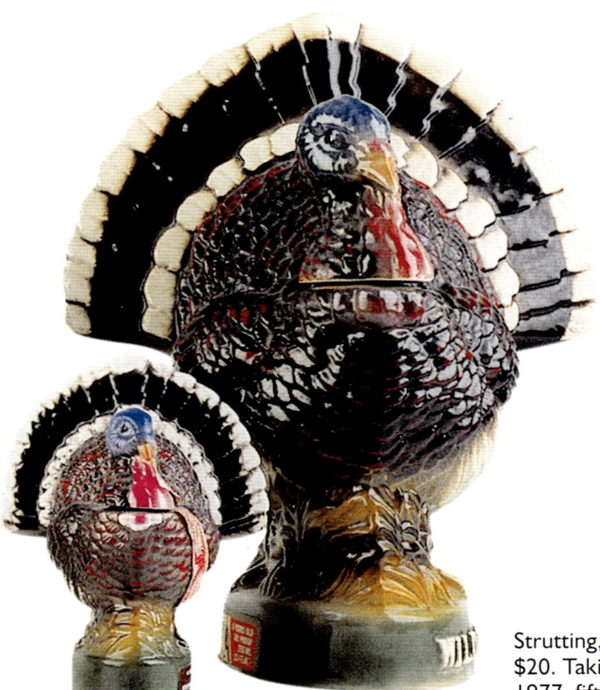

Strutting, 1978, $15-20, mini $20. Taking Off, (not shown) 1977, fifth $15-20, mini $20.

Turkey Series #2

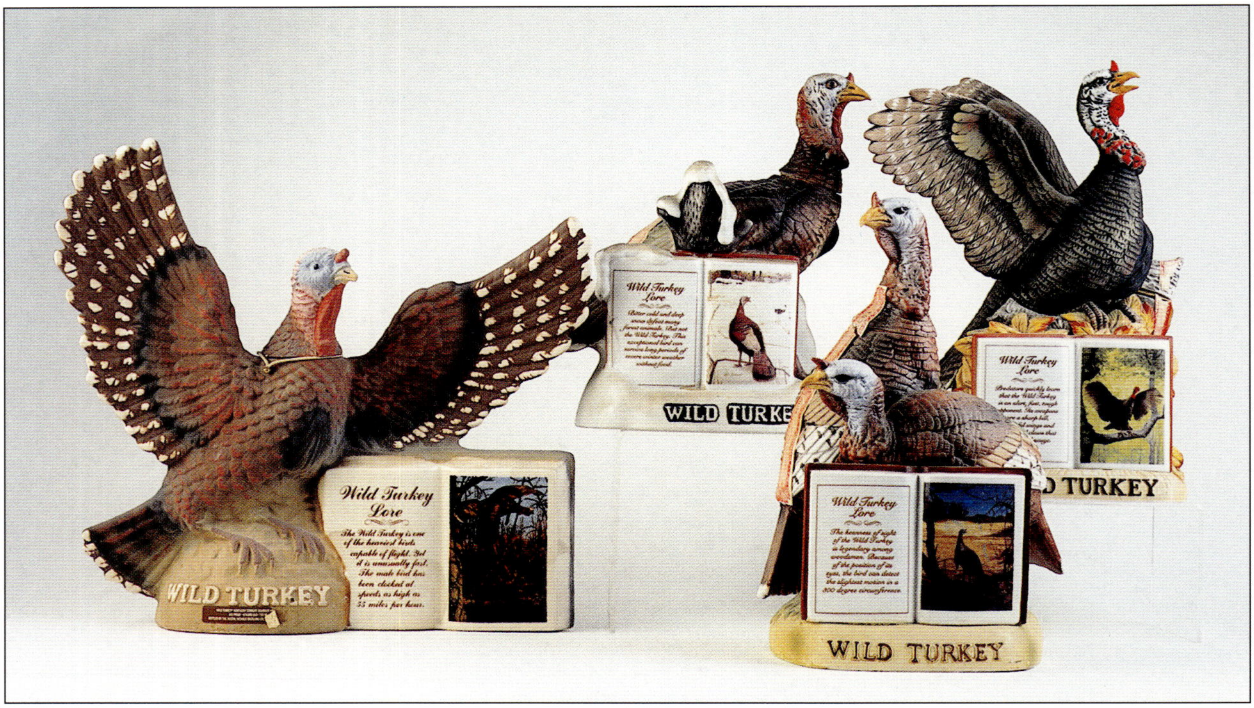

Lore #1, 1979, $25-30; Lore #2, $25-30; Lore #3, $25-30; Lore #4, $35-40.

Turkey Series #3

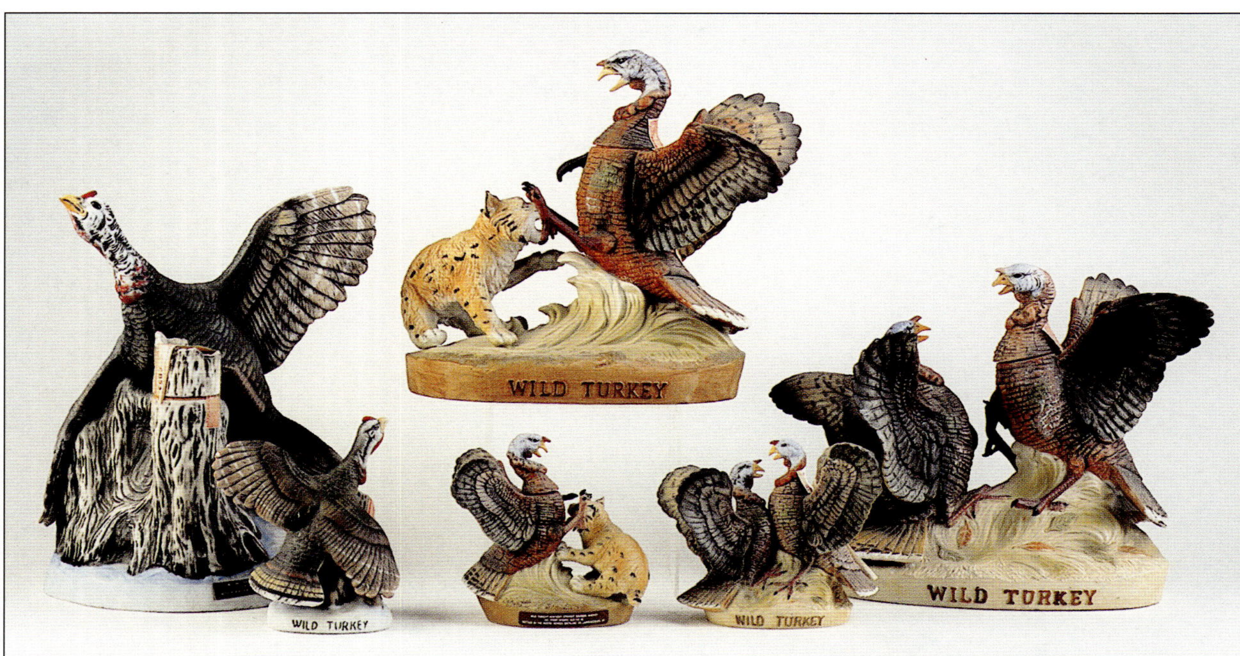

Turkey in Flight, 1983, fifth $75-85, mini $25-30; Turkey and Bobcat, 1983, fifth $85-95, mini $25-30; Turkey Fighting, 1983, fifth $75-85, mini $25-30.

Turkey Series #4

Turkey and Eagle, 1984, fifth $85-95, mini (not shown) $45-50; Turkey and Raccoon, 1984, fifth $75-85, mini (not shown) $20-25; Turkey and Poults, 1984, fifth $75-85, mini $20-25.

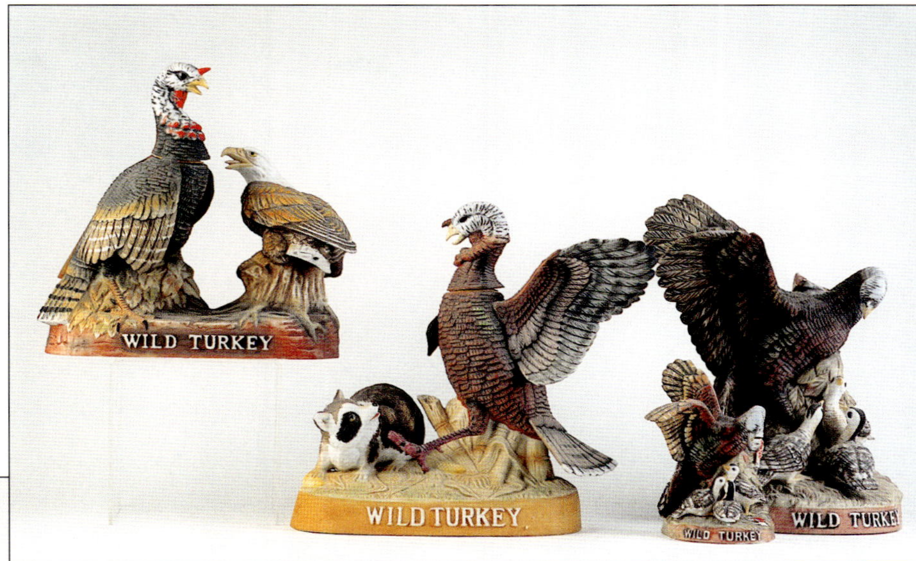

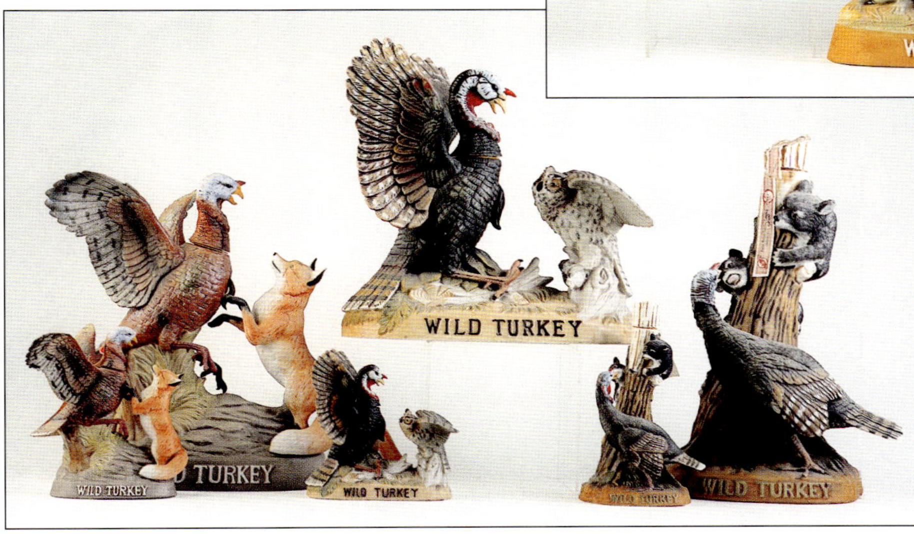

Turkey and Fox, fifth $75-80, mini $20-25; Turkey and Owl, fifth $85-95, mini $25-30; Turkey and Bears, fifth $85-95, mini $25-30.

Turkey and Coyote, 1986, fifth $65-75, mini $20-25; Wild Turkey and Falcon, 1986, fifth $75-85, mini $25-30; Turkey and Skunks, 1986, fifth $75-85, mini (not shown) $25-25.

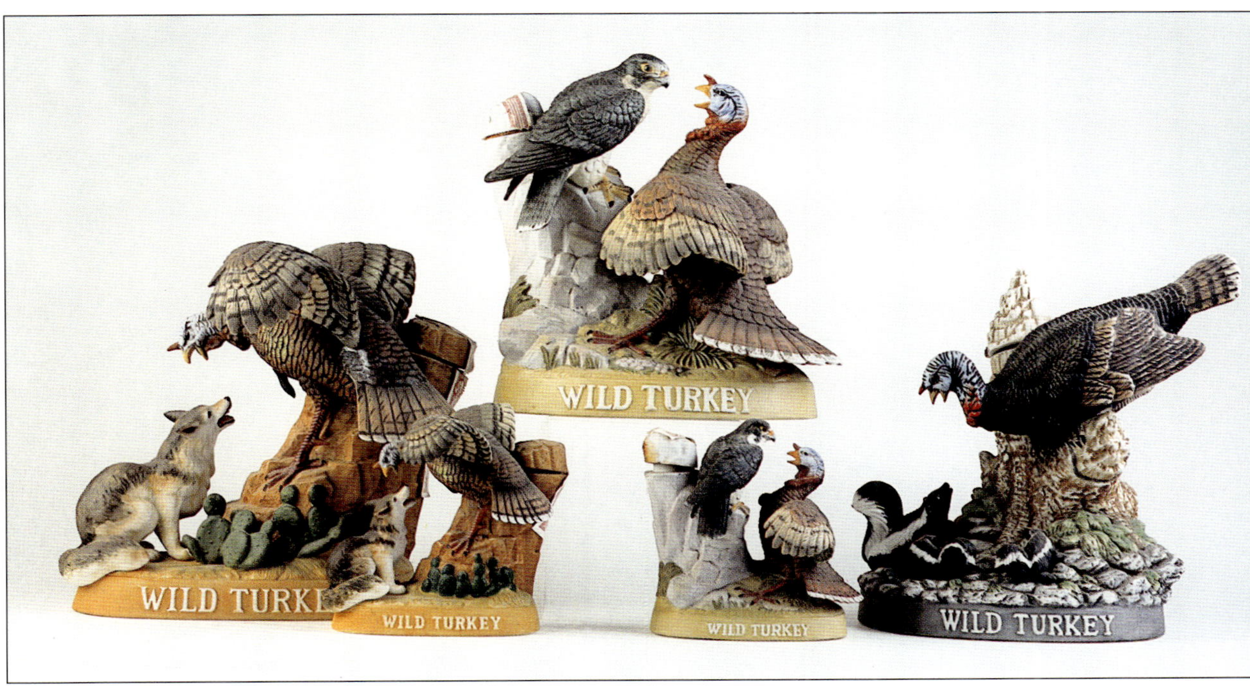

Miscellaneous Wild Turkey

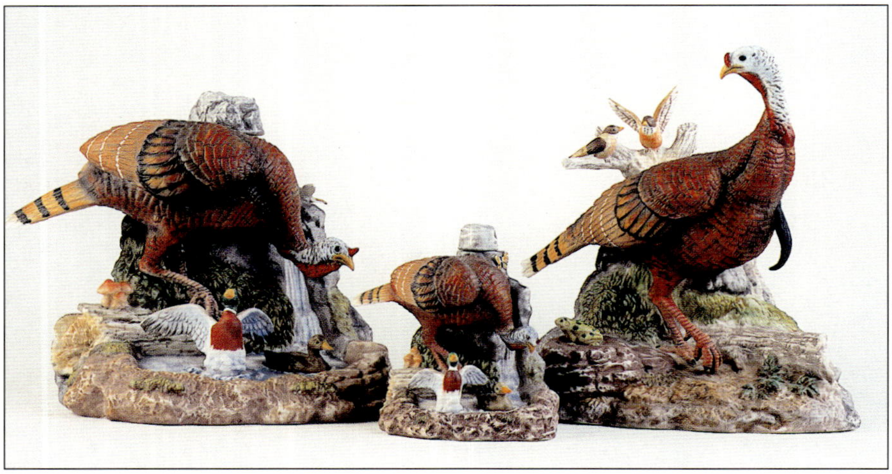

Habitat I-A, 1988, fifth $125-135, mini $65-75; Habitat I-B, 1989, fifth $145-150, mini (not shown) $70-75.

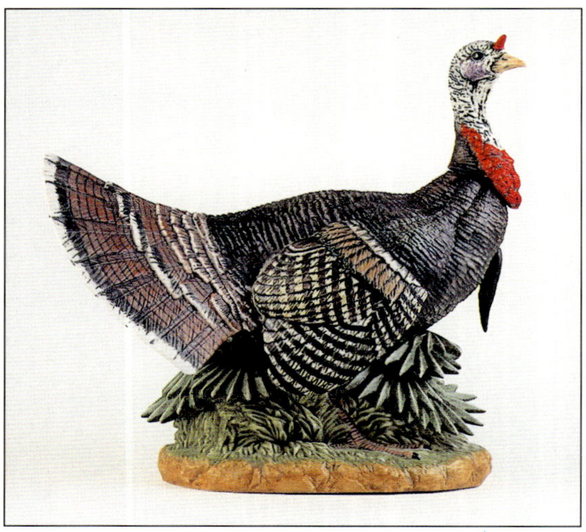

Wild Turkey 1/2 gallon, $250-295.

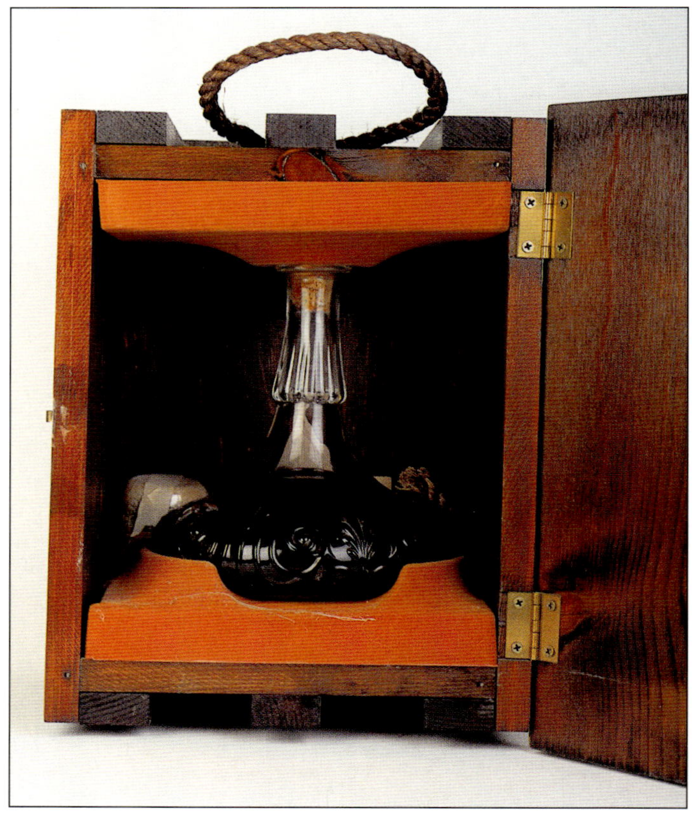

Capitan's Chest with Baccarat Crystal Decanter, 1979, $149-175.

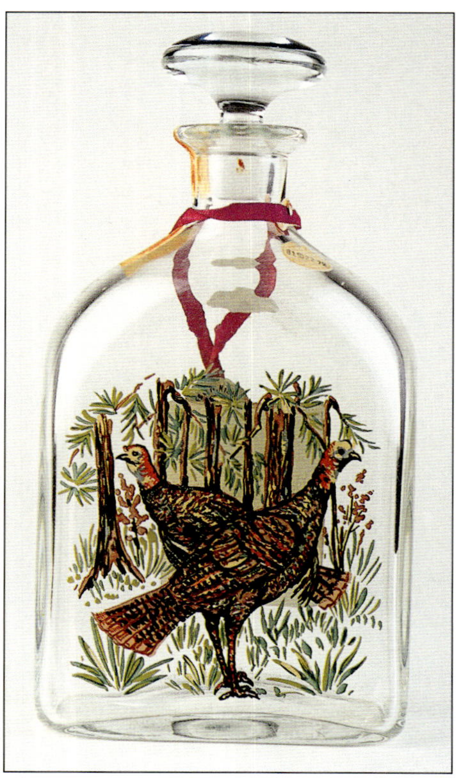

Crystal Anniversary Decanter, 100th Anniversary of Wild Turkey, 1955, $850-900.

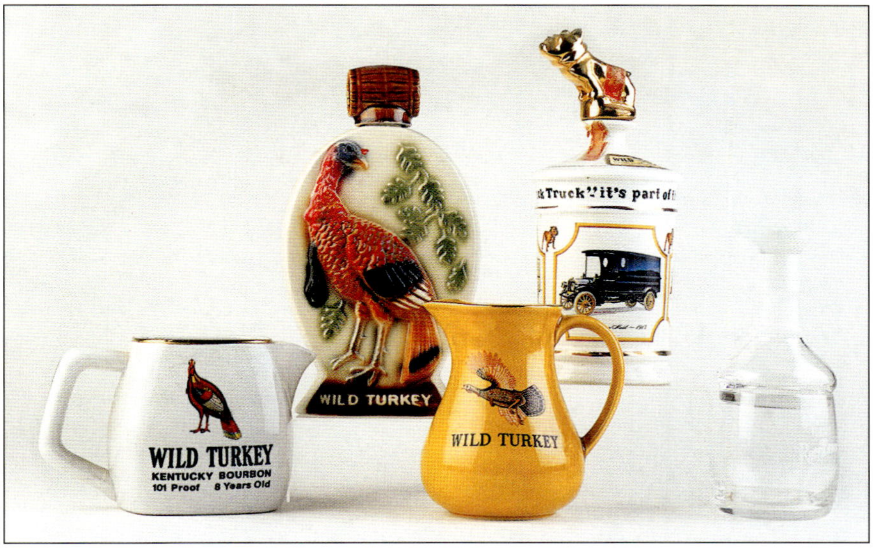

Wild Turkey pitcher, $20-25. Charleston Centennial decanter, 1974, $45-50. Mack Truck, 1975 first issue limited edition, $20-25. Staffordshire Pottery Wild Turkey pitcher, $20-25. Rare Breed decanter, $35-40.

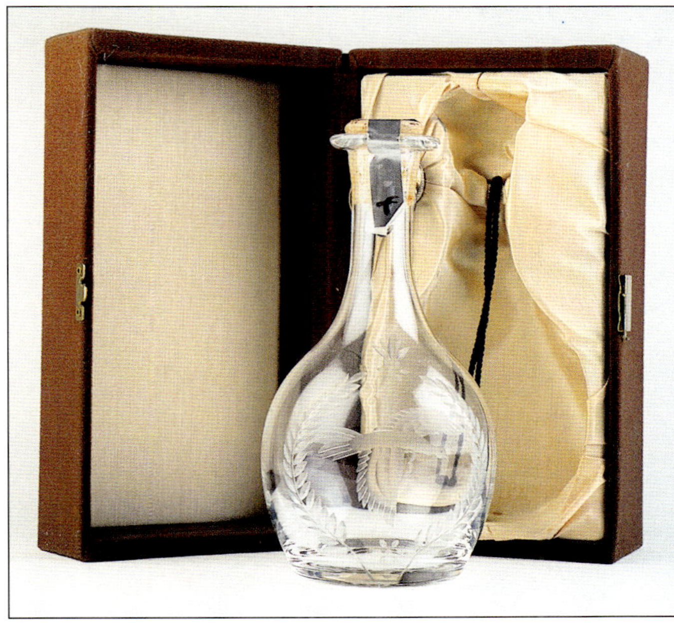

Wild Turkey crystal decanter and case, $35-40.

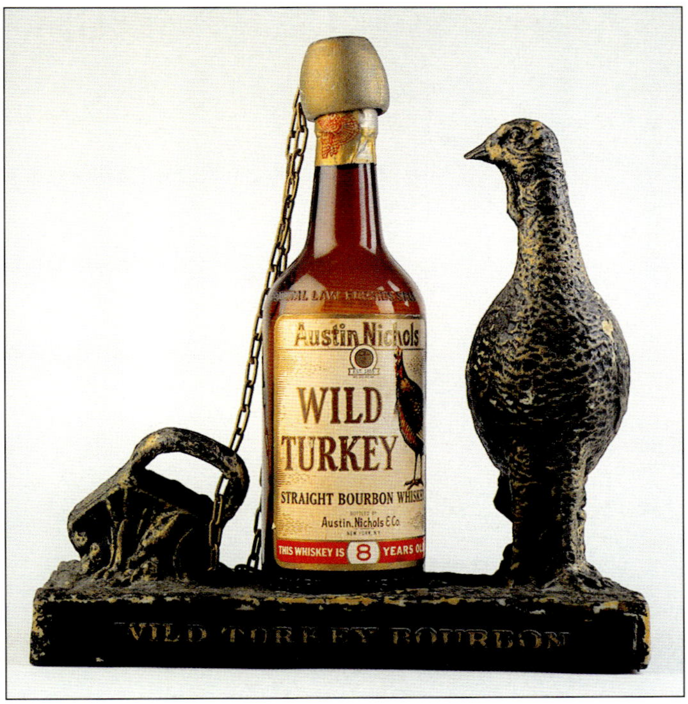

Wild Turkey Back Bar Piece, $45-50.

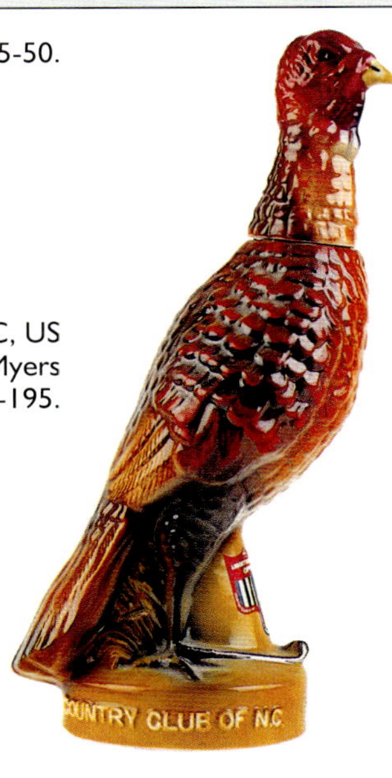

Collectors Club of NC, US Championship Liggett &Myers Open, 1972, $175-195.

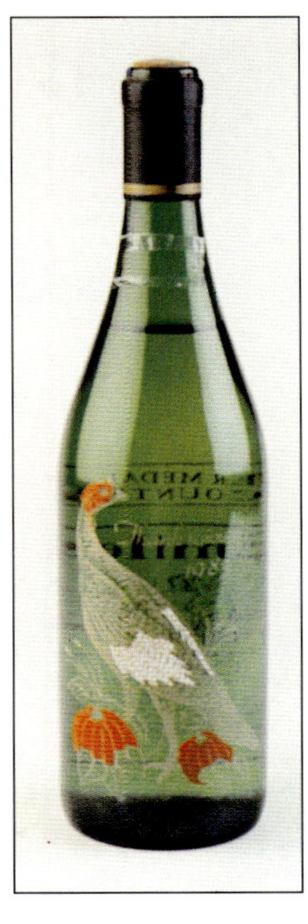

Thanksgiving Wine, Wild Turkey, $20-25.

Lewis and Clark

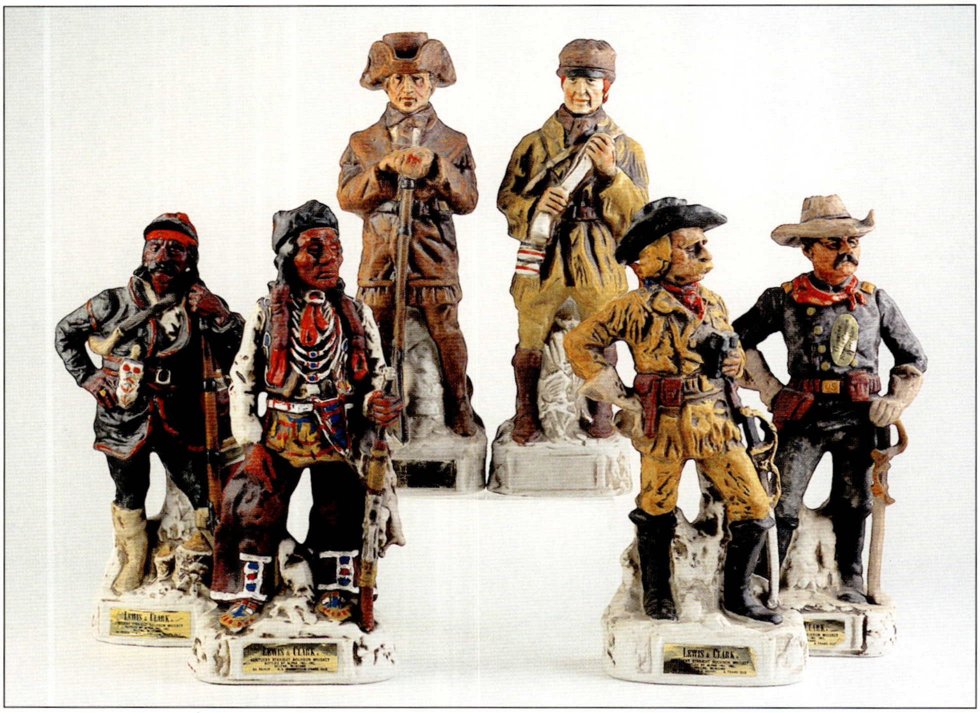

Charbonneau, 1972, fifth $25-35. Curlee Scout, 1974, fifth $20-25. Lewis, 1971, fifth $20-25. Clark, 1971, fifth $20-25. General Custer, 1974, fifth $20-25. Major Reno, 1975, fifth $20-25.

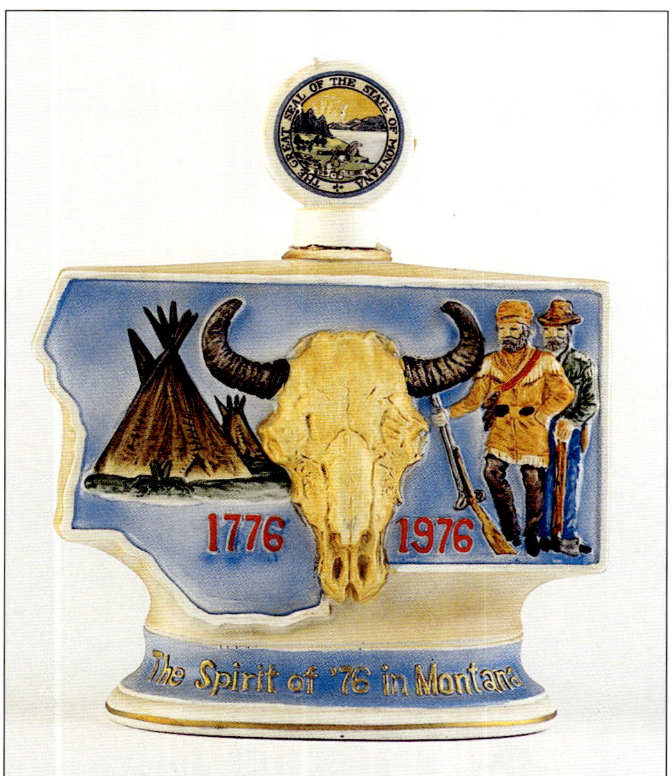

Montana State, 1976, $30-35.

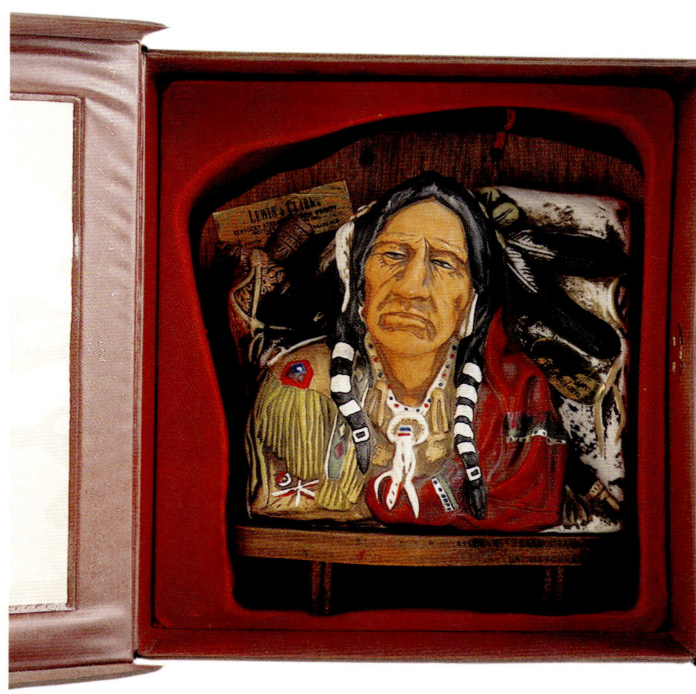

Indian Peacepipe in display box, 1978, $35-40.

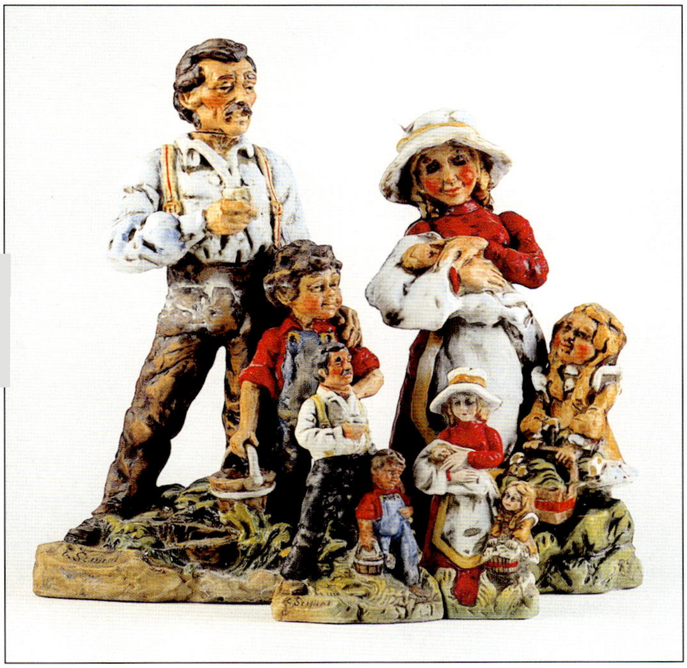

Pioneer Family (pair), 1978, fifth $70-75, mini $20-25.

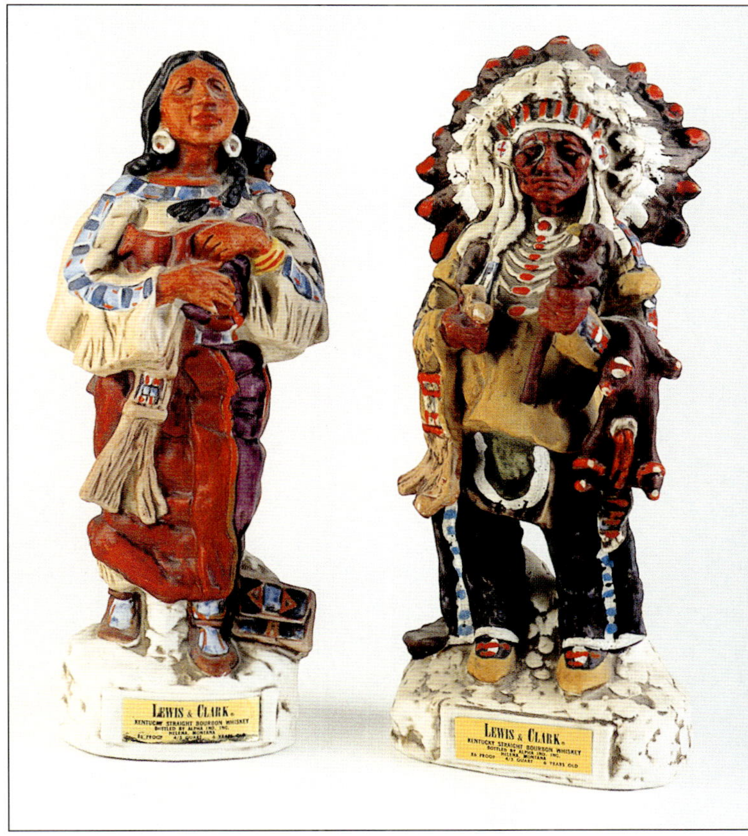

Sacagawea, 1972, $40-45. Sitting Bull, 1976, $65-75.

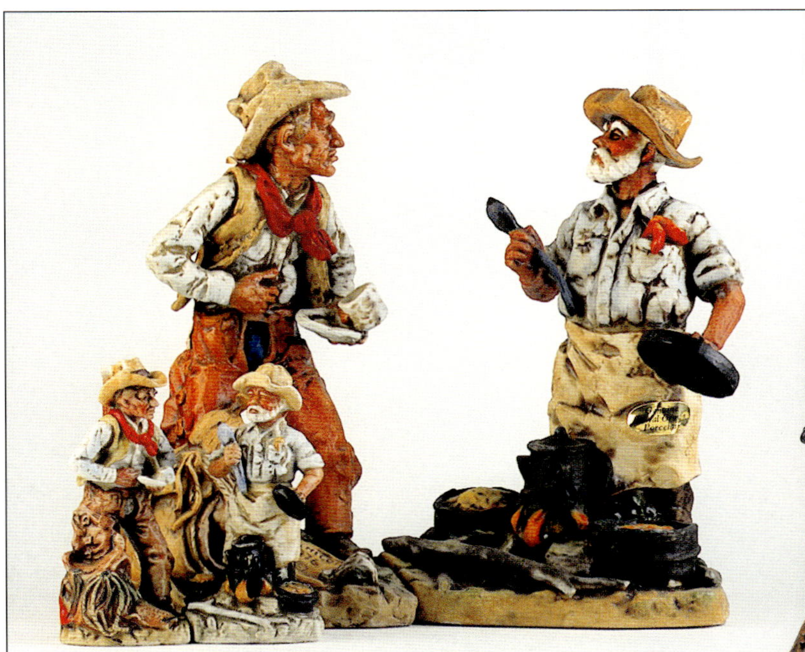

Son of a Gun Stew (pair), 1977, fifth $30-35, mini $10-15.

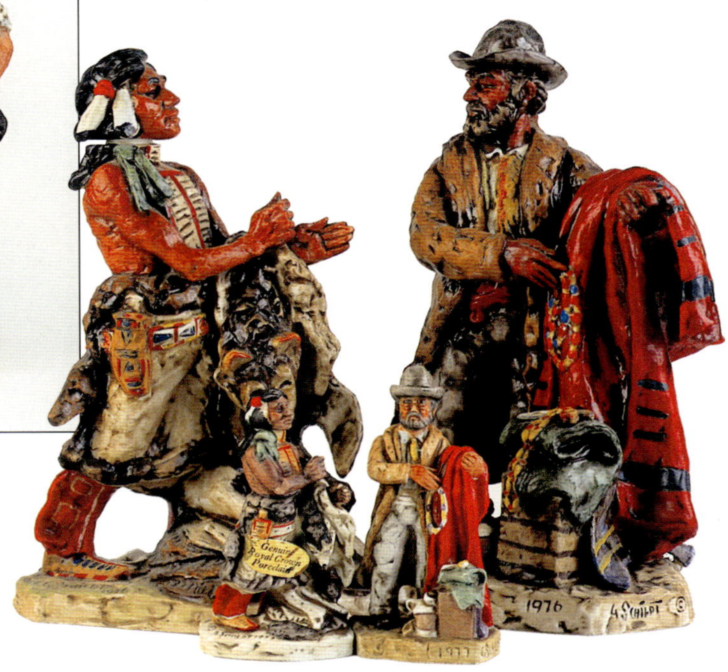

Striking a Bargain (pair), 1978, fifth $30-35, mini $15-10.

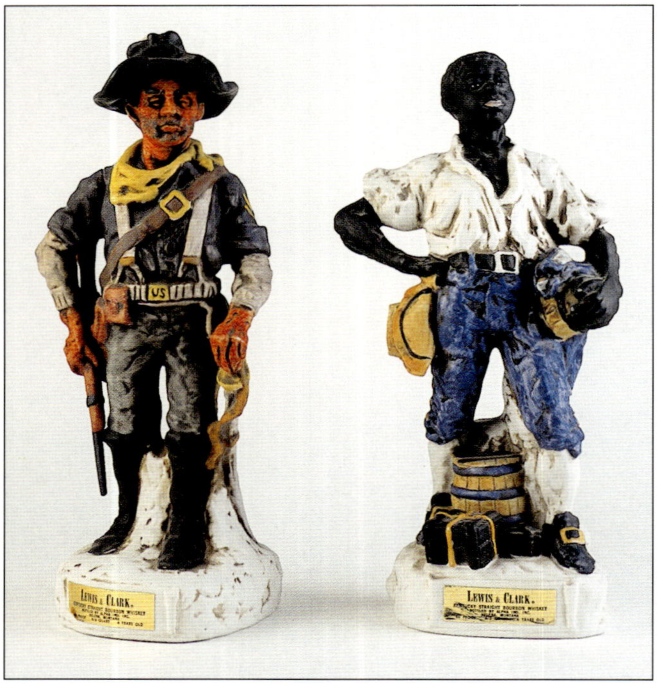

Trooper, 1975, $30-35. York, 1972, $30-35.

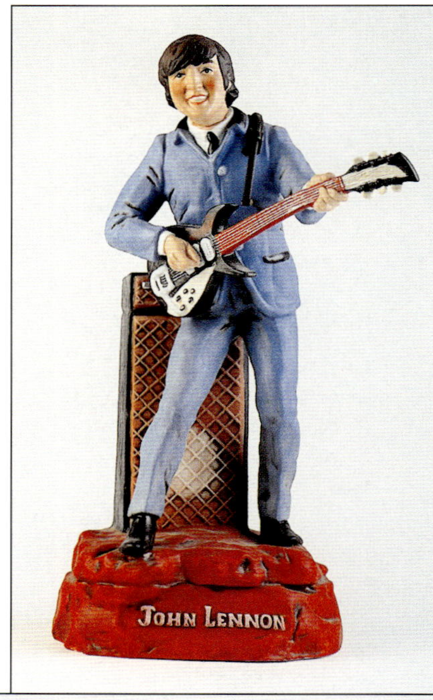

John Lennon, 1981, $125-135.

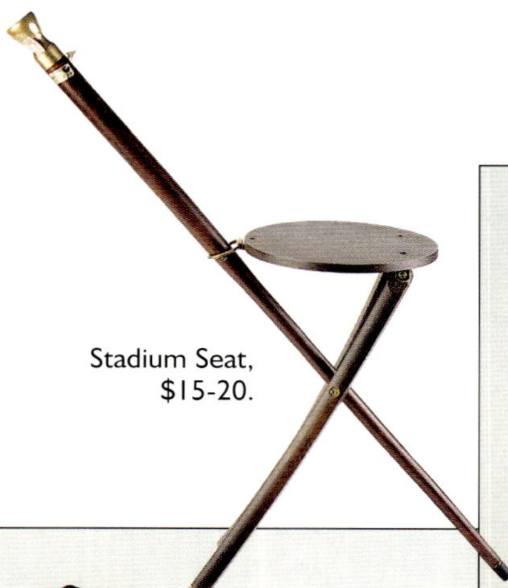

Stadium Seat, $15-20.

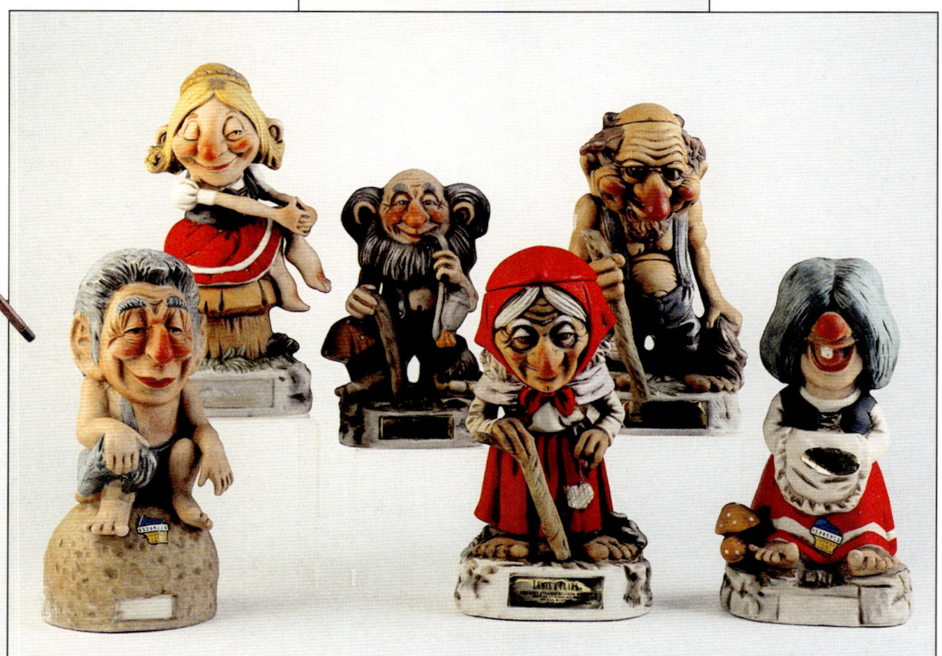

Cousin Troll, 1979, $10-15. Daughter Troll, 1978, $10-15. Grandfather Troll, 1978, $10-15. Grandmother Troll, 1979, $10-15. Mr. Troll, 1978, $10-15. Mrs. Troll, 1979. $10-15.

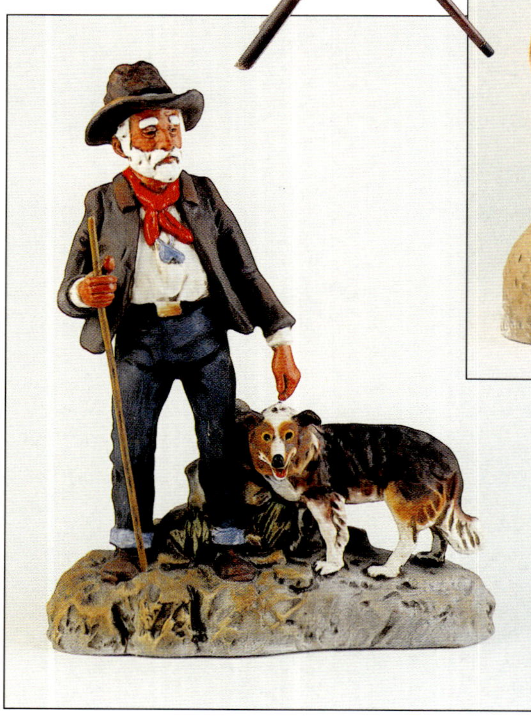

Sheep Herder, 1980, $20-25.

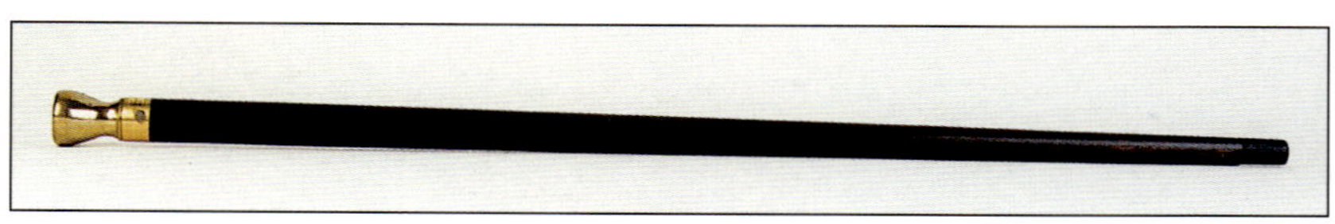

Walking Stick, $10-15.

Lionstone

Transportation Series

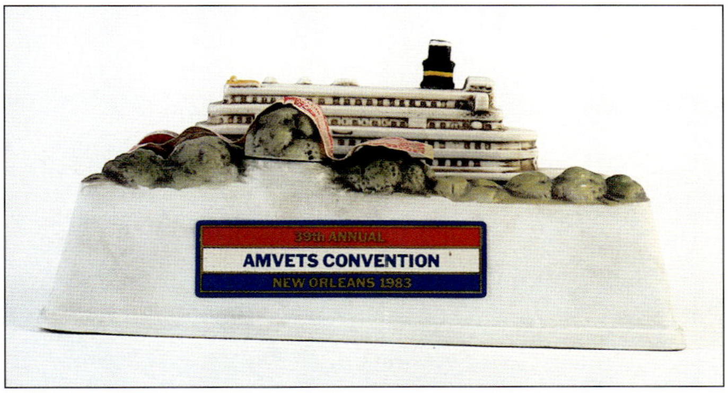

Amvets Convention Riverboat, 1983, fifth $10-15.

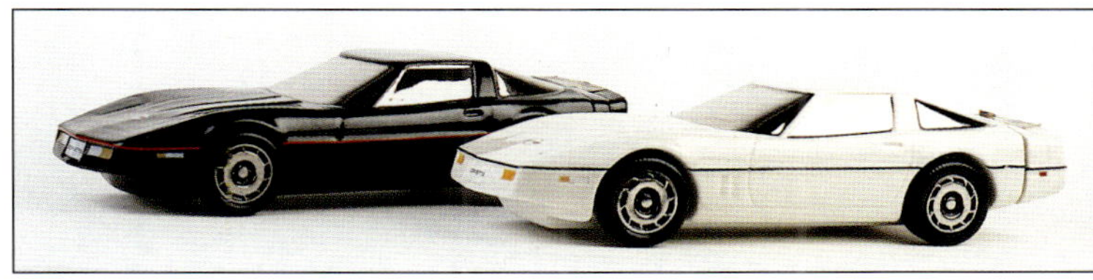

1984 Corvette (black), 1984, $50-60.
1984 Corvette (white), 1984, $50-60.

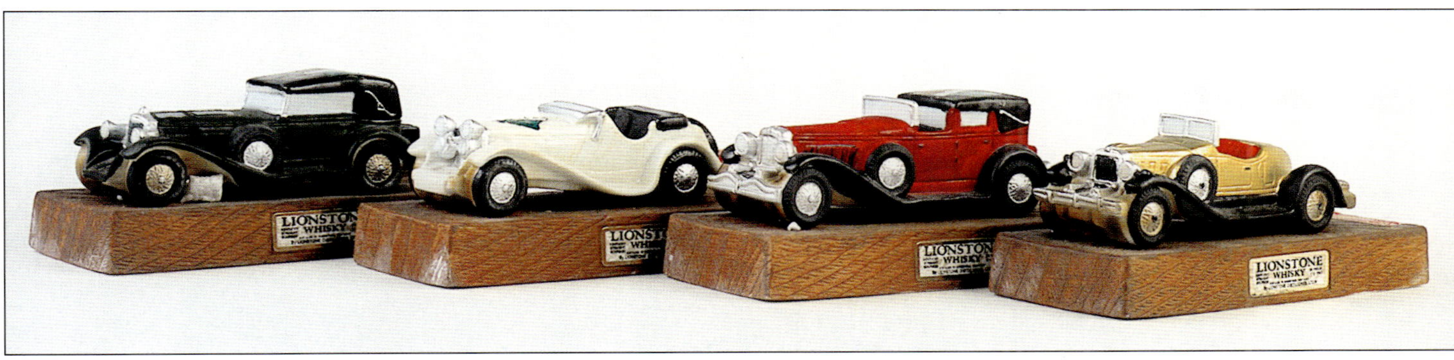

Duesenberg, 1974, mini $15-20. Jaguar, 1978, mini $15-20.
Mercedes, 1978, mini $15-20. Stutz Bearcat, 1978, mini $15-20.

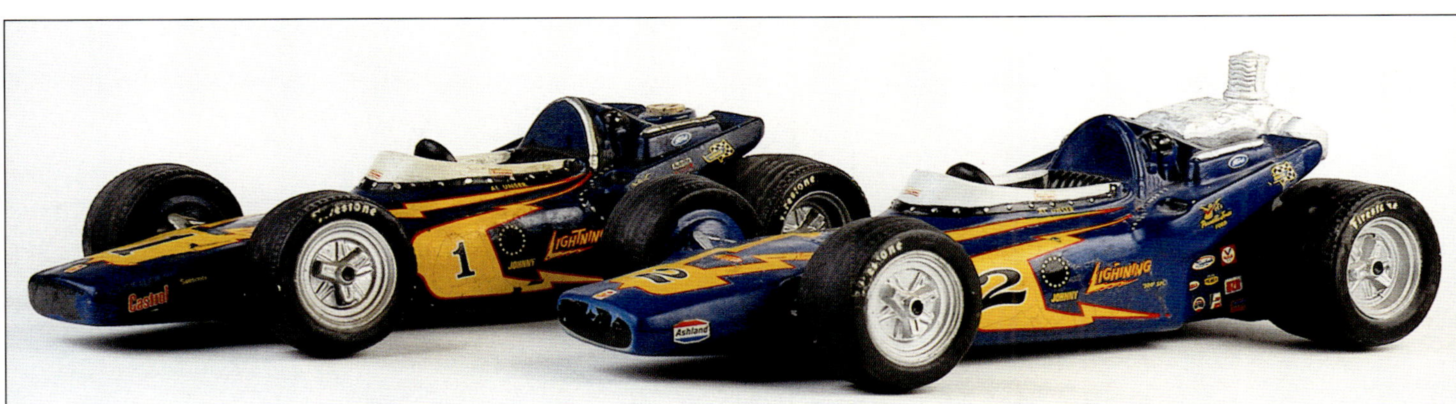

Johnnie Lightning #1, 1972, fifth $60-70. Johnnie Lightning #2, 1973, fifth $55-65.

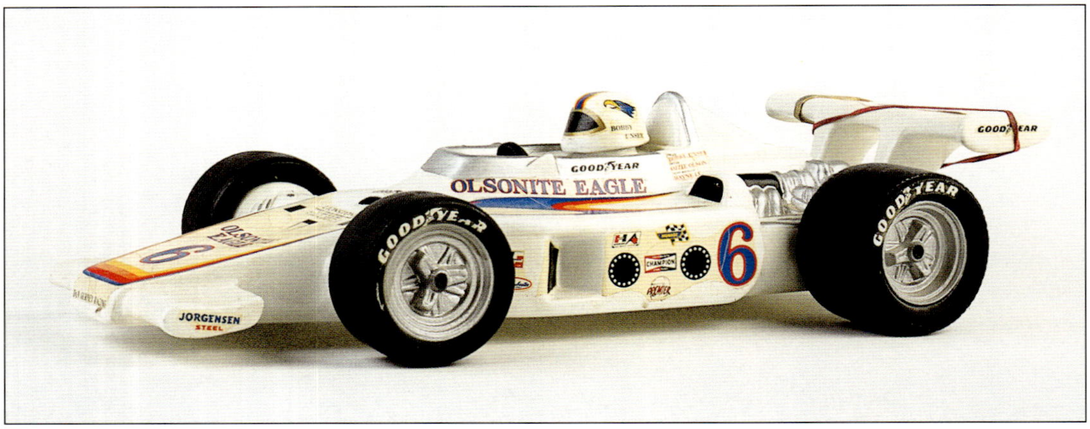

Olsonite Eagle #6, 1973, fifth $65-75.

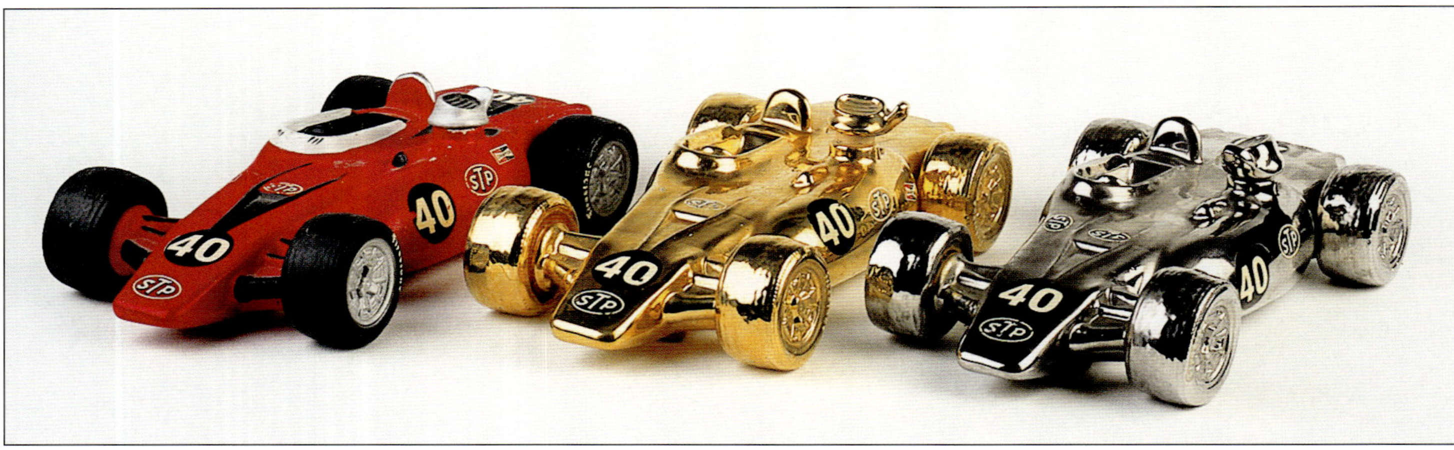

STP Turbo Car, 1972, red $30-35, gold $100-110, platinum $100-110.

Bicentennial Series

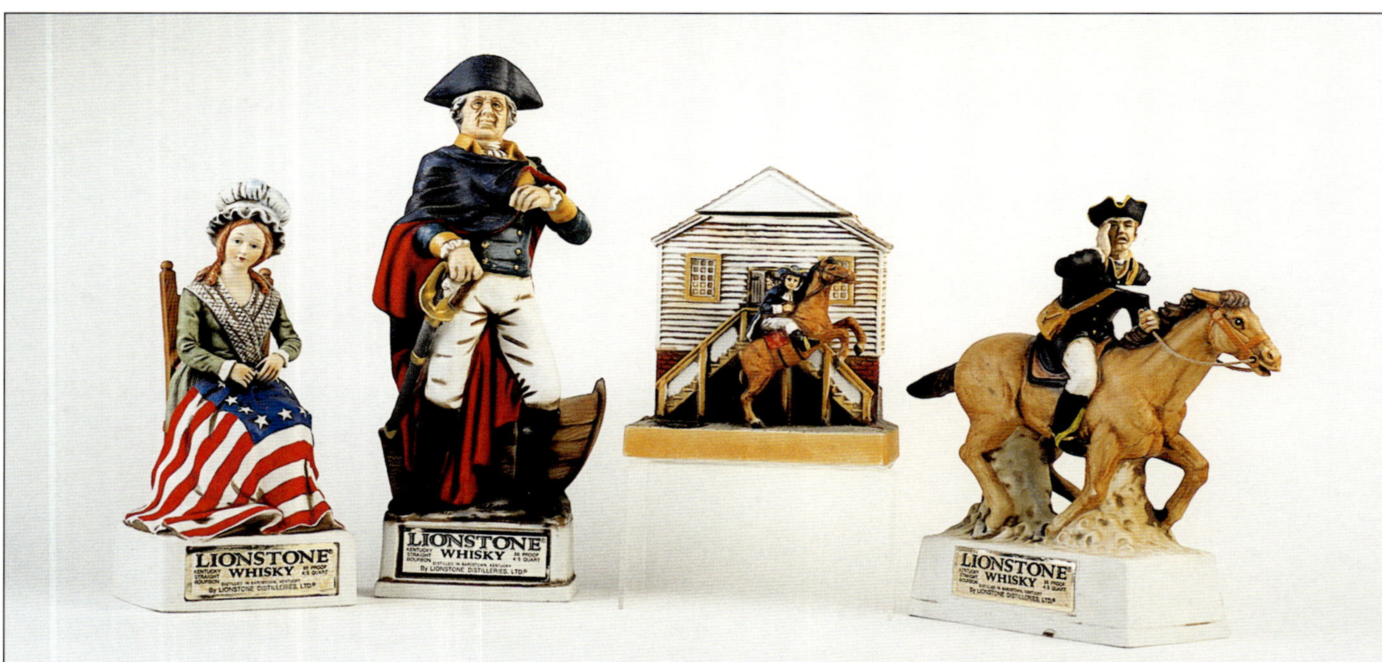

Bicentennial series: Betsy Ross, 1975, $15-20. George Washington, 1975, $10-15. Mecklenburg, 1975, $10-15. Paul Revere, 1975, $15-20.

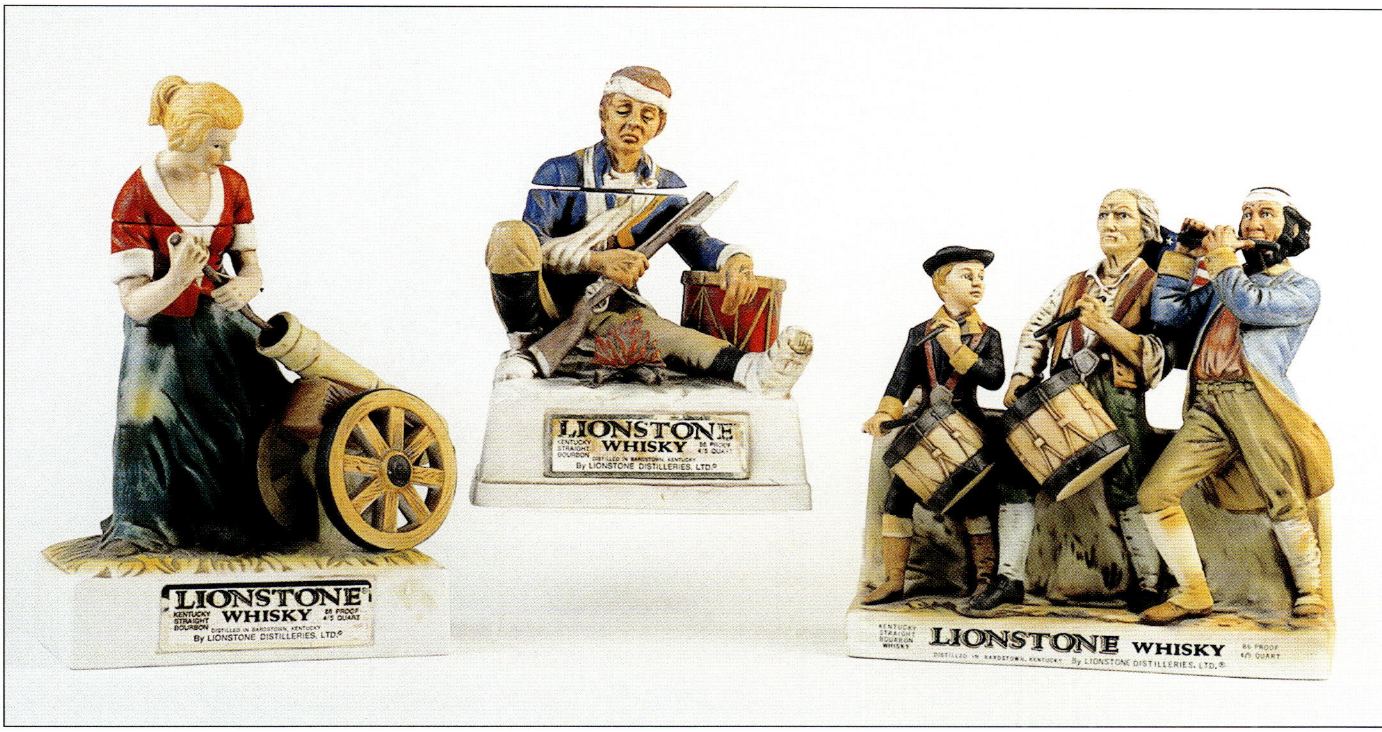

Bicentennial series: Molly Pitcher, 1975, $10-15. Valley Forge, 1975, $15-20. Sons of Freedom, 1975, $20-25.

Bird Series

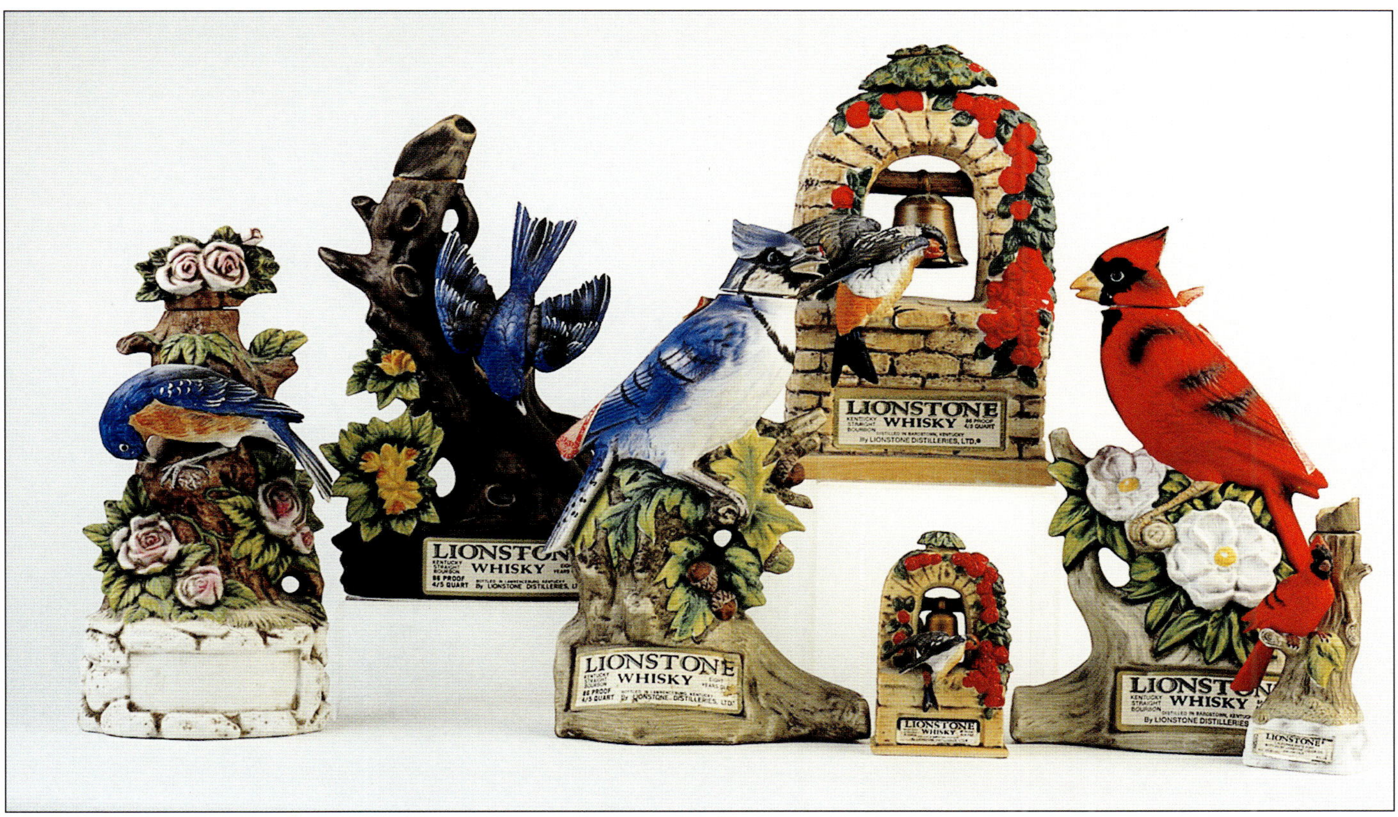

Eastern Blue Bird, 1972, $10-15. Western Blue Bird, 1972, $10-15. Capistrano Swallow, 1972, fifth $10-15, mini (1974) $5-10. Cardinal, 1972, fifth $10-15, mini $5-10.

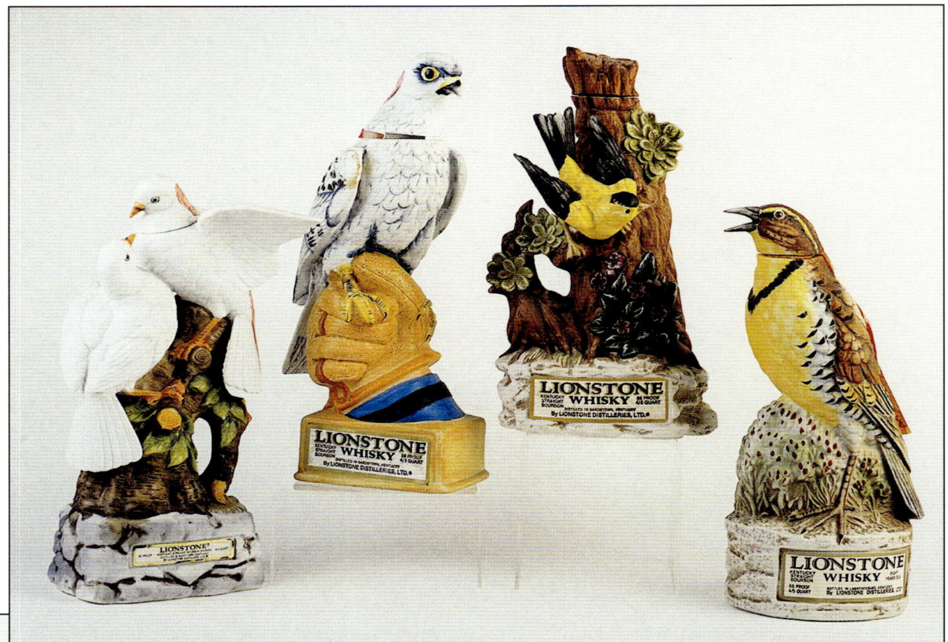

Doves of Peace, 1977, $20-25. Falcon, 1973, $20-25. Goldfinch, 1972, $20-25. Meadowlark, 1969, $15-20.

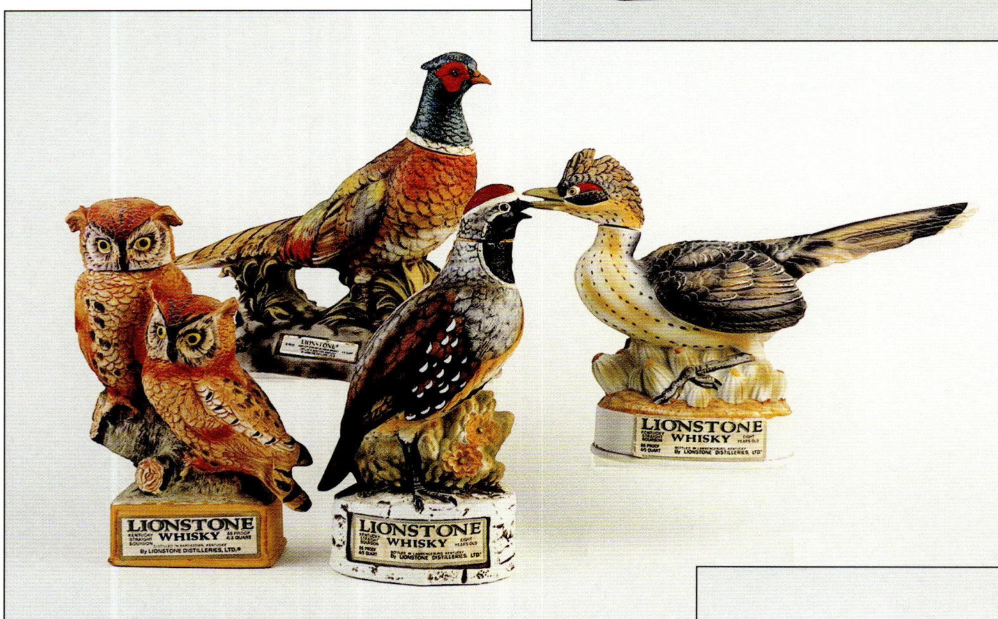

Owls, 1973, $15-20. Pheasant, 1977, $25-30. Quail, 1969, $15-20. Roadrunner, 1969, $15-20.

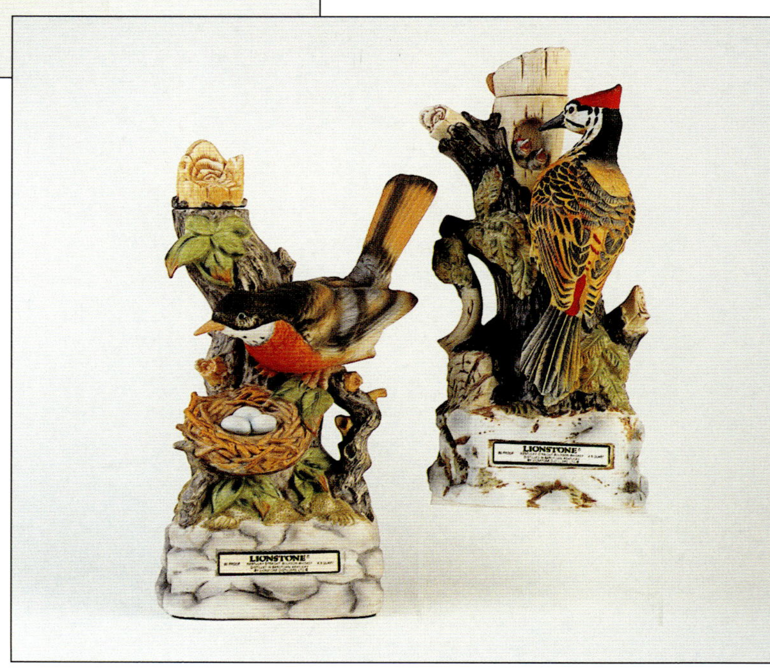

Robin, 1975, $15-20. Woodpecker, 1975, $15-20.

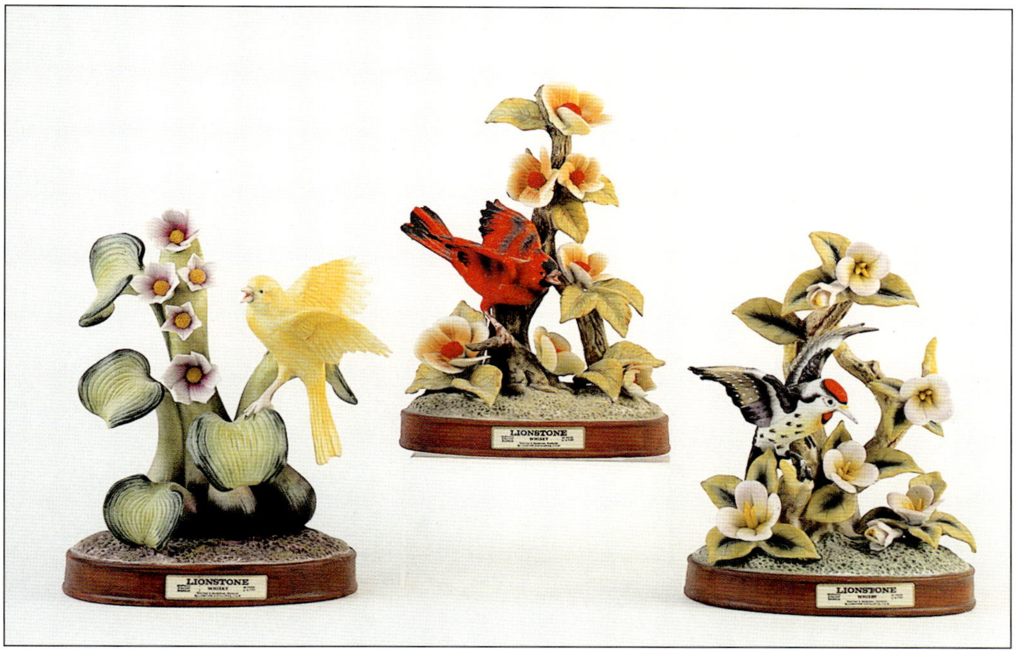

Fancy birds – Canary, 1973, $20-25. Cardinal, 1973, $20-25. Oriental Woodpecker, 1973, $20-25.

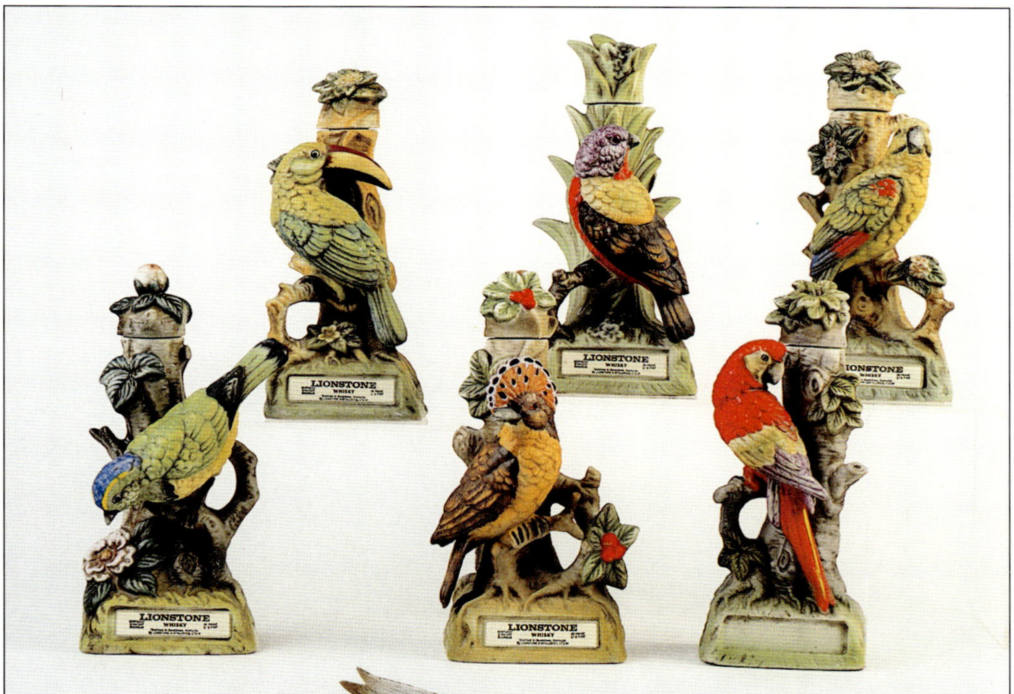

Tropical birds – Blue Crowned Chiorophonia, 1974, mini $10-15. Emerald Toucanet, 1974, mini $10-15. Northern Royal Flycatcher, 1974, mini $10-15. Painted Bunting, 1974, mini $15-20. Scarlet Macaw, 1974, mini $10-15. Yellow Head Amazon, 1974, mini $10-15.

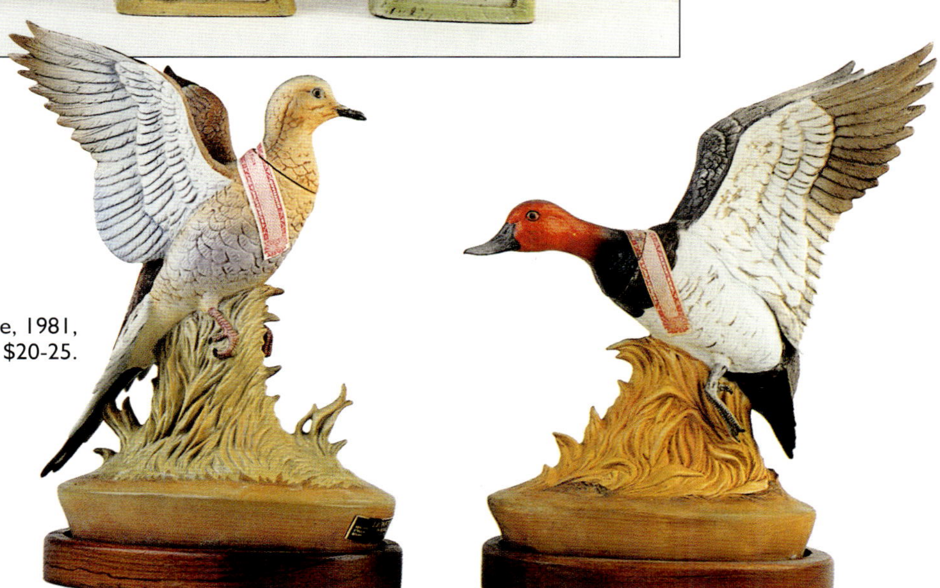

Wildlife birds – Mourning Dove, 1981, $25-30. Canvasback Duck, 1981, $20-25.

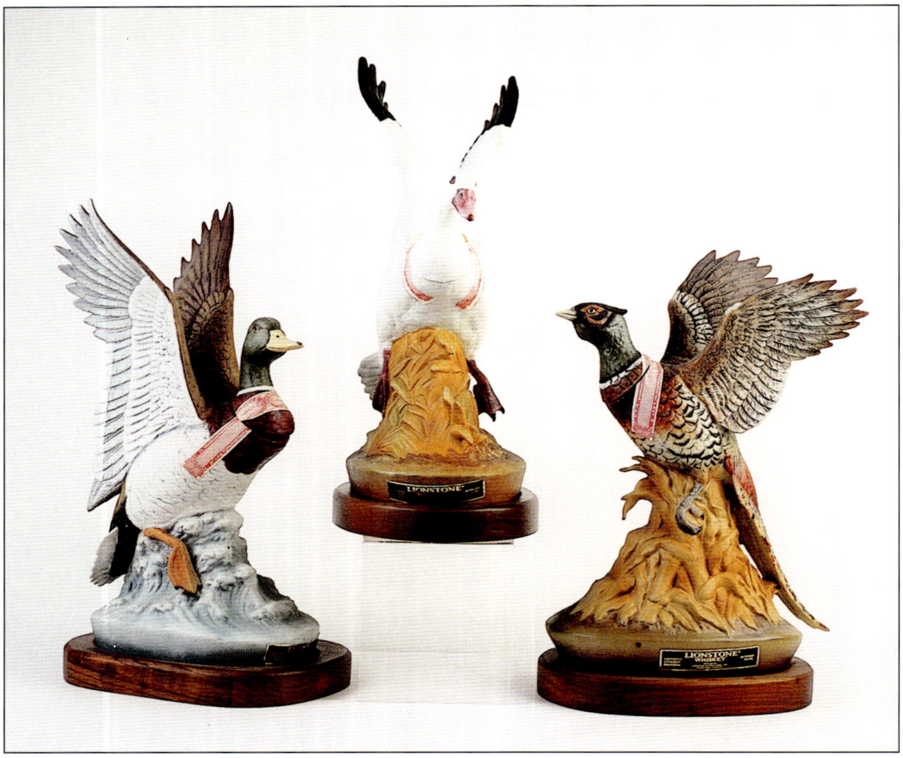

Mallard Duck, 1981, $20-25. Snow Goose, 1981, $25-30. Pheasant, 1981, $30-35.

Miscellaneous Lionstone

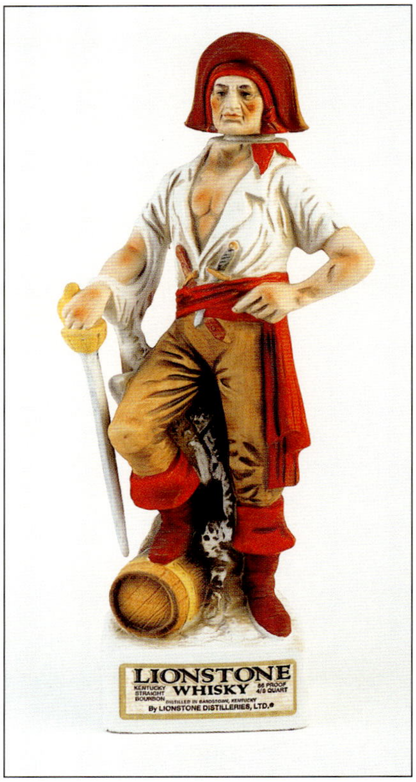

Buccaneer, 1983, $20-25.

Circus Series

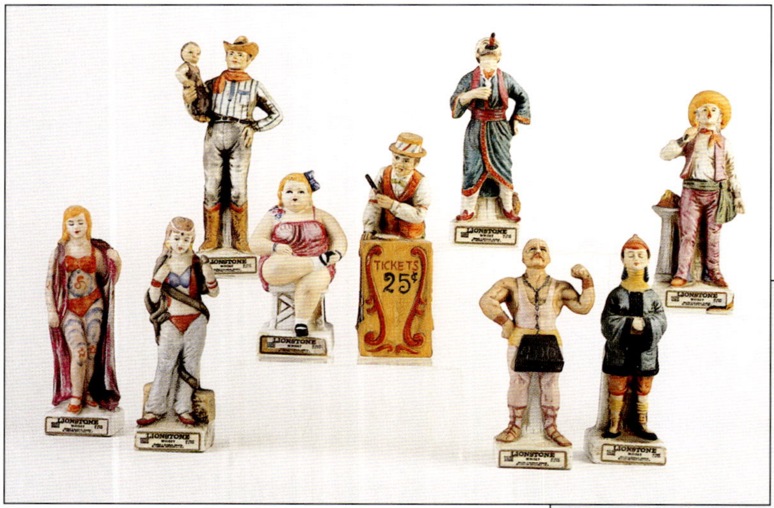

1973: Tattooed Lady, mini $10-15; Burmese Girl, mini $10-15; Giant with Midget, mini $10-15; Fat Lady, mini $10-15; Barker, mini $10-15; Sword Swallower, mini $10-15; Strong Man, mini $10-15; Snake Charmer, mini $10-15; Fire Eater, mini $10-15.

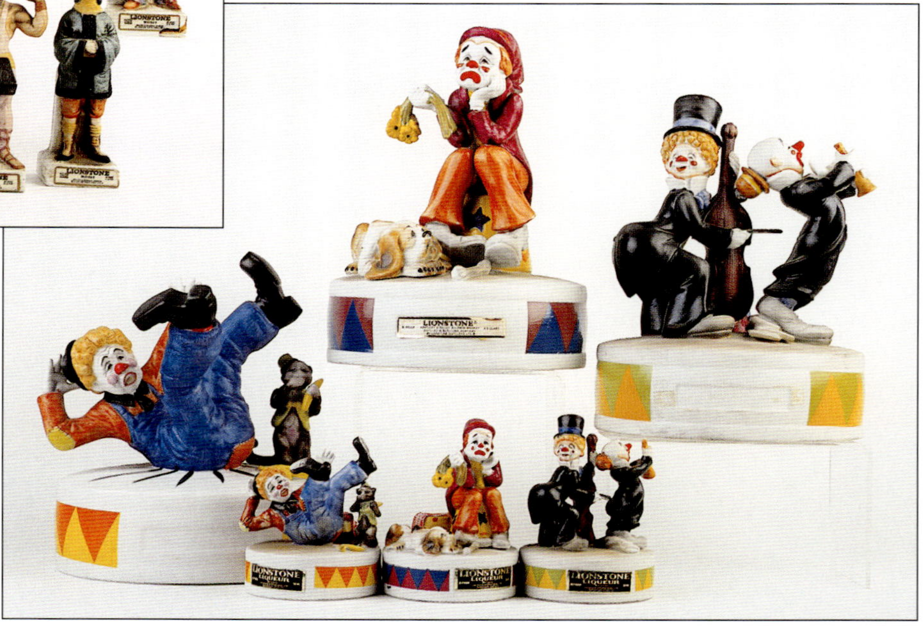

Monkey Business, 1987, fifth $20-25, mini $10-15; Sad Sam, 1978, fifth $20-25, mini $10-15; Say it With Music, 1978, fifth $20-25, mini $10-15.

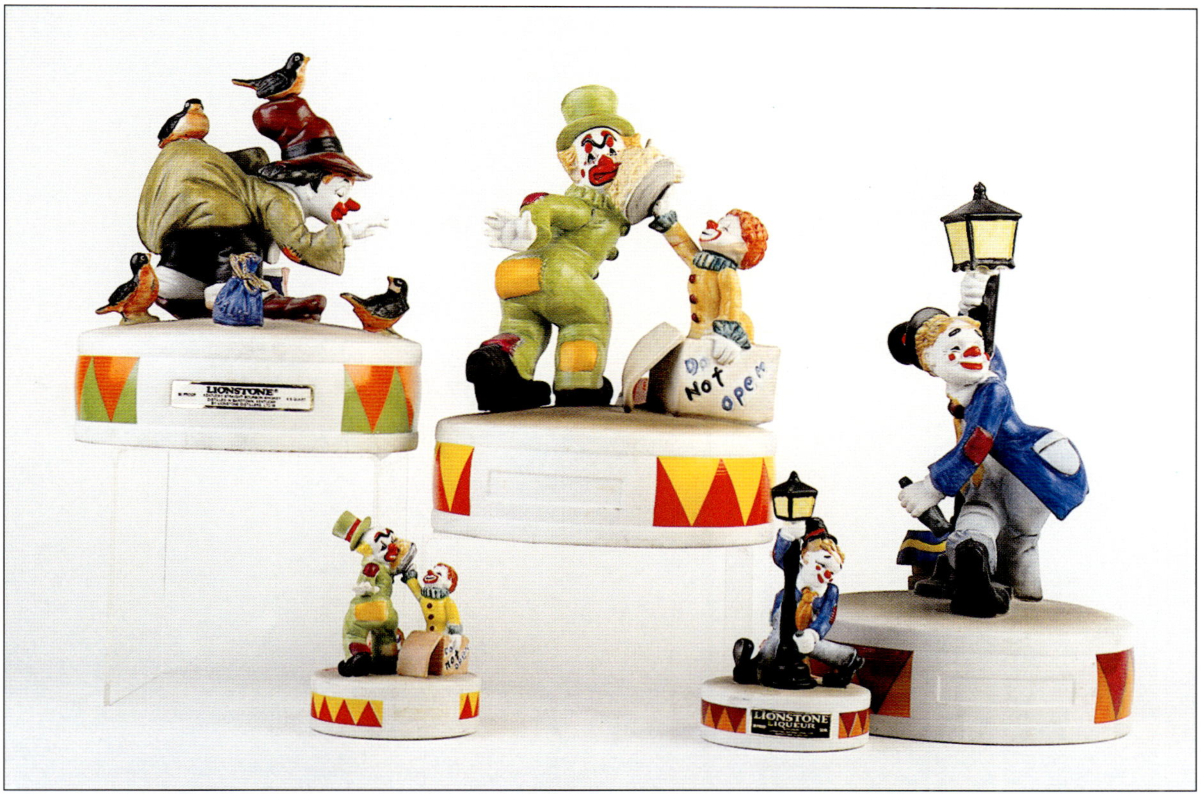

Salty Tails, 1978, fifth $20-25, mini $10-15; Pie Face, 1979, fifth $20-25, mini $10-15; Lampy, 1979, fifth $20-25, mini $10-15.

Dog Series

#1: British Pointer, 1975, mini $10-15; British Rough Collie, 1975, mini $10-15; Cocker Spaniel, 1975, $10-15; French Poodle, 1975, $10-15; German Boxer, 1975, $10-15. German Shepherd, 1975, $10-15.

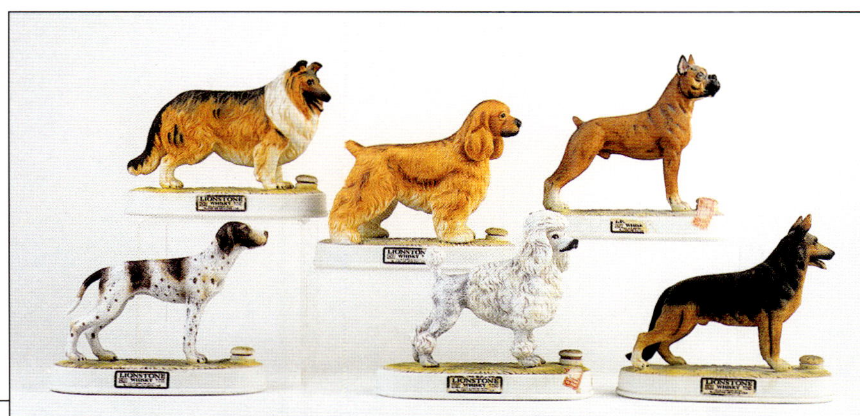

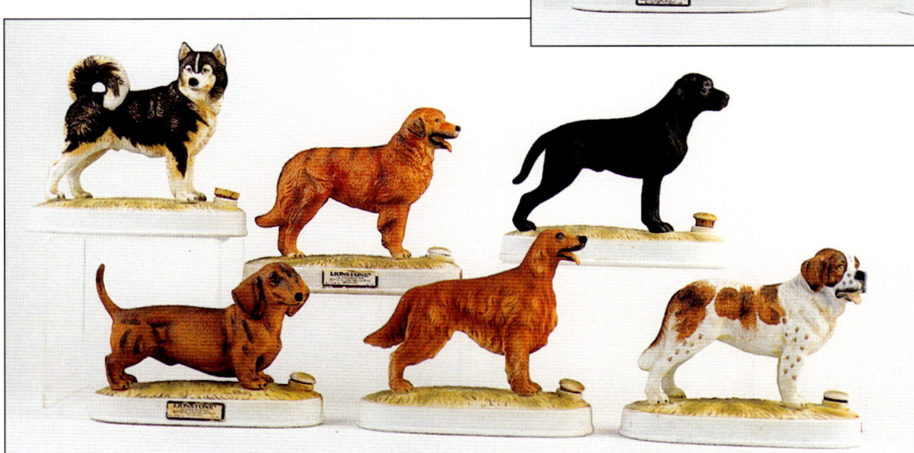

#2: Alaskan Malamute, 1977, mini $10-15; German Dachshund, 1977, mini $10-15; Golden Retriever, 1977, mini $10-15; Irish Setter, 1977, mini $10-15; Labrador Retriever, 1977, mini $10-15; St. Bernard, mini $10-15.

Miscellaneous Lionstone

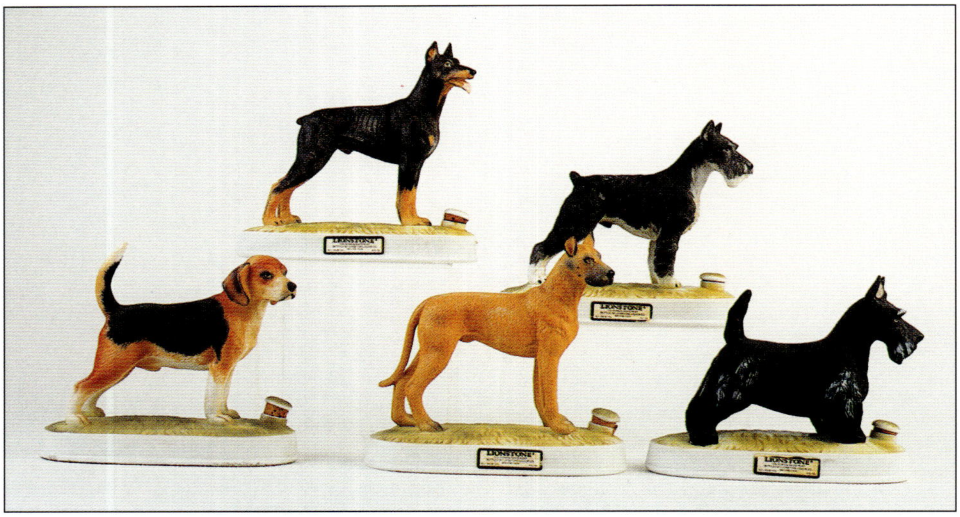

#3: Beagle, 1977, mini $10-15; Doberman, 1977, mini $10-15; Great Dane, 1977, mini $10-15; Schnauzer, 1977, mini $10-15; Scottish Terrier, 1977, mini $10-15.

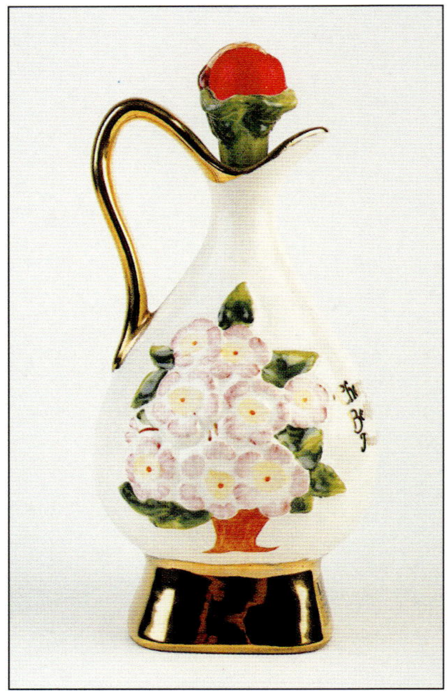

Cherry Valley Bottle Club (gold), 1971, $10-15.

Firefighter Series

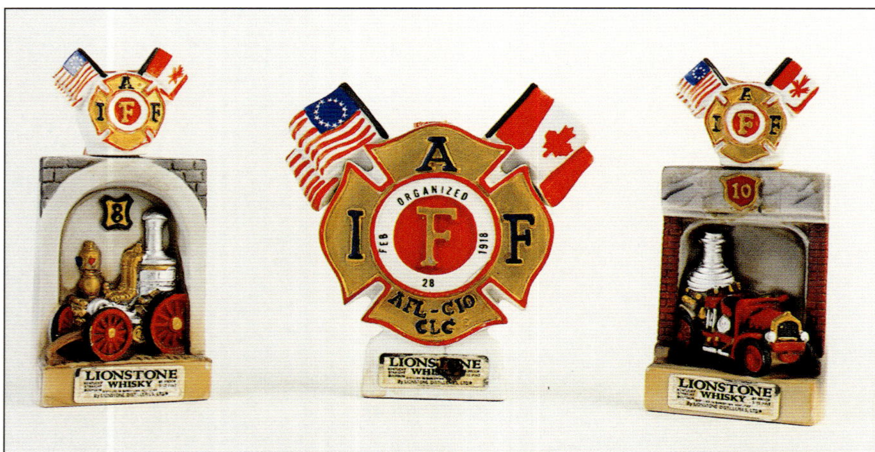

Fire Equipment Set, 1976, mini $45-50 set.

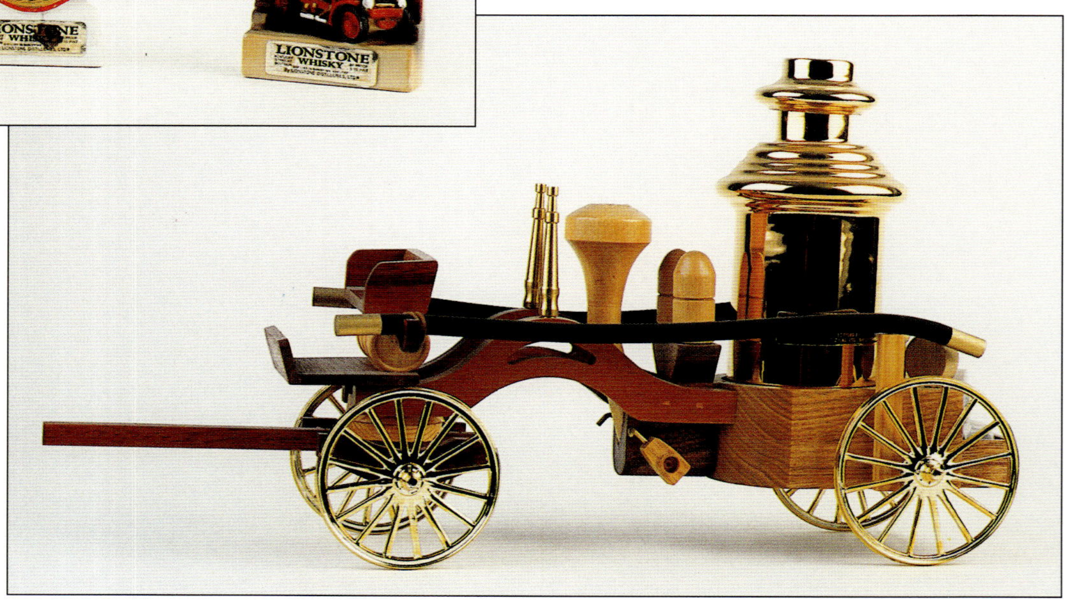

Horse Drawn Pumper, only eleven produced, $125-135.

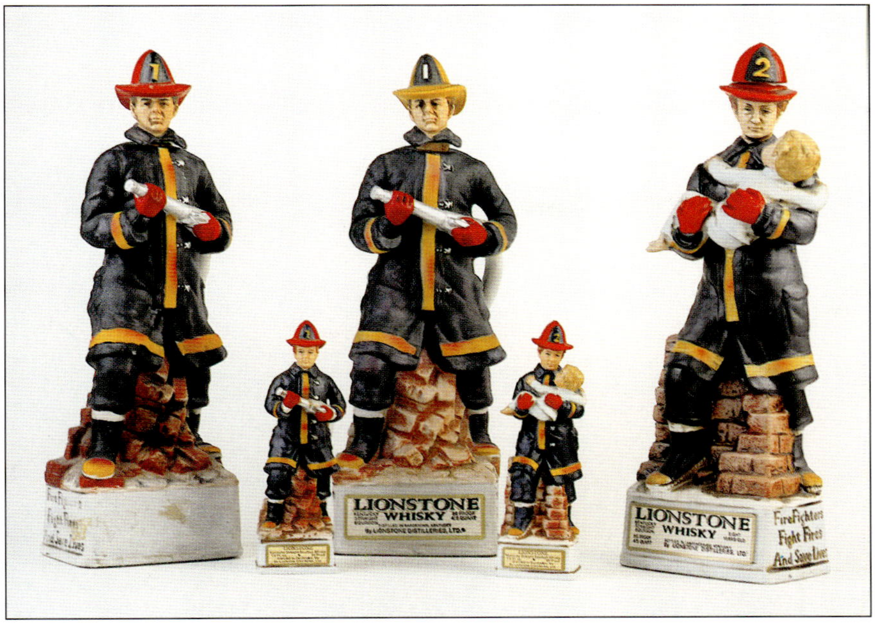

Fireman with red hat #7, 1972, fifth $75-85, mini $25-30. Fireman with yellow hat, 1972, fifth $110-125. Fireman with child, 1974, fifth $65-75, mini $25-30.

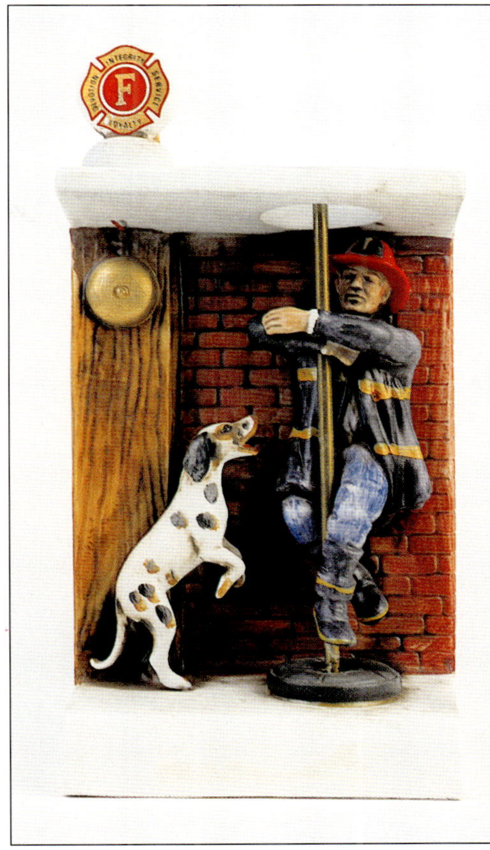

Fireman down pole, 1975, fifth $65-75.

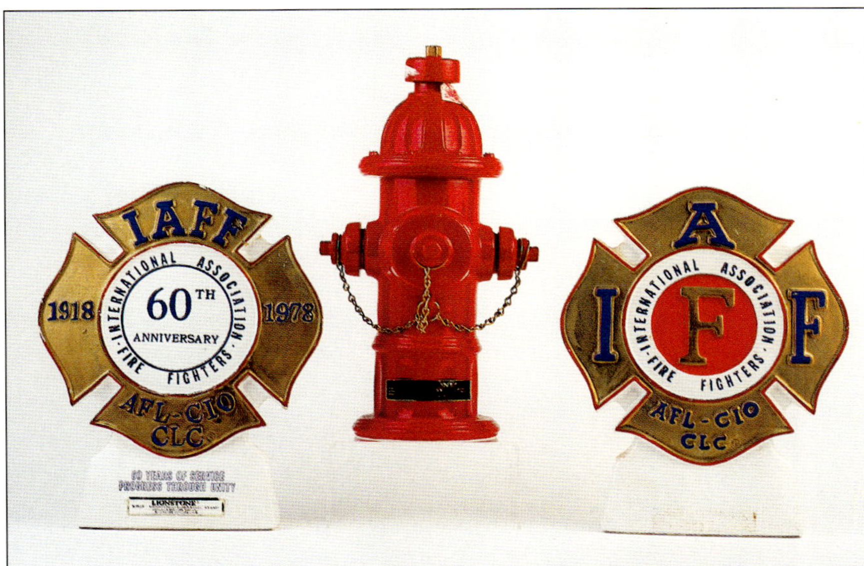

Fireman Emblem 60th Anniversary, 1979, fifth $20-25. Fire Hydrant, 1981, fifth $65-75. Fireman Emblem, 1978, fifth $20-25.

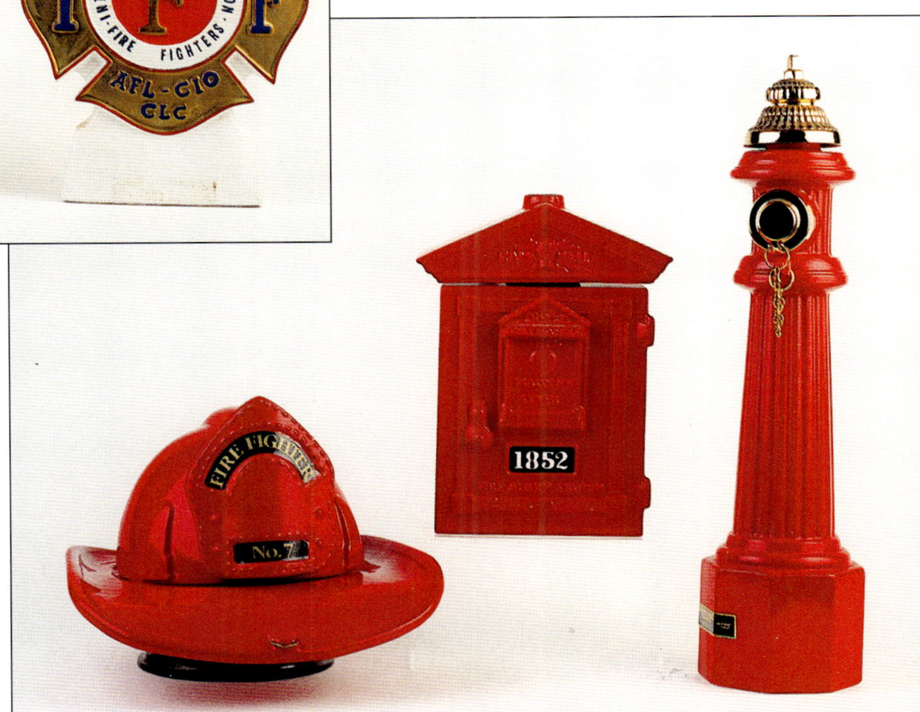

Fireman Hat, 1982, fifth $65-75. Fire Alarm Box, fifth $65-75. Fire Extinguisher, 1983, fifth $65-75.

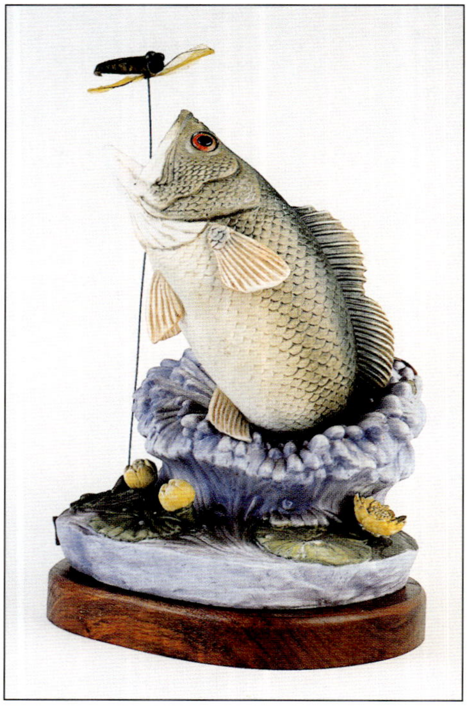

Large Mouth Bass #2 with Dragonfly, 1982, fifth $55-65.

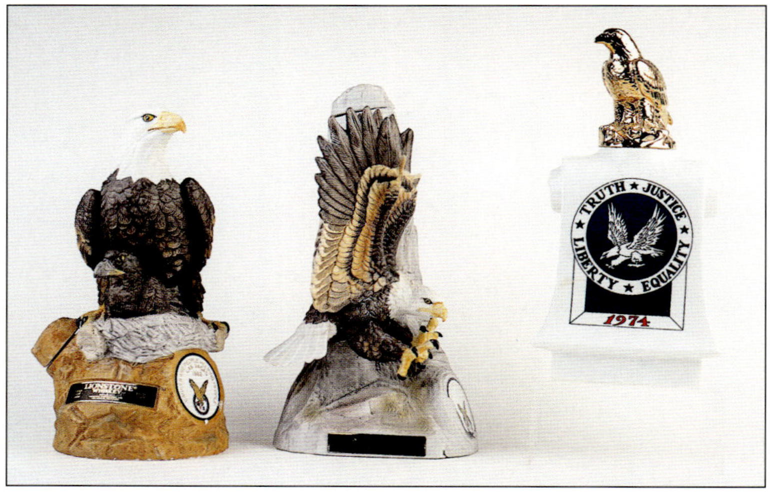

F.O.E. Eagles: Eagle #1, 1982, fifth $15-20; Eagle #2, 1983, fifth $15-20; Eagle #3, 1983, fifth $10-15.

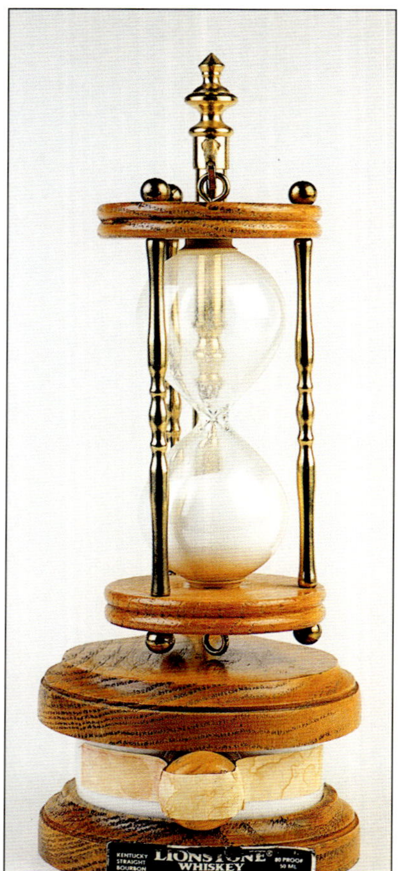

Hour Glass, very rare, $75-85.

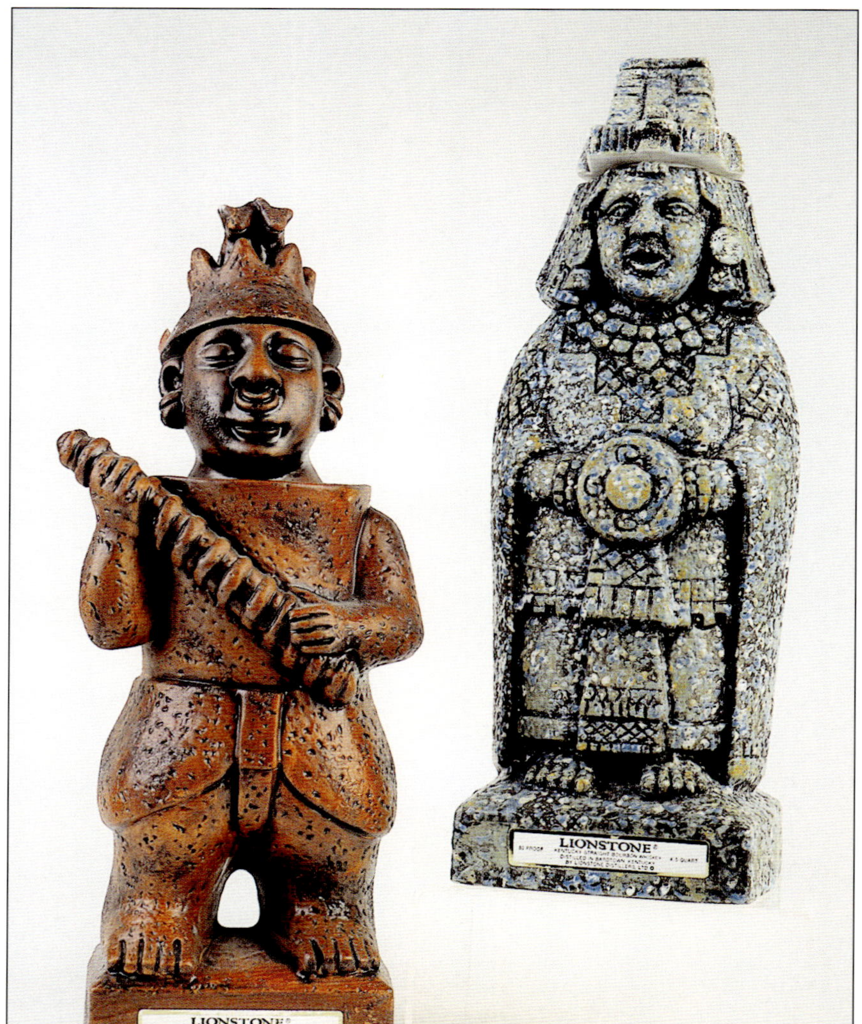

God of War, 1978, fifth $10. Goddess of Love, 1988, fifth $10.

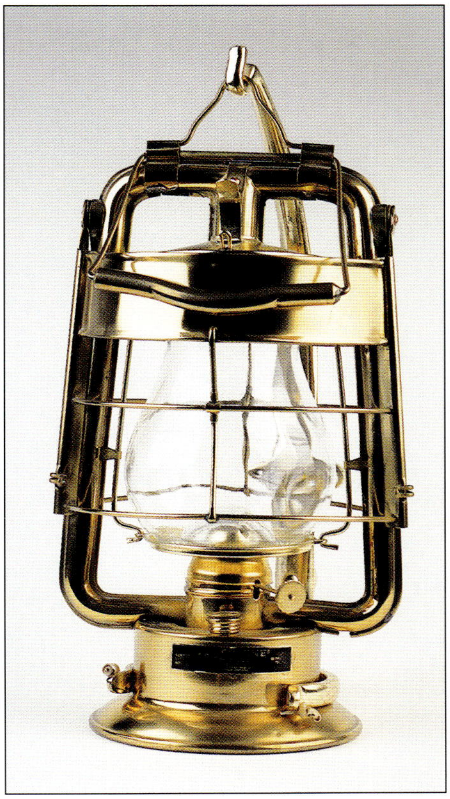

Lantern, rare, fifth $65-75.

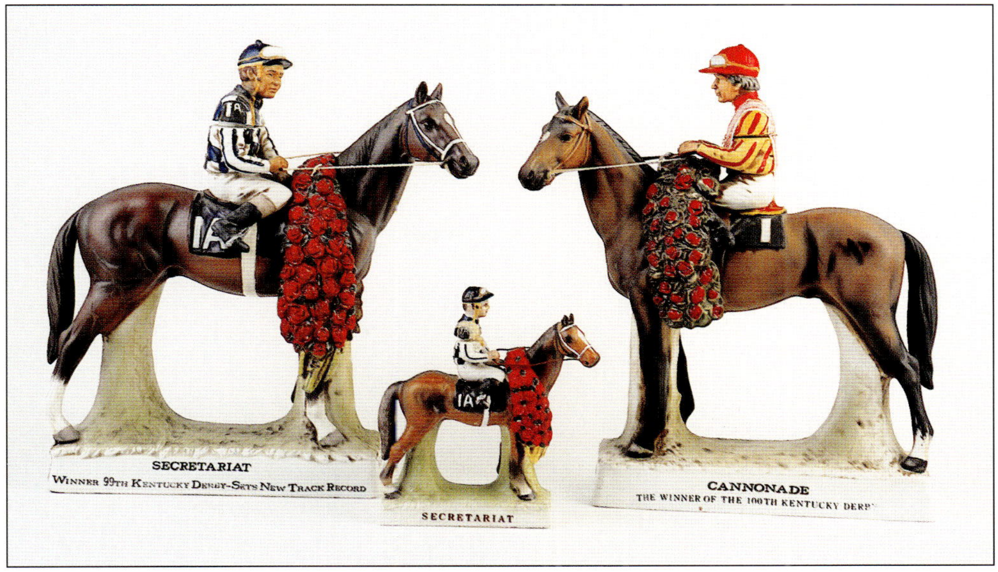

Secretariat, 1977, fifth $125-150, mini $45-50. Cannonade, 1976, fifth $90-100.

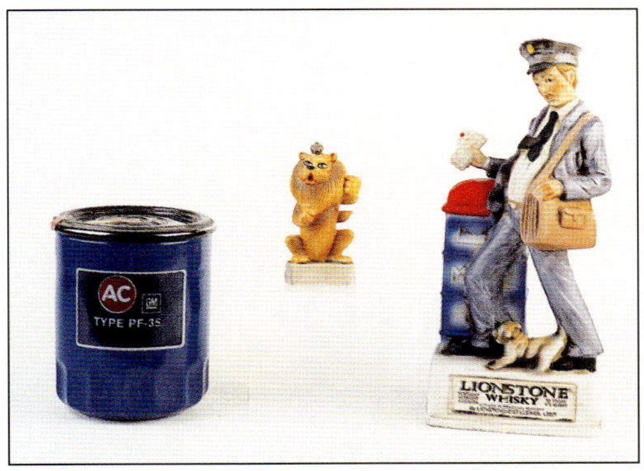

Delco Oil Filter, $35-40. Lion, 1.6 oz. $10-15. Mailman, 1974, $20-25.

Old West Series

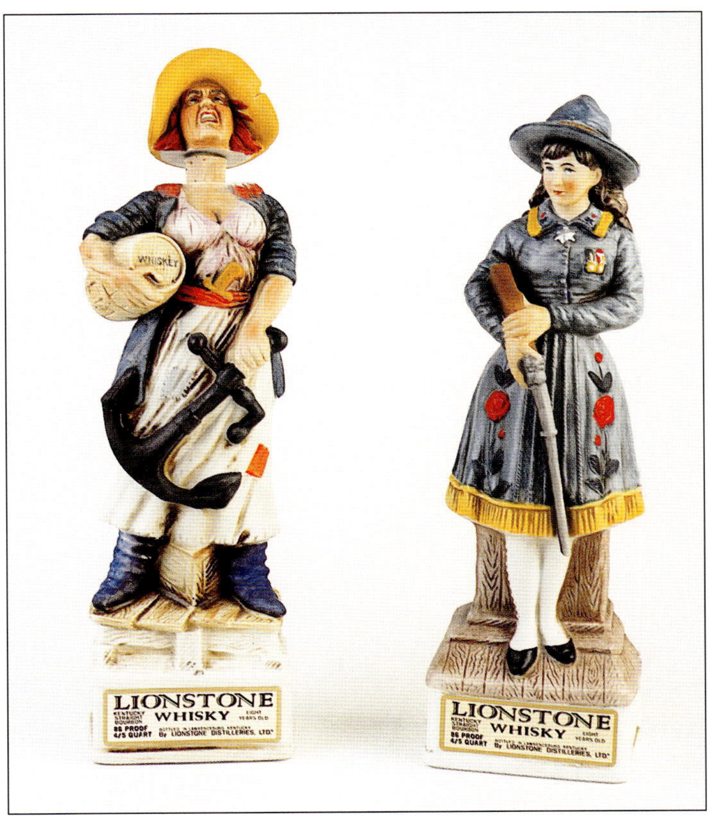

Annie Christmas, 1969, fifth $10-15. Annie Oakley, 1969, fifth $10-15.

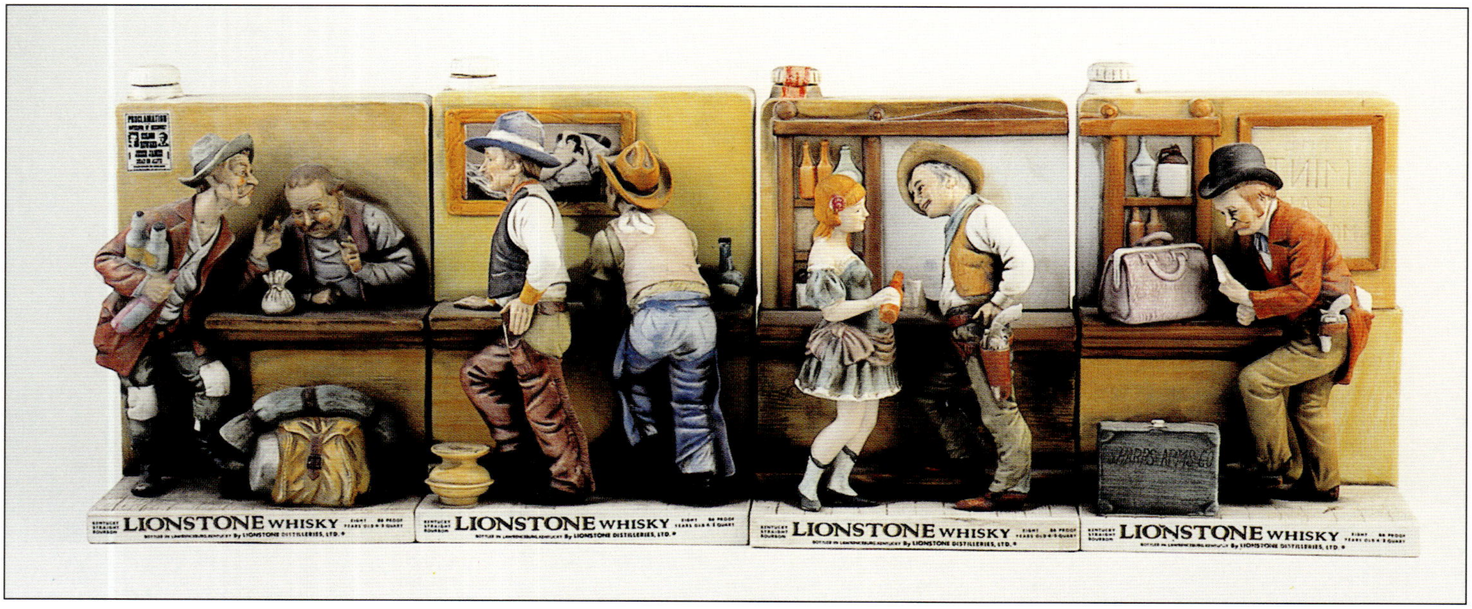

Bar Scene with nude lady, 1970, set $300-350. This set was also produced without nude painting, set $250-300.

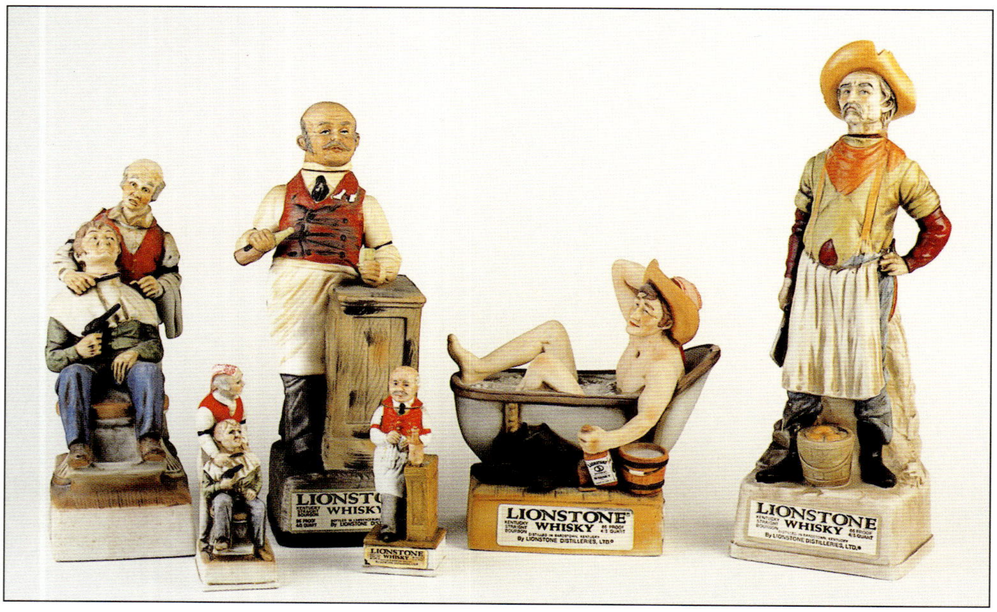

Barber, 1976, fifth $15-20, mini $10-15. Bartender, 1969, fifth $25-30, mini $15-20. Bath, 1976, $20-25. Belly Robber, 1969, fifth $25-30.

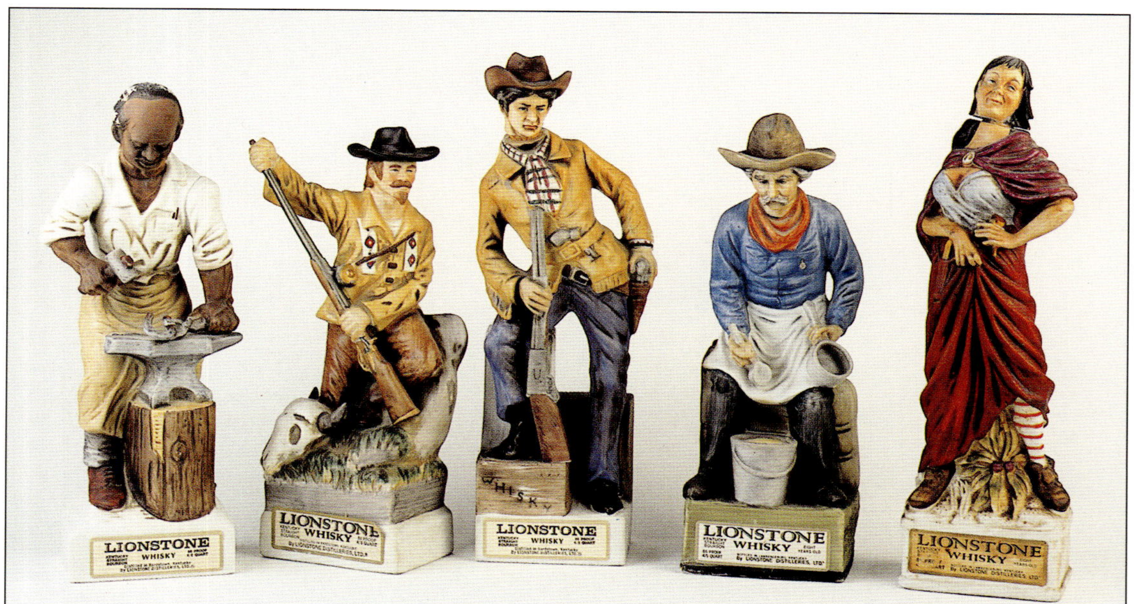

Blacksmith, 1973, $15-20. Buffalo Bill, 1973, fifth $25-30. Calamity Jane, 1973, fifth $15-20. Camp Cook, 1969, fifth $10-15. Camp Follower, fifth $10-15.

Cavalry Scout, 1969, fifth $10-15, mini (1979) $50-10. Chinese Laundry Man, 1969, fifth $10-15. Country Doctor, 1969, fifth $10-15. Cowboy, 1969, fifth $10-15, mini (1970) $5-10. Cowgirl, 1973, fifth $10-15.

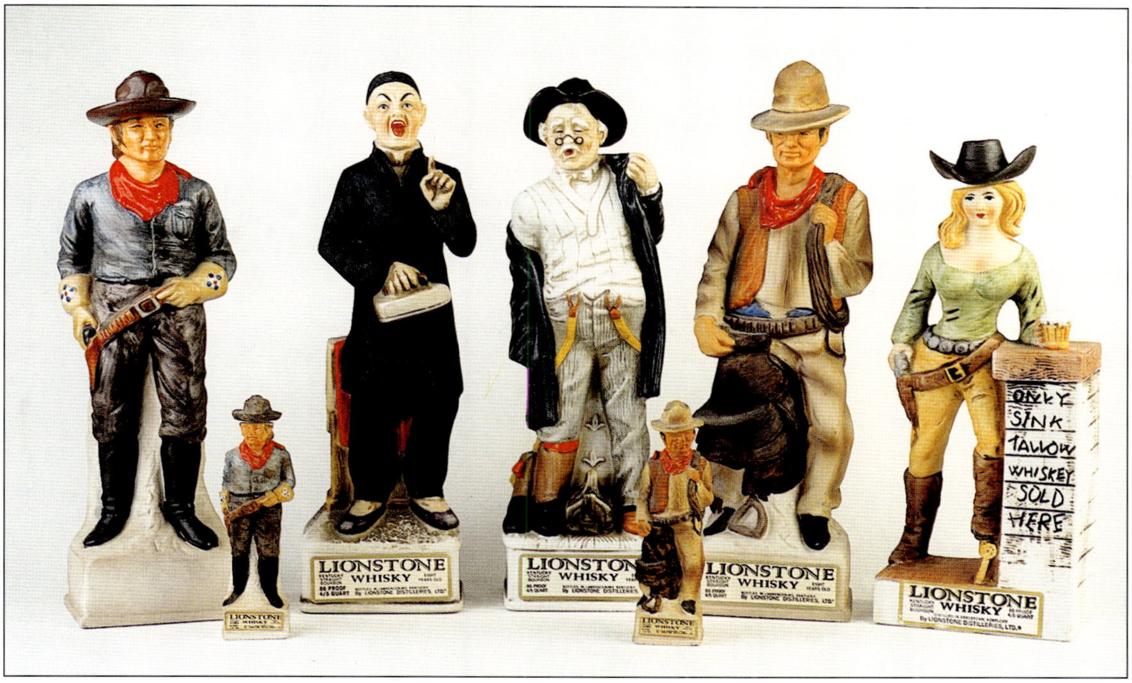

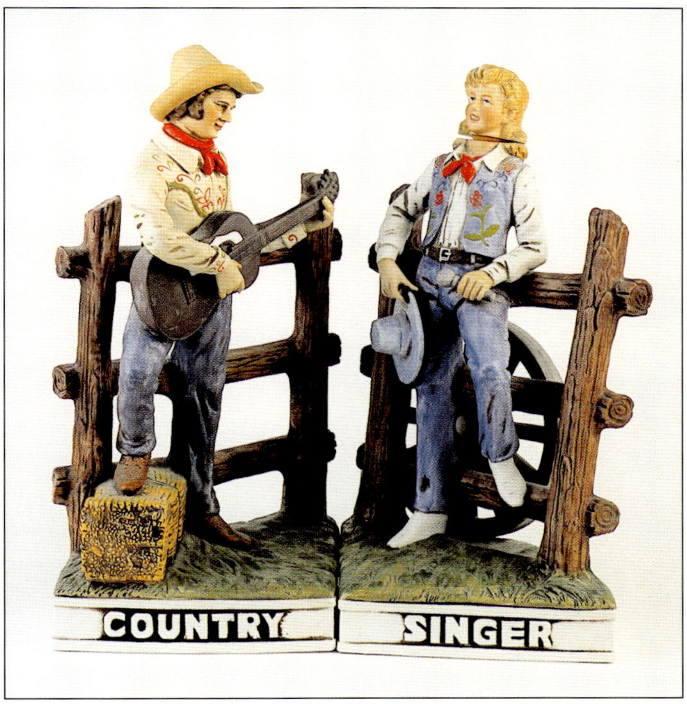

Country Singers, possible one-of-a-kind, $125-150.

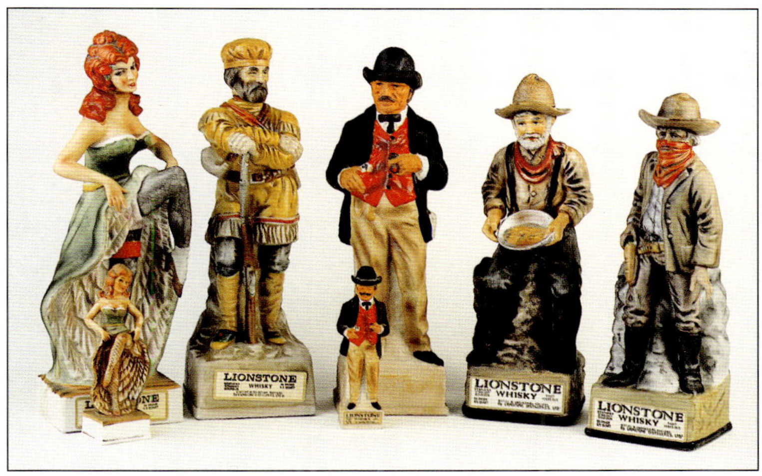

Dancehall Girl, 1973, fifth $20-35, mini $10-15. Frontiersman, 1969, fifth $10-15. Gambler, 1969, fifth $10-15, mini $5-10. Gold Panner, 1969, fifth $20-25. Highway Robber, 1969, fifth $10-25.

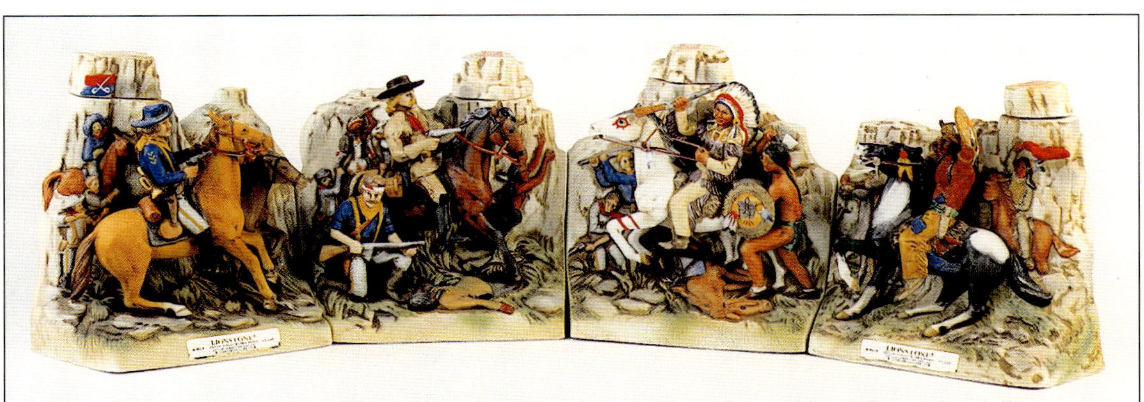

Custer's Last Stand, 1979, four piece set $300-325.

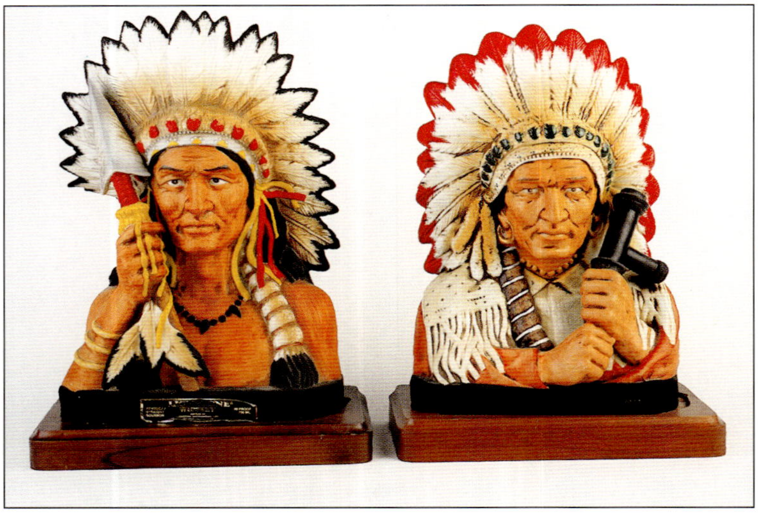

Indian Bust #1, 1980, $25-30. Indian Bust #2, $25-30.

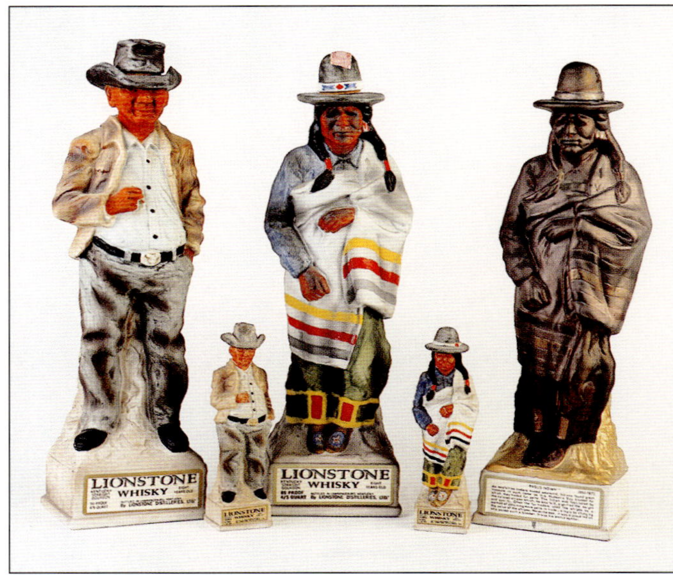

Indian casual, 1969, fifth $10-15, mini $10-15. Proud Indian, 1969, fifth $10-15, mini (1979) $10-15. Proud Indian, bronze mock-up, fifth $45-50.

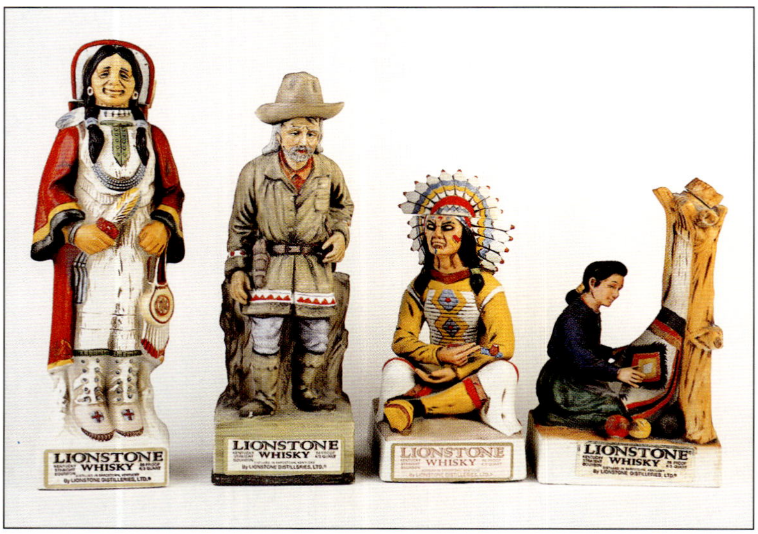

Indian Squaw, 1973, fifth $10-15. Indian Squawman, 1969, fifth $10-15. Indian Tribal Chief, 1973, fifth $15-20. Indian Weaver, 1976, fifth $15-20.

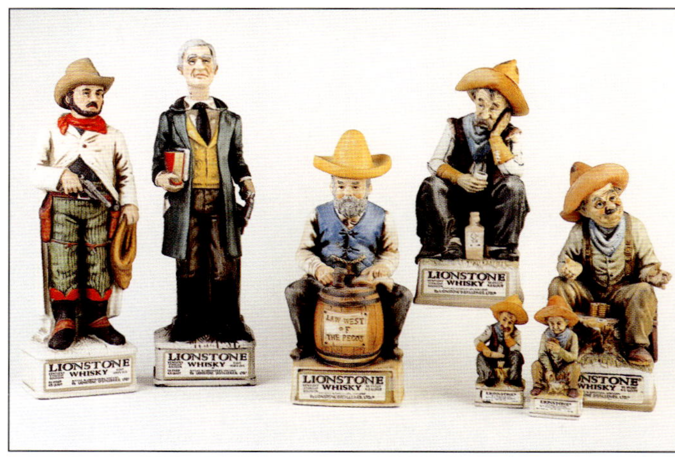

Jesse James, 1969, fifth $15-20. Judge Circuit Riding, 1969, fifth $10-15. Judge Roy Bean, 1973, fifth $10-15. Lonely Luke, 1974, fifth $10-15, mini (1975) $10-15. Lucky Buck, 1974, fifth $10-15, mini (1975) $10-15.

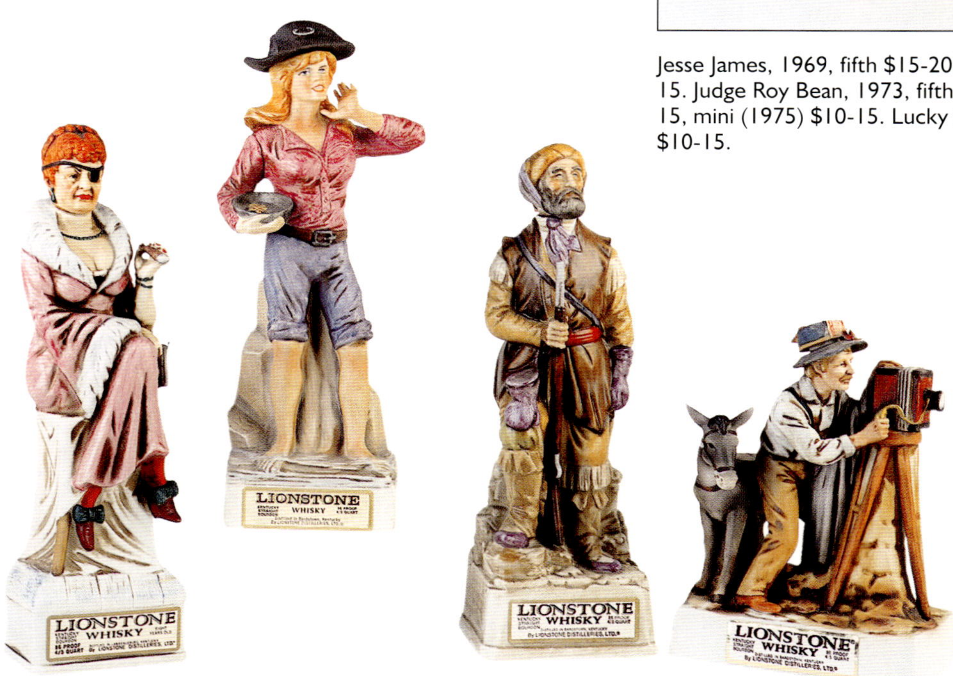

Madame, 1969, fifth $25-30. Molly Brown, 1973, fifth $10-15, Mountain Man, 1969, fifth $10-15, Photographer, fifth, $40-45, mini $15-20.

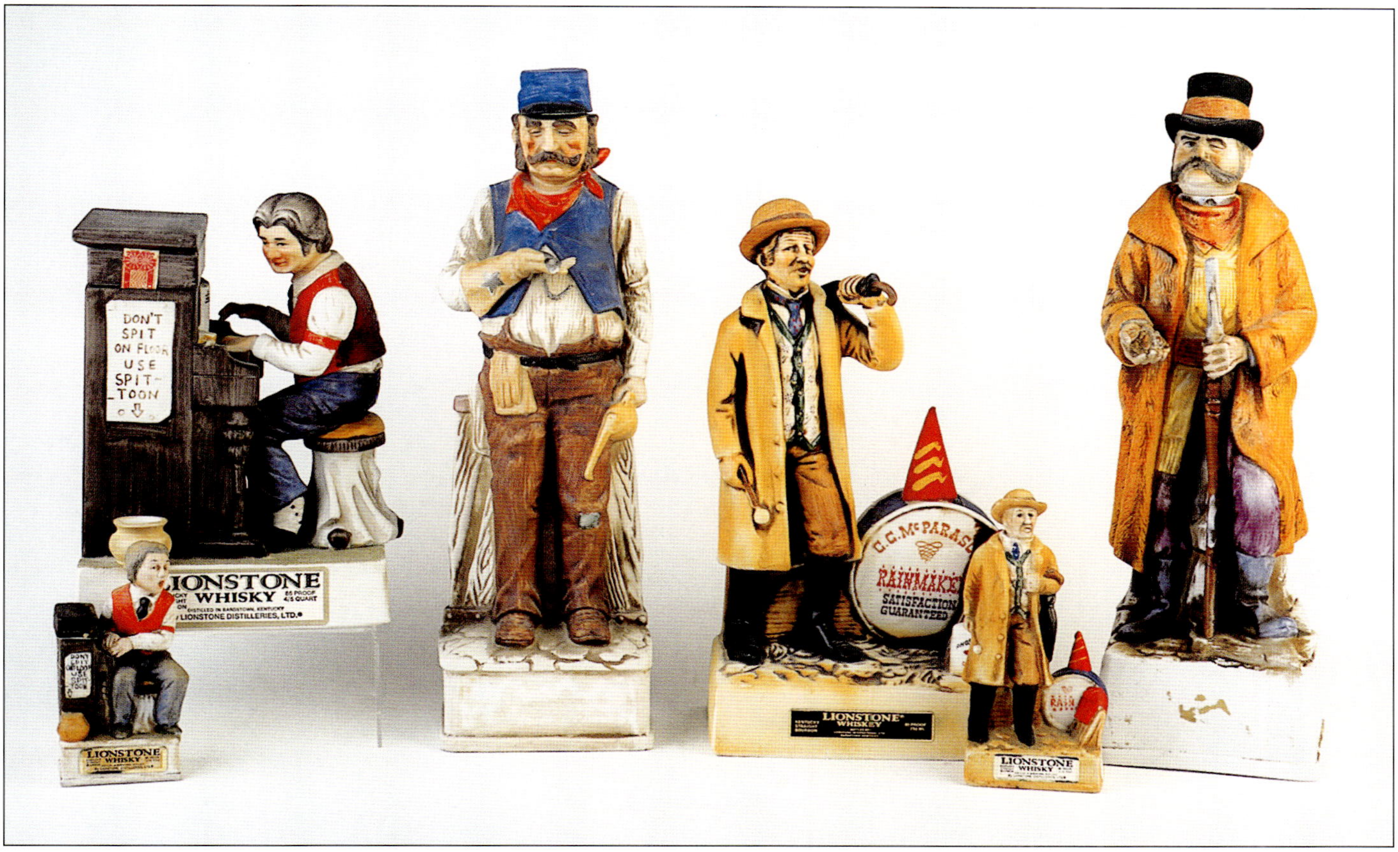

Professor (piano player), 1973, fifth $20-25, mini $10-15. Railroad Engineer, 1969, fifth $10-15. Rain Maker, 1976, fifth $15-20, mini $10-15. Renegade Trader, 1969, fifth $10-15.

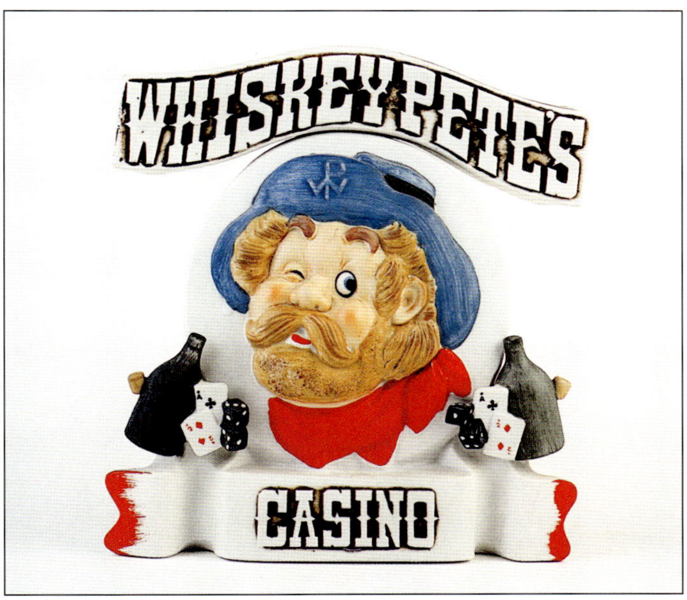

Whiskey Pete's Casino, $45-55.

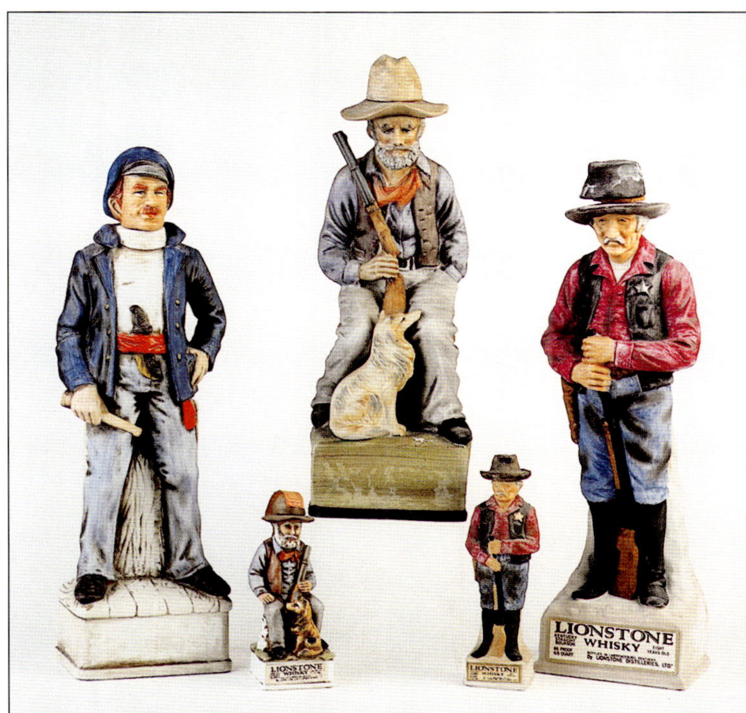

Riverboat Captain, 1969, fifth $10-15. Sheepherder, 1969, fifth $10-15, mini $5-10. Sheriff, 1969, fifth $15-20, mini $10-15.

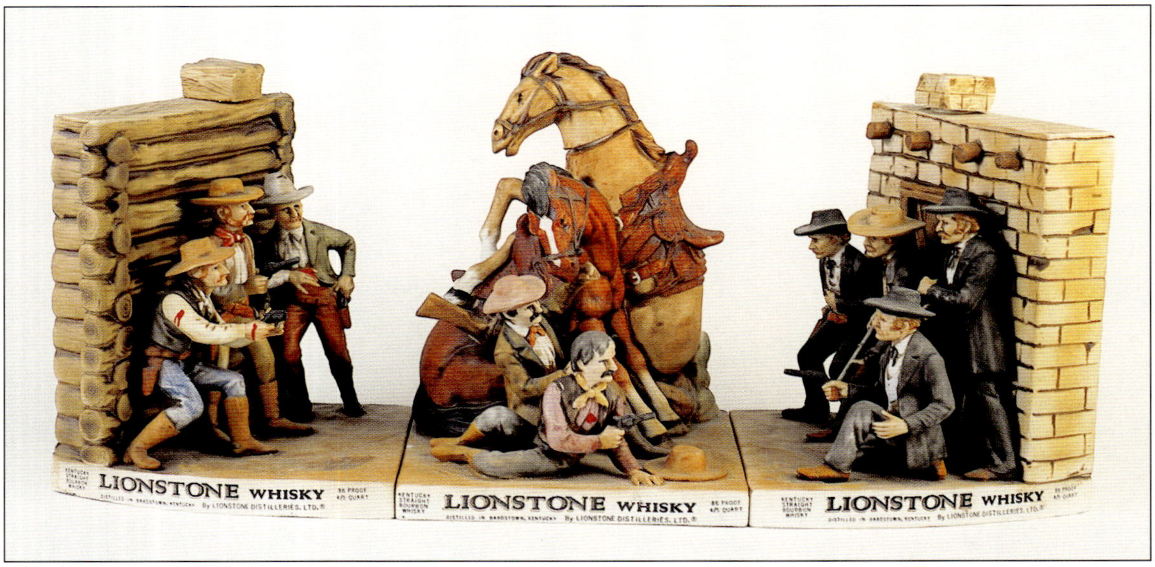

Shootout at the OK Corral, 1971, set of three fifths $175-200.

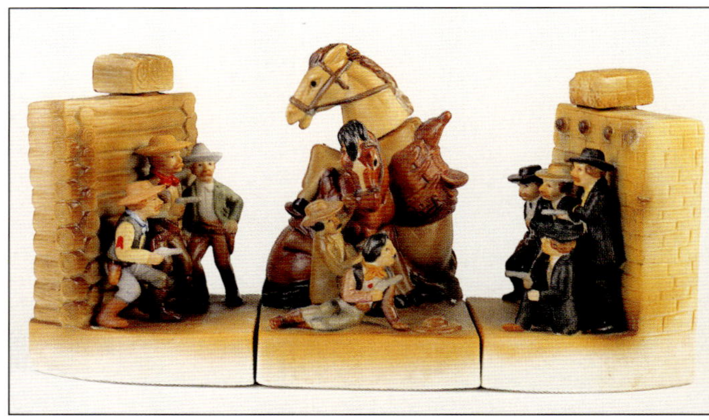

Shootout at the OK Corral, 1971, set of three minis $125-150.

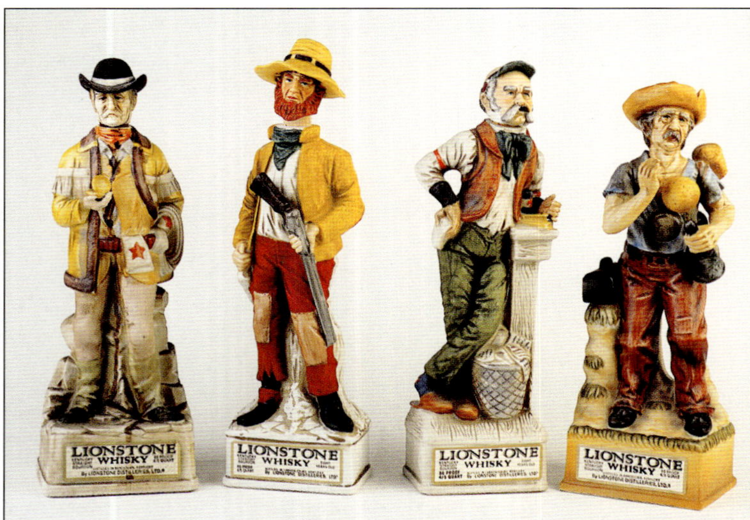

Sodbuster, 1969, fifth $10-15. Stage Driver, 1969, fifth $10-15. Telegrapher, 1969, fifth $10-15. Tinker, 1974, fifth $10-15.

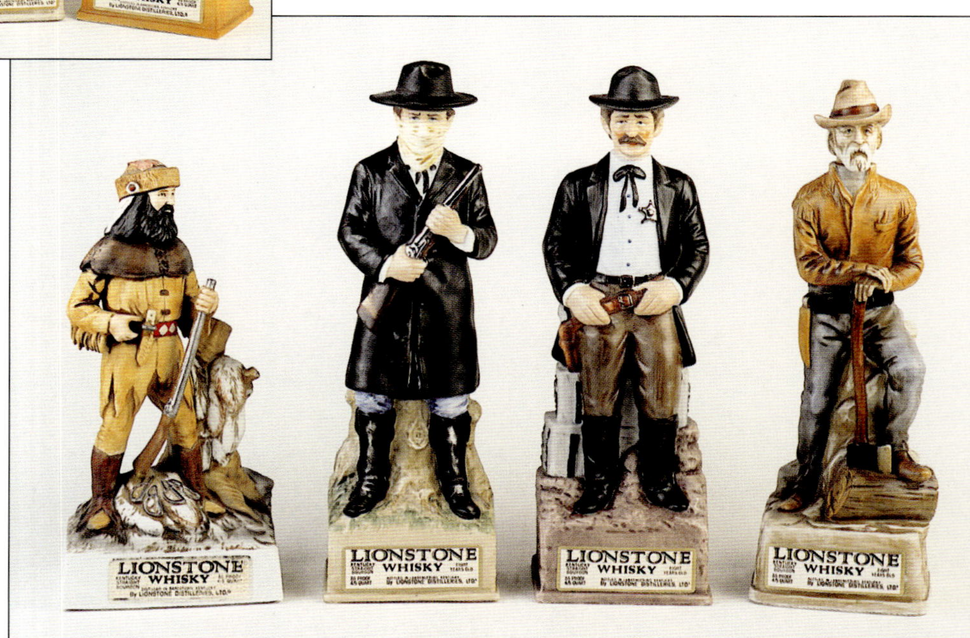

Trapper, 1976, fifth $10-15. Vigilante, 1969, fifth $10-15. Wells Fargo Man, 1969, fifth $10-15. Woodhawk, 1969, fifth $10-15.

Miscellaneous Lionstone

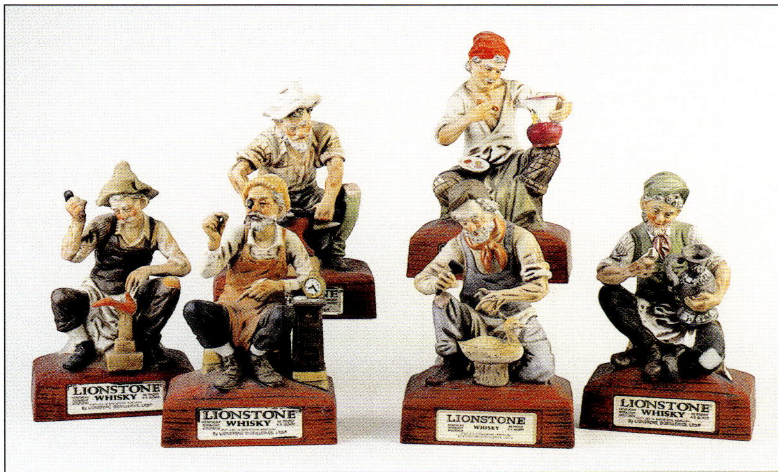

European Workers – Shoemaker, Watchmaker, Blacksmith, Potter, Woodcarver, Silversmith, $15-20 ea.

Asian Workers – Basket Weaver, Egg Merchant, Gardener, Sculptor, Tea Vendor, Timekeeper, $15-20 ea.

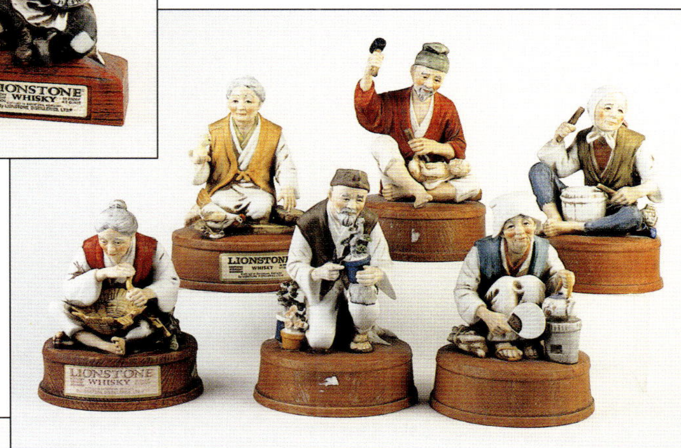

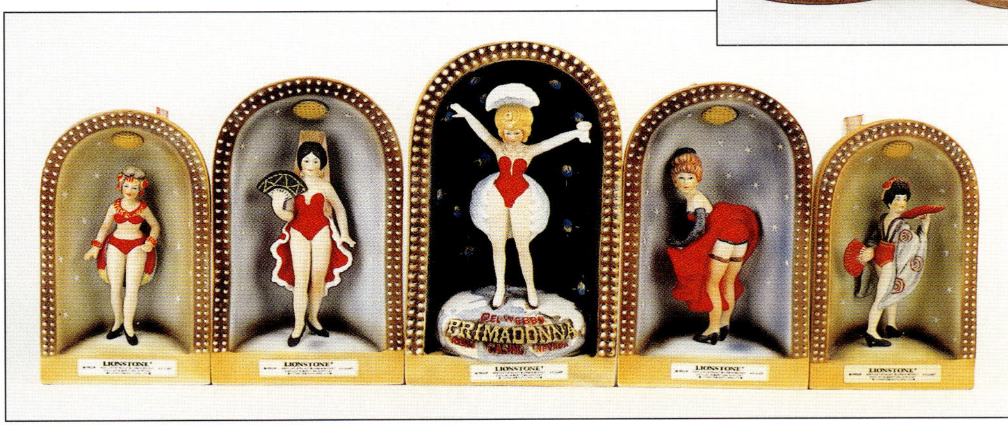

Primadonna Club, 1978, set of 5 $250-300.

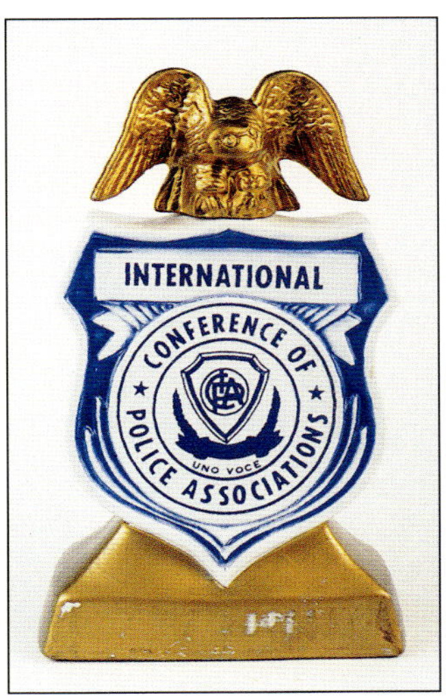

International Police Association Convention, 1980, $15-25.

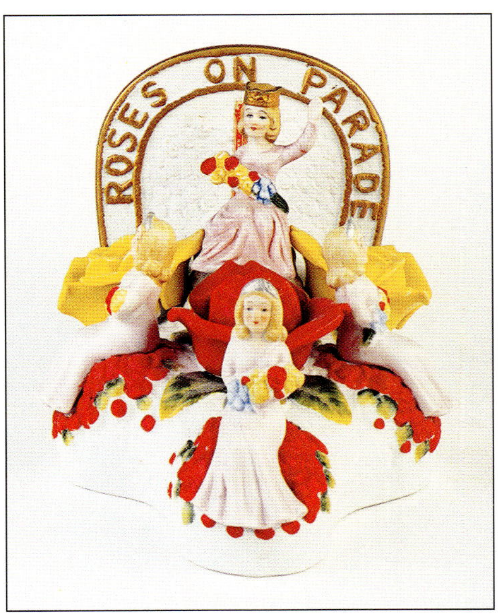

Rose Parade, 1973, $10-15.

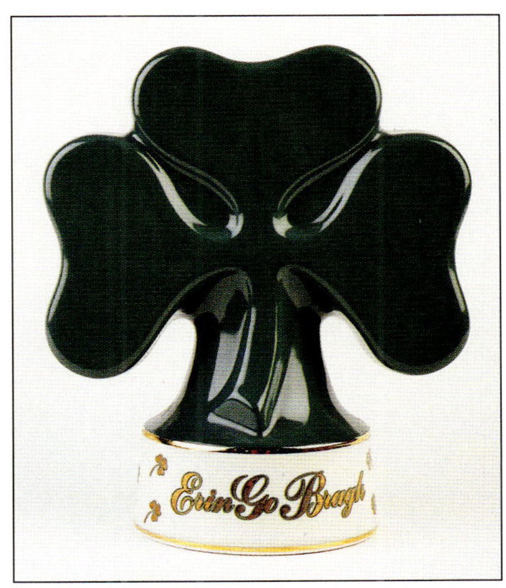

Shamrock, music box (plays "When Irish Eyes Are Smiling"), 1983, $20-25.

Safari Series

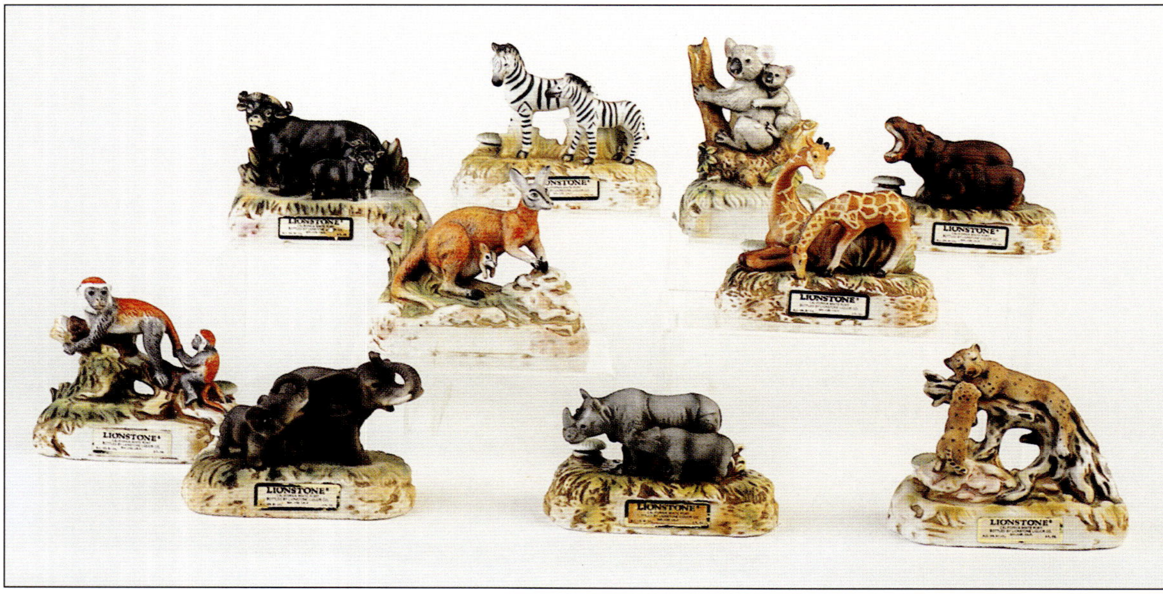

Safari series, 1977: monkeys, cape buffalo, elephant, kangaroo, zebra, rhinoceros, koala bears, hippopotamus, leopard, $10-15 each. Complete set of 10 minis $75-85. (Gazelles not shown.)

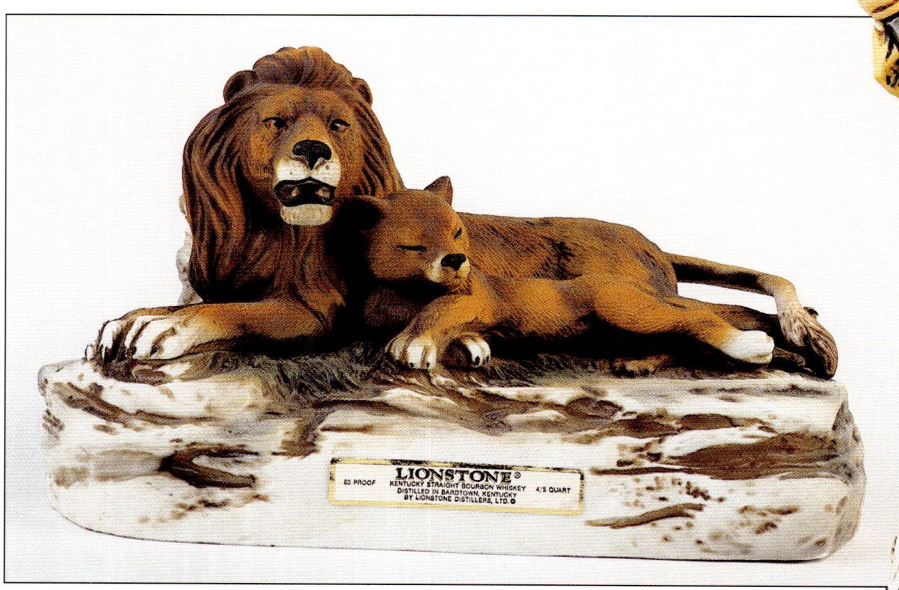

Lions, 1977 limited edition, $15-20.

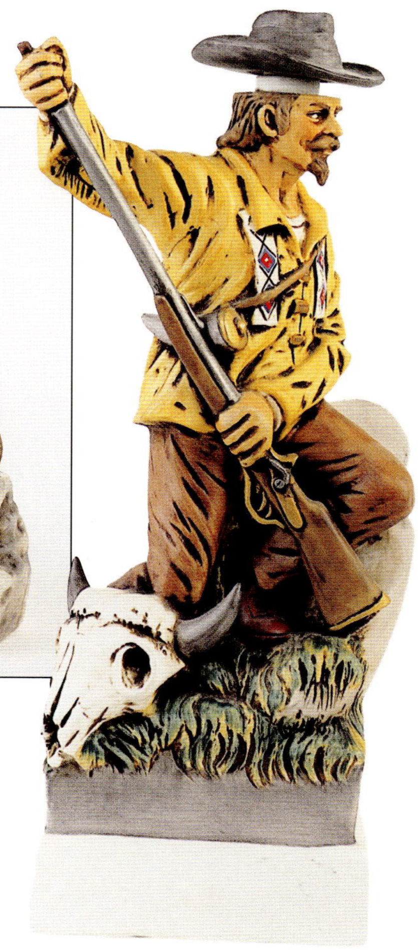

Buffalo Bill, one-of-a-kind prototype, $95-125.

Sports Series

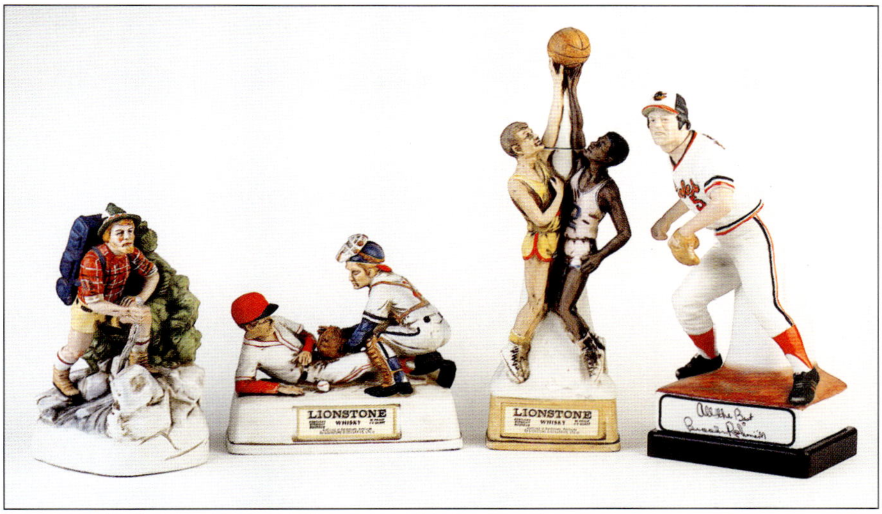

Backpacker, 1980, $20-25. Baseball player, $50-60. Basketball Players, $35-40. Brooks Robinson (signed), 1983, $225-250.

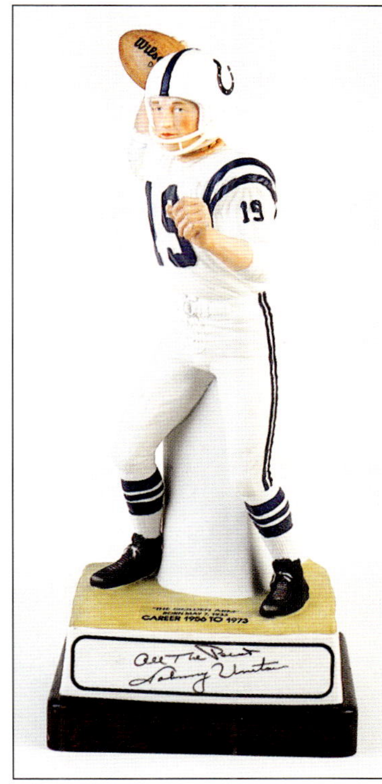

Johnny Unitis (signed), $245-275.

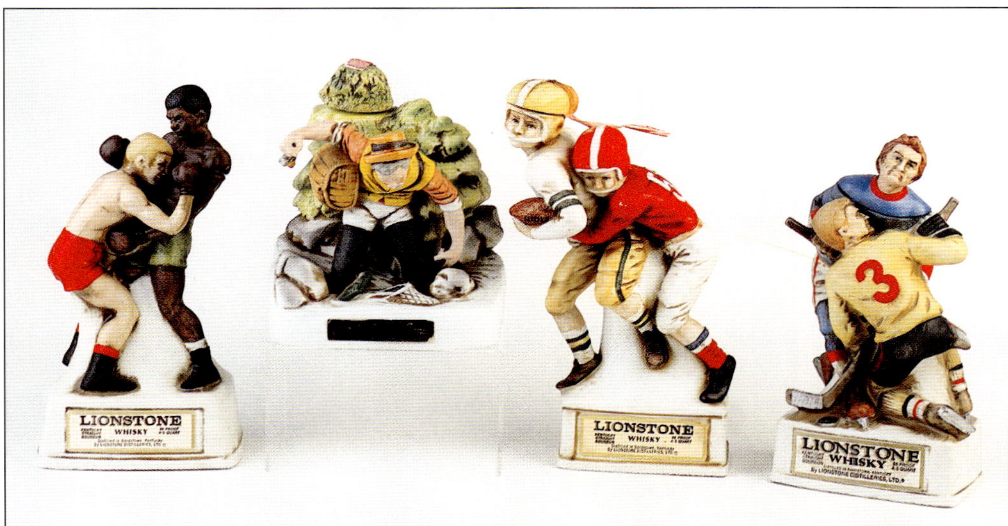

Boxer, 1974, $35-40. Fisherman, 1980, $25-30. Football players 1974, $45-50. Hockey Players, 1974, $40-45.

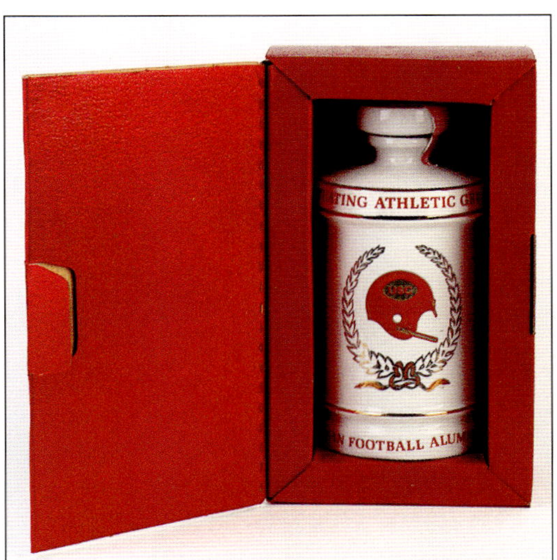

Trojan Football Alumni, University of Southern California, $25-30.

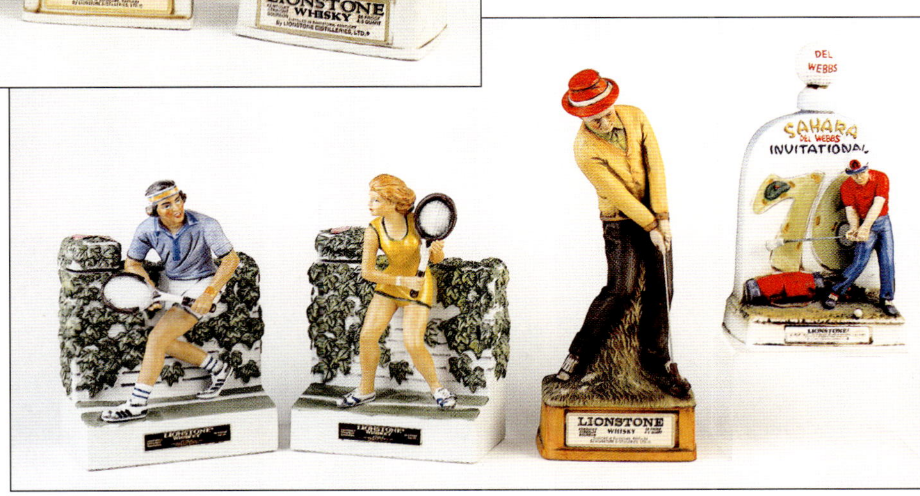

Tennis Players, set $20-25. Golfer, $45-60. Del Webb's Sahara Invitational, $40-60.

Ezra Brooks

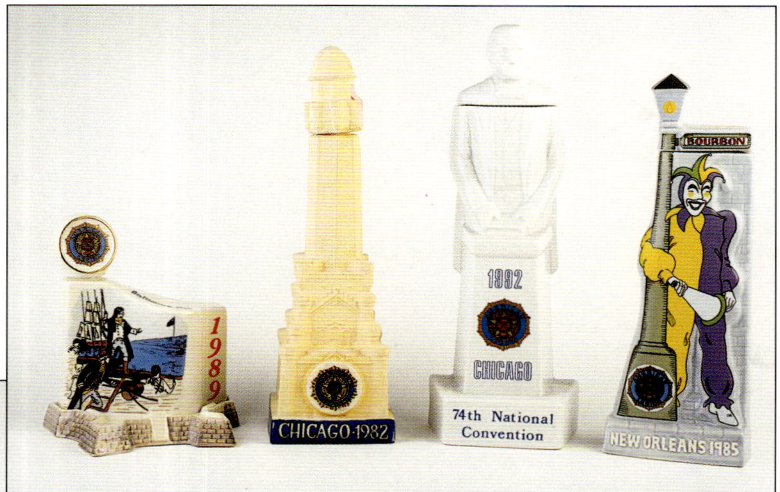

American Legion National Convention – Baltimore 1989, $10-15. Chicago 1982, $10-15. Chicago 1992, $10-15. New Orleans 1985, $10-15.

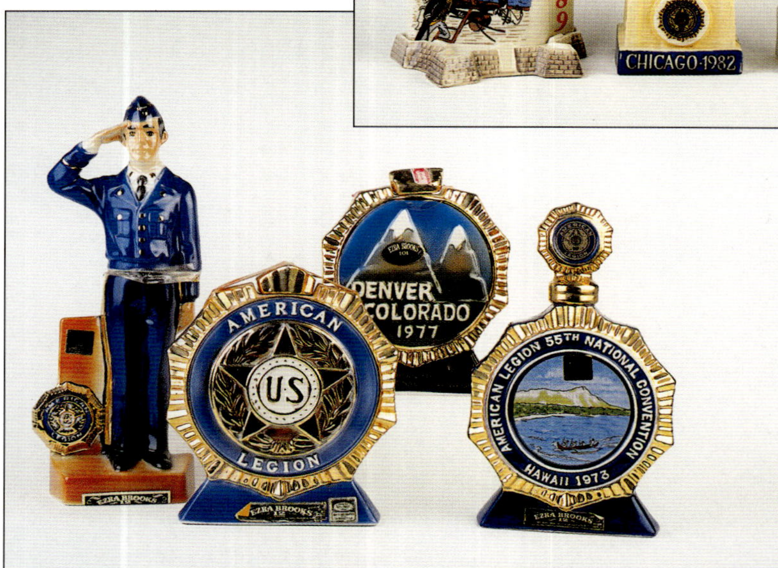

American Legion National Convention – Chicago 1972, $25-30. Texas 1971, $20-25. Colorado 1977, $10-15. Hawaii 1973, $10.

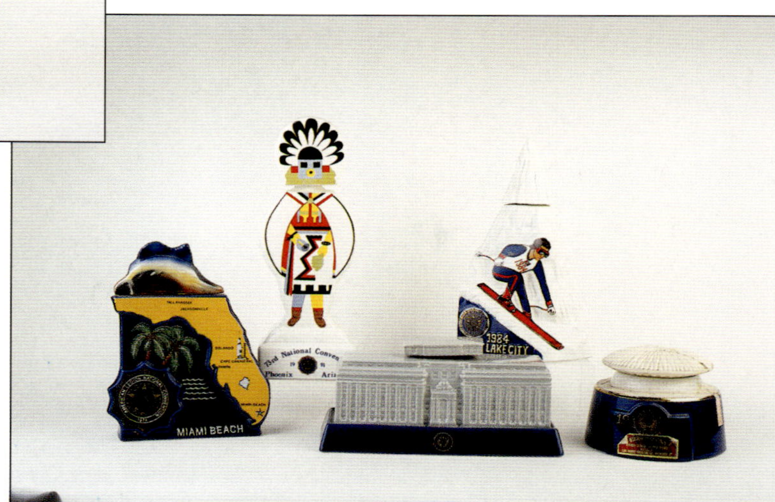

American Legion National Convention – Miami Beach 1974, $10-15. Phoenix 1991, $20-25. Indianapolis 1990, $10-15. Salt Lake City 1984, $10-15. Champaign/Urbana (Illinois) 1983, $10-15.

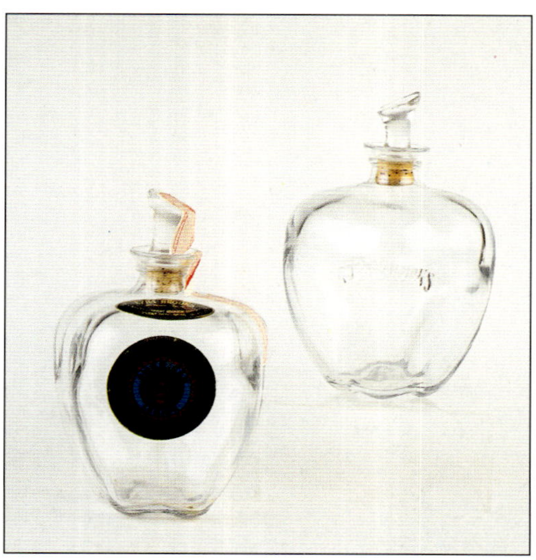

American Legion National Convention – Seattle 1983, value undetermined. Apple Bottle, value undetermined.

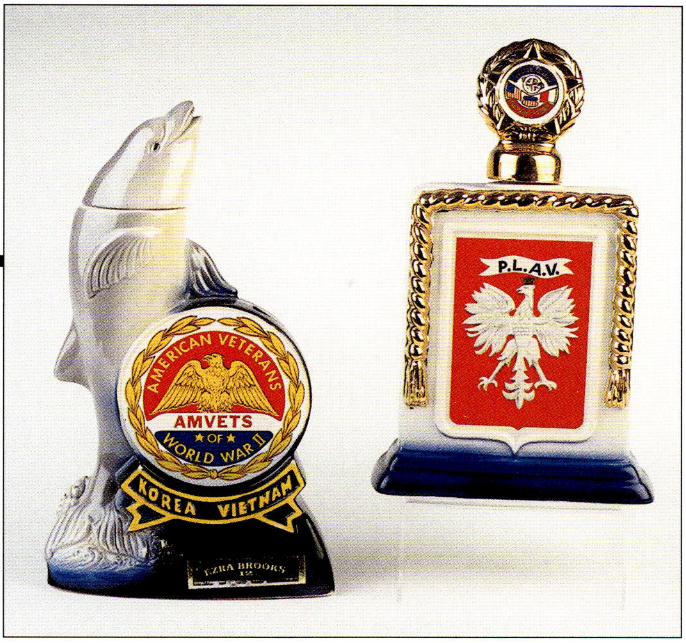

American Veterans Association, 30th National Convention, Hollywood, Florida, 1974 $10-15. Polish Legion of American Veterans and Ladies Auxiliary, Las Vegas, Nevada, 1984, $???.

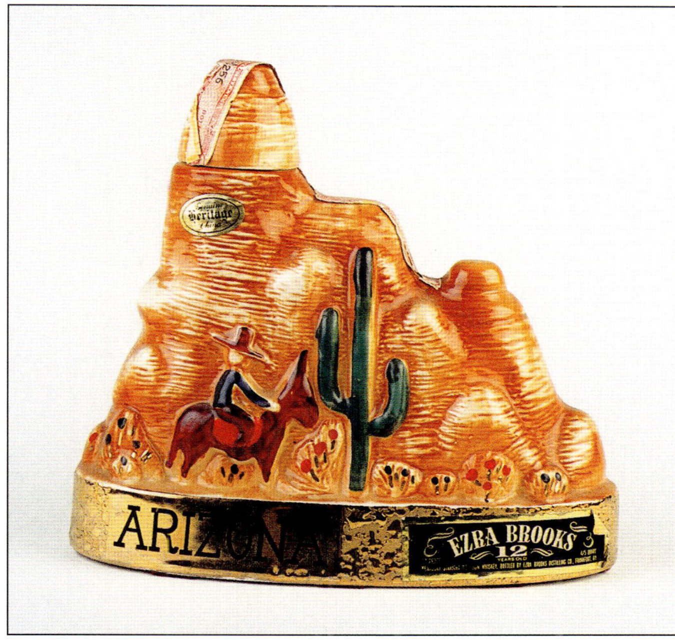

Arizona, 1969, $10.

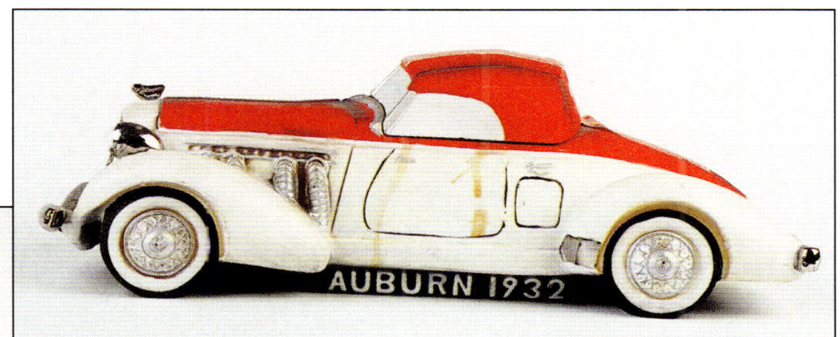

1932 Auburn Boat Tail, 1978, $10-15.

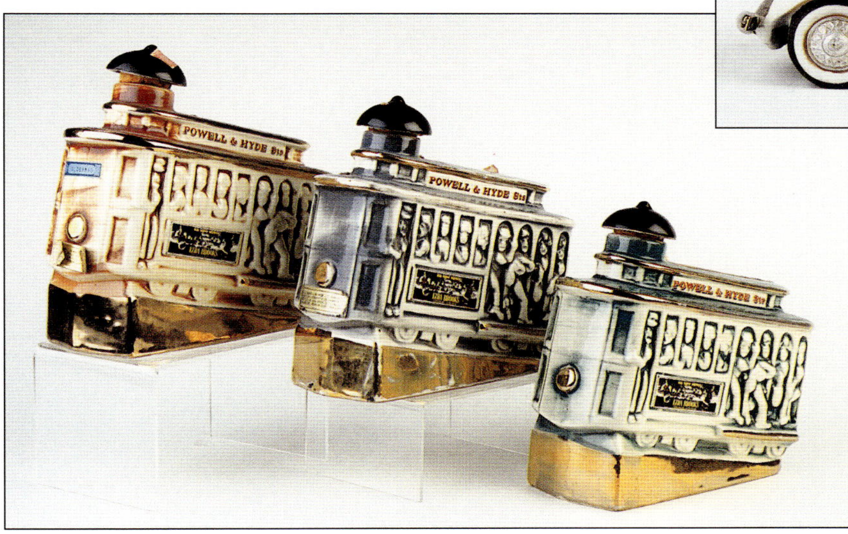

Cable Cars, 1968, brown $5; gray $5; green $5.

1957 Corvette, 1976, blue $40-50; yellow $40-50.

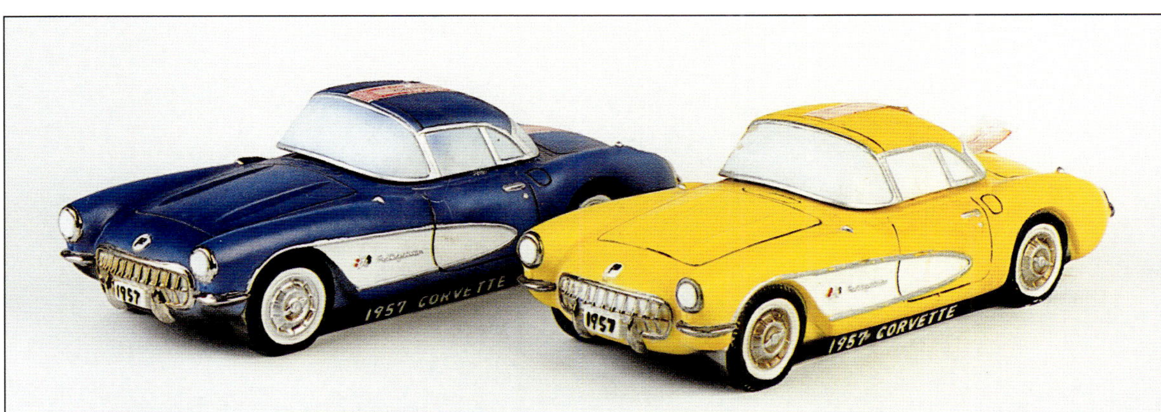

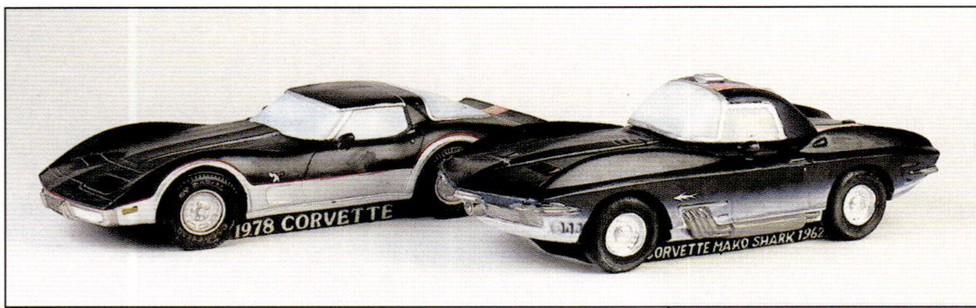

1978 Corvette Indy Pace Car, 1978, $45-55.
1962 Corvette Mako Shark, 1979, $45-55.

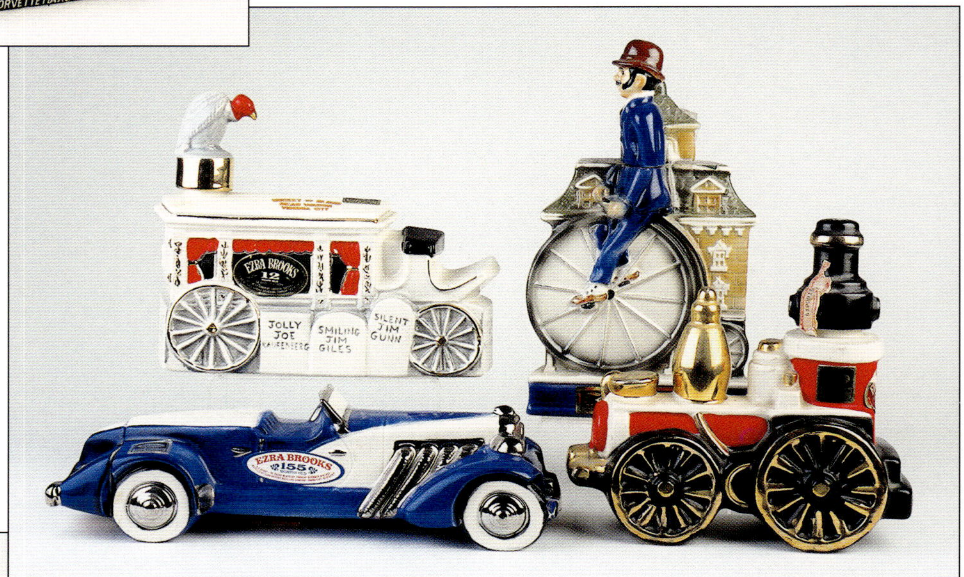

Deadwagon, 1970, $10-15. Duesenberg, 1971, $15-20. Farthington Bike, 1972, $10-15. Fire Engine, 1971, $15-20.

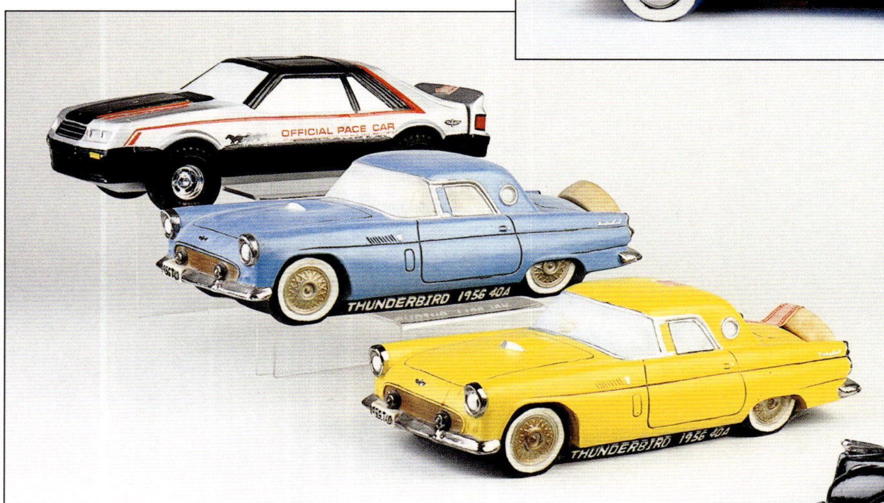

Ford Mustang Indy Pace Car, 1979, $45-50. 1956 Ford Thunderbird, 1976, blue $35-45; yellow $35-45.

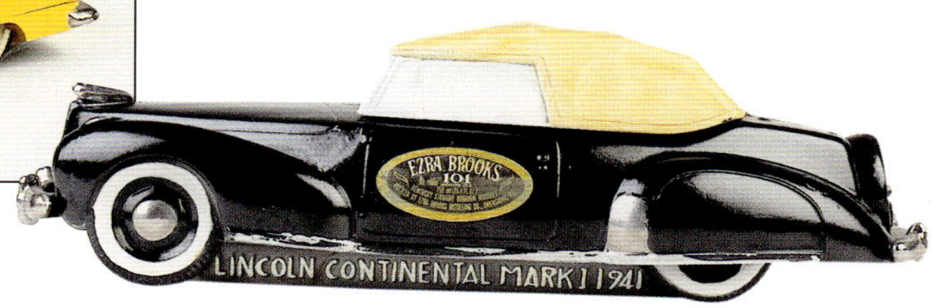

1941 Lincoln Continental, 1979, $15-20.

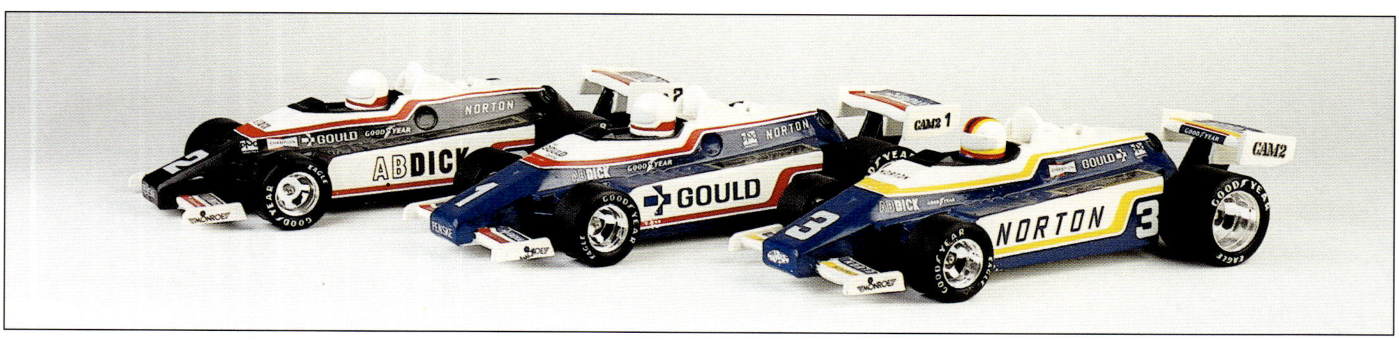

Indy Pace Car, AB Dick #2, 1982, $65-75. Indy Pace Car, Gould Charger #1, $65-75. Indy Race Car, Norton Spirit #3, $65-75.

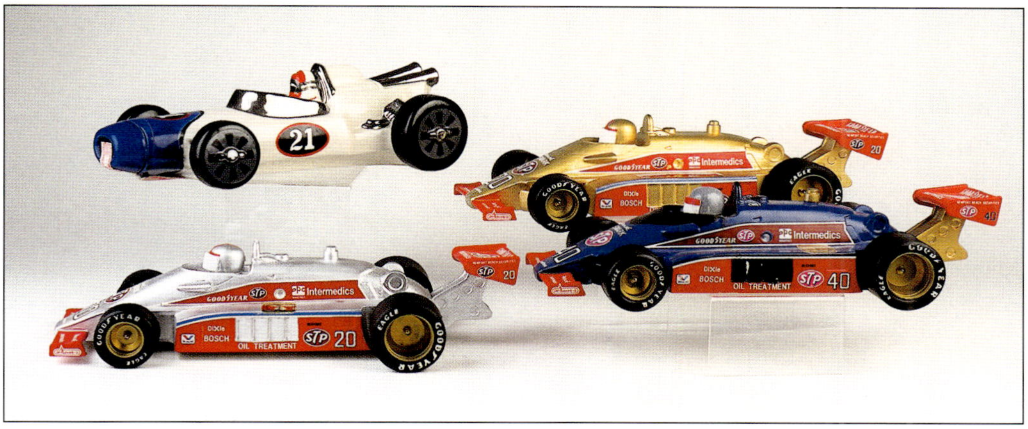

Indy Racer #21, 1970, $20-25. Indy STP #20 G. Johncock, 1983, silver $110-125; gold $110-125. Indy STP #40 Mario Andretti, 1982, $65-75.

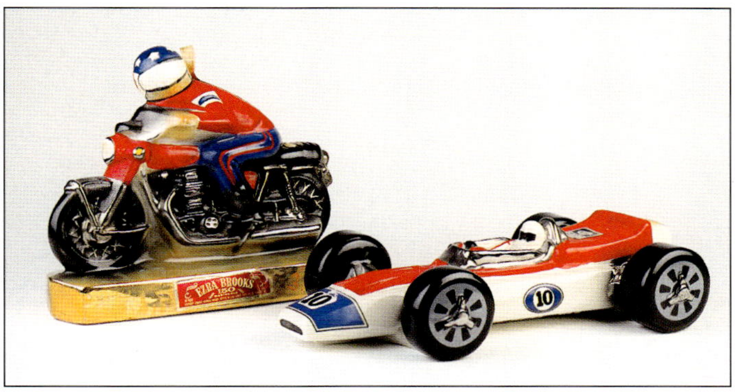

Motorcycle, 1971, $10. Ontario Racer #10, 1970, $10-15.

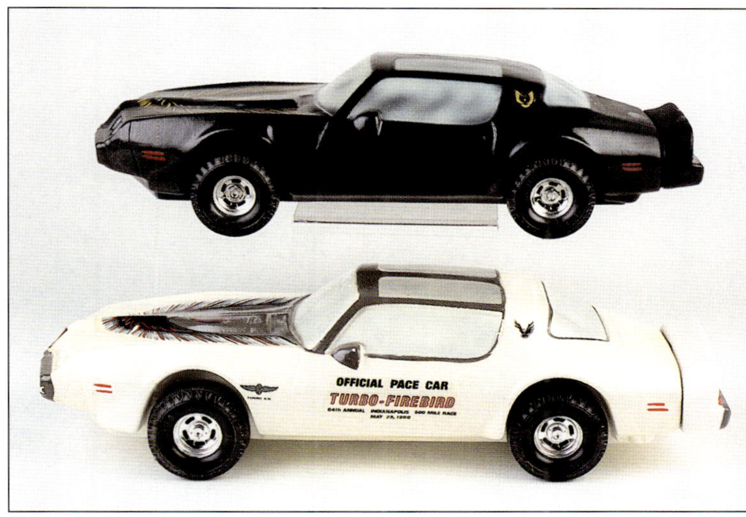

Pontiac Firebird, 1980, black, $20-25.
Pontiac Indy Pace Car, 1980, $20-25.

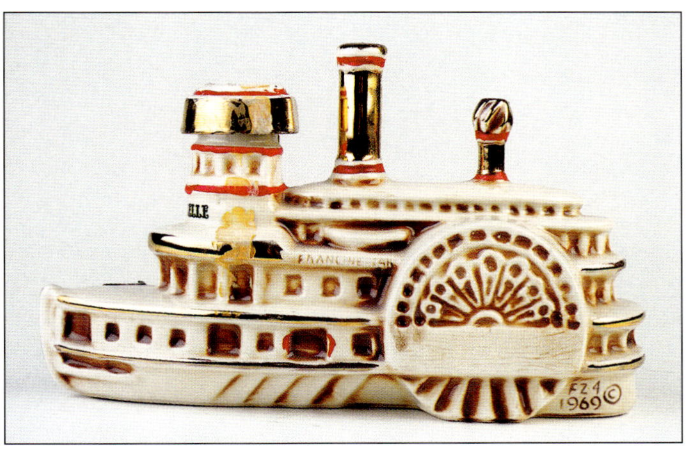

Delta Belle Riverboat, 1969, $10.

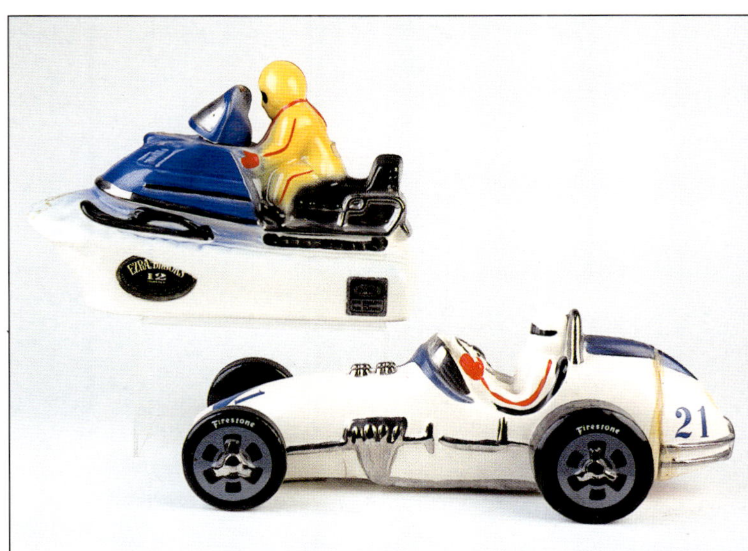

Snowmobile, 1972, $10. Spirit Racer #21, 1971, $25-35.

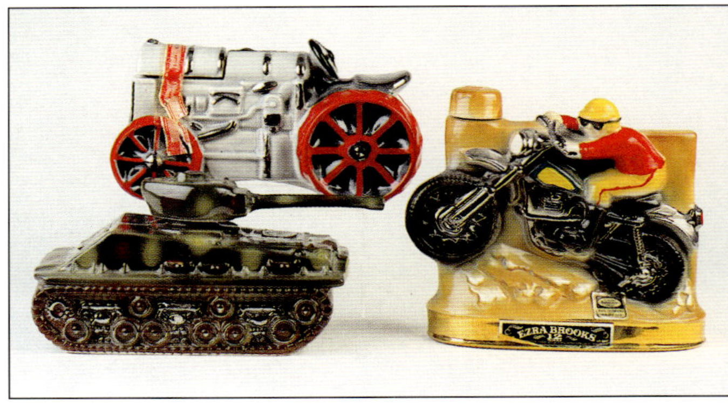

Tank, 1971, $20-25. Fordson Tractor, 1971, $15-20. Trail Bike, 1972, $10-15.

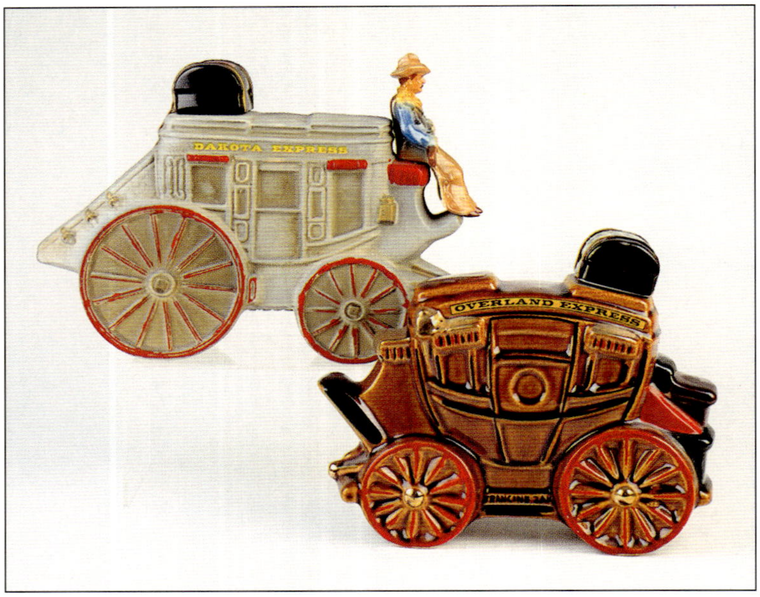

Stagecoach, Dakota Express, 1977, $10. Stagecoach, Overland Express, 1969, $25-30.

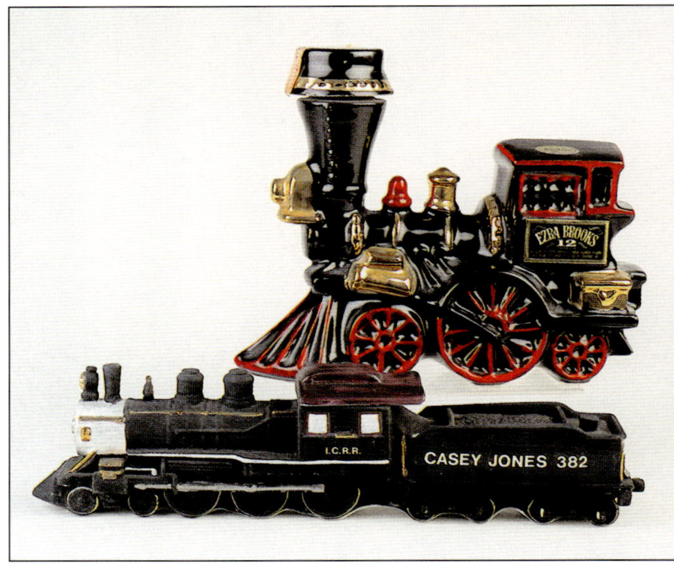

Train, Casey Jones #1, 1980, $15-20. Train, Iron Horse, 1969, $10-15.

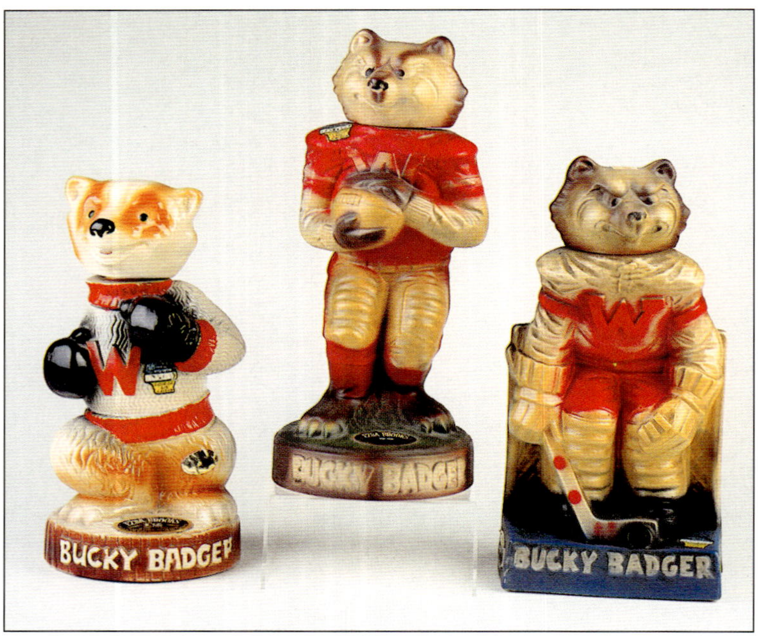

Badger Boxer, 1973, $20-25. Badger Football, 1974, $25-30. Badger Hockey, 1974, $20-25.

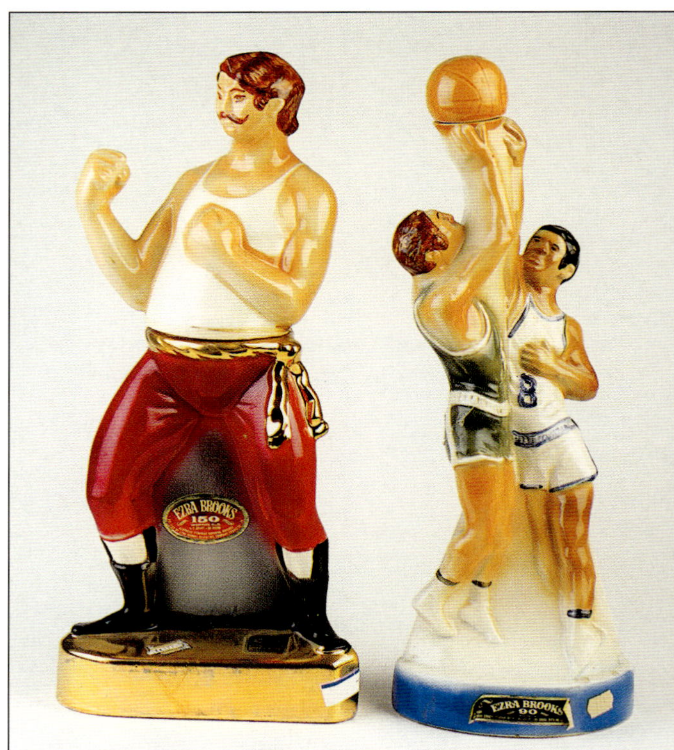

Bareknuckle Fighter, 1971, $20-25. Basketball Players, 1974, $20-25.

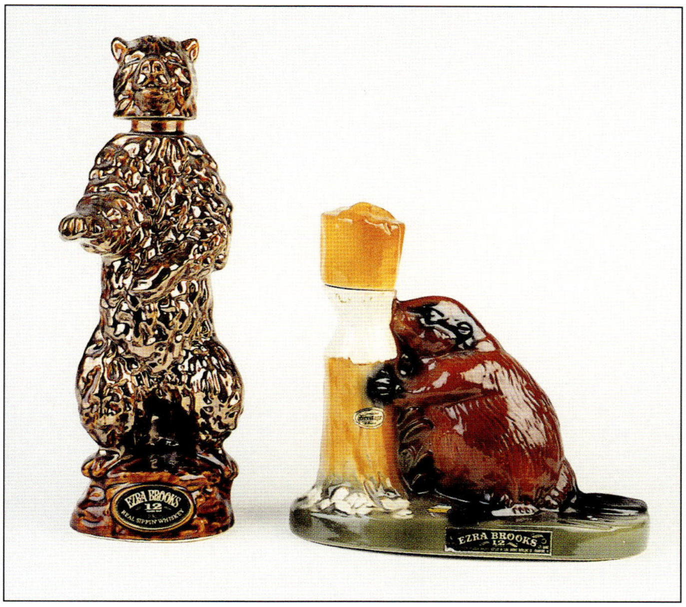

Bear, 1968, $5. Beaver, 1972, $5.

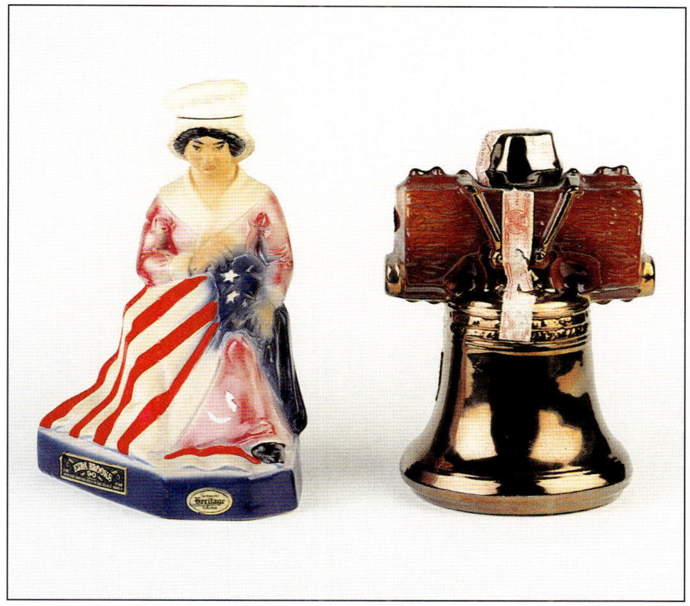

Liberty Bell, 1969, $5. Betsy Ross, 1975, $10-15.

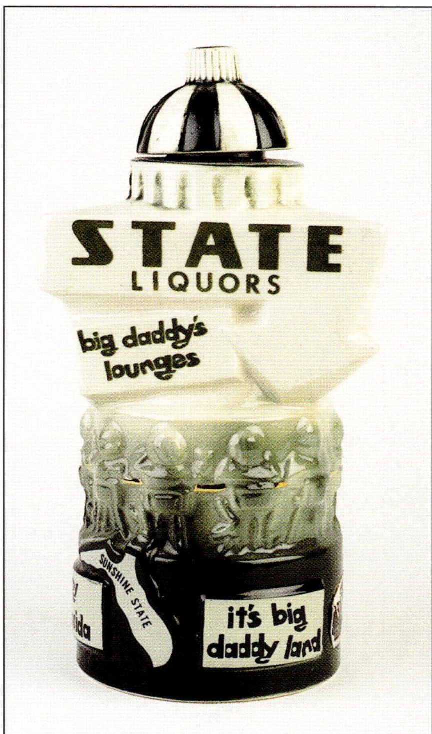

State Liquors, Big Daddy's Lounges, 1969, $5.

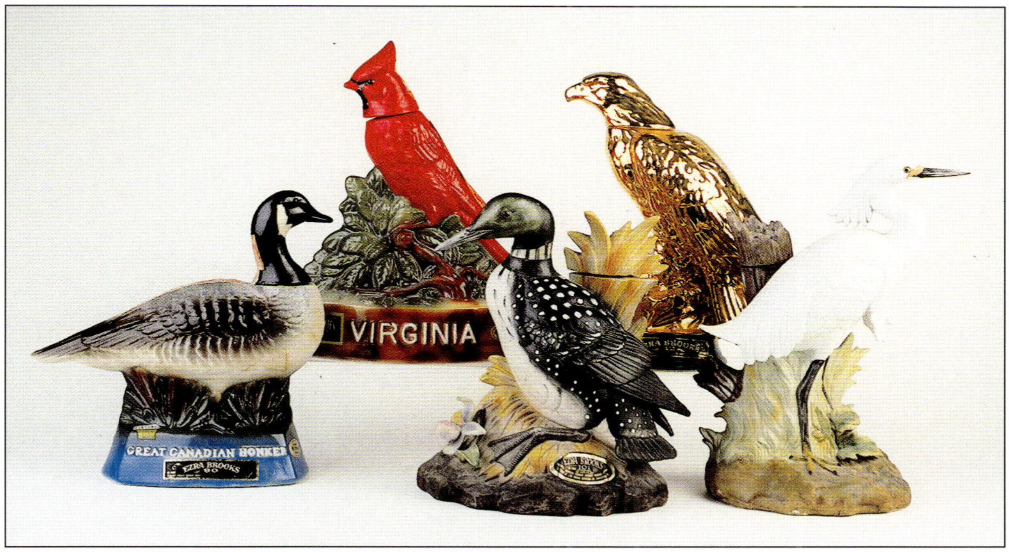

Canadian Goose, 1975, $10-15. Cardinal, 1972, $10-15. Canadian Loon, 1979, $25-35. Gold Eagle, 1971, $15-20. Snowy Egret, 1980, $10-15.

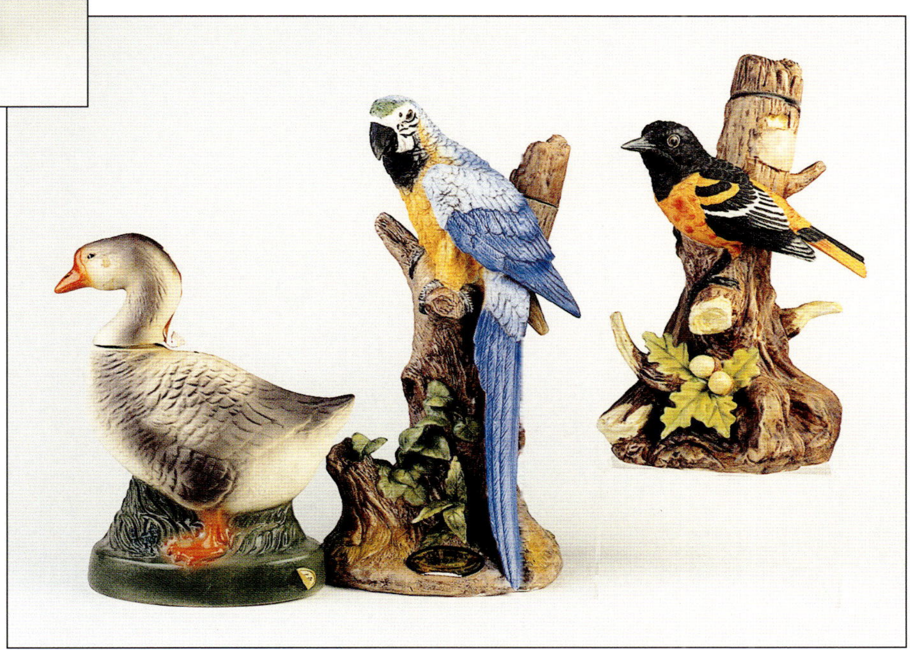

Goose, 1974, $10-15. Macaw, 1980, $15-20. Baltimore Oriole, 1979, $10-15.

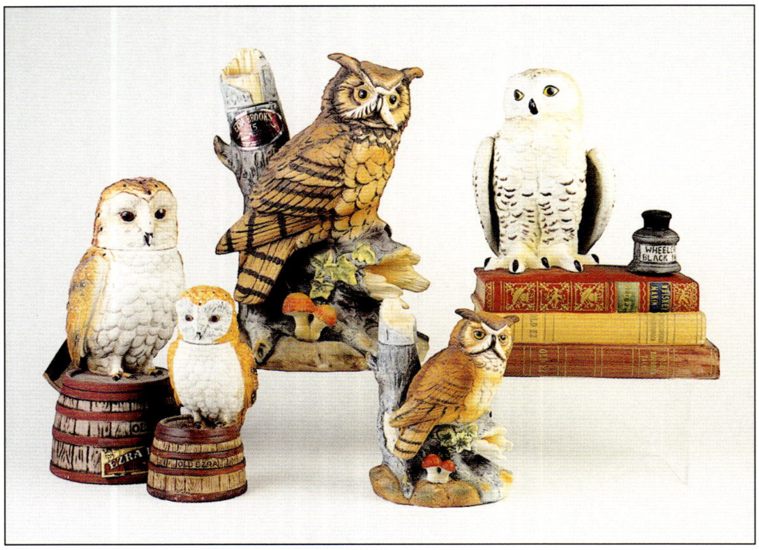

Owl #1 EZ Owl, 1977, fifth, $15-20, mini (1980) $10-15. Owl #2, 1978, fifth $20-25, mini (1981) $10. Snowy Owl #3, 1979, $10-15.

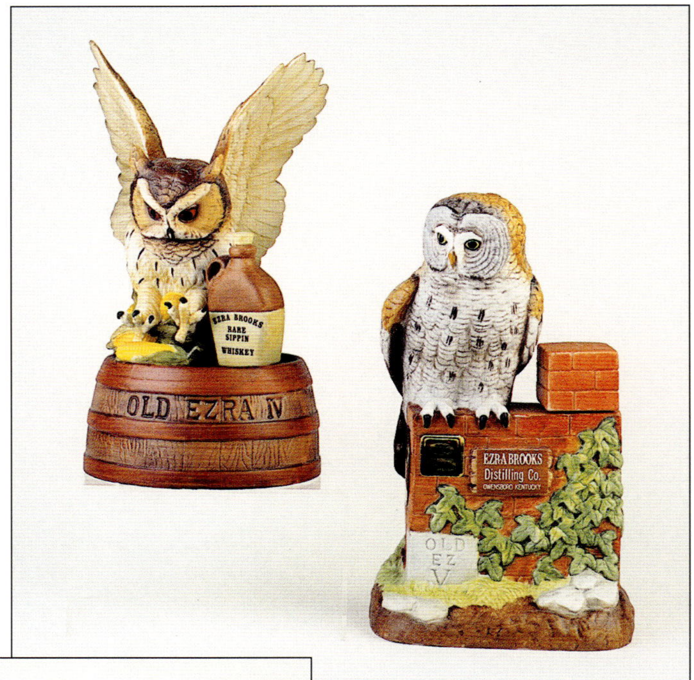

Owl #4, 1981, $15-20. Owl #5 Great Grey Owl, 1982, $15-20.

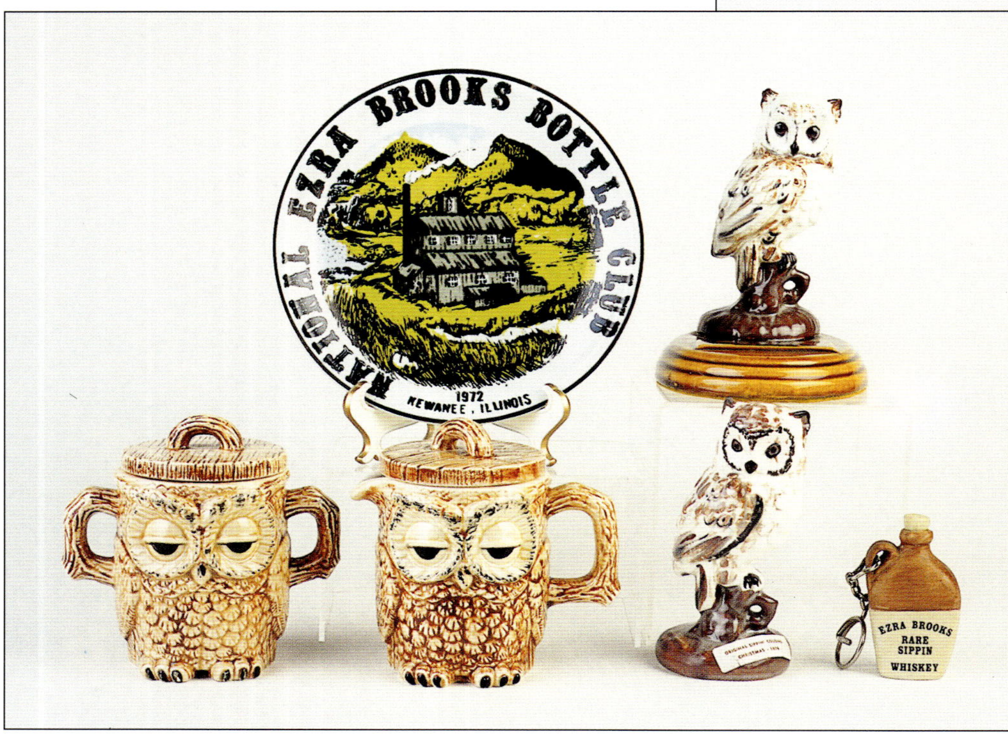

Ezra Brooks Club give-aways, sugar and creamer, 1980, $25-30. Plate 1972, Kiwanee, Il, $5-10.Club 10th birthday, $10-15. Christmas 1979, $10-15. Keychain $5.

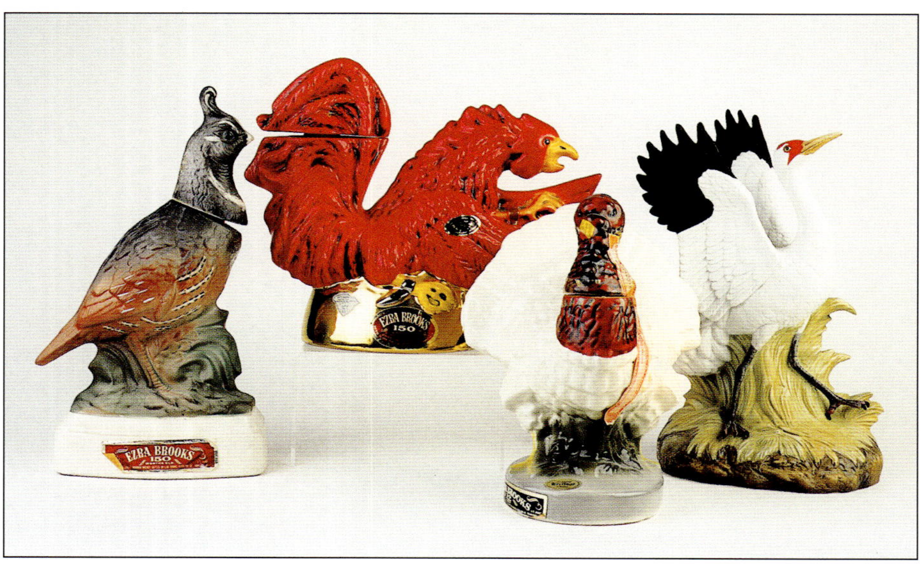

Quail, 1979, $5. Fighting Gamecock, 1970, $5. White Turkey, 1971, $5-10. Whooping Crane, 1982, $10-15.

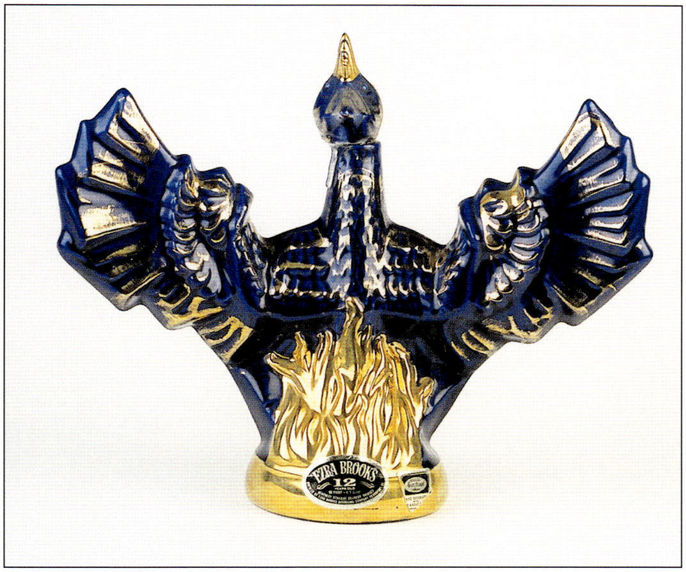

Phoenix Bird, 1971, $5.

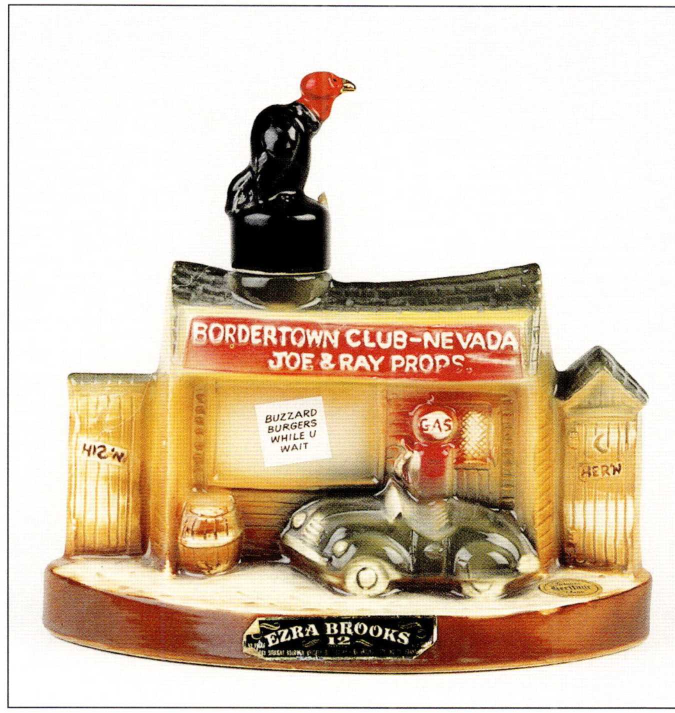

Bordertown Club, Nevada, 1970, $5.

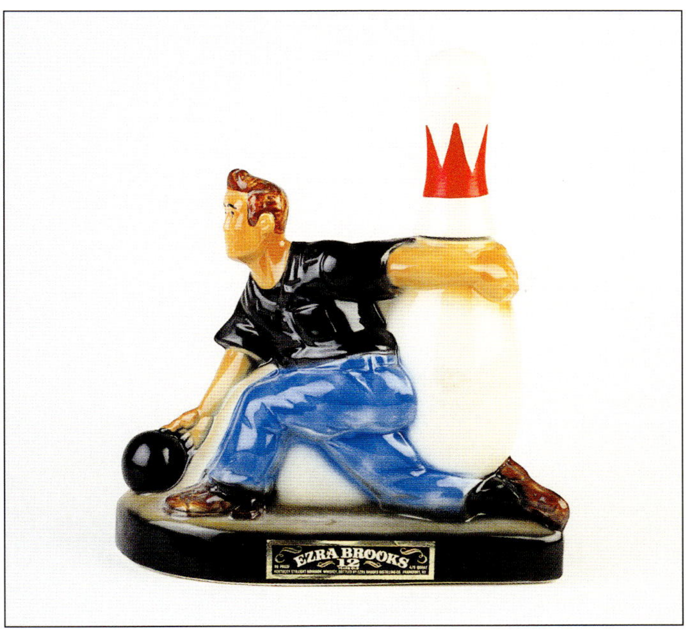

Bowler, 1973, $5-10.

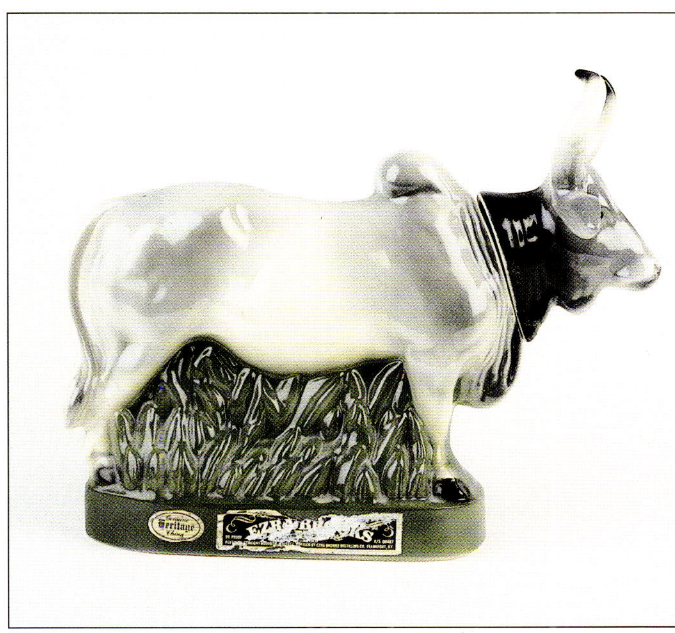

Brahma, 1971, $10-15.

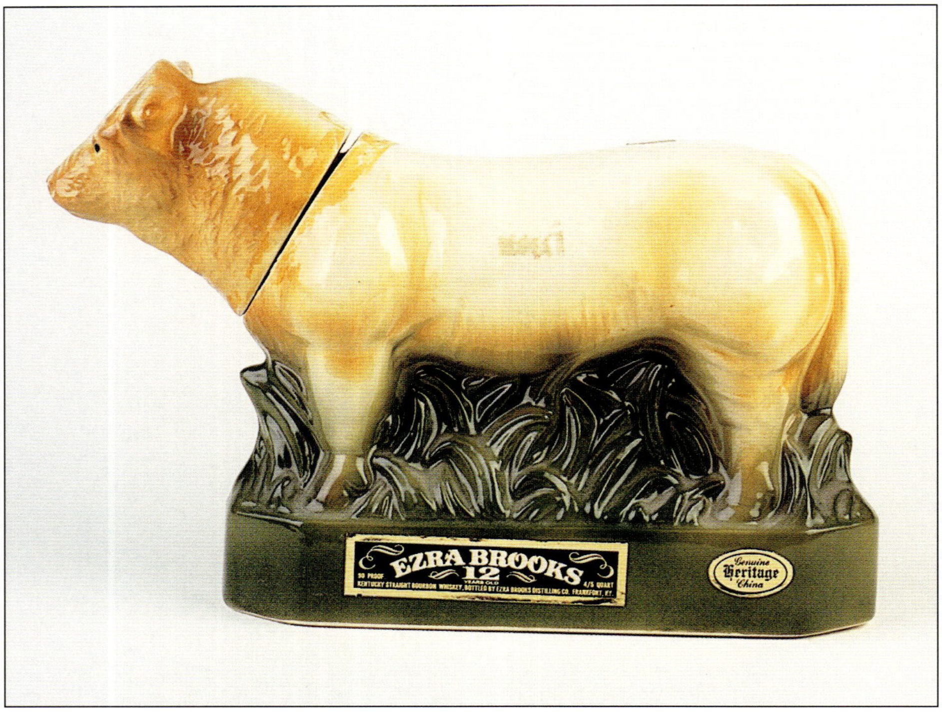

Charolais, 1972, $10-15.

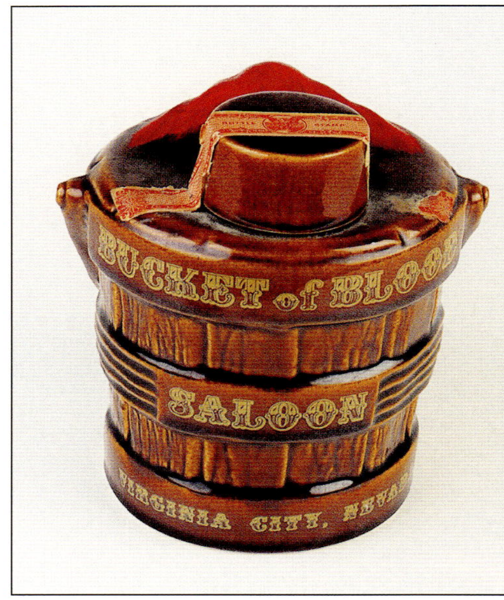

Bucket of Blood Saloon, 1970, $5.

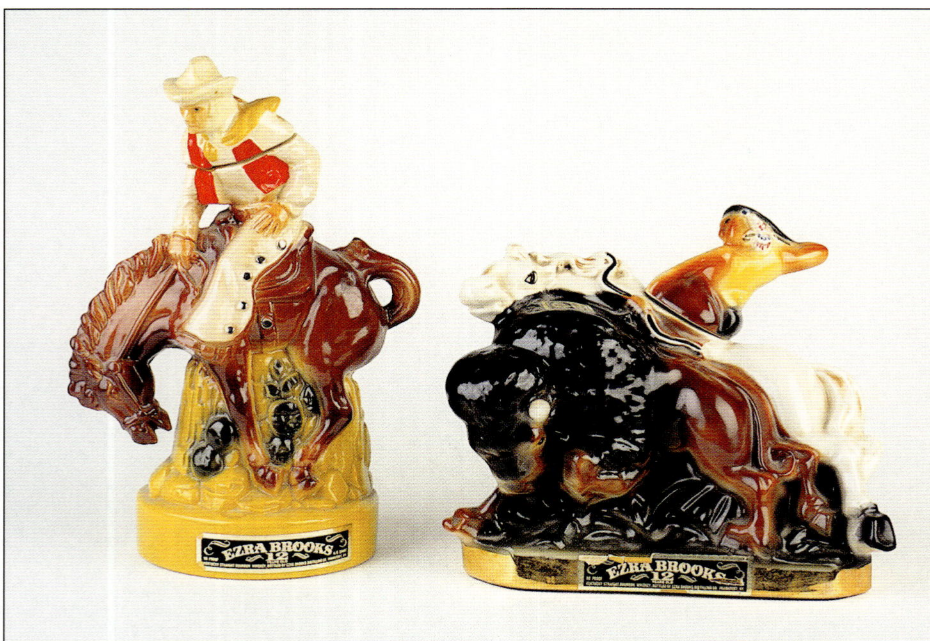

Bucking Bronco, 1973, $50-10.
Buffalo Hunt, 1971, $5-10.

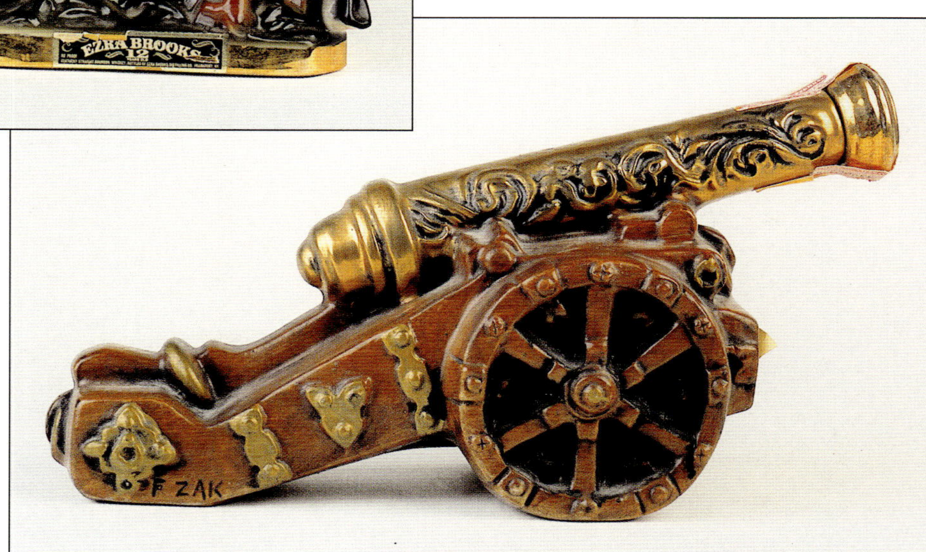

Antique Cannon, 1969, $5.

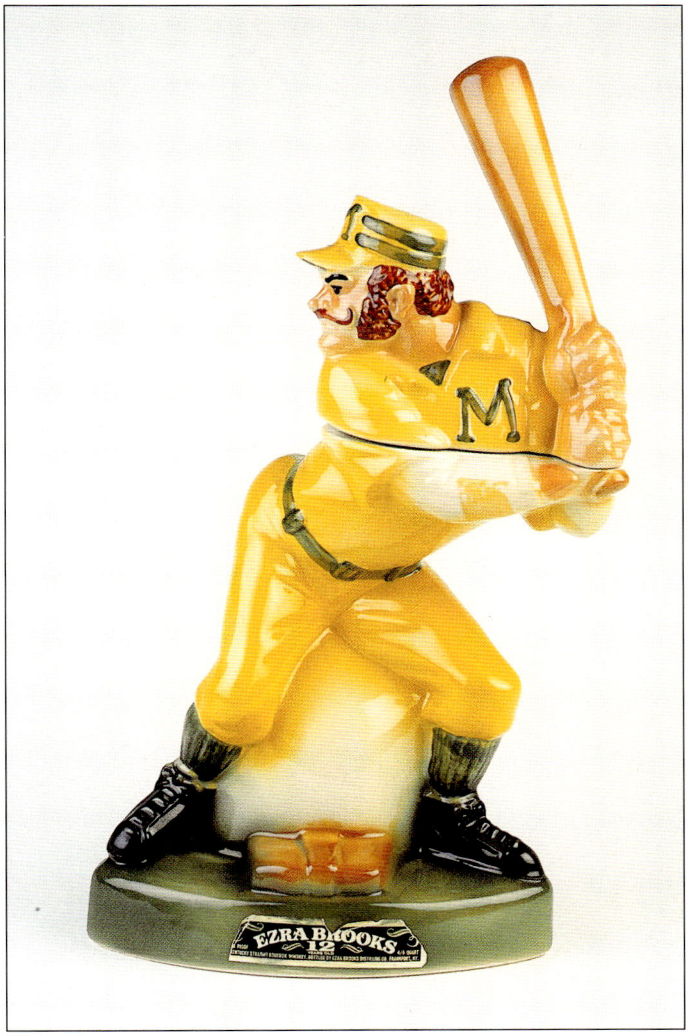

Casey at Bat, 1973, $25-30.

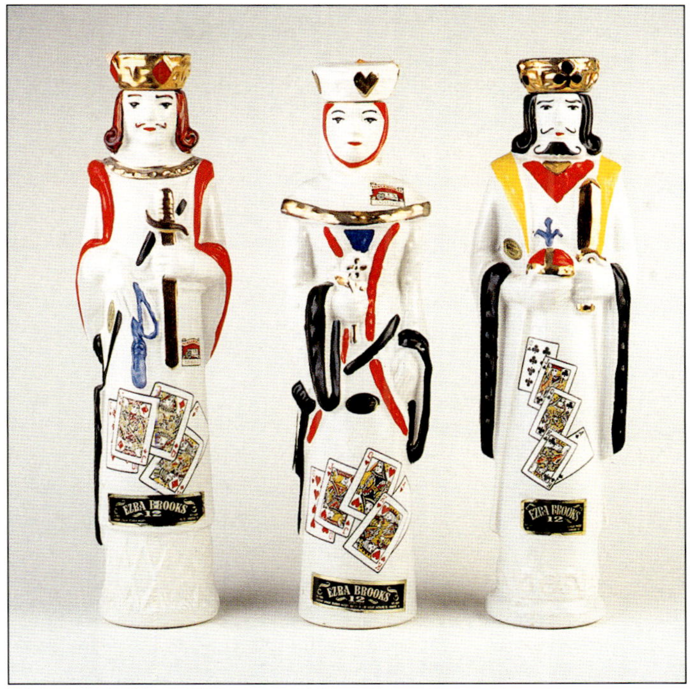

Jack of Diamonds, 1969, $10-15. Queen of Hearts, 1969, $10-15. King of Clubs, 1969, $10-15.

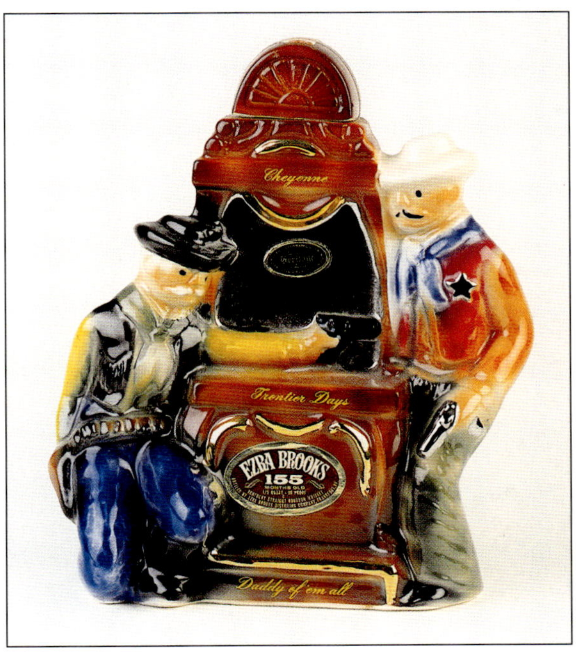

Cheyenne Shootout, 1970, $5.

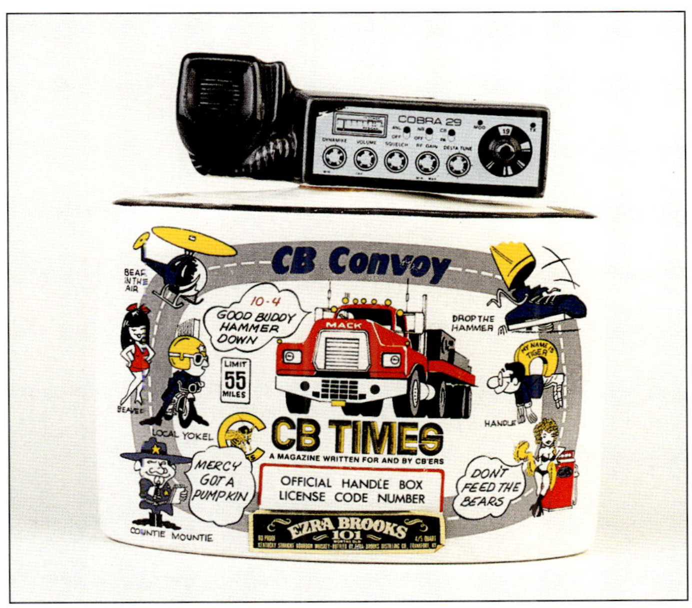

C. B. Convoy. 1976, $5.

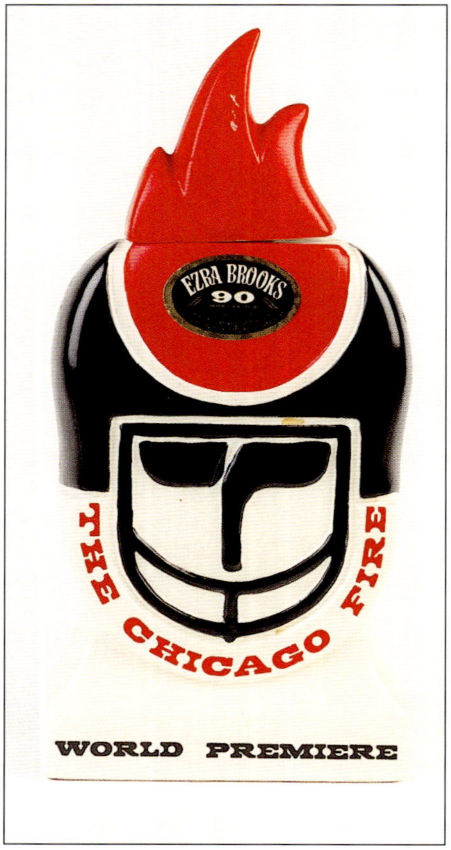

Chicago Fire, 1974, $25-30.

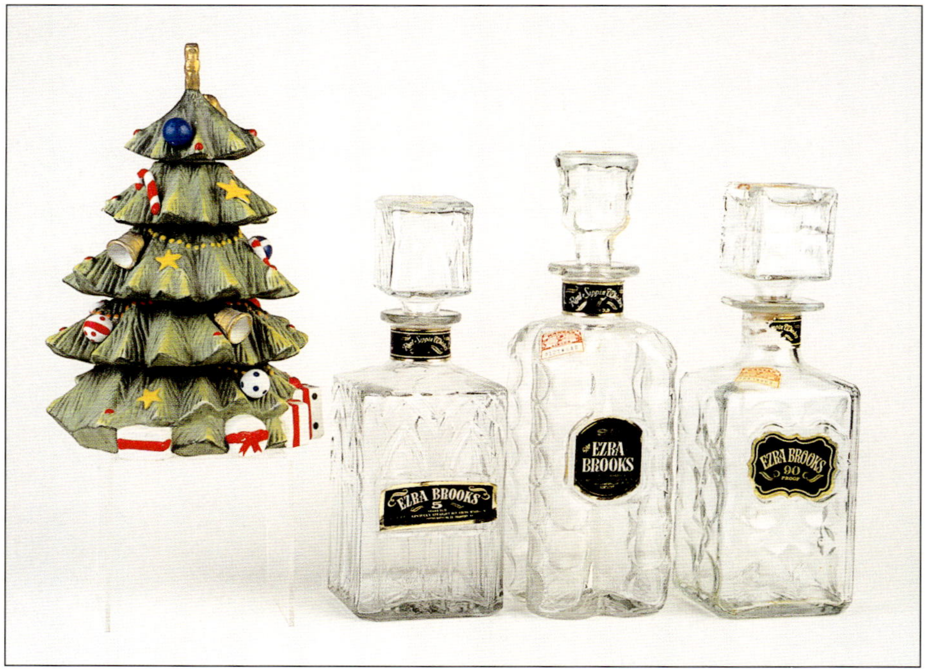

Christmas Tree, 1979, $10-15. Christmas Decanter 1966, $10-15. Christmas Decanter 1967, $10-15. Christmas Decanter 1969, $10-15.

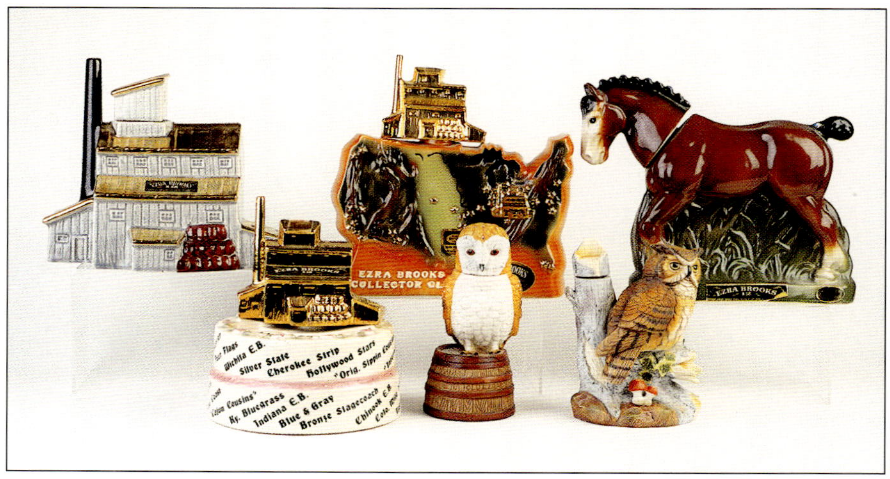

Club #1, Distillery, 1970, $10-15. Club #2, Birthday Cake, 1971, $10. Club #3, USA Map, 1972. $10. Club #4, Old EZ Owl, 1980, mini $10. Club #5, Eagle Owl, 1981, $10. Clydesdale, 1974, $15-20.

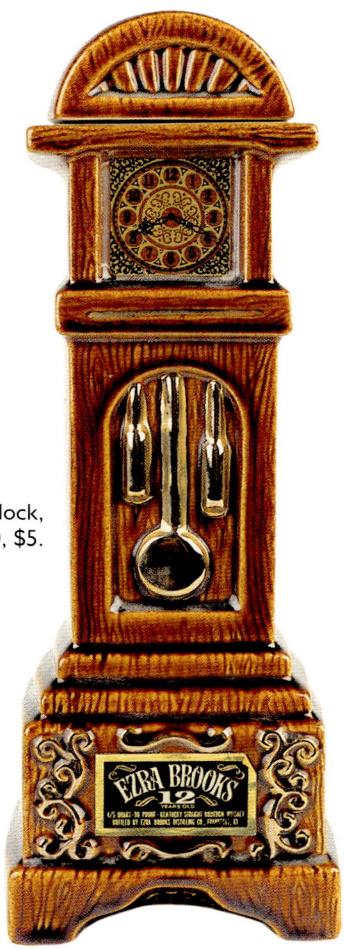

Grandfather Clock, 1970, $5.

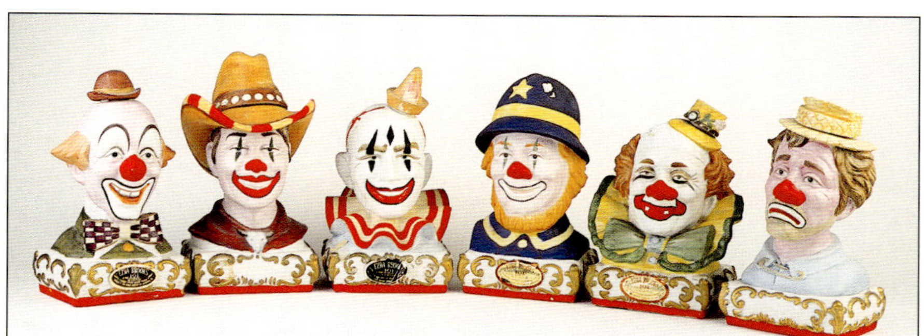

Clown Bust #1, Smiley, 1979, $20-25. Clown Bust #2, Cowboy, 1979, $20-25. Clown Bust #3, Pagliacci, 1979, $20-25. Clown Bust #4, Keystone Cop, 1980, $20-25, Clown Bust #5, Cuddles, 1980, $20-25. Clown Bust #6, Tramp, 1980, $20-25.

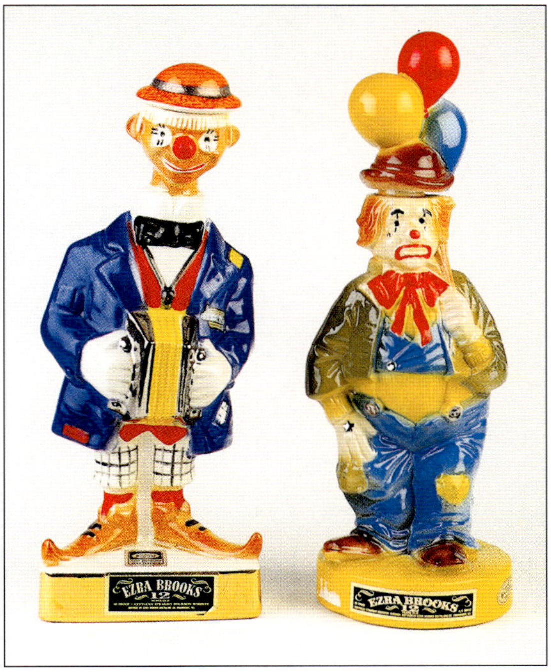

Clown with Accordion, 1971, $10-15. Clown with Balloons, 1973, $10-15.

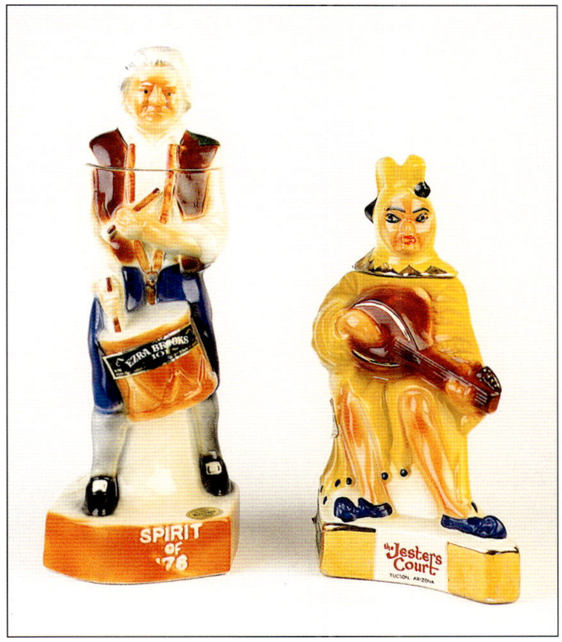

Colonial Durmmer, 1974, $10-15. Court Jester, 1971, $10-15.

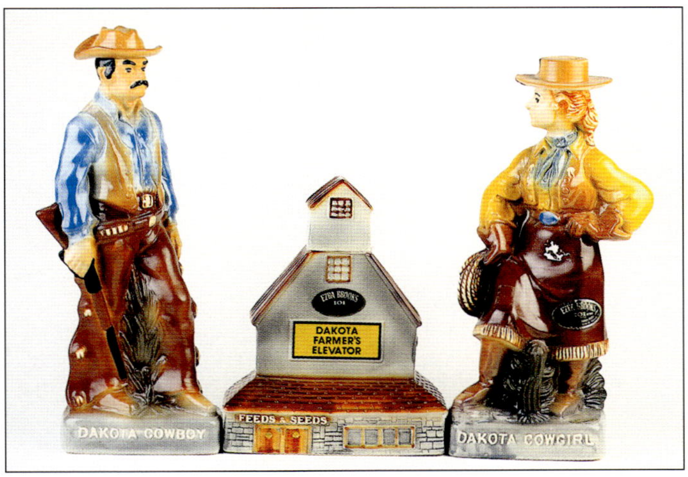

Dakota Cowboy, 1975, $10. Dakota Farmers Elevator, 1978, $10. Dakota Cowgirl, 1978, $10.

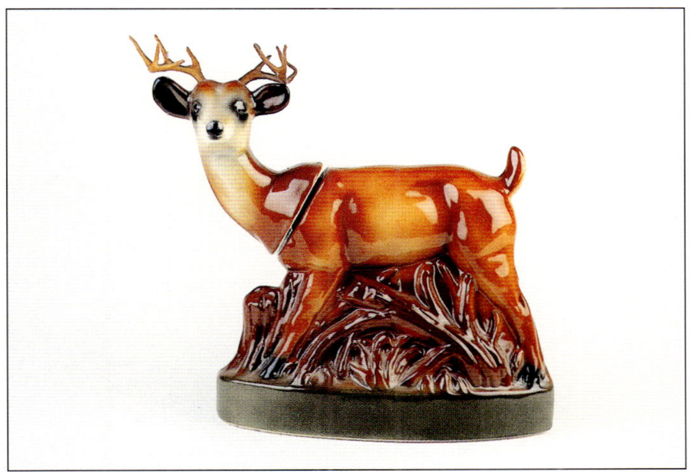

White Tail Deer, 1974, $10-15.

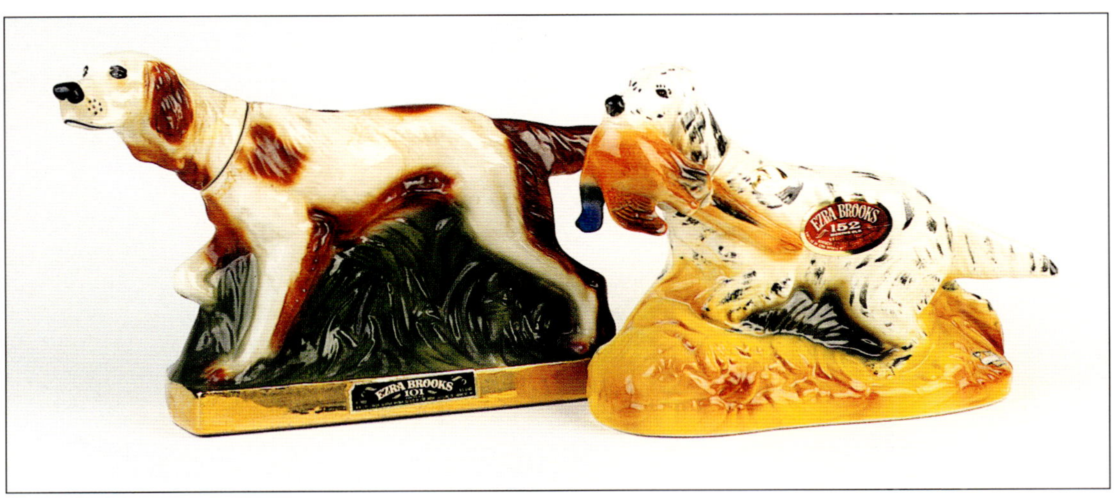

Setter, 1974, $10; Setter with bird, 1970, $10.

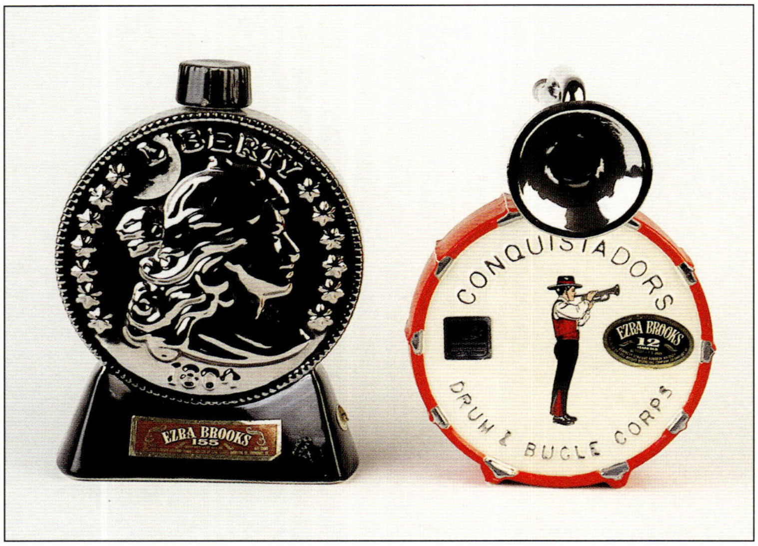

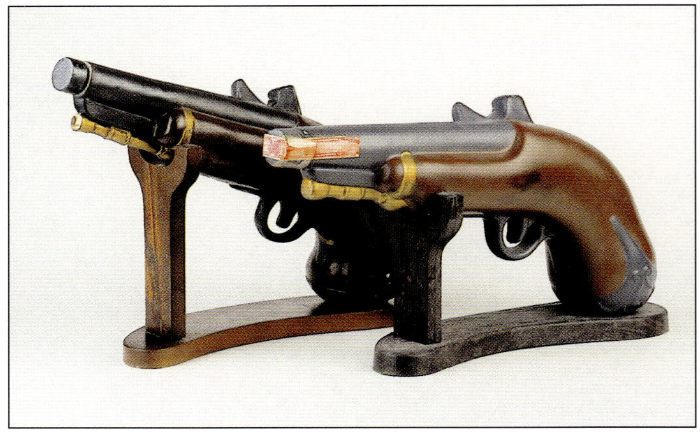

Dueling Pistol, 1968, $10. Japanese Dueling Pistol, 1968, $10.

Silver Dollar, black bottom, 1969, $5. Drum and Bugle, Conquistador, 1971, $5.

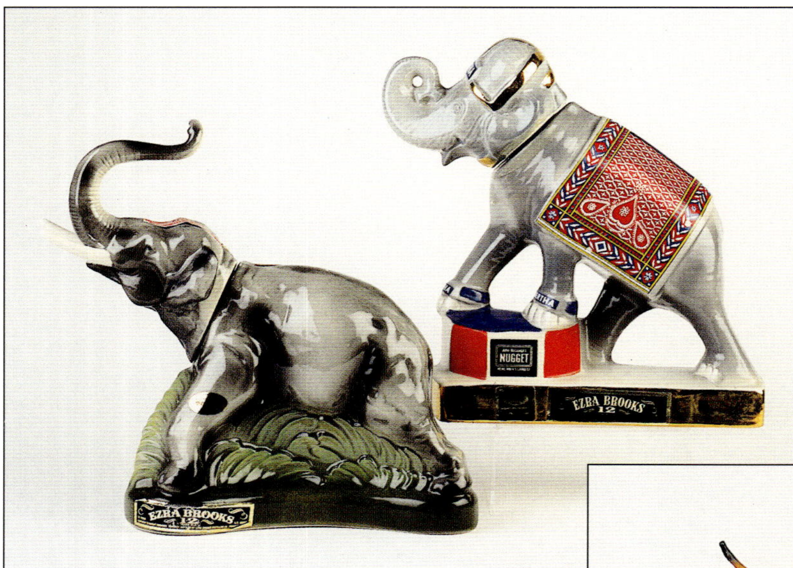

Asian Elephant, 1973, $10-15.
Big Bertha, 1970, $10-15.

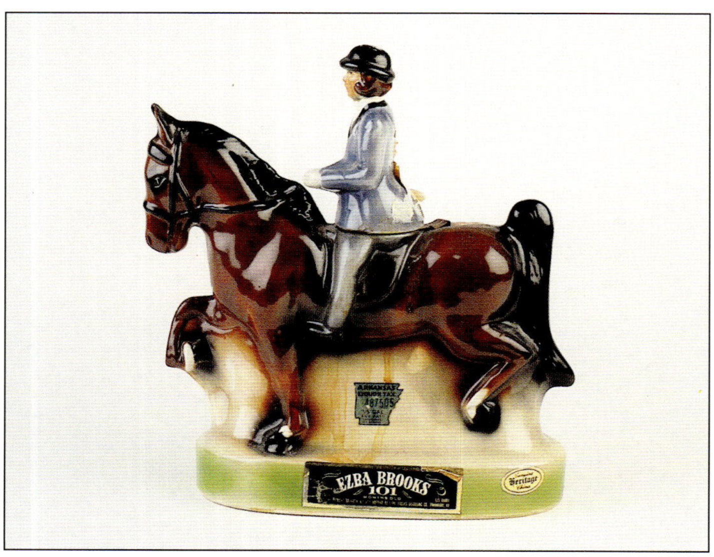

Equestrian, 1974, $10-15.

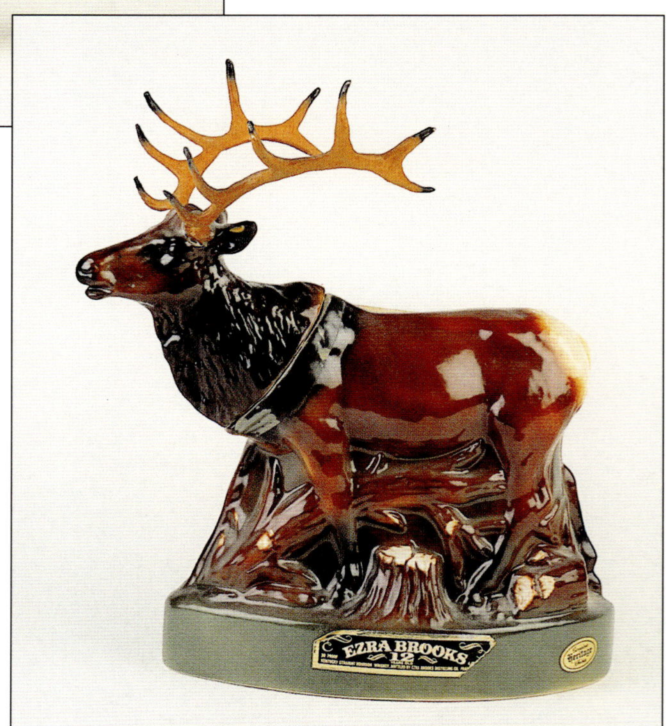

Elk, 1972, $10-15.

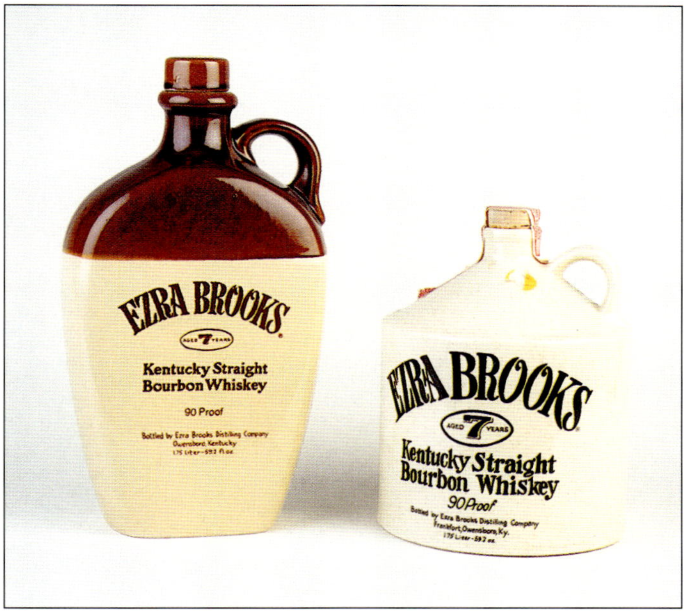

EZ Jug #1, 1977, $5. EZ Jug #2, 1980, $5.

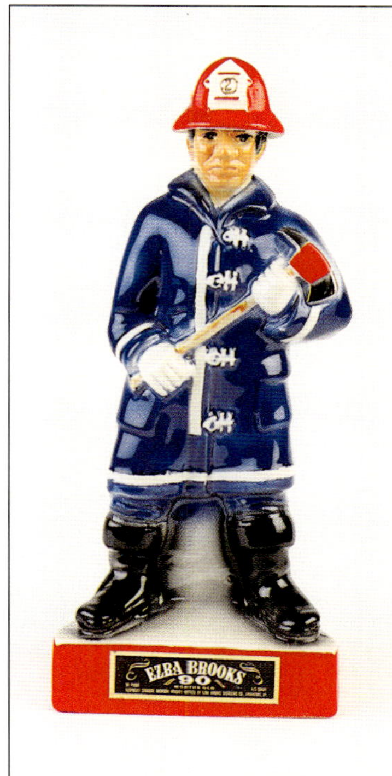

Fireman, 1975. $20-25.

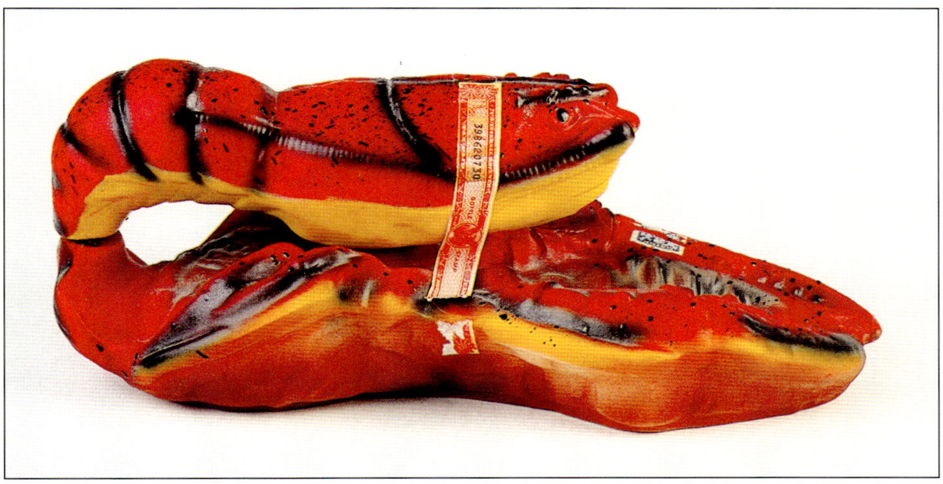

Maine Lobster, 1970, $5.

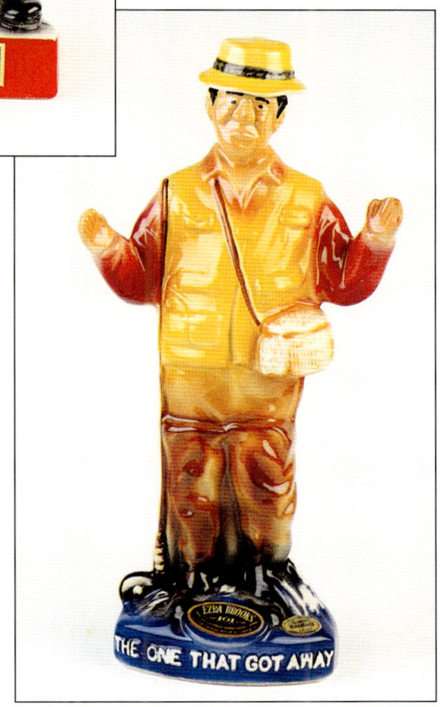

Fisherman, 1974, $10.

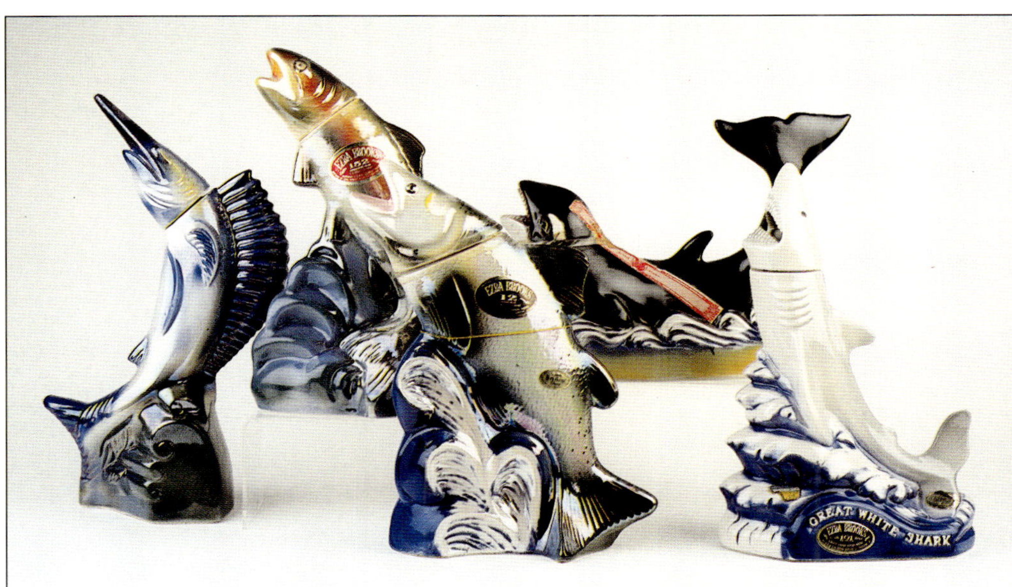

Sailfish, 1970, $10-15. Trout and Fly, 1970, $10-15. Washington King Salmon, 1971, $10-15. Washington Whale, 1972, White Shark, 1977, $10-15.

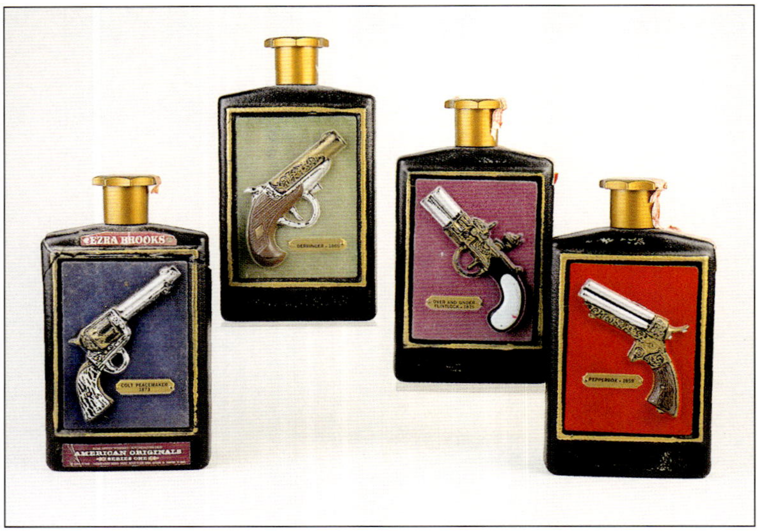

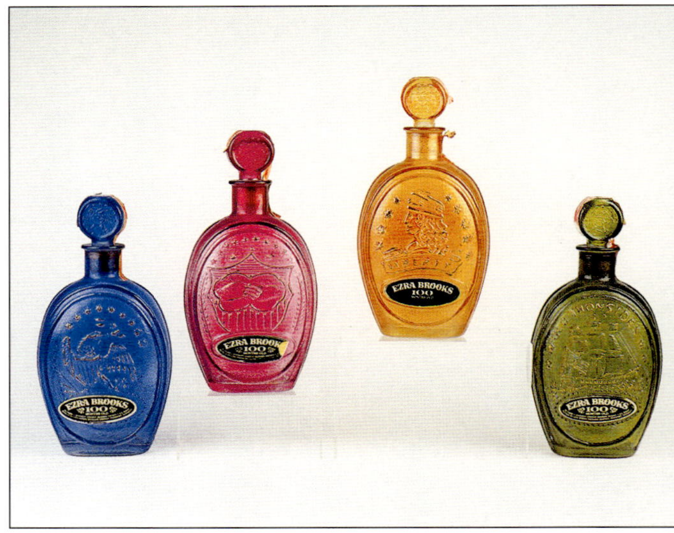

Gun Flasks, 1969: Colt Peacemaker, $5; Derringer, $5; Over/Under Flintlock, $5; Pepperbox $5.

Historical Flasks, 1970: Eagle (blue), $5; Flagship (purple), $5; Liberty (amber), $5; Old Ironside (green), $5.

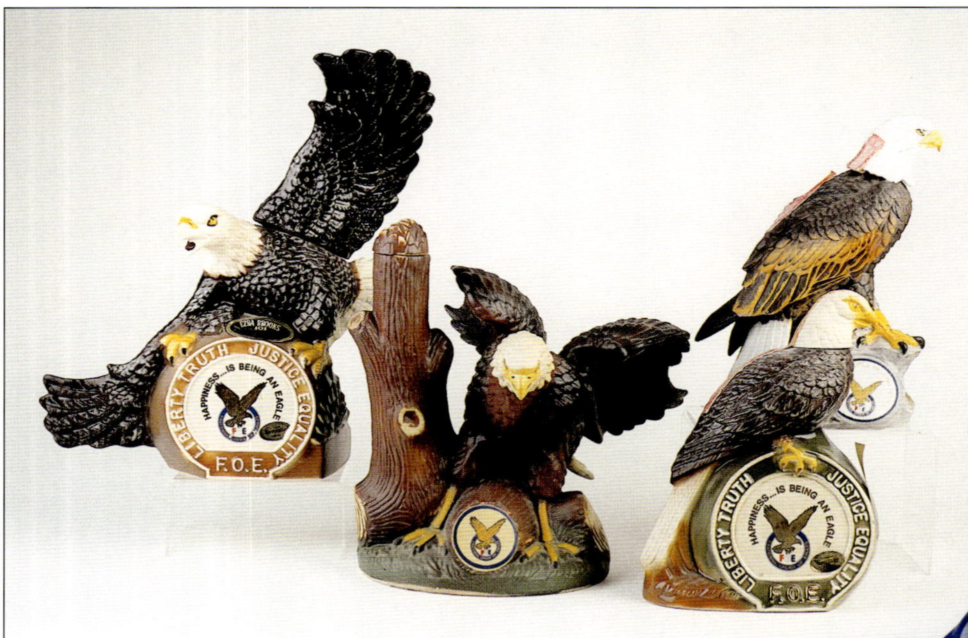

F.O.E. Eagle, 1982, $20-25. F.O.E. Eagle, 1980, $20-25. F.O.E. Eagle, 1978, $15-20. F.O.E. Eagle, 1978, $15-20.

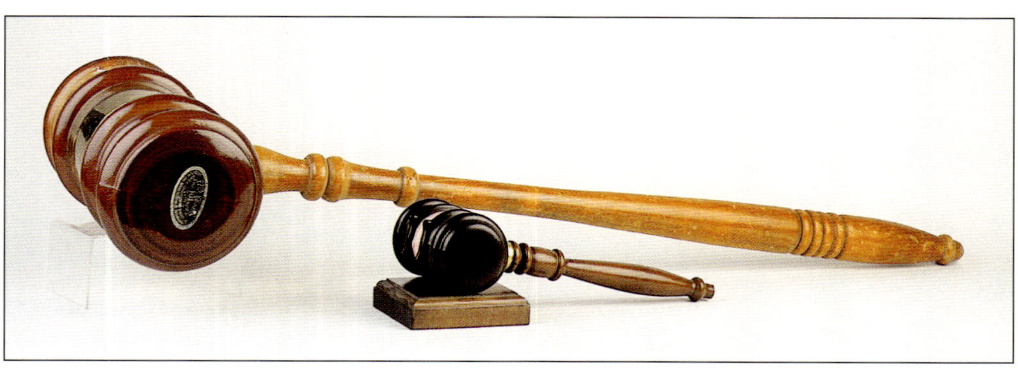

Gavels, The V.I.P., 1982, 200 ml $10-15.
The Chairman, 1982, 1.75 ml $20-25.

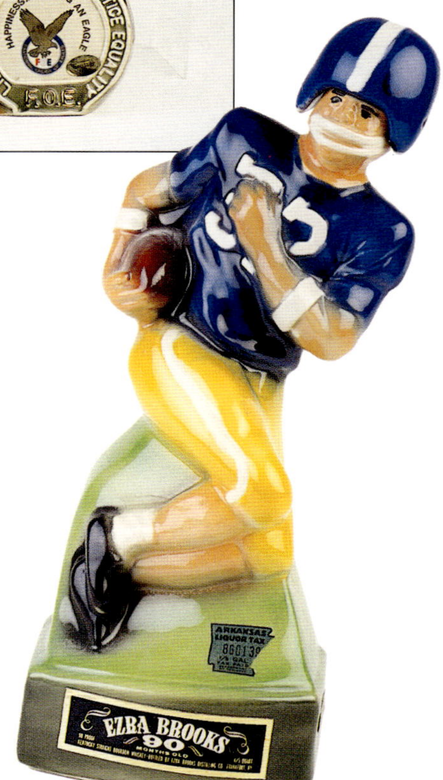

Football Player, 1974, $20-25.

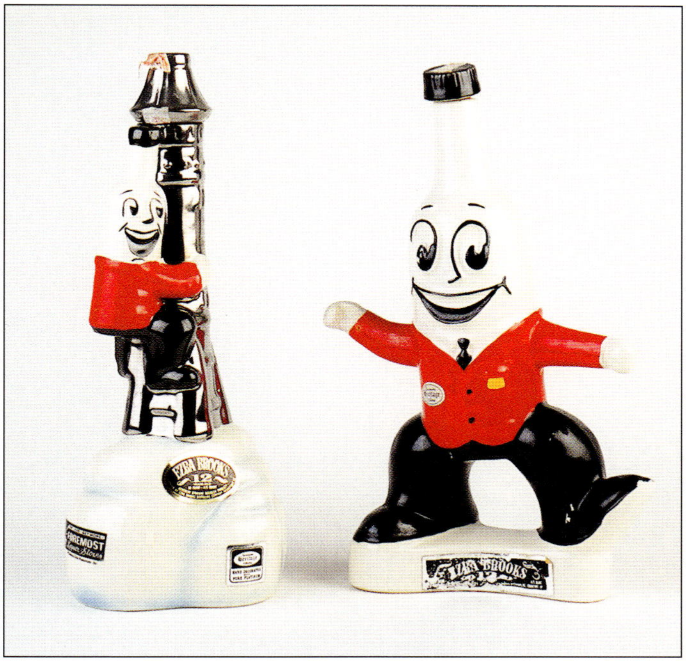

Foremost Astronaut, 1970, $10-15.
Foremost Dancing Man, 1969, $10-15.

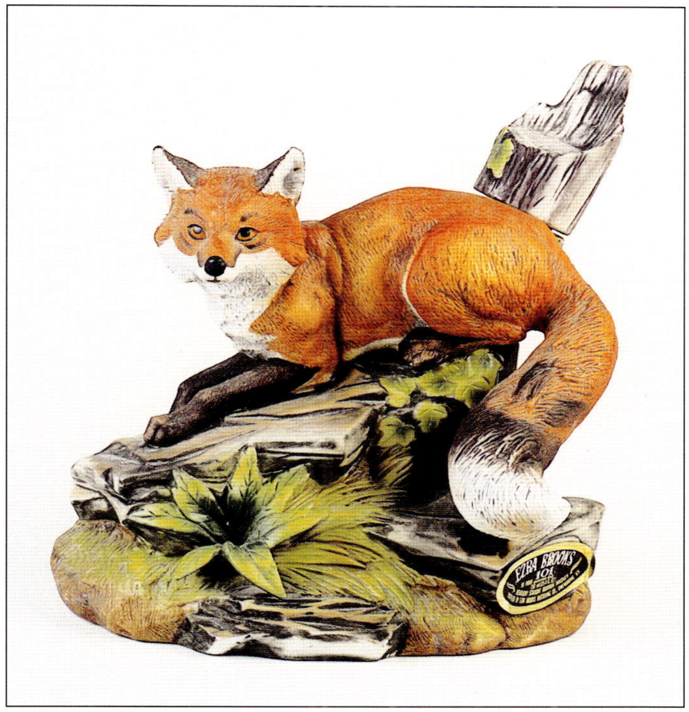

Redtail Fox, 1979, $20-25.

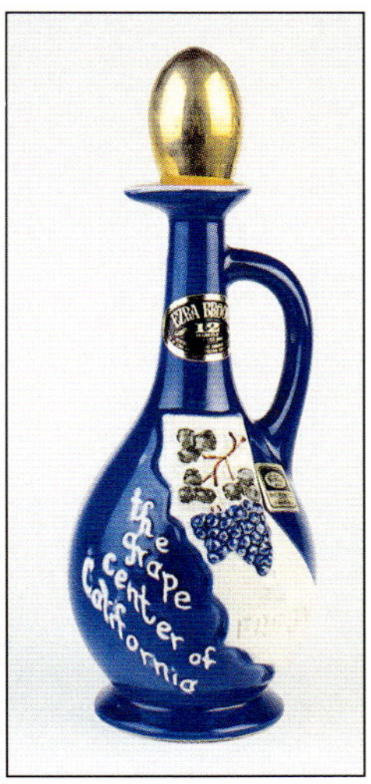

Fresno Grape wine bottle, 1970, $5.

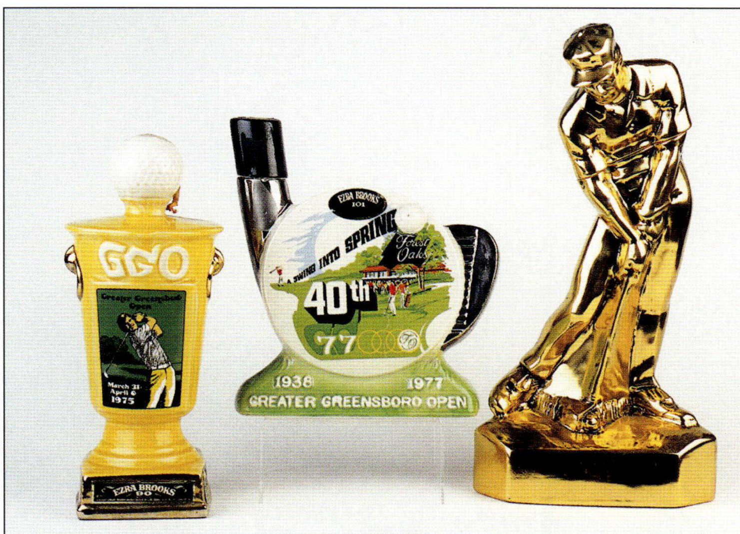

Greensboro Open, 1975, cup, $20-25. Club and ball, 1977, $15-20. Gold golfer, $45-65.

Greensboro Open 1972: green $15-20, gold $45-50; map $15-20; golfer $25-30.

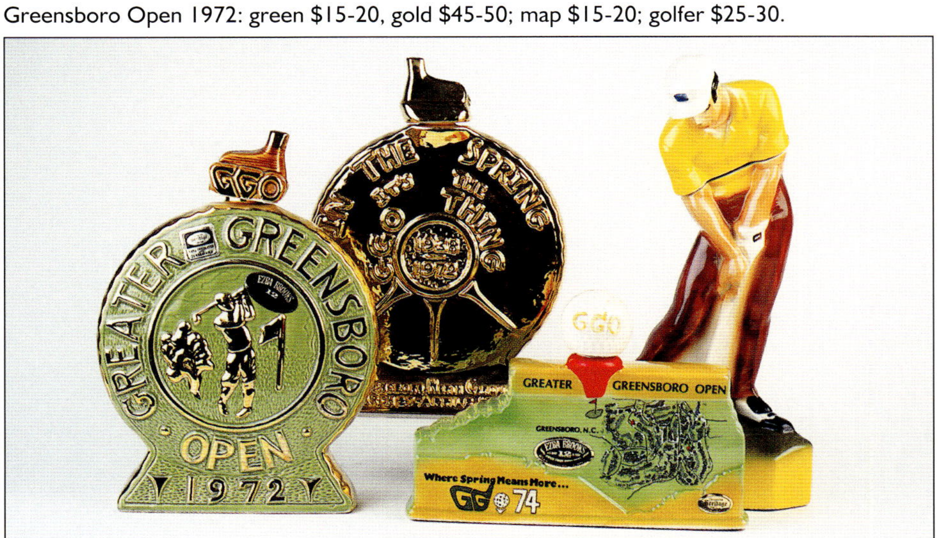

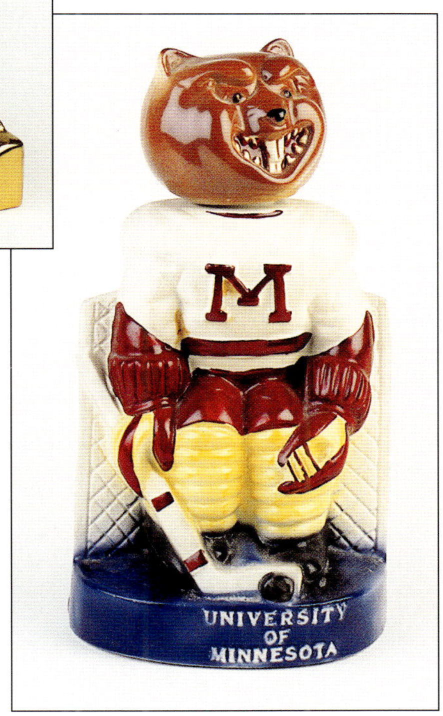

Minnesota Gopher Hockey Player, 1985, $20-25.

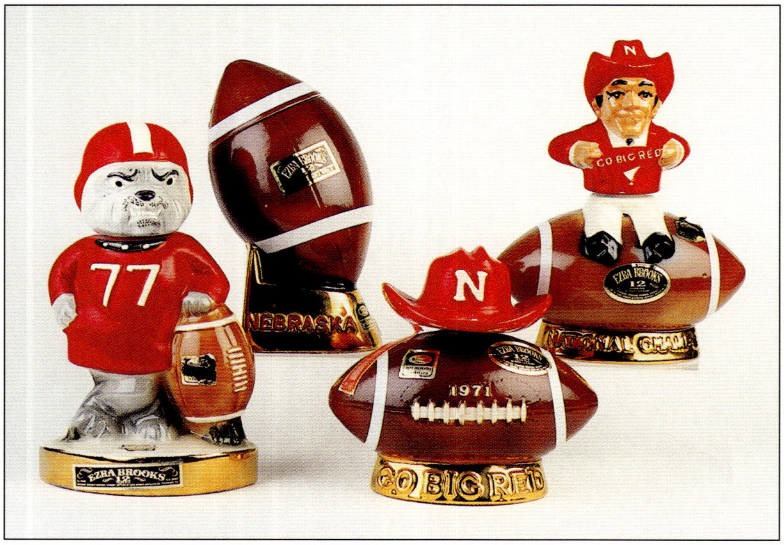

Georgia Bulldog, 1971, $20-30. Go Big Red Football, 1970, $25-30. Red Hat, 1971, $20-30. Big Red Fan, 1972, $30-35.

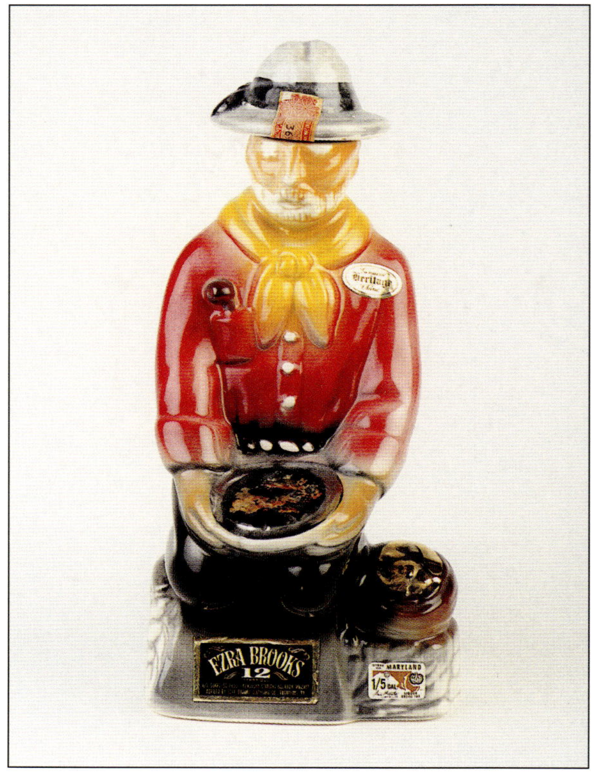

Gold Panner, 1969, $5.

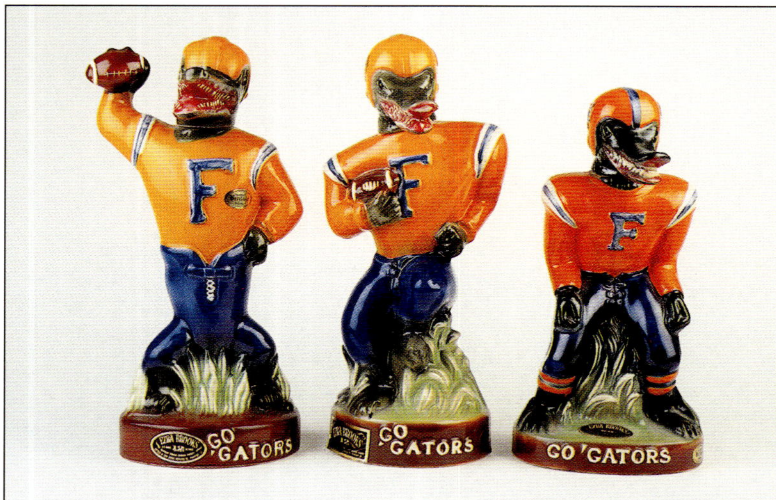

Florida Gator #1 (passing), 1972, $125-150. Gator #2 (running), 1973, $100-125. Gator #3 (blocker), 1975, $125-150.

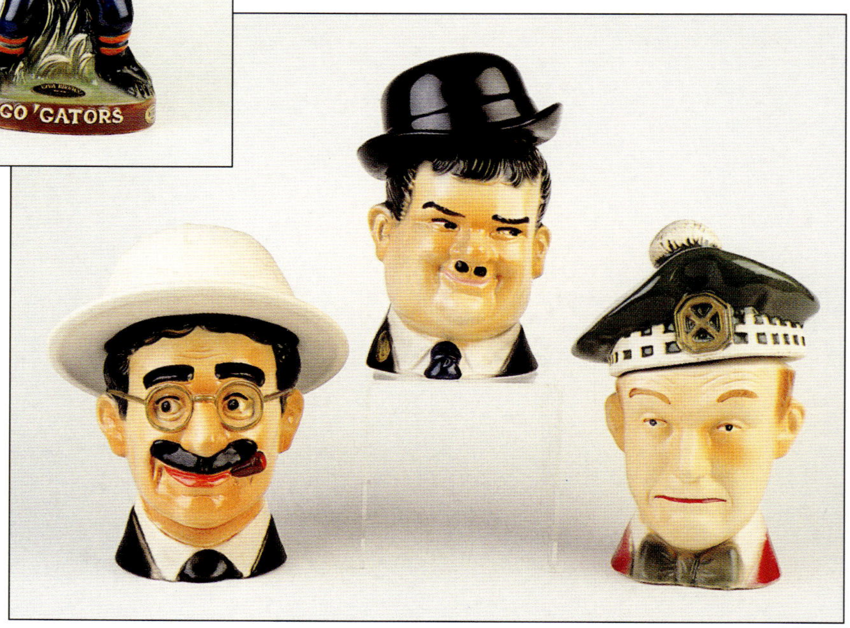

Groucho Marx, 1977, $35-45. Oliver Hardy, 1976, $35-40. Stan Hardy, 1976, $35-40.

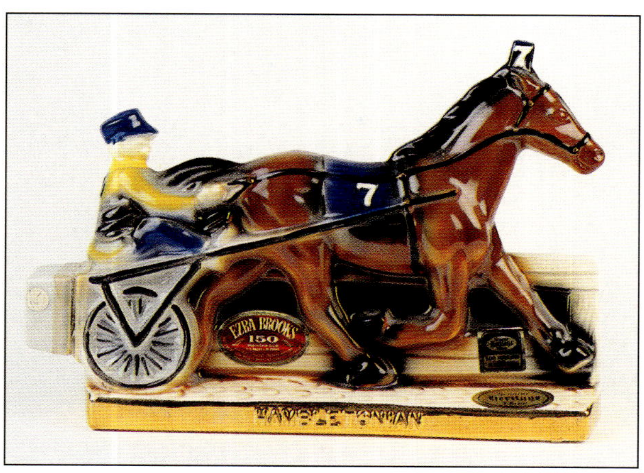

Hambletonian, 1970, $15-20.

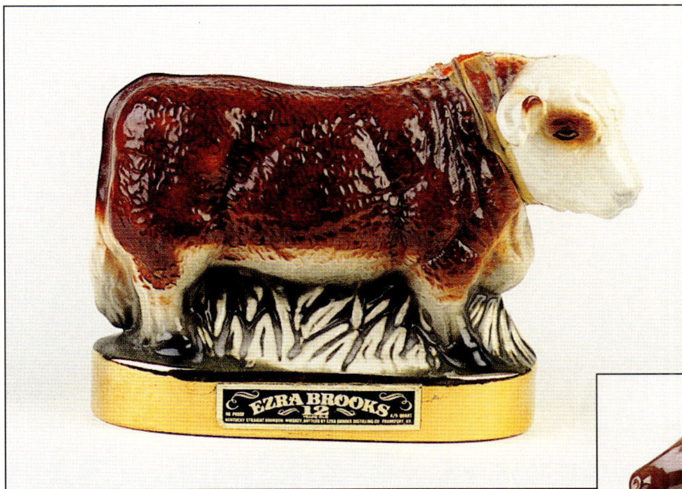

Hereford, 1971, $10.

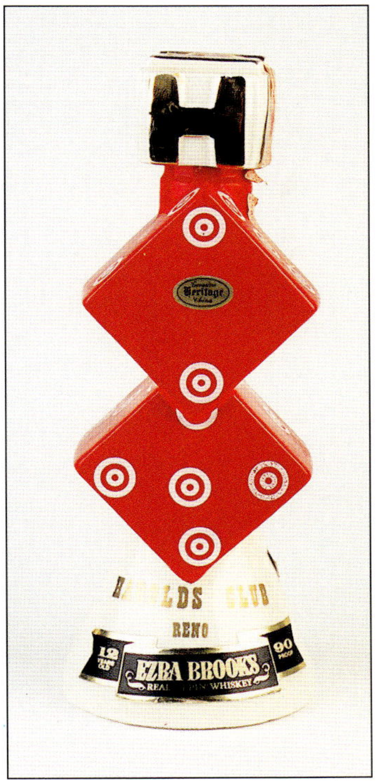

Harolds Club Dice, 1968, $15-20.

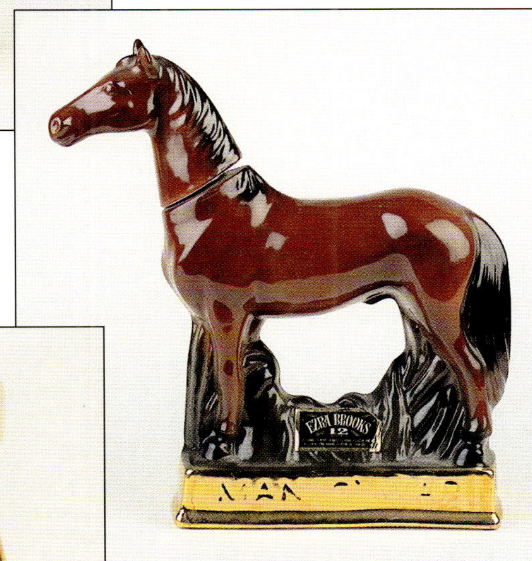

Man O' War, 1969, $10-15.

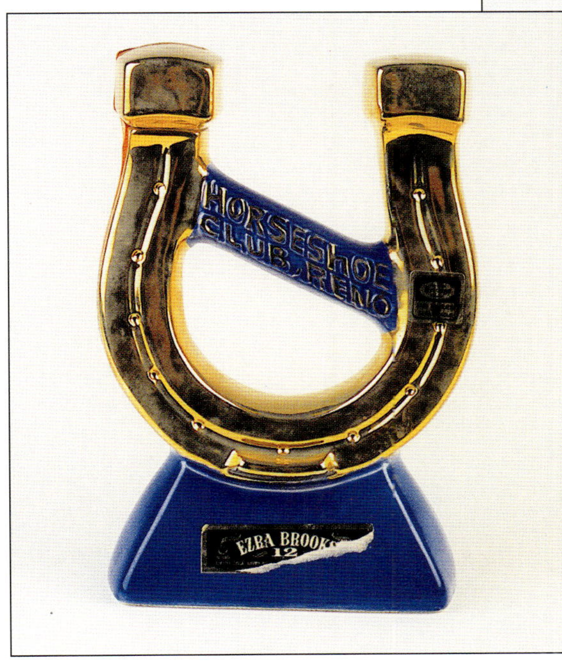

Horseshoe Club, Reno, 1970, $15-20.

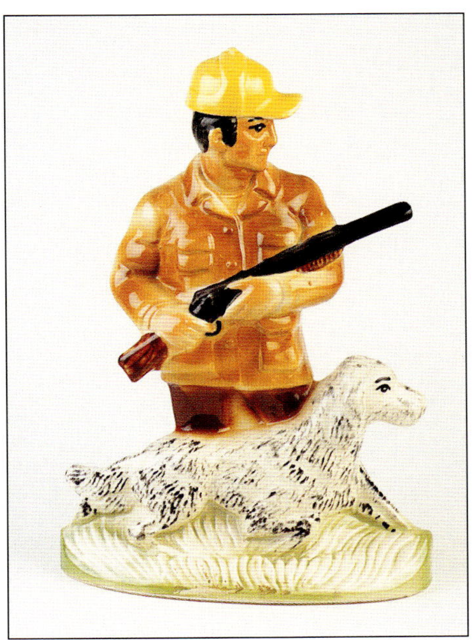

Hunter and Dog, 1973, $10-15.

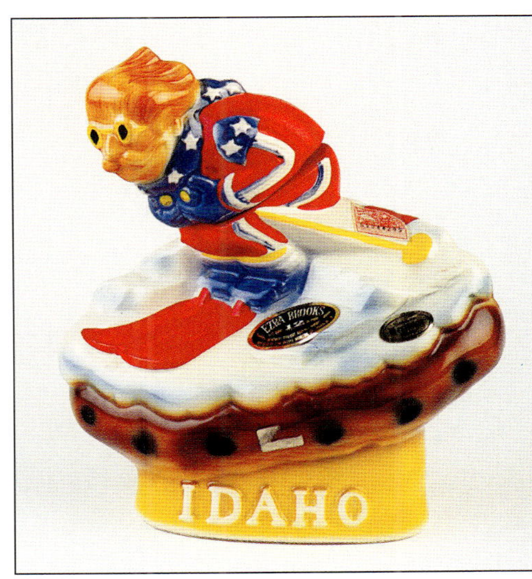

Idaho Skier, 1972, $5.

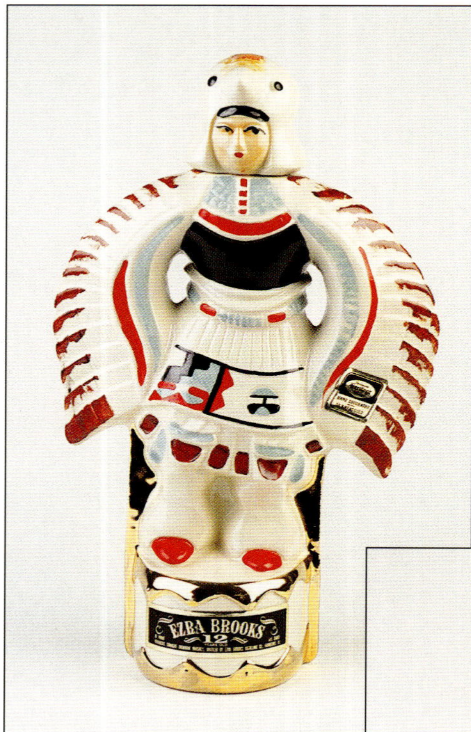

Ceremonial Indian, 1970, $10-15.

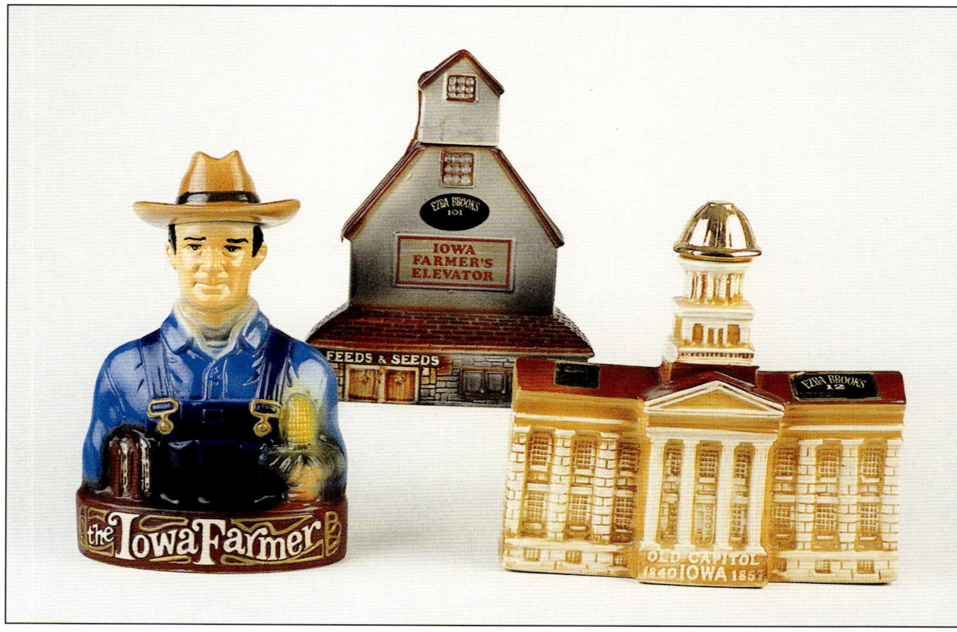

Iowa Farmer, 1977, $10. Iowa Farmers Elevator, 1978, $10-15. Iowa Statehouse, 1971, $15-20.

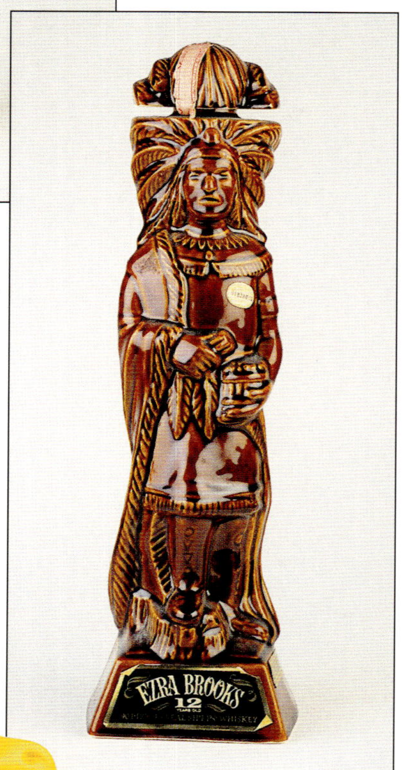

Cigar Store Indian, 1968, $10.

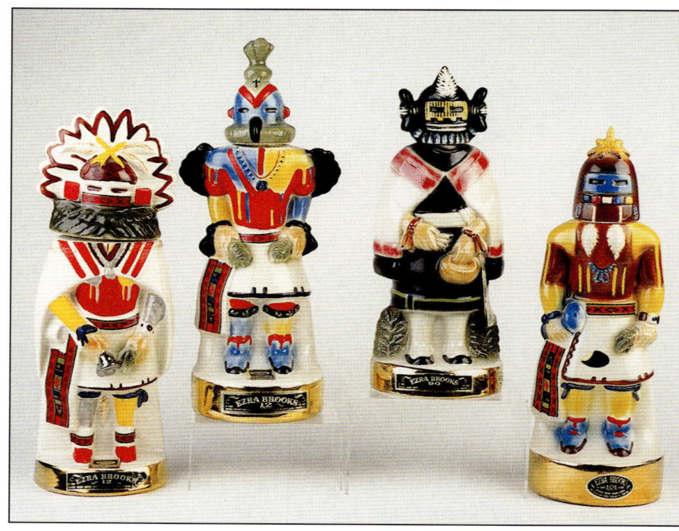

Kachina series: #1 Morning Singer, 1971, $45-50; #2 Hummingbird, 1973, $45-50; #4 Maiden, 1975, $20-25; #5 Longhair, 1976, $30-35.

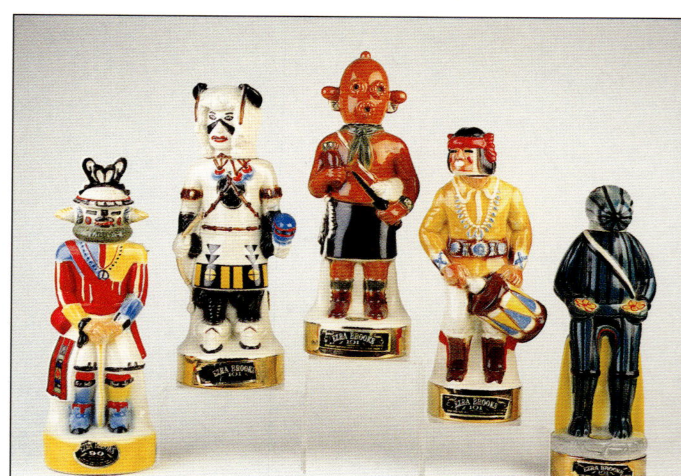

#3 Antelope, 1974, $40-45; #6 Buffalo Dancer, 1977, $30-35; #7 Mudhead, 1978, $30-35; #8 Drummer, 1979, $40-45; #9 Rattlesnake watermelon, 1980, $20-25.

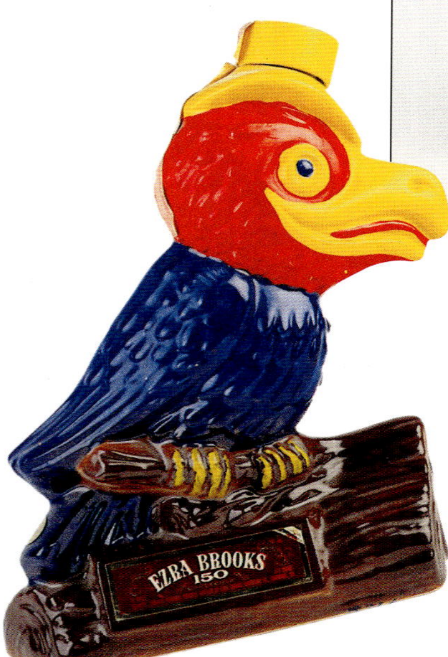

Kansas Jayhawk, 1969, $15-20.

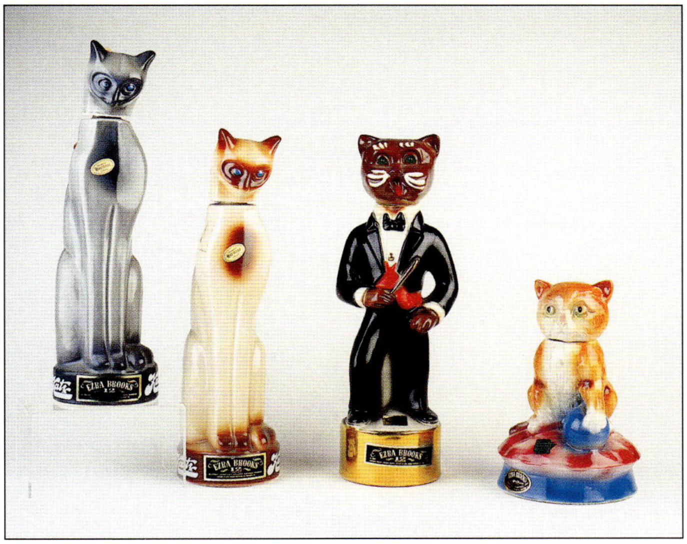

Katz Cat, 1969: gray $5; tan $5. Katz Philharmonic, 1970, $5. Kitten on a Pillow, 1975, $5.

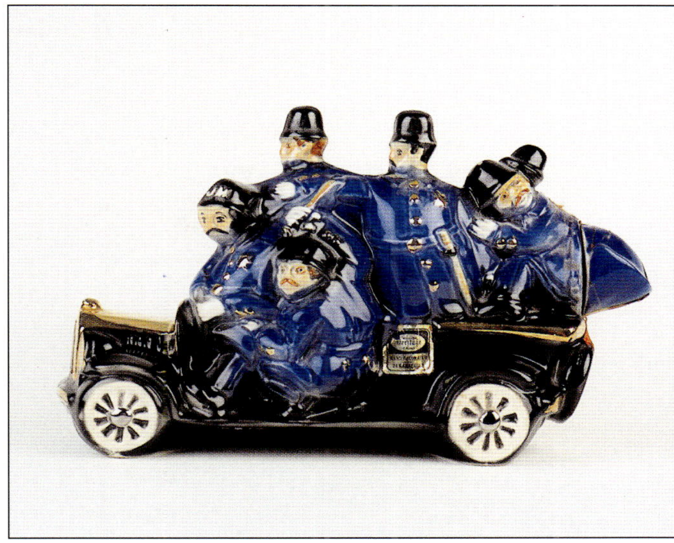

Keystone Cops, 1971, $35-45.

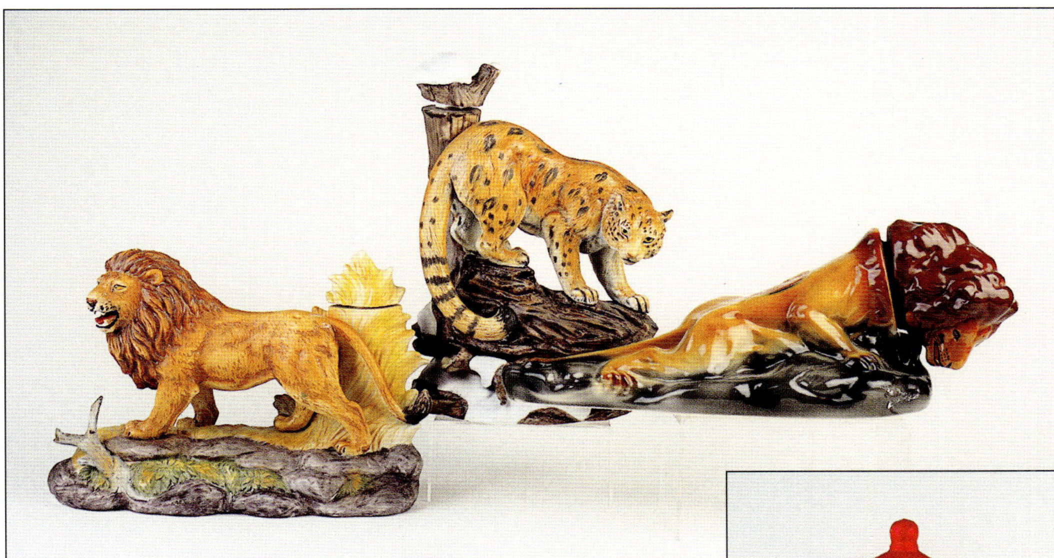

Snow Leopard, 1980, $20-25. African Lion, 1980, $15-20. Lion on a Rock, 1971, $10.

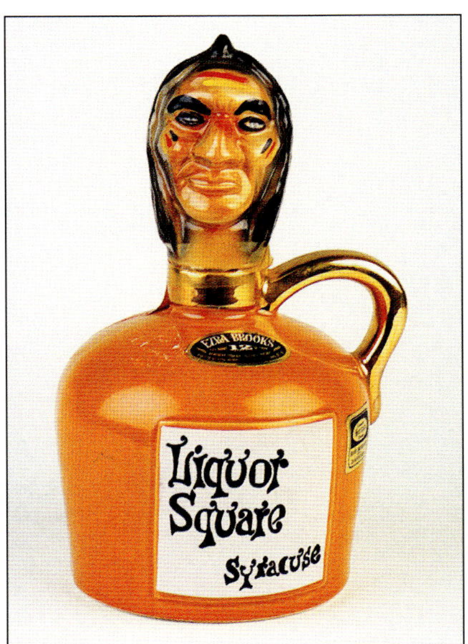

Liquor Square, 1972, $5.

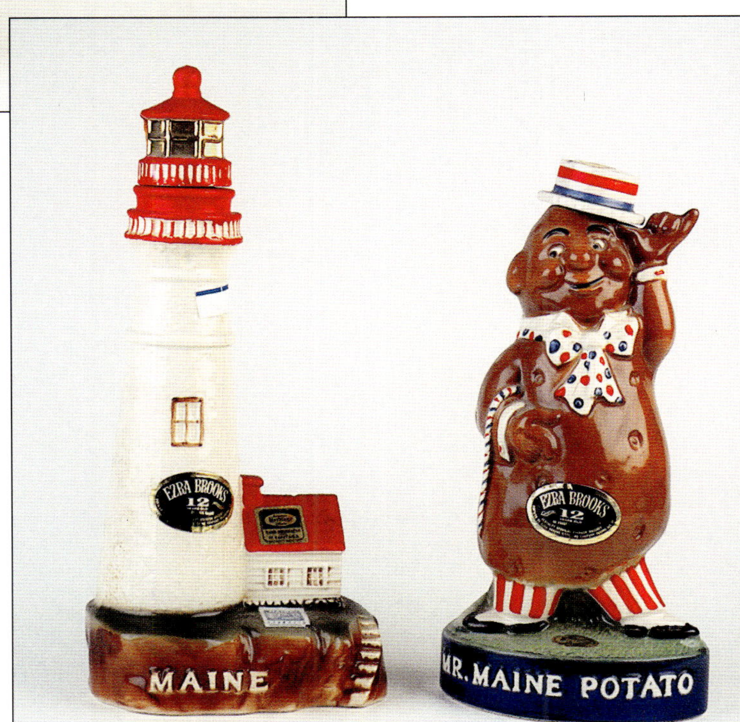

Maine Lighthouse, 1971, $10. Maine Potato, 1973, $10.

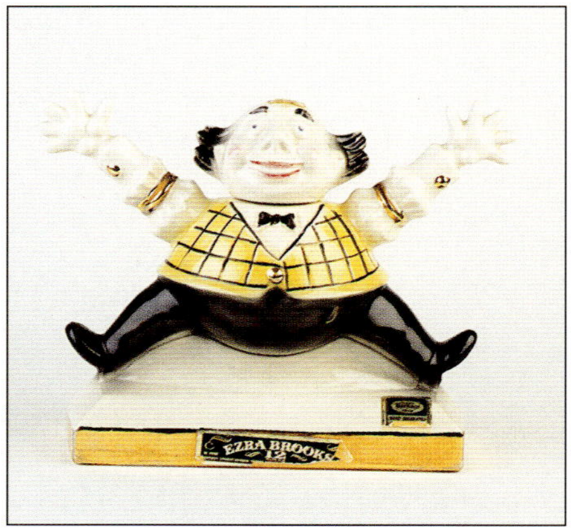

Mr. Merchant, 1970, $5.

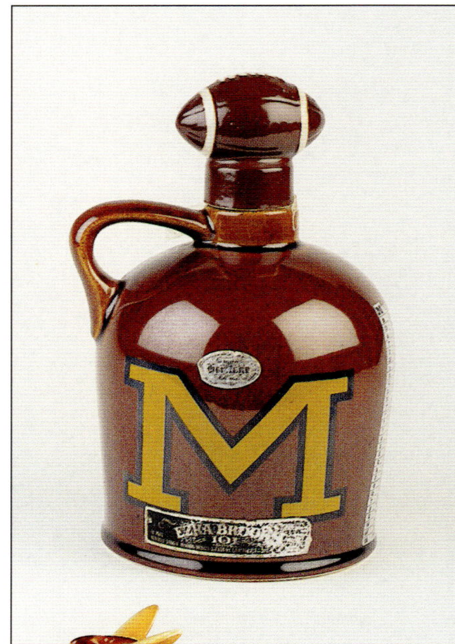

Minnesota and Michigan
Jug, 1974, $10.

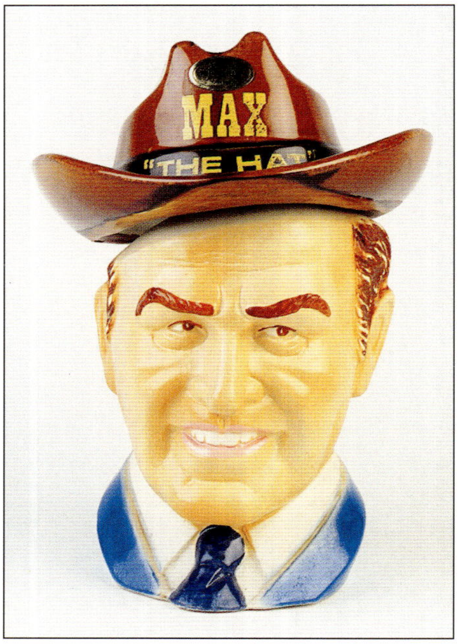

Max "The Hat" Zimmerman, 1976, $10.

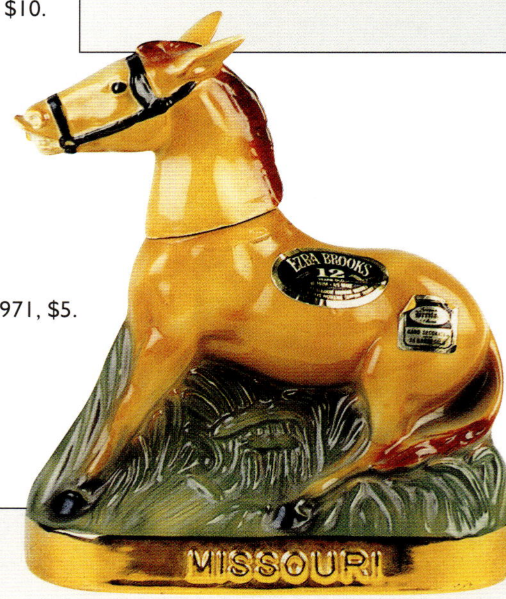

Missouri Mule, 1971, $5.

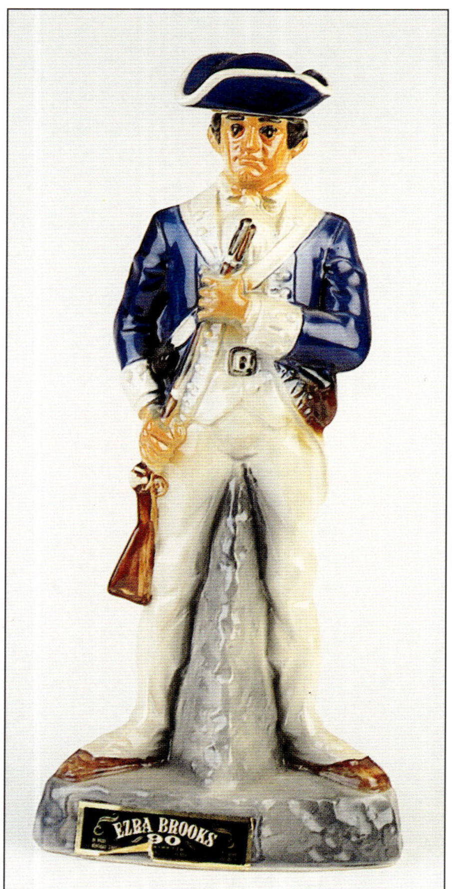

Minuteman, 1975, $10.

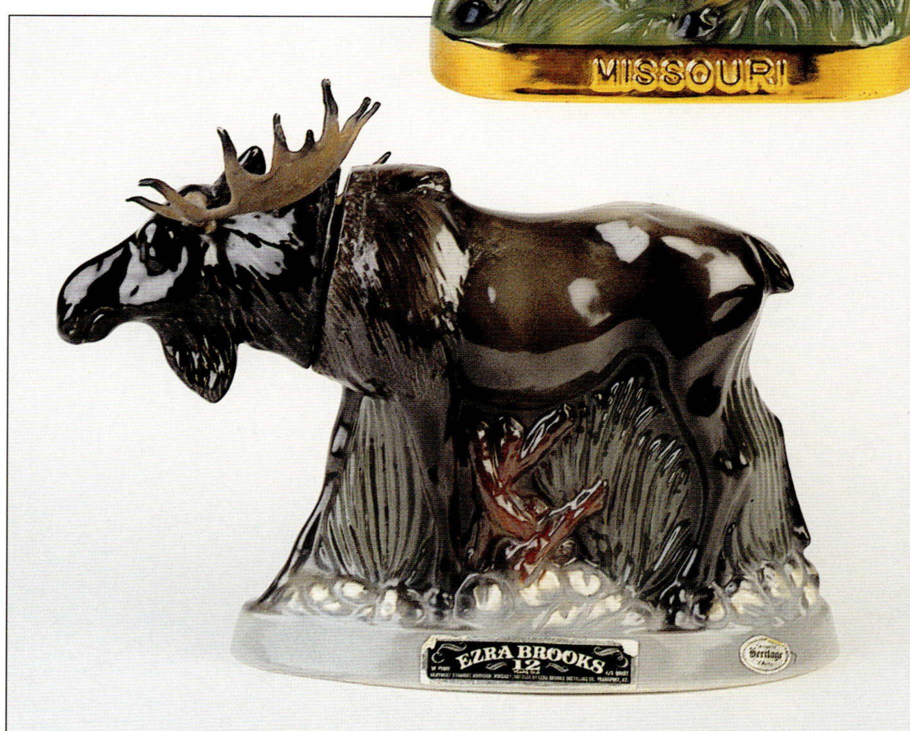

Moose, 1972, $10.

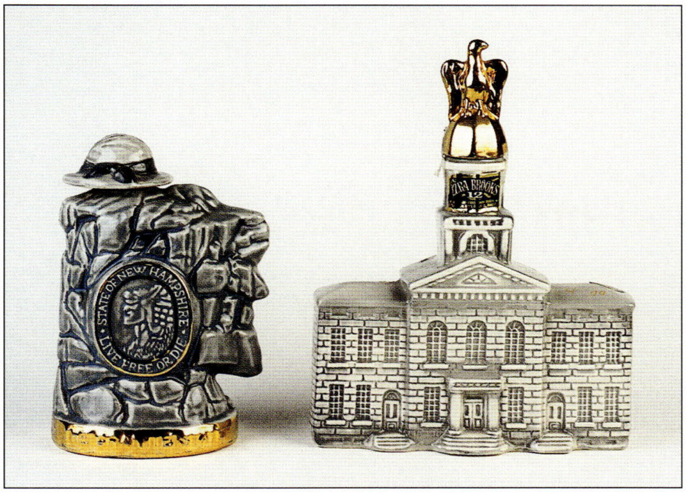

New Hampshire Man on Mountain, 1970, $5.
New Hampshire State House, 1969, $5.

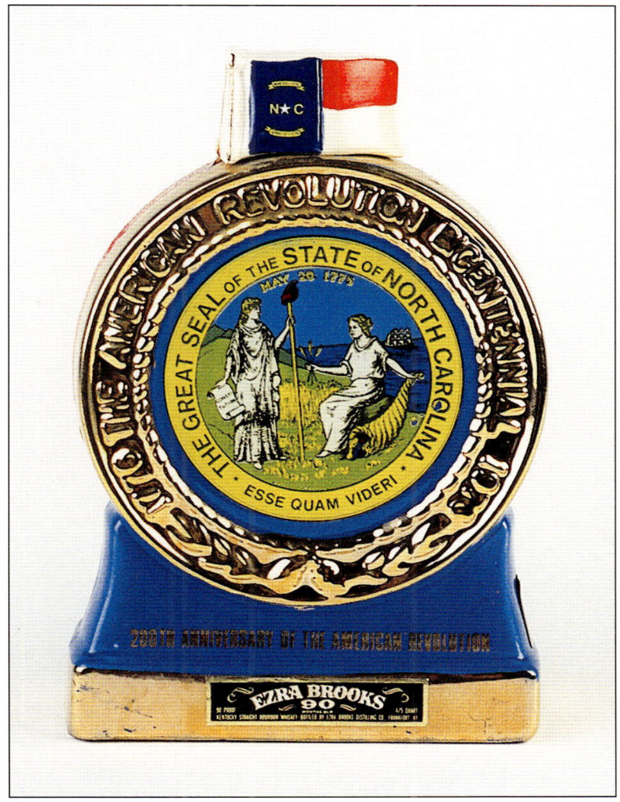

North Carolina Bicentennial, 1975, $10.

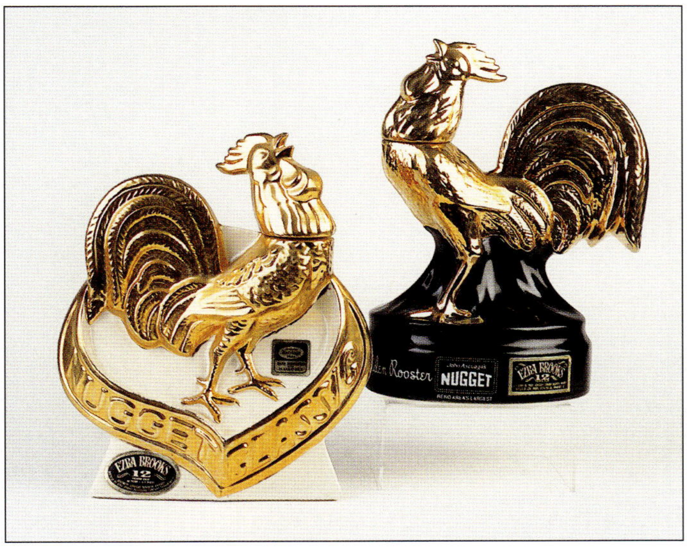

Casino bottles: Nugget Classic, 1970, $10-15; Nugget Rooster, 1969, $10-15.

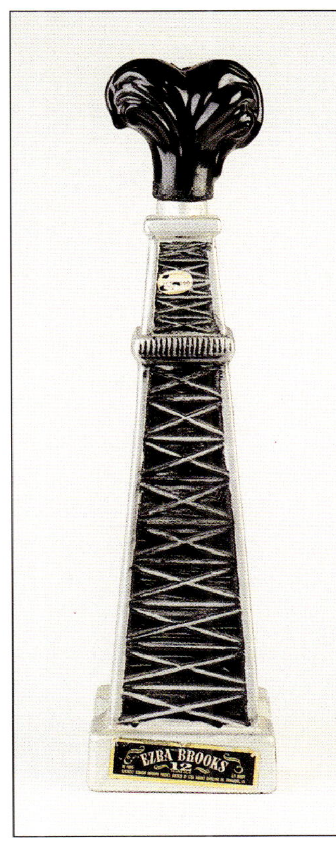

Oil Gusher, 1969, $5.

Panda, 1972, $10. Penguin, 1973, $10. Phonograph, 1970, $5. Pirate, 1971, $10.

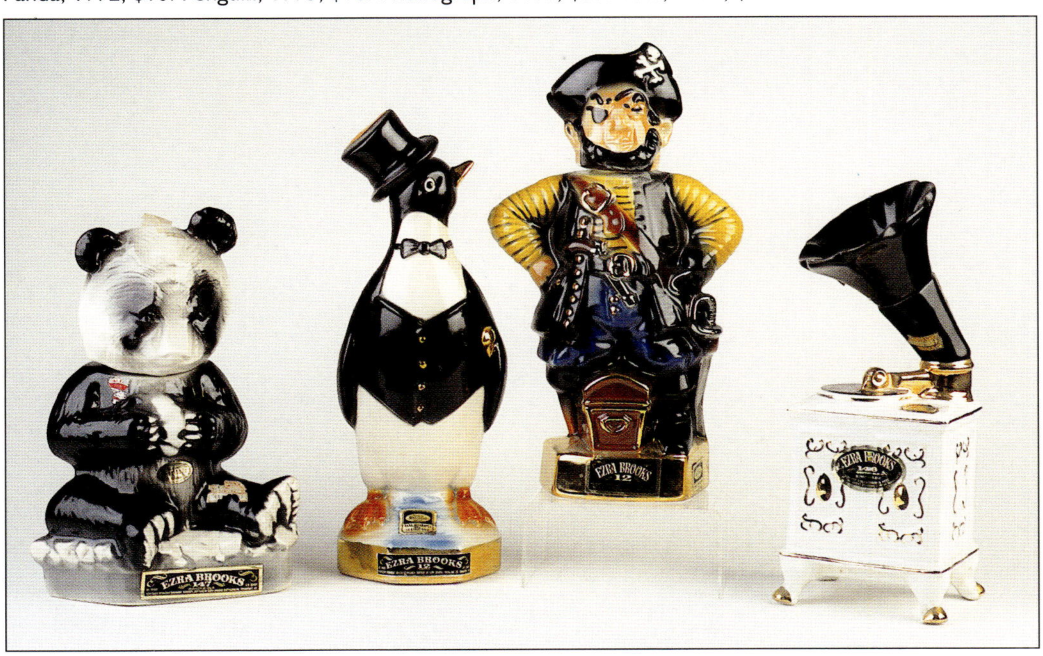

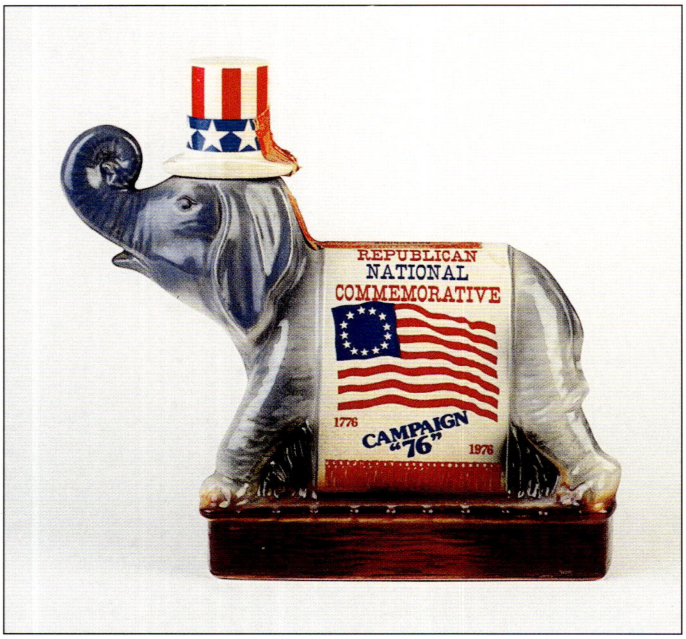

Political Elephant, Kansas City, 1976, $10. Political Donkey, New York (not shown), 1976, $10.

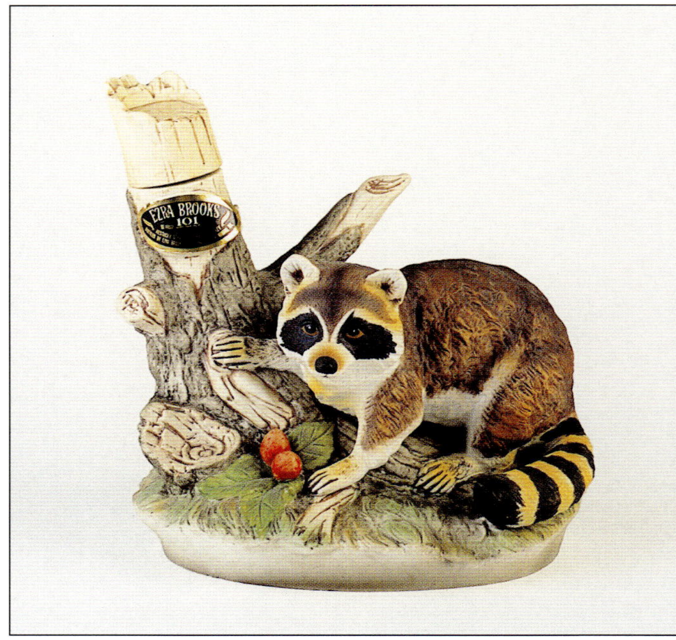

Northern Raccoon, 1978, $10-15.

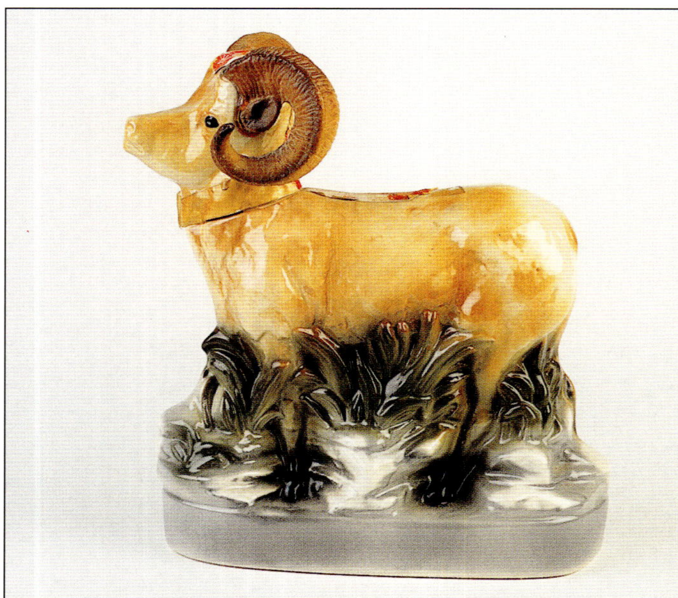

Ram, 1972, $10.

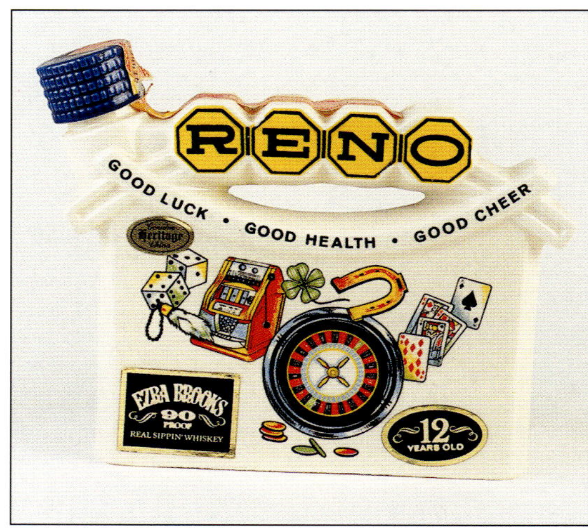

Casino series: Reno Arch, 1968, $10.

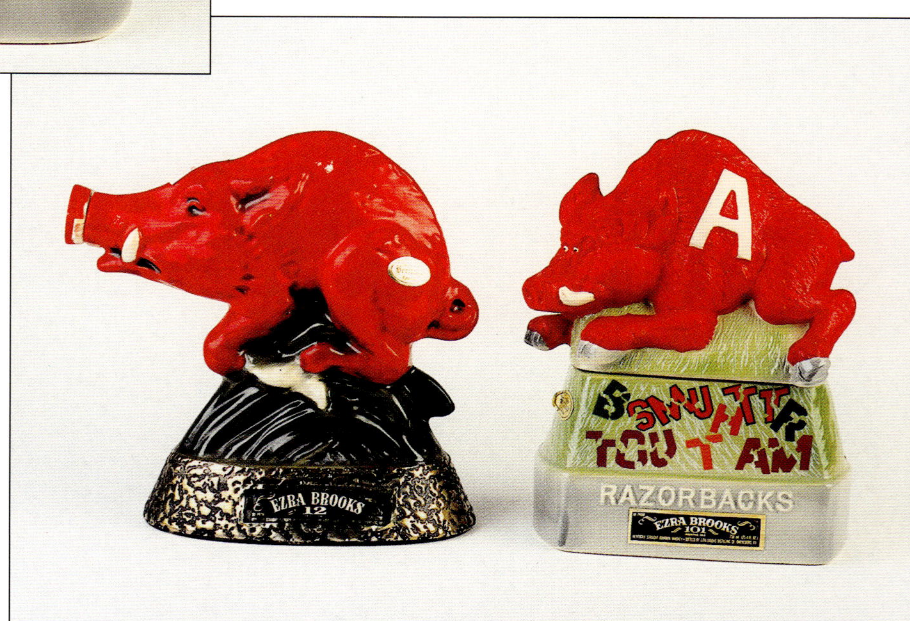

Razorback Hog, 1969, $10. Arkansas Razorback, 1979, $10.

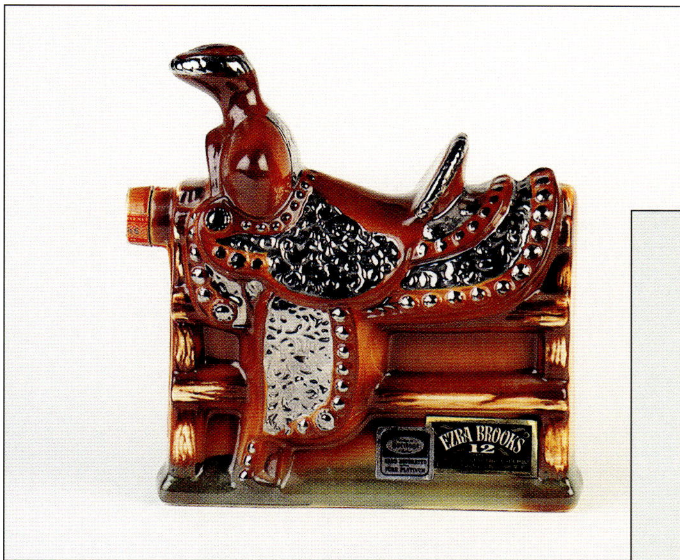

Saddle (silver), 1972, $10.

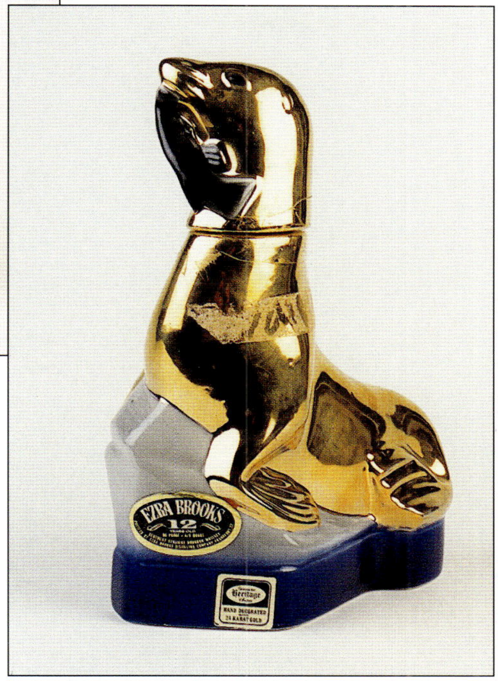

Seal (gold), 1972, $10.

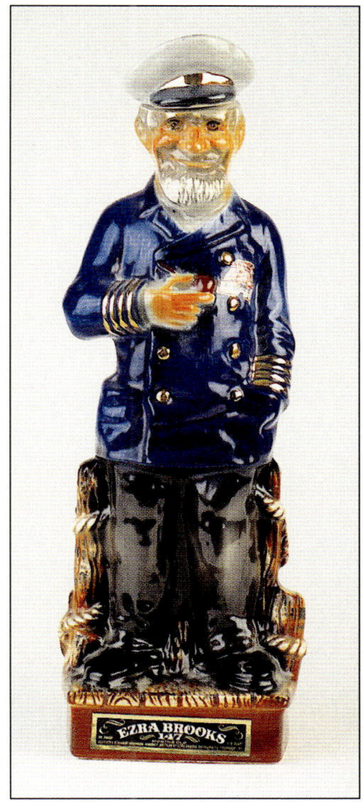

Sea Captain, 1971, $10.

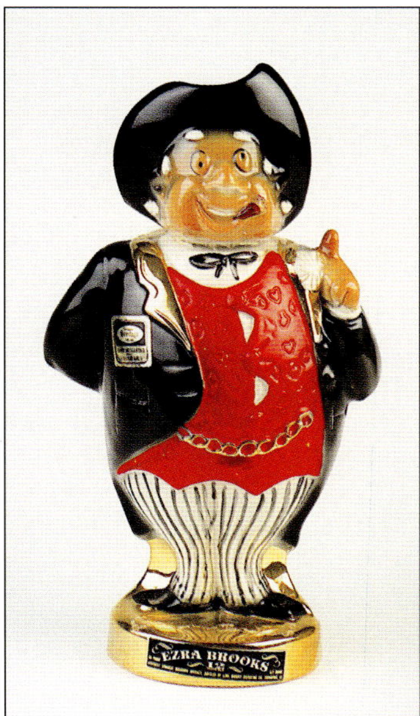

Senator, 1971, $10.

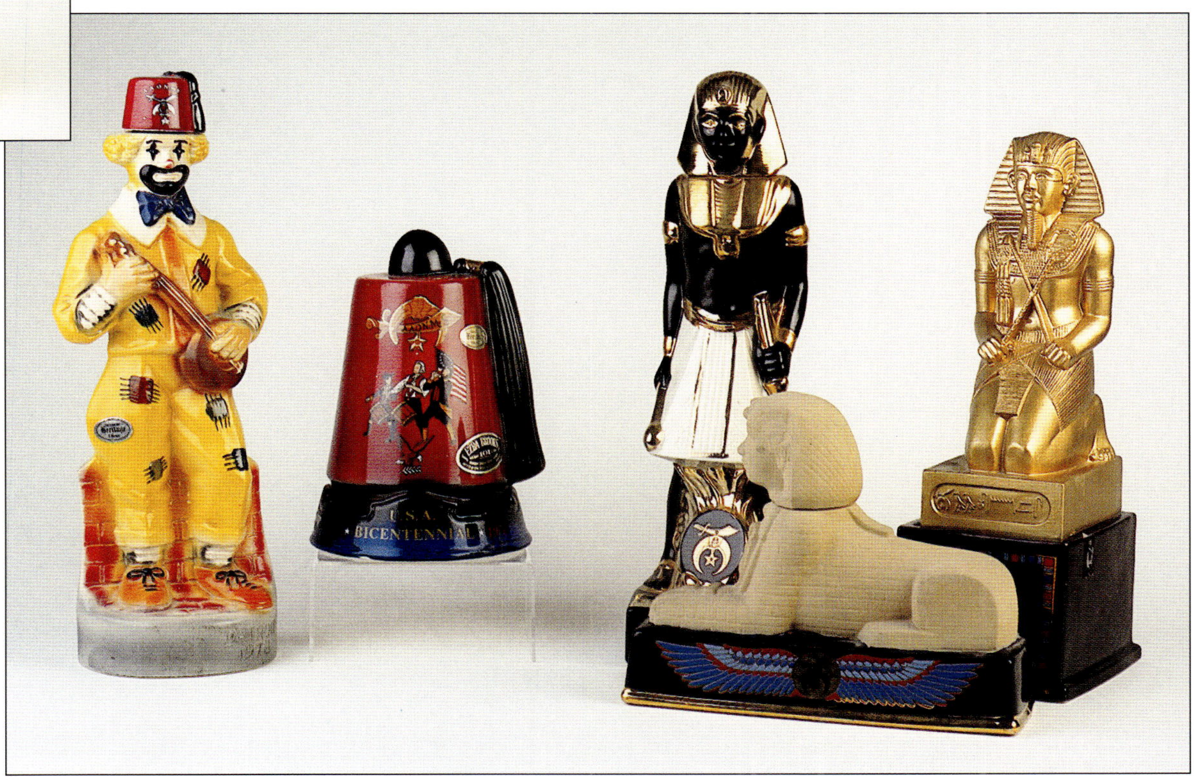

Clown, 1976, $15-20; Fez, 1976, $15-20; Golden Pharaoh, 1981, $20-25; King Tut Guard, 1979, $20-25; Sphinx, 1980, $15-20.

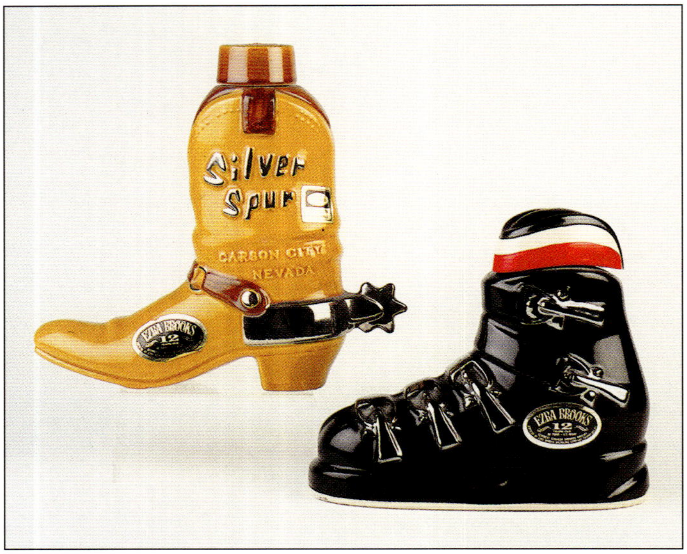

Silver Spur Boot, 1971, $10. Ski Boot, 1972, $5.

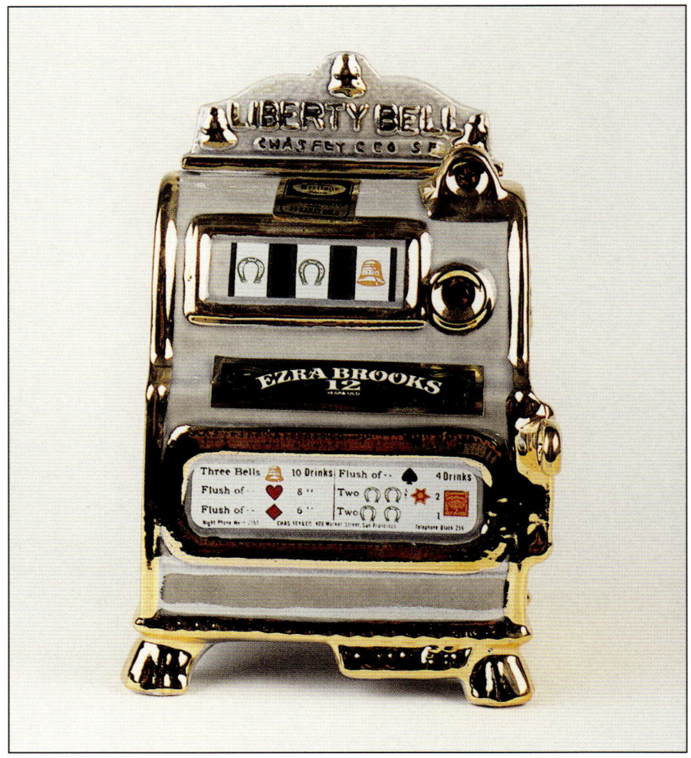

Slot Machine, 1971, $10-15.

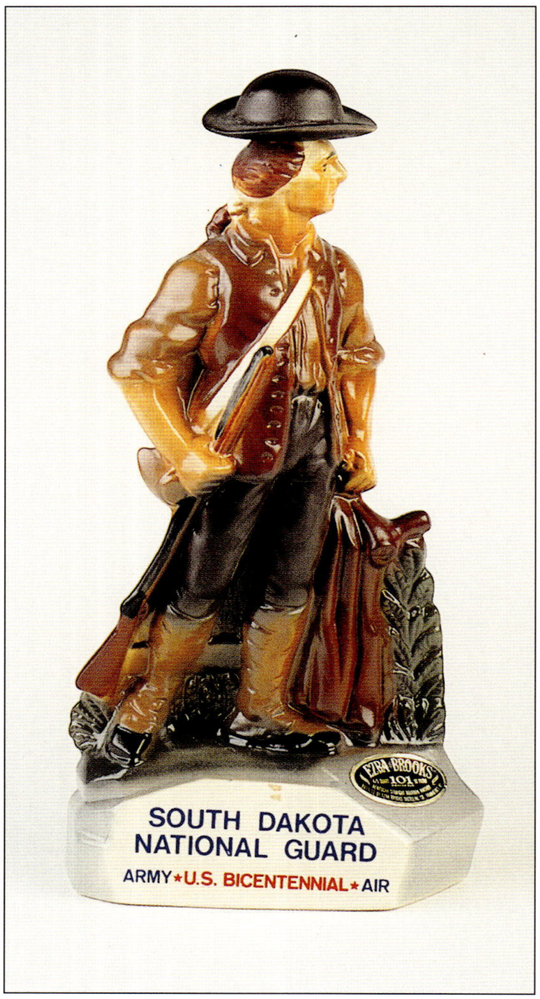

South Dakota National Guard, 1976, $10.

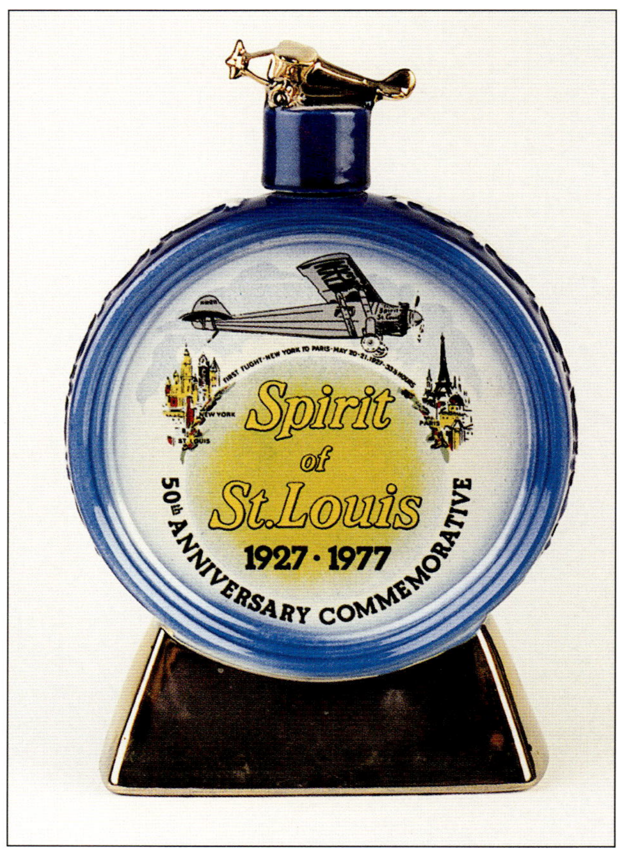

Spirit of St. Louis, 1977, $20-25.

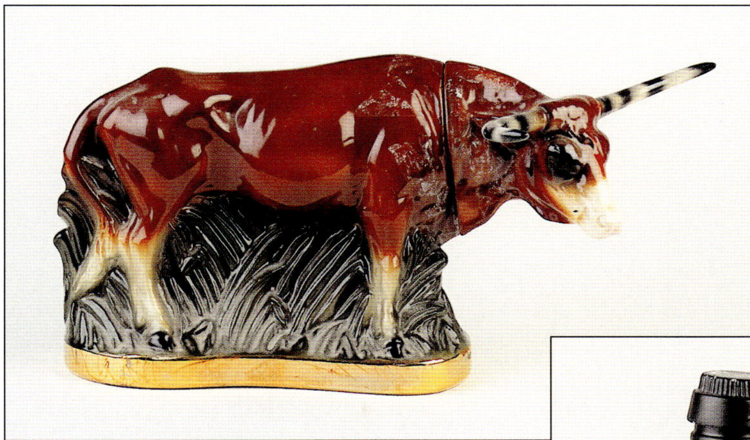

Longhorn Steer, 1971, $10-15.

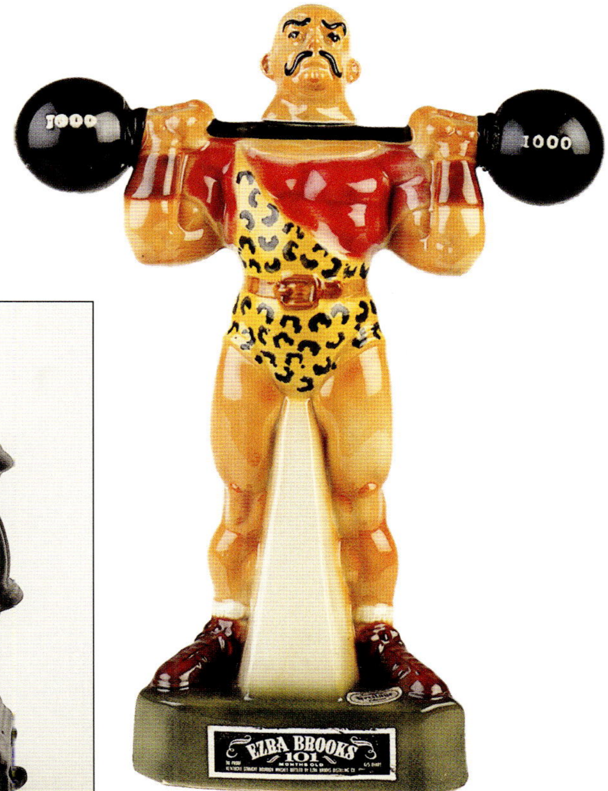

Strongman, 1974, $15-20.

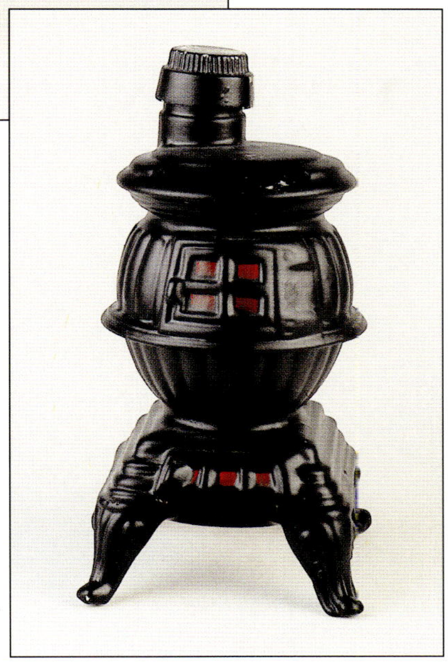

Pot Belly Stove, 1968, $5.

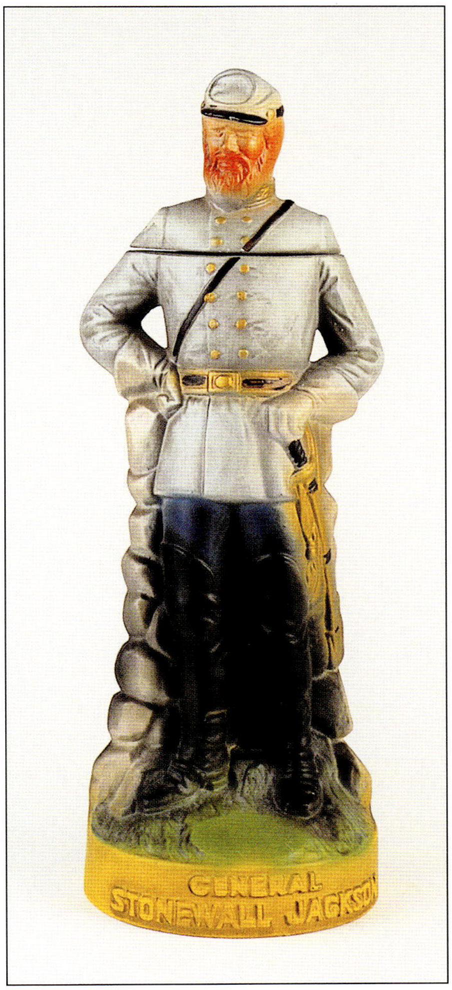

Stonewall Jackson, 1974, $15-20.

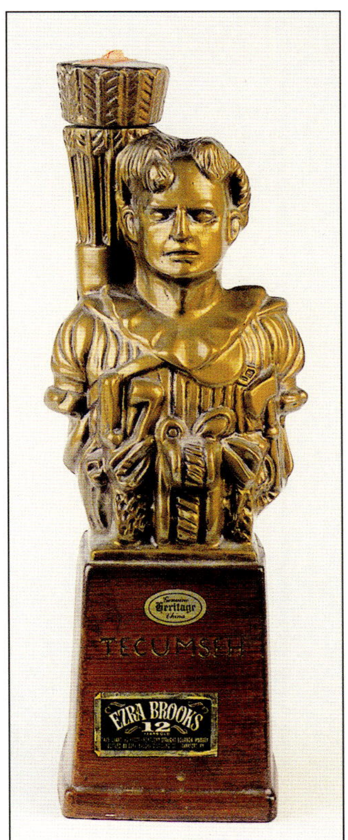

Tecumseh, 1969, $5.

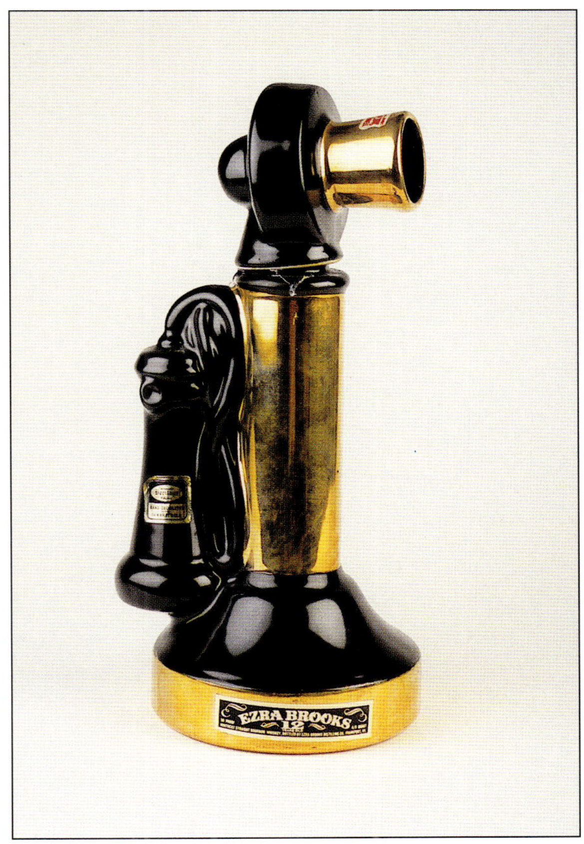

Telephone, 1974, $10.

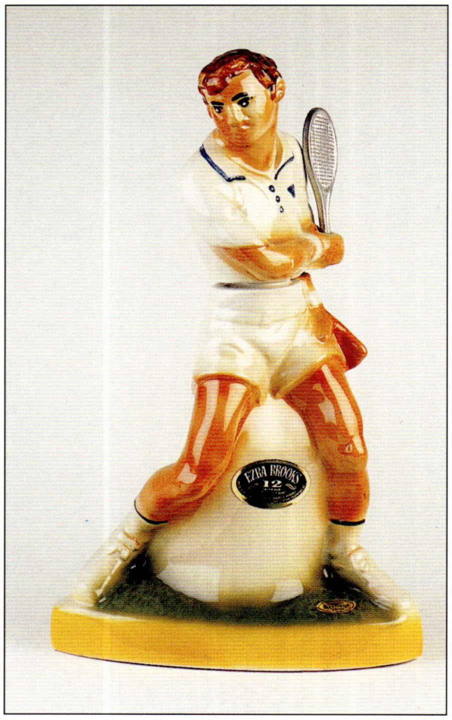

Tennis Player, 1973, $10-15.

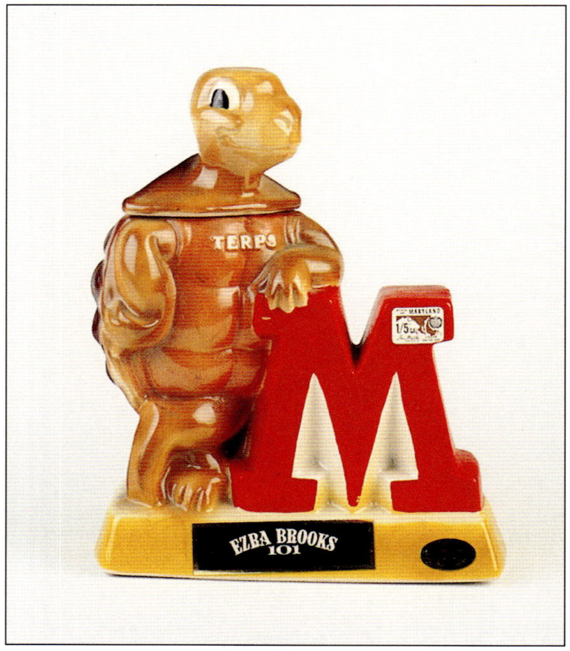

Maryland Terps, 1974, $20-25.

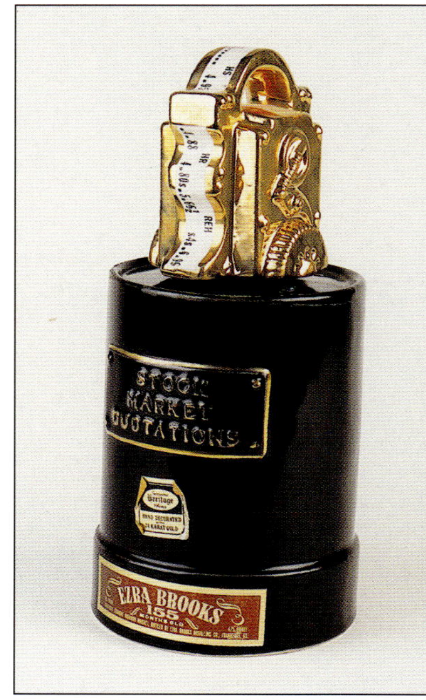

Ticker Tape, 1970, $5.

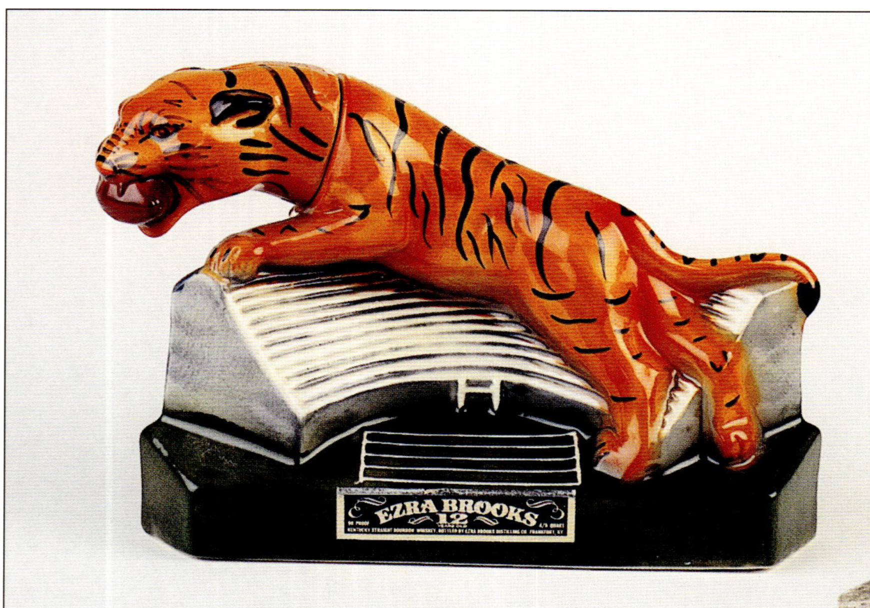

Tiger on a Stadium, 1973, $20-25.

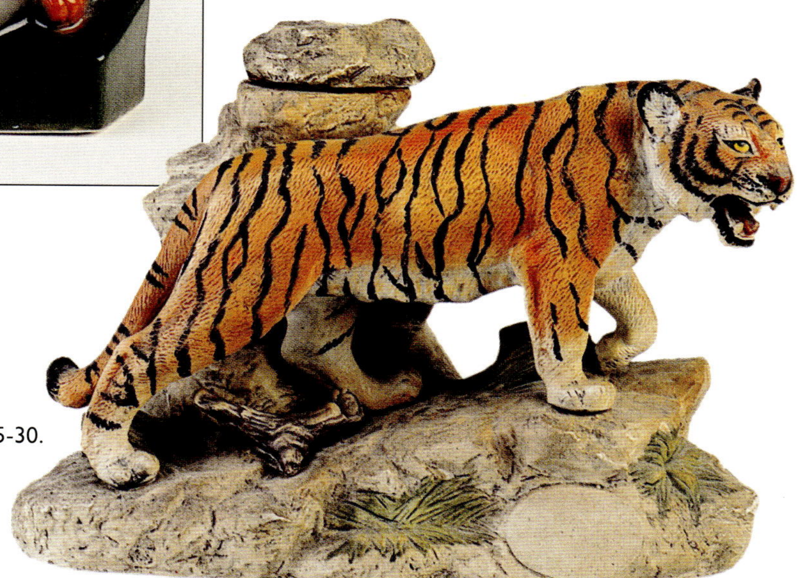

Bengal Tiger, 1979, $25-30.

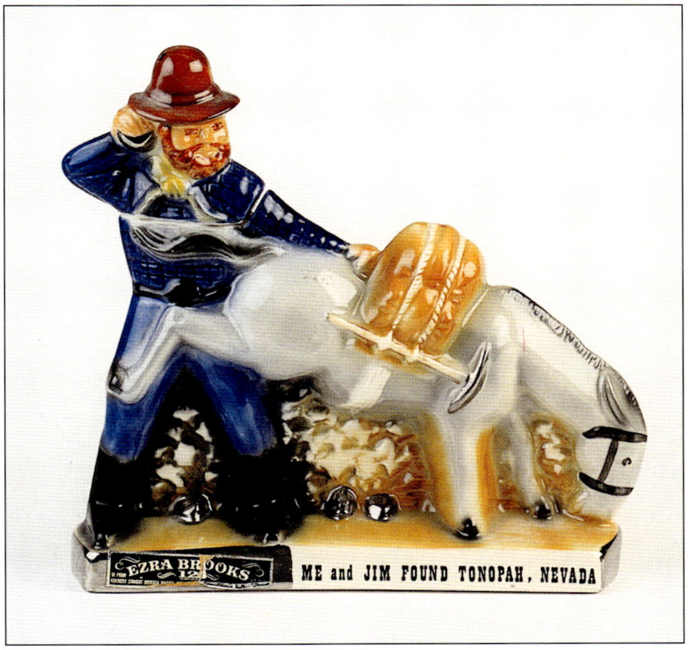

Tonopah, Nevada, 1972, $10.

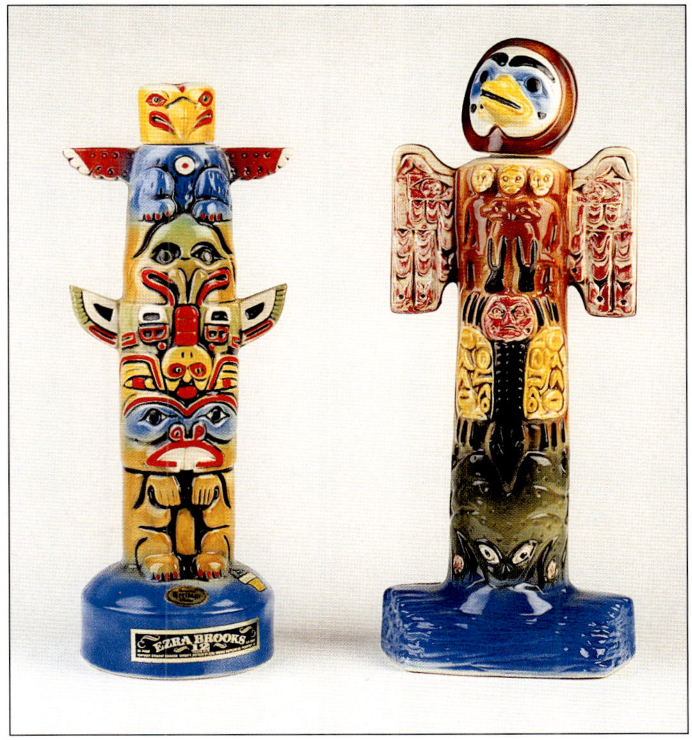

Totem Pole #1, 1972, $10-15. Totem Pole #2, 1973, $10-15.

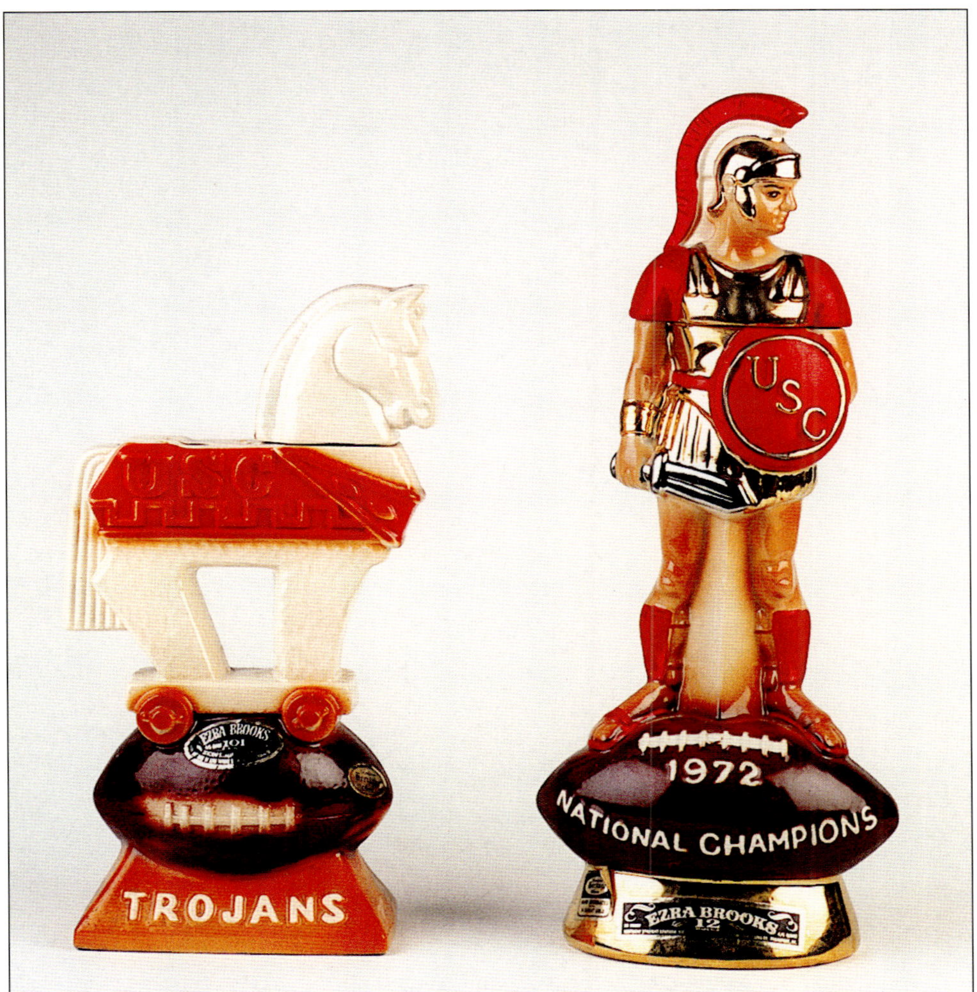

Trojan Horse, 1974, $25-30. USC Trojan, 1973, $25-30.

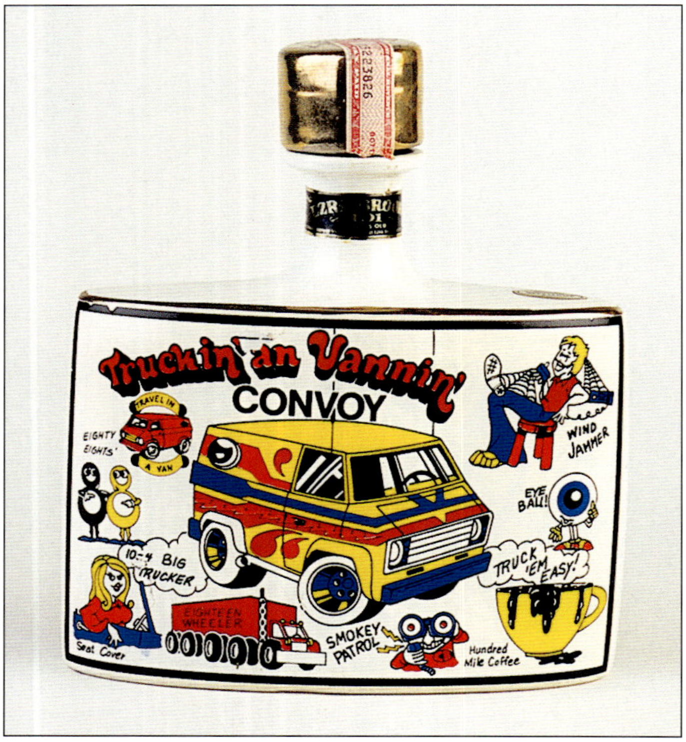

Convoy, Truckin' an Vannin', 1976, $5.

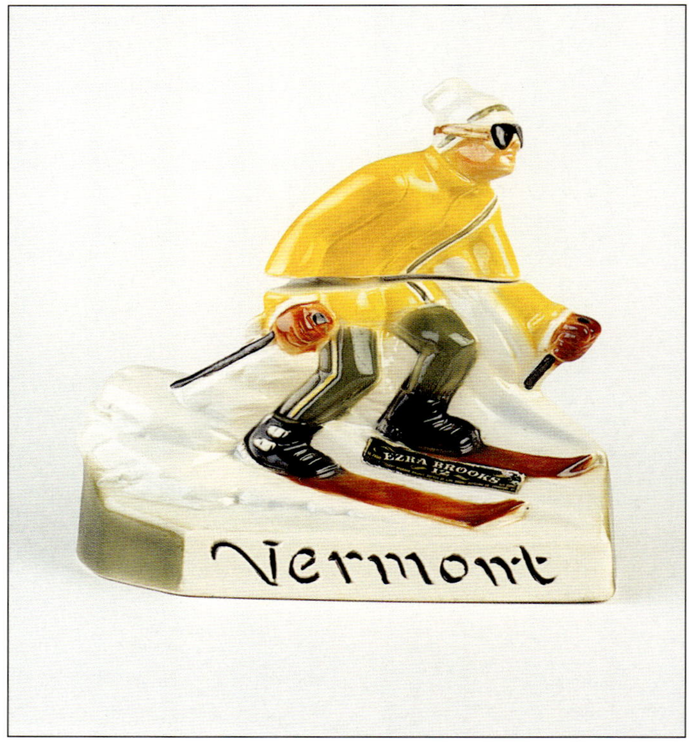

Vermont Skier, 1972, $10.

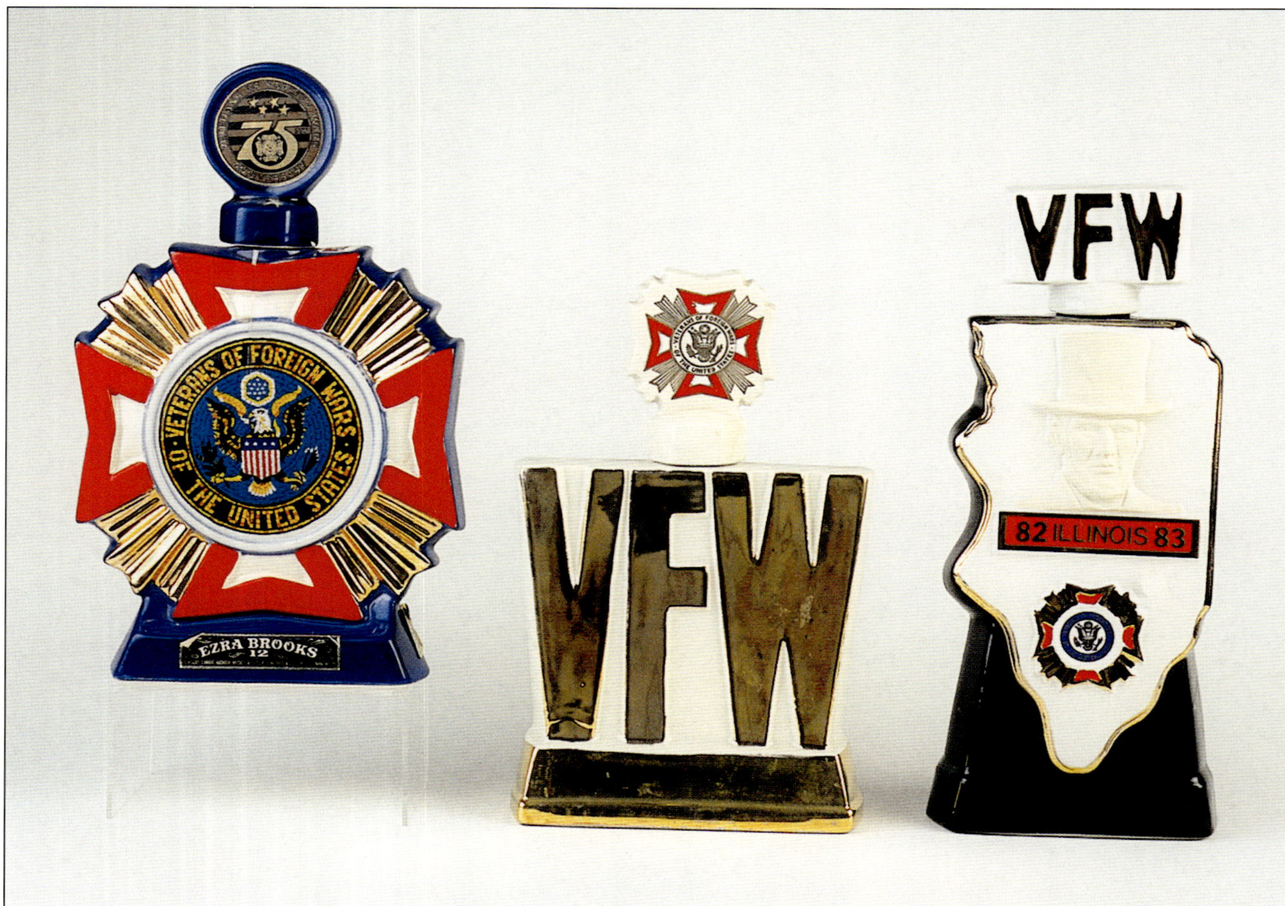

V.F.W., 1973, $10. V.F.W., 1974, $10. V.F.W., 1983, $10. Illinois (not shown), 1982, $10.

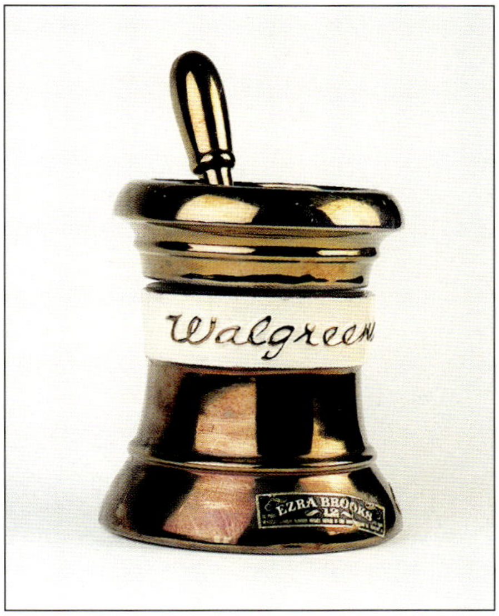

Walgreen Drugs, 1973, $5.

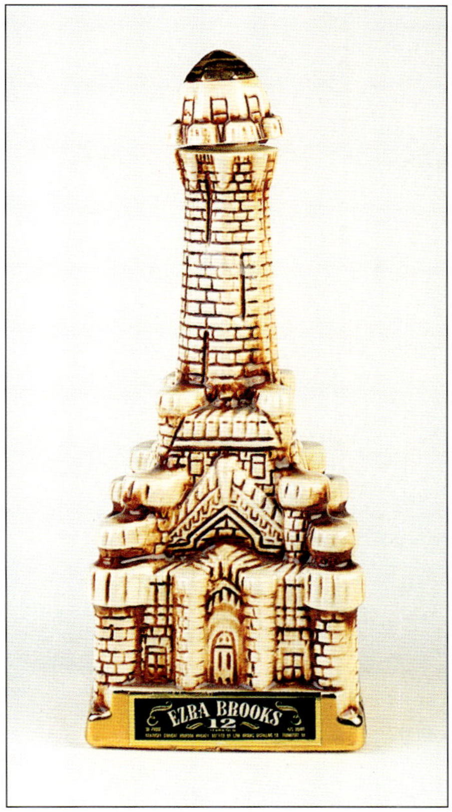

Water Tower, Chicago, 1969, $10.

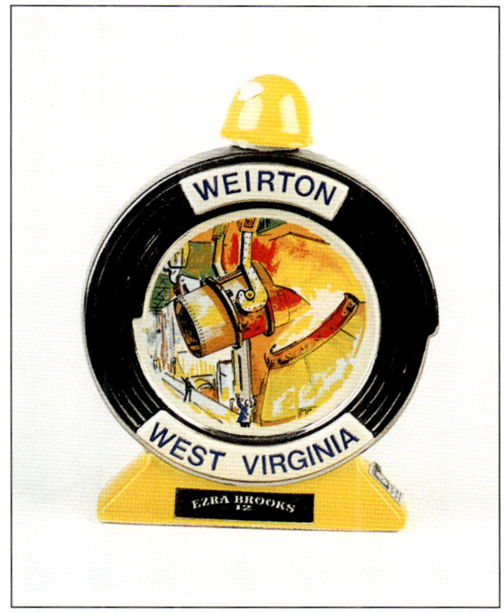

Weirton Steel, 1973, $5.

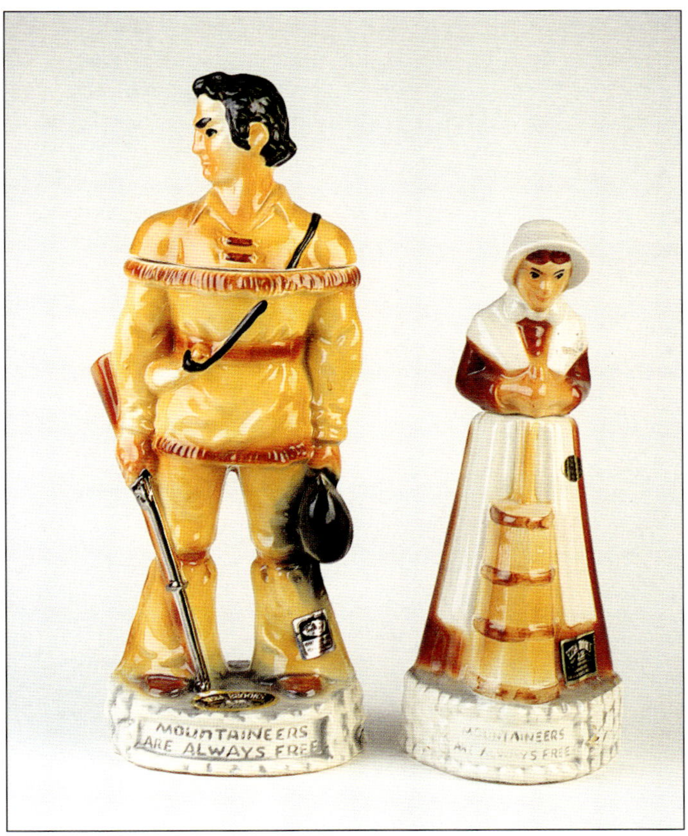

West Virginia Man, 1972, $20-25. West Virginia Woman, 1970, $10.

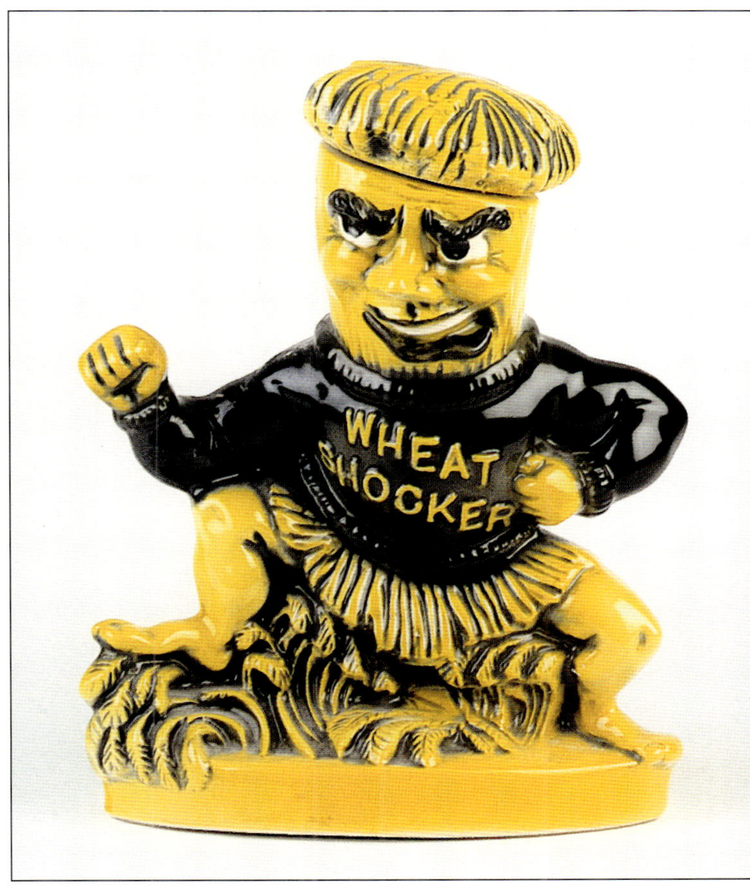

Kansas Wheat Shocker, 1971, $10.

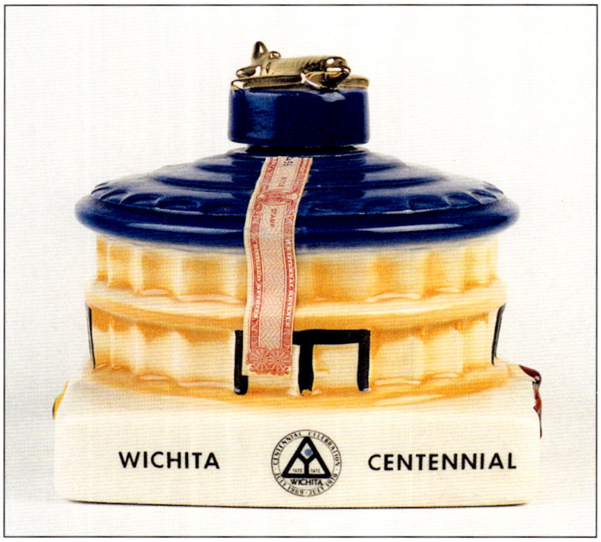

Wichita Centennial, 1970, $10.

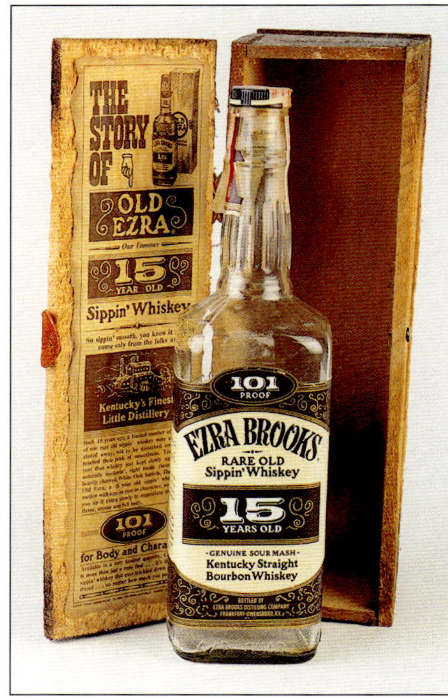

Ezra Brooks Sippin' Whiskey, 1976, $10.

Winston Churchill, 1969, $10.

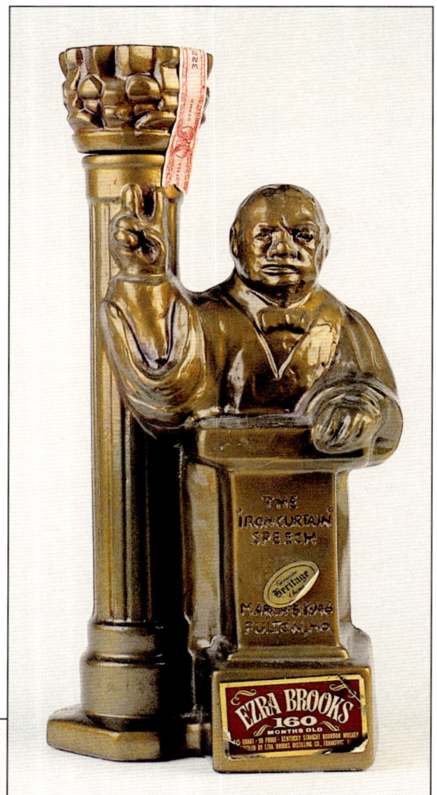

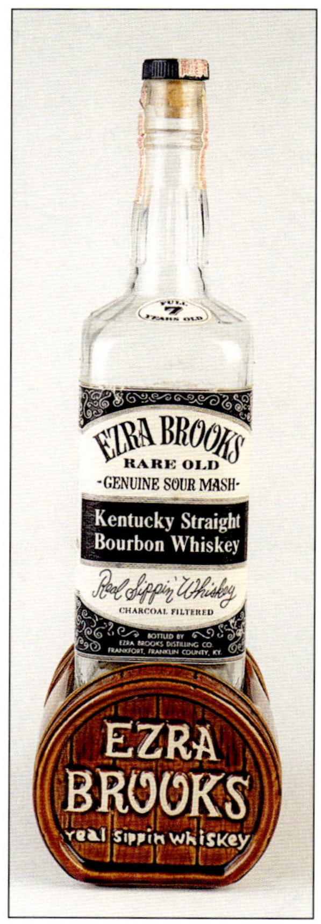

Ezra Brooks, back bar piece, $20-25.

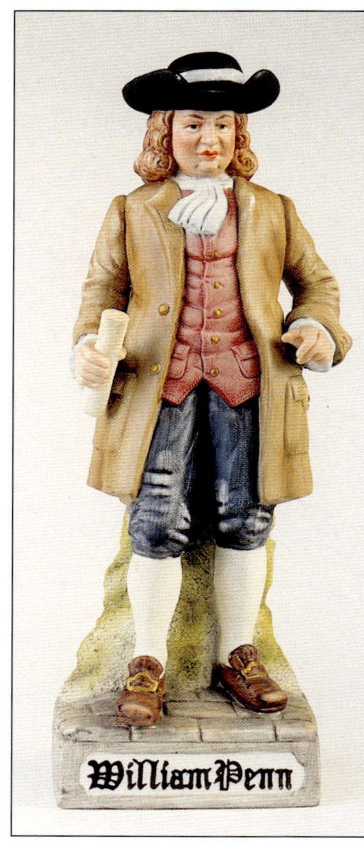

William Penn 1981, $10-15.

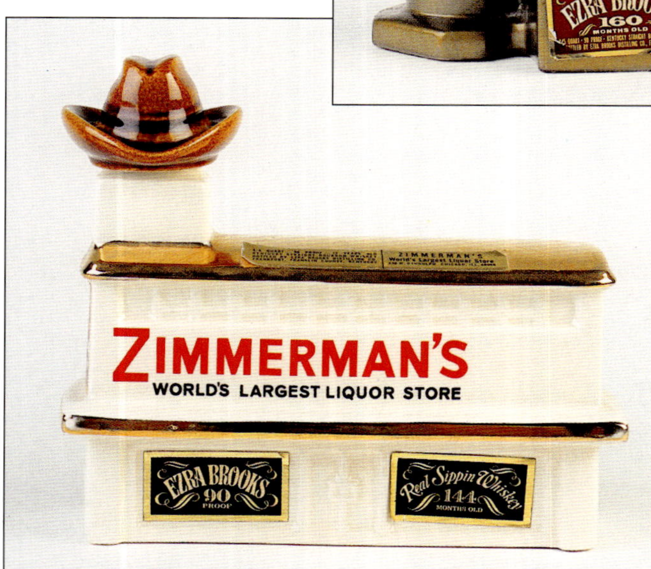

Zimmerman Top Hat, 1968, $10.

Dugs Nevada Brothels

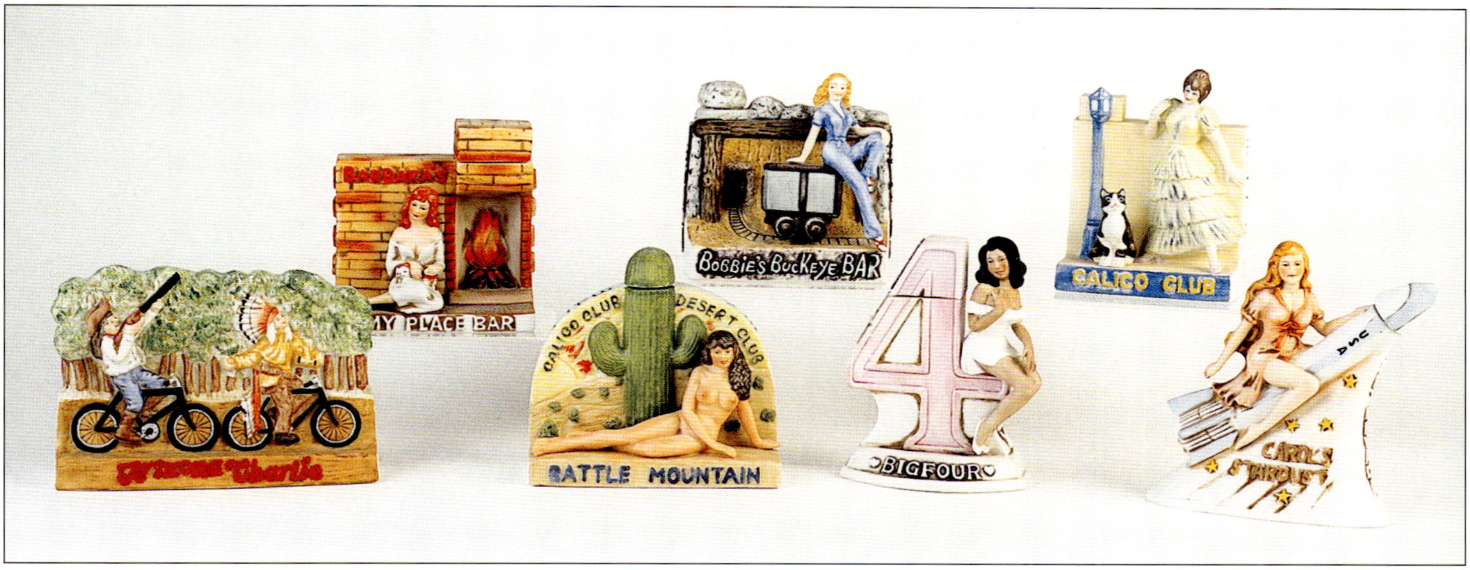

Arizona Charlie's, 1993, $20-25. BarBara's My Place, 1981, $15-20. Battle Mountain, 1989, $40-45. Bobbies Buckeye Bar, 1982, $15-20. Big Four, 1983, $15-20. Calico Club Battle Mountain, 1985, $15-20. Carol's Stardust, 1981, $40-45.

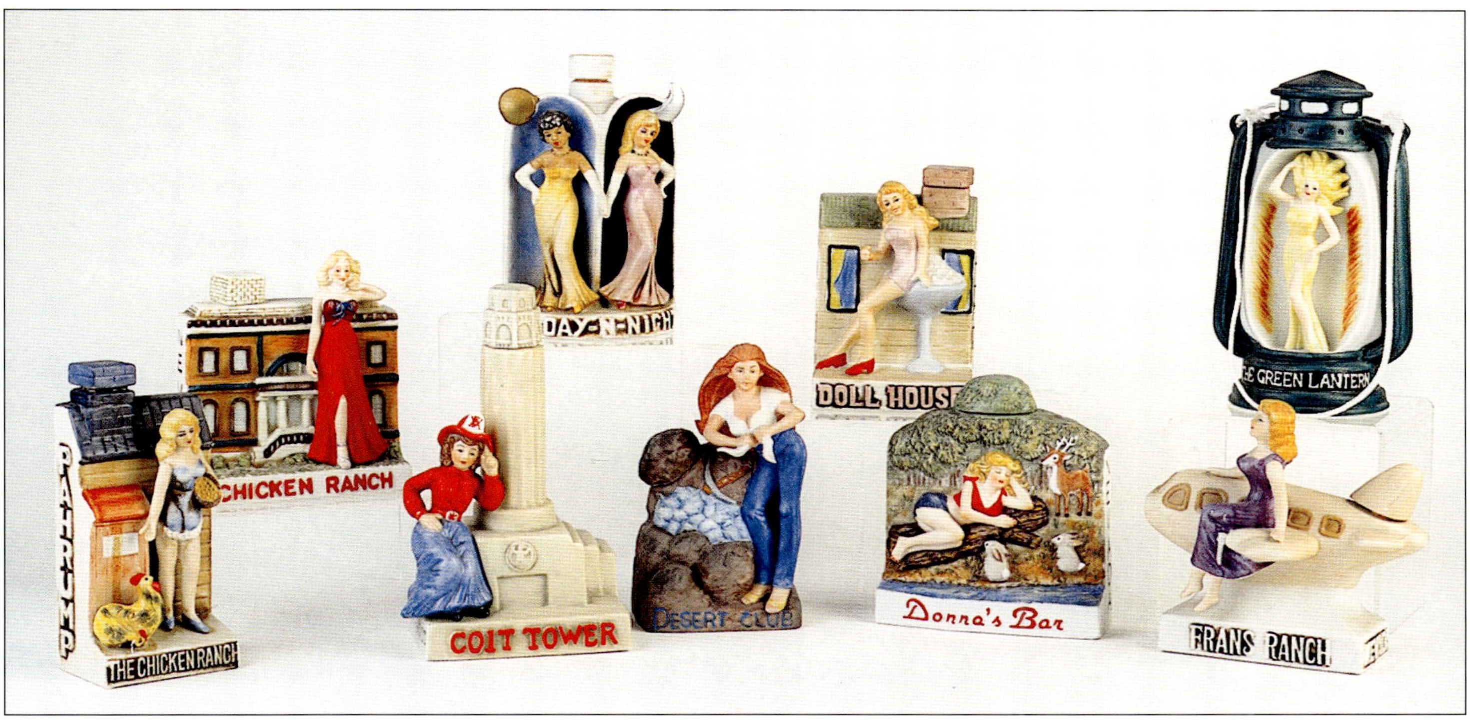

Chicken Ranch, 1979, $65-70. Chicken Ranch, 1986, $30-35. Coit Tower, 1994, $15-20. Billie's Day 'n Night, 1979, $75-80. Desert Club, 1982, $45-50. Doll House, 1981, $15-20. Donna's Bar, 1987 $15-20. Fran's Ranch, no date, $65-70. Green Lantern, 1984, $25-30.

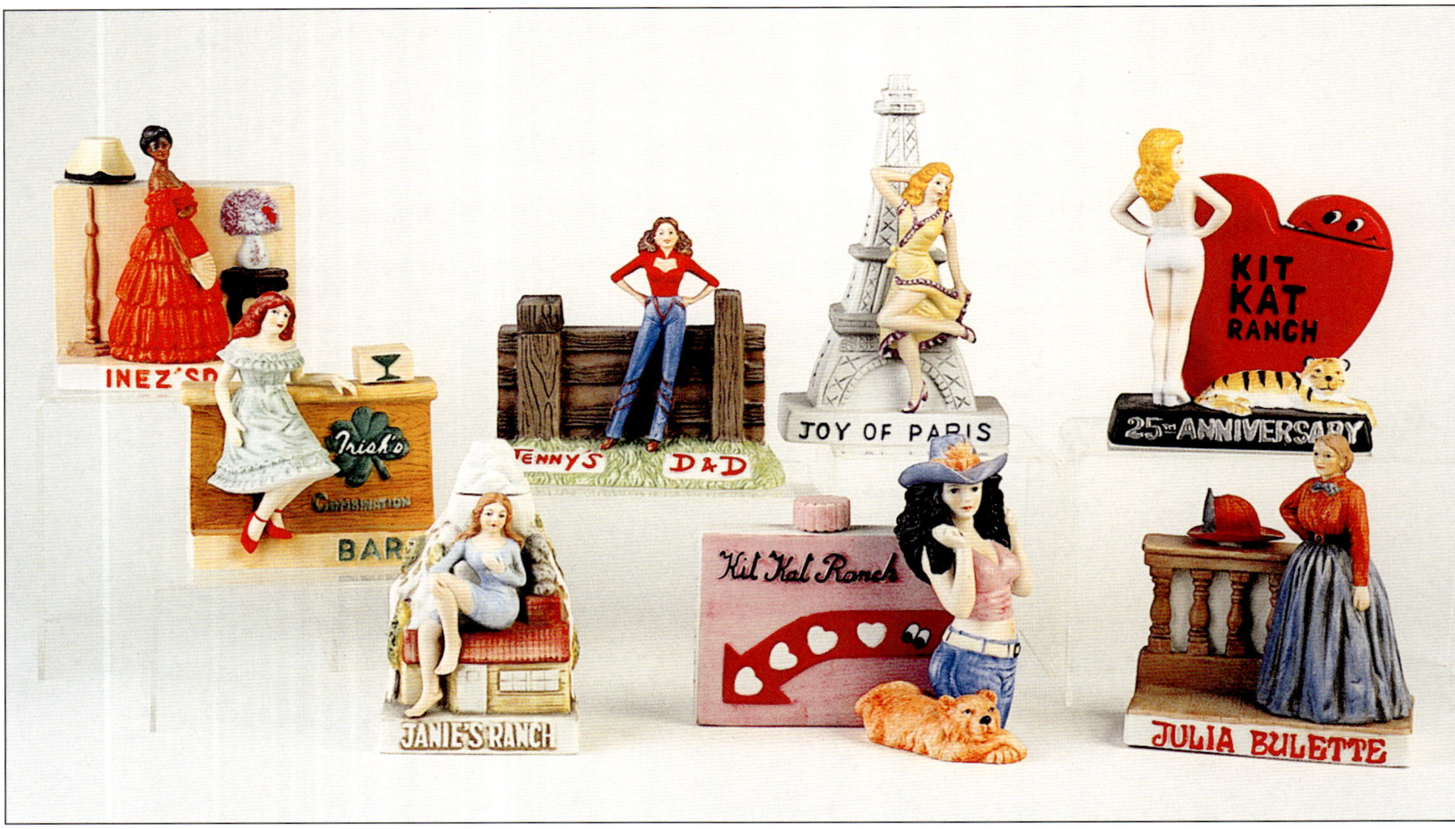

Inez's D&D, 1987, $20-25. Irish's Combination Bar, 1985, Janie's Ranch, 1982, $15-20. Jenny's D&D, 1984, $15-20. Joy of Paris, 1983, $15-20. Kit Kat Ranch, 1984, $70-75. Kit Kat Ranch, 1993, $15-20. Julia Bulette, $20-25.

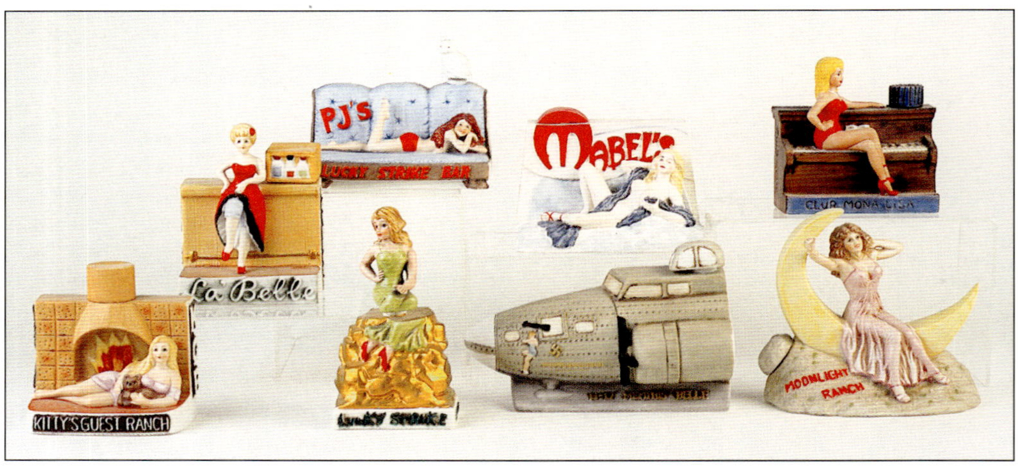

Kitty's Guest Ranch, 1983, $15-20. La Belle, $15-20. Lucky Strike,1987, $15-20. PJ's, $15-20. Mabel's, 1992, $15-20. Memphis Belle, 1996, $20-25. Club Mona Lisa, 1981, $15-20. Moonlight Ranch, 1991, $20-25.

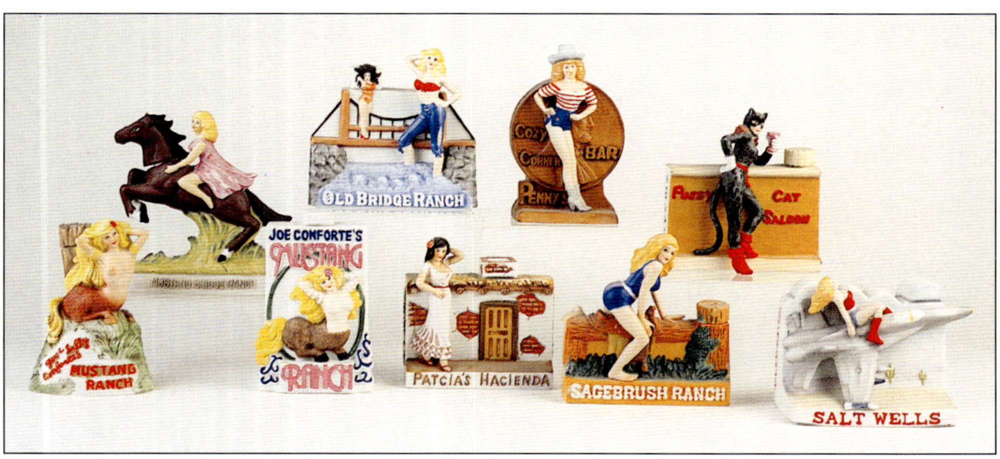

Mustang Ranch, $100-110. Mustang Bridge Ranch, 1981, $80-85. Mustang Ranch, 1986, $40-45. Old Bridge Ranch, 1984, $15-20. Patcia's Hacienda, 1981, $15-20. Penny's Cozy Corner Bar, $15-20. Pussy Cat Saloon, 1986, $15-20. Sage Brush Ranch, 1985, $15-20. Salt Wells, 1994, $15-20.

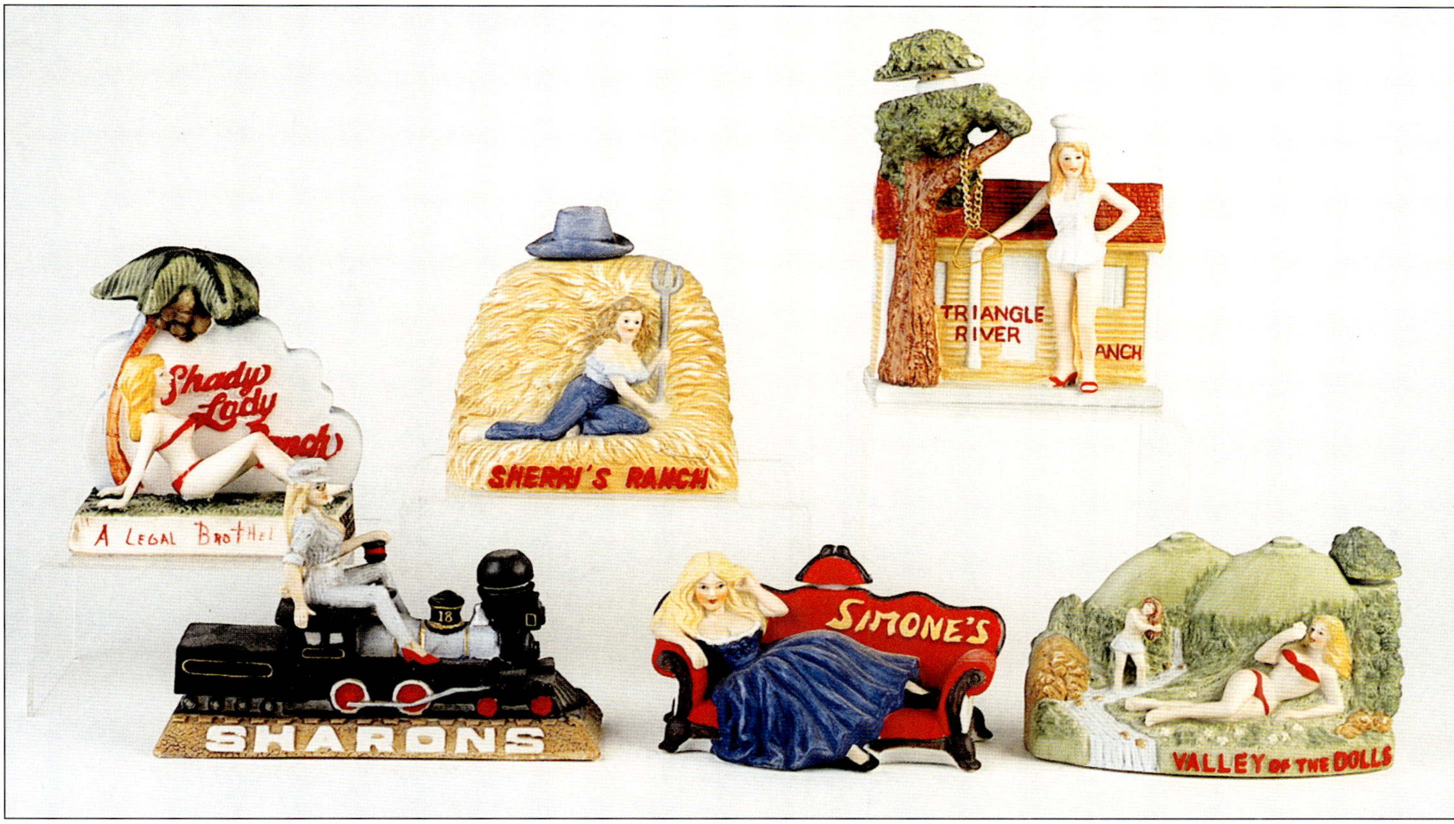

Shady Lady Ranch, 1999, $55-60. Sharon's, 1991, $30-35. Sherri's Ranch, 1989, $15-20. Simone's, 1988, $20-25. Triangle River Ranch 1988, $15-20. Valley of the Dolls, 1990, $20-25.

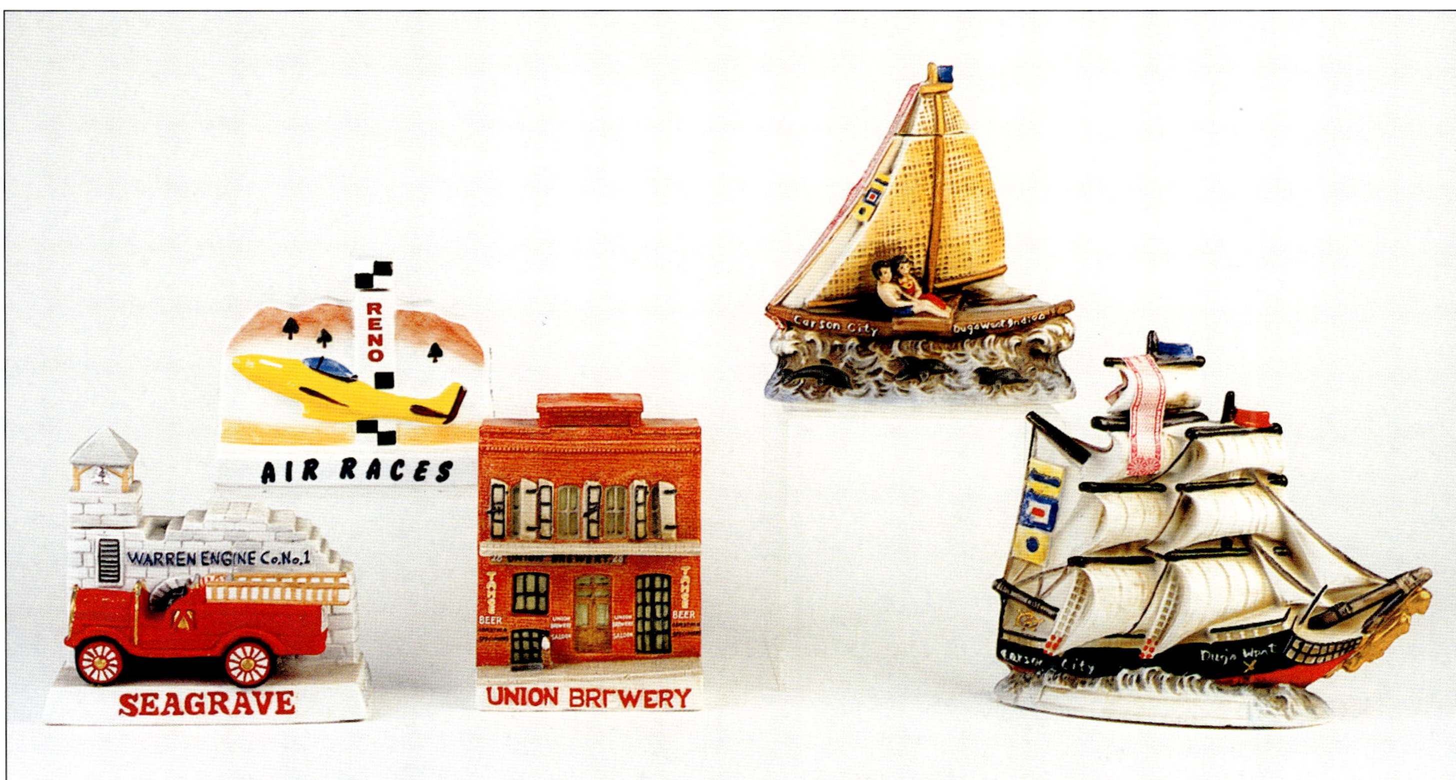

Miscellaneous Dugs: Seagrave, 1993, $20-25. Union Brewery, 1990, $20-25. Reno Air Races, 1993, $20-25. Dugs West Indies raft, 1975, $10. Dugs West Indies ship, 1974, $10.

Kontinental

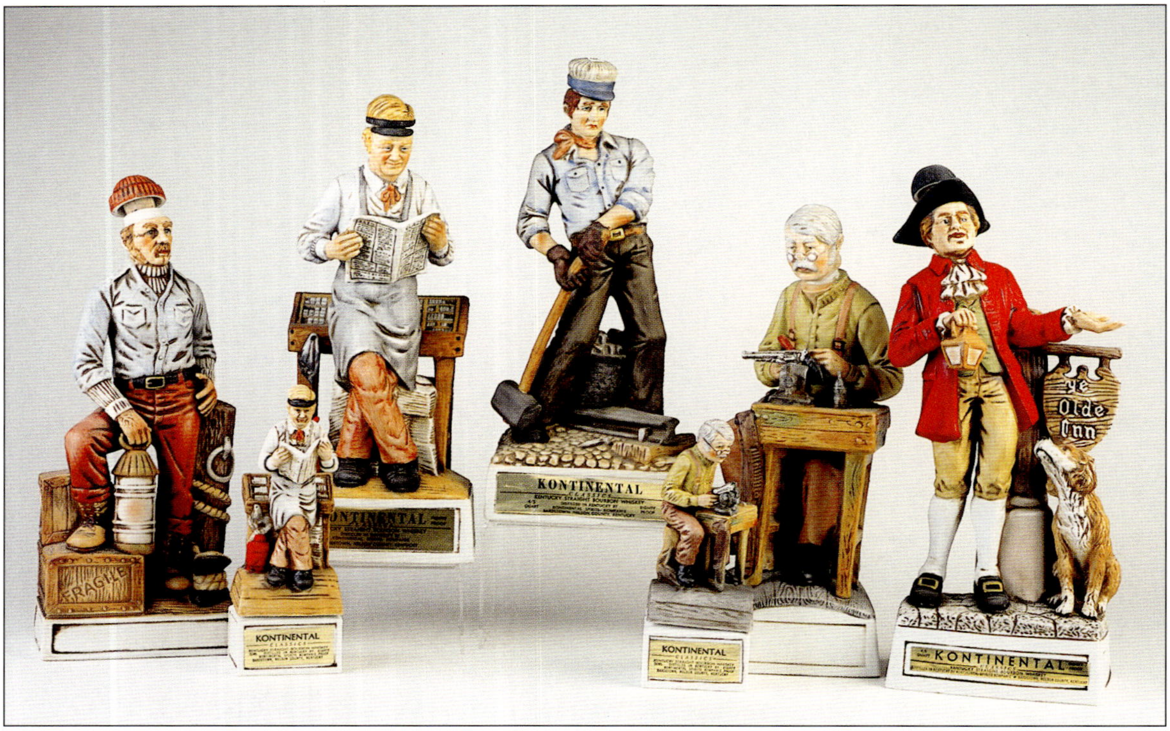

Dock Worker, 1979, $10-15. Editor, 1976, $10-25, mini $10-15. Gandy Dancer, 1976, $10-15. Gunsmith, 1977, $15-20, mini $10-15. Innkeeper, 1978, $10-15.

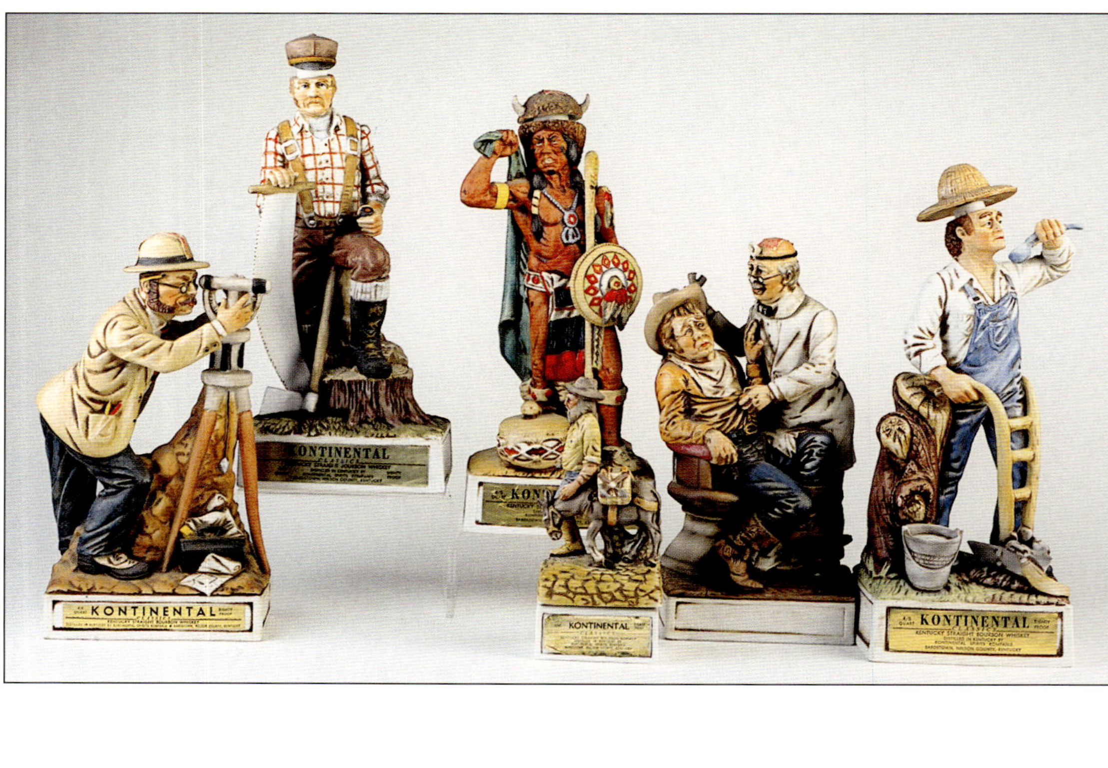

Land Surveyor, 1978, $15-20. Lumber Jack, 1978, $10-15. Medicine Man, 1977, $15-20. Pioneer Dentist, 1978, $10-15. Pioneer Farmer, 1978, $10-15. Prospector and Burro, 1977, mini, $10.

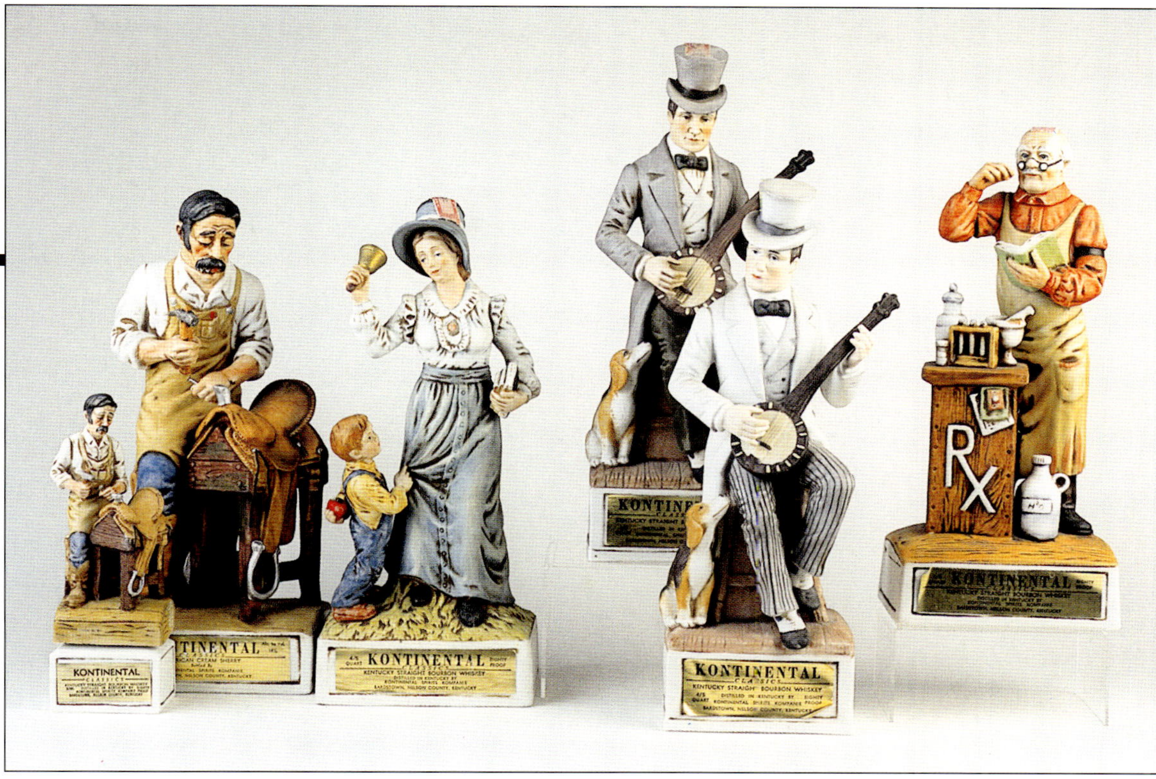

Saddle Maker, 1977, fifth $10-15, mini $5-10. School Marm, 1977, $10-15. Stephen Foster (gray coat), 1975, $20-25. Stephen Foster (white coat), 1976, $40-45. Village Pharmacist, 1977, $10-15.

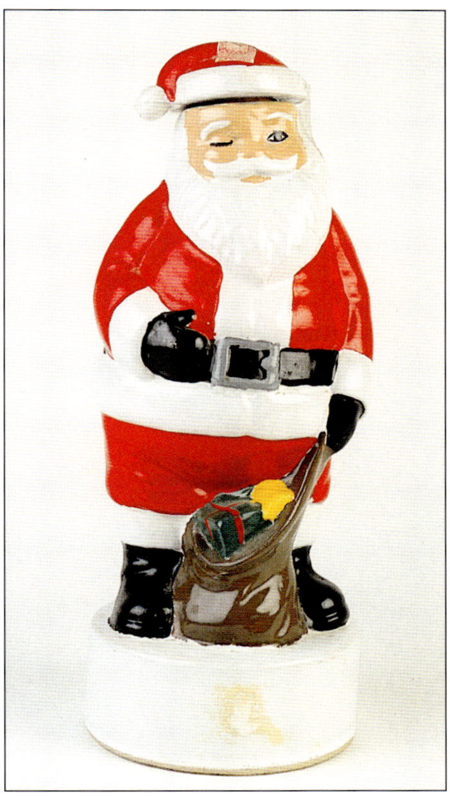

Santa Claus, $15-20.

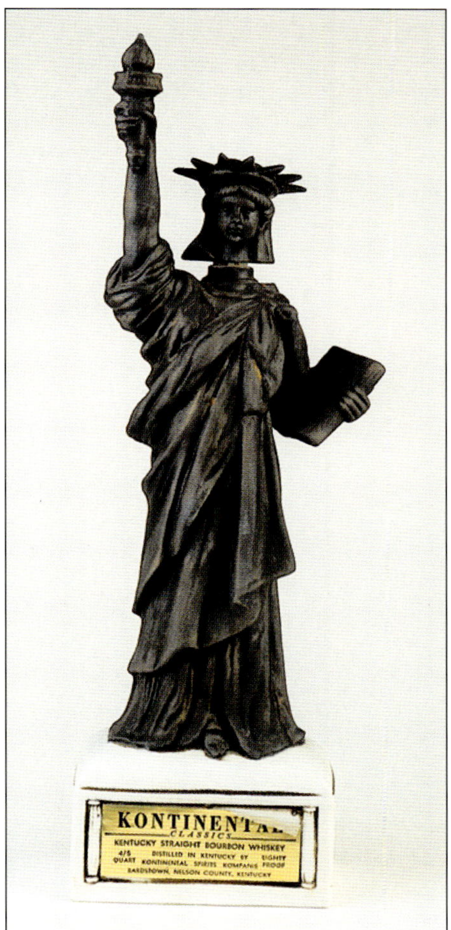

Statue of Liberty, 1976, $10-15.

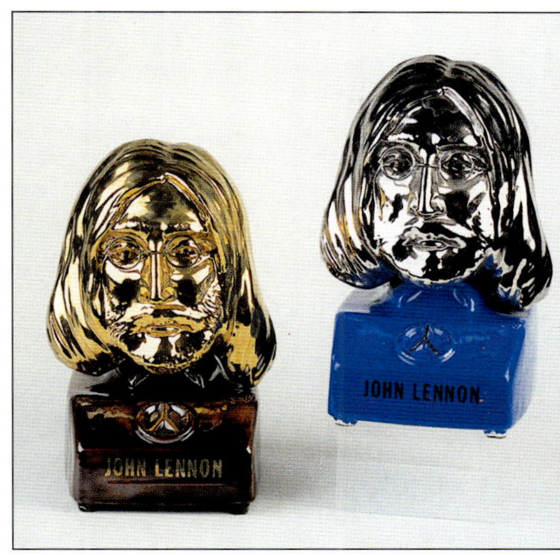

John Lennon (gold), 1981, $20-25. John Lennon (silver), 1981, $20-25.

Daviess County

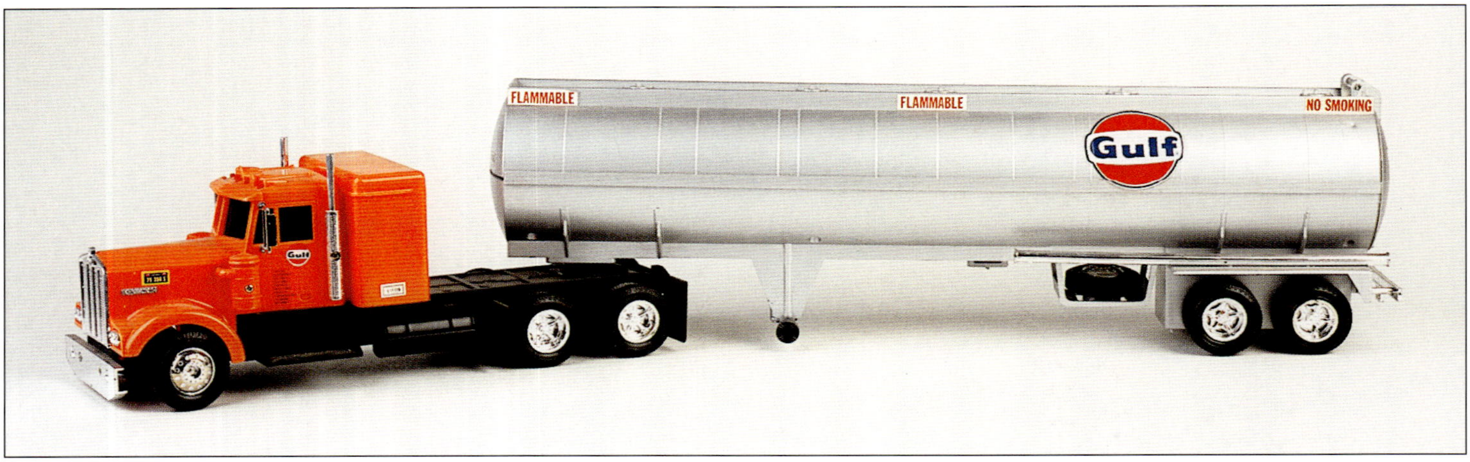

Kenworth Tractor 18 wheel Gulf Tanker, 1979, $45-55.

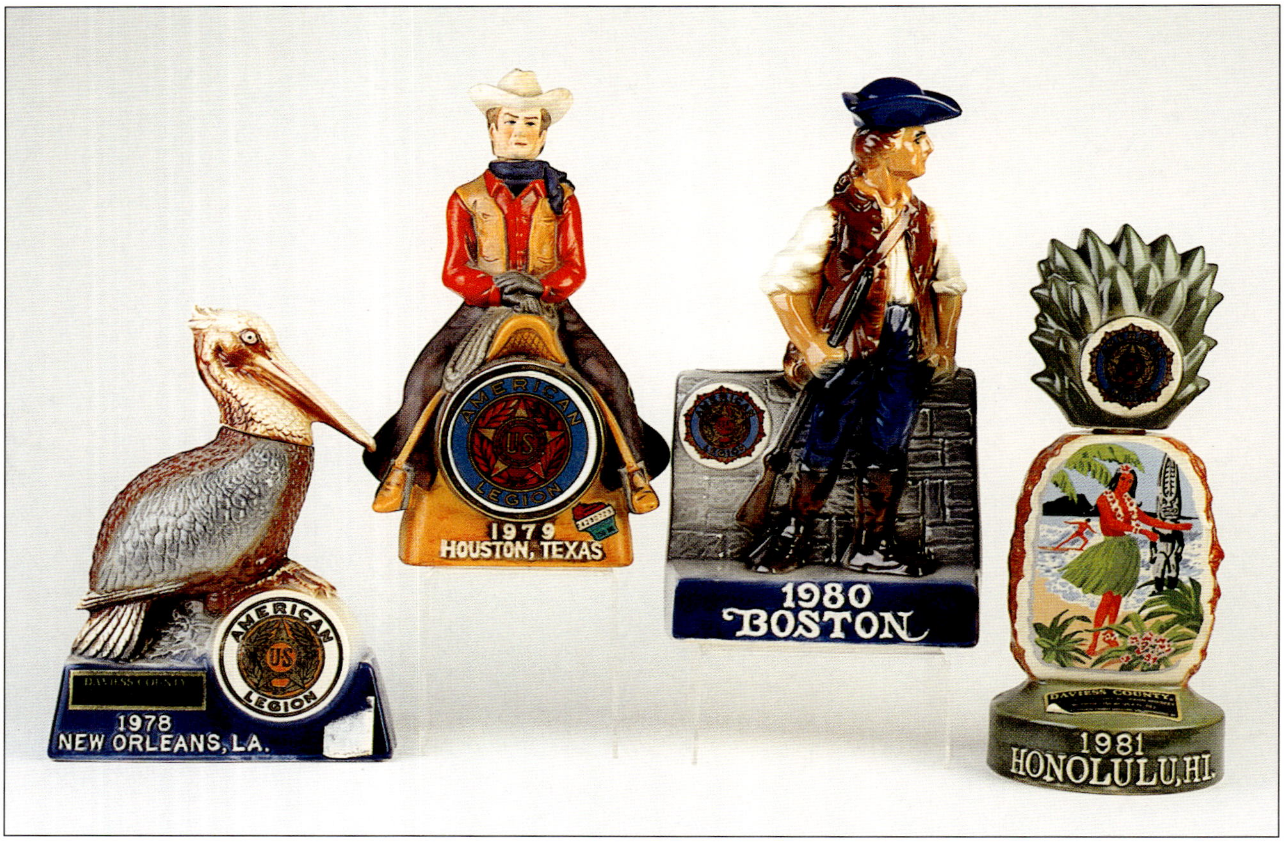

American Legion, New Orleans, 1978, $10-15. American Legion, Houston, 1979, $10-15. American Legion, Boston, 1980, $10-15. American Legion, Hawaii, 1981, $10-15.

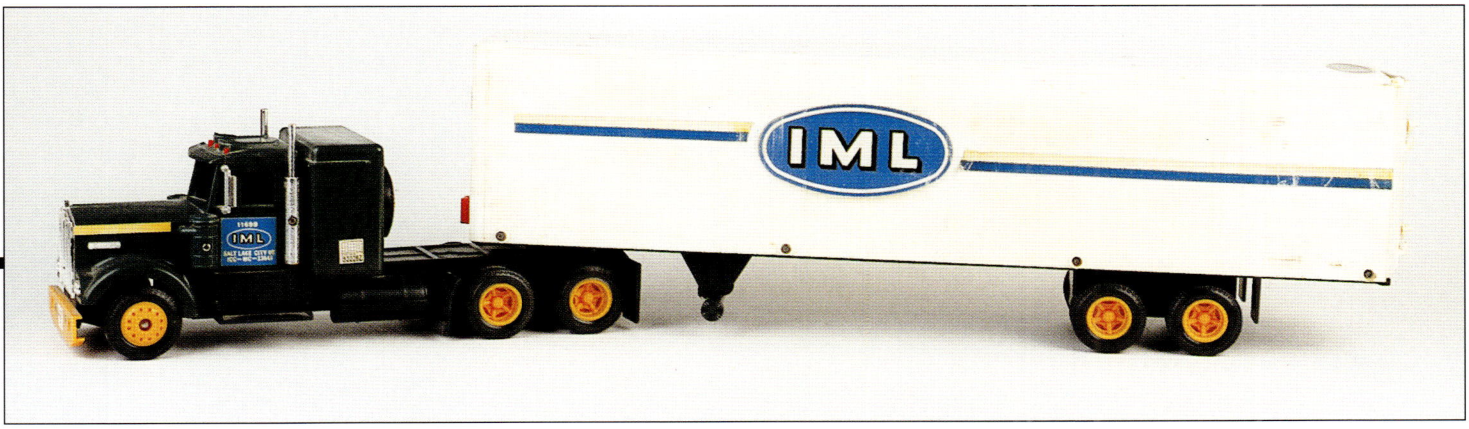

Peterbilt Tractor, 18 wheel IML, 1979, $25-30.

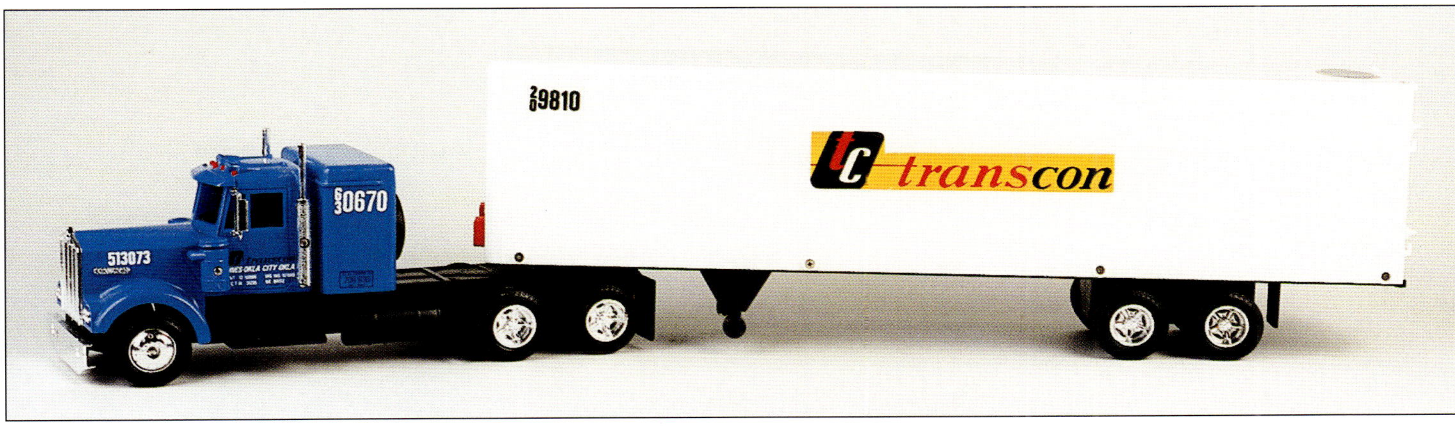

18 wheel Kensworth Transcon, 1979, $30-35.

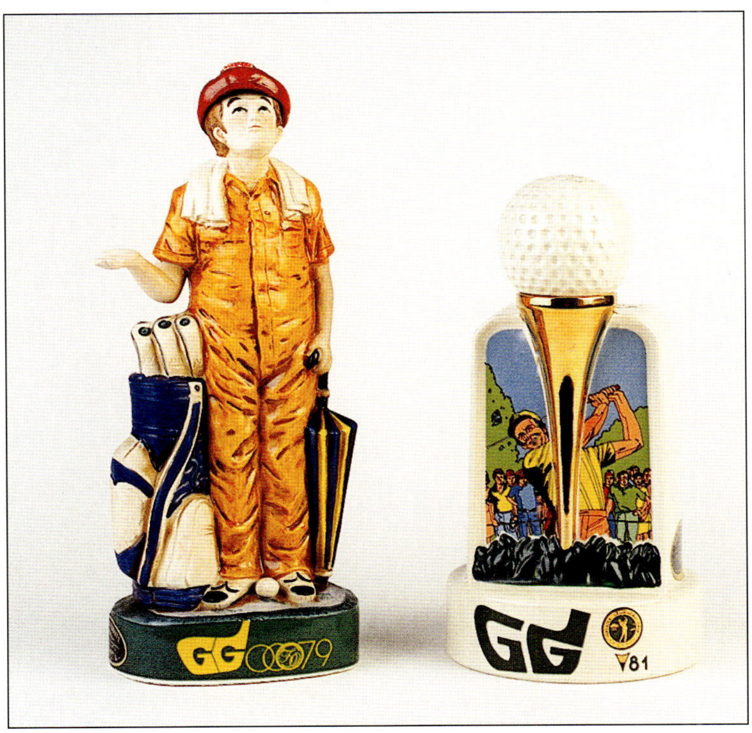

Greensboro Caddie, 1979, $25-30. Greensboro Golf Ball and Tee, 1981, $15-20.

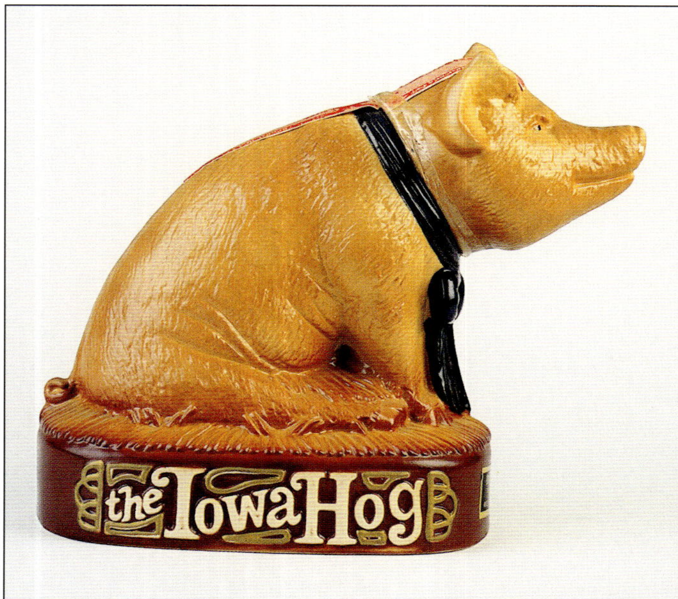

Iowa Hog, 1978, $15-20.

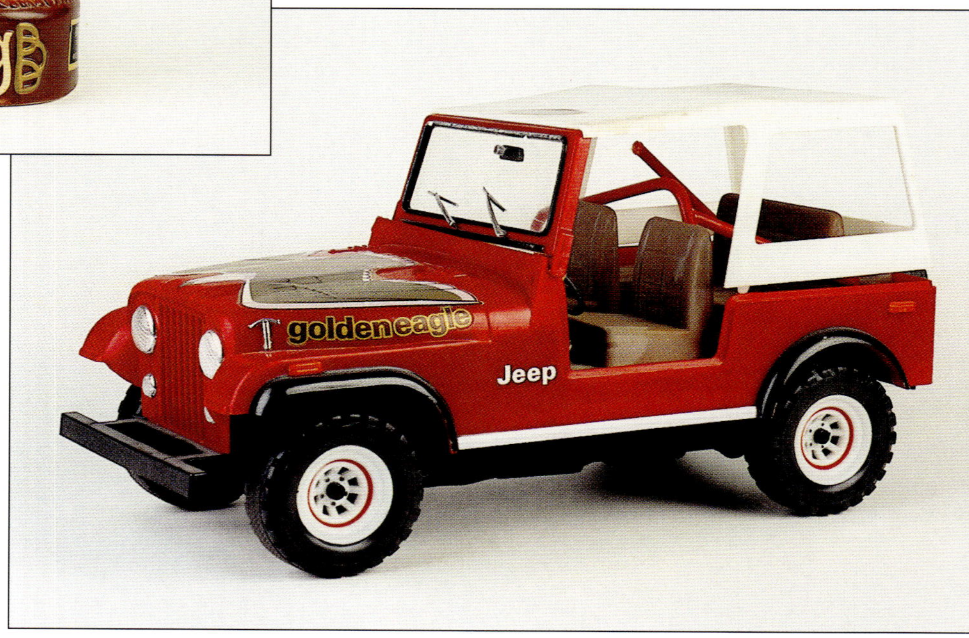

Jeep CJ 7 (red), 1979, $35-40.

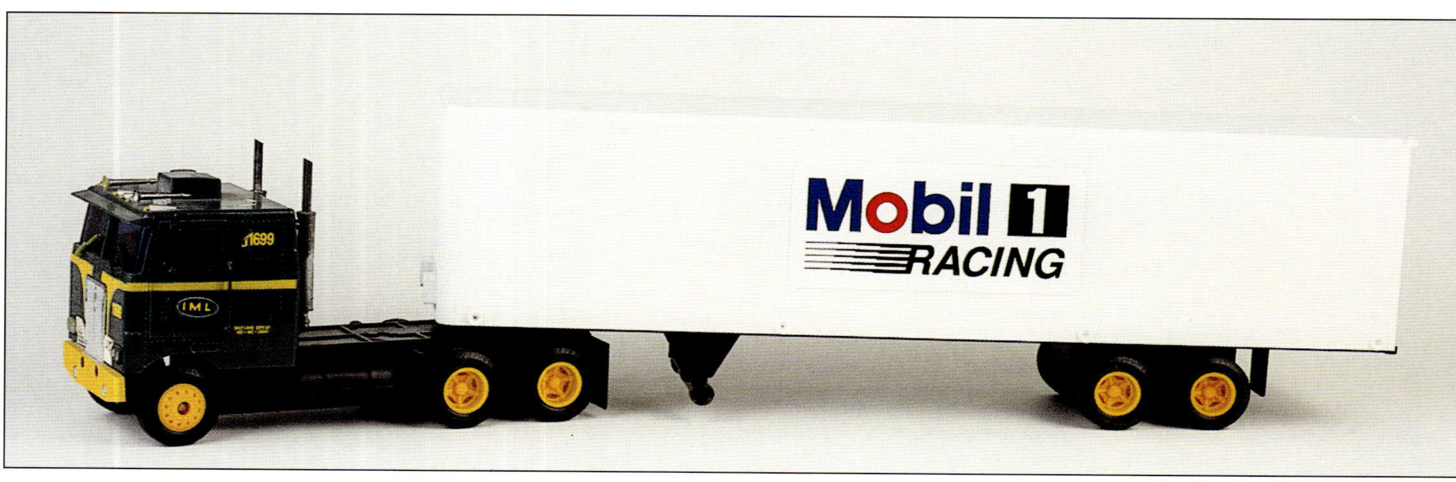

Mobile 1 Racing Tractor-Trailer, possible prototype, value undetermined.

Jeep CJ 7 (yellow), 1979, $35-40.

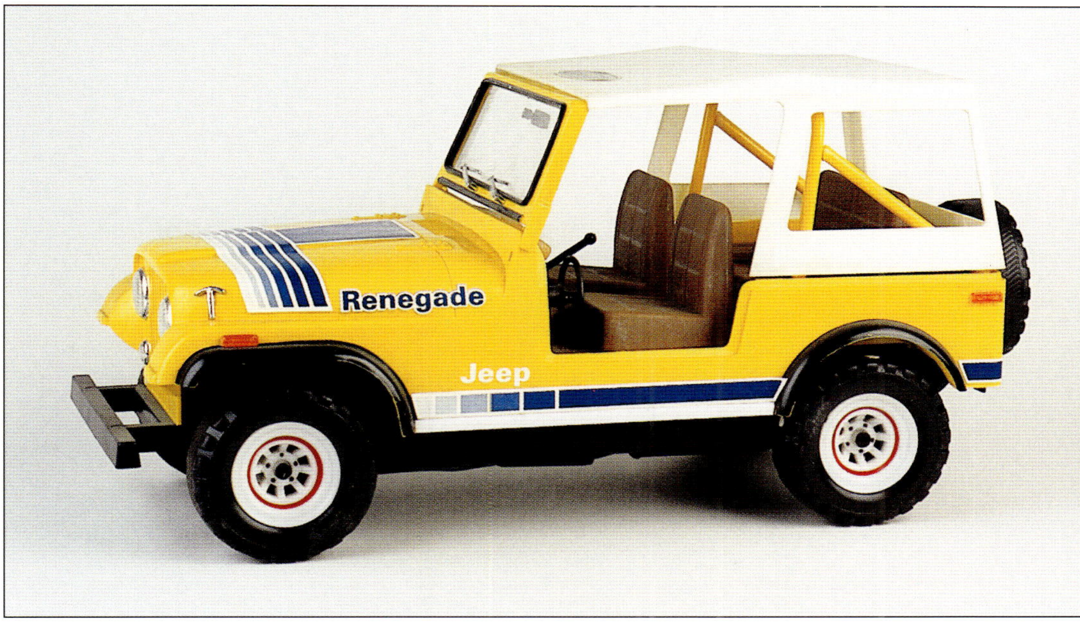

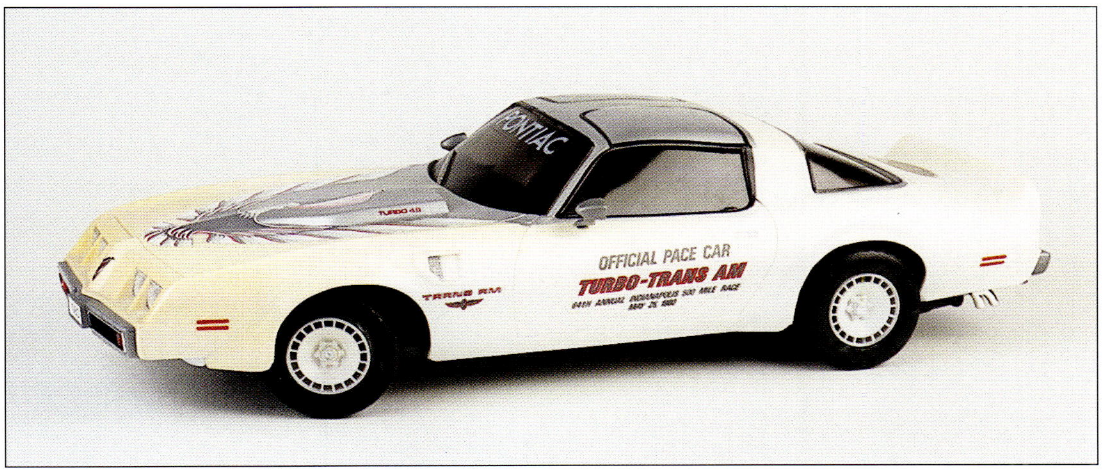

Pontiac Trans AM, 1980, $35-40.

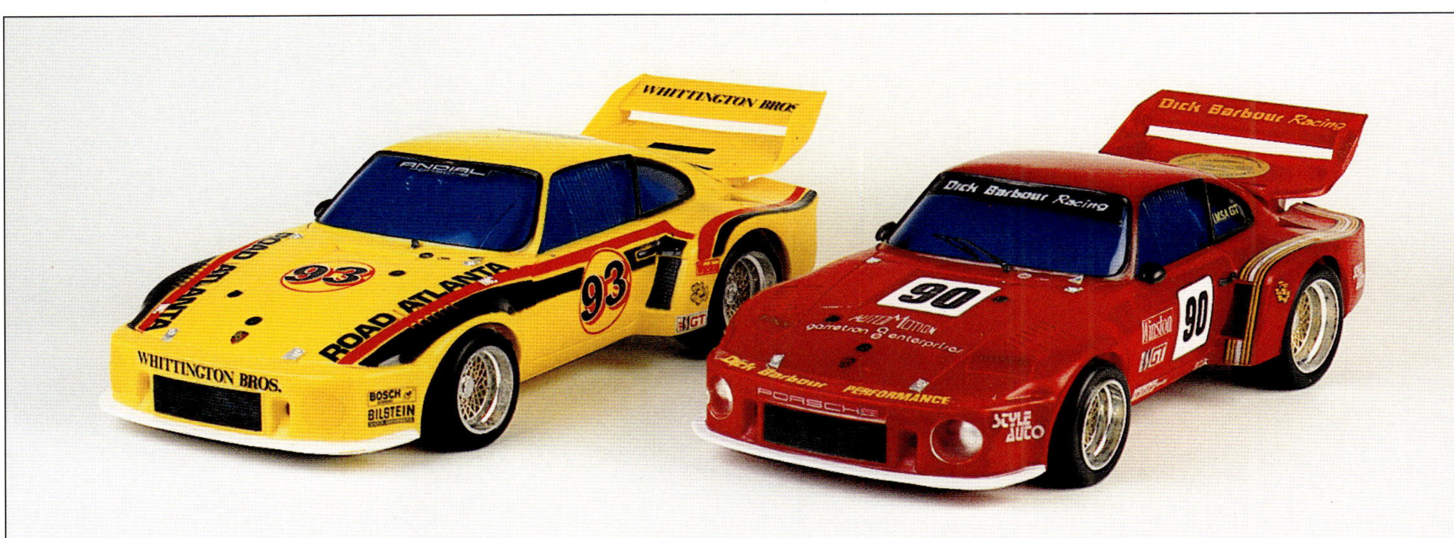

Porsche 935, 1979 Whittington Bros. #93 (yellow), $20-25. 1979 Dick Barbour #90 (red), $20-25.

Pancho Villa

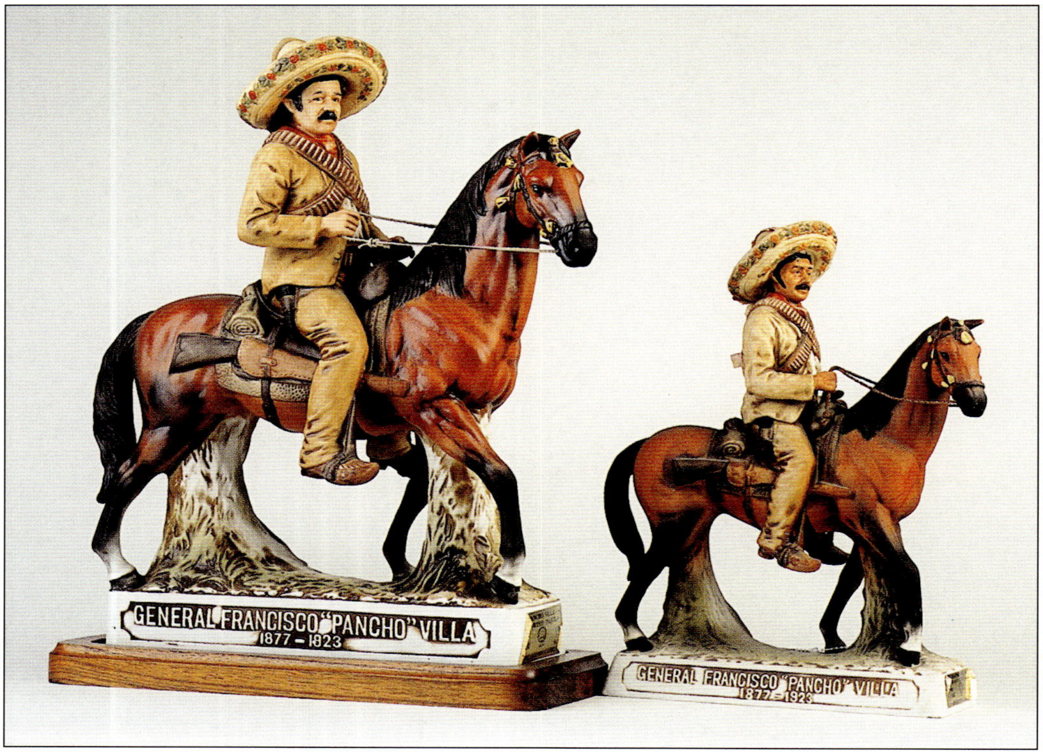

Pancho Villa on Horseback, 1975, 1.75 liter, $75-80, fifth $25-30.

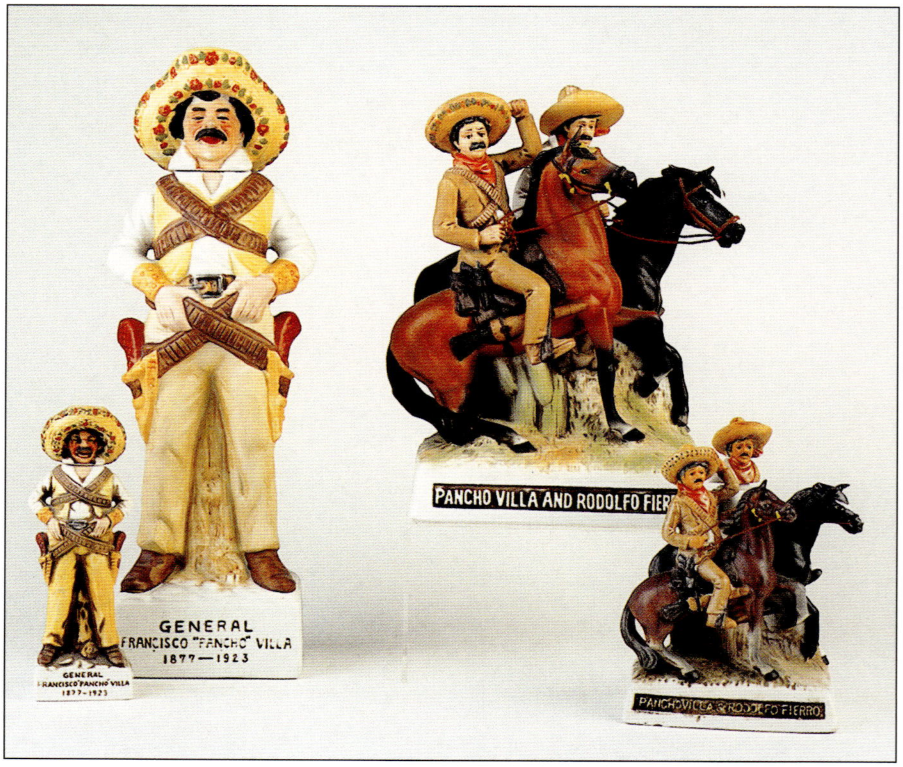

Pancho Villa (standing), $15-20, mini $10. Pancho Villa and Fierro, $10-15, mini $10.

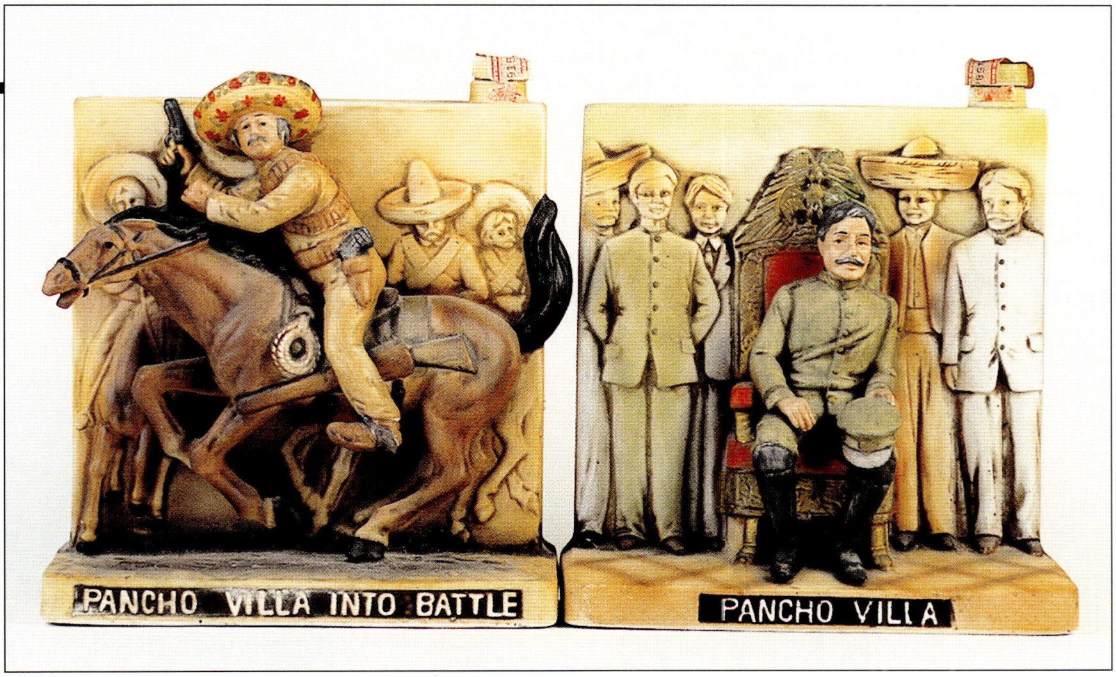

Pancho Villa and Obercon, 1976, $15-20. Pancho Villa at Palacio, 1976, $12-15.

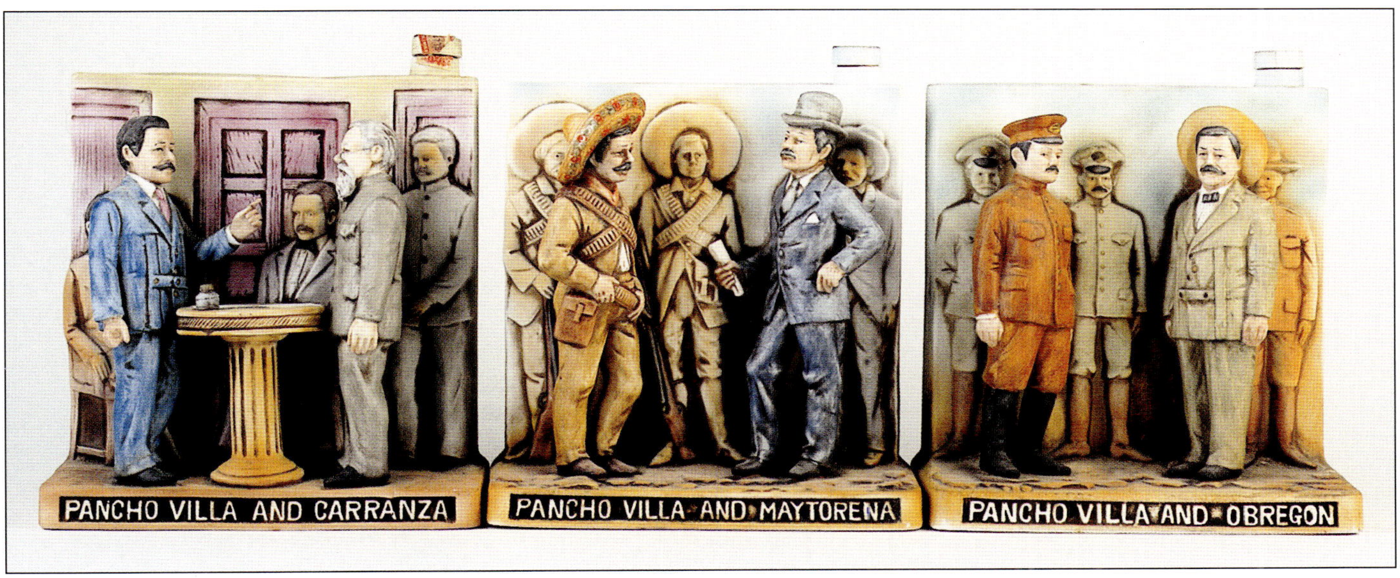

Pancho Villa and Carranza, 1976, $15-20. Pancho Villa and Maytorena, 1976, $15-20. Pancho Villa into Battle, 1976, $15-20.

Potters

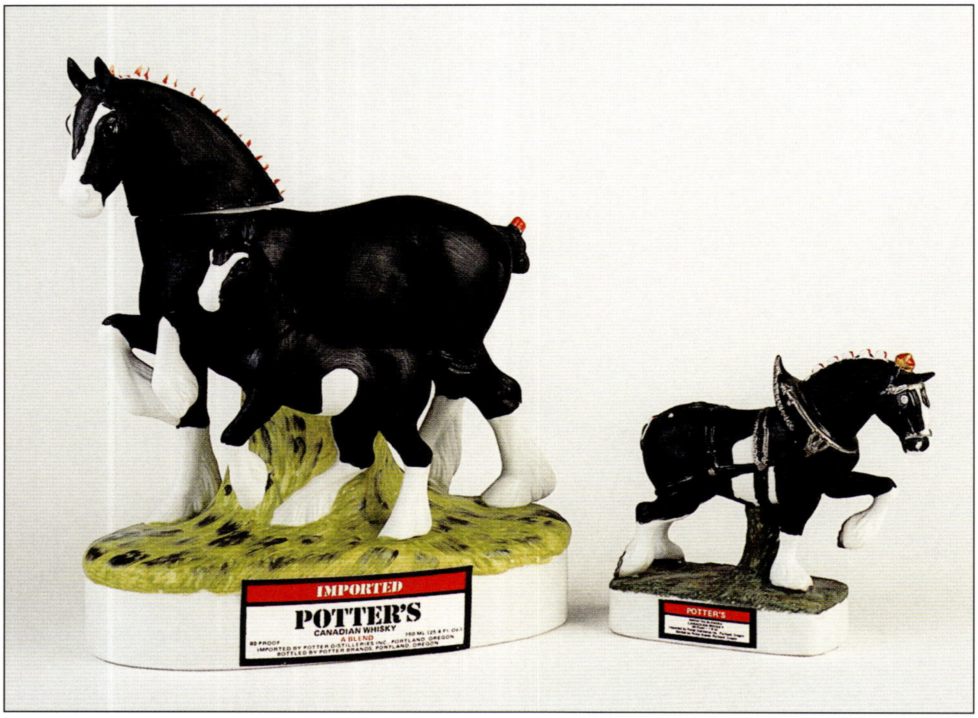

Clydesdale with colt, 1979, $40-45.
Clydesdale, 1978, mini $10.

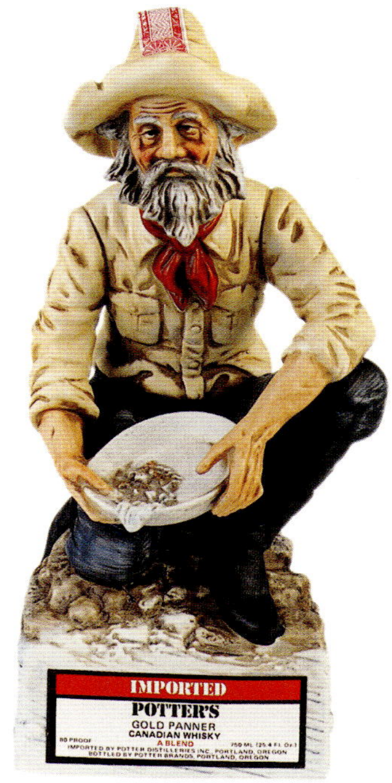

Gold Panner, $10-15.

Eskimo Dog Sled, 1977, mini $50-60.

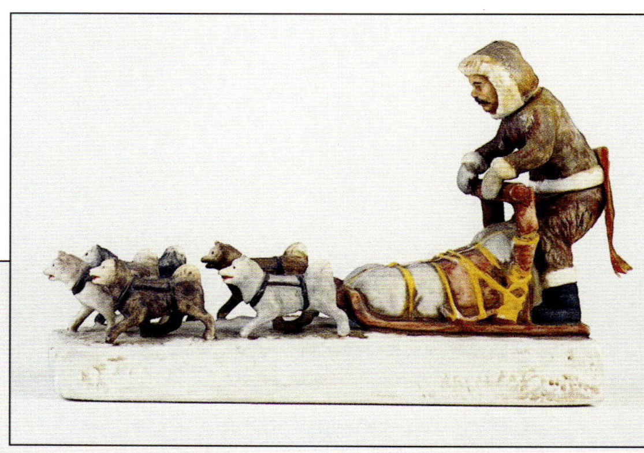

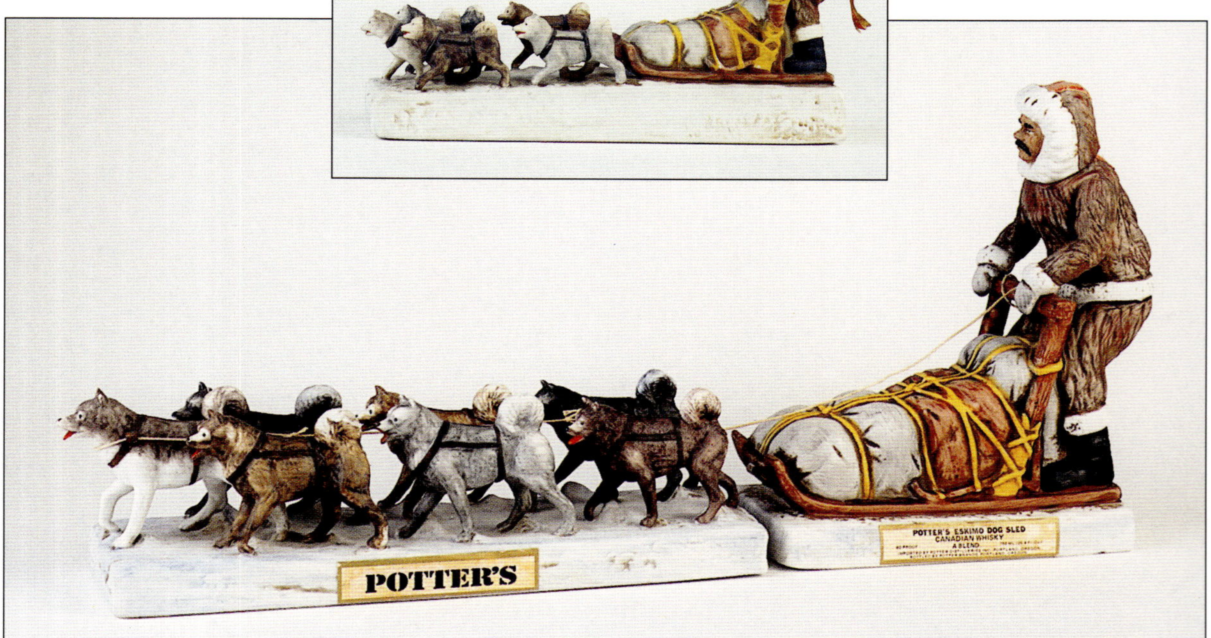

Eskimo Dog Sled, 1977, $125-135.

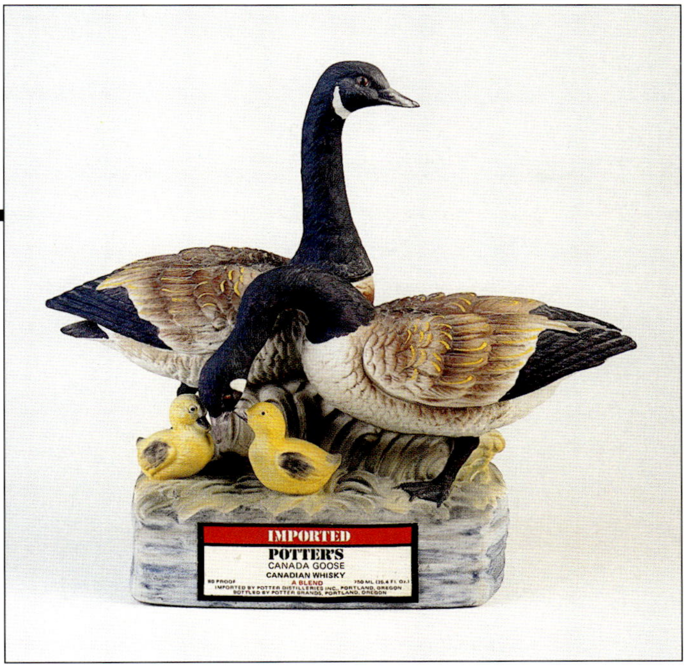

Canadian Geese, 1978, $20-25.

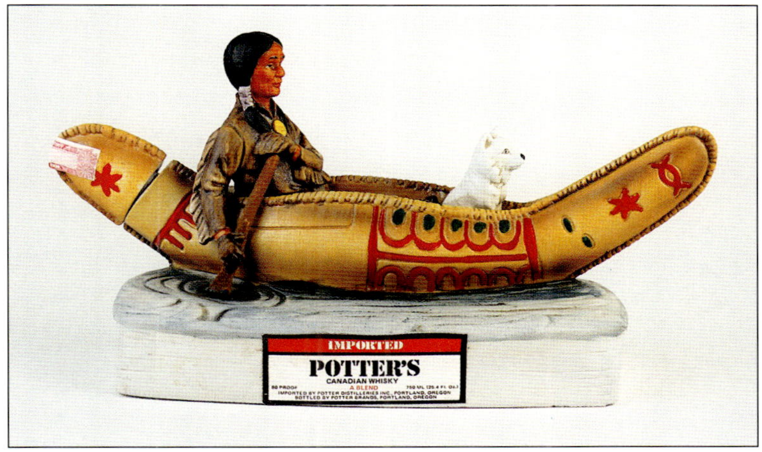

Indian in Canoe, 1979, $20-25.

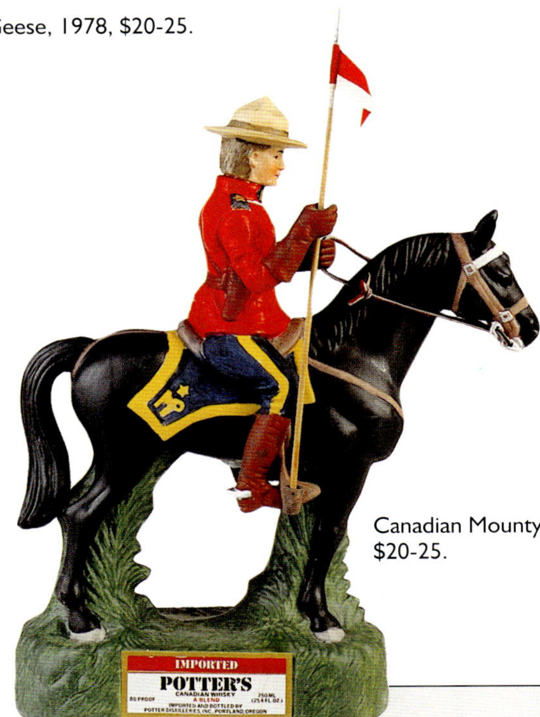

Canadian Mounty, 1980, $20-25.

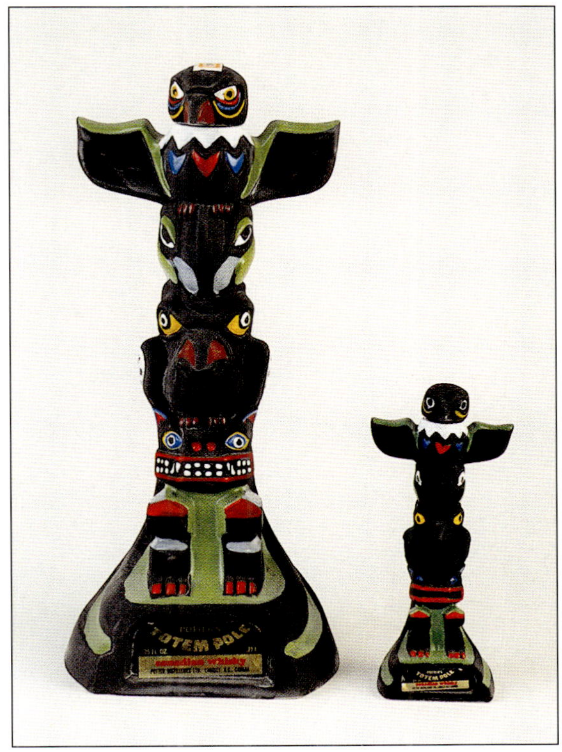

Totem Pole, 1971, $15-20, mini $5-10.

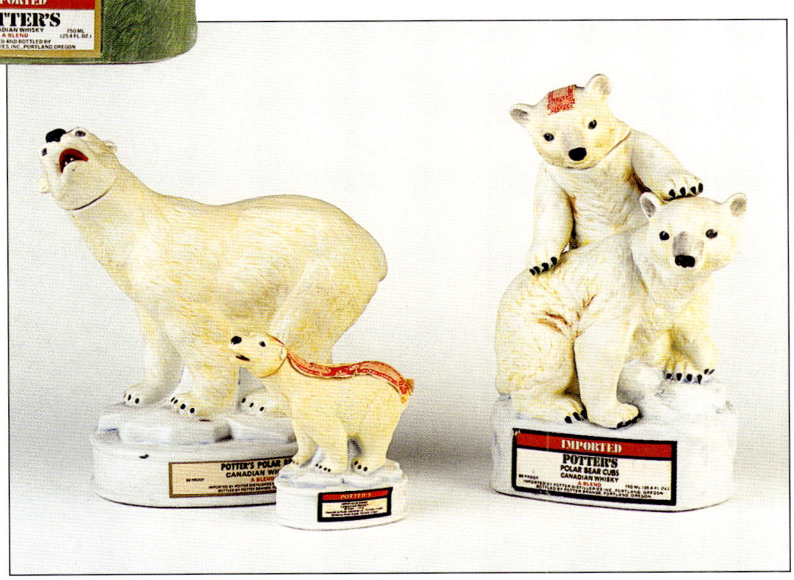

Polar Bear, 1977, $15-20, mini $10-15. Polar Bear Cubs, 1977, $15-20.

Hoffman

Aesops Fables Series

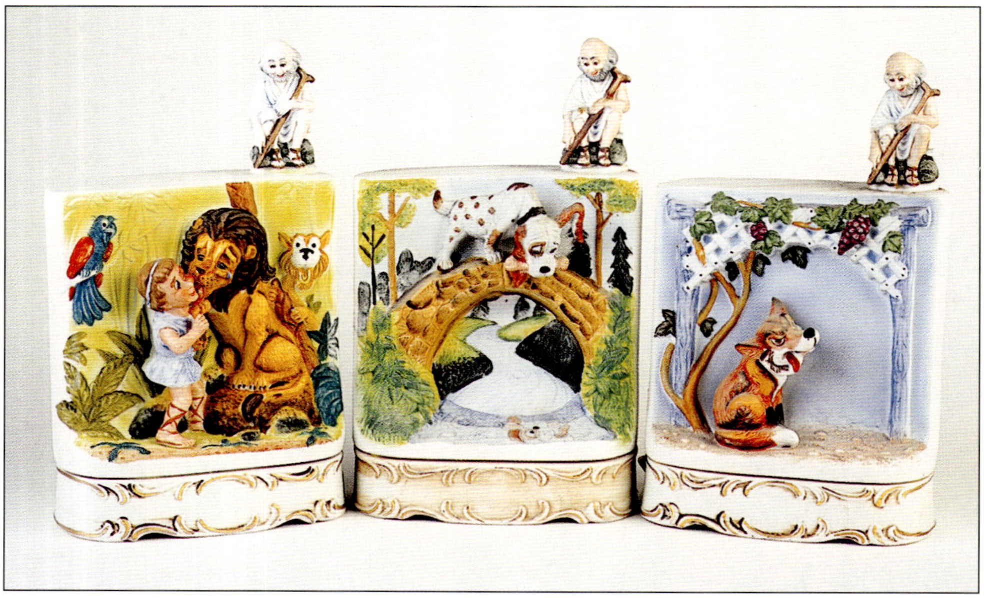

Music boxes: Androcles and the Lion, 1978, $10-15; Dog and his Shadow, 1978, $10-15; Fox and the Grapes, 1978, $10-15.

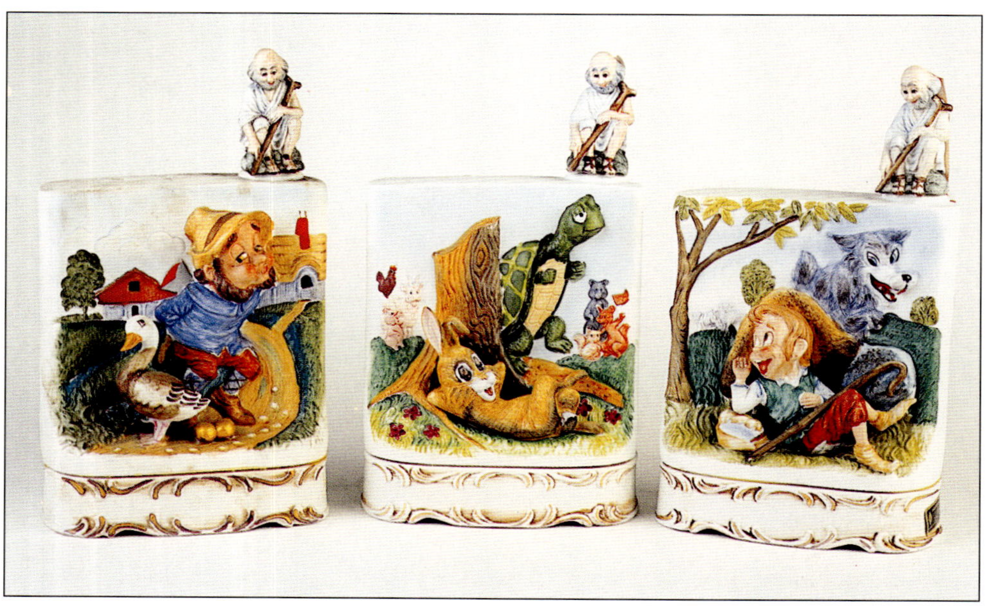

Goose with the Golden Egg, 1976, $10-15. Tortoise and the Hare, 1978, $10-15. Shepherd Boy (The Boy Who Cried Wolf), 1978, $10-15.

Miscellaneous Hoffman

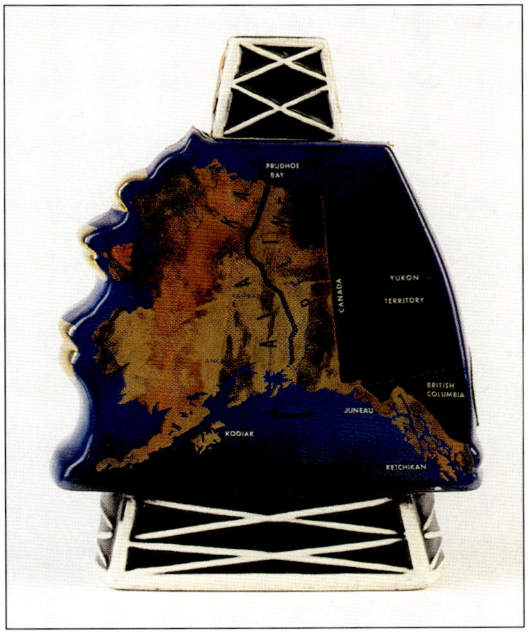

Alaska Pipeline, 1975, $10-15.

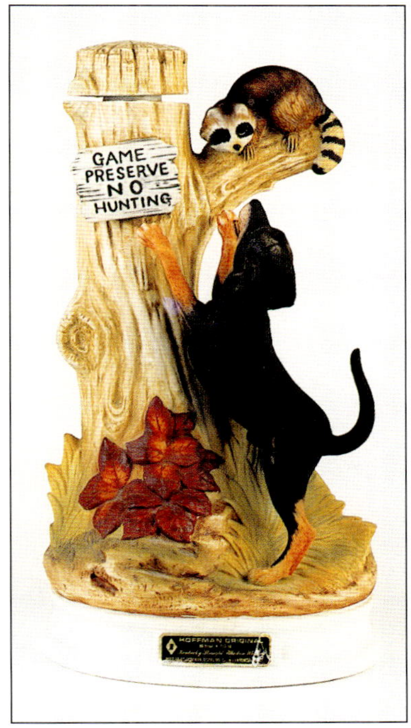

Dog and Raccoon, 1978, $20-25.

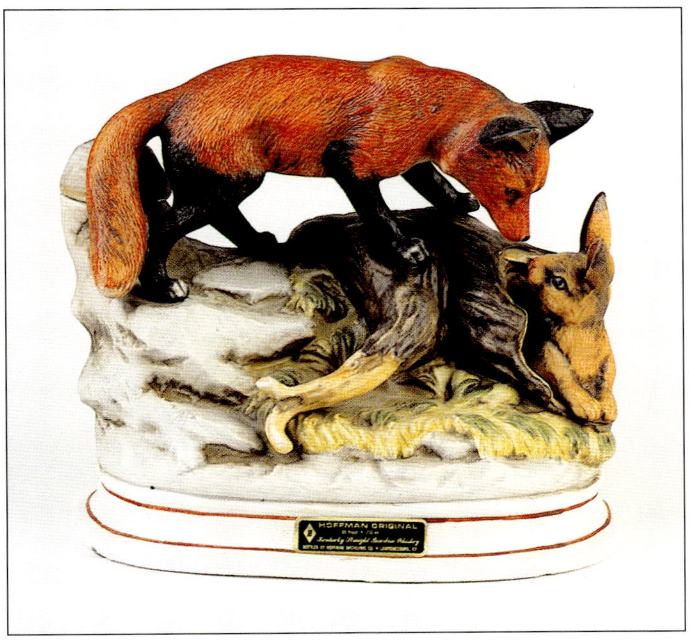

Fox and rabbit, music box, 1981, $20-15.

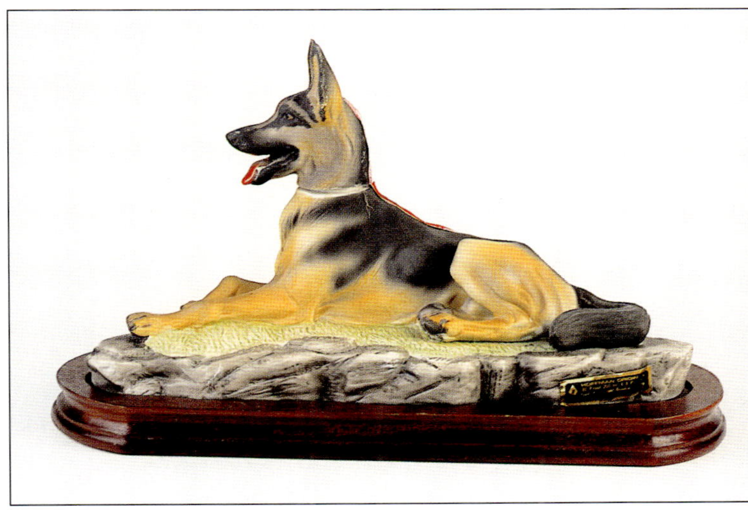

The Shepherd 1980, $20-25.

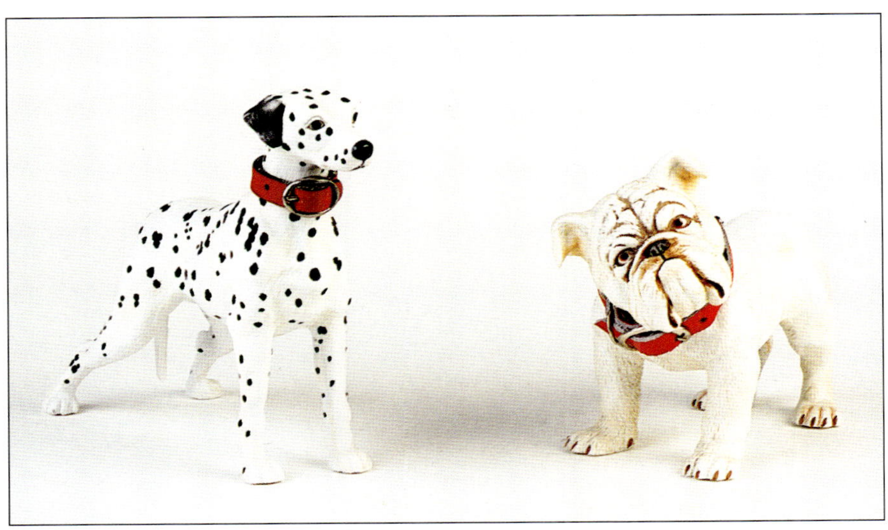

Dog Set #1: Dalmatian, $10-15; Bull Dog, 1981, $45-55.

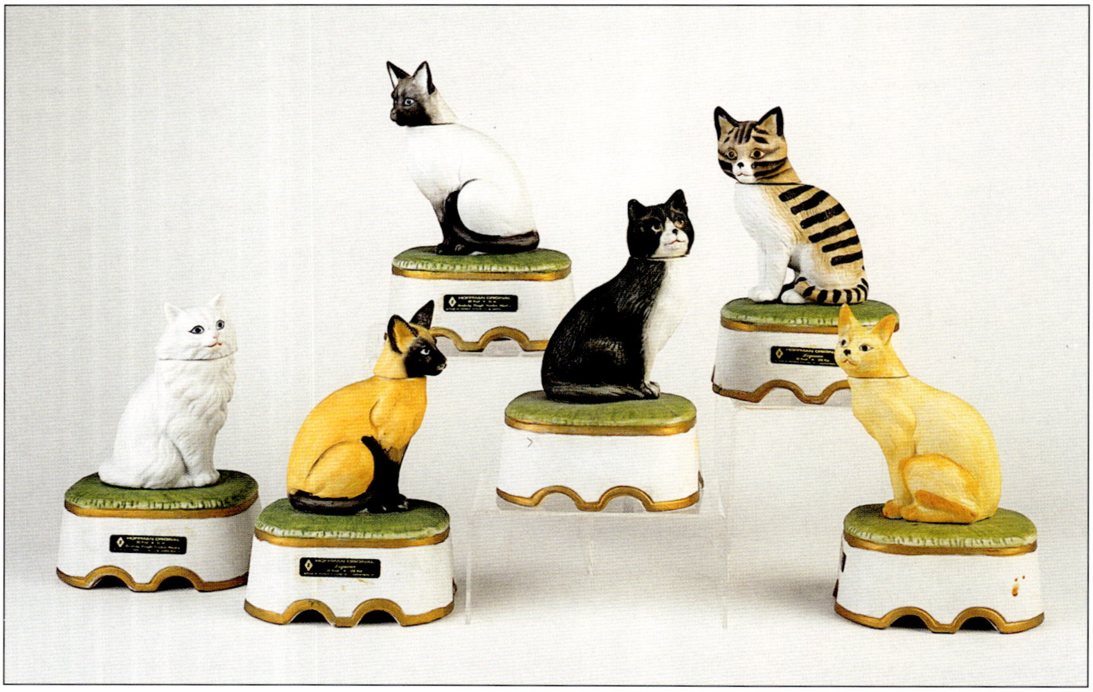

Perry Persian, 1981, $5-7. Sammy Siamese, 1981, $5-7. Suzie Siamese, 1981, $5-7. Tom Cat, 1981, $5-7. Terry Tiger, 1981, $5-7. Tillie Shorthair, 1981, $5-7.

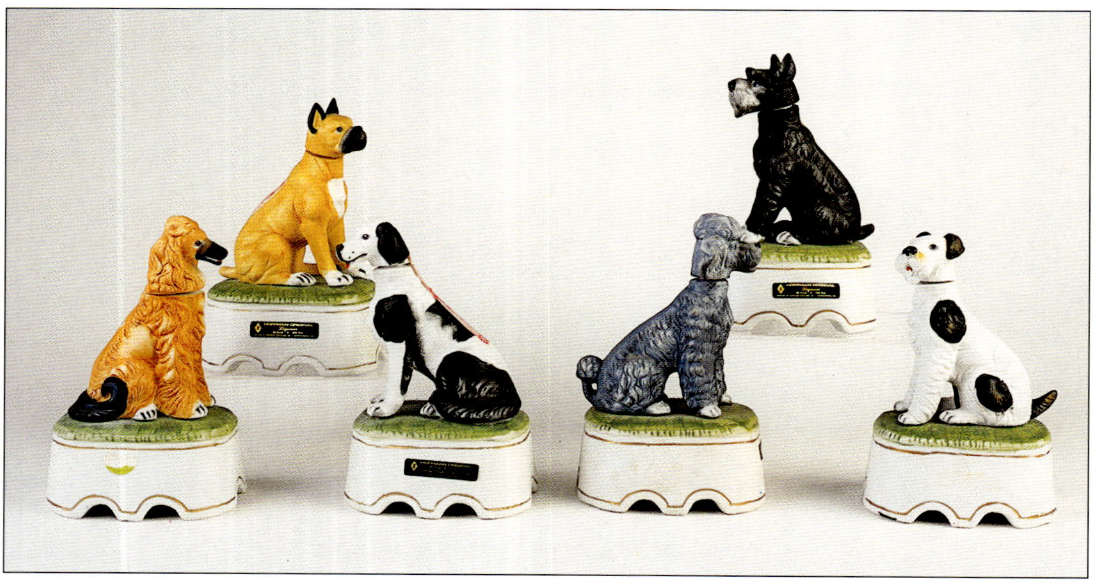

Ally Afghan, 1981, $10. Billy Boxer, 1981, $10. Fanny fox, 1981, $10. Percy Poodle, 1981, $10. Scotty Terrier, 1981, $10, Terry Terrier, 1981, $10.

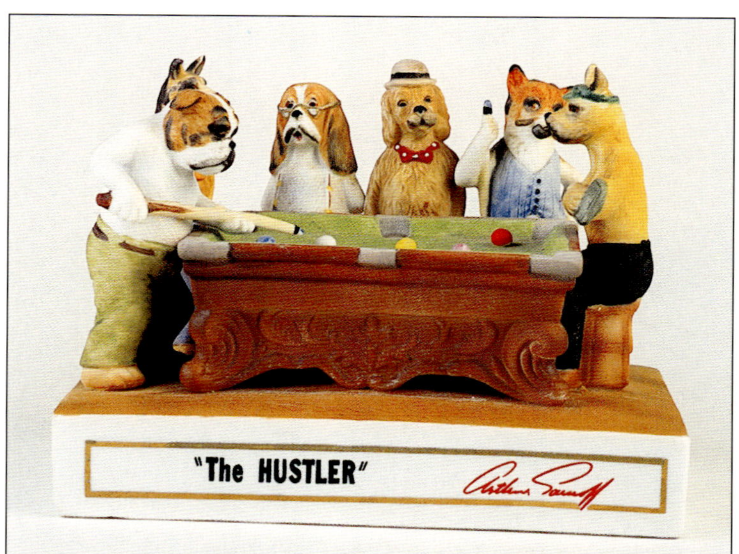

The Hustler, 1979, $150-175.

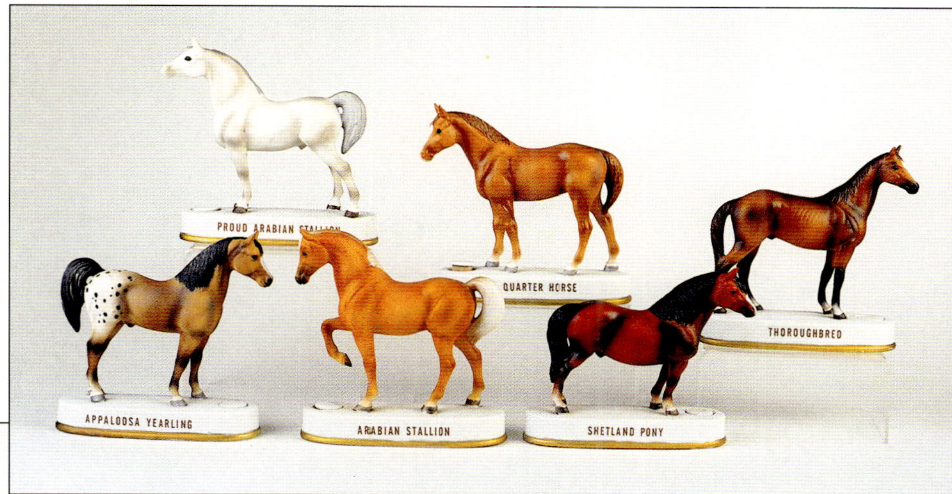

Appaloosa Yearling, 1979, mini $10. Arabian Stallion, 1979, mini $10. Proud Arabian Stallion, 1979, mini $10. Quarter Horse, 1979, mini $10. Shetland Pony, 1979, mini $10. Thoroughbred, 1979, mini $10.

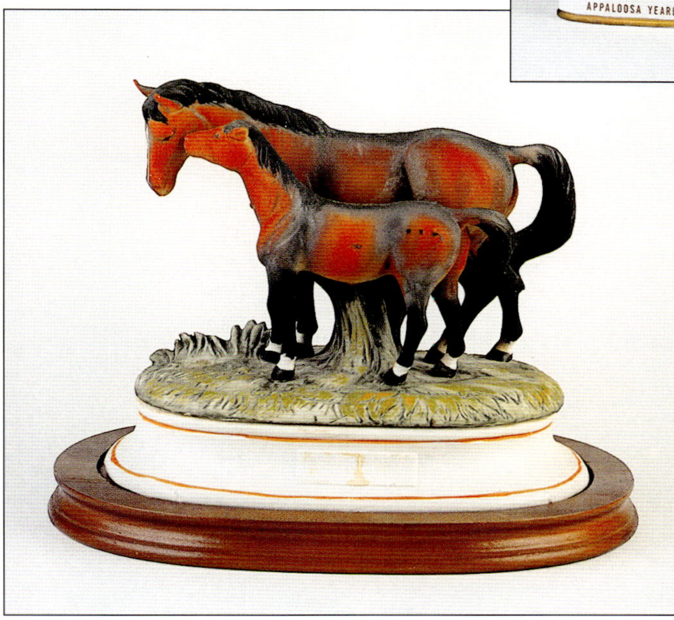

Mare and Colt, 1979, $20-25.

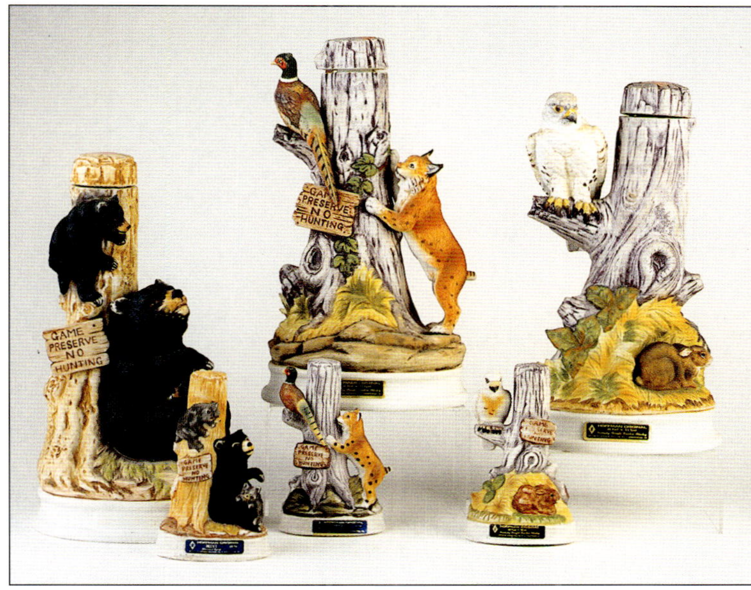

Bear and Cub, 1978, $30-35, mini $10. Bobcat and Pheasant, 1978, $25-30, mini $10. Falcon and Rabbit, 1978, $25-30, mini $10.

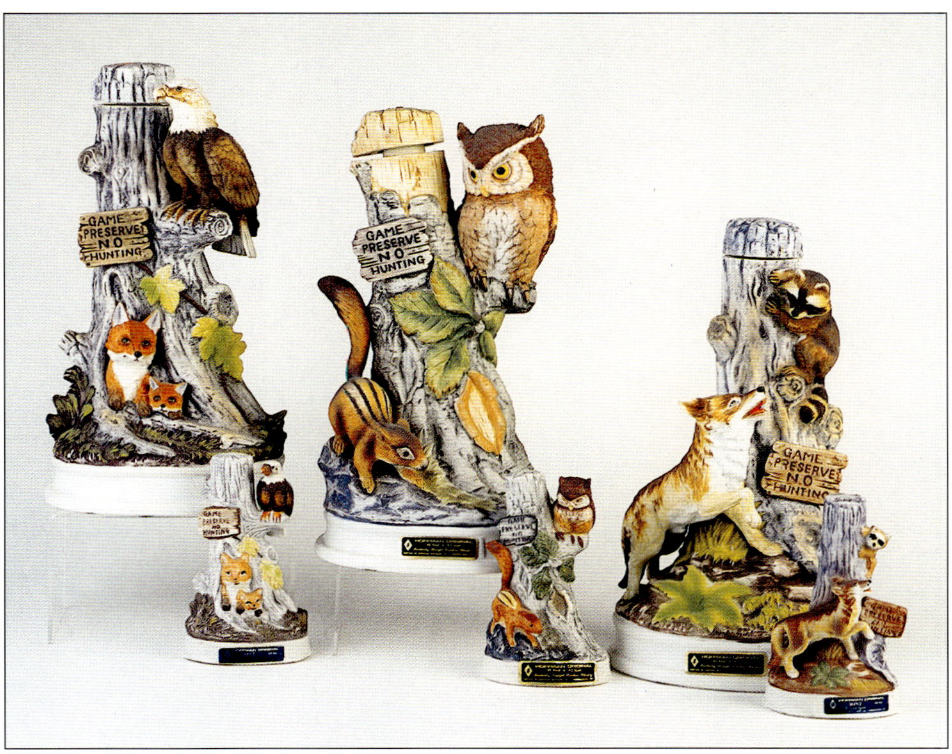

Fox and Eagle, 1978, $20-25, mini $10. Owl and Chipmunk, 1978, $25-30, mini $10. Wolf and Raccoon, 1978, $20-25, mini $10.

Miguer Series

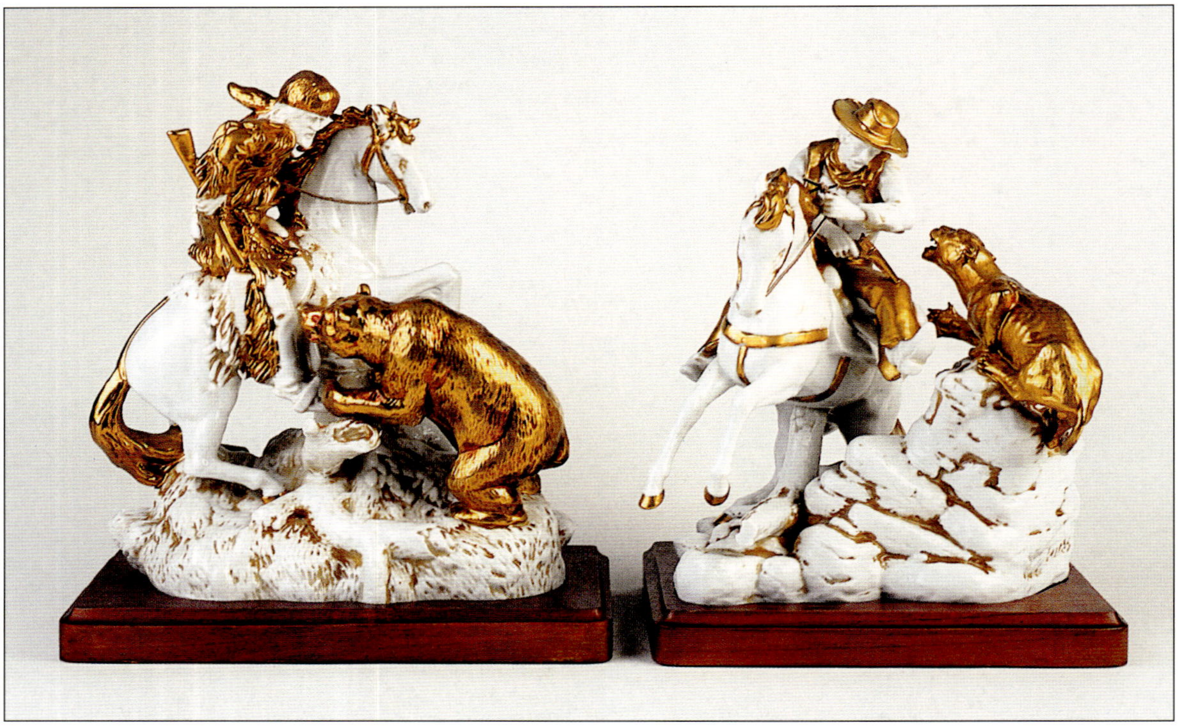

Big, Big Trouble on the Trail, 1981, $200-225; Stranger, This Land is Mine, 1981, $200-225.

100th Commemorative: Only 100 sets made to commemorate the Anniversary of Hoffman Distillery. Limited Edition, numbered and certified, accented in 24 k gold.

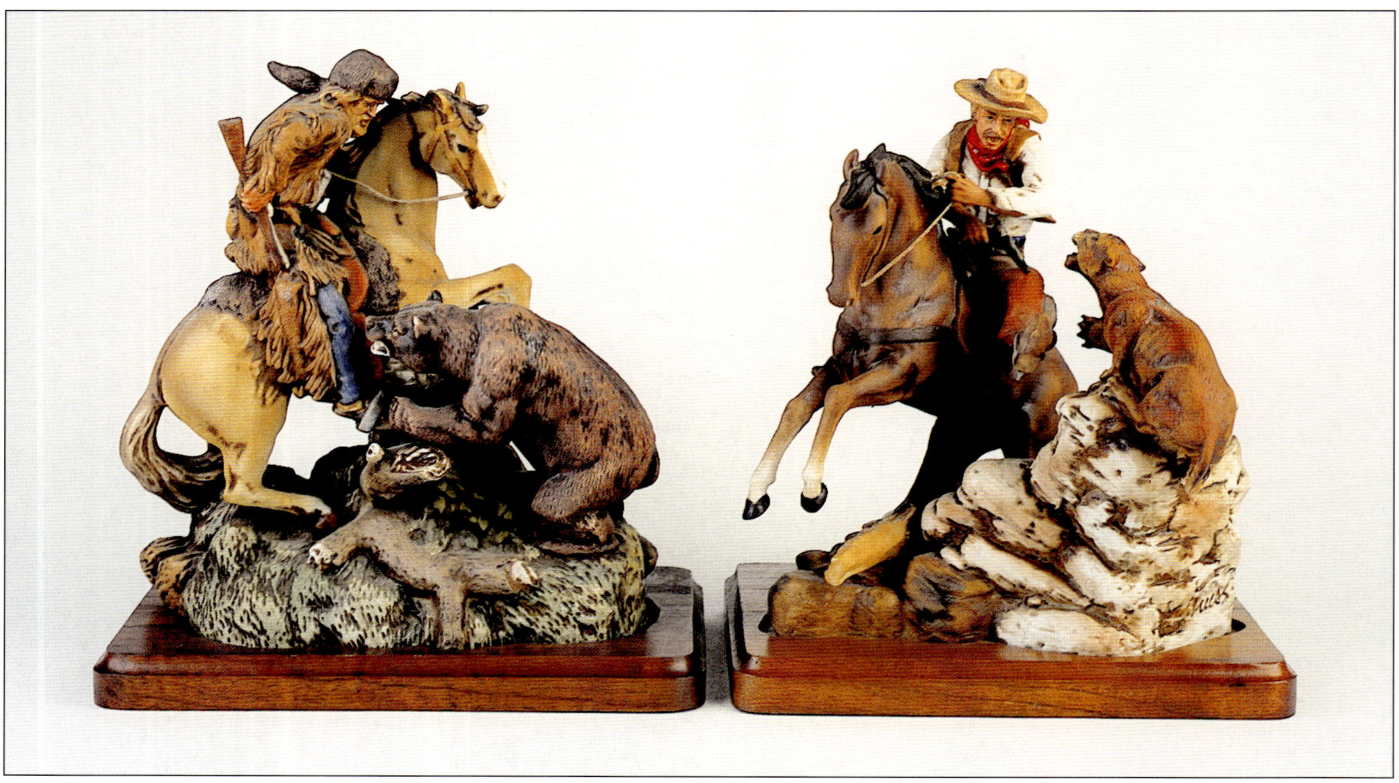

Big, Big Trouble on the Trail, 1981, $100-125; Stranger, This Land is Mine, 1981, $100-125.

Ohrman Wildlife Series

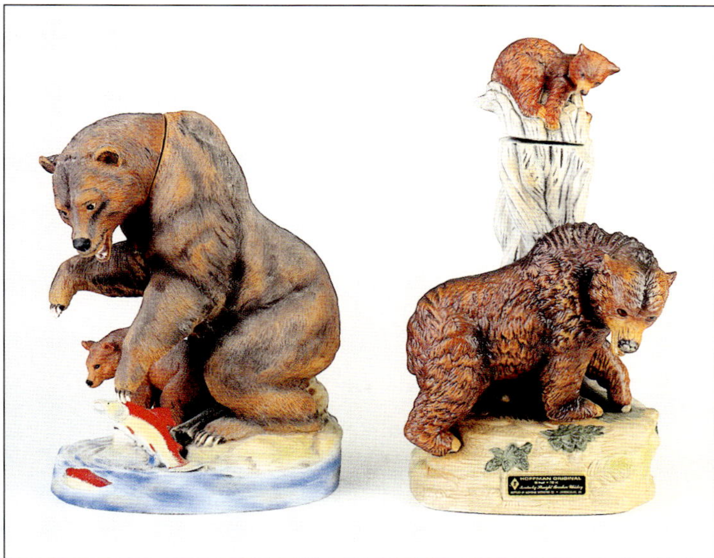

Bear and Cub Fishing, 1981, $30-35; Bear and Cub in a Tree, 1978, $20-25.

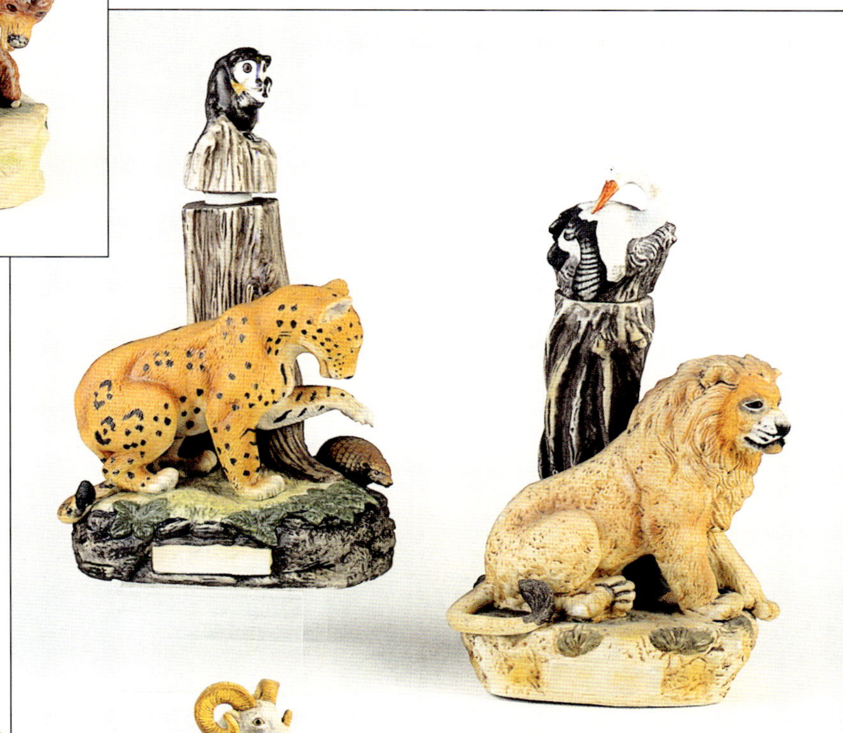

Jaguar and Possum, 1978, $10-15; Lion and Crane, 1978, $10-15.

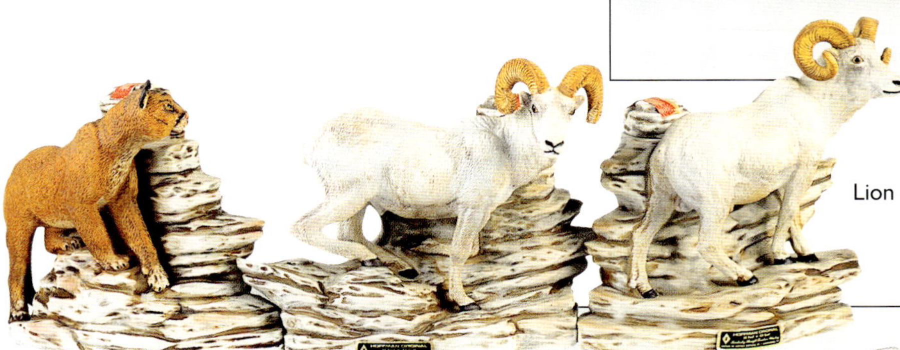

Lion and Dall Sheep set, 1977, $75-85.

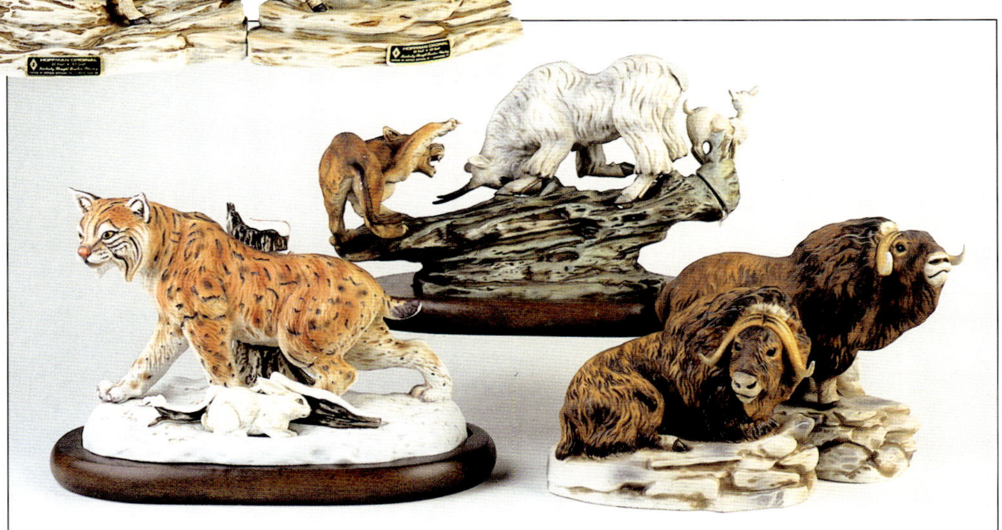

Lynx and Rabbit, 1981, $45-50; Mountain Goat and Puma, 1981, $60-70; Musk Ox Pair, 1979, $60-70.

Wildlife Richardson Series

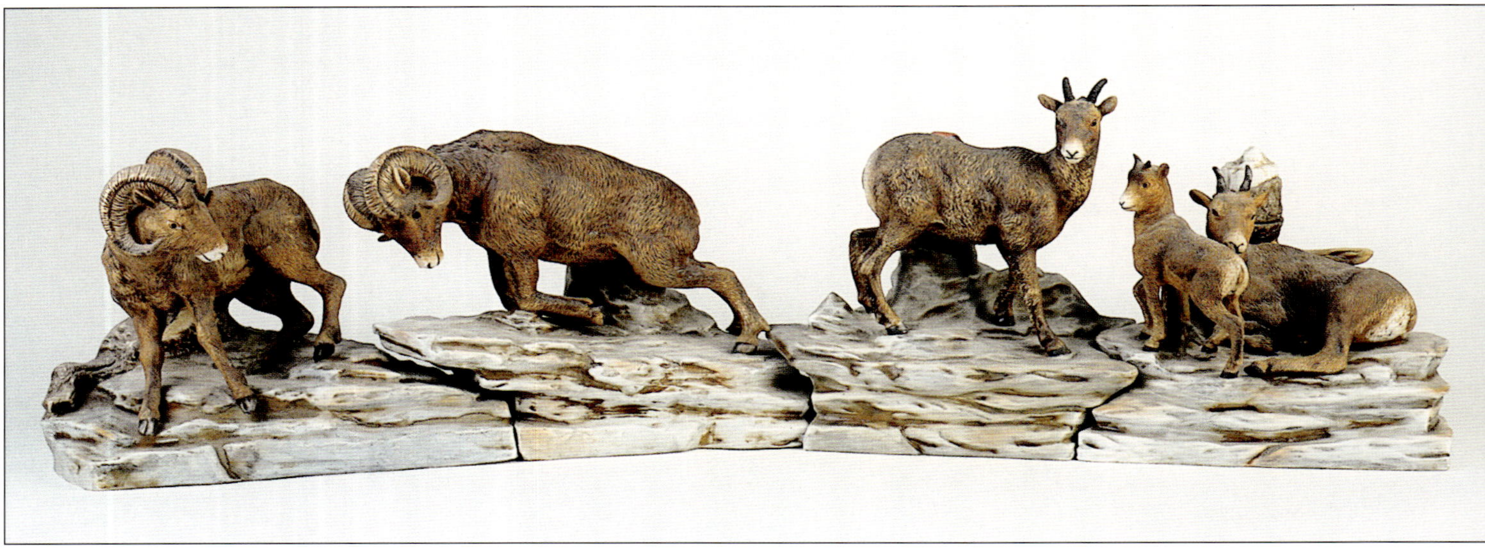

Fighting Rams Set, 1977, $175-195.

Miscellaneous Wildlife

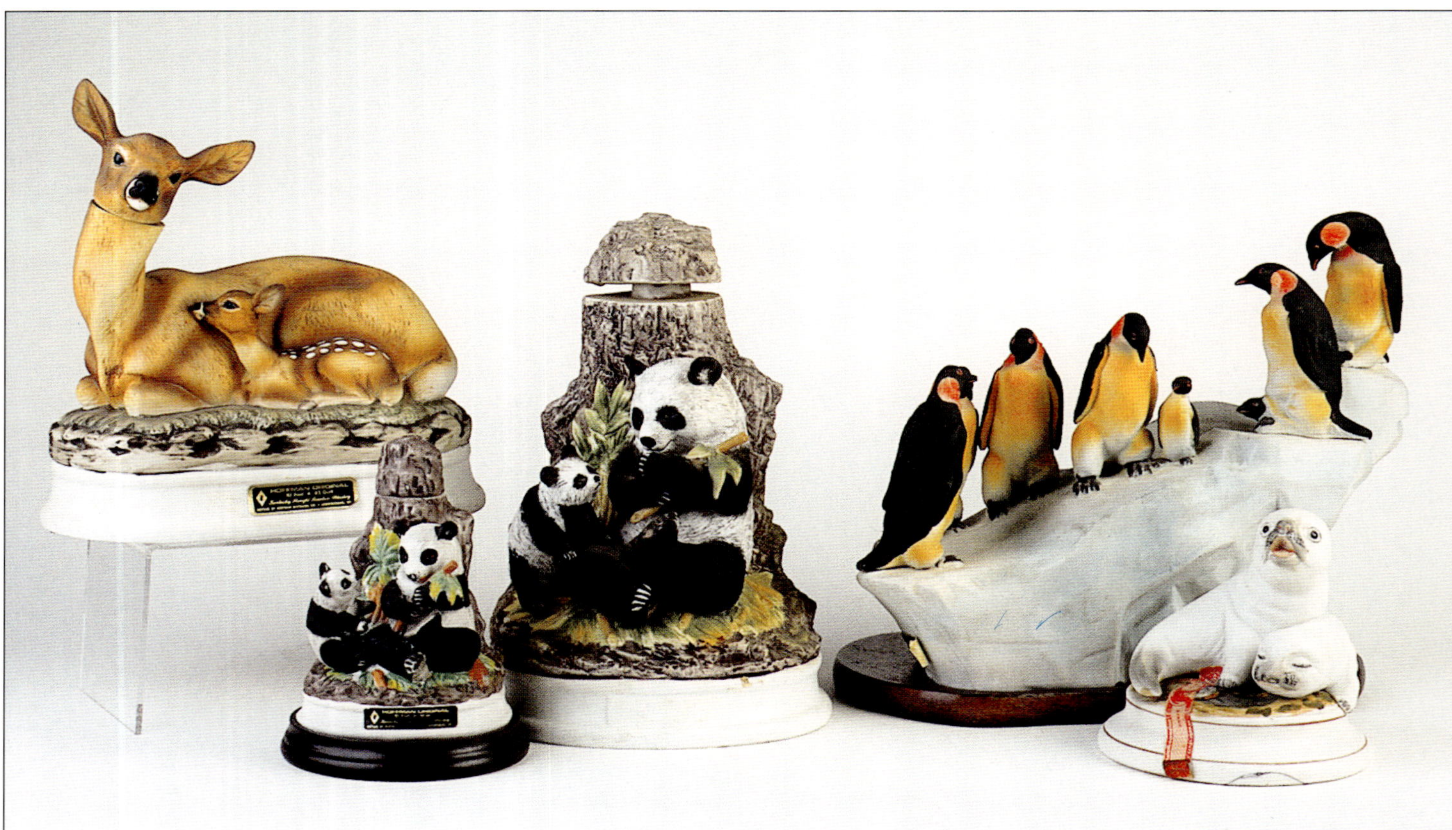

Doe & Fawn, 1975, mini $20-25. Panda, 1976, $20-25, mini $10.
Penguins, 1979, $20-25. Seal pups, 1979, $15-20.

Automotive and Transportation

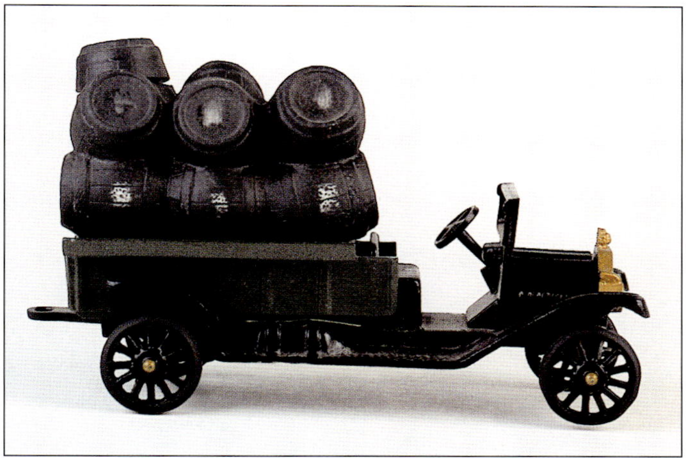

Distillery Truck, 1981, 200ml $35-40.

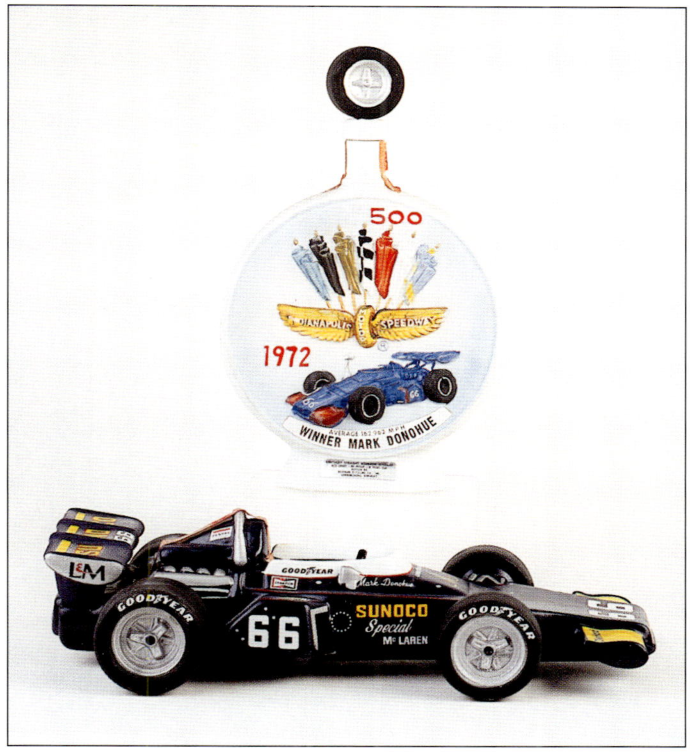

Mark Donahue Commemorative, 1972, $20-25.
Donahue Sunoco, #66, 1972, $65-75.

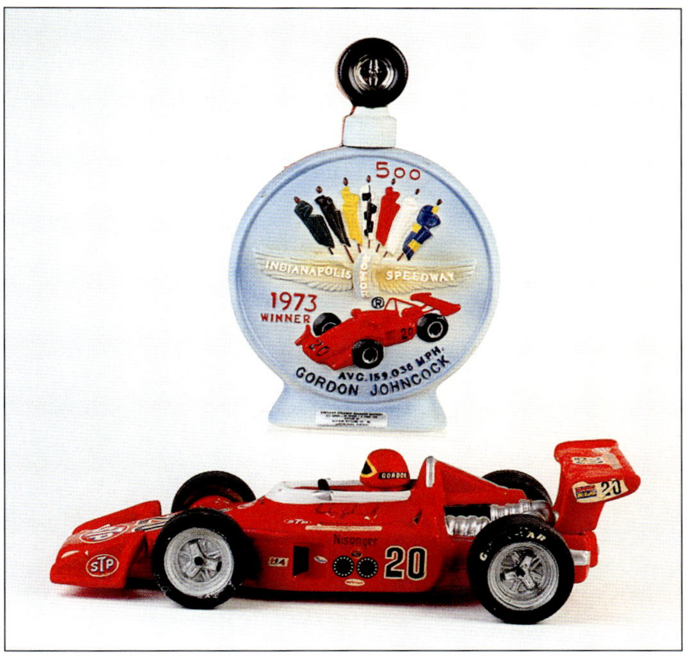

Gordon Johncock Commemorative, 1973, $25-30. Johncock #20, 1974, $35-40.

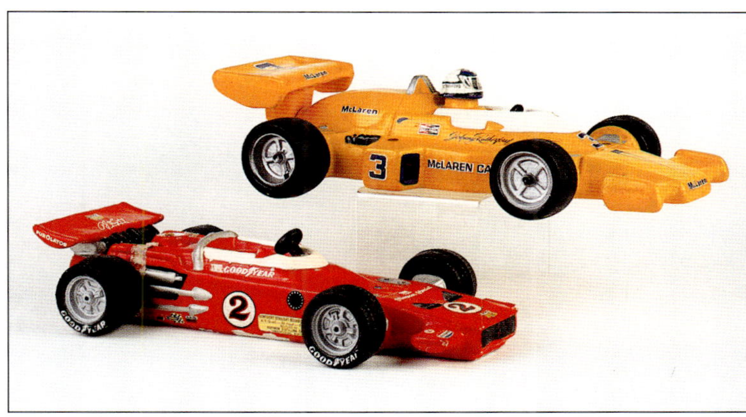

A.J. Foyte #2, 1972, $65-75. Rutherford #3, 1974, $50-60.

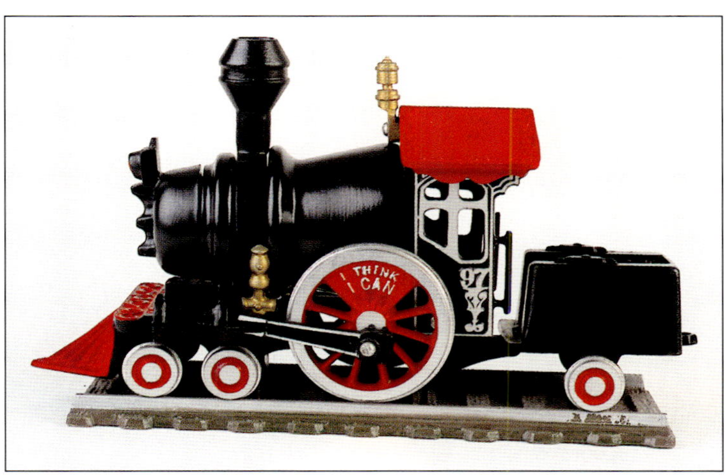

Locomotive, 1981, $35-40.

Band Street Swingers Series

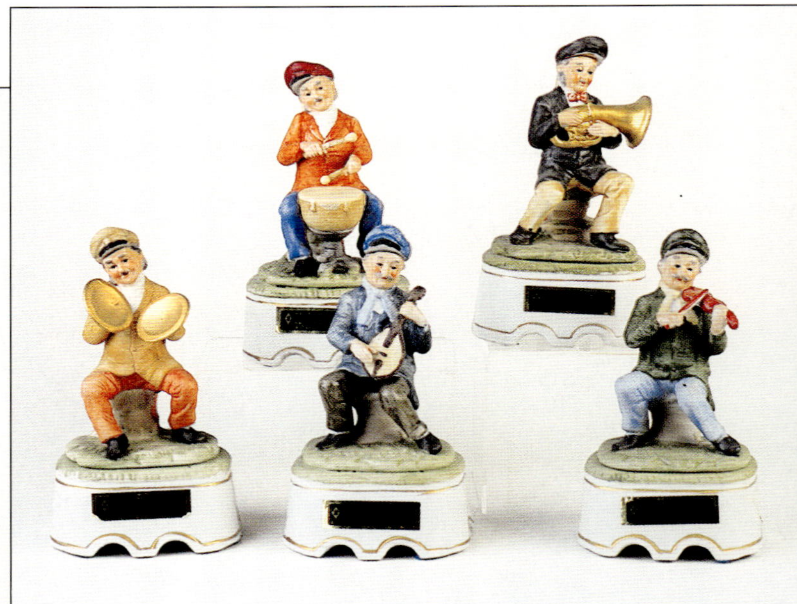

#1, Bass Player, 1979 (not shown) $10-15. Cymbal Player, 1979, $10-15. Drummer, 1979, $10-15. Mandolin Player, 1979, $10-15. Tuba Player, 1979, $10-15. Violin, 1979, $10-15. All the Band Sreet Swingers are music boxes.

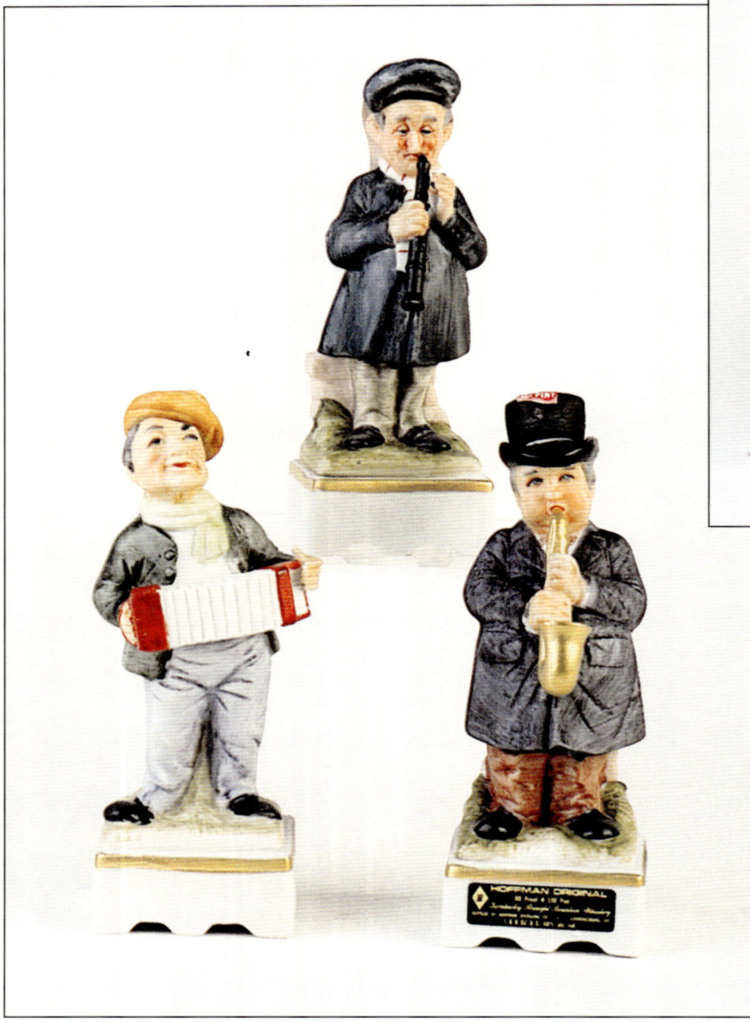

#2, Accordion Player, 1978, $10-15. Clarinet Player, 1978, $10-15. Cymbal Player, 1978 (not shown), $10-15. Fiddler, 1978 (not shown), $10-15. Saxophone Player, (not shown), $10-15. Tuba Player, 1978 (not shown), $10-15. All the Band Sreet Swingers are music boxes.

Miscellaneous Hoffman

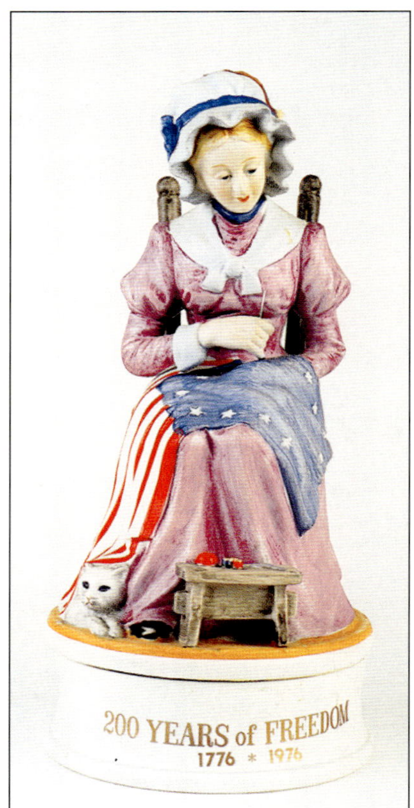

Betsy Ross, 1974, $15-20.

Hoffman Birds

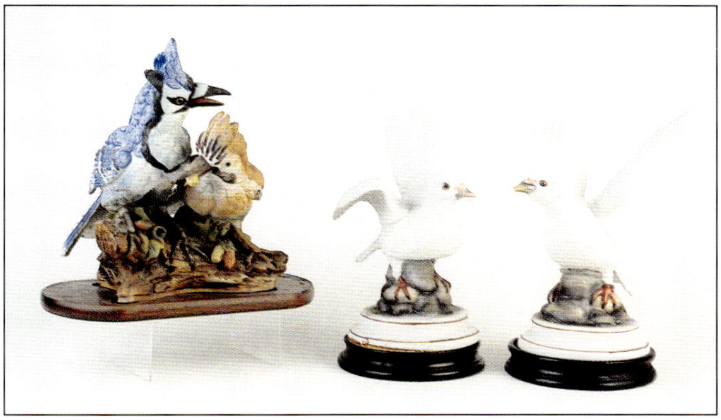

Blue Jay pair, 1979, $15-20. Closed Wing Dove, 1979, $10-15. Open Wing Dove, 1979, $10-15.

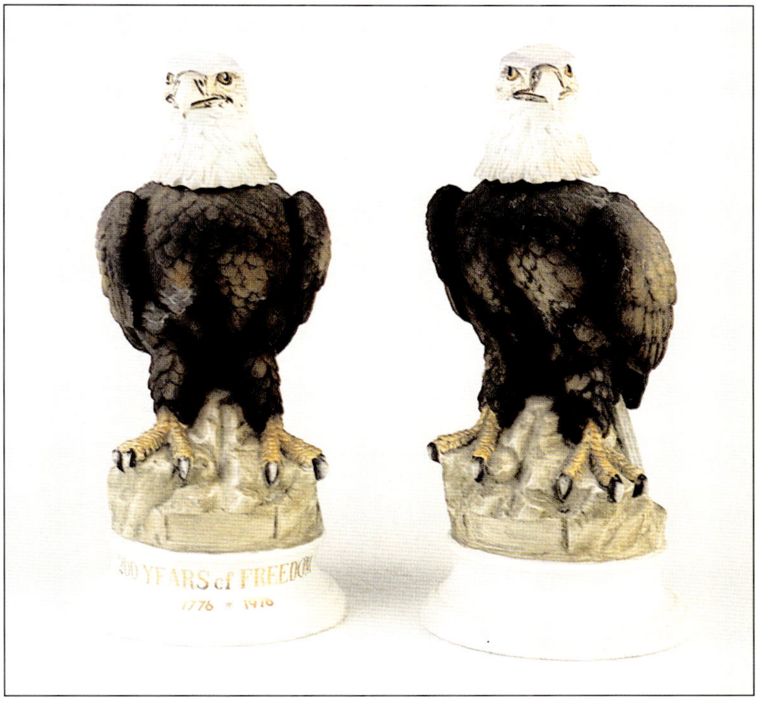

Eagle, 200 years of freedom, music box, 1976, $15-20. Eagle, music box, $20-25.

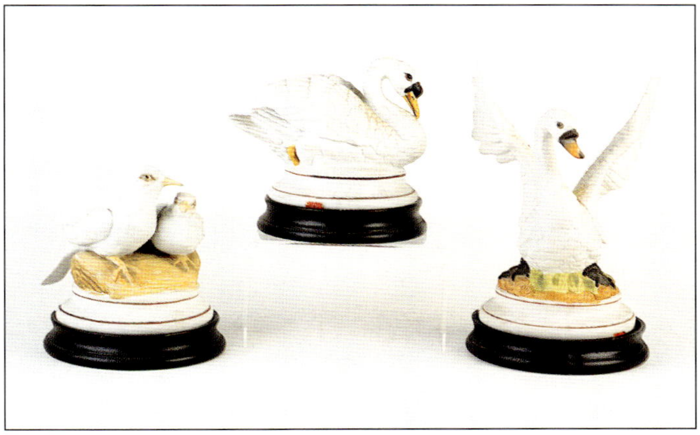

Love Birds, 1979, 1/2 pint $10. Closed wing swan, 1980, 200 ml $10. Open wing swan, 1980, 200 ml $10.

Open Wing Eagle, 1979, mini $10. Baby Egret, 1979, 200 ml $10. Canada Geese pair, 1980, 200 ml $10. Geese pair, 1980, 1/2 pint $10. Canadian goose decoy, 1977, 8 oz $10.

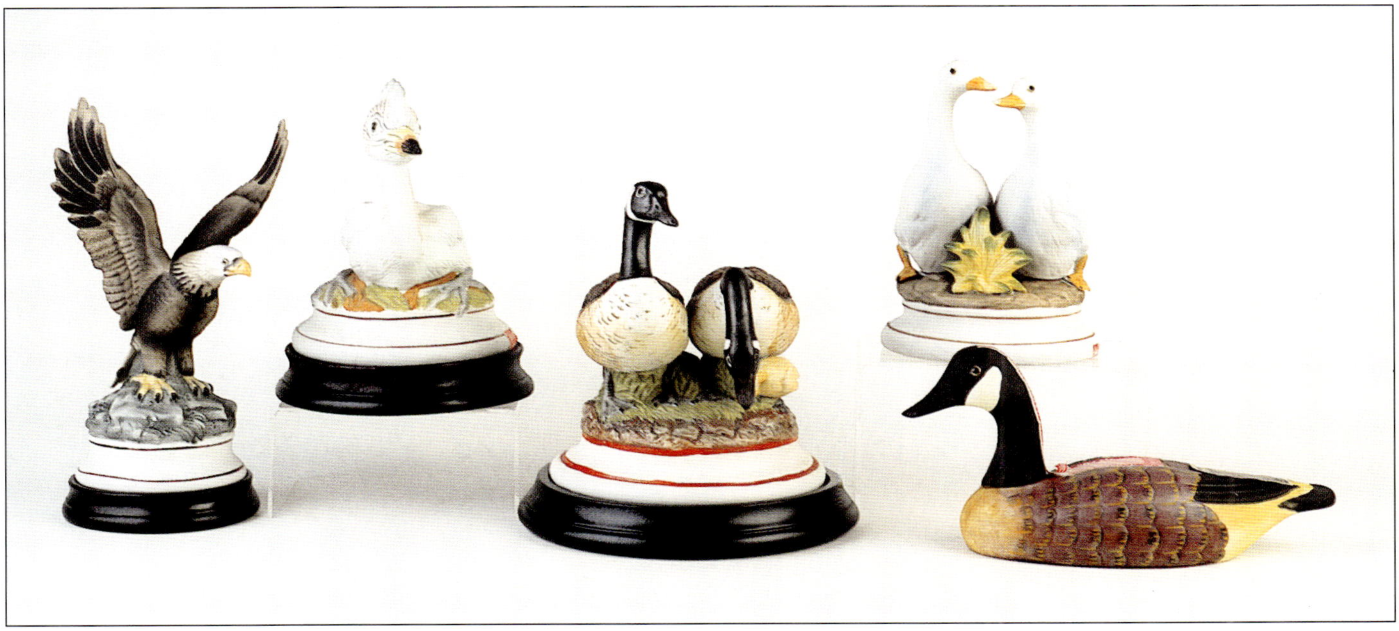

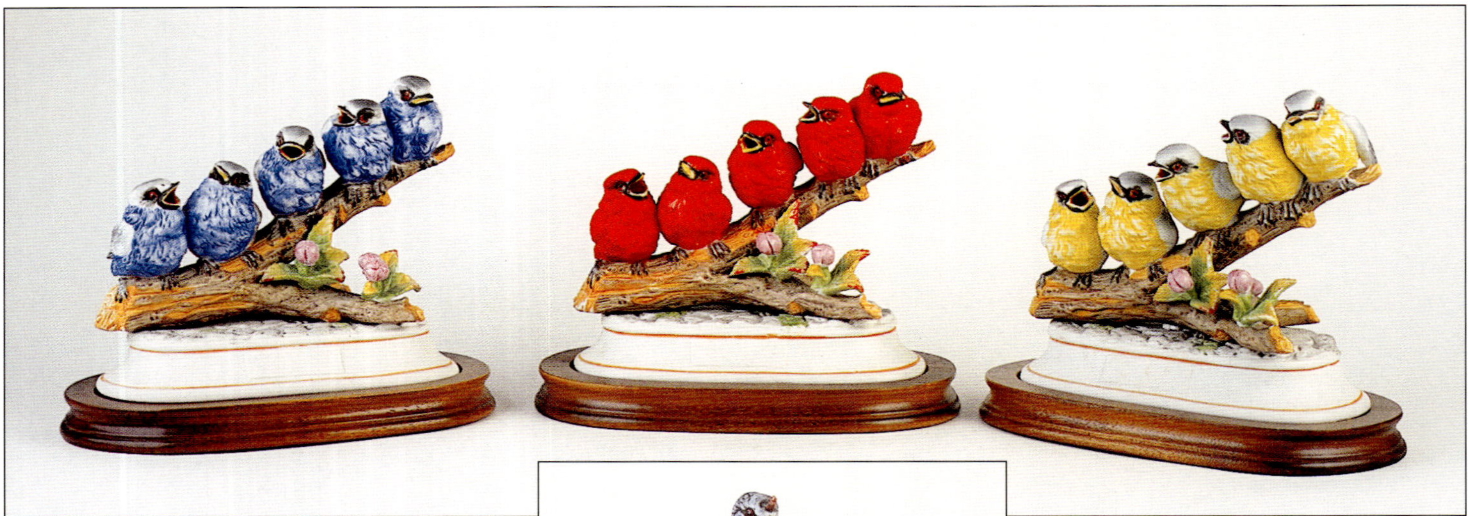

Baby Titmice, 1979: blue $15-20; red $15-20; yellow $15-20.

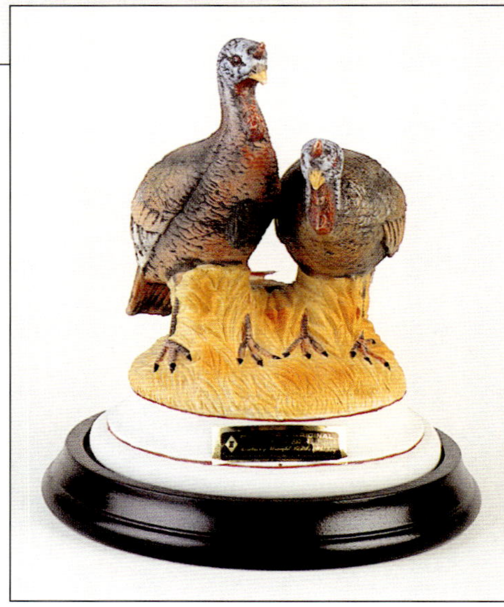

Turkeys, 1980, 200 ml $20-25.

Children of the World Series

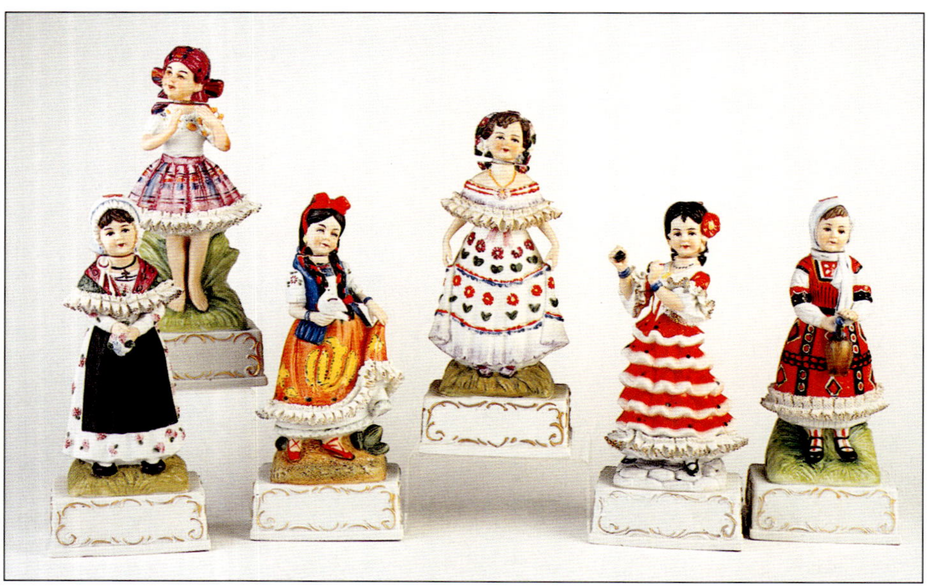

France 1979, 8 oz $10-15. Jamaica 1979, 8 oz $10-15. Mexico 1979, 8 oz $10-15. Panama 1979, 8 oz $10-15. Spain 1979, 8 oz $10-15. Yugoslavia 1979, 8 oz $10-15.

Hoffman Ducks

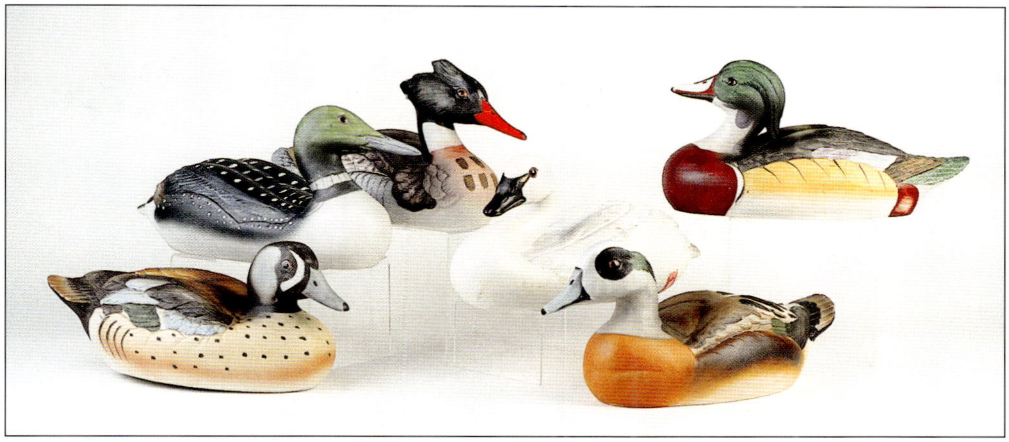

Duck Decoys: Blue Wing Teal, 1978, $10-15; Loon, 1978, $15-20; Merganzer, 1978, $10-15; Swan, 1978, $10-15; Widgeon, 1978, $10-15; Wood Duck, 1978, $15-20.

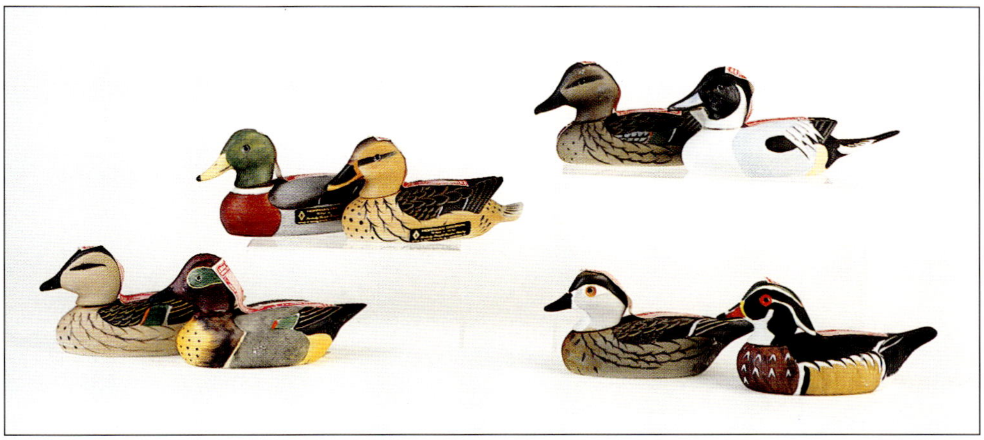

Duck Decoys pairs: Green Wing Teal, 1977, mini $10; Mallards, 1977, mini $10; Pintail, 1977, mini $10; Red Head, 1977, mini $10.

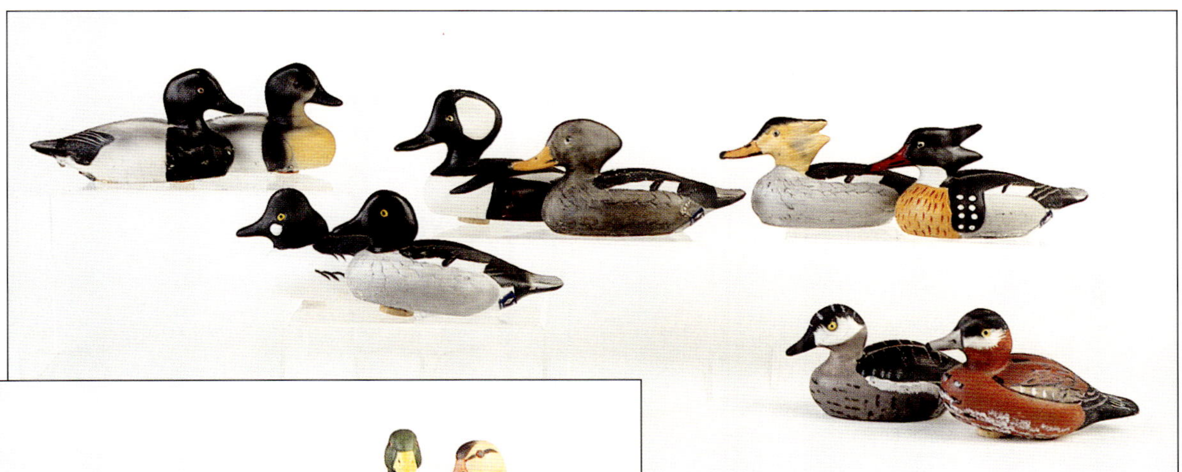

Canvas Back, 1978, mini $10. Golden Eye, 1978, mini $10. Hooded Mergnazer, 1978, mini $10. Red Breasted Merganzer, 1978, mini $10. Ruddy Duck, 1978, mini $10.

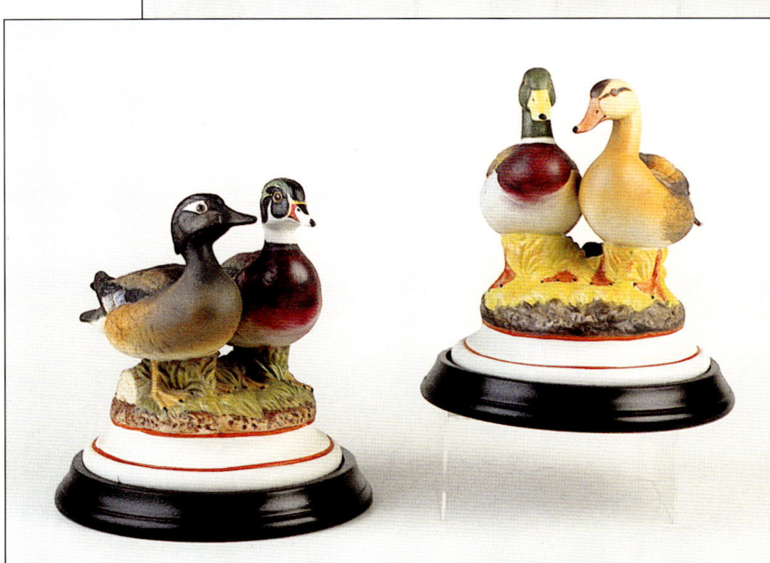

Closed wing Mallards, 1982, $10-15. Open wing Mallards, 1980, $10-15.

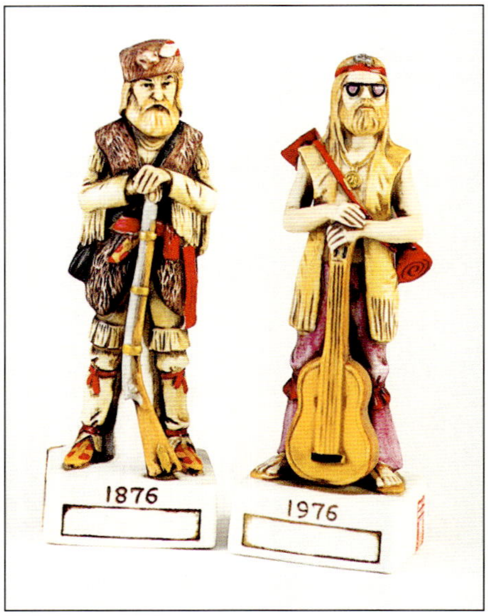

Generation Gap 1876-1976, 1976,
mini pair $10.

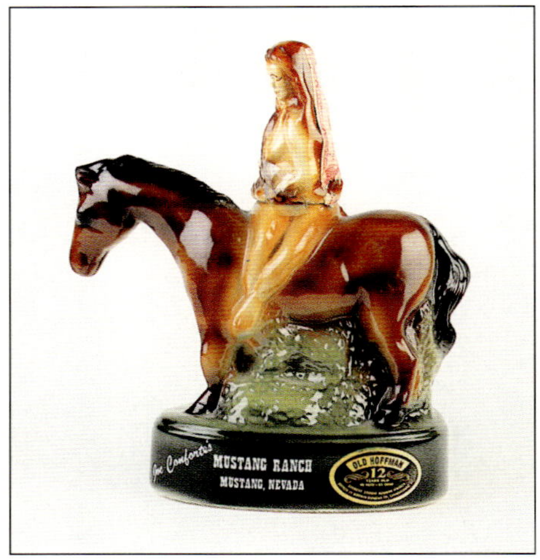

Lady Godiva, 1974, $65-75

Mr. Lucky Series

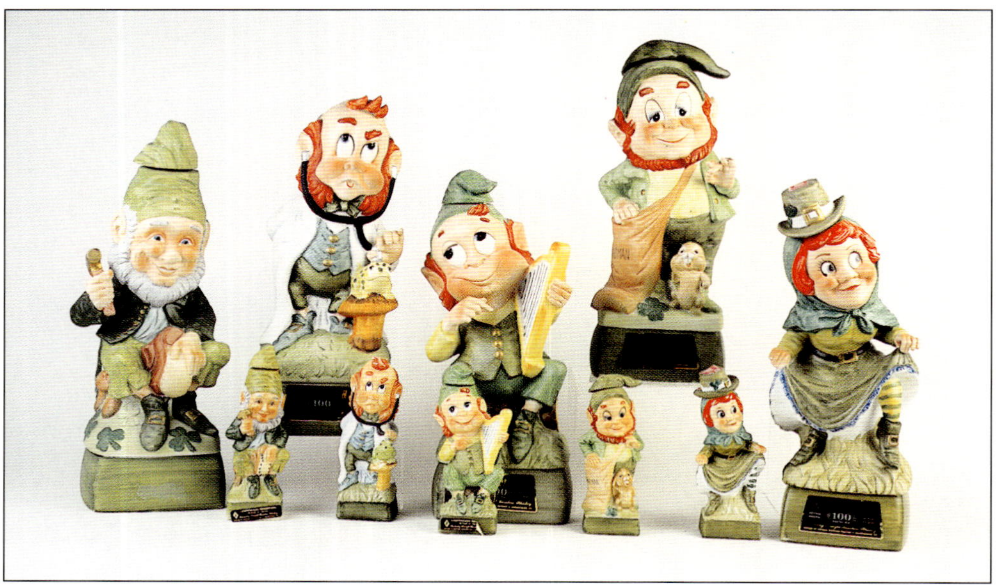

Cobbler, 1973, $15-20, mini $10. Doctor, 1974, $15-20, mini $10. Harpist, 1974, $10-15, mini $10. Sandman, 1974, $10-15, mini $10. Mrs. Lucky, $10-15, mini $10. All fifth size decanters are music boxes.

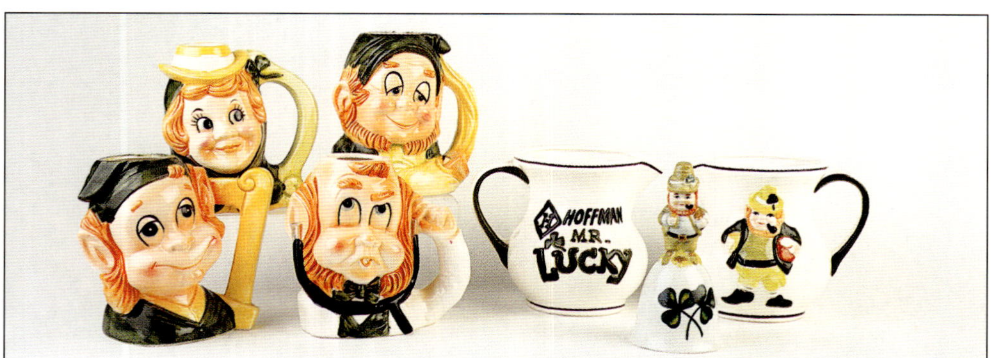

Mr. Harpist, 1979, $10-15. Mrs. Lucky, 1979, $10-15. Mr. Sandman, 1979, $10-15. Mr. Doctor, 1979, $10-15. Mr. Lucky Pitcher, 1978, $10-15. Mr. Lucky Pitcher, 1978, $10-15.

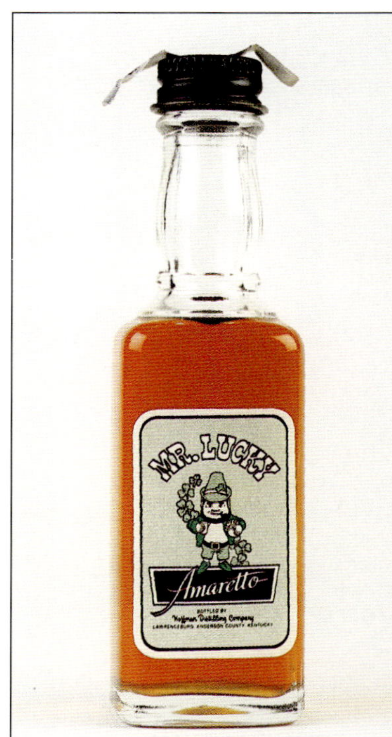

Mr. Lucky Amaretto, mini $5.

Charmer, 1974, $10-15, mini $10. Dancer, 1974, $15-20, mini $10. Fiddler, 1974, $10-15, mini $10. Policeman, 1975, $35-40, mini $10-15. Saxophonist, 1975, $15-20, mini $10. All fifth size decanters are music boxes.

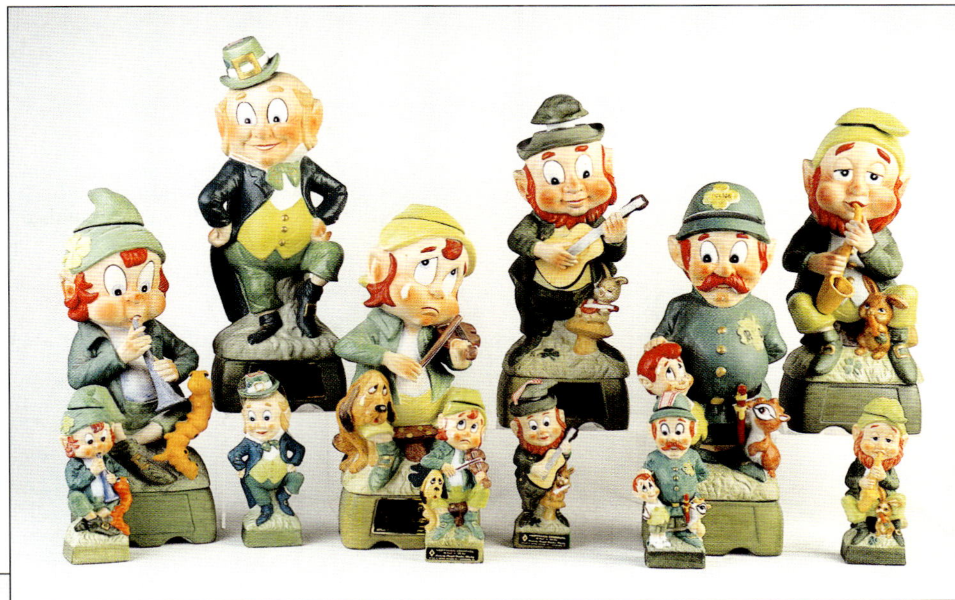

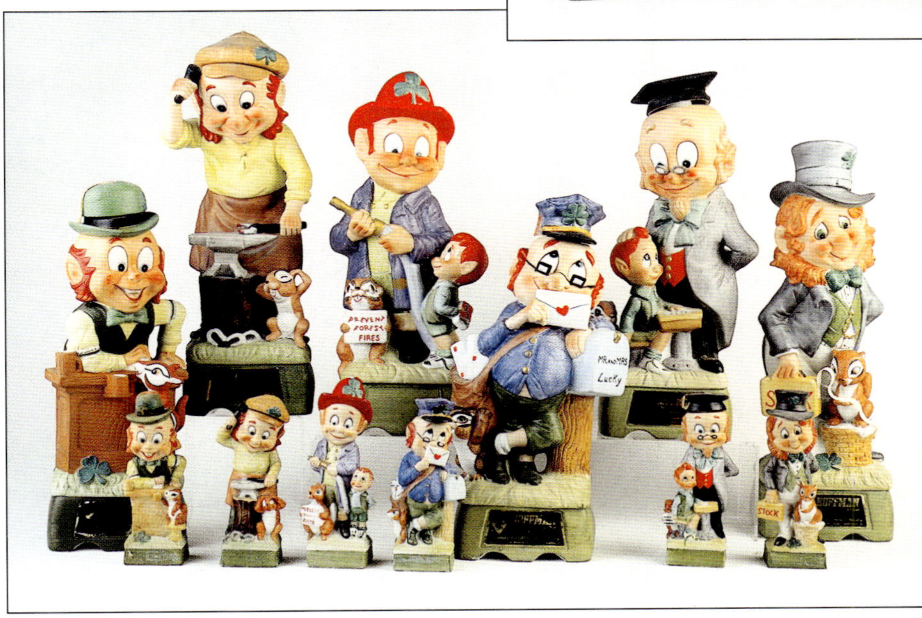

Bartender, 1975, $20-25, mini $10. Blacksmith, 1976, $10-15, mini $10. Fireman, 1976, $45-50, mini $15-20. Mailman, 1976, $25-30, mini $15-20. School Teacher, 1976, $15-20, mini $10. Stockbroker, 1976, $15-20, mini $10. All fifth size decanters are music boxes.

Butcher, 1979, $10-15, mini $10. Carpenter, 1979, $15-20, mini $10. Electrician, 1978, $15-20, mini $10. Mechanic, 1979, $15-20, mini $10. Plumber, 1978, $15-20, mini $10. Tailor, 1979, $10-15, mini $10. All fifth size decanters are music boxes.

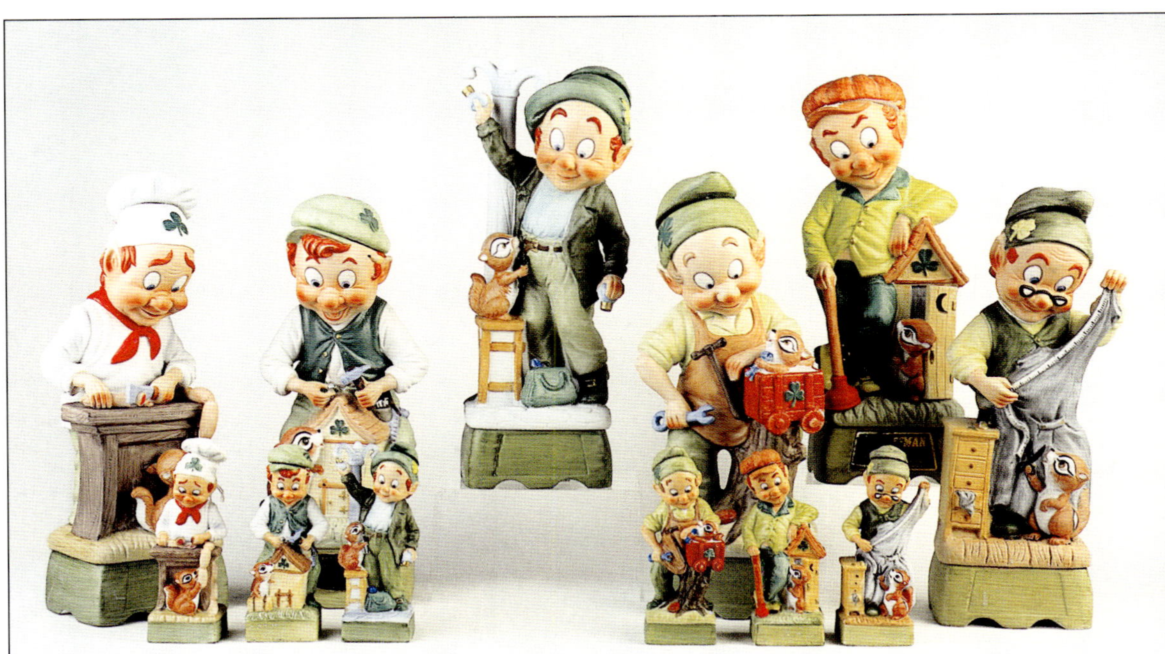

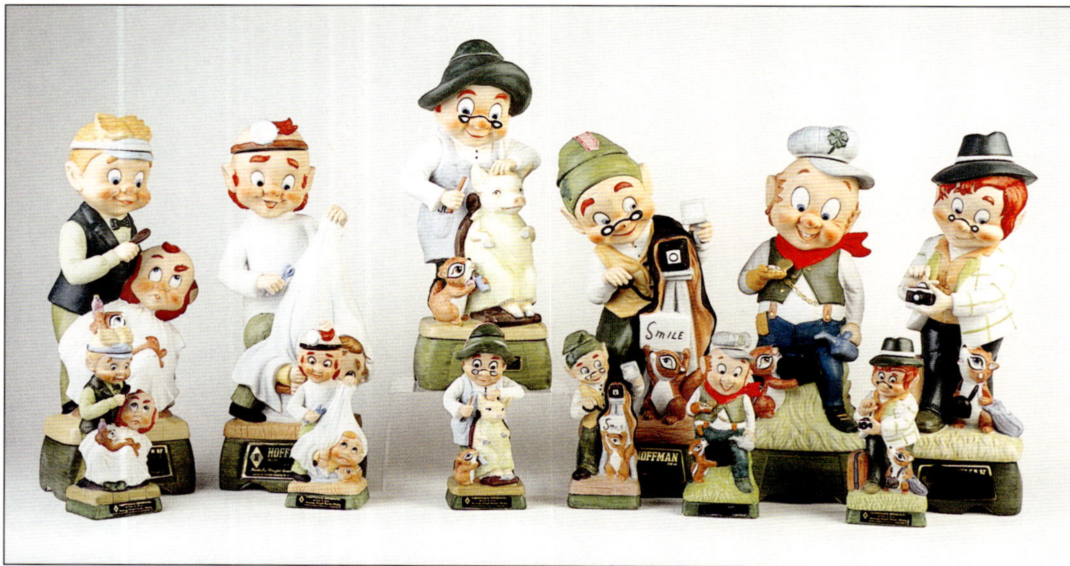

Barber, 1980, $10-15, mini $10. Dentist, 1980, $15-20, mini $10. Farmer, 1980, $10-15, mini $10. Photographer, 1980, $20-25, mini $15. Railroad Engineer, 1980, $15-20, mini $10. Tourist, 1980, $15-20, mini $10. All fifth size decanters are music boxes.

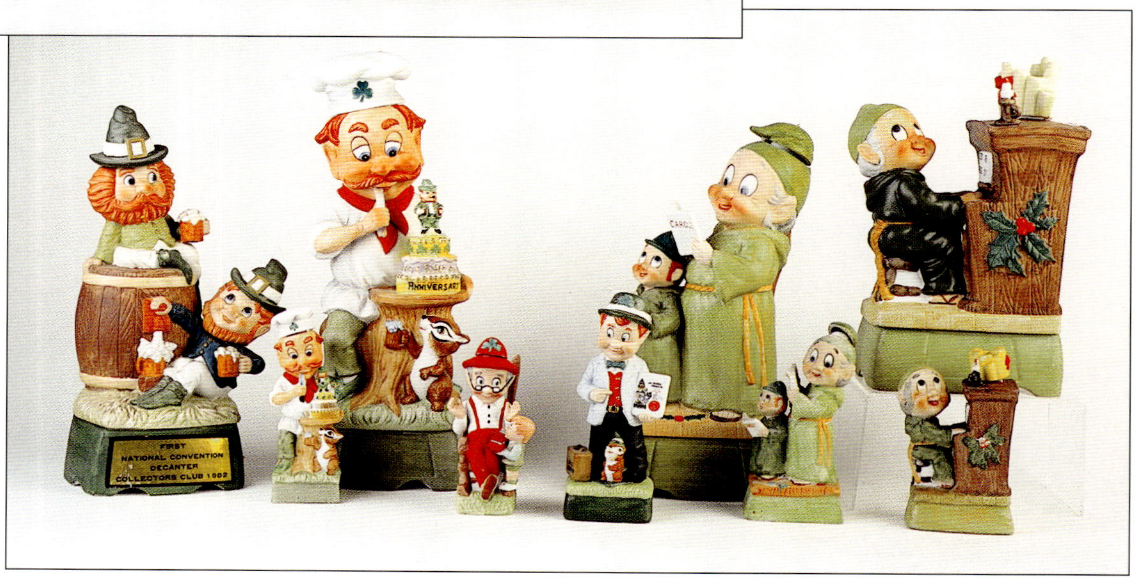

Leprechaun on a Barrel, convention decanter, 1982, $15-20. Carolers, 1979, $15-20, mini $10. Baker, 1978, $15-20, mini $10. Mr. Fireman retired, 1983, mini $15-20. Salesman, 1982, mini $10-15. Organ Player, 1979, $10-15, mini $10. All fifth size decanters are music boxes.

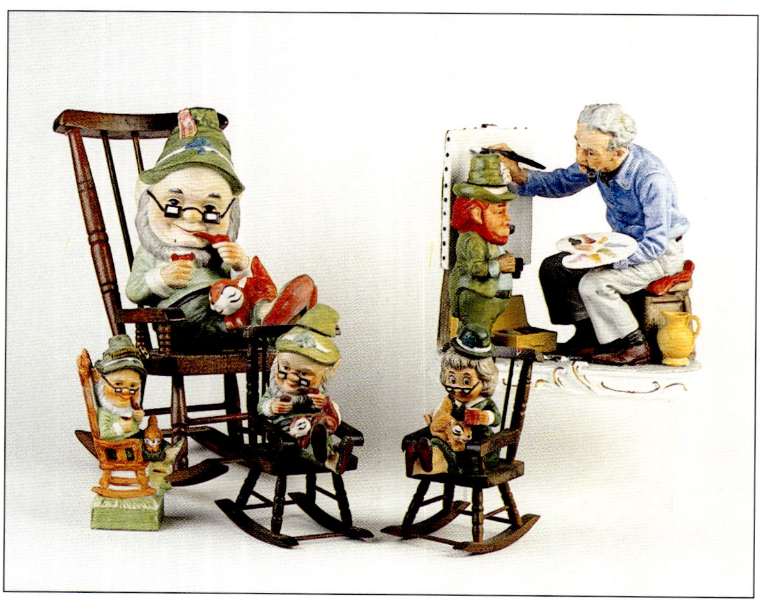

Lucky retired with wooden chair, 1981, $25-30. Lucky retired, 1978, mini $15-20. Lucky retired with wooden chair, 1981, mini $10-15. Mrs. Lucky retired with wooden chair, 1981, mini $10-15. Lucky and Norman Rockwell, 1980, $45-50.

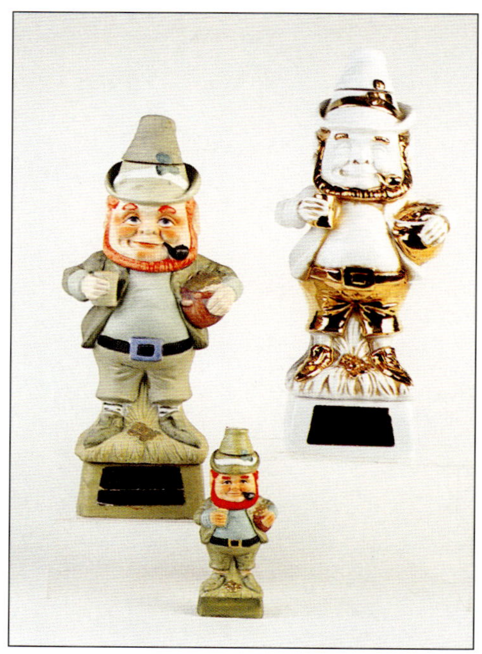

Lucky, 1973, $20-25, mini $10. Lucky (white and gold), 1981, $75-95.

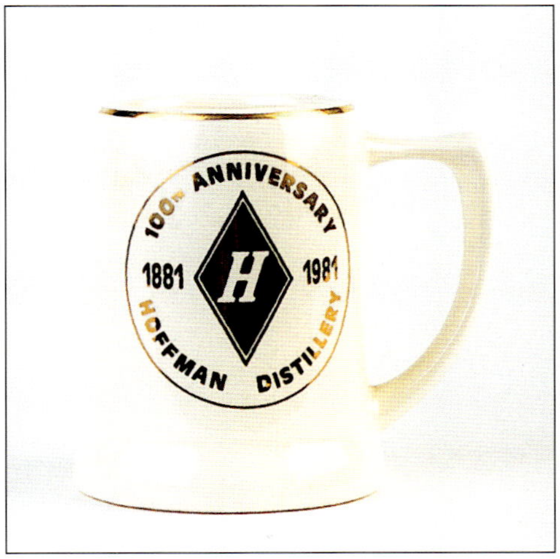

100th Anniversary Hoffman Distillery, 1981, mug $5.

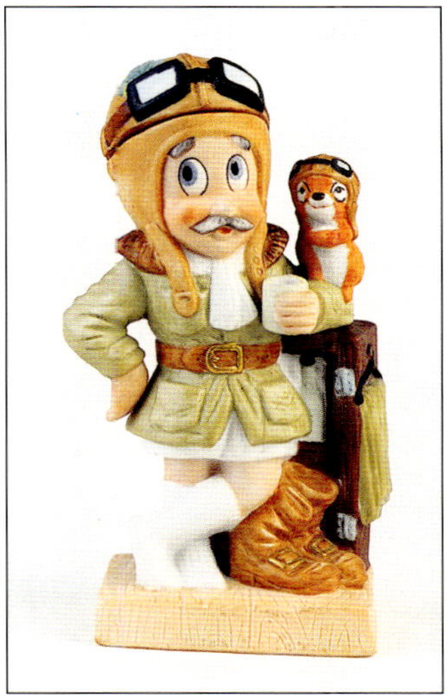

Aviator, 1989, mini $10-15.

Pistol Series

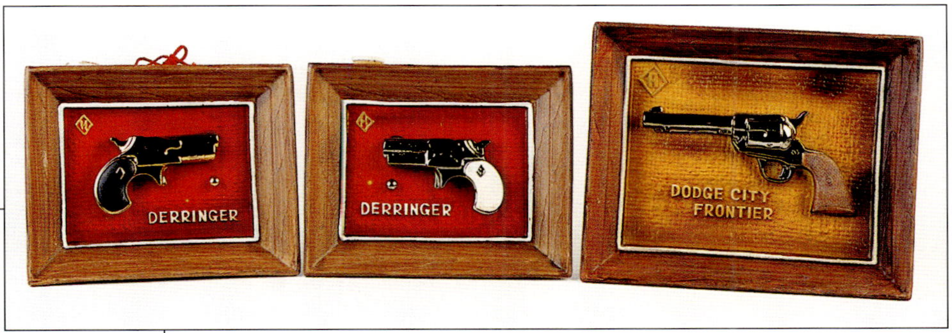

Framed Pistols: Derringer Gold, 1979, pint $10-15. Derringer Silver, 1979, pint $10-15. Dodge City Frontier, 1978, pint $10-15.

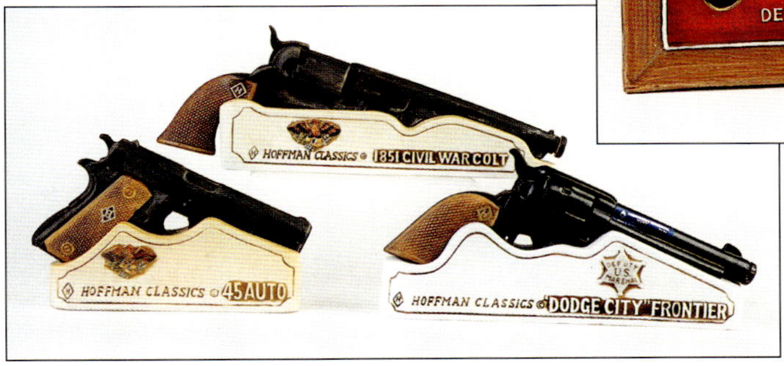

With stand: 45 Automatic, 1975, mini $10. Civil War Colt, 1975, mini $10. Dodge City Frontier, 1975, mini $10.

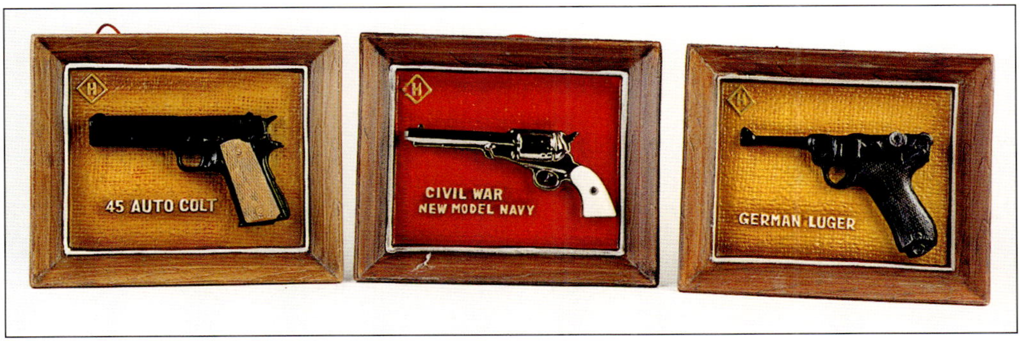

Framed Pistols: 45 Automatic, pint $10-15; Civil War Colt, 1978, pint $10-15; German Lugar, 1978, pint, $10.

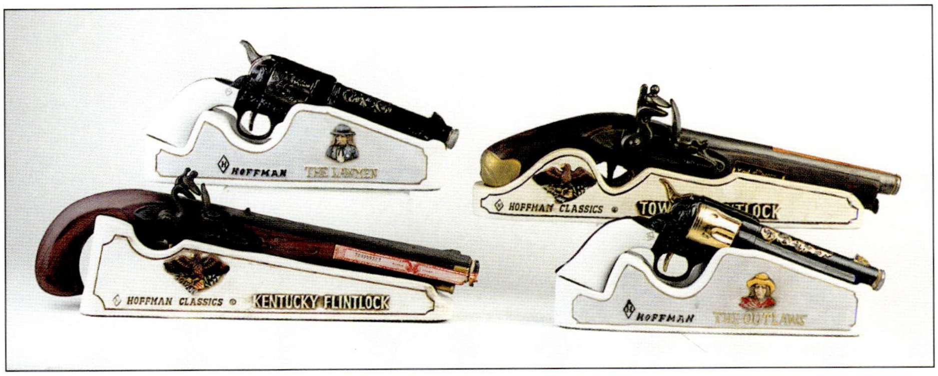

With stand: Kentucky Flintlock, 1975, 8 oz. $10. The Lawman, 1978, mini $10-15. The Outlaw, 1978, mini $10-15. Tower Flintlock, 1975, 8 oz. $10.

Rodeo Series

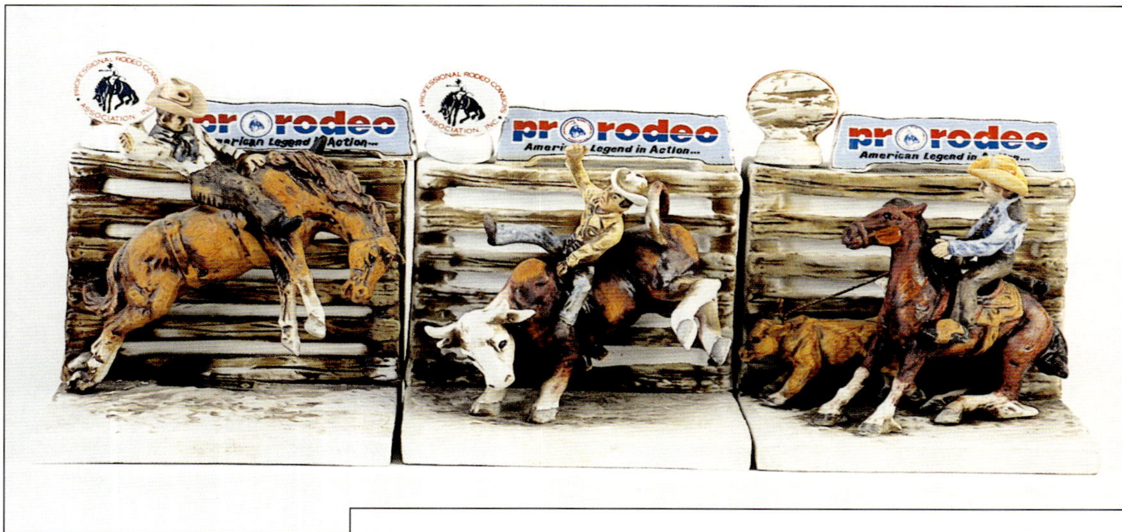

Bareback Rider, 1978, $10-15. Brahma Bull Riding, 1978, $10-15. Calf Roping, 1978, $10-15.

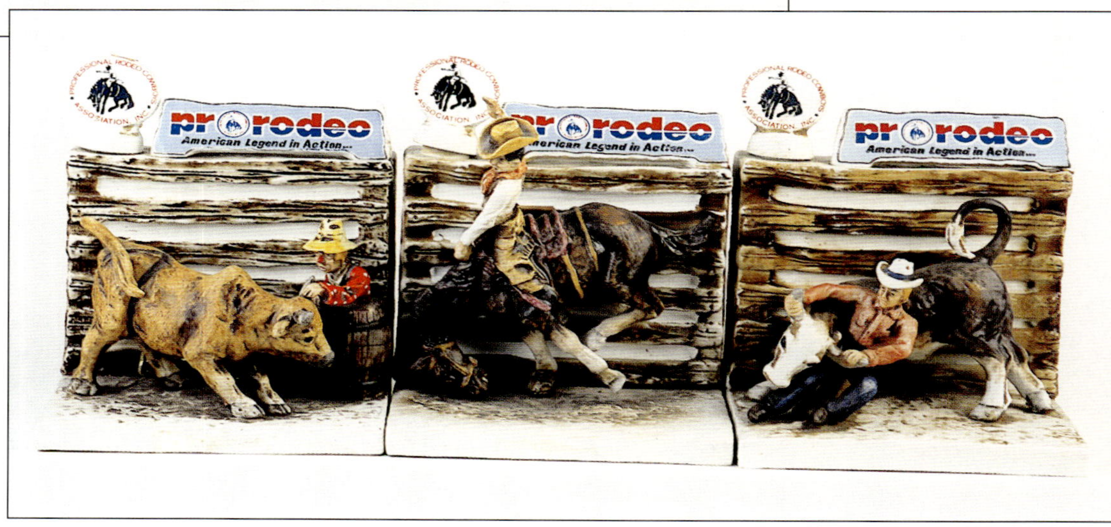

Clown, 1978, $10-15. Saddle Bronc Riding, 1978, $10-15. Steer Wrestling, 1978, $10-15.

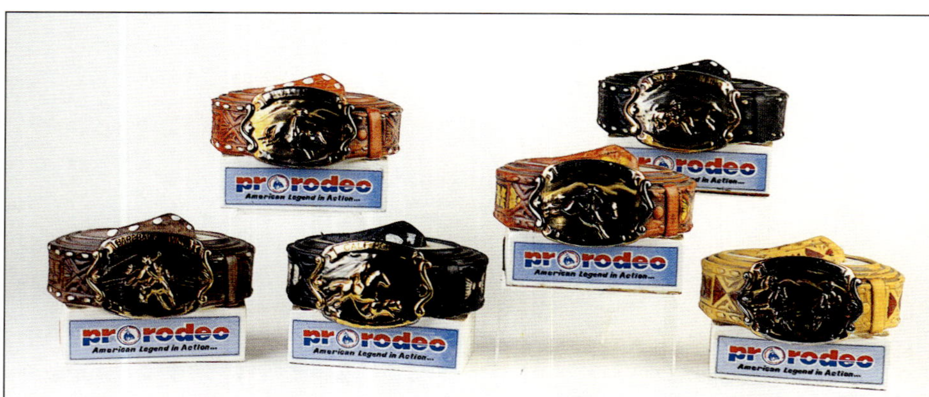

Belt Buckles: Bareback Riding, 1979, $10. Bull Riding, 1979, $10. Calf Roping, 1979, $10. Saddle Bronc Riding, 1979, $10. Steer Wrestling, 1979, $10. Team Roping, 1979, $10.

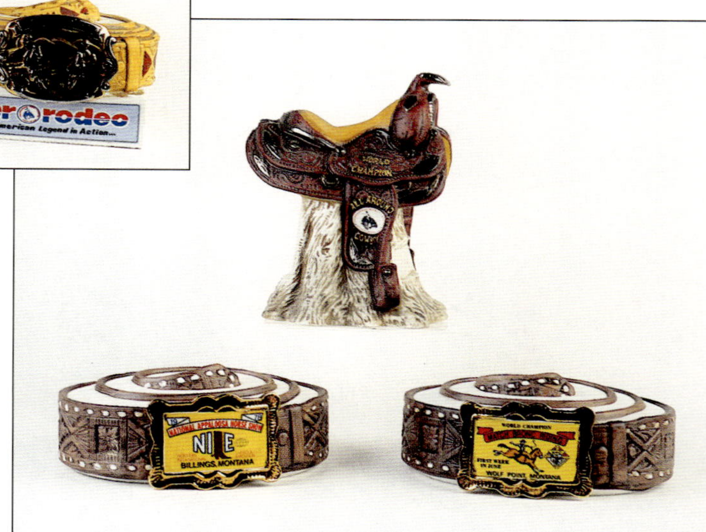

Belt Buckles: Billings Montana, National Appaloosa Horse Show, 1978, $10-15. Wolf Point Montana, Match Point Riding, 1978, $10-15. Rodeo Championship Saddle, 1978, $30-35.

C.M. Russell Series

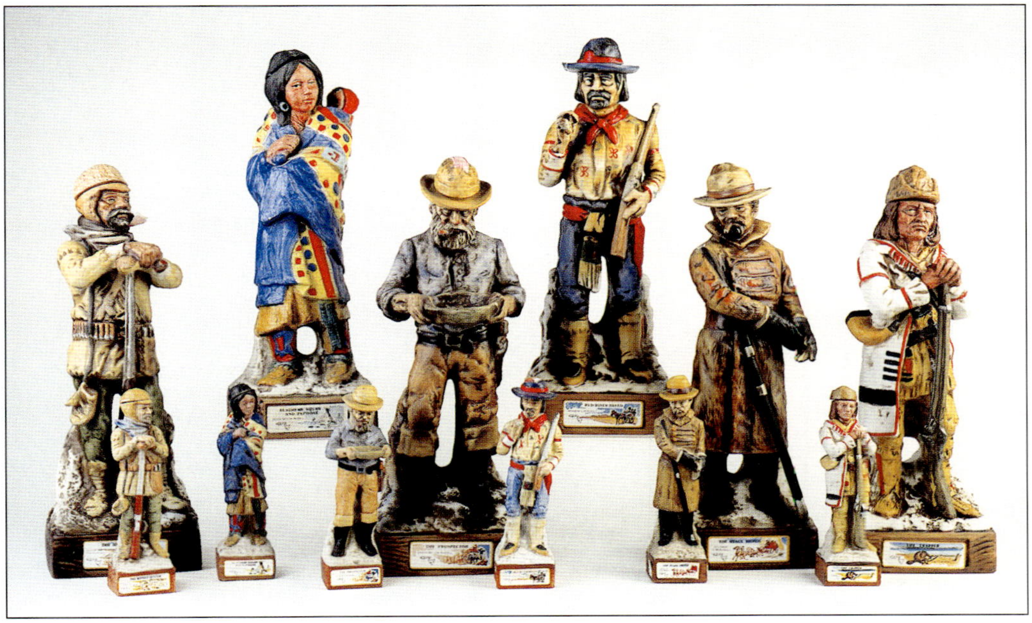

Buffalo Man, 1978, $20-25, mini $10; Flat Head Squaw, 1978, $20-25, mini $10; Prospector, 1978, $15-20, mini $10; Red River Breed, 1978, $15-20, mini $10; Stagecoach Driver, 1978, $15-20, mini $10; Trapper, 1978, $15-20, mini $10.

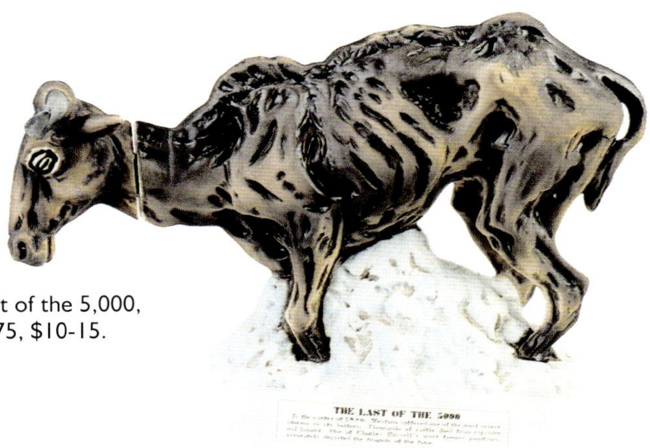

Last of the 5,000, 1975, $10-15.

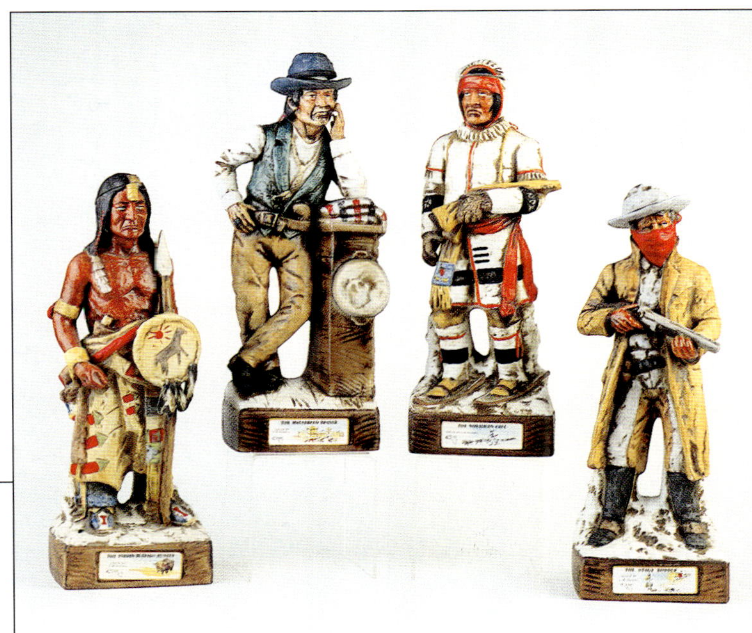

Buffalo Hunter, 1978, $20-25. Half Breed Traitor, 1978, $20-25. Northern Cree, 1978, $15-20. Stage Coach Robber, 1978, $20-25. Not shown: Cowboy, 1978, $15-20; Scout, 1978, $15-20.

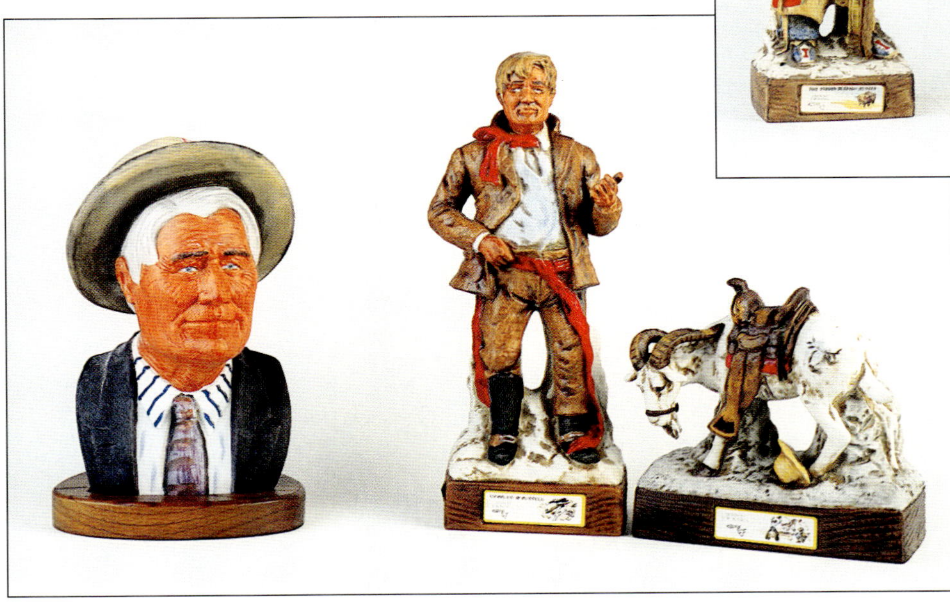

Bust of Charlie Russell, signed, 1978, $25-30. "I Rode Him" (pair), 1978, $20-25.

Miscellaneous Hoffman

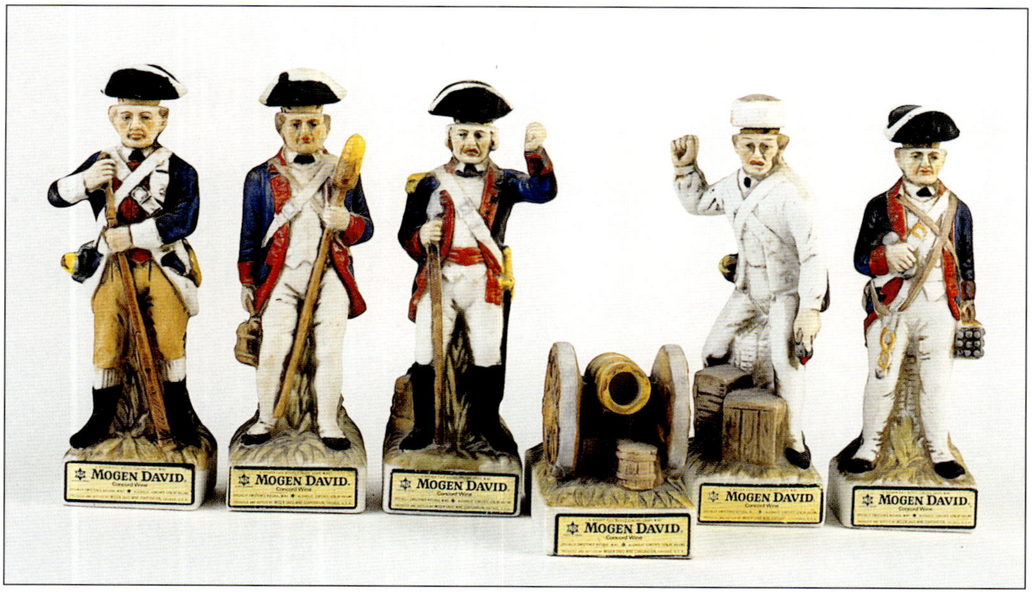

Concord Soldiers, 1973, set of 6 minis $35-40.

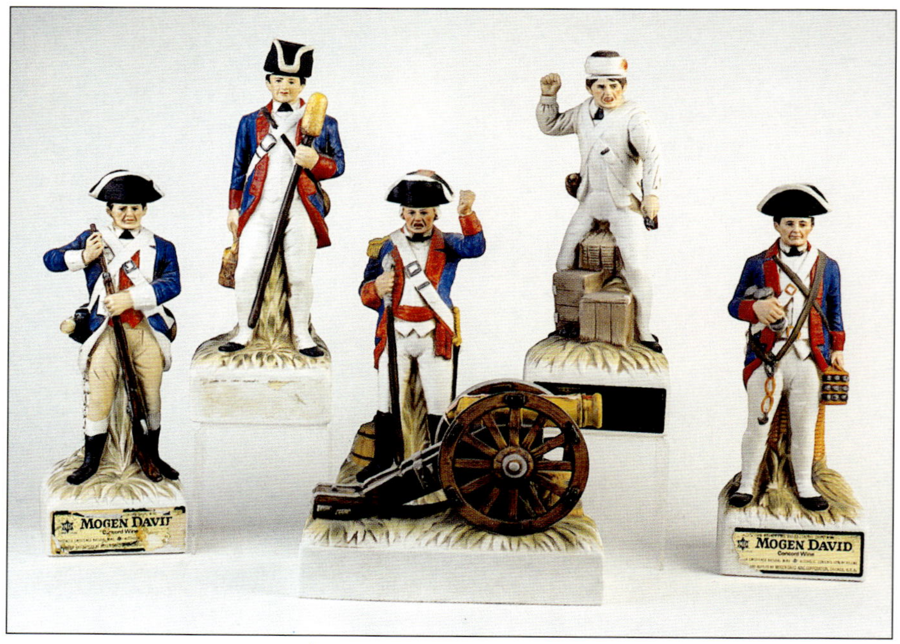

Concord Soldiers, 1973, set of 6 $75-85.

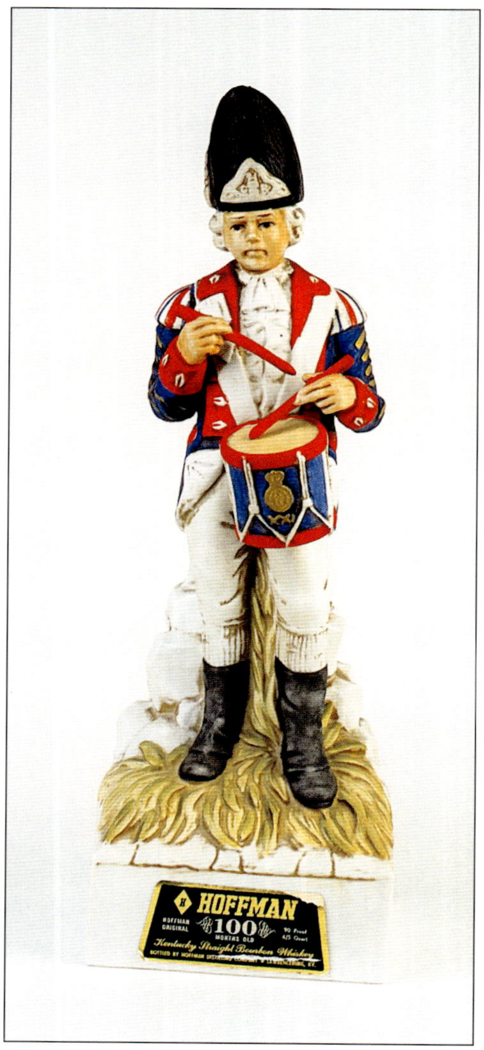

Drummer, $10-15.

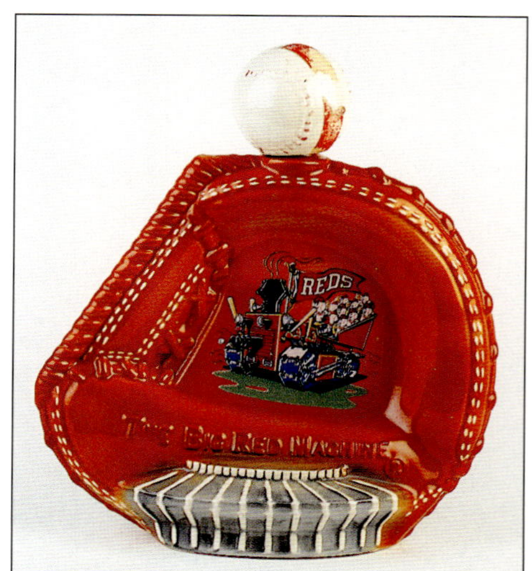

Big Red Machine, 1973, $65-75.

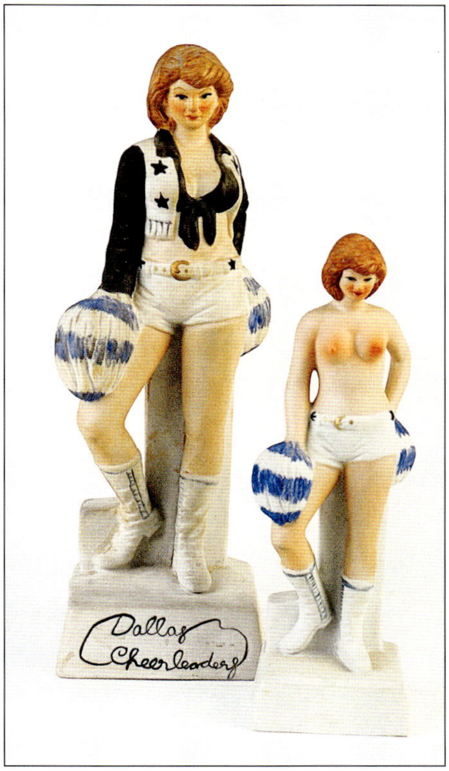

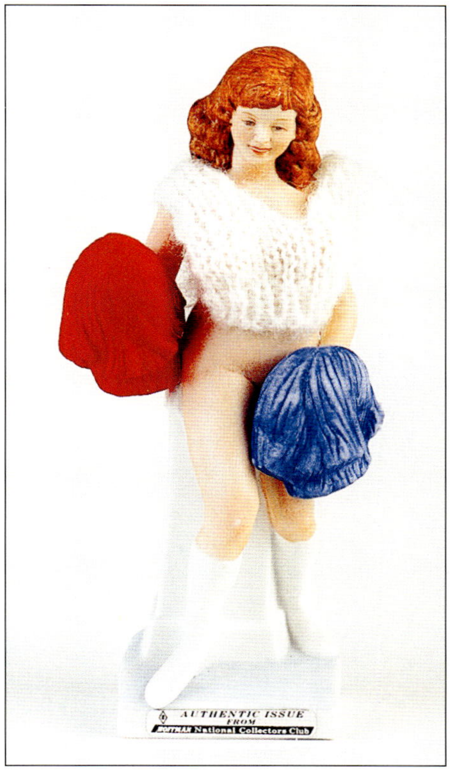

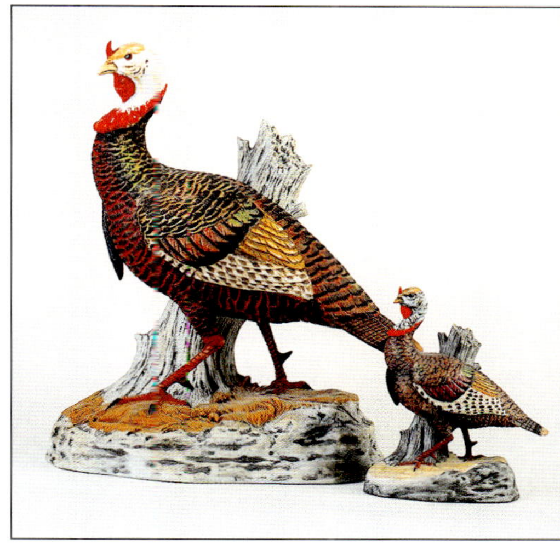

Turkeys, 1980, $70-80, mini (1987) $20-25.

Dallas Cowboy Cheerleaders, 1978, 8 oz $30-35. Cheerleader, topless, 1978, $65-75.

Lucky Lindy, nude with cover-up, 1984, $75-85.

Clemson Tigers, 1981, $30-35. Cincinnati Bengal's fan, 1982, $25-30. Go Tigers Go, music box, $20-25. LSU, music box, $20-25.

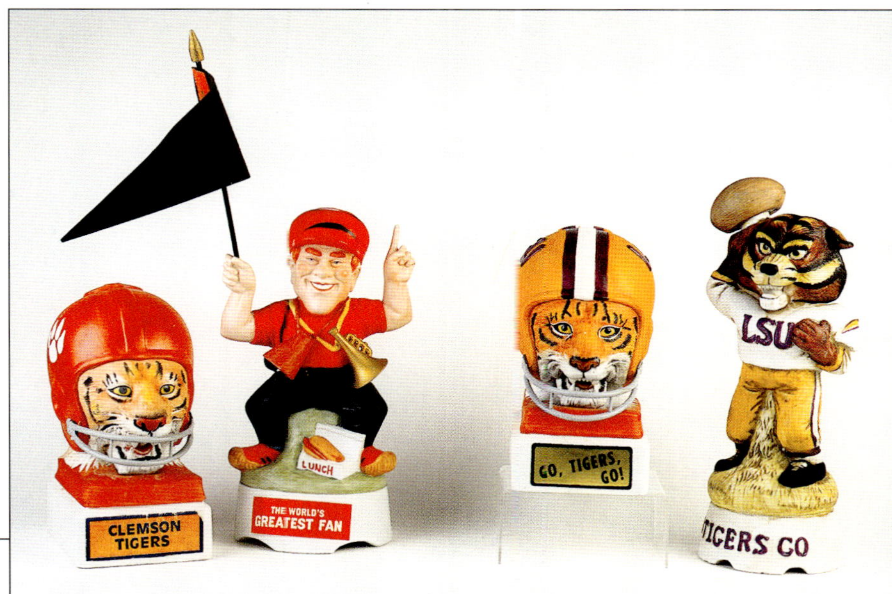

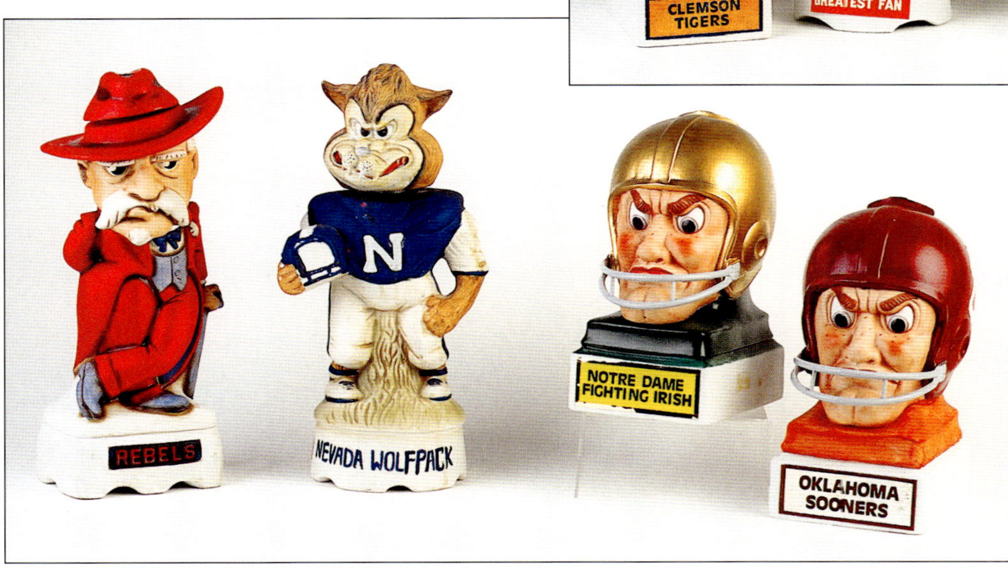

Mississippi Rebels, music box, 1977, $40-45. Nevada Wolfpack, music box, 1979, $40-45. Notre Dame Fighting Irish, music box, $40-45. Okalahoma Sooners, music box, 1981, $40-45.

Bibliography

Higgins, Molly. *Jim Beam Figural Bottles: An Unauthorized Collector's Guide*, 2nd Edition. Atglen, PA: Schiffer Publishing, Ltd., 2004.

Montague, H.F. *Montague's Modern Bottle Identification and Price Guide, 3rd Edition*. Overland Park, KS: H.F. Montague Enterprises, Inc., 1984.

http://www.ka.net/heartlandky/subdir/decantersandsteinslist.htm

http://www.jimbeamclub.com/aboutus/info.html